American Women
Civil Rights Activists

American Women Civil Rights Activists

Biobibliographies of 68 Leaders, 1825–1992

by
GAYLE J. HARDY

McFarland & Company, Inc., Publishers
Jefferson, North Carolina, and London

A portion of the research for this work was made possible by grants from the University at Buffalo Libraries Faculty and Professional Staff Development Committee, and the New York State/United University Professions Professional Development and Quality of Working Life Committee.

British Library Cataloguing-in-Publication data are available

Library of Congress Cataloguing-in-Publication Data

Hardy, Gayle J., 1942–
    American women civil rights activists : biobibliographies of 68
leaders, 1825–1992 / by Gayle J. Hardy.
        p.   cm.
    Includes bibliographical references and index.
    ISBN 0-89950-773-5 (lib. bdg. : 50# alk. paper) ∞
    1. Women civil rights workers — United States — Biography.   2. Women
civil rights workers — United States — History.   3. Women civil rights
workers — United States — Bibliography.   I. Title.
JC599.U5H273   1993
323′.092′273 — dc20
    [B]   92-56649
                                                                 CIP

Manufactured in the United States of America

McFarland & Company, Inc., Publishers
  Box 611, Jefferson, North Carolina 28640

To Cecil,
a most unique husband
and individual

CONTENTS

ACKNOWLEDGMENTS

So many people contributed in so many ways to this book, and I am most grateful to them all. Family, friends, and my exceptionally kind and patient colleagues lent emotional support, time, ideas and encouragement.

Special thanks to Judith Adams, director of Lockwood Library, who was always there, ready to help and advise; to Don Hartman for the countless number of times he assisted me, especially with his computer knowledge; to Loss Glazier for sharing his facility for language in this and other projects; to Laura Hartman for her technical assistance; to Marilyn Haas for her expertise in several areas; to Gemma DeVinney for her help in the conceptual development of this project; and to Marcie Dudek, Linda Gould, and most especially Cindy Kloss, for so many things it would take pages to list them all!

Thanks also to the amazing interlibrary loan staff who obtained countless numbers of books and articles, and to the scholars who contributed wonderful entries and submitted to my questions and suggestions with good grace.

Thanks also to the graduate students from the School of Information and Library Studies at the State University at Buffalo who assisted in the bibliographic searching: Kristine Olsen, Julie Wash, Marsha Nigro, William Hersch, Mavis Schedel, Sharon A. Gadawski, Jill Feine and Kristen Hunt were careful and cheerful during this tedious task. Heartfelt thanks go to their professor Judith Schiek Robinson for her immeasurable help in many ventures.

And to Cecil Davis, my husband, who kept our lives together during the long process of bringing an idea to fruition: no words can fully express my gratitude.

Thanks so much to all of you — we did it!

PREFACE

As a reference librarian, I know firsthand the frustration of searching endlessly for information that is strewn far and wide. This book provides access to formerly widely dispersed information about women prominent in civil rights activities in the United States. The arrangement lends itself to quick reference as well as extensive and in-depth research use, and the information will be useful to the scholar, the student, the researcher, the general reader and librarians in academic and public libraries.

This book introduces 68 historical and contemporary American women with descriptions of their civil rights activism. "Civil rights" is used in its broadest sense to encompass activities promoting the rights, privileges, and protection of all people. Groups and concerns represented include Native Americans/Indigenous peoples, African Americans, Hispanic Americans, children, lesbians and gays, adoptees, older adults, differently abled people, prisoners, political reform, health issues, economic opportunity, education and many others. Although women's rights and women's suffrage are not a special focus, many of the women profiled were also active in these areas.

This work compiles information and outlines important facts. Not every aspect or detail of each woman's life and career is presented; instead the entries provide the highlights of their lives. The extensive bibliographies will guide the reader to other sources for further information.

These women were, of course, products of their times, and their actions and beliefs are not judged in this book. Indeed, history may have proved some of them "wrong" in light of later developments. Some policies and actions that were viewed as helpful to certain groups at the time may now be seen as harmful.

More than 60 print and online sources, over 150 monographs, and numerous catalogs, articles, documents and individuals were consulted to identify names and material for inclusion. Some of the biographees were also contacted personally.

Included are women in the United States who are nationally known for their work with civil rights. Their activities span the period from the early

1800s to the present. Some of the women were not born in the United States, but all spent the majority of their lives living and working there. The entries are arranged alphabetically by the biographee's last name. Compound surnames are alphabetized by final name (i.e., you will find Helen Maria Fiske Hunt Jackson, who was married twice, under the "J's").

It was quickly discovered when sample searches were conducted that information about many of the subjects would be found under various names. Women are referred to by their maiden name, pseudonym, hyphenated name, married name, and so on, regardless of the name they wished to be known by, or used themselves. For example, Elizabeth Cochrane Seaman's pseudonym was Nellie Bly. Information concerning her was found not only under Seaman, but also under Bly, Cochrane, and Cochran.

Every attempt was made to check all forms of names during the research phase of this work. (This is an important point for researchers to remember—check every conceivable variation in each source consulted. Consistency within and between sources should not be expected because consistency does not exist. Variations occur in last names, first names, middle initials, and middle names, so a keen eye is essential so that the information is not overlooked.) To assist the reader with the name variations, there are cross references in the index and in Appendix F. In addition, these alternate names can be found in the "Also known as" category in the *Background Information* section of each entry.

Each entry includes a biography and a bibliography. *Biographical Information* has two sections. The first is the *Chronological Biography* which highlights the major events year-by-year of the biographee. *Background Information* is the second section and gives a range of information from personal data (parents, children, etc.) to historical sites associated with the biographee. *Bibliographical Information* cites works by and about the subject as well as primary source materials.

The comprehensive index and appendices provide a variety of access points including occupation, ethnicity, last name, civil rights activity, birthplace, pseudonym, religion, schools attended, tribal membership, organizations, important names, and books written by the subjects. Biographees are indexed in as many ways as possible and topics were deliberately interpreted broadly to enhance access. The *Appendices* will be helpful as well for an overview of a particular area of interest.

Notes About Biographical Information

If a woman profiled in this book is referred to in another entry, the notation referring the reader to the appropriate entry number will be found after the mention.

When conflicting information was found concerning dates in the *Chronological Biography* section, the following rules were used:

ca. = the date was uncertain or approximate
or = the date was known to be one of two years
? = the date was probable

Parents: Includes information concerning occupation, religion, etc. If nothing is known about her parents, "Not known" is stated. The subject's mother's maiden name appears in parentheses.

Siblings: When known, numbers and names are given. "None" is used when there were no siblings and "None known" is used when it is unclear whether there were siblings.

Children: When known, numbers and names are given. "None" is used when there were no children and "None known" is used when it is unclear whether there were children.

Influences: Lists people who significantly influenced, supported, or assisted in the biographee's civil rights activities. The person could be a family member, friend, husband, mentor, life-partner, teacher, or anyone. "None" is used when there were no notable influences and "None known" when it is unclear whether there were notable influences.

Ethnicity: Lists subject's ethnicity when known (e.g., Italian American, African American). "Not known" is used when ethnicity is unknown.

Also known as: Lists subject's pseudonyms and alternate forms of her names. "None known" is used when no alternate names are known.

Historical sites, landmarks, etc.: Lists gravesites, places named after subjects, and the like. "None known" is used when no appropriate material was identified.

Notes About Bibliographical Information

Print and nonprint sources (films, audio and video recordings, filmstrips, and recordings) are included, in addition to dissertations and theses, and primary sources. Citations to both scholarly and popular materials in English are included.

Citations within each category of the bibliographical section are arranged alphabetically by the first element (i.e., last name of author or editor, or first word of title if appropriate) and are as consistent as possible with regard to elements presented (dates, volume and issue numbers), given the number and variety of places from which they were gleaned. Items in the *Primary Source Materials* category are listed alphabetically by the first word of the collection — "Alice Dunbar-Nelson. Papers." is under "A."

In the *Books by* or *Books About* categories, an item is included if it is a stand-alone piece, regardless of length. Therefore, a 16 page pamphlet is considered to be a book. Further, the original and the most recent reprint or edition of a book is included. If another reprint or edition was special or important in some way, it, too, is noted.

A collection of a biographee's work edited by another person is entered in the *Books by* category with the editor's name included.

The *Shorter Works by* and *Shorter Works About* categories include articles or parts of books. If the biographee was a regular contributor to, or editor of, a publication, not every article she wrote is listed; instead there is a note stating this fact with inclusive years if available.

The ERIC (Educational Resources Information Center) documents are identified by ED number [ED306427].

United States federal government publications are identified by a Superintendent of Documents number [C3.2: M57].

Exclusions to the Bibliographies

Foreign language works are excluded unless they were unique or especially important.

Materials about the subject intended for children or young adults are not generally included unless there was little else available; however, it must also be remembered that there is not always agreement about the targeted audience so some inclusions may be borderline. (Materials written *by* the biographee intended for these audiences *are* included.)

Newspaper articles are usually omitted unless little else could be found concerning the biographee or the article contained information not readily found elsewhere.

Book reviews written by the subjects or reviews about items the subjects authored were excluded unless there was something very special that warranted their inclusion.

Very brief mentions in monographs were not included.

Not every primary source was included; listed are large collections and those pointing up unique, important, or especially interesting aspects of the subject's activities.

CONTRIBUTORS

Thirteen invited scholars contributed 20 entries to this work. The contributors are listed here in alphabetical order with their respective articles.

Jane E. Ashwill   (DOROTHY DAY)
Learning Resource Center
Erie Community College
Buffalo, New York

Kathy A. Burock   (ROSA PARKS)
James L. Crane Branch
Buffalo and Erie County Public
  Library
Buffalo, New York

Renee D. Chapman
(EMMA GOLDMAN)
Olin Library
Cornell University
Ithaca, New York

Amy DiBartolo Rockwell
(SARAH ELIZABETH VAN DE VORT
  EMERY; MARY ELIZA CHURCH
  TERRELL; IDA BELL
  WELLS-BARNETT)
E. H. Butler Library
State University College at Buffalo
Buffalo, New York

Carol A. Gloss
(ELIZABETH COCHRANE SEAMAN)
Library

Mohawk Correctional Facility
Rome, New York

Levirn Hill
(SHIRLEY CHISHOLM; CORETTA
  SCOTT KING)
E. H. Butler Library
State University College at Buffalo
Buffalo, New York

Glendora Johnson-Cooper
(ANGELA DAVIS)
Silverman Undergraduate Library
State University of New York at
  Buffalo
Buffalo, New York

Kathryn M. Kerns
(BELVA ANN BENNETT MCNALL
  LOCKWOOD)
J. Henry Meyer Memorial Library
Stanford University
Stanford, California

Barbara L. Morgan
(ELIZABETH GURLEY FLYNN;
  FANNIE LOU TOWNSEND HAMER;
  KATE RICHARDS O'HARE)
University Library
University of Massachusetts
Amherst, Massachusetts

Sharon C. Murphy
(ELIZABETH BLACKWELL)
Health Sciences Library
State University of New York at
  Buffalo
Buffalo, New York

Cynthia L. Seitz
(BARBARA JORDAN)
Lockwood Memorial Library
State University of New York at
  Buffalo
Buffalo, New York

Dorothy S. Tao
(DONALDINA MACKENZIE CAMERON;

LILLIAN D. WALD)
National Center for Earthquake
  Engineering Research
State University of New York at
  Buffalo
Buffalo, New York

Lillian S. Williams
(MARY FRANCES BERRY;
  MARY BURNETT TALBERT
Women's Studies Department and
  Africana Studies Department
State University of New York at
  Albany
Albany, New York

CHRONOLOGY

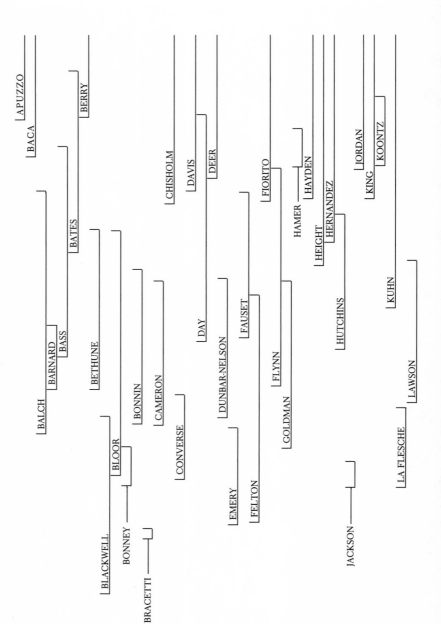

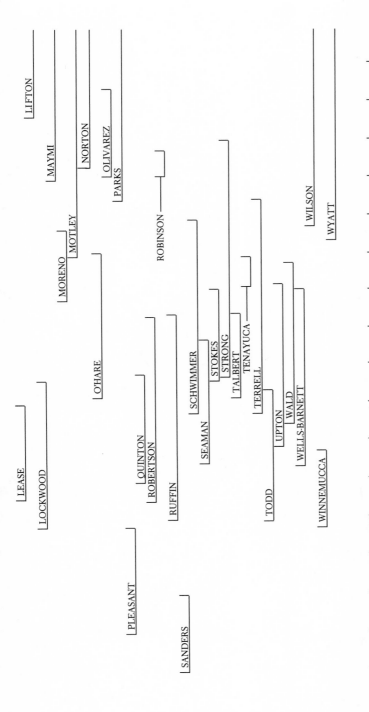

|1820–29|1830–39|1840–49|1850–59|1860–69|1870–79|1880–89|1890–99|1900–09|1910–19|1920–29|1930–39|1940–49|1950–59|1960–69|1970–79|1980–89|1990—

American Women
Civil Rights Activists

1. Virginia M. Apuzzo
(1941–   )

Advocate for lesbian and gay rights and
human rights; lecturer; and feminist

BIOGRAPHICAL INFORMATION

Chronological Biography

Born June 26, 1941. Grew up in Bronx, New York, as oldest daughter in a very ethnic environment. Her strong feelings about many issues, especially the idea of fairness in all matters, are a direct result of upbringing and school teachings. Excellent student in public grammar school and Catholic high school. Received bachelors degree in history and education; also earned graduate credits.

196?: Tenured chair of social studies department of upstate New York school.   1967?: At age 26, entered convent and became nun in Sisters of Charity Order so that she could examine her life and determine what direction to take.   1969: Left convent with commitment to work for those who are oppressed and to empower them by helping them realize how much power they have. Began teaching at Brooklyn College.   1976: Coordinated National Gay Task Force's effort to obtain gay rights plank in Democratic party platform. Task Force, formed in 1973, is country's oldest and largest gay civil rights organization, dedicated to elimination of prejudice against persons based on sexual orientation.   1978: Ran unsuccessful, but highly praised, campaign for New York State Assembly.   1979: Obtained leave of absence from Brooklyn College to accept position of Assistant Commissioner for Operations in New York City Department of Health. Responsible for running six bureaus, including District Health Services, which functioned as largest ambulatory health care operation in country. Served briefly as Executive Director of New York City Office of Administrative Trials and Hearings. Asked by Anne Wexler, special assistant to President Carter, to work on 1980 presidential campaign.   1980: Delegate to Democratic party national convention, co-authoring first gay rights plank to be accepted by any United States national political convention.   1982: Served as one of the openly gay delegates to the midterm Democratic party convention in Philadelphia.   1982?: Executive director of Fund for Human Dignity, educational affiliate of National Gay Task Force.   1982–?: Executive director of National Gay Task Force, later named National Gay and Lesbian Task

Force. **January 1983:** Held press conference to issue statement on national blood donor policy and AIDS (Acquired Immune Deficiency Syndrome); fifty gay community organizations and representatives participated. Stressed importance of screening blood instead of barring high-risk groups from donating. **May 1983:** Testified before federal House Appropriations Subcommittee on funding and priorities of departments of Labor, Health and Human Services, and Education, calling for $100 million to be appropriated by Congress to fight AIDS. Also wrote Margaret Heckler, U.S. Health and Human Services Secretary, urging coordinated federal effort against AIDS, accurate information in media and requesting meeting. **June 1983:** Testified before U.S. Conference of Mayors AIDS Task Force. Met with Judy Buckalew, special assistant to President Reagan for health issues in Office of Public Liaison. **July 1983:** Urged Conference of Local Health Officers to be especially sensitive to high-risk groups in their response to AIDS crisis. Witness at Senate hearing regarding presidential nominations to Civil Rights Commission. **August 1983:** Spoke before House Subcommittee on Intergovernmental Relations and Human Resources, characterizing federal response to AIDS as uncoordinated, and proposing jointly with Lambda Legal Defense and Education Fund to protect confidentiality of research subjects. Founded in 1973, Lambda Fund's mission is to defend civil rights of gay persons in employment, housing, child custody, etc. Met with assistant secretary for health, Dr. Edward Brandt, to discuss federal AIDS efforts; ten days later Secretary Margaret Heckler increased her budget request for AIDS from $17 to $39 million. **October 1983:** New York State Executive Chamber citation recognized her work as founding member of Lambda Independent Democrats of Brooklyn. **November 1983:** Met with Dr. James O. Mason on his first day as director of Centers for Disease Control. **April 1984:** Appeared before federal Senate and House appropriations subcommittees calling for increased AIDS funding. HTLV-III virus identified as probable cause of AIDS. **May 1984:** Joined by three AIDS service organization representatives, met with commissioner of Social Security Administration in effort to discuss needs of people with AIDS, resulting in streamlining of disability review procedures. **June 1984:** Named by New York Governor Mario Cuomo to 12-member panel to investigate discrimination against homosexuals by New York in areas of state employment, services and benefits. City of Boston Proclamation received. **August 1984:** San Francisco Board of Supervisors Certificate of Honor presented. **September 1984:** Assisted by representatives from Lambda Legal Defense and Education Fund and American Association of Physicians for Human Rights, successfully negotiated model consent form for AIDS-related research funded by Public Health Service; form was subsequently recommended by Dr. Brandt, assistant secretary of health, for national use. Citation received from Alice B. Toklas Democratic Club of San Francisco. **October 1984:** Led lobbying effort that resulted in setting aside of federal monies for direct grants to community-based organizations to conduct education among groups at risk to AIDS. Approximately $140,000 was made available through U.S. Conference of Mayors. Virginia M. Apuzzo Day proclaimed in Houston, Texas. **November 1984:** Met with Secretary Margaret Heckler, first meeting between Reagan administration cabinet officer and lesbian/gay leader. **1984:** As member of platform committee of Democratic convention, helped broaden scope and strength of party's commitment to lesbian and gay civil rights. **January 1985:** Organized coalition of national gay/lesbian and AIDS service organizations to issue joint statement responding to licensing of test for HTLV-III antibodies. Testified in opposition to confirmation of Edwin Meese for attorney general. **April 1985:** Gay Men's Health Crisis Special Citation awarded. Honored by National Gay Task Force Resolution. **May 1985:** Howard J. Brown award presented by National Gay Task Force Fund for Human Dignity. **October 1985:** Lambda Independent Democrats of Brooklyn Citation of Honor. Woman of Year award from Christopher Street West Association. **December 1985:** New York State Center for Women in Government award presented. **1985–ᅠ:** Tapped by Governor Cuomo to become deputy executive director of New York State Consumer Protection Board, consumer advocacy organization. She is in charge of running programs and operations of board and has been responsible for several state investigations into cost of FDA approved drugs, and products which fraudulently claim to cure or prevent AIDS. Charles Gormley award presented by Dignity New York organization. **January 1986:** New York Civil Liberties Union Special Citation. **May 1986:** Asked by New York State Governor Cuomo to serve as his liaison to lesbian/gay community. **October 1986:** Honored by California State Assembly Resolution. **Mid–1980s:** Named by Cuomo as vice chair of New York State AIDS Advisory Council. Began working directly with Cuomo to formulate comprehensive AIDS program for New York state. **June 1987:** Greater Gotham Business Council award given. **June 1988:** Honorary Doctor of Laws Degree, Queens College, City University of New York Law School conferred. **June 24, 1989:** Keynote speaker in Central Park, New York City, at commemoration of 20th anniversary of Stonewall Rebellion, 1969 police raid on Greenwich Village gay bar which began gay rights movement. **Present–ᅠ:** Continues to work closely with Cuomo, his Counsel Unit, and the New York State Lesbian and Gay Lobby, for passage of inclusive, language-specific legislation to protect all New Yorkers from bias-motivated violence. According to Apuzzo, despite strong support from Cuomo and the state assembly, the state senate failed to pass the bill while it contained reference to lesbians and gay men; continues to work on behalf of its passage. Believes that AIDS crisis has helped to solidify gay community and that positive changes in health insurance, social security, etc. brought about by their efforts will benefit other groups who may be discriminated against, i.e. older Americans, disabled, etc. Has lectured extensively at Yale, Harvard, Princeton and Cornell universities, the Kennedy Institute for Policy Studies, etc. Has spoken at numerous gatherings nationwide regarding basic civil rights and dignity for all Americans, and has appeared on network programs such as "Nightline," "The McNeil-Lehrer Report," "CBS Morning News," "20/20," and the "Phil Donahue Show."

Background Information

Parents: Mother worked as family finances required as a waitress, in retail sales and in a factory. Father owned gas station in Bronx.   **Siblings:** Number not known (no known names). **Children:** None. **Influences:** None. **Ethnicity:** Italian American.   **Also known as:** Ginny.   **Historical sites, landmarks, etc.:** None known.

BIBLIOGRAPHICAL INFORMATION

Shorter Works by Virginia M. Apuzzo

"Grace to Empower." In *Lesbian Nuns: Breaking Silence,* edited by Rosemary Curb and Nancy Manahan. Tallahassee: Naiad, 1985.
Vida, Ginny, ed. *Our Right to Love: A Lesbian Resource Book.* Englewood Cliffs, NJ: Prentice-Hall, 1978.

Shorter Works About Virginia M. Apuzzo

Barron, James. "Homosexuals See 2 Decades of Gains, but Fear Setbacks." *New York Times* (June 25, 1989): 1.
Basler, Barbara. "Diverse Groups Woo Primary Voters." *New York Times* (April 2, 1984): 7.
Biederman, Marcia. "N.Y. Targets Quackery in AIDS Medicine Chest." *Crain's New York Business* (June 29, 1987): 14.
Blow, Richard. "Those Were the Gays: What Now for the Gay Movement." *New Republic* (November 2, 1987).
Braun, Stephen. "The Trouble with Terrigno; When West Hollywood's First Mayor Was Driven from City Hall, She Took Part of the Dream of a 'Gay Camelot' with Her." *Los Angeles Times* (June 1, 1986): 17.
_____. "West Hollywood: Vote May Make It First Gay-Run City; Issue Forges Alliance Between Homosexuals, Older Jewish Residents." *Los Angeles Times* (October 14, 1984): 1.

Cincotti, Joseph A. "Some Pharmacies Quote Prices Far Over Cost for AIDS Drug, New York Study Finds." *New York Times* (August 21, 1987): 4.

Clendinen, Dudley. "AIDS Spreads Pain and Fear Among Ill and Healthy Alike." *New York Times* (June 17, 1983): 1.

_____. "Book on Lesbian Nuns Upsets Boston, Delighting Publisher." *New York Times* (April 12, 1985): 12.

_____. "Throughout the Country; Homosexuals Increasingly Flex Political Muscle." *New York Times* (November 8, 1983): 26.

"Community News (Another Open Lesbian)." *Lesbian Feminist* (October 1978): 9.

"Confrontation: Black/White (Interview with Ginny Apuzzo and Betty Powell)." *Quest* 3 (Spring 1977): 34–46.

Cotter, Kitty. "Ginny Apuzzo, a Lesbian Feminist Politician." *Lesbian Feminist* (June 1977): 8+.

"Court Ruling Spurs Homosexuals' Antidiscrimination Effort." *New York Times* (September 2, 1984): 26.

"Dan J. Bradley, 47, Dies of AIDS; Ex-Head of Legal Services Agency." *New York Times* (January 9, 1988): 34.

Duggan, Dennis. "Career Fears Opened Closet Door for Failla." *Newsday* (December 4, 1988): 20.

"Effort on AIDS Called Faulty." *New York Times* (August 2, 1983): 10.

Glaberson, William. "Ruling Stretches Legal Concept of Family." *New York Times* (July 8, 1989): 25.

Guttenplan, D. D. "Going to the Chapel of Law." *Newsday* (June 25, 1989): 8.

"Homosexual Bias Unit Named." *New York Times* (June 24, 1984): 37.

Humm, Andrew, and Betty Santoro. "If We Gay Men and Lesbians Stand Up." *New York Times* (November 1, 1980): 25.

Japenga, Ann. "Lesbian Nuns Break Their Silence; Former, Current Sisters Discuss Religious Life in Book." *Los Angeles Times* (May 1, 1985): 1.

Jehl, Douglas. "Issue Hurt Mondale in 1984; Dukakis Bluntly Evading Special-Interest Pitfalls." *Los Angeles Times* (June 11, 1988): 1.

Johnson, Julie. "Washington Talk: Lobbies; Homosexual Groups and the Politics of AIDS." *New York Times* (October 6, 1988): 16.

"Justice Department Plays Doctor." *New York Times* (February 4, 1985): 18.

Klemesrud, Judy. "For Homosexuals' Parents, Strength in Community." *New York Times* (October 10, 1983): 9.

Lindgren, Kristina. "Fear of AIDS Leads Red Cross to Cancel Lesbian Blood Drive." *Los Angeles Times* (January 9, 1985): 1.

_____. "Lesbian Center Plan Called a 'Mistake'; Red Cross Cites Its Image in Canceling Blood Drive." *Los Angeles Times* (January 10, 1985): 1.

Lowe, David M. "A Dream of Ginny's: Virginia Apuzzo Speaks Up for Us." *Sentinel* (July 4, 1986): 6+.

McBee, Susanna, with Jeannye Thornton, Patricia A. Avery, and Alvin P. Sanoff. "Growing Voter Blocs Flex Their Muscles." *U.S. News & World Report* (July 16, 1984): 84.

Mandell, Jonathan. "'Clearly, We're Seen As a Constituency'." *New York Newsday* (June 15, 1989): 3+.

Molotsky, Irvin. "Democratic Platform Committee Hears Koch Plea." *New York Times* (June 14, 1980): 8.
Morgan, Thomas. "Amid AIDS, Gay Movement Grows but Shifts." *New York Times* (October 10, 1987): 1.
Norman, Michael. "Homosexuals Confronting a Time of Change." *New York Times* (June 16, 1983): 1.
Pear, Robert. "Health Chief Calls AIDS Battle 'No. 1 Priority'." *New York Times* (May 25, 1983): 1.
"Portrait." *Lesbian Tide* 7 (September–October 1977): 7.
Robinson, Julie. "Noble Politics: Won't Run for Re-election." *Lesbian Tide* 7 (1977): 7+.
Russell, Christine. "Mysterious Lethal Disease Spreads in U.S.; Government Health Officials Fearful the Pace Is Accelerating." *Washington Post* (February 7, 1983): 5.
Slade, Margot, and Wayne Biddle. "Ideas & Trends in Summary; Immune Disease Given Priority." *New York Times* (May 29, 1983): 8.
Smothers, Ronald. "Mondale Tells Homosexual Group Reagan Record Is Biased on Rights." *New York Times* (September 30, 1982): 16.
"Top Health Officials Refute Bias Charge in Combating AIDS." *New York Times* (August 3, 1983): 18.
Weaver, Warren, Jr., and James F. Clarity. "Briefing." *New York Times* (June 22, 1983): 22.
Whitmore, George. "Reaching Out to Someone with AIDS." *New York Times* (May 19, 1985): 68.
Yoshihashi, Pauline. "170 Homosexual Officials Confer on Tactics and National Platform." *New York Times* (November 25, 1985): 16.

2. *Polly B. Baca*
(1941–   )

State legislator; advocate for Hispanic American education, economic opportunity, minority rights, and women's rights

BIOGRAPHICAL INFORMATION

Chronological Biography

Born February 13, 1941. Pauline Celia (Polly) is fourth generation Coloradan, one of three daughters and three sons born to Leda (Sierra) and José Manuel Baca in LaSalle, Weld County, five miles from Greeley in northern Colorado. Strongly influenced by father's deep sense of social consciousness and fighting spirit, as well as by mother's fierce independence and belief that a woman must be her own person. Encouraged by parents to pursue education and not marry early. Father was farm worker and Mexican American family was subject to much racism and segregation in conservative town; grew up with feelings of inferiority as result. **Mid 1940s–1958:** Performed well scholastically; highly motivated by the discrimination she experienced, she set out to prove she was as good as anyone else. Desire to change things sparked ambition to enter law and politics, but discouraged when she learned it was unlikely women would be accepted in legal profession. Turned instead to physics, mathematics and chemistry with Madame Curie as inspiration and model. Although high school principal attempted to intimidate her, ran successfully for secretary of student body. Active in Adlai Stevenson Young Democrats Club. Awarded joint honor scholarship from Greeley High School to attend college. **1958–1962:** Began college with major in physics, but returned in sophomore year to interest in law and politics. Active in campus politics; vice president and president of school's Young Democrats; secretary of freshman class. Participated in congressional campaigns. Served as state college coordinator of Colorado Viva (John F.) Kennedy Clubs; worked as Colorado Democratic Party intern. Elected secretary of student body in junior year. Graduated from Colorado State University at Fort Collins with B.A. in political science and education and minor in mathematics. One of 11 students, and first Mexican American, to win Pacemaker Award for outstanding graduates, the school's highest award. Began graduate work but decided to seek employment instead. **December 1962–December 1965:** At age 21, took position in Washington, D.C., as editorial assistant in department of research and education at International Brotherhood of Pulp, Sulphite and Paper Mill Workers, AFL-CIO. Greatly aided and encouraged by supervisor. Won International Labor Press Association award in 1963, 1964, and 1965 for work on monthly newspaper with circulation of 100,000. **January 1966–September 1967:** Remained in Washington as editor of *Airline News* magazine for Brotherhood of Railway and Airline Clerks of AFL-CIO, researching and writing all news articles, supervising magazine layout and design. Additionally, was assistant director of research and education department, developing materials for use in organizing campaigns, congressional testimony and legislative lobbying. **1966–1967:** Studied for master's degree in public relations at American University in Washington, D. C. **September 1967–March 1968:** Public information officer for Interagency Committee on Mexican Americans, first cabinet committee on opportunities for Spanish-speaking people. Working out of White House, oversaw communication with media and public, supervised media arrangements for 1967 hearings, promoted visits of Committee's chair to Hispanic communities throughout country, and coordinated press relations with Secret Service for presidential and vice presidential presentations. **March 1968–June 1968:**

National deputy director, Viva Kennedy Division, of Robert F. Kennedy's national campaign for president. Operating out of Washington, supervised development of public relations materials focused on Hispanic community and organized "Viva Kennedy" clubs. **September 1968–September 1970:** Moved to Phoenix, Arizona, to accept position as director of research services and information for National Council of La Raza; responsibilities again encompassing public relations and communication activities. Met husband-to-be Miguel Barragan, Chicano activist and former priest. Divorced several years later. **September 1970–December 1984:** With husband, founded public relations firm, Bronze Publications in Phoenix, later moving to Denver. Served as president and director specializing in media communications. Company produced materials for wide range of organizations including National Institute of Mental Health, National Urban Coalition, Colorado State University Chicano Studies Program, Democratic National Committee, and VISTA. **1971:** First of two children, daughter Monica, born. **December 1971–August 1972:** Recognized for expertise, creativity and dedication, named first director of division of Spanish-Speaking Affairs, and special assistant to chair of Democratic National Commitee. Primary responsibility concerned public relations programs focused on national Hispanic community. Supervised staff at 1972 Miami Democratic Convention. **November 1972–November 1973:** Relocated to Denver, accepting position as director of Colorado Committee on Mass Media and the Spanish-Surnamed, Inc. Directed all programs and coordinated media efforts of member organizations, agencies and individuals state-wide. **January 1975–December 1978:** Elected in November 1974 on Democratic ticket, served as representative from district 34, Adams County, to Colorado State legislature, one of very few Chicana women elected to state office in country. Constituents were primarily low and lower-middle class working people. Extremely successful in introducing bills which were later signed into law, a feat unusual for freshman legislators. Among concerns were actions regarding housing, consumer protection, elderly tax credits, bilingual and bicultural education, sexual assault victims, child abuse and unemployment benefits for pregnant women. Sponsored or co-sponsored 156 pieces of legislation that became law. Earned respect of colleagues and governor for leadership skills and efforts to reform laws to make electoral process equally available to all citizens. First woman chair of House Democratic Caucus, vice chair of house rules committee, and member of committees regarding labor and school finance, among others. **July 3, 1975:** Son, Miguel, born. **November 1978:** One of eight state legislators selected nation-wide by American Council of Young Political Leaders for study tour of Soviet Union. **1978:** Vice chair of procedures and rules committee of Democratic National Committee. **January 1979–December 1986:** With election as state senator from district 34, became first Chicana elected to Colorado senate. Chaired

Senate Democratic Caucus and served on numerous committees including those relating to education, health and environment. First Hispanic woman in any state senate in United States to serve in leadership position. (Easily reelected in 1982.)   **March 1979:** White House guest at signing of Egyptian-Israeli Peace Treaty.   **July 1979:** Participated in Camp David Domestic Summit.   **November 1979:** Named one of ten "Women of the Future" by *Ladies' Home Journal.*   **December 1979:** Selected by *Ms.* magazine for inclusion on list of "Women to Watch in the 80s."   **March 1980:** One of the leaders at the first National Hispanic Feminist Conference in San Jose, California, attended by nearly 1,000 women of Cuban, Puerto Rican, Latin American, and Mexican ancestry. Conference was financed by federal government to determine priorities for Hispanic women in 1980s. **1980–1981:** Member of national advisory council of Federal Savings and Loan Association.   **January 1981–February 1989:** Vice chair of Democratic National Committee. Special emphasis on liaison program with women and minority state legislators nationwide.   **May 1981:** One of 15 Americans chosen to take part in foreign policy seminar with 16 Europeans in Brussels, Belgium; sponsored by German Marshall Fund and European Cooperative Fund.   **August 1982:**One of 20 North American women selected to participate in Jerusalem Women's Seminar in Israel, Egypt and Lebanon. **December 1984:** Participant in West Berlin, Germany, seminar on impact of 1984 American elections; sponsored by Aspen Institute Berlin. **May 1985–September 1989:** Founded Sierra Baca Systems in Thornton, Colorado, a management consulting firm specializing in problems of minorities in higher education, leadership and development programs for minority women, analysis of political issues in relation to minority community, etc. Left organization, now headed by her sister, to assume position at Colorado Institute for Hispanic Education and Economic Development.   **1985:** Cochair of National Democratic Fairness Commission.   **July 1986:** Attended symposium on world economics and defense in Brussels, Belgium, sponsored by Konrad Adenauer Foundation of West Germany.   **1986:** Unsuccessfully ran for U.S. Congress. Had she won, would have been first minority woman in Congress.   **August 1987:** One of 12 women leaders invited by Center for Global Education to participate in fact-finding delegation to Honduras, El Salvador and Nicaragua during Central American peace initiatives.   **1987 and 1988:** Received Certificate of Achievement in Media.   **January 1988:** Participated in Alumni Conference on Soviet-American relations in Moscow, cosponsored by American Council of Young Political Leaders and Soviet Committee of Youth Organizations. **May 1988:** Led special delegation on study tour of Bulgaria.   **April–May 1989:** Under auspices of U.S. Information Agency, lectured in Japan and Philippines regarding role of women, racial and ethnic Americans in U.S. socio-political-economic systems.   **May 1989:** Received honorary Doctor of Laws degree from

Wartburg College.   **October 1989–**   : Appointed second executive director, and first woman, of Colorado Institute for Hispanic Education and
Economic Development in Denver. Non-profit policy action organization
begun in 1987, it is joint effort of various educational institutions, including
University of Colorado at Denver, as well as Hispanic community. Seeks to
facilitate policies and programs to enhance opportunities for Hispanics,
create jobs, and support those seeking to enter private business as well as the
corporate world. Memberships on boards, commissions, and committees
continue to be extensive and diverse. Has received numerous awards and
honors for community activism, efforts at social change, and championing of
minority advancement and women's rights, and is one of original 14 members
to be inducted into National Hispanic Hall of Fame. Lives in Thornton, Colorado, with her two children.

Background Information

Parents: Leda (Sierra) and Jose Manuel Baca. Father was farm worker.
Great great uncle was one of founders of Trinidad, Colorado, and had served
in Colorado Territorial Legislature.   **Siblings:** Five (known names: Bettie
Baca Rodriguez, head of Sierra Baca Systems; and Fernie, assistant vice
chancellor for research at University of Colorado at Denver).   **Children:**
Two (Monica and Miguel [Mike]).   **Influences:** None.   **Ethnicity:** Hispanic
American.   **Also known as:** Baca-Barragan; Barragan.   **Historical sites,
landmarks, etc.:** None known.

BIBLIOGRAPHICAL INFORMATION

Biographical Sketches About Polly B. Baca

"In Honor of Polly B. Baca." *Congressional Record* 135 (November 16, 1989).
Meier, Matt S. *Mexican American Biographies: A Historical Dictionary, 1836–1987.*
     New York: Greenwood, 1988. (Listed as Baca-Barragan, Polly.)
————, and Feliciano Rivera. *Dictionary of Mexican American History.*
     Westport, CT: Greenwood,1981. (Listed as Baca-Barragan, Polly).
Telgen, Diane, and Jim Kamp, eds. *Notable Hispanic American Women.* Detroit:
     Gale Research, 1993.
Who's Who of American Women. Wilmette, IL: Marquis Who's Who, 1986.

Shorter Works About Polly B. Baca

"All But 3 Democratic Caucuses Stripped of Official Recognition." *Los Angeles
     Times* (May 18, 1985): 3.

"Baca Barragan, Polly, Richard Hamner, and Lena Guerrero." *National Hispanic Journal* 1 (Winter 1982): 8–11.

"Baca, Chavez Announce Plans." *Nuestro* 10 (March 1986): 11.

Ben-Itzak, Paul. "Feminist Education in the 80's Explored." *New York Times* (July 1, 1984): 15.

Brozan, Nadine. "State Legislature: Center Stage for Women." *New York Times* (November 18, 1985): B8.

Chavez, Lucy, and Julio Moran. "Latina Legislators: Few and Far Between: Colorado's Polly Baca-Barragan: New York's Olga Aran Mendez." *Nuestro* 4 (April 1980): 18–20.

Clarity, James F., and Warren Weaver, Jr. "Briefing; Democrats Revamping." *New York Times* (April 12, 1985): A14.

Clymer, Adam. "Democrats Open Parley by Assailing Reagan." *New York Times* (June 26, 1982): 1.

―――――. "Democrats Select Manatt as Chairman." *New York Times* (February 28, 1981): 7.

―――――. "Votes by Women in G.O.P. Attacked." *New York Times* (July 12, 1981): 16.

"Colorado Governor May Be Drafted as Favorite Son." *Los Angeles Times* (December 28, 1987): 4.

"Colorado May Declare an Official State Fossil." *New York Times* (February 1, 1981): 15.

"Congress: The Match-ups in this Year's Open-Seat Races." *National Journal* (October 4, 1980): 1652.

Cummings, Judith. "Hispanic Democratic Leaders Discuss Strategy for '84." *New York Times* (May 7, 1983): 12.

"Election USA: Arizona, California, Colorado, New Mexico." *La Luz* 3 (November 1974): 21–25.

Espinosa, Ann. "Hispana—Our Resources for the Eighties." *La Luz* 8 (October, November 1979): 10–13.

Gailey, Phil. "Talking Politics: Images, Old and New." *New York Times* (October 8, 1986): A30.

Hollie, Pamela G. "Hispanic Group Sets Priorities for the 1980's." *New York Times* (April 1, 1980): B17.

"Hispanas Conocidas." *La Luz* 6 (November 1977): 31.

Johnson, Richard. "Polly Baca Clears Paths to Hispanic Achievement." *Denver Post* (October 25, 1989): C1.

"Kirk, Ex-Kennedy Aide, New Democratic Chairman." *Los Angeles Times* (February 3, 1985): 1.

Kirschten, Dick. "The Hispanic Vote—Parties Can't Gamble That the Sleeping Giant Won't Waken." *National Journal* (November 19, 1983): 2410.

Merry, George B. "Democrats Unlikely to Challenge 'Early' Votes in Iowa, N.H." *Christian Science Monitor* (May 4, 1984): 5.

"*Ms.* Magazine Selects Its 'Women to Watch'." *New York Times* (December 20, 1979): 17.

"N.A.L.E.O.'s 'Fiesta '83'." *Caminos* 4 (November 1983): 28–29.

"New Mexico Governor Picked as Leader of Hispanic Lobby." *New York Times* (February 21, 1983): A15.

"Politics—Top Campaign Officials." *National Journal* (January 5, 1980): 13.

"Polly Baca-Barragan." In *Politicians for the People: Six Who Stand for Change,* by Elizabeth Levy and Mara Miller. New York: Dell, 1981.

"Polly Baca-Barragan: A Woman on the Move." *La Luz* 9 (August–September 1981): 14.

"Polly Baca Barragan: She Belongs in the House." *Nuestro* 4 (November 1980): 24.

"Polly Baca's Back." *Congressional Record* 135 (November 21, 1989).

Quigley, Eileen V. "Washington's Movers and Shakers; Fair's Fair." *National Journal* (June 29, 1985): 1536.

_____. "Washington's Movers and Shakers; Political Stripes." *National Journal* (April 20, 1985): 876.

Raines, Howell. "Democrats Pick a Kennedy Ally as Party's Chief." *New York Times* (February 2, 1985): 6.

Riehle, Thomas. "People: Washington's Movers and Shakers; With the Commissions and Committees." *National Journal* (December 31, 1983): 2709.

Steinbach, Carol. "Washington Update; People; They Came to Camp David." *National Journal* (July 21, 1979): 1224.

Sulzberger, A. O., Jr. "More Women than Ever May Win Congress Seats." *New York Times* (September 1, 1980): A1.

"A Tribute to Polly Baca." *Congressional Record* 135 (November 8, 1989).

"2 Democrats Seek Party Chairmanship." *New York Times* (February 20, 1981): A21.

"Washington Update: Policy and Politics in Brief." *National Journal* (March 7, 1981): 402.

Weaver, Warren, Jr. "Schroeder Will Run for President If Her Campaign Can Pay for Itself." *New York Times* (June 20, 1987): 8.

Wittenauer, Cheryl. "New Players in an Old Game." *Hispanic Business* 6 (March 1984): 8 + .

3. *Emily Greene Balch*
(1867–1961)

Nobel Peace Prize winner; sociologist; feminist; economist; and advocate for peace

BIOGRAPHICAL INFORMATION

Chronological Biography

Born January 8, 1867, in Jamica Plain, near Boston, Massachusetts, to Ellen Maria (Noyes) and Francis Vergnies Balch. Third of seven daughters and one son in warm, loving family. Parents were liberal New England Unitarians who taught children selflessness and service; Emily pledged herself to service at age ten. Parents both believed in advanced education for women.

1880–1884: Attended secondary school at Miss Catherine Ireland's in Boston where she showed strong leadership abilities. 1884: When Balch was 17, mother, who had been chief influence and center of her life, died. From then on, father was guide and model. 1886–1889: Attended Bryn Mawr College, women's college founded by Quakers, at first studying classics, philosophy, and modern languages, but finding her niche and earning an A.B. in economics as member of first graduating class in 1889. First recipient of school's highest honor, European Fellowship. 1890–1891: Used fellowship to study political economy at Sorbonne in Paris, France. Wishing to gain actual experience, returned to United States to become social worker with Children's Aid Society in Boston. 1892–1893: Became friends with Jane Addams, Katharine Coman, and Vida D. Scudder, at Felix Adler's Summer School of Applied Ethics. Worked for a year as social worker, her work greatly influenced by that of Jane Addams. Helped to found Denison House, one of America's first settlement houses, in Dorchester, Massachusetts, with Vida Scudder, among others. Ran house, which offered camps, clubs, clinics, and other services for neighborhood, from December 1892 until former college classmate, Helena Stuart Dudley, became head in 1893. About this time, having worked closely with those in labor movement, joined Federal Labor Union, part of American Federation of Labor. 1893: Research results from Sorbonne studies, *Public Assistance of the Poor in France*, published by American Economic Association. One of earliest sociological studies of care of poor and disabled. 1893–1896: Having decided she could have more affect on motivation and training of young women to work for social betterment by teaching at college level, resumed education. Financial assistance from father enabled her to study at Harvard Annex (forerunner of Radcliffe) and University of Chicago. One of few women students while at University of Berlin, she travelled for time with Mary Kingsbury Simkhovitch. 1896: Began working part-time at Wellesley College, grading papers for Katharine Coman's economics course. By following semester, was teaching. Promoted to instructor in 1897. Organized school's first sociology class in 1900. Outstanding, innovative teacher in Department of Economics and Sociology who believed in practical investigation as well as classroom work. During years at Wellesley, introduced study of immigrant problems as well as socialism and economic roles of women (advocated that women not drop out of work force entirely when marrying). Made significant contributions to development of sociology in United States. June 1897–October 1898: Member of Boston Municipal Board of Trustees for Children. 1902: Co-founder and president of Boston Women's Trade Union League. 1903:

Promoted to associate professor at Wellesley. **1904–1905:** Studied Slavic emigration areas in Austria-Hungary. **1905–1906:** Visited major Slavic settlements in United States. **1906:** Declared herself a socialist. **1908–1909:** Served on Massachusetts State Commission on Industrial Education. **1909:** Organized socialist conference in Boston with Vida Scudder. **1910:** *Our Slavic Fellow Citizens,* much-acclaimed major study on immigration, published. First major sociological work on immigration. Had done research for work during two year leave (1904–1906). **1912:** Member of Progressive party's committee on immigration. **1913:** Eventually promoted to full professor and chair of political economy and political and social science at Wellesley at age 46 and given a five year appointment. Slow ascent was caused by activities outside classroom which were often unfavorably looked upon by college. Reputation as social scientist, however, was firmly established by this time due to work and well-received writings. Chaired Massachusetts' Minimum Wage Commission which drafted first minimum wage law in country. **1913–1914:** Member of Massachusetts State Commission on Immigration. **1914–1917:** Served on Boston City Planning Board. **1915:** Joined Woman's Peace party after its founding in January. Invited to be part of American delegation to International Congress of Women at The Hague to discuss international peace. She, Jane Addams and 40 other Americans participated, and she was chosen to travel to Scandinavia and Russia to call on statesmen with a proposal for conference of neutral states to act as mediators. Despite all efforts, President Wilson declined to sanction suggestions. **January 1916–1917:** Participated in International Committee on Mediation in Stockholm, supported by Henry Ford, stepping in for an ill Addams. Wrote two proposals for conference. Some of her ideas later were reflected in League of Nations Covenant. Returned to New York City later that year and took unpaid leave from teaching, working with various groups which opposed American intervention in war. One of founders of Emergency Peace Federation and supporter of succeeding organization, People's Council of America. New group was much more radical, calling for new social order, and was increasingly viewed as disloyal. **April 1917:** Testified before House Committee on Judiciary hearings on Espionage and Interference with Neutrality. **May 1919:** Five year appointment had run out in 1918 and, due to pacifist activities, Wellesley trustees refused to renew contract despite faculty and student protest. She did not resist action, although some urged her to prepare civil liberties case on grounds of academic freedom, choosing instead to work for radical magazine, *The Nation,* for about a year to earn living and continue activities. Women's International League for Peace and Freedom (WILPF), formed to study causes of and find alternatives to war, was established by Addams and Balch's help. An outgrowth of International Congress of Women held in Zurich, and also grew from Women's International Committee for Permanent Peace, which had met at 1915 Hague conference, and which Balch had also helped found. Addams was elected president. Balch assumed paid position in new organization as international secretary-treasurer, serving until 1922. Served without pay for 18 months from 1934 to 1935. Edited *Pax et Libertas,* official publication of organization.   1921: Third international congress of WILPF, organized by Balch, held in Vienna. Joined London Society of Friends, Quaker group whose views complemented her own. During this period, moved away from socialism finding it had become too closely identified with Marxism and she did not agree with many Marxist theories.   1922–1925: Resigning from WILPF office due to ill health, continued to actively participate in organization on volunteer basis, developing WILPF branches in over 50 countries, working on disarmament, mediation, etc. While living mainly in Geneva, she also maintained a home in Wellesley, Massachusetts. Due to financial constraints, she occupied wing of house owned by college friends, which she referred to as her domichek ("little house"). Lived frugally while there on little money with occasional help from friends.   1926–1927: Travelled to Haiti under auspices of WILPF with five other Americans, two of them black women, to study conditions in country which had been under U.S. Marine occupation since 1915. Primarily responsible for subsequent report, *Occupied Haiti,* published in 1927, which was highly influential in eventual troop withdrawal.   1931: Became president of American section of WILPF succeeding Jane Addams.   1935: Invited by Wellesley College to be Armistice Day speaker.   1937: Elected honorary international president of WILPF after death of Addams.   **World War II Years:**   Despite pacifist beliefs, supported war against Germany because, having worked with and helped Jewish refugees, felt that Hitler had to be stopped. Worked for rights of interned Japanese Americans. One of 542 signers of letter to President Truman in 1947 urging amnesty for conscientious objectors.   1946: At age 79, awarded Nobel Peace Prize for life work and dedication to peace and justice, thereby also acknowledging role of women in effecting social change. Shared award with John R. Mott, ecumenical leader. Second American woman to win prize, first having been close associate, Jane Addams, who was 1931 recipient. Like Addams, donated most of $17,000 prize money to WILPF and related causes.   **Post World War II:** Continued to work for peace, developing proposals for international administration of air and sea, polar regions, etc., believing that social and economic international cooperation could be extended to political issues and world government, leading to planetary civilization.   1955: Wrote *A Letter to the Chinese People,* a poem about love overcoming differences, in effort to narrow gulf between United States and People's Republic of China. It was translated into Chinese and she was invited to come to China. At age 88, felt she was too old to be useful and so declined.   1959: Cochaired celebration of hundredth anniversary of birth of Jane Addams.   **January 9, 1961:** Her dream of international unity not yet realized, she died in Cambridge, Massachusetts, of pneumonia, on the day after her 94th birthday in Vernon Nursing Home. Had lived there since December 1956, due to old age and lack of money.

> If married women could work some hours a day, or some days a week, or some months a year, or some years and not others, as circumstances indicated ... it would seem advantageous, in more ways than one, for them not to drop out of industry at marriage. Both marriage and employment might become sufficiently universal to make it usual to train every girl for both...
> — Emily Greene Balch, "The Education and Efficiency of Women," Proceedings of the Academy of Political Science. 1, 1910

Background Information

Parents: Ellen Maria (Noyes) and Francis Vergnies Balch. Mother, advanced student at Ipswich Female Academy, was school teacher before marriage. Father successful, distinguished, Harvard educated, Boston lawyer, had been secretary to Charles Sumner, Massachusetts senator and peace leader. **Siblings:** Seven (Catie [died before Emily was born], Bessie, Ellie, Francis, Alice, Annie, Elizabeth). **Children:** None. **Influences:** Jane Addams. **Ethnicity:** English American. **Also known as:** None known. **Historical sites, landmarks, etc.:** None known.

BIBLIOGRAPHICAL INFORMATION

Biographical Sketches About Emily Greene Balch

Garraty, John A., ed. *Dictionary of American Biography.* New York: Charles Scribner's Sons, 1981.
Mainiero, Lina, ed. *American Women Writers.* New York: Frederick Ungar, 1979.
Sicherman, Barbara, and Carol Hurd Green, eds. *Notable American Women: The Modern Period: A Biographical Dictionary.* Cambridge, MA: Belknap Press of Harvard University Press, 1980.
Trattner, Walter I., ed. *Biographical Dictionary of Social Welfare in America.* New York: Greenwood, 1986.
Whitman, Alden, ed. *American Reformers: An H. W. Wilson Biographical Dictionary.* New York: H. W. Wilson Company, 1985.

Books by Emily Greene Balch

Addams, Jane, Emily G. Balch, and Alice Hamilton. *Women at The Hague: The International Congress of Women and Its Results, by Three Delegates to the Congress from the United States, Jane Addams, Emily G. Balch, Alice*

Hamilton. New York: Macmillan, 1915. Reprint. With a new introduction for the Garland edition by Mercedes M. Randall. New York: Garland, 1972.

Approaches to the Great Settlement. Published for the American Union Against Militarism. New York: B. W. Huebsch, 1918.

Balch, Emily Greene, ed. *Occupied Haiti: Being the Report of a Committee of Six Disinterested Americans Representing Organizations Exlusively American, Who, Having Personally Studied Conditions in Haiti in 1926, Favor the Restoration of the Independence of the Negro Republic.* New York: The Writers Publishing Company, 1927. Reprint. With a new introduction for the Garland edition by Mercedes M. Randall. New York: Garland, 1972.

Beyond Nationalism: The Social Thought of Emily Greene Balch. Edited by Mercedes M. Randall. New York: Twayne, [1972].

Manual for Use in Cases of Juvenile Offenders and Other Minors in Massachusetts 1895, Revised 1903 and 1908. Boston: Conference of Child-Helping Societies, 1908.

The Miracle of Living. New York: Island, 1941.

Our Slavic Fellow Citizens. New York: Charities Publication Committee, 1910. Reprint, New York: Arno, 1969.

Outline of Economics. Cambridge: Co-Operative Press, 1899.

Public Assistance of the Poor in France. [Baltimore]: American Economic Association, 1893.

Statement of Facts Concerning the Women's International League in Regard to Certain Misrepresentations. Washington, D. C.: Women's International League, [192?].

The Strike of the Shoe Workers in Marlboro, Mass., November 14, 1898–May 5, 1899: A Report, Prepared for the Civic Department of the Twentieth Century Club of Boston, by the Following Committee: F. Spencer Baldwin, Emily G. Balch, William L. Rutan. [N.p.]: n.p., 1899?]. Reprint. Boston: Boston Co-operative, n.d.

A Study of Conditions of City Life, With Special Reference to Boston. Boston: Geo. H. Ellis Company, 1903.

Toward Human Unity or Beyond Nationalism: [Nobel Lecture, Delivered at Oslo, April 7th, 1948]. Stockholm: P. A. Norstedt, 1949.

A Venture in Internationalism. Geneva: Maison Internationale, 1938.

Vignettes in Prose. Philadelphia: Women's International League for Peace and Freedom, 1952.

Books About Emily Greene Balch

Randall, John Herman. *Emily Greene Balch of New England, Citizen of the World.* Washington, D. C.: Women's International League for Peace and Freedom, [1946?].

Randall, Mercedes (Moritz). *Improper Bostonian: Emily Greene Balch, Nobel Peace Laureate, 1946.* New York: Twayne, 1964.

Shane, Martha P. *Papers of Emily Greene Balch, 1875–1961: Guide to the Scholarly Resources.* Wilmington, DE: Scholarly Resources, 1988.

Shorter Works by Emily Greene Balch

Addams, Jane. *Peace and Bread in Time of War*. New York: King's Crown, 1945.
(New introductory essay by John Dewey and new appendix by Emily Greene
Balch and Mercedes Randall.)
Addams, Jane, and E. G. Balch. "Is a United Peace Front Desirable?" *Survey
Graphic* 23 (February 1934): 60 + .
"Apponyi and the Slovak Demonstrations." *Survey* 26 (May 13, 1911): 271–72.
"Economic Rule of the Housewife." *Home Progress* 4 (September 1914): 620–24.
"Education and Efficiency of Women." *Proceedings of the Academy of Political
Science* 1 (October 1910): 61–71.
"Flag Speaks; poem." *Christian Century* 49 (May 25, 1932): 666.
"French Women and Peace." *Nation* 103 (October 26, 1916): 396–97.
"Getting Some Reading Done." *Home Progress* 3 (February 1914): 291–97.
"Housework, English and Immigrants." *Journal of Home Economics* 6 (December
1914): 447–49.
"In the Balance." *Survey* 37 (February 17, 1917): 565–66.
"International Congress of Women at The Hague." *Home Progress* 5 (November
1915): 110–13.
"The Lesson of the Past, the Challenge of the Future." *Four Lights* 5 (May 1945).
"Letter to China; poem." *Nation* 180 (May 14, 1955): 418.
"The Life of Helena Stuart Dudley." In *A Heart That Held the World: An Appraisal
of the Life of Helena Stuart Dudley and a Memorial to Her Work*. Boston: n.p.,
1939.
"Little Neighbor Haiti." *Survey* (March 15, 1930): 708.
"Myth of Military Security." *World Tomorrow* 10 (December 1927): 496–97.
"One Europe; with biographical note. *Survey Graphic* 36 (February 1947):
148–51 + .
"Our Slavic Fellow Citizens." Parts 1–8. *Charities and the Commons* 18, 19 (April 6,
May 4, June 1, July 6, September 7, October 5, November 2, December 7,
1907): 11–22, 166–69, 259–67, 365–77, 676–90, 773–84, 969–79, 1162–74.
"Peace Delegates in Scandinavia and Russia." *Survey* 34 (September 4, 1915): 506–
08.
"Peace Must Be Waged." *Collier's* 136 (December 23, 1955): 31.
"Peasant Background of Our Slavic Fellow Citizens." *Survey* 24 (August 6, 1910):
666–77.
"Polar Regions as Part of One World." *Survey Graphic* 37 (September 1948): 392–
93.
"Public Assistance of the Poor in France." *American Economic Association Publi-
cations* 8 (July and September 1893): 263–451.
"Racial Contacts and Cohesions." *Survey* 33 (March 6, 1915): 610–11.
"Shepherd of Immigrants." *Charities and the Commons* 13 (December 3, 1904):
193–94.
"Slav Emigration at its Source." Parts 1–8. *Charities and the Commons* 15, 16
(January 6, February 3, March 3, April 7, May 5, June 2, July 7, September
1, 1906): 438–41, 591–602, 832–39; 71–79, 171–83, 321–28, 435–43, 541–49.

"Stockholm Conference." *New Republic* 8 (September 9, 1916): 141–42.
"Tax Reform in France." *Nation* 52 (January 15, 1891): 47–48.
"Time to Make Peace." *Survey* 35 (October 2, 1915): 24–25.
"True Story of a Bohemian Pioneer." *Chautauquan* 49 (February 1908): 397–403.
"UN and the Waters of the World." *Survey Graphic* 36 (October 1947): 529–30.
"War in its Relation to Democracy and World Order." *Annals of the American Academy of Political and Social Science* 72 (July 1917): 28–31.
"Western Civilization and the Birth-rate." *American Journal of Sociology* 12 (March 1907): 623–26.
"What the Poor Need Is Income." *Survey* 30 (September 27, 1918): 755–56.
"Why Cooperation Is Not Enough." *Co-operation* 11 (November 1925): 208–10.
"Women for Peace and Freedom." *Survey Graphic* 35 (October 1946): 358–60.
"Yelia Hertzka—In Memoriam." *Four Lights* 8 (February 1949).

Shorter Works About Emily Greene Balch

"A for Effort; Nobel Awards." *Time* 48 (November 26, 1946): 33.
Abrams, Irwin. *The Nobel Peace Prize and the Laureates: An Illustrated Biographical History, 1901–1987.* Boston: G. K. Hall, 1988.
"Article on the Fund and its Status." *Four Lights* 16 (January 1957): 4.
Baker, Adelaide N. "Planetary New Englander." *New-England Galaxy* 13 (1971): 46–52.
"Biography." *Current Biography* 8 (January 1947): 3–5.
Bussey, Gertrude Carman, and Margaret Tims. *Women's International League for Peace and Freedom, 1915–1965: A Record of Fifty Years' Work.* London: Allen & Unwin, 1965.
Deegan, Mary Jo. "Sociology at Wellesley College: 1900–1919." *Journal of the History of Sociology* 5 (1983): 91–117.
"Emily Greene Balch Number." *Four Lights* (January 1947).
"The First Lady of the WIL." *Four Lights* 11 (January 195?): 1+.
Gillmor, Dan. "Emily Balch, Crusader." *Nation* 180 (May 14, 1955): 417–18.
Gray, Tony. *Champions of Peace: The Story of Alfred Nobel, the Peace Prize and the Laureates.* [New York]: Paddington, 1976.
"Miss Balch on the Ford Peace Conference." *Survey* 36 (July 29, 1916): 444.
"Nobel Lecture, April 7, 1948." *Bulletin of the Atomic Scientists* 35 (April 1979): 1.
"Obituary." *Americana Annual 1962* (1962): 847.
"Obituary." *Newsweek* 57 (January 23, 1961): 63.
"Obituary." *Time* 77 (January 20, 1961): 78.
Opfell, Olga S. *The Lady Laureates: Women Who Have Won the Nobel Prize.* Metuchen, NJ: Scarecrow, 1986.
"Pioneer for Peace." *Bryn Mawr Alumnae Bulletin* (Winter 1956): 2–4.
"Portrait." *Senior Scholastic* 49 (December 2, 1946): 16.
Randall, J. H., Jr. "Emily Greene Balch; Awarded the Nobel Peace Price." *Nation* 164 (January 4, 1947): 14–15.
"Seventh Annual Unitarian Award: Emily Greene Balch." *Christian Register* (July 1955): 20.

"She Lived for Humanity." *Christian Century* 78 (January 25, 1961): 101.
"Surprise, Surprise." *Newsweek* 34 (October 21, 1974): 49.
"A Tribute to Emily Greene Balch." *Four Lights* 16 (January 1957): 2–3.
"Where Are They Now?" *Newsweek* 49 (February 11, 1957): 20.
White's Biographical Bulletin 9 (November 1946).

Other Works About Emily Greene Balch

Theses

Cook, Blanche Wiesen. "Woodrow Wilson and the Antimilitarists, 1914–1917."
    Ph. D. diss., Johns Hopkins University, 1970.
Huber, Lois Elaine. "Three Studies in English: Evidence of Chaucer's Learning
    in the House of Fame; Bertrand Russell: A letter to Emily Greene Balch;
    Freneau's Deism: Princeton and Thereafter." Master's thesis, Pennsylvania
    State University, 1971.
Palmieri, Patricia Ann. "In Adamless Eden: A Social Portrait of the Academic
    Community at Wellesley College 1875–1920." EDD diss., Harvard Univer-
    sity, 1981.
Steinson, Barbara Jean. "Female Activism in World War I: The American
    Women's Peace, Suffrage, Preparedness, and Relief Movements, 1914–1919."
    Ph.D. diss., University of Michigan, 1977.

Primary Source Materials Relating to Emily Greene Balch

Emily Greene Balch. Papers. 1842–1979. Extent of collection: 25.75 lin. ft. Find-
    ing aids: Checklist available in repository. Location: Swarthmore College,
    Peace Collection, Swarthmore, Pennsylvania 19081. Scope of collection:
    Correspondence (1875–1961); diaries (1876–1955); books and poetry by Balch;
    draft of autobiography and interviews with Mercedes M. Randall (1951); ar-
    ticles about Balch including Nobel Peace Prize publicity; research notes and
    subject files. Microfilm available.
Emily Greene Balch. Papers. 1915–1947 (inclusive). Extent of collection: 2 folders.
    Finding aids: Unpublished finding aid. Location: Schlesinger Library, Rad-
    cliffe College, Cambridge, Massachusetts 02138. Scope of collection: "Index
    to Civic Organizations in Boston, 1915" by Balch and typed letter, 1947.
Erin-Go-Bragh. Records. 1894–1953 (inclusive). Extent of collection: .5 lin. ft. Find-
    ing aids: Unpublished finding aid. Location: Schlesinger Library, Radcliffe
    College, Cambridge, Massachusetts 02138. Scope of collection: Club founded
    in 1889 by women who had studied at Miss Ireland's school, including Emily
    Greene Balch.
Jane Addams. Papers. 1838–1959. Extent of collection: 59 ft. Finding aids: Catalog
    of correspondence and checklist in library. Location: Friends Historical
    Library, Swarthmore College, Peace Collection, Swarthmore, Pennsylvania
    19081. Scope of collection: Correspondence, manuscripts of writings, pam-
    phlets, and clippings relating to the Women's International League for Peace

and Freedom, rights of women and children, some material on Hull House.

John Herman Randall. Papers. 1911-1977. Extent of collection: ca. 25,400 items. Finding aids: Not listed. Location: Columbia University Libraries, 116th St. and Broadway, New York, New York 10027. Scope of collection: Mercedes Randall's papers include material relating to her work with Women's International League for Peace and Freedom and her book, *Improper Bostonian: Emily Greene Balch* (1946).

Massachusetts Peace Society. Records. 1911-1917. Extent of collection: ca. 6 ft. Finding aids: Not listed. Location: Swarthmore College, Peace Collection, Swarthmore, Pennsylvania 19081. Scope of collection: Includes correspondence (1915-1917) of Emily Greene Balch relating to the Society.

Women's International League for Peace and Freedom. Records. 1915-ca. 1976. Extent of collection: ca. 234 ft. Finding aids: Published guide and detailed inventory. Location: Swarthmore College, Peace Collection, Swarthmore, Pennsylvania 19081. Scope of collection: Records of international office of WILPF 1920-1976, material concerning all congresses to 1965, and archives of U.S. section. Microfilm available.

4. *Kate Barnard*
(1874?-1930)

First U.S. woman to win election to state office; labor organizer; and advocate for Native American rights and child welfare

BIOGRAPHICAL INFORMATION

Chronological Biography

Born May 23, 1874/5, in Geneva, Nebraska, only child of Rachel (Shiell) and John P. Barnard; christened Catherine Ann. Mother had been widowed and had two sons by former marriage.

January 1876/7: Mother and week-old newborn died; 18-month-old Kate and two step-brothers were sent by father to live with relatives, probably maternal grandparents, in Kansas.   **1880?-1903:** Rejoined father after his remarriage. Father's wife left him about two years later. When she was about 14, father left her, supposedly with strangers, to pursue land in Oklahoma Territory, newly opened to white settlers. Rejoined father at age 16 and lived on 160 acre farm outside Oklahoma City. Graduated from St. Joseph's Academy, parochial high school in Oklahoma City, and taught in rural public schools for three years. About this time she and father were living in slum district of Oklahoma City where she was exposed to effects of unemployment and poverty. Later took short business course and worked as stenographer in city. Introduction to politics came when she was chosen to be assistant to chief clerk to Democratic minority of territorial legislature at Guthrie; during this time she made valuable political friendships. **1904:** While working at World's Fair in St. Louis as hostess and secretary for Oklahoma Territory's pavilion, wrote light letters for *Daily Oklahoman,* local paper back home, thus coming to attention of paper's editor, Roy Stafford, who proceeded to support her career. Having seen negative side of industrialization and urbanization while in St. Louis — child labor, poor working conditions, etc. — began reform efforts by again writing letters to *Daily Oklahoman,* this time dealing with need for Oklahoma to move to prevent such conditions; with Stafford's help, letters received much attention. **1905–1907:** Due to interest generated by letters, appointed matron in charge of United Provident Association of Oklahoma City in December. Through this charitable organization, supported by business and church leaders, she not only directed relief efforts, but also campaigned for higher city workers' wages. Formed Federal Labor Union of city's jobless citizens and was elected to represent it in Oklahoma City Trades and Labor Assembly. Union, affiliated with American Federation of Labor, was effective in municipal elections. Organized and became secretary of Oklahoma chapter of Women's International Union Label League; group sought to educate people and to urge them to buy union products. Believed that elimination of poverty and suffering could only be accomplished through unionization, higher wages and use of union-made products, in addition to education of children. **1906:** To help gain public support for social reform legislation in Oklahoma, Stafford sent Barnard to eastern United States to interview and obtain written endorsements from leading social reformers, such as Jane Addams, to print in his newspaper. Became more well-known through her actions as an AFL delegate at "Shawnee Convention," a meeting held by various union groups to send their suggestions for consideration at state constitutional convention, pushing through planks on child labor and compulsory education; ideas were subsequently incorporated into Democratic platform. In addition, elective office of Commissioner of Charities and Corrections, also her plan, (she referred to it as "his or her office"), was created; resigned her Provident Association office to campaign for post. Women's suffrage plank, in which she had no interest, was defeated. **1907:** Conducted vigorous campaign, winning votes with strong, emotional speeches and attractive appearance; received more votes than any other candidate, despite fact that women could not yet vote in state. Elected first Commissioner of Charities and Corrections for state of Oklahoma; at 32 became first woman in United States elected to major state office. Speaker at National Conference of Charities and Correction. **1908:** Oklahoma had been sending its prisoners to Kansas, paying fee for housing them rather than building its own prisons. Hearing reports of brutality and exploitation, she paid unannounced visit to Kansas State Penitentiary in Lansing. Her scathing report of appalling conditions brought about much needed prison reform in Kansas, building of prisons in Oklahoma, and reform in Arizona in 1911 as well. Later succeeded in having first time offenders separated from repeaters and effected other prison reforms. Addressed national audience in Atlanta at fourth annual meeting of National Child Labor Committee. Continued to lecture widely on national level responding to invitations from unions, schools, social workers, prison officials, reform and charity conventions, etc., throughout tenure as commissioner. Spoke at Sixth International Congress on Tuberculosis in Washington, D. C., in fall of year regarding harm to children working in cotton mills, etc. **1909:** Oklahoma's Child Labor Law was passed; she had written legislation implementing the law. Elected first vice president of newly formed Southern Conference on Woman and Child labor. Father died in May. **1910:** Ordered to rest; spent some time in Colorado Rockies. Reelected commissioner of Charities and Corrections, again winning more votes than any other candidate. Spoke at National Editorial Association in New Orleans, and Southern Textile Conference in Memphis. **1911:** American delegate to International Prison Congress in Rome. **1911–1913:** Began investigation of defrauding of Native American orphans by white guardians. Her office secured the return in 1912 of almost $950,000 to 1,361 minors. This intrusion into a sensitive area led directly to her downfall as her formerly supportive political friends deserted her and legislature cut heavily into her funds, staff and support, early in 1913. Lost much time to illness, nearly six months in 1911 and a number of months in 1912. Suffered complete nervous breakdown in 1913. **1912:** First Southern Sociological Congress was organized by governor of Tennessee at her suggestion to promote racial understanding and progressive legislation. Speaker at Governors' Conference in Richmond, Virginia; advocated uniform child labor law. **1913:** Addressed National Governors' Conference. American delegate to International Tuberculosis Congress in Copenhagen. **1914:** As result of harassment by legislature and ill health, she did not seek reelection, instead retiring at age 39 as commissioner, although number of labor groups sought to employ her as Washington, D. C., lobbyist. Organized People's Lobby to influence government policy; group campaigned successfully against many candidates who were against her reform measures. Had been highly effective commissioner, instituting reforms in mental health care, widows' pensions, union blacklisting, labor legislation, prison reform, and compulsory education. Her success in accomplishing so much in short period of time can be traced to her pattern of persuading experts to draft bills, gaining the support of the affected groups, lobbying for public support, and then presenting proposals to legislature for action. She was never a supporter of woman suffrage, due to father's opposition and her own feeling of never having needed it since she had been able to achieve her goals without it, working on those with it, until they abandoned her. Managed real estate properties left to her by father.   **March 1915:** Spoke on floor of Oklahoma senate, first woman ever to do so, pleading cause of Native American minors. 1915–1922: Employed in Denver by longtime judge friend as juvenile court case worker. Became ill and retired.   **February 23, 1930:** Found dead at age 54 in hotel in which she lived in Oklahoma City; cause of death was not recorded but she suffered from heart trouble and had also spent much time in hospitals and clinics for treatment of hay fever and unspecified, disfiguring skin disease. On day of funeral, state flag was lowered to half-mast and all seven men who had been governor of Oklahoma were honorary pallbearers. She was buried in unmarked grave next to father's grave in Oklahoma City's Rosehill Cemetery, with 1400 people at funeral mass.   **1982:** Small stone bearing the inscription "Intrepid pioneer leader for social ethics in Oklahoma" placed on her grave by group wanting to honor her service to state.

Background Information

Parents: Rachel (Shiell) and John P. Barnard. Father was lawyer and surveyor of Irish descent, originally from Mississippi. Parents were married in Canada. **Siblings:** Two (No known names). **Children:** None. **Influences:** Roy Stafford. **Ethnicity:** Irish American. **Also known as:** None known. **Historical sites, landmarks, etc.:** Grave, Rosehill Cemetery, Oklahoma City, Oklahoma.

BIBLIOGRAPHICAL INFORMATION

Biographical Sketches About Kate Barnard

James, Edward T., ed. *Notable American Women 1607–1950: A Biographical Dictionary.* Cambridge, MA: Belknap Press of Harvard University Press, 1971.
Lamar, Howard R., ed. *The Reader's Encyclopedia of the American West.* New York: Thomas Y. Crowell, 1977.
McHenry, Robert, ed. *Famous American Women.* New York: Dover, 1980.
Trattner, Walter I., ed. *Biographical Dictionary of Social Welfare in America.* New York: Greenwood, 1986.
Whitman, Alden, ed. *American Reformers: An H. W. Wilson Biographical Dictionary.* New York: H. W. Wilson Company, 1985.
Zophy, Angela Howard, ed. *Handbook of American Women's History.* New York: Garland, 1990.

Shorter Works by Kate Barnard

"Fighting the Lease System with Pardons." *Survey* 29 (January 1913): 457–58.
"For the Orphans of Oklahoma." *Survey* 33 (November 7, 1914): 154–55.
"Human Ideals in Government." *Survey* 23 (October 2, 1909): 16–20.
"The New State and Its Children." In *Child Labor and Social Progress, Proceedings of the Fourth Annual Meeting of the National Child Labor Committee.* Philadelphia: American Academy of Political and Social Science, 1908.
"Shaping the Destinies of the New State." In *Official Proceedings of the National Conference of Charities and Corrections at the Thirty-Fifth Annual Session.* Fort Wayne: Fort Wayne Printing Company, 1908.
"'Stump' Ashby Saves the Day." *Journal of the West* 12 (1973): 296–306.
"Through the Windows of Destiny: How I Visualized My Life Work." *Good Housekeeping* 55 (November 1912): 600–06.
"Working for the Friendless." *Independent* 63 (November 28, 1907): 1307–08.

Shorter Works About Kate Barnard

Bennett, Helen Christine. *American Women in Civic Work.* New York: Dodd, Mead, and Company, 1915.
Bryant, Keith L., Jr. "The Juvenile Court Movement: Oklahoma as a Case Study." *Social Science Quarterly* 49 (September 1968): 368–76.
_____. "Kate Barnard, Organized Labor, and Social Justice in Oklahoma During the Progressive Era." *Journal of Southern History* 35 (1969): 145–64.
_____. "Labor in Politics: The Oklahoma State Federation of Labor During the Age of Reform." *Labor History* 2 (Summer 1970): 260–64.
Conley, John A. "Revising Conceptions about the Origin of Prisons: The Importance of Economic Considerations." *Social Science Quarterly* 62 (June 1981): 247–58.
Eaton, C. "Breaking a Path for the Liberation of Women in the South." *Georgia Review* 28 (Summer 1974): 195–96.
Hougen, Harvey R. "The Impact of Politics and Prison Industry on the General Management of the Kansas State Penitentiary, 1883–1909." *Kansas Historical Quarterly* 43 (1977): 297–318.
_____. "Kate Barnard and the Kansas Penitentiary Scandal, 1908–1909." *Journal of the West* 17 (January 1978): 9–18.
Hunt, W. P. "Appreciation of Miss Barnard." *Good Housekeeping* 55 (November 1912): 606–07.
Johnson, A. "Commissioner of Charities in Oklahoma." *Survey* 30 (April 26, 1913): 138–39.
Leavitt, J. "Man in the Cage." *American Magazine* 73 (March 1912): 538–42.
McKelway, A. J. "'Kate', the 'Good Angel' of Oklahoma." *American Magazine* 66 (October 1908): 591+.
_____. "'Kate', the 'Good Angel' of Oklahoma." In *Lives to Remember,* edited by Leon Stein. New York: Arno, 1974.

Peavy, Linda S. *Women Who Changed Things.* New York: Scribner, 1983.
"Portrait." *World To-Day* 13 (October 1907): 965.
"She Is Uplifting Oklahoma." *Literary Digest* 46 (January 11, 1913): 108.
"Sketch." *Charities and the Commons* 18 (July 6, 1907): 389–91.
Thoburn, Joseph Bradfield. *Standard History of Oklahoma.* Chicago: American Historical Society, 1916.
Truman, Margaret. *Women of Courage.* New York: Bantam, 1977.

Other Works About Kate Barnard

Theses

Conley, John A. "History of the Oklahoma Penal System, 1907–1967." Ph.D. diss., Michigan State University, 1977.
Short, Julia A. "Kate Barnard: Liberated Woman." Master's thesis, University of Oklahoma, 1970.

Primary Source Materials Relating to Kate Barnard

Charles L. Daugherty. Papers. 1907–1913. Extent of collection: .66 ft. Finding aids: Not listed. Location: Western History Collections, University of Oklahoma, 630 Parrington Oval, Room 452, Norman, Oklahoma 73019. Scope of collection: Correspondence, circulars, pamphlets, and labor regulations while Daugherty was serving as Oklahoma's first Commissioner of Labor.

Fayette Copeland. Papers. 1841–1961. Extent of collection: 5.5 ft. Finding aids: Inventory available in repository. Location: Western History Collections, University of Oklahoma, 630 Parrington Oval, Room 452, Norman, Oklahoma 73019. Scope of collection: Research notes concerning Barnard. Also contains notes Barnard planned to use in a book about early Oklahoma history and her own life.

J. B. A. (James Brooks Ayers) Robertson. Papers. 1903–1938. Extent of collection: 4 ft. Finding aids: Inventory available in repository. Location: Western History Collections, University of Oklahoma, 630 Parrington Oval, Room 452, Norman, Oklahoma 73019. Scope of collection: Governor of Oklahoma. Correspondence regarding the Oklahoma Constitutional Convention of 1906, etc.

John Robert Williams. Papers. 1906–1910. Extent of collection: .45 ft. Finding aids: Inventory available in repository. Location: Western History Collections, University of Oklahoma, 630 Parrington Oval, Room 452, Norman, Oklahoma 73019. Scope of collection: Political campaign manager. Correspondence, telegrams, publications, regarding election campaigns for governorship of Oklahoma, etc.

Julee A. (Julia A.) Short Collection. Extent of collection: 5 cu. ft. Finding aids:

Not listed. Location: Oklahoma Department of Libraries, Archives and Records Division, 200 Northeast 18th St., Oklahoma City, Oklahoma 73105-3298. Scope of collection: Includes primary and secondary historical materials regarding Barnard. Prior written permission from donor is required before viewing. Microfilm available.

Kate Barnard Collection. Extent of collection: Not listed. Finding aids: Not listed. Location: Archives and Manuscripts Division, Oklahoma Historical Society, Wiley Post Historical Building, Oklahoma City, Oklahoma 73105. Scope of collection: Not listed.

Oklahoma Department of Charities and Corrections. Records. 1907–1949. Extent of collection: 16 cu. ft. Finding aids: Guide in repository. Location: Oklahoma Department of Libraries, Archives and Records Division, 200 Northeast 18th St., Oklahoma City, Oklahoma 73105-3298. Scope of collection: Administrative files of department pertaining to meetings, inspections, and investigations. Bulk of records document work of Barnard.

Walter Lowrie Fisher. Papers. 1879–1936. Extent of collection: 19 ft. (ca. 14,000 items). Finding aids: Indexed in part. Published register. Location: Library of Congress, Manuscript Division, Washington, D. C. 20540. Scope of collection: Includes material relating to Oklahoma Indians. Correspondents include Barnard.

5. *Charlotta A. Spears Bass*
(1880?–1969)

Editor; journalist; publisher; 1952 Progressive party
vice presidential candidate; and advocate for African American rights

BIOGRAPHICAL INFORMATION

Chronological Biography

Born October 1880?, in Sumter, South Carolina, to Kate and Hiram Spears, sixth of 11 children, third of four daughters.

Before 1890: Moved to Providence, Rhode Island, to live with oldest brother, Ellis. Employed by local newspaper, *Providence Watchman*, as office clerk and advertising solicitor. **September 10, 1910:** Relocated to Los Angeles for health reasons, planning to stay for two years, but remained lifelong resident of California. **1910–1912:** Hired at salary of $5 per week by Los

Angeles newspaper, *The Eagle*, to collect and solicit subscriptions. Publication was oldest black paper on West Coast, started in 1879 by John Neimore. As Neimore's health declined, she began to run the paper. **May 1912:** Captain G. W. Hawkins, second-hand store owner, bought paper for $50 when it was sold at auction after Neimore died. Hawkins gave newspaper to her to publish; she was to repay him in future. Began including social news to attract subscribers from rival paper, but primary focus remained on issues important to black community such as discrimination, police mistreatment, corruption, etc. Suffered extreme financial hardship but continued to publish paper. **1912–1934:** Joseph B. Bass became editor of paper; had been one of founders of Kansas paper, *Topeka Plaindealer.* Paper's name was changed to *California Eagle* to reflect broadening coverage. Spears and Bass were married; she assumed duties of managing editor, and they increased fight against segregation, discrimination in housing and employment against blacks and other minorities, etc. **1916:** Called for making of the film *Birth of a Nation* to stop, believing it would adversely affect race relations. **1917:** Spoke out against injustice to black soldiers in Houston race riots. Backed creation of Progressive Educational Association, one of first interracial organizations to defend rights of blacks and other minorities. **1919:** Attended Pan-African Conference in Paris. **Early 1920s:** Co-president of Los Angeles division of Marcus Garvey's United Negro Improvement Association. **1925:** As longtime, vigorous opponents of the Ku Klux Klan, the Basses were charged with libel, but *California Eagle* was vindicated in trial. **1930s:** Helped to organize Industrial Business Council to fight discrimination in employment and encourage blacks to enter business. West Coast promoter of "Don't Buy Where You Can't Work" campaign. **1934–1951:** Joseph Bass died. She continued to run paper, stepping up civil rights efforts in mid-forties, waging war on Klan, fighting for fair employment practices and crusading against southern lynchings. **1940:** Western regional director for Republican presidential candidate Wendell Willkie's campaign. **World War II:** Christened ship named *James Weldon Johnson.* **1943:** First black to serve on county grand jury. **1945:** Helped to found, and served as chair of, Home Protective Association, militant integrated organization which worked to defend right of blacks to live in formerly all-white neighborhoods and to end restrictive covenants. Due to activities, was brought in June before Tenney Committee, California version of House Committee on Un–American Activities. Calling for black representation on Los Angeles City Council, ran unsuccessfully in seventh district as an independent "people's candidate." **1947–1948:** Republican up to now, but because of her disenchantment with Republican and Democratic parties regarding civil rights and peace issues, was one of founding members of Progressive Party. One of three co-chairs of national "Women for Wallace," campaigned for the Progressive Party's Wallace/Taylor 1948 ticket. **October 27, 1949:** Named one of ten most outstanding women in area by Hadassah; the first black woman to be honored.   **1950:** Opposed the Korean War along with others in Progressive Party. Member of Defenders of the Peace Committee of World Congress in Paris and Prague, supporting "Stockholm Appeal" which called for banning of atomic bomb. Delegate to World Student Congress in Prague; visited Soviet Union. Failed to win seat in race for Congress in 14th District of Los Angeles on Progressive Party ticket.   **April 26, 1951:** Retired from *California Eagle*. Had provided jobs and training for many young blacks during her tenure to encourage them to enter journalism profession. Later, in garage of her Los Angeles home, maintained library for neighborhood youths.   **1952:** National chair of organization of black women (Sojourners for Truth and Justice) protesting racial violence in South. At age 62, unanimously nominated vice presidential candidate of Progressive Party, becoming first black and first woman to run for this office in the United States. Vincent Hallinan, California attorney noted for civil liberties cases, was presidential candidate. One of her campaign themes was "Win or lose, we win by raising the issues," another was "Let my people go." Received only 140,023 popular votes, 0.2 percent of votes cast. Some votes may have been lost as many felt voting for third party to be "waste" of their vote. Campaign, however, was a significant one as many important issues were addressed, including those regarding civil rights (equal job opportunities for minorities, equal pay for women, federal anti-poll tax and anti-lynching laws, etc.), and foreign affairs (end to war in Korea and recognition of People's Republic of China, among others). Third party was seen by many in media as being "leftist"; majority of their support came from more radical elements of country. One article called slate "shocking pink," and vigorously conducted campaign drew comments as she attacked records and activities of Richard Nixon and John Sparkman, two other vice presidential candidates.   **1960:** Published autobiography, *Forty Years: Memoirs from the Pages of a Newspaper*, which also discusses her paper's role in public events between 1912 and 1951.   **1965:** *California Eagle* ceased publication.   **April 12, 1969:** Died in Los Angeles from stroke suffered in 1967. Buried in Evergreen Cemetery. Had been active community leader and member of many black organizations, including National Association for the Advancement of Colored People (NAACP), Pan-African Congress and Council of African Affairs.

Background Information

Parents: Kate and Hiram Spears.   **Siblings:** Ten (Known names: Ellis, Edmond, Lillian Spears Carter).   **Children:** None.   **Influences:** Joseph B. Bass.   **Ethnicity:** African American.   **Also known as:** None known.   **Historical sites, landmarks, etc.:** Grave, Evergreen Cemetery, Los Angeles, California.

BIBLIOGRAPHICAL INFORMATION

Biographical Sketches About Charlotta A. Spears Bass

Morris, Dan, and Inez Morris. *Who Was Who In American Politics.* New York: Hawthorn, 1974.

Page, James A., and Jae Min Roh, comps. *Selected Black American, African, and Caribbean Authors: A Bio-Bibliography.* Littleton, CO.: Libraries Unlimited, 1985.

Ploski, Harry A., and James Williams, eds. and comps. *The Negro Almanac: A Reference Work on the African American.* Detroit: Gale Research, 1989.

Sicherman, Barbara, and Carol Hurd Green, eds. *Notable American Women: The Modern Period.* Cambridge, MA: Belknap Press of Harvard University Press, 1980.

Smith, Jessie Carney, ed. *Notable Black American Women.* Detroit: Gale Research, 1992.

Books by Charlotta A. Spears Bass

Forty Years: Memoirs from the Pages of a Newspaper. Los Angeles: Charlotta A. Bass, 1960.

Shorter Works About Charlotta A. Spears Bass

"Charlotta A. Bass Final Rites Friday." *Los Angeles Sentinel* (April 17, 1969): 1 + .

"Charlotta Bass: 'It Is the Call of All My People and to My People'." *National Guardian* 4 (April 2, 1952): 3.

Gill, Gerald R. "'Win or Lose—We Win': The 1952 Vice Presidential Campaign of Charlotta A. Bass." In *The Afro-American Woman: Struggles and Images,* edited by Sharon Harley and Rosalyn Terborg-Penn. Port Washington, NY: Kennikat, 1978.

"Hallinan Assails 'Imperialist' War." *New York Times* (October 28, 1952): 17.

"Hallinan Opens His '52 Campaign." *New York Times* (September 7, 1952): 46.

"I Accept This Call." In *Black Women in White America,* edited by Gerda Lerner. New York: Vintage, 1973.

"Progressive Candidates: Hallinan, West Coast Attorney, is Proposed for President." *New York Times* (March 7, 1952): 12.

"Progressive Rally Held." *New York Times* (March 24, 1952): 17.

"Progressives Get Place on Ballot." *New York Times* (March 24, 1952): 17.

Schmidt, Karl M. *Henry A. Wallace, Quixotic Crusade 1948.* [Syracuse, NY]: Syracuse University Press, 1960.

"Shocking Pink." *Time* 59 (March 17, 1952): 20.

Primary Source Materials Relating to Charlotta A. Spears Bass

California Eagle. Records. 1920–1965. Extent of collection: Not listed. Finding aids: No guide. Location: Southern California Library for Social Studies and Research, 6120 S. Vermont Ave., Los Angeles, California 90044. Scope of collection: Includes copies of *California Eagle*.

Calvin Benham Baldwin. Papers. 1933–1975. Extent of collection: 30 ft. Finding aids: Unpublished inventory. Location: University of Iowa Libraries, Iowa City, Iowa 52242-1098. Scope of collection: Baldwin was national secretary of Progressive Party. Correspondents include Bass.

Charlotta Bass. Extent of collection: Not listed. Finding aids: Not listed. Location: Schomburg Center for Research in Black Culture, 515 Malcolm X Blvd., New York, New York 10037. Scope of collection: Clipping file.

Charlotta Bass. Extent of collection: Not listed. Finding aids: Not listed. Location: Moorland-Spingarn Research Center Library, 500 Howard Pl. NW, Washington, D.C. 20059. Scope of collection: Clipping file.

6. *Daisy Bates*
(1920?–   )

Advocate for African American rights; journalist; and publisher

BIOGRAPHICAL INFORMATION

Chronological Biography

1920?: Grew up in small sawmill town of Huttig in southeast Arkansas. Learned at age eight that biological mother had been raped and murdered by white men after refusing their sexual demands, and that father had left her in care of his closest friends, the Gatsons, and disappeared. Foster parents shielded her from discrimination as long as possible then tried to help her to understand and accept situation. When she became deeply angry and rebellious due to harsh treatment by whites, parents sent her on trip to northern cities and Canada so that she could experience blacks and whites living in different, more harmonious circumstances. Attended school for blacks in rundown building in hometown; continued education in Memphis. 1939: Foster father died of cancer. Had influenced her to channel her anger and work toward solutions, rather than to hate all whites indiscriminately. 1941: At about 17, married family friend Lucius Christopher (L. C.) Bates, insurance agent many years her senior; moved to Little Rock. Husband had been born in Mississippi, grew up in Ohio, and majored in journalism at

Wilberforce College; had worked for a number of newspapers and wished to resume career. Couple founded and edited weekly newspaper, *Arkansas State Press*, and began crusade against discrimination, segregation, police brutality, etc. Readership grew rapidly; paper became very influential with both black and white readers; Bateses gained prominence and financial security. Attended Shorter and Philander Smith colleges in Little Rock while husband took business courses at Shorter College. She eventually became affiliated with 22 organizations. Both joined National Association for the Advancement of Colored People (NAACP); she was co-chair of its State Conference's Committee for Fair Employment Practices. **March 1942:** Her vivid article detailing killing of black soldier from nearby military post galvanized black community; black leaders organized protest meetings. White store owners, benefitting from soldiers' business, attempted to suppress incident. Despite losing most advertising revenue, and in danger of closure, Bateses persisted and stepped up publicity. Circulation finally began to rise as blacks found voice in paper; some small advertisers resumed support. **July 8, 1945–1954:** Readership increased and couple was able to buy new equipment and move to larger building. Regularly reported court cases won by NAACP. Continued involvement in community, persuading white business owners to advertise. Several university professors joined NAACP, as did Harry Ashmore, editor of largest Little Rock newspaper. When interracial Human Relations Committee was formed, she was invited to join. **1946:** Couple convicted of contempt of court for criticizing Circuit Court trial in newspaper; conviction later reversed by Arkansas State Supreme Court. **1952:** Elected president of Arkansas State Conference of NAACP Branches, an office she held until November 1961. **1954–1955:** United States Supreme Court ruled public school segregation unconstitutional on May 17th in Brown vs. Board of Education case. *Arkansas State Press* and hundreds of other newspapers applauded decision. Governor Francis A. Cherry stated Arkansas would comply; integration began or was planned in several towns. Prodded by newspapers and Committee on Human Relations, Little Rock school board proposed three-phase integration plan to be implemented slowly, with possible starting date of fall 1957 and full integration to be accomplished within six years. She was optimistic that all would go well as state had only 25 percent black population. **1956–1957:** City's integration plan was scaled down, dates extended; Bates and NAACP assisted black parents in filing suit, winning partial victory as date was reinstated; city school officials decided to comply. Harrassment against Bateses for their activities, which had begun earlier, continued. **Spring 1957:** Four prosegregation bills introduced in state legislature. Met Orval E. Faubus, governor since January 1955, while part of group who talked with him to enlist support to defeat measures. One bill would require her as the head of the state NAACP to submit organization's financial statement and membership list.

Despite efforts by NAACP, religious leaders and labor groups, bills passed. **1957–1959:** Georgia politicians held meeting attacking desegregation decision and praising the Arkansas groups who were fighting the ruling. In August 1957, large rock hurled through Bates' front window with note threatening "dynamite next." Newly formed Mother's League of Little Rock Central High School successfully sued to prevent integration but federal judge overruled. On September 2, 1957, Faubus refused to comply, stating fear of violence, and surrounded school with National Guard of Arkansas. Events escalated with Bates playing major role in strategy, counseling students, etc. Helped by blacks and some whites, and despite many threats, explosions, ˉcross-burnings and other violence, Bates, with her husband's assistance, eventually succeeded in gaining federal intervention to integrate school and came to national attention as events were televised. Nine students were constantly harassed and physically attacked by some whites. Many parents and other supporters, black and white, lost their jobs and were harassed until they moved, etc. **1957:** Honored as Outstanding Citizen of the Year, 1957, by National Organization of American Council on Human Rights, and by Editors of Associated Press as one of top nine news personalities of world for 1957. **July 11, 1958:** Bates and nine students awarded Spingarn Medal of NAACP, one of scores of awards and honors she would receive in years to come. **1958–59:** Joined Martin Luther King, Jr., and others in April 18, 1959, second Youth March for Integrated Schools; 26,000 high school and college students participated in Washington, D. C., march. Governor Faubus closed all city schools; most whites attended private school, but blacks were unable to do so. Many whites finally acted to reopen school, electing new school board, etc. **October/November 1959:** Bateses forced to close newspaper; loss of revenue was caused by whites refusing to advertise in paper, harrassment of newsboys, threats of violence to those who continued to advertise, etc. In anticipation, L. C. had already agreed to become Field Secretary of NAACP in Arkansas. **1959:** Awarded honorary degree from Lincoln University. **1960:** Supreme Court (Bates vs. Little Rock) unanimously reversed conviction for refusal to furnish NAACP membership lists to Little Rock officials. Bateses moved to New York City so that she could write book. Received achievement award from New York Negro Business and Professional Women's Club. **November 1961:** Resigned as head of Arkansas NAACP but remained active in organization. **1962:** Autobiographical *The Long Shadow of Little Rock: A Memoir* published. Book's foreward was written by Eleanor Roosevelt. **1963–1964:** Worked with National Committee of Democratic party in Washington, D. C., on voter education projects. Despite numerous job offers elsewhere, the Bateses preferred to remain in South and continue civil rights work. Worked with underprivileged people in Arkansas Office of Economic Opportunity Training Program. **1968?:** Member of National Board of Directors of NAACP. **1968–**

1972: Founded "Bootstraps," Office of Economic Opportunity Self Help Project to help improverished town of 600 people, Mitchellville, Arkansas. As project director, enlisted help of local university and NAACP, obtained federal grants and loans, etc. Adult education classes begun, sewage system designed, etc. **1972:** Led fight against President Nixon's cutting OEO funds for Mitchellville program, calling it economic genocide. **March 1974:** Bates and Little Rock Nine honored by National Black Political Convention. **1980:** Tutored group of children who were reading below their grade level in her home. Husband died. **March 1981:** Honored for achievements by National Newspaper Publishers Association. **April 1984:** Resumed publication of *Arkansas State Press.* First issue was dedicated to late husband. Coverage of paper continued to focus on black issues throughout state. Awarded honorary degrees from University of Arkansas and Washington University. **1987:** Southwestern Bell Foundation established "The Daisy and The Late L. C. Bates Scholarship Award" and presented scholarships to first recipients in Mrs. Bates' home in Little Rock. New school in southwest Little Rock named "Daisy Bates Elementary School" 24 days before 30th anniversary of school integration crisis. School enrolled 650 students, evenly divided among blacks and whites, with black female principal. Received American Black Achievement Award from *Ebony* magazine. **1988:** Sold *Arkansas State Press,* state's only black-oriented newspaper, to managing editor. Continues to live in Little Rock; serves on numerous boards in community organizations.

BACKGROUND INFORMATION

Parents: Foster father Orlee Gatson worked as lumber-grader in local sawmill. **Siblings:** None. **Children:** None. **Influences:** L. C. Bates. **Ethnicity:** African American. **Also known as:** None known. **Historical sites, landmarks, etc.:** Daisy Bates Elementary School, Little Rock, Arkansas. The Daisy and the Late L. C. Bates Scholarship Award, Southwestern Bell Foundation.

BIBLIOGRAPHICAL INFORMATION

Biographical Sketches About Daisy Bates

Low, W. Augustus, ed. *Encyclopedia of Black America.* New York: McGraw-Hill, 1981.

Ploski, Harry A., and James Williams, eds. *The Negro Almanac: A Reference Work on the African American.* Detroit: Gale Research, 1989.

Robinson, Wilhelmena S. *Historical Negro Biographies.* New York: Publishers Company, 1969.

Schoenebaum, Eleanora W., ed. *Political Profiles: The Eisenhower Years.* New York: Facts On File, 1977.

Smith, Jessie Carney, ed. *Notable Black American Women.* Detroit: Gale Research, 1992.

Books by Daisy Bates

The Long Shadow of Little Rock: A Memoir. New York: David McKay, 1962. (Forward by Eleanor Roosevelt.)

The Long Shadow of Little Rock: A Memoir. Fayetteville: University of Arkansas Press, 1987. (Contains new photographs and new preface.)

Shorter Works by Daisy Bates

(All of the following are excerpts from *The Long Shadow of Little Rock.*)

Alexander, Rae Pace, comp. *Young and Black in America.* New York: Random, 1970.

David, Jay, ed. *Growing Up Black.* New York: Morrow, 1968.

_____, and Elaine Crane, eds. *Living Black in White America.* New York: Morrow, 1971.

Grant, Joanne, ed. *Black Protest: History, Documents, and Analysis.* Greenwich, CT: Fawcett, 1968.

"I Did Not Really Understand What It Meant to Be a Negro." In *Black Women in White America,* edited by Gerda Lerner. New York: Vintage, 1973.

"The Ordeal of the Children." In *Black Women in White America,* edited by Gerda Lerner. New York: Vintage, 1973.

Shorter Works About Daisy Bates

"At the Point of a Bayonet." In *I Have a Dream,* by Emma Gelders Sterne. New York: Alfred A. Knopf, 1965.

Bennett, Lerone, Jr. "First Lady of Little Rock." *Ebony* 13 (September 1958): 17–20 + .

"Daisy Bates: Firebrand of Little Rock." In *Portraits in Color: The Lives of Colorful Negro Women,* by Gwendolyn Cherry, Ruby Thomas, and Pauline Willis. New York: Pageant, 1962.

"Daisy Bates Resumes Publication of Black Newspaper in Arkansas." *Jet* 66 (April 30, 1984): 30.

"Daisy Bates Sells Her Little Rock Newspaper." *Jet* 73 (February 15, 1988): 32.

"Daisy Gatson Bates." In *Profiles of Negro Womanhood,* by Sylvia G. L. Dannett. Yonkers: Educational Heritage, 1966.

Garland, Phyl. "Builders of a New South." *Ebony* 21 (August 1966): 27 + .
"Gets Achievement Award from N.Y. Negro Business and Professional Women's Club." *Jet* (May 12, 1960): 4.
Harrington, M. "Whence Comes Their Passion." *Reporter* 27 (November 22, 1962): 55–56.
Hughes, Langston. *Fight for Freedom*. New York: W. W. Norton, 1962.
Lanker, Brian. *I Dream a World: Portraits of Black Women Who Changed America*. New York: Stewart, Tabori & Chang, 1989.
"Little Rock NAACP Plans Happy 1986 for Civil Rights Veteran Daisy Bates." *Jet* 69 (January 13, 1986): 12.
Manuel, R. D. "Essence Woman." *Essence* 16 (Feburary 1986): 32.
"People of the Week." *U.S. News & World Report* 43 (October 4, 1957): 17.
Rankin, Edwina L. "After 20 Years, Daisy Bates and the 'Little Rock Nine' Still Keep in Touch." *Jet* 52 (September 15, 1977): 6–7.
"Scholarships Given in Honor of Daisy Bates and Her Late Husband." *Jet* 72 (August 3, 1987): 23.
"School Named for Daisy Bates in Little Rock." *Jet* 72 (September 21, 1987): 22.
"Student Power Lifts Mitchellville." *Crisis* 75 (May 1968): 161–66.
Trescott, Jacqueline. "Daisy Bates: Before and After Little Rock." *Crisis* 88 (1981): 232–35.
"What Happened to Daisy Bates?" *Negro Digest* 11 (May 1962): 76–82.
"Whatever Happened to Daisy Bates?" *Ebony* 39 (September 1984): 92 + .
"Whatever Happened to the Little Rock 9?" *Ebony* 27 (February 1972): 136–38.

Other Works About Daisy Bates

Play

Hamilton, Denise, "Parallax (In Honor of Daisy Bates)." In *Women Heroes: Six Short Plays from the Women's Project*, edited by Julia Miles. New York: Applause Theatre Book Publishers, 1986.

Media Materials About Daisy Bates

Video Recordings

Eyes on the Prize: America's Civil Rights Years: Fighting Back 1957–1962. Alexandria, VA: PBS Video, 1986. Videocassette; VHS; sound; color with black and white segments; 60 min.
Missing Pages, A Moment in Black History. Washington, D. C.: WETA-TV, 1980. Videocassette; ¾ in; sound; color with black and white sequences.
The Second American Revolution, Pt. 2. Washington, D. C. : PBS Video, 1983. Videocassette; ¾ or ½ in; 58 min; sound; color.

Primary Source Materials Relating to Daisy Bates

Daisy Bates. Papers. 1946–1966. Extent of collection: 2.2 cu. ft., 6 reels microfilm, 4 tape recordings. Finding aids: Register. Location: State Historical Society of Wisconsin, Archives Division, 816 State Street, Madison, Wisconsin 53706. Scope of collection: General correspondence, speeches, research files, portions of an interview with Bates, etc. Microfilm available.

Nimrod Booker Allen. Papers. 1876–1977. Extent of collection: 4.75 cu. ft. Finding aids: Not listed. Location: Ohio Historical Society, Archives Library, 1985 Velma Avenue, Columbus, Ohio 43211. Scope of collection: Personal papers and records of various black organizations.

Southern Women After Suffrage. Oral History. 1972–1976. Extent of collection: ca. 4000 pp. Finding aids: Unpublished guide. Location: University of North Carolina, Southern Oral History Program, Walter Royal Davis Library, Chapel Hill, North Carolina 27599. Scope of collection: Interviews with 60 women including Bates.

7. *Mary Frances Berry*
(1938–)
Advocate for human rights; historian; lawyer;
lecturer; educator; and administrator

BIOGRAPHICAL INFORMATION

Chronological Biography

Born February 17, 1938, in Nashville, Tennessee, second of three children, to Frances (Southall) and George Ford Berry.

1954: Graduated with honors from Pearl High School in Nashville; mentored by teacher Minerva Hawkins.   **1961:** Received Bachelor of Arts degree in Philosophy from Howard University in Washington, D. C. (had begun college at Fisk University and transferred). Worked in hospital laboratories throughout graduate and undergraduate years.   **1962:** Granted Masters of Arts degree in History from Howard University.   **1962–1963:** Was a teaching fellow in American History at Howard University.   **1965–1966:** Was a teaching assistant at University of Michigan, Ann Arbor. Received Civil War Round Table Dissertation Fellowship Award.   **1966:** Awarded Doctorate of Philosophy in American Constitutional History from University of Michigan.   **1966–1968:** Assistant professor in department of history at Central Michigan University in Mount Pleasant.   **1968–1970:** Assistant and associate professor in department of history at Eastern Michigan University in Ypsilanti.   **1969–1976:** Associate professor in department of history at University of Maryland, College Park.   **1970:** Earned Juris Doctor degree from University of Michigan.   **1970–1971:** Adjunct associate professor of history at University of Michigan.   **1970–1972:** Acting director of Afro-American studies program, University of Maryland, College Park.   **1972–**

1974: Interim chair of division of behavioral and social sciences at University of Maryland, College Park. 1974–1976: Provost of division of behavioral and social sciences at University of Maryland, College Park. 1976–1977: Chancellor of University of Colorado at Boulder, first black woman to head major research university. 1976–1980: Professor of history and law at University of Colorado at Boulder. 1977: Recipient of Athena Distinguished Alumni Award from University of Michigan. 1977–1980: First black woman to serve as assistant secretary for education in U.S. Department of Health, Education, and Welfare. Advocated establishment of Department of Education; created Graduate and Professional Opportunities Program to expand opportunities for racial minorities and women. 1979: Honorary member of Delta Sigma Theta public service sorority. 1980: Member of Tuskegee University Board of Directors. 1980–: United States Commission of Civil Rights commissioner. 1980–1982: Vice chair of United States Commision on Civil Rights. 1980–1985: Senior fellow at Institute for the Study of Educational Policy. 1980–1989: Professor of history and law at Howard University. 1983: Received National Association for the Advancement of Colored People (NAACP) Image Award. Recipient of Roy Wilkins Civil Rights Award from NAACP. 1984: When President Ronald Reagan fired her, and other outspoken critics of his policies, from the United States Commission on Civil Rights, she sued him and Federal District Court reinstated her. Founded Free South Africa Movement (FSAM) with District of Columbia Congressman Walter Fauntroy, Randall Robinson of Trans-Africa, and historian Roger Wilkins. On day before Thanksgiving, arrested along with Fauntroy and Robinson for anti-apartheid demonstration outside South African Embassy. 1985: Received Rosa Parks Award from Southern Christian Leadership Conference. President's Award recipient from Congressional Black Caucus Foundation. FSAM generated more than 20 anti-apartheid organizations by summer of 1985. 1986: Member of United Nations University council. Honored as one of "Women of the Year" by *Ms.* magazine. Awarded Hubert H. Humphrey Civil Rights Award from Leadership Conference on Civil Rights. 1987: Member of National Advisory Council of American Civil Liberties Union. 1988: Member of Editorial Board of Frederick Douglass Papers at Yale University. Member of Board of Directors of National Wildlife Federation. 1990–1991: President of Organization of American Historians. Has received 19 honorary doctorate degrees throughout past several years. **Present–:** Geraldine R. Segal Professor of Social Thought and professor of history at University of Pennsylvania.

Background Information

Parents: Frances (Southall) Wiggins and George Ford Berry. **Siblings:** Two (George F. and half-brother Troy Merritt). *Children:* None.

Influences: Minerva Hawkins. **Ethnicity:** African American. **Also known as:** None known. **Historical sites, landmarks, etc.:** M. F. Berry Womyn's Center, Reeve Union, University of Wisconsin, Oshkosh, Wisconsin.

BIBLIOGRAPHICAL INFORMATION

Biographical Sketches About Mary Frances Berry

Lanker, Brian. *I Dream a World: Portraits of Black Women Who Changed America.* New York: Stewart, Tabori & Chang, 1989.
Ploski, Harry A., and James Williams, comps. and eds. *The Negro Almanac: A Reference Work on the African American.* Detroit: Gale Research, 1989.
Smith, Jessie Carney, ed. *Notable Black American Women.* Detroit: Gale Research, 1992.

Books by Mary Frances Berry

Black Resistance, White Law: A History of Constitutional Racism in America. New York: Appleton-Century-Crofts, 1971.
Military Necessity and Civil Rights Policy: Black Citizenship and the Constitution, 1861–1868. Port Washington, NY: Kennikat, 1977.
Stability, Security, and Continuity: Mr. Justice Burton and Decision-Making in the Supreme Court, 1945–1958. Westport, CT: Greenwood, 1978.
Toward Freedom and Civil Rights for the Freedmen: Military Policy Origins of the Thirteenth Amendment and the Civil Rights Act of 1866. Washington: Department of History, Howard University, 1975.
Why ERA Failed: Politics, Women's Rights, and the Amending Process of the Constitution. Bloomington: Indiana University Press, 1986.
Berry, Mary Frances, and John W. Blassingame. *Long Memory: The Black Experience in America.* New York: Oxford University Press, 1982.

Shorter Works by Mary Frances Berry

"Affirmative Action and the Court." *Point of View* (Fall 1986): 3–4.
"Black Visions of Educational Improvement." *History of Education Quarterly* 24 (Winter 1984): 597–600.
"Blacks in Predominantly White Institutions of Higher Learning." In *The State of Black America 1983*, edited by James D. Williams. N.p.: National Urban League, 1983.
"Civil Rights Under Siege." *Peace and Freedom* 45 (September / October 1985): 18–19.
"The Concept of Excellence." *Phi Delta Kappan* 60 (November 1978): 196S–197S.
"The Constraints and Opportunities for Black Women in the 1980s." *Creative Woman* 5 (Fall 1981): 18–21.

"Deliberately Fraught with Difficulties: New Light on the History of Constitutional Amendments and the Prospects for Women's Rights." *Women's Studies Quarterly* 13 (Spring 1985): 2–7.

"The Federal Role in Increasing Equality of Educational Opportunity — Responses." *Harvard Educational Review* 52 (November 1982): 462–66.

"Forum — the Future of Title VII Over the Next 20 Years." *BNA's Employee Relations Weekly* 3 (September 30, 1985): 1205–06.

"Forum — Hiring Goals in Historical Perspective." *BNA's Employee Relations Weekly* 2 (October 8, 1984): 1235–36.

"How Hard It Is to Change: Amending the Constitution." *New York Times* (September 13, 1987): Sec. 6, 93.

"Increasing Women's Influence in Government and Politics: The Inclusion of Women of Color." *Proteus* 3 (Fall 1986): 1–5.

"Keynote Address: Cleo Tenth Anniversary Symposium. Notes." *Howard Law Journal* 22 (1979): 409–15.

"A Liberal-Integrating Prospectus." In *Blacks in the Year 2000*, edited by Joseph R. Washington, Jr. Philadelphia: University of Pennsylvania Press, 1981.

"Lincoln and Civil Rights for Blacks." *Papers of the Abraham Lincoln Association* 2 (1980): 46–57.

"A Love-Hate Relationship with the National Archives." In *Afro-American History: Sources for Research*, edited by Robert L. Clarke. Washington, D. C.: Howard University Press, 1981.

"Negro Troops in Blue and Grey: The Louisiana Native Guards, 1861–1863." *Louisiana History* 8 (Spring 1967): 165–90.

"New Emphases in Federal Policy on Education." *Phi Delta Kappan* 59 (October 1977): 122–26.

"Overinvolvement of the Federal Government in Higher Education: Fact or Fiction." *National Conference on Public Service and the Federal-University Partnership: Proceedings, June 21–23, 1978*. Athens: University of Georgia Center for Continuing Education, 1979.

"The Pressing Need for Environmental Education." *USA Today* 107 (May 1979): 50–52.

"Qualified Praise for Liberal Learning." *Harvard Educational Review* 53 (November 1983): 393–97.

"Raising Questions About Public Policy and the Status of Women." *AHA Newsletter* 19 (October 1981): 6–8.

"Relevance to American Needs." In *China's Schools in Flux: Report by the State Education Leaders Delegation [and] National Committee on United States-China Relations*, edited by Ronald N. Montaperto and Jay Henderson. White Plains, NY: M. E. Sharpe, 1979.

"Reparations for Freedmen, 1890–1919: Fraudulent Practices or Justice Deferred?" *Journal of Negro History* 57 (July 1972): 219–30.

"Repression of Blacks in the South, 1890–1945: Enforcing the System of Segregation." In *The Age of Segregation: Race Relations in the South, 1890–1945*, edited by Robert Haws. Jackson: University Press of Mississippi, 1978.

[Review Essay] *Afro-Americans in New York Life and History* 6 (January 1982): 55–59.

[Review Essay] *Louisiana History* 24 (1983): 325–27.
"Slave Behavior in Eighteenth-Century Virginia." *Reviews in American History* 1 (June 1973): 192–95.
"The Slave Community: A Review of the Reviews." In *Revisiting Blassingame's the Slave Community: The Scholars Respond*, edited by Al-Tony Gilmore. Westport, CT: Greenwood, 1978.
"Slavery in the Courtroom: An Annotated Bibliography of American Cases." *Afro-Americans in New York Life and History* 10 (July 1986): 65.
"Student Competency Testing." *High School Journal* 62 (January 1979): 166–72.
"Taming the Civil Rights Commission." *Nation* 240 (February 2, 1985): 106–08.
"Turning Back the Clock on Women and Minority Rights: The Reagan Record." *Negro History Bulletin* 46 (July–September 1983): 82–84.
"Twentieth-Century Black Women in Education." *Journal of Negro Education* 51 (Summer 1982): 288–300.
Berry, Mary Frances, and John W. Blassingame. "Africa, Slavery, and the Roots of Contemporary Black Culture." *Massachusetts Review* 18 (Autumn 1977): 501–16.
_____, and Albert Shanker. "The Politics of Thinking About China [text of speech by Berry and response of Shanker]." *Change* 10 (1978): 36–39 + .

Shorter Works About Mary Frances Berry

Barthel, Joan. "Mary Frances Berry, Civil Rights Commissioner." *Ms.* 15 (January 1987): 68–70 + .
Bradley, David. "Where Mary Berry Is Coming From." *Pennsylvania Gazette* 88 (April 1990).
"Dr. Berry Quits Education Post After Carter's Snub." *Jet* 57 (December 13, 1979): 5.
Duvall, Henry. "Dr. Mary Frances Berry: Educator-Activist Beats Drum for Civil Rights." *About Time* 14 (November 1986): 16–17.
Fields, C. M. "Washington's Top Two in Education." *Chronicle of Higher Education* 14 (July 11, 1977): 3.
"50 Faces for America's Future." *Time* 114 (August 6, 1979): 37.
Glastris, P. "The Powers That Shouldn't Be: Five Washington Insiders the Next Democratic President Shouldn't Hire." *Washington Monthly* 19 (October 1987): 39–46 + .
Jones, Marsha. "Dr. Mary Frances Berry: Championing Social Justice." *About Time* 16 (January 1988): 18–21.
Molotsky, I. F. "A Conversation with Mary Frances Berry." *Academe* 72 (September/ October 1986): 27–30.
Neill, G."Carter Installs New Team to Run Education Agencies." *Phi Delta Kappan* 58 (March 1977): 582–83.
Pinderhughes, Dianne M. "Black Women and National Educational Policy." *Journal of Negro Education* 51 (Summer 1982): 301–08.
Poinsett, Alex. "Colorado University's Chancellor." *Ebony* 32 (January 1977): 58–60 + .
Reynolds, B. A. "Black America Under Reagan." *Essence* 15 (October 1984): 12 + .

Simmons, J. "She Helped to Pluck the E Out of HEW." *Black Enterprise* 10 (February 1980): 75–76 + .

Slacum, Marcia A. "Essence Women: Mary Frances Berry." *Essence* 7 (November 1976): 10.

Smith, Carol Hobson. "Black Female Achievers in Academe." *Journal of Negro Education* 51 (Summer 1982): 318–41.

United States. Congress. Senate. Committee on Human Resources. *Nominations: Hearing Before the Committee on Human Resources, United States Senate, Ninety-Fifth Congress, First Session, On Dr. Mary Frances Berry, of Boulder, Colorado, to be Assistant Secretary of Education, and Dr. Ernest Leroy Boyer, of Albany, New York, to be U.S. Commissioner of Education, March 25, 1977.* Washington, D. C.: U.S. GPO, 1977.

"University of Maryland Names Black to Top Post." *Jet* 46 (July 11, 1974): 29.

"Women in Government: A Slim Past, But a Strong Future." *Ebony* 32 (August 1977): 89–92 + .

Other Works by Mary Frances Berry

Theses

"The Negro Soldier Movement and the Adoption of National Conscription, 1652–1865." Ph.D. diss., University of Michigan, 1966.

Primary Source Materials Relating to Mary Frances Berry

Mary Frances Berry. Papers. Extent of collection: Not listed. Finding aids: Not listed. Location: Moorland-Spingarn Research Center, Howard University, 500 Howard Place, Washington, D. C. 20059. Scope of collection: Includes correspondence, reports and speeches which document years as assistant secretary of education, chancellor of University of Colorado at Boulder, and U.S. Commission on Civil Rights commissioner.

(THE ABOVE ENTRY WAS CONTRIBUTED BY LILLIAN S. WILLIAMS)

8. *Mary McLeod Bethune*
(1875–1955)

*Educator; government official; and advocate for
African American rights and African American women's rights*

BIOGRAPHICAL INFORMATION

Chronological Biography

Born July 10, 1875, in Mayesville, South Carolina, probably second to last of 17 children, ten girls and seven boys. First free-born child of former slaves

Patsy (McIntosh) and Samuel McLeod. Parents had purchased small amount of land and built a cabin; family farmed, picked rice and cotton, etc. No early education as schools were unavailable in area for black children and parents could not read or write. Parents instilled strong work ethic and religious beliefs and encouraged her leadership abilities.

1886–1888?: At age 11 began attending newly opened Presbyterian Mission School about five miles from home. Teacher was young, black, Northern woman. Excelled in studies; taught younger students and family as she learned. Assisted local farmers in keeping their accounts. 1888?–1894: Provided with scholarship by white Quaker dressmaker in Denver, Colorado, to continue studies. Attended Scotia Seminary in Concord, North Carolina, which stressed religion and industrial education. White teachers at Presbyterian school for black girls helped her to understand that not all whites were against black education. Worked in school laundry and kitchen to contribute to family's finances. Graduated and was qualified to begin teaching. 1893?–1895: Aspiring to become a missionary in Africa, studied on scholarship funds at Bible Institute for Home and Foreign Missions in Chicago, one of two black students. Presbyterian Mission Board would not send her to Africa. Reasons are not clear, but some reasons put forth were her youthfulness, the fact that there were no openings in Africa for black missionaries, or that they did not send black missionaries to Africa. 1895–1896?: Senior instructor at Haines Normal and Industrial Institute in Augusta, Georgia. Inspired by school's dynamic black founder and principal, Lucy Laney, decided to continue teaching in life-long effort to provide educational opportunities for black children, especially girls. Started Sunday School for black children, giving lessons, teaching hymns and organizing the choral group. Continued to send money home to pay off parents' mortgage. (May also have taught previously for one year at Mayesville Mission School.) 1896?–1898: Taught at Kindell Institute in Sumter, South Carolina. The funds she sent home helped to send two sisters to Scotia Seminary. May 6, 1898: Married Albertus L. Bethune, teacher then businessman, five years older than she. Moved to Savannah. 1899: Only child, Albert McLeod, born. 1899–1903: Family moved to Florida so she could teach at Palatka Mission School. Felt it essential that blacks learned academic subjects, as well as vocational and other living skills, in order for them to survive and advance. Desire to open own school intensified as she felt existing schools did not meet these needs. Bethunes separated during this period, possibly because husband did not share intense devotion to her career. 1904: Taking son with her, moved to Daytona Beach where there was large black population and no public education existed for these children. With only $1.50 in savings and an abiding faith, began efforts to open own private school for black girls. Rented run-down four room cottage in September by promising to pay by end of month. Eloquent speaker, solicited funds at churches and other gatherings, and from individuals, poor and rich, black and white. **October 3, 1904:** Opened Daytona Normal and Industrial Institute for Negro Girls, modeled after Scotia Seminary, with five girls, aged eight to twelve, and her son as pupils and with a tuition of fifty cents per week. School's motto was "Enter to learn; depart to serve." With children, gathered boxes for desks, burned logs and used charred splinters for pencils, mashed elderberries for ink. Gleaned linens, broken chairs, and kitchen items from city dump and hotel refuse. Made sleeping mats from sacks filled with moss for overnight pupils. Used experiences of cleaning and mending to teach skills. **1905–1929:** Continued to solicit resources to expand school by making speeches, training girls to sing and taking them to resort hotels, etc. Wealthy whites in community and elsewhere, such as John D. Rockefeller, contributed funds, and pupils' parents and community assisted in building and supplies. Friends from Scotia Seminary and Bible Institute for Home and Foreign Missions sent books and supplies as did Lucy Laney from Haines Institute. In less than two years there were 250 students, and adult evening classes had been added; there were a number of paid teachers, many volunteer workers, and the school had outgrown its original cottage and a rented hall next door. Decided to build college and bought swampy dump called Hell's Hole for $5 down with $200 balance to be paid in two years, raising the down payment by selling sweet potato pies and ice cream to construction workers. Redoubled fund-raising efforts by making speeches, ringing doorbells, writing articles, and pleading with workers to donate building skills. Added high school, then college courses. Emphasized moral and religious values while teaching academics and practical skills, all the while concentrating on black girls, who she felt had fewer educational opportunities than boys. **1911:** Opened two-bed hospital as none existed for blacks in area. Grew to 20 beds staffed by black and white physicians and student nurses from her college. City took over hospital in 1927 and ran it until 1931. **1917–1924:** President of Florida Federation of Colored Women. **October 22, 1918:** Husband died. **1919:** One of the founding members of Commission on Interracial Cooperation. Organization was begun to reduce racial tensions, improve status of black population, and educate races in mutual tolerance, understanding, and cooperation. **1920:** Ignoring Ku Klux Klan threats, headed voter registration drive for black women. Founded and headed precursor to Southeastern Federation of Colored Women. **1923–1948:** School merged in 1923 with all-male Cookman Institute of Jacksonville after obtaining sponsorship of Methodist Episcopal Church, North. The name changed to Daytona Cookman Collegiate Institute. In 1929, name changed to Bethune-Cookman College at request of school trustees. Junior college curriculum was developed and pre-college courses reduced. By 1932 it was accredited as a junior college. In 1936, high school curriculum was discontinued. First four-year students in teacher education graduated in 1943. By 1948 school had grown to a four-year liberal arts college.   1924–1928: Served two terms as president of National Association of Colored Women 10,000 member organization. Funds were raised during this period to purchase building in Washington, D. C., for a permanent national headquarters and to preserve Frederick Douglass home. 1927: Met Eleanor Roosevelt while only black woman to attend meeting of National Council of Women of United States; the beginning of their long friendship. She educated and advised President and Mrs. Roosevelt on black affairs and concerns for many years.   November 1930: Invited by President Hoover to White House Conference on Child Health and Protection.   1931: Attended President's Conference on Home Building and Home Ownership. August 1935: Asked by President Franklin D. Roosevelt to serve on National Advisory Committee of National Youth Administration, one of two blacks to do so.   1935: On December 5th, awarded Spingarn Medal of National Association for the Advancement of Colored People (NAACP) for outstanding contributions to advancement of her race. In December, founded National Council of Negro Women, coalition of major national black women's organizations. Served as president until December, 1949. The council worked to provide national voice for betterment of black women. Established permanent headquarters in Washington, D. C., and began *Aframerican Woman's Journal*.   June 1936: Appointed Director of Negro affairs in National Youth Administration, one of highest-placed blacks and only black woman in Roosevelt's administration. Served as special adviser on minority affairs. First black woman to receive major federal appointment.   August 1936: Founded Federal Council on Negro Affairs. Referred to as "black cabinet" it met weekly at her home and worked to advance blacks in government jobs, obtain job training funds, function as racial adviser to government, end discrimination, etc. Succeeded in gaining federal support for 1937 and 1939 National Negro Conferences which focused attention on black conditions in United States and enabled policy recommendations to be made to federal government. 1936: Received Frances A. Drexel Award for distinguished service. Became president of Carter G. Woodson's publishing house, founded to publish books on black subjects.   1936–1951: President of Association for Study of Negro Life and History.   February 1937: Testified as president of National Council of Negro Women before Senate Committee on Education and Labor regarding federal aid to education.   1938: Formed Museum-Archives Department in National Council of Negro Women.   January 1939: Appointed director of Division of Negro Affairs of National Youth Administration. Instrumental in establishment of Negro college and graduate fund disbursing $610,000 over seven years to more than 4,000 black students. 1940–1955: Vice president of National Association for the Advancement of Colored People and of National Urban League.   Spring 1942: Loaned by National Youth Administration to act as special assistant to secretary of war to aid in selection of first Women's Army Corps officer candidates. **December 1942:** Resigned from presidency of Bethune-Cookman College, but remained a trustee until her death. **1942:** Awarded Thomas Jefferson Medal by Southern Conference for Human Welfare. **1943:** Representing National Council of Negro Women, appeared before Senate and House Committees on Public Lands concerning George Washington Carver National Monument in Missouri on February 5th, and in November / December before Senate Committee on Banking and Currency considering Commodity Credit Corporation. **1944:** National Youth Administration was disbanded. **1944–1946:** Testified before federal committees regarding Fair Employment Practices Act, Federal Aid for Education, and General Housing Act, again representing National Council of Negro Women. **April 1945:** Delegate to founding conference of United Nations in San Francisco. Spoke at nationwide memorial program following President Roosevelt's death. Mrs. Roosevelt later presented her with President's cane which she used until her death. **1946–1947:** Again served as president of Bethune-Cookman College for one year. **1949:** Was a witness representing National Council of Negro Women at a hearing considering the taxes on and the coloring of oleomargarine in March and, later in year, regarding Housing Amendments of 1949. Retired from presidency of National Council of Negro Women and returned to Daytona Beach. Received Haitian Medal of Honor and Merit. **January 1952:** Represented country at Liberian President William Tubman's second inaugural proceedings. **April 1952:** Englewood, New Jersey, Board of Education cancelled scheduled speech she was to make when some whites labeled her a communist. She spoke instead at local church. **1953:** Presented with Robert S. Abbott Memorial Award. **May 18, 1955:** Died of heart attack at age 79 at home in Daytona Beach and was buried on Bethune-Cookman College campus. Recipient of many awards and honorary degrees, revered as most influential black woman of her time, champion of civil rights and education, and role model for black women.

Background Information

Parents: Patsy (McIntosh) and Samuel McLeod. Mother was from Africa. **Siblings:** 16 (Known names: Marjorie). **Children:** One (Albert McLeod). **Influences:** None. **Ethnicity:** African American. **Also known as:** Mary Jane. **Historical sites, landmarks, etc.:** Mary McLeod Bethune Elementary School, Atlanta, Georgia; Mary McLeod Bethune Home, Campus of Bethune-Cookman College, 2nd Avenue, Daytona Beach, Florida (proclaimed National Historic Landmark on December 2, 1974); Mary McLeod Bethune Junior High School, Los Angeles, California; Marker Near Site of Birthplace, Mayesville, South Carolina; Bethune is honoree in Hall of Fame, South Carolina Hall of Fame, Myrtle Beach Convention Center, 21st Avenue N. and Oak Street, Myrtle Beach, South Carolina; Bethune is honoree in Hall of Fame, National Women's Hall of Fame, 76 Fall Street, Seneca Falls, New York; Bethune Dormitory, Howard University, 4th and College Streets N.W., Washington, D.C.; Statue in Lincoln Park, East Capitol at 12th Street S.E., first monument to an African American or a woman, erected on public land in Washington, D.C.; Mary McLeod Bethune Council House and Bethune Museum and Archives, designated National Historic Site in 1985; U.S. Postage Stamp, eighth in U.S. Postal Service's Black Heritage USA Series.

BIBLIOGRAPHICAL INFORMATION

Biographical Sketches About Mary McLeod Bethune

Block, Maxine, ed. *Current Biography: Who's News and Why 1941.* New York: H. W. Wilson Company, 1942.

Garraty, John A., ed. *Dictionary of American Biography.* New York: Charles Scribner's Sons, 1977.

Ohles, John F., ed. *Biographical Dictionary of American Educators.* Westport, CT: Greenwood, 1978.

Sicherman, Barbara, and Carol Hurd Green, eds. *Notable American Women: The Modern Period: A Biographical Dictionary.* Cambridge, MA: Belknap Press of Harvard University Press, 1980.

Smith, Jessie Carney, ed. *Notable Black American Women.* Detroit: Gale Research, 1992.

Whitman, Alden, ed. *American Reformers: An H. W. Wilson Biographical Dictionary.* New York: H. W. Wilson Company, 1985.

Books by Mary McLeod Bethune

Mary McLeod Bethune: Her Own Words of Inspiration. Edited by Florence Johnson Hicks. Washington, D. C.: Nuclassics and Science Publishing, 1975.

Books About Mary McLeod Bethune

Anderson, LaVere. *Mary McLeod Bethune, Teacher with a Dream.* Champaign, IL: Garrard, 1976.

Burt, Olive (Woolley). *Mary McLeod Bethune: Girl Devoted to Her People.* Indianapolis: Bobbs-Merrill, [1970].

Carruth, Ella Kaiser. *She Wanted to Read: The Story of Mary McLeod Bethune.* Nashville: Abingdon, 1966.

Greenfield, Eloise. *Mary McLeod Bethune.* New York: Crowell, 1977.

Halasa, Malu. *Mary McLeod Bethune.* New York: Chelsea House, 1989.

Hardiman, Jim, ed. *Moral Re-armament Presents the Crowning Experience: Technicolor Book of the Film.* New York: Random House, [1960].

Holt, Rackham. *Mary McLeod Bethune: A Biography.* Garden City, NY: Doubleday, 1964.

Johnson, Jan. *Mary Bethune and Her Somedays: A Story About Mary McLeod Bethune.* Minneapolis: Winston, 1979.

McKissack, Pat. *Mary McLeod Bethune: A Great American Educator.* Chicago: Children's Press, 1985.

Massie, Dorothy C. *The Legacy of Mary McLeod Bethune.* Washington: National Education Association, [1974].

Meltzer, Milton. *Mary McLeod Bethune: Voice of Black Hope.* New York: Viking Kestrel, 1987. Reprint. New York: Puffin, 1988.

Peare, Catherine Owens. *Mary McLeod Bethune.* New York: Vanguard, [1951].

Radford, Ruby Lorraine. *Mary McLeod Bethune.* New York: Putnam, [1973].

Selected Resources: Mary McLeod Bethune. New York: Black Christian Education Resources Center, [between 1974 and 1977].

Sterne, Emma Gelders. *Mary McLeod Bethune.* New York: Knopf, 1957.

Shorter Works by Mary McLeod Bethune

"Adaptation of the History of the Negro to the Capacity of the Child." *Journal of Negro History* 24 (January 1939): 9–13.

"A Century of Progress of Negro Women." In *Black Women in White America,* edited by Gerda Lerner. New York: Vintage, 1973.

"Certain Unalienable Rights." In *What the Negro Wants,* by M. M. Bethune and Others, edited by Rayford Whittingham Logan. New York: Agathon Press, 1969.

"Clarifying Our Vision with the Facts." *Journal of Negro History* 23 (January 1938): 10–15.

"A College on a Garbage Dump." In *Black Women in White America,* edited by Gerda Lerner. New York: Vintage, 1973.

"Educational Values of the College-bred." *Southern Workman* 63 (July 1934): 200–04.

"Faith that Moved a Dump Heap." *Who, the Magazine About People* 1 (June 1941): 32+.

Finkelstein, Louis. *American Spiritual Autobiographies, Fifteen Self-Portraits.* New York: Harper, [1948].

"God Leads the Way, Mary." *Christian Century* 69 (July 23, 1952): 851–52.

"I'll Never Turn Back No More." *Opportunity* 16 (November 1938): 324–26.

"An Introduction." In *Black Women in White America,* edited by Gerda Lerner. New York: Vintage, 1973.

"My Last Will and Testament..." *Ebony* 41 (November 1985): 172–74+.

"My Last Will and Testament; reprint from *September* 1963 issue.' *Ebony* 31 (November 1975): 44–50.

"My Last Will and Testament; reprint of 1955 article." *Ebony* 18 (September 1963): 150–56.

"My Last Will and Testament; reprint of September 1963 issue." *Ebony* 29 (November 1973): 84–88 + .

"My Secret Talks with FDR." In *The Negro in Depression and War; Prelude to Revolution 1930–1945*, edited by Bernard Sternsher. Chicago: Quadrangle, 1969.

"Negro in Retrospect and Prospect." *Journal of Negro History* 35 (January 1950): 9–19.

"The Torch Is Ours." *Journal of Negro History* 36 (January 1951): 9–11.

"Which Way America." *Aframerican Woman's Journal* (Summer-Fall 1947): 3 + .

Shorter Works About Mary McLeod Bethune

"Amazon of God." In *13 Against the Odds*, by Edwin Rogers Embree. New York: Viking, 1944.

"America's Ten Most Powerful Negroes." *Our World* 10 (April 1955): 48–**55**.

"Be a Daniel!" *Time* 65 (May 30, 1955): 44 + .

Bennett, Lerone, Jr. "Chronicles of Black Courage." *Ebony* 38 (December 1982): 136 + .

————. "The 50 Most Important Figures in Black American History." *Ebony* 44 (February 1989): 176 + .

Berry, Mary Frances. "Twentieth-Century Black Women in Education." *Journal of Negro Education* 51 (Summer 1982): 288–300.

"Bethune Memorial Fund." *Telefact* (November 1960).

Bickerstaff, Joyce, and Wilbur C. Rich. "Mrs. Roosevelt and Mrs. Bethune: Collaborators for Racial Justice. *Social Education* 48 (November–December 1984): 532–35.

"The Black Cabineteers." In *New World A-Coming*, by Roi Ottley. New York: Arno Press and the New York Times, 1968.

Brawley, Benjamin Griffith. *Women of Achievement*. Chicago: Woman's American Baptist Home Mission Society, 1919.

"Break Ground for Bethune Statue in D. C. Park." *Jet* 4 (July 8, 1971): 21.

Brewer, William M. "Mary McLeod Bethune." *Negro History Bulletin* 19 (November 1955): 48 + .

Brokaw, Joel. "Mary McLeod Bethune: An Organizational Legacy." *About Time* 13 (February 1985): 18–20.

Byron, Dora. "From 'A Cabin in the Cotton': A Biographical Sketch of a Remarkable Personality." *Opportunity: Journal of Negro Life* 14 (April 1936): 106–7 + .

Carruth, E. K. "Magnificent Mary." *Negro Digest* 11 (Summer 1962): 11–18.

Carter, Elmer Anderson. "A Modern Matriarch." *Survey Graphic* 25 (October 1936): 573–74.

"Chicago Black Women Honor Dr. Bethune." *Jet* 49 (January 1, 1976): 14–15.

"College Built on Faith." *Reader's Digest* 39 (July 1941): 47–50.

"College Started with '$1.50, Five Little Girls and Faith in God' Marks 100th Year." *Jet* 42 (May 18, 1972): 18–19.

"Cotton Picker, LL.D." In *They Did Something About It*, by Robert Merrill Bartlett. New York: Association Press, 1943.

"D. C. Fete Honors Bethune with New Postage Stamp." *Jet* 68 (March 25, 1985): 18.

Daniel, Sadie Iola. *Women Builders*. Washington, D. C.: Associated Publishers, 1931.

Dannett, Sylvia G. L. *Profiles of Negro Womanhood*. Yonkers: Educational Heritage, 1964.

Davis, Elizabeth Lindsay. *Lifting As They Climb*. Washington, D. C.: National Association of Colored Women, 1933.

"Doctorate of Humanities." *Nation* 168 (February 26, 1949): 227.

Edmunds, Lavinia. "An Archive of Personal Treasures." *Ms.* 14 (August 1985): 22.

"Englewood, Our Town in Turmoil." *Nation* 174 (May 3, 1952): 415.

"Faith in a Swampland." *Newsweek* 45 (May 30, 1955): 47.

"First for a First." *Time* 53 (March 7, 1949): 44.

For the Dignity of Humanity. Washington, D. C.: U.S. GPO, 1979. [ED175782]

Fosdick, Franklin, pseud. "War Among the Women." *Negro Digest* 8 (February 1950) 21–25.

"Founder President of Bethune-Cookman College, Daytona Beach, Florida and Dr. Frank P. Graham, President of University of North Carolina Received the Thomas Jefferson Award, April 20, 1942, for Outstanding Service to the South." *Jet* (April 21, 1960): 9.

Henry, Linda J. "Promoting Historical Consciousness: The Early Archives Committee of the National Council of Negro Women." *Signs* 7 (1981): 251–59.

Herrick, Genevieve Forbes. "Loved, Feared, and Followed." *Collier's* 126 (September 23, 1950): 26 + .

―――――. "Queen Mary: Champion of Negro Women." *Negro Digest* 9 (December 1950): 32–39.

"Honorary Degree from Rollins College." *Journal of the National Education Association* 39 (March 1950): 230.

"House of Representatives and Senate Pass Bill Authorizing Secretary of Interior to Grant Authority to the National Council of Negro Women to Erect on Public Grounds a Memorial in Honor of the Late Dr. Bethune; Memorial Will Be Located in Washington, D. C., Near a Statue of Abraham Lincoln." *Jet* (April 21, 1960): 9.

Ihle, Elizabeth L. *Black Women's Academic Education in the South*. Harrisonburg, VA: James Madison University, 1986. [ED281959]

Jackson, George F. *Black Women, Makers of History: A Portrait*. Oakland, CA: GRT Printing, 1985.

Leffall, Dolores C., and Janet L. Sims. "Mary McLeod Bethune—The Educator; Also Including a Selected Annotated Bibliography." *Journal of Negro Education* 45 (Summer 1976): 342–59.

Lewis, J. G. "Statue That Struggle Built." *Ms.* 3 (December 1974): 20.

"Life of Mary McLeod Bethune." *Our World* 5 (December 1950): 32–35.

Ludlow, Helen W. "The Bethune School." *Southern Workman* (March 1912): 144–54.

Macdonald, Fiona. *A Chance to Learn.* New York: Hampstead, 1989.

McGlynn, M. M. "Lady Who Left Us Hope." *Look* 35 (February 9, 1971): 57.

McMillan, Terri L. "Mary McLeod Bethune Memorial Dedication." *Essence* 5 (November 1974): 17 + .

"Mary McLeod Bethune." In *Great American Negroes,* by Ben Albert Richardson. New York: Crowell, 1945.

"Mary McLeod Bethune." In *In Spite of Handicaps,* by Ralph W. Bullock. New York: Association Press, 1927. Reprint. Freeport, NY: Books for Libraries Press, 1968.

"Mary McLeod Bethune." *Journal of Negro History* 40 (October 1955): 393–95.

Masso, Clara Bodian. "Mary McLeod Bethune and the National Council of Negro Women." *Freedomways* 14 (1974): 51–53.

"Matriarch." *Time* 48 (July 22, 1946): 55.

Mays, Benjamin E., and others. "Most Extraordinary Black Woman I Have Ever Known: Four Prominent Black Men Pay Tribute to Four Pioneers." *Ebony* 32 (August 1977): 139–40.

"Memorable Woman." *Christianity Today* 15 (March 12, 1971): 39.

"Mrs. Bethune: Spingarn Medalist." *Crisis* 8 (December 1980): 543–45.

"Mrs. Bethune's Death Marks Changing Negro Leadership." *Christian Century* 72 (June 8, 1955): 676.

"My Last Will and Testament; As Life Drew to a Close." *Ebony* 10 (August 1955): 105–10.

"National Council of Negro Women Have Authorization from Congress to Build a Monument in Lincoln Park in Memory of Dr. Bethune." *Jet* 21 (December 28, 1961): 3.

"Negro Angel: College Founder Sees Bright Future for Her Race." *Literary Digest* 123 (March 6, 1937): 8–9.

"Obituary." *Crisis* 90 (June–July 1983): 30.

"Obituary." *Journal of Negro History* 40 (October 1955): 393–95.

Picott, J. R. "Editorial Comment." *Negro History Bulletin* 37 (August 1974): 275.

"Pioneers in the Struggle Against Segregation." *Survey Graphic* 36 (January 1947): 91.

"Portrait." *Saturday Evening Post* 210 (June 4, 1938): 15.

"Retired." *Survey* 86 (January 1950): 36.

Reynolds, Moira Davison. *Women Champions of Human Rights: Eleven U.S. Leaders of the Twentieth Century.* Jefferson, NC: McFarland, 1991.

Ross, B. Joyce. "Mary McLeod Bethune and the National Youth Administration: A Case Study of Power Relationships in the Black Cabinet of Franklin D. Roosevelt." *Journal of Negro History* 60 (January 1975): 1–28.

Scole, Evan. "Mary McLeod Bethune." In *Something More than Human: Biographies of Leaders in American Methodist Higher Education,* edited by Charles E. Cole. Nashville: United Methodist Church Board of Higher Education and Ministry, Division of Ordained Ministry, 1986.

Sloan, Robert L. "The Miracle Years of Mrs. Bethune." *Christian Century* 73 (February 1, 1956): 140–41.

Smith, Elaine M. "Mary McLeod Bethune and the National Youth Administration." In *Clio Was a Woman: Studies in the History of American Women*, edited by Mabel E. Deutrich and Virginia C. Purdy. Washington, D. C.: Howard University Press, 1980.

"Son Albert Bethune, Jr., Speaks at Moral Re-Armament World Assembly, Crux, Switzerland." *Jet* 20 (June 22, 1961): 18.

Stanton, Joyce B. *Living the Vision: A Program.* (N.p.: n.p.], 1982.

"Three Black Women Earn Place in New Hall of Fame." *Jet* 44 (September 13, 1973): 7.

Tobias, C. H. "Some Outstanding Negro Christians." *Missionary Review of the World* 59 (June 1936): 298–99.

"True Leadership Is Timeless." *Negro History Bulletin* 13 (May 1950): 173.

Walworth, D. "Unforgettable Character." *Reader's Digest* 60 (February 1952): 146–51.

Wilson, Beth P. *Giants for Justice: Bethune, Randolph, and King.* New York: Harcourt Brace Jovanovich, 1978.

"Women Who Have Led in Education." In *Negro Builders and Heroes*, by Benjamin Griffith Brawley. Chapel Hill: University of North Carolina Press, 1937. Reprint. [Alexandria, VA]: Chadwyck-Healey, [1987].

Other Works About Mary McLeod Bethune

Theses

Blackwell, Barbara Grant. "The Advocacies and Idelogical Commitments of a Black Educator: Mary McLeod Bethune, 1875–1955." Ph.D. diss., University of Connecticut, 1978.

Kifer, Allen Francis. "The Negro Under the New Deal, 1933–1941." Ph.D. diss., University of Wisconsin-Madison, 1961.

Kirby, John Byron. "The New Deal Era and Blacks: A Study of Black and White Race Thought, 1933–1945." Ph.D. diss., University of Illinois at Urbana-Champaign, 1971.

Newsome, Clarence G. "Mary McLeod Bethune in Religious Perspective: A Seminal Essay." Ph.D. diss., Duke University, 1982.

Rawick, George Philip. "The New Deal and Youth: The Civilian Conservation Corps, The National Youth Administration, and The American Youth Congress." Ph.D. diss., University of Wisconsin-Madison, 1957.

Roane, Florence Lovell. "A Cultural History of Professional Teacher Preparation at Bethune-Cookman College." Ed.D. diss., Boston University, 1965.

Young, Jacqueline Ann. "A Study of the Educational Philosophies of Three Pioneer Black Women and Their Contributions to American Education." Ph.D. diss., Rutgers University, 1987.

Media Materials About Mary McLeod Bethune

Films

A Rock in a Weary Land. Jacksonville, FL: Barton Film Co., 1968. 16mm film; 27 min; optical sound; color.

Filmstrips

Mary McLeod Bethune. Chicago: Society for Visual Education, Inc., 1964. Filmstrip with cassette; 48 frames; color.

Slides

Portraits of Outstanding Americans of Negro Origin. New York: Harmon Foundation, Inc., 1975. 2 × 2 slides with script; 32 frames; color.

Sound Recordings

Celebrated American Women. WEBZ, Chicago, IL. (Journeys), 1980. Sound tape reel; 60 min; 3 ¾ ips; mono; 7 ¼ in. tape

Hughes, Langston. *The Glory of Negro History*. Folkways Records FC 7752, 1958. 12 in; 33.3 rpm; script included. Reprint. Folkways Records FC 7752, 1966. Disc; script with bibliography.

Video Recordings

Mary McLeod Bethune. Reston, VA: Sylvestre C. Watkins Co., 1985. Videocassette; 30 min; ¾ or ½ inch; color.

Primary Source Materials Relating to Mary McLeod Bethune

Commission on Interracial Cooperation. Records. 1919–1943. Extent of collection: 61,967 items. Finding aids: Unpublished guide. Location: Atlanta University, Trevor Arnett Library, Negro Collection, 111 James P. Brawley Dr. S.W., Atlanta, Georgia 30314. Scope of collection: Bethune is among founding and guiding members of original organization.

Mary Jane (McLeod) Bethune. Papers. 1923–1942. Extent of collection: ca. 1 ft. (505 items). Finding aids: Unpublished register in repository. Location: Amisted Research Center, Tulane University, 6825 St. Charles Ave., New Orleans, Louisiana 70118. Scope of collection: Correspondence, diaries, speeches, writings, invitations, programs, clippings, photos and other papers. Microfilm available.

National Association for the Advancement of Colored People. Records. 1909–1969. Extent of collection: ca. 1,000,000 items. Finding aids: Published guide. Location: Library of Congress, Manuscript Division, Independent Ave. at First St. S.W., Washington, D. C. 20540. Scope of collection: Includes correspondence of Bethune.

National Council of Negro Women. Records. 1935–1978. Extent of collection: ca. 200 ft. Finding aids: In repository. Location: National Archives for Black Women's History, Bethune Museum, 1318 Vermont Ave. N.W., Washington, D.C. 20005. Scope of collection: Contains council records which include all aspects of the organization.

National Youth Administration. Records. 1934–1944. Extent of collection: 993 cu. ft. Finding aids: Published and unpublished guides. Location: National Archives and Records Administration, National Archives Library, Pennsylvania Ave. at Eighth St. N.W., Washington, D. C. 20408. Scope of collection:

Includes records of director Bethune which include general subject file, reports of state directors of Negro affairs, and final report of division.
Theodore R. McKeldin and Lillie May Jackson. Oral history. 1976–1977. Extent of collection: 98 tapes and 40 transcripts. Finding aids: Unpublished guide. Location: Maryland Historical Society, Oral History Office, 201 W. Monument St., Baltimore, Maryland 21201. Scope of collection: One of Jackson's daughters discusses her acquaintance with Bethune and Eleanor Roosevelt.

9. *Elizabeth Blackwell*
(1821–1910)

First woman to earn medical degree in United States;
pioneer of women's medical education; abolitionist;
and advocate for women's rights and
health care for women, girls and poor

BIOGRAPHICAL INFORMATION

Chronological Biography

Born February 3, 1821, to Hannah (Lane) and Samuel Blackwell in Counterslip, near Bristol, England. Third daughter of 13 children, four of whom died in infancy.

October 8, 1826: Birth of sister Emily, who followed in her footsteps and also became physician.   **August 1832:** Emigrated at age 11 with family on merchant ship "Cosmos" to New York due to rioting in Bristol and father's concern for future of sugar refinery business. Early childhood spent in New York City and Jersey City where she enrolled in school. Family friends included Harriet Beecher Stowe, Henry Ward Beecher and William Lloyd Garrison.   **August 1838:** Father died from intestinal ailment four months after relocating family to Cincinnati, Ohio, to help revive failing sugar business. Family left financially destitute, but survived by taking in boarders and opening successful private school, "Cincinnati English and French Academy for Young Ladies." Taught private pupils after school closed in 1842.   **March 1843:** Relocated to Henderson in slave state of Kentucky and taught at girl's school for one year. Her opposition to slavery was bolstered after she witnessed it firsthand.   **August 1844:** Returned to Cincinnati where dying friend, who wished to have been treated by woman physician, suggested she study medicine. Rejected marriage as a personal option.   **June 1845:** Raised money to finance education by teaching music in an Asheville, North Carolina, school. Began medical education under the Rev. John Dickson, principal and clergyman, who had previously practiced medicine. Interest in religion and abolition increased. **January 1846:** After Asheville School closed, continued teaching music while pursuing medical studies in South Carolina under Dickson's brother, Dr. Samuel Henry Dickson, professor at Charleston Medical College. **May 1847:** Returned to Philadelphia, at time one of the nation's centers of medical learning. Lodged with Dr. and Mrs. William Elder and continued studies, including private course of dissection and midwifery under Dr. Joseph Warrington and Dr. Jonathan Allen. Began applying to medical schools in the United States but encountered strong prejudice. Advised to study in Paris and to don masculine attire. **October 20, 1847:** Accepted by unanimous student vote into Geneva Medical College (later Hobart and William Smith Colleges) in Geneva, New York, after being rejected by at least 12 other medical colleges, including ones in Boston, New York and Philadelphia. Dean of school, unable or unwilling to make decision on admission, had put it to student vote with surprising result. Also received acceptance from Castleton Medical College in Vermont. **1848:** Spring and summer breaks spent at hospital attached to Blockley Almshouse in Philadelphia to gain clinical experience. Persevered even when young resident physicians walked out of wards when she entered. Hospital experience shaped belief in hygiene, preventive medicine and public health. Outbreak of typhus among Irish immigrant patients became subject of her thesis. **January 23, 1849:** Granted Doctor of Medicine from Geneva Medical College at age 27 at head of class. Although hailed by Horace Greeley's *New York Tribune*, *Boston Medical and Surgical Journal* contained scathing comments. **February 1849:** Graduate thesis, "Ship Fever," published in the *Buffalo Medical Journal and Monthly Review*. Editor Austin Flint, professor at Geneva during her first term, followed her progress favorably. **Spring 1849:** Traveled to England, then Paris, to practice medicine and obtain clinical experience but met resistance and opposition. Enrolled as student in midwifery at Hôpital de la Maternité, large state institution. **Fall 1849:** Severe infection developed when she was splashed while irrigating newborn's eye for treatment of purulent ophthalmia, resulting in blindness of her left eye. Subsequent water cure in Austria unsuccessful and eye was later removed in Paris, ending aspiration to become surgeon. **October 1850:** Practiced all branches of medicine at St. Bartholomew's Hospital in London but denied access to female diseases department. Worked with pathologist and surgeon Sir James Paget. **April 1851:** Met Florence Nightingale and developed lasting friendship. **July 26, 1851:** Returned to New York City but prevented from starting practice due to resistance and hostility. Presented well received lectures on physical education of girls to Quaker women. **1852:** Published first major work *The Laws of Life with Special Reference to the Physical Education of Girls,* which stemmed from her lectures. Chapters included "The Criticism of Education" and "Reform of Education." **1853:** Organized and opened New York Dispensary for Poor Women and Children in East side slums after being turned down for position at public clinic for poor. Mission of institution was to provide medical aid for the sick and poor (especially women and children) to secure the services of well qualified women physicians, and to form a training school for nurses. Advocated cleanliness, exercise, fresh air and wholesome food. **1854:** Invited midwife Marie Elizabeth Zakrzewska to join Dispensary. Adopted seven-year-old Irish orphan, Katherine "Kitty" Barry, who remained lifelong companion. Sister Emily, rejected by Geneva Medical College, graduated from Western Reserve Medical College in Cleveland. **1856:** Began planning for opening of hospital for poor women and children. Enlisted support of Emily Blackwell, recently returned from additional training in Europe, and Marie Zakrzewska, now physician. **May 12, 1857:** Established and served as director of 16-bed New York Infirmary for Indigent Women and Children at 64 Bleeker Street in Greenwich Village. First hospital by and for women; served as model for six others to come in next 25 years. Florence Nightingale's birthdate was chosen for opening date as tribute to their friendship. Henry Ward Beecher spoke. Among those present were Horace Greeley, James Gordon Bennett and Charles Dana. Emily Blackwell, a surgeon, taught obstetrics, and Marie Zakrzewska served as resident and instructor. **1859:** First woman to have name placed on Medical Register of Great Britain. An extended lecture tour in 1858–59 helped advance cause of women in medicine in Great Britain. Initiated Sanitary Visitor Program at her infirmary run by Dr. Rebecca Cole, first black graduate of the Woman's Medical College of Pennsylvania and second regularly trained black female physician in United States. **1860:** Published *Medicine as a Profession for Women.* A decade after obtaining her degree, there were 300 licensed female physicians in United States. Impending outbreak of Civil War postponed plans to open medical college for women in New York City. Initiated 13-month course for nurses. **April 1861:** Organized meeting that resulted in formation of Women's Central Association of Relief. Chaired the registration committee, responsible for nurses' training and duty assignment for war front. **May 1866–October 1866:** Extended stay in England. **November 2, 1868:** Official opening of Woman's Medical College of New York Infirmary which established educational standards far above norm for time, and it advanced cause of medical education for women. Three year program instead of usual one year, required entrance examinations ten years before they were mandatory in the United States; first to have independent Board of Examiners. Prevention stressed over cure. Served as first chair of hygiene and offered nurses training. **July 1869:** Returned to England where she resided permanently. Emily Blackwell succeeded her as dean of college. **1871:** Sought after as lecturer on health, hygiene and sanitation. Helped organize National Health Society whose motto was "Prevention Is Better Than Cure." **1872:** Appointed professor of gynecology at London School of Medicine for Women but activities curtailed after one year due to ill health. Began to write prolifically in pursuit of moral reform. **May 1879:** Settled permanently at Rock House in Hastings, England, with Kitty. **May**

1880: Presiding officer of the Association of Registered Medical Women. Goal of organization to advance interests of medical women in Great Britain. 1884: Published *The Human Element in Sex* which rejected Victorian code of silence on sexuality and argued against prostitution and double standard. Became vocal opponent of vaccination after inoculation resulted in child's death. Dubious toward bacteriology and germ theory, and persistently questioned rationale for and number of gynecologic surgical procedures performed. Worked for establishment of Leigh Brown Trust to sponsor original research in biological sciences without vivisection.   1892: Wrote essays in medical sociology promoting Home Colonization Idea which visualized drawing neighborhoods together in cooperative units, joint land ownership, profit-sharing from community industry and equal morality between men and women.   1895: Published partial autobiography, *Pioneer Work in Opening the Medical Profession to Women*.   1899: Woman's Medical College of New York Infirmary closed when Cornell Medical College admitted women and goal of coeducation realized. College had graduated 368 women physicians, including two nieces: Edith Brown Blackwell and Ethel Blackwell. Infirmary continued to flourish.   Summer 1906: Made final visit to America at age 85 to see brother Henry and celebrate sister Emily's 80th birthday. Took first and last automobile ride. Attended political meetings and visited New England Hospital.   1907: Never fully recovered from fall sustained at summer home in Argyllshire, Scotland, where she had summered since 1902. Cared for by Kitty.   May 31, 1910: Died at Rock House in Hastings, England, at age 89, six days after suffering a stroke. Buried in Argyllshire, Scotland. Grave marked by Celtic cross and inscription, "The first woman in modern times to qualify in medicine (1849)."

Background Information

Parents: Hannah (Lane) and Samuel Blackwell, married in Bristol, England, on September 27, 1815. Mother, a milliner and abolitionist, was daughter of jeweler and watchmaker. Father (1790–1838) was sugar refiner, religious dissenter, abolitionist and proponent of equal education of sexes. Siblings: 12 (Known names: Anna [1816–1900], Marian [1818–1897], Samuel Charles [1823–1901], Henry Brown [1825–1909], Emily [1826–1910], Sarah Ellen [1828–1901], John Howard, George Washington [1832–1912]). Four other brothers died in infancy.   Children: One (Katherine "Kitty" Barry [1848?–1936], adopted daugher).   Influences: None.   Ethnicity: English. Also known as: None known.   Historical sites, landmarks, etc.: Grave, Argyllshire, Scotland; Blackwell Hall, Dormitory, Hobart and William Smith Colleges, Geneva, New York; Portrait in London School of Medicine for Women, London, England; New York Infirmary — Beekman Downtown Hospital, 170 William Street, New York, New York. Outgrowth of original New

York Infirmary founded by Blackwell; Elizabeth Blackwell Health Center for Women, 1124 Walnut Street, Philadelphia, Pennsylvania; Blackwell is honoree in National Women's Hall of Fame, 76 Fall Street, Seneca Falls, New York; Elizabeth Blackwell Street, Syracuse, New York; Elizabeth Blackwell Award granted annually since 1949 by American Medical Women's Association to women physicians who have made most outstanding contribution to cause of women in field of medicine; Elizabeth Blackwell Award granted annually since 1958 by Hobart and William Smith Colleges to outstanding women for service to humanity in arts and sciences; U.S. Postage Stamp, 18-cent Elizabeth Blackwell Commemorative Postage Stamp. Purple in color, bears portrait and words "First Woman Physician." Issued January 23, 1974.

BIBLIOGRAPHICAL INFORMATION

Biographical Sketches About Elizabeth Blackwell

Bullough, Vern L., Olga Maranjian Church, and Alice P. Stein, eds. *American Nursing: A Biographical Dictionary.* New York: Garland, 1988.

Garraty, John A., ed. *Encyclopedia of American Biography.* New York: Harper & Row, 1974.

James, Edward T., ed. *Notable American Women 1607–1950: A Biographical Dictionary.* Cambridge, MA: Belknap Press of Harvard University Press, 1971.

Johnson, Allen, ed. *Dictionary of American Biography.* New York: Charles Scribner's Sons, 1929.

Kauffman, Martin, Stuart Galishoff, and Todd L. Savitt, eds. *Dictionary of American Medical Biography.* Westport, CT: Greenwood, 1984.

McHenry, Robert, ed. *Famous American Women: A Biographical Dictionary from Colonial Times to the Present.* New York: Dover, 1983.

Ogilvie, Marilyn Bailey. *Women in Science: Antiquity Through the Nineteenth Century: A Biographical Dictionary with Annotated Bibliography.* Cambridge, MA: MIT Press, 1986.

Whitman, Alden, ed. *American Reformers: An H. W. Wilson Biographical Dictionary.* New York: H. W. Wilson Company, 1985.

Books by Elizabeth Blackwell

Address on the Medical Education of Women. New York: Baker & Duyckinck, 1856.

Christian Duty in Regard to Vice. A Letter Addressed to the Brussels International Congress Against State Regulation of Vice. London: Moral Reform League, 1891.

Christian Socialism: Thoughts Suggested by the Easter Season. Hastings: D. Williams, 1882.

Christianity in Medicine. London: Moral Reform League, 1891.

Christianity in Medicine: An Address Delivered Before the Christo-Theosophical Society, December 18th, 1890. Privately printed, 1890.

Counsel to Parents on the Moral Education of Their Children. New York: Bretano's Literary Emporium, 1879.

Criticism of Grenlund's Co-operative Commonwealth; Chapter X — Woman. St. Leonards: J. F. Nock, 1892.

Essays in Medical Sociology. London: Bell, 1902. Reprint. New York: Arno, 1972.

How to Keep a Household in Health. London: W. W. Head, 1870.

Human Element in Sex: A Consideration of Facts in Relation to the Physical and Mental Organisation of Men and Women: Addressed to Students of Medicine. London: McGowan's Steam Printing, 1880.

The Human Element in Sex. Being a Medical Inquiry into the Relation of Sexual Physiology to Christian Morality. London: Churchill, 1884. Reprint. London: Churchill, 1894.

The Influence of Women in the Profession of Medicine. Address Given at the Opening of the Winter Session of the London School of Medicine for Women. London: George Bell & Sons, 1889.

The Laws of Life with Special Reference to the Physical Education of Girls. New York: G. P. Putnam, 1852. Reprint. Rothman, David J., and Sheila M. Rothman, eds. *Women and Children First.* New York: Garland, 1986.

Lectures on the Laws of Life. London: Sampson Low, Son, & Marston, 1871.

A Medical Address on the Benevolence of Malthus, Contrasted with the Corruptions of Neo-Malthusianism. London: T. W. Danks & Co., 1888.

On the Decay of Municipal Representative Government: A Chapter of Personal Experience. London: Moral Reform League, 1888.

On the Humane Prevention of Rabies. St. Leonards: J. F. Nock, 1891.

Pioneer Work in Opening the Medical Profession to Women: Autobiographical Sketches. London and New York: Longmans, Green, 1895. Reprint without the bibliography but with a new introduction. New York: Schocken Books, 1977.

The Purchase of Women: The Great Economic Blunder. London: John Kensit, 1887.

The Religion of Health. Edinburgh and Glasgow: J. Menzies, 1878.

Rescue Work in Relation to Prostitution and Disease. New York: Fowler and Wells, 1882.

Rescue Work in Relation to Prostitution and Disease: An Address Given at the Conference of Rescue Workers Held in London, June 1881. London: T. Danks, 1881.

Responsibility of Women Physicians in Relation to the Contagious Diseases Acts: Address Given to a Medical Meeting in London, April 27th, 1897. Privately printed, 1897.

Scientific Method in Biology. London: Eilliot Stock, 1898.

A Serious Protest Sent to the Alumnae Association of the Women's Medical College of the New York Infirmary. St. Leonards: J. F. Nock, 1890. Reprinted as *Erroneous Method in Medical Education.* London: Women's Printing Society, 1891.

Why Hygienic Congresses Fail: Lessons Taught by the International Congress of 1891. London: G. Bell & Sons, 1892.

Wrong and Right Methods of Dealing with Social Evil As Shown by English Parliamentary Evidence. New York: Bretano, 1883.

_____, and Emily Blackwell. *Address on the Medical Education of Women.* New
York: Baptist & Taylor, Book and Job Printers, 1864.
_____, and _____. *Medicine as a Profession for Women.* New York: Tinson,
1860.

Books About Elizabeth Blackwell

Baker, Rachel (Mininberg). *The First Woman Doctor: The Story of Elizabeth
Blackwell, M.D.* New York: Messner, 1944.
Chambers, Peggy. *A Doctor Alone: A Biography of Elizabeth Blackwell, the First
Woman Doctor 1821–1910.* New York: Abelord-Schuman, 1958.
Fischoff, Ephraim. *Elizabeth Blackwell: First Woman M.D.* Springfield, IL: Pro-
duced for the department of medical humanities, Southern Illinois Univer-
sity School of Medicine by the division of biomedical communications,
Medical Illustration, 1981.
Johnson, Malcolm Sanders. *Elizabeth Blackwell and Her Alma Mater: The Story
in the Documents.* Geneva, NY: Humphrey, 1947.
McFerran, Ann. *Elizabeth Blackwell, First Woman Doctor.* New York: Grosset &
Dunlap, 1966.
The New York Infirmary: A Century of Devoted Service, 1854–1954. New York:
New York Infirmary, 1954.
Ross, Ishbel. *Child of Destiny: The Life Story of the First Woman Doctor.* New
York: Harper, 1949.
Sahli, Nancy Ann. *Elizabeth Blackwell, M.D., (1821–1910): A Biography.* New York:
Arno, 1982.
Wilson, Dorothy Clarke. *Lone Woman: The Story of Elizabeth Blackwell, the First
Woman Doctor.* Boston: Little, Brown, 1970.

Shorter Works by Elizabeth Blackwell

Brownlee, W. Elliot, and Mary M. Brownlee, eds. *Women in the American
Economy: A Documentary History, 1675 to 1929.* New Haven, CT: Yale
University Press, 1976.
Cott, Nancy F., ed. *Root of Bitterness: Documents of the Social History of
American Women.* New York: E. P. Dutton, 1972.
"Cruelty and Lust — Appeal to Women." *Philanthropist* 6 (December 1891): 1–3.
"English Experience and Purity Work." *Philanthropist* 11 (June 1896): 2–4.
"Legal Enactments in Relation to Vice." *Philanthropist* 9 (September 1893): 1–3.
Lerner, Gerda, ed. *The Female Experience: An American Documentary.* In-
dianapolis: Bobbs-Merrill, 1977.
"Letter to Young Ladies Desirous of Studying Medicine." *English Woman's Jour-
nal* 4 (January 1860): 329–32.
"Lyndhurst." *Columbian Lady's and Gentleman's Magazine* 5 (June 1846): 274–78.
"Medicine and Morality." *Modern Review* 2 (October 1881): 750–61.
"Position of Women." *Philadelphia Press* (August 25, 1847).

Tanner, Leslie Barbara, comp. *Voices from Women's Liberation.* New York: New American Library, 1971.

Shorter Works About Elizabeth Blackwell

Abram, Ruth J. "Will There be a Monument?: Six Pioneer Women Doctors Tell Their Own Stories." In *"Send Us a Lady Physician": Women Doctors in America, 1835–1920,* edited by Ruth J. Abram. New York: W. W. Norton, 1985.

Antler, Joyce. "Medical Women and Social Reform—A History of the New York Infirmary for Women and Children." *Women and Health* 1 (1976): 11–18.

Bell, Enid Hester Chataway Moberly. *Storming the Citadel: The Rise of the Woman Doctor.* London: Constable, 1953. Reprint. Westport, CT: Hyperion, 1983.

Bendiner, Elmer. "Elizabeth Blackwell, 'Heresy with Intelligence.'" *Hospital Practice* 15 (1980): 109–28.

Blackwell, Alice Stone. "The First Woman Doctor." *Woman Citizen* (February 12, 1921): 986 + .

Blake, John B. "Women and Medicine in Ante-Bellum America." *Bulletin of the History of Medicine* 39 (1965): 99–123.

Buckmaster, Henrietta. *Women Who Shaped History.* New York: Collier, 1966.

Catt, Carrie Lane Chapman. "The First Woman Physician." *Woman's Press* (May 1942): 232–33.

Crovitz, Elaine, and Elizabeth Buford. *Courage Knows No Sex.* North Quincy, MA: Christopher, 1978.

"Doctors Blackwell: First Women Physicians." *Survey* 25 (1911): 795–96.

"Elizabeth Blackwell Celebration." *Journal of the History of Medicine* 29 (1974): 238–39.

Fancourt, Mary St. J. *They Dared to Be Doctors: Elizabeth Blackwell, Elizabeth Garrett Anderson.* London: Longmans, 1965.

"Female Physicians." *Buffalo Medical Journal and Monthly Review* 3 (January 1848): 494–96.

Fleming, Thomas P. "Dr. Elizabeth Blackwell on Florence Nightingale." *Columbia Library Columns* (November 1956): 37–43.

Forster, Margaret. *Significant Sisters: The Grassroots of Active Feminism, 1839–1939.* New York: Knopf, 1985.

"Founding Mothers." *Vogue* 155 (1970): 112–13.

Gillie, Annis. "Elizabeth Blackwell and the 'Medical Register' from 1858." *British Medical Journal* 5107 (1958): 1253–57.

Guion, Connie M. "Contribution of Medical Women to Society." *Journal of the American Medical Women's Association* 15 (1960): 764–70.

Hays, Elinor Rice. *Those Extraordinary Blackwells.* New York: Harcourt, Brace & World, 1967.

Horn, Margo. "Sisters Worthy of Respect: Family Dynamics and Women's Roles in the Blackwell Family." *Journal of Family History* 8 (1983): 367–82.

In Memory of Dr. Elizabeth and Dr. Emily Blackwell: January Twenty-Fifth MDCCCCXI. New York: Academy of Medicine, 1911.

Justin, Meryl S. "The Entry of Women into Medicine in America: Education and Obstacles, 1847–1910." *Synthesis* 4 (1978): 31–46.

Knaster, I. H. "Student No. 130." *Today's Health* 30 (1952): 72.

"The Lady Doctor from Geneva." *Journal of the American Medical Association* 178 (1961): 126–27.

Lentz, John. "America's First Woman Physician." *Today's Health* 42 (1964): 36–37 +.

L'Esperance, Elise S. "Influence of the New York Infirmary on Women in Medicine." *Journal of the American Medical Women's Association* 4 (1949): 255–61.

Link, Eugene P. "Elizabeth Blackwell, Citizen and Humanitarian." *Woman Physician* 26 (1971): 451–58.

Lovejoy, Esther Pohl. *Women Doctors of the World.* New York: Macmillan, 1957.

McCormick, E. "Trail Blazer in Medicine." *Independent Woman* 27 (1948): 325–26 +.

McNutt, S. J. "Dr. Elizabeth Blackwell, Her Character and Personality." *Medical Record* 100 (1921): 922–26.

Melin, G. H. "Elizabeth Blackwell, Pioneer." *Instructor* 74 (1956): 52 +.

"Memorial Meeting, Dr. Elizabeth Blackwell and Dr. Emily Blackwell." *Woman's Medical Journal* 21 (1911): 21–27.

Montiero, Lois A. "On Separate Roads: Florence Nightingale and Elizabeth Blackwell." *Signs: The Journal of Women in Culture and Society* 9 (1984): 520–33.

Morantz, Regina Markell. "Feminism, Professionalism, and Germs: A Study of the Thought of Mary Putnam Jacobi and Elizabeth Blackwell." In *Women and the Structure of Society: Selected Research from the Fifth Berkshire Conference on the History of Women,* edited by Barbara J. Harris and JoAnn K. McNamara. Durham, NC: Duke University Press, 1984.

————, Cynthia Stodola Pomerleau, and Carol Hansen Fenichel, eds. *In Her Own Words: Oral Histories of Women Physicians.* Westport, CT: Greenwood, 1982.

Morantz-Sanchez, Regina. "The Female Student Has Arrived: The Rise of the Women's Medical Movement." In *"Send Us a Lady Physician": Women Doctors in America, 1835–1920,* edited by Ruth J. Abram. New York: W. W. Norton, 1985.

O'Neill, Lois Decker, ed. *Women's Book of World Records and Achievements.* New York: Doubleday, 1979.

Ostler, F. J. "America's First Woman Doctor." *Coronet* 25 (1949): 177–80.

Pizer, Irwin H. "A Brief History of the State University of New York Upstate Medical Center." *Minnesota Medicine* 49 (1966): 1923–30.

Roth, Laurence G. "Elizabeth Blackwell, 1821–1910." *Yale Journal of Biology and Medicine* 20 (1947): 1–18.

Roth, Nathan. "The Personalities of Two Pioneer Medical Women: Elizabeth Blackwell and Elizabeth Garrett Anderson." *Bulletin of the New York Academy of Medicine* 47 (1971): 67–79.

Sahli, Nancy. "A Stick to Break Our Heads With: Elizabeth Blackwell and Philadelphia Medicine." *Pennsylvania History* 44 (1977): 335–47.

Sanes, Samuel. "Elizabeth Blackwell, Her First Medical Publication." *Bulletin of the History of Medicine* 16 (1944): 83–88.

Shelgrove, E. E. "First Woman Doctor." *Hygeia* 27 (1949): 534–35.

Shipler, G. E. "Elizabeth Blackwell." *Saturday Review* 35 (1952): 27.

Smith, Dean. "A Persistent Rebel." *American History Illustrated* 15 (1981): 28–35.

Smith, Elizabeth C. "Heirs to Trotula: Early Women Physicians in the United States." *New York State Journal of Medicine* 77 (1977): 1142–65.

Smith-Rosenberg, Carroll. "A Richer and Gentler Sex." *Social Research* 53 (1986): 283–09.

Something Hard: The Life of Elizabeth Blackwell, M.D., the first Woman Doctor, 1821–1910. London: Sheldon, 1949.

Soriano, Victor. "The Exemplary Life of Elizabeth Blackwell, First Woman Medical Doctor in the World." *International Journal of Neurology* 9 (1974): 192–97.

Tabor, Margaret E. *Pioneer Women: Elizabeth Fry, Elizabeth Blackwell, Florence Nightingale, Mary Slessor.* New York: Macmillan, 1925.

"To Honor the World's First Woman Doctor." *Independent Woman* 26 (1947): 322.

Tripp, Wendell. "Dr. Elizabeth Blackwell's Graduation—An Eye Witness Account by M. M. DeLancey." *New York History: Quarterly Journal of the New York State Historical Association* 43 (1962): 182–85.

Vaughan, E. "The Early Days of Elizabeth Blackwell." *Fortnightly Review* 94 (1913): 976–85.

Waite, Frederick C. "Two Early Letters by Elizabeth Blackwell." *Bulletin of the History of Medicine* 21 (1947): 110–12.

Wood, Ann Douglas. "'The Fashionable Diseases': Women's Complaints and Their Treatment in Nineteenth-Century America." *Journal of Interdisciplinary History* 4 (1973): 25–52.

Other Works by Elizabeth Blackwell

"Ship Fever. An Inaugural Thesis, submitted for the Degree of M.D., at Geneva Medical College, Jan. 1849." *Buffalo Medical Journal and Monthly Review* 4 (February 1849): 523–31.

Other Works About Elizabeth Blackwell

Score

In Celebration: Elizabeth Blackwell. Music by Patsy Rogers, words by Eve Merriam, 1976. One ms. score (40 leaves), bound, 22 × 28 cm. For SAB chorus, piano, and 4 percussionists.

Theses

Henderson, Janet Karen. "Four Nineteenth Century Professional Women." Ed. D. diss., Rutgers University, 1982.

Horn, Margo Ellen. "Family Ties: The Blackwells, a Study in the Dynamics of Family Life in Nineteenth Century America." Ph.D. diss., Tufts University, 1980.
Sahli, Nancy Ann. "Elizabeth Blackwell, M.D., (1821–1910): A Biography." Ph.D. diss., University of Pennsylvania, 1974.

Media Materials About Elizabeth Blackwell

Filmstrips

Elizabeth Blackwell. Chicago: International Film Bureau, 1975. 36 frame filmstrip; with cassette.
Elizabeth Blackwell: First Woman Doctor. Chicago: Society for Visual Education, 1974. 56 frame filmstrip; color; 35mm. plus phonodisc; 1 s.; 12 in.; 33⅓ rpm; (16 min.) or cassette; plus teacher's guide.

Slides

Elizabeth Blackwell, M.D. Anacortes, WA: Outdoor Pictures, 1975. 40 slides; color; 2 × 2 slide with cassette.

Sound Recordings

Dr. Elizabeth Blackwell. New York: Center for Cassette Studies, 1972. Audio tape cassette; 1⅞ ips; mono; 22 minutes.
Elizabeth Blackwell. San Francisco: Mind's Eye, 1986. Audio tape cassette; 1⅞ ips; stereo.
Elizabeth Blackwell. South Holland, IL: Wilcom, 1986. Audio tape cassette; 1⅞ ips; stereo.
Elizabeth Blackwell: The First Woman Doctor. Boulder, CO: National Center for Audio Tapes, 1961. 1 track audio tape; 3¾ ips; mono; 30 min.

Primary Source Materials Relating to Elizabeth Blackwell

Alma Lutz Collection on Abolitionists and Women's Rights Activists. 1775–1943. Extent of collection: 0.5 lin. ft. Finding aids: Unpublished finding aid. Location: Schlesinger Library, Radcliffe College, Cambridge, Massachusetts 02138. Scope of collection: Correspondence of leading abolitionists and 19th and early 20th century feminists on antislavery and women's rights, including letters from Blackwell. Microfiche available.
Anthony-Avery Papers. 1882–1908, 1887–1898 (bulk). Extent of collection: 267 items. Finding aids: Register. Location: University of Rochester, Rush Rhees Library, Department of Rare Books, Manuscripts and Archives, Rochester, New York 14627. Scope of collection: Correspondence of Susan B. Anthony and Rachel Foster Avery concerning cause of woman suffrage; includes letters from Blackwell.
Blackwell Family Papers. 1784–1960 (inclusive), 1832–1939 (bulk). Extent of collection: 40 lin. ft. Finding aids: Unpublished finding aid. Location: Schlesinger Library, Radcliffe College, Cambridge, Massachusetts 02138. Scope of collection: Blackwell and adopted daughter, Katherine (Kitty) Barry Blackwell, are heavily represented in wide variety of materials that include

correspondance, journals, diaries, memoirs, memorabilia, photos, biographical and autobiographical materials and other items. Portions available on microfilm.
Blackwell Family Papers. 1830–1950. Extent of collection: 40 lin. ft. (ca. 29,000 items). Finding aids: Register. Location: Library of Congress, Manuscript Division, Washington, D. C. 20540. Scope of collection: Contains family and general correspondence, diaries, biographical data, speeches, articles, book files and miscellaneous papers. Portions available on microfiche.
Elizabeth Blackwell. Letters. 1850–1884. Extent of collection: 152 items. Finding aids: Not listed. Location: Columbia University, Rare Book and Manuscript Library, New York, New York 10027. Scope of collection: Letters to close friend Barbara Smith Bodichon describing Blackwell's work in America and England, including her fight against prejudice towards women in medical profession, work in Civil War and efforts to improve sanitary conditions. Includes three letters from sister Emily. Microfilm available.
Elizabeth Blackwell Collection. 1847–1979, ca. 1945 (bulk). Extent of collection: 0.4 cu. ft. Finding aids: Item list. Location: Geneva Historical Society Museum, 543 South Main Street, Geneva, New York 14456. Scope of collection: Manuscripts and correspondance of Malcolm S. Johnston concerning Blackwell's career, two letters of Samuel Craddock, student at Geneva Medical College, 1847, copies of documents of and about Blackwell, photographs and numerous articles and clippings.
Elizabeth Blackwell Research Collection. 1847–1981. Extent of collection: 0.8 cu. ft. Finding aids: Not listed. Location: State University of New York Health Science Center at Syracuse, Health Science Library, Syracuse, New York 13210. Scope of collection: Mostly photocopies. Contains research collection of articles pertaining to life and career, 1848–1965; copies of Blackwell's letter seeking admission to Castleton Medical College in Vermont, 1947; letter from Margaret Murray DeLancey describing Blackwell's graduation from Geneva Medical College, 1849; and facsimile of Geneva diploma, 1849, and other materials.
Woman's Rights Collection. 1853–1958 (inclusive). Extent of collection: 38 lin. ft. Finding aids: Unpublished finding aid. Location: Schlesinger Library, Radcliffe College, Cambridge, Massachusetts 02138. Scope of collection: Includes materials on Blackwell in collection of manuscripts concerning men and women involved in women's rights movement.

(THE ABOVE ENTRY WAS CONTRIBUTED BY SHARON C. MURPHY)

10. *Ella Reeve Bloor*

(1862–1951)

Founding member of U.S. Communist party; journalist;
labor organizer; and advocate for women's rights and suffrage

BIOGRAPHICAL INFORMATION

Chronological Biography

Born July 8, 1862, near Mariners Harbor, Staten Island, New York. Oldest of 12 children (five girls and seven boys) of Harriet Amanda (Disbrow) and Charles Reeve. Family moved to Bridgeton, New Jersey; upbringing was conservative, in affluent neighborhood; mother active in community affairs, father successful drugstore owner. Attended local public school and one unhappy year at finishing school, Ivy Hall Seminary; afterwards, starting at age 14, tutored at home by mother. Especially enjoyed reading biographies of women.

1879: Took over care of siblings and home after mother died at age 38 giving birth to a premature child. Father would not allow her to attend college because he did not consider it proper. Affected in early life by mother and extensive reading, especially of Walt Whitman's works. Great uncle Dan Ware, active abolitionist and freethinker, was strong influence on intellectual development when she became interested in social and political reform as teenager; introduced her to writings of agnostic Robert Ingersoll. **1881–1892:** Father remarried. At age 19, married Lucien Ware, son of Dan Ware. Moved to New Jersey, living first in Camden, then Haddonfield and Woodstown, settling in Woodbury, New Jersey, near Philadelphia, where great uncle also lived; continued to study with him. Husband was aspiring lawyer and had been court stenographer at trial of the Molly Maguires, radical miners who had been accused of conspiracy. Six children, three girls and three boys, born during 11 year marriage: Pauline, 1882; Charles, 1883; Grace, 1885; Helen, 1887; Harold, 1889; Hamilton Disbrow, 1892. **1882–1894?:** Influenced by Quakers and Unitarians while living in Woodbury. Began working for women's suffrage and equality, organizing women to vote in school board elections. Established local chapter of Woman's Christian Temperance Union, serving as president. Joined Ethical Culture Society of Philadelphia. Read Marx and Engels. Assisted in unionizing Philadelphia streetcar workers after 1890 strike in which she had participated. Wrote about political issues for local periodicals to earn money to pay for tutoring in subjects she had wanted to take in college. **1884?:** Joined local Knights of Labor. **1886:** Daughter Pauline and son Charles died on same day. **1887:** Joined Prohibition party. **Mid 1890s:** After separation from Lucien Ware, attended University of Pennsylvania in 1895–1896 after moving to West Philadelphia. Studied science, history, philosophy and took teacher's training courses. Contributed articles to various newspapers. Joined weaver's union to help organize women after becoming aware women earned one quarter of men's wages. Met socialist leader Eugene V. Debs in 1895. Lived for short time in an Arden, Delaware, an utopian community formed by single-taxers and socialists; while there became acquainted with novelist Upton Sinclair.

1895: *Three Little Lovers of Nature,* textbook for use in nature studies in grade schools, published. First of two children's books written to help support family.   1896: Following separation caused by her political activities, the Wares were divorced.   1897: Searching for organization that reflected her increasingly radical views, especially regarding labor issues, joined Social Democratic Party of America formed that year by Eugene V. Debs and Victor L. Berger. Wrote young people's column in party's publication, *Social Democrat.* Married socialist Louis Cohen, associate of Daniel DeLeon and his Socialist Labor Party; had two sons, Richard, born in 1898, and Carl in 1900.   1898: Switched to more radical Marxist-oriented Socialist Labor Party headed by DeLeon after disagreement with Debs; wrote for organization's *Weekly People* and *Daily People,* and assisted in pre-publication editing of writings of Karl Kautsky and other socialists. Son Richard Cohen born. 1899: *Talks About Authors and Their Work,* second book for children, published.   October 12, 1900: Last child, son Carl Cohen, born.   1900: Elected to general executive board of Socialist Trade and Labor Alliance.   1902– 1919: Returned to Debs, and Socialist party which was formed in 1901, becoming state labor organizer in Pennsylvania. Increased labor and women's rights activities, organized strike and striker-relief activities among miners, hatters, steelworkers, etc. In effort to maintain family ties while travelling throughout country for party's causes, often took two young sons with her during early years, placing other children in boarding schools at times; in later years occasionally took along one of granddaughters. Worked in Ohio, West Virginia, Illinois, Colorado, Michigan, etc. Bestowed honorary membership in United Mine Workers of America for efforts in coal fields. Formulated plans for cooperative kitchen and nursery for working mothers. Taught English to foreign students at University of Pennsylvania in Philadelphia. Cohens separated in about 1902 and later divorced.   1903: To enable women to have both careers and families, advocated communal sharing of basic housekeeping expenses by groups of families living together cooperatively in *Wilshire's Magazine* article entitled "Rational Housekeeping."   1905: Served as Socialist party's state labor organizer for Connecticut from 1905 to 1910. Encouraged working women to join suffrage clubs. Fired from newspaper *Waterbury* (Conn.) *American* after making speech revealing harsh child labor practices in state; had been writing column entitled "Facts and Fancies About Fashions." Edited *Musical Waterbury* monthly magazine. 1906: Asked by Upton Sinclair to gather information to present to presidential commission to document charges he raised in *The Jungle.* Accompanied to Chicago by Socialist party pottery worker, Richard Bloor, for safety reasons. Knowing that public would be outraged at unmarried couple travelling together, used alias of "Mrs. Richard Bloor" or "Ella Bloor" in written reports. Because of recognition she received from investigation, continued to use "Bloor" rest of life, although denied any romantic involvement with him. Later affectionately called "Mother Bloor." Returned to Chicago later in year to investigate compliance with Pure Food and Drug Act. Travelled with Dan Ryan, editor of *New York Evening Telegram* which was employing her. Worked in several packing houses and found that laws were not being enforced, but newspaper owner would not allow them to print findings. Used gathered material in subsequent speeches and articles.   **1908:** Became first woman to run for state office in Connecticut in unsuccessful bid for secretary of state post on Socialist party ticket.   **1910:** Participated in establishment of National Women's Committee of Socialist party and advocated involvement of socialist women in suffrage movement. Chaired Department of Working Women of party.   **April–late Summer, 1912:** Travelled to London, Germany, and Hungary to see daughter, Helen, who had become engaged while living in Budapest studying violin; Helen was married while Bloor was there.   **1913:** Took part in mass demonstration of suffragists at President Wilson's inauguration; active in Ohio referendum campaign for woman suffrage amendment.   **December 1913:** Participated in Calumet, Michigan, copper miners' strike. During children's Christmas Eve party she organized, 72 children were crushed to death trying to escape after an ally of the mine owners falsely reported wooden building was on fire. She revealed details of tragedy to newspapers and testified during Congressional investigation. **1914:** Took part in miner's strike in Ludlow, Colorado, and witnessed state militiamen setting fire to tents in which women and children were sleeping, killing 13 children and one pregnant woman, shooting them as they fled. Brought national attention to mine conditions with speeches, fund-raisers, and by leading a march of 1,000 women in Colorado. Helped found National Woman's party in Connecticut; later withdrew support and opposed its Equal Rights Amendment as she felt it would hurt women by repealing all laws that limited exploitation of women.   **1916–1919:** Worked with hatter unions in New York State, Toronto, and St. Louis, and with machinists in Boston. In opposition to World War I, helped Elizabeth Gurley Flynn (see entry 25) and others establish Workers' Defense Union, raising money and supporting conscientious objectors and those arrested for antiwar activities. **1918:** Unsuccessfully ran as Socialist party candidate for lieutenant governor of New York state.   **1919:** At age 57, was one of founding members of U.S. Communist party (called Communist Labor party until 1923), Socialist party having expelled radical faction she participated in who opposed World War I and supported Russian Revolution. Signed up Earl Browder as charter member and helped to run his paper, *The Worker's World,* while he was in prison. He later led U.S. Communist party from 1935 to 1945 and was party's presidential candidate in 1936 and 1940.   **1921:** Helped form and was field organizer for Workers' party in Los Angeles.   **1921–1922:** Part of U.S. trade union delegation to First and Second Red International of Labor Unions conventions in Moscow. Also attended Third World Congress of Comintern taking place at same time. Felt American women should model themselves after Communist women. **1921-1924**: National organizer for International Defense. **1925**: At 63 years old, hitchhiked from New York City to San Francisco to recruit new members, sell subscriptions to party's *Daily Worker*, and raise money for striking workers. Worked with International Labor Defense in vain attempt to free Sacco and Vanzetti. **1925-1927**: Organizer for United Front Committee of Textile Workers in several cities. **1927**: Duplicated 1925 cross-country trek. **1929**: Stayed with Browder's group after party leadership clashes. **1930s**: Continued party activities in her seventies, campaigning for candidates and recruiting new members. Participated in hunger marches and unemployed demonstrations, made speeches, campaigned for women's rights. Worked with Midwest farmers in five states, organizing United Farmers' League. **1932**: Married for third time, to Andrew Omholt, Communist organizer, farmer, and candidate for Congress in North Dakota. Participated in organization of First Farmers' National Relief Conference in nation's capital. Elected regional secretary for farmers in Midwest, led farmer's strikes. **1932-1948**: Wrote for party's *The Communist* and *Party Organizer*, and was member of Central Committee. **Summer 1934**: Worked with American League Against War and Fascism in 1930s. Led American delegation to Paris for Women's International Congress Against War and Fascism; took group to German Embassy there to protest imprisonment and treatment of German women in concentration camps run by Nazis. **1934-1940**: Chaired commission to equalize status for women in Communist party. **February 1935**: Witness representing executive committee of Farmers National Committee for Action before House Committee on Labor proceedings on unemployment, old age, and social insurance. **April 1935**: Testified before House Committee on Immigration and Naturalization, representing national executive committee of Communist party. **1935**: Son Harold Ware killed in automobile accident. **1936**: Served 30 day jail sentence at age 72 in Nebraska after farmers' mass protest meeting. **July 18, 1937**: *Mother Bloor 75th Birthday Souvenir Book* issued and *Mother Bloor Song* by Fritz West sung at celebration in her honor at Grant City Park, Staten Island. Festivities were chaired by Elizabeth Gurley Flynn. **1937**: Honored guest in Soviet Union at 20th anniversary celebration of Bolshevik revolution. **1938**: Unsuccessfully ran for office of governor of Pennsylvania on Communist ticket. Pamphlet, *Women in the Soviet Union* published, praising communism's positive effect on women and motherhood. Honored on International Women's Day. **World War II**: Opposed war until Germany invaded Soviet Union, then actively supported American efforts after United States allied with Russia, travelling nationally during her final major campaign, speaking against fascism in person and on radio. **1940**: Autobiography, *We Are Many*, published. **1941**: Travelled coast to coast publicizing autobiography, recruiting new party members and soliciting subscriptions to party papers.   **1941–1947:** Headed Pennsylvania Communist party. **Post World War II:** Withdrew from active leadership in late 1940s and retired to "April Farms," apple orchard near Coopersburg in eastern Pennsylvania. She and Omholt had been living there since about 1940; she referred to it as "her first real home."   **August 10, 1951:** Died of cerebral hemorrhage at age 89 in convalescent home in Richlandtown, Pennsylvania. A warm, caring person, she was an activist rather than theoretician and had endured scores of arrests, threats and harrassment during her many years of activity.

Background Information

Parents: Harriet Amanda (Disbrow) and Charles Reeve. Mother's French and English ancestors came to Connecticut in 17th century. Father's Dutch and English ancestors settled on Staten Island in 18th century. Father was in Seventh New York Regiment in the Civil War when Bloor was born and owned successful drugstore in Bridgeton, New Jersey, where he had moved in 1860.   **Siblings:** 11 (No known names)   **Children:** Eight (Pauline, Charles, Grace, Helen, Harold, Hamilton Disbrow, Richard and Carl)   **Influences:** None.   **Ethnicity:** Dutch American, English American, French American.   **Also known as:** Ware; Cohen; Omholt; Reeve.   **Historical sites, landmarks, etc.:** Song, *Mother Bloor Song,* by Fritz West, sung at 1937 celebration.

BIBLIOGRAPHICAL INFORMATION

Biographical Sketches About Ella Reeve Bloor

Fink, Gary M., ed. *Biographical Dictionary of American Labor Leaders.* Westport, CT: Greenwood, 1974.
Garraty, John A., ed. *Dictionary of American Biography.* New York: Charles Scribner's Sons, 1977.
Johnpoll, Bernard K., and Harvey Klehr, eds. *Biographical Dictionary of the American Left.* New York: Greenwood, 1986.
Sicherman, Barbara, and Carol Hurd Green, eds. *Notable American Women: The Modern Period.* Cambridge, MA: Belknap Press of Harvard University Press, 1980.
Whitman, Alden, ed. *American Reformers: An H. W. Wilson Biographical Dictionary.* New York: H. W. Wilson, 1985.

Books by Ella Reeve Bloor

Talks About Authors and Their Work. Chicago: A. Flanagan, 1899. (Written under name of Ella Reeve Ware)

Three Little Lovers of Nature. Chicago: A. Flanagan, 1895. (Written under name
   of Ella Reeve Ware)
We Are Many: An Autobiography by Ella Reeve Bloor. New York: International,
   1940. (Introduction by Elizabeth Gurley Flynn)
Women in the Soviet Union. [New York: Workers Library Publishers, 1938].

Books About Ella Reeve Bloor

Barton, Ann. *Mother Bloor: The Spirit of '76*. New York: Workers Library, 1935.
Mother Ella Reeve Bloor Forty-fifth Anniversary Banquet: Friday, January 24, 1936.
   Hotel Lismore, New York. [New York: n.p., 1936].
Todes, Charlotte, and Sashsa Small eds. *Mother Bloor 75th Birthday Souvenir
   Book July 1937*. [New York]: Mother Bloor Celebration Committee, 1937.

Shorter Works by Ella Reeve Bloor

"The American Woman." *The Communist* (September 1939): 829–35.
_____, and Elizabeth Gurley Flynn. "Women in the National Front Against
   Hitler." *The Communist* (October 1941): 887–909.
"International Woman's Day." *Party Organizer* (February 1937): 19–22.
"Lenin Is Here, Lenin Is Here!" *New World Review* 38 (Winter 1970): 62–65.
"Rational Housekeeping." *Wilshire's Magazine* (July 1903): 14. (Written under
   name of Eleanor Reeve)
"Unity of Farmers and Workers." *Party Organizer* (August-September 1933):
   86–87.
"We Are Many." In *Female Liberation: History and Current Politics*, edited by
   Roberta Salper. New York: Alfred A. Knopf, 1972.

Shorter Works About Ella Reeve Bloor

*Birthday Celebration: Ella Reeve Bloor, Anita Whitney, Emmett Patrick Cush:
   August 30, 1942*. [Pittsburgh?: n.p.], 1942.
Draper, Theodore. *The Roots of American Communism*. New York: Viking, 1957.
Flynn, Elizabeth Gurley. *Daughters of America: Ella Reeve Bloor, Anita Whitney*.
   New York: Workers Library, [1942].
_____. *The Rebel Girl: An Autobiography, My First Life (1906–1926)*. New York:
   International, 1973.
Kipnis, Ira. *The American Socialist Movement, 1897–1912*. New York: Columbia
   University Press, 1952.
"Milestones." *Time* 58 (August 20, 1951): 69.
"Obituary." *Americana Annual* 74 (1952).
"Obituary." *New York Times* (August 11, 1951): 11.
"Obituary." *Newsweek* 38 (August 20, 1951): 60.
"Old Fashioned Radical." *Time* 58 (August 20, 1951): 15.
Patterson, B. "Funeral of Mother Bloor." *American Mercury* 73 (November 1951):
   63–70.

"Portrait." *Time* 31 (January 17, 1938): 25.

Raymond, Anan. "Prairie Fire: A Footnote to Contemporary History." *American Bar Association Journal* 38 (November 1952): 911–14.

Sinclair, Upton. *The Autobiography of Upton Sinclair.* New York: Harcourt, Brace & World, 1962.

"Trouble into Trouble." *Time* 26 (November 11, 1935): 13.

"United States Fascism and Communism." *Life* 3 (July 26, 1937): 19–27.

Vorse, Mary Heaton. "Mother Bloor: An Appreciation." *Woman Today* (July 1937): 14.

Weinstein, James. *The Decline of Socialism in America, 1912–1925.* New York: Monthly Review Press, 1967.

Other Works About Ella Reeve Bloor

Theses

Brown, Kathleen A. "Ella Reeve Bloor: Suffagist, Trade-Unionist, Socialist, and Revolutionary in the Making, 1862–1919." Master's thesis, San Francisco State University, 1987.

Scholten, Pat Creech. "Militant Women for Economic Justice: The Persuasion of Mary Harris Jones, Ella Reeve Bloor, Rose Pastor Stokes, Rose Schneiderman, and Elizabeth Gurley Flynn." Ph.D. diss., Indiana University, 1978.

Primary Source Materials Relating to Ella Reeve Bloor

Anna Rochester. Papers. 1880–1965. Extent of collection: 2 ft. Finding aids: Inventory and supplement to published guide. Location: University of Oregon Library, Special Collections, Eugene, Oregon 97403-1299. Scope of collection: Includes correspondence with Bloor.

Elizabeth Gurley Flynn. Papers. 1896–1964. Extent of collection: 8 lin. ft. Finding aids: Guide available from library. Location: Tamiment Institute Library, New York University Libraries, 70 Washington Square South, New York, New York 10012. Scope of collection: Bulk of collection covers Flynn's years in Communist party and includes material on Bloor. Microfilm available.

Ella Reeve Bloor. Papers. 1890–1972. Extent of collection: 6 lin. ft. (18 document boxes). Approximately 2100 items. Finding aids: Available in repository. Location: Sophia Smith Collection, Smith College, Northampton, Massachusetts 01063. Scope of collection: Personal and professional correspondence, pamphlets, clippings, memorabilia and printed ephemera. Microfilm available.

Grace Hutchins. Papers. 1898–1954. Extent of collection: 1.5 ft. Finding aids: Inventory and supplement to published guide. Location: University of Oregon Library, Special Collections, Eugene, Oregon 97403-1299. Scope of collection: Includes correspondence with Bloor.

Mary Marvin (Heaton) Vorse. Papers. 1841–1966. Extent of collection: 77 ft. Finding aids: Published guide. Location: Wayne State University, Archives of

Labor and Urban Affairs, Archives, 5401 Cass Avenue, Detroit, Michigan 48202. Scope of collection: Papers contain information on Bloor.

New York Bureau of Legal Advice. Records. 1917–1919. Extent of collection: 5.5 lin. ft. (13 boxes). Finding aids: Unpublished guide. Location: Tamiment Institute Library, New York University Libraries, 70 Washington Square South, New York, New York 10012. Scope of collection: Correspondents include Bloor.

Oscar Ferdinand Hawkins and Madge (Ytrehus) Hawkins, and Family. Papers. 1888–1963. Extent of collection: 11 boxes. Finding aids: Unpublished guide. Location: Minnesota Historical Society, Library and Archives, 1500 Mississippi St., St. Paul, Minnesota 55101. Scope of collection: Includes speeches, newsletters and pamphlets by Bloor.

Victor Jeremy Jerome. Papers. 1923–1967 (inclusive). Extent of collection: 16 lin. ft. (40 boxes). Finding aids: Unpublished guide in repository. Location: Manuscripts and Archives, Yale University Library, Box 1603A Yale Station, New Haven, Connecticut 06520. Scope of collection: Bloor is one of important correspondents.

11. *Mary L. Bonney*
(1816–1900)
Advocate for Native American rights; educator

BIOGRAPHICAL INFORMATION

Chronological Biography

Born June 8, 1816, in Hamilton, Madison County, New York, to Lucinda (Wilder) and Benjamin Bonney, fourth of six children. Only she and younger brother survived infancy.

1835: Graduated from Emma Willard's Troy (New York) Female Seminary. Previously attended private school nearby as well as local Hamilton Academy. **1835?–1850:** Taught school in New Jersey, New York, South Carolina and Pennsylvania at various secondary schools, including Troy Seminary and Miss Phelp's School in Providence, Rhode Island. Principal of Academy in DeRuyter, New York, for a time. **September 1850:** In order to provide home for mother, established secondary school for girls, Chestnut Street Female Seminary in Philadelphia with Harriette A. Dillaye, former colleague at Troy Seminary. School was dedicated to producing clear, independent, principled thinkers. **1850s +:** Activities on behalf of others included service as officer of Philadelphia branch of Woman's Union Missionary Society of America for Heathen Lands which she had helped to found, and heading Woman's Home Missionary Committee of First Baptist Church to assist Native Americans. Also provided financial assistance to enable young women to become missionaries to Orient, for education of five young men, one white and four black, to become ministers, for relief of homeless Armenian children, etc. **1879:** Outraged by American government's actions toward Native Americans, she and Amelia Stone Quinton (see entry 50), close friend of many years standing, began to circulate petition to arouse public opinion and to gain legislative action in favor of Native Americans. This was beginning of Women's National Indian Association (WNIA), although it was not formally named that until 1883. **February 14, 1880:** Bonney and two companions presented 300 foot long petition, prepared by Quinton, with 13,000 signatures to President Rutherford B. Hayes and Congress calling for honoring of land treaties with Native Americans. **1880:** In May, she, Quinton, and two other women from church missionary circle designated themselves Committee of Ways and Means and continued to distribute leaflets regarding Native Americans' plight. Later that year group was reorganized becoming Central Indian Committee, and in 1881, Indian Treaty-Keeping and Protective Association, and still later National Indian Association. Finally, after male-led Indian Rights Association was founded in 1882, group became Women's National Indian Association in 1883. Became president few months later, after original president resigned. **January 27, 1881:** Henry L. Dawes, senator from Massachusetts presented Committee's 50,000 signature petition to U.S. Senate urging protection of Native American lands and strict observance of all treaties. **February 1882:** Third WNIA petition of over 100,000 signatures pressing for allotment of tribal lands to individual Native Americans, granting of U.S. citizenship, guaranteed school education, etc. was presented to President Chester A. Arthur by Quinton and five others. It was introduced in Senate by Dawes. This became official policy of United States for next 50 years through Dawes Act of 1887. **1883:** Moved Chestnut Street Female Seminary to Ogontz, Pennsylvania, suburb of Philadelphia, renaming it Ogontz School for Young Ladies. The WNIA expanded and began to focus attention on training and education, especially of Native American women; establishment of missions, schools and libraries; building of homes; granting of loans, etc., in attempt to assimilate Native Americans into American society. Attended annual Lake Mohonk [New York] Conference of Friends of the Indian which also advocated land allotment. **November 1884:** Resigned as president of WNIA, continuing as honorary president and as executive board and missionary committee member. Had contributed more than $1,600 of personal funds to organization and continued to do so until her death. **1888:** Retired from Ogontz School as senior principal. **June 1888:** Attended Centenary Conference on Protestant Missions of World in London, England, as delegate of either WNIA or Women's Union Missionary Society. While there, became re-acquainted with and married the Reverend Dr. Thomas Rambaut. He had assisted in her conversion from Episcopalian to Baptist 40 years previously and was retired president of William Jewell College in Missouri. After travelling in England and Ireland, they settled in Hamilton, New York. **October 1890:** Husband died. Continued to live in Hamilton with brother until her death. **July 24, 1900:** Died at home in Hamilton, New York, at age 84. Amelia Stone Quinton was among those attending funeral. Baptist Education Society of State of New York was chief beneficiary of estate.

Background Information

Parents: Lucinda (Wilder) and Benjamin Bonney. Mother was teacher before marriage. Father was prosperous farmer; had served in War of 1812 and was colonel in New York State Militia. He died while she was young (date unknown). **Siblings:** Five (Known names: Benjamin Franklin). **Children:** None. **Influences:** Amelia Stone Quinton (see entry 50). **Ethnicity:** Not known. **Also known as:** Rambaut; Bonney-Rambaut. **Historical sites, landmarks, etc.:** None known.

BIBLIOGRAPICAL INFORMATION

Biographical Sketches About Mary L. Bonney

Fairbanks, Mrs. A. W., ed. *Emma Willard and Her Pupils or Fifty Years of Troy Female Seminary 1822–1872.* New York: Mrs. Russell Sage, 1898.

James, Edward T., ed. *Notable American Women 1607–1950: A Biographical Dictionary.* Cambridge, MA: Belknap Press of Harvard University Press, 1971.

Johnson, Rossiter, ed. *The Twentieth Century Biographical Dictionary of Notable Americans.* Boston: Biographical Society, 1904. (Listed as Rambaut, Mary Lucinda Bonney)

Logan, Mrs. John A. *The Part Taken by Women in American History.* Wilmington, DE: Perry-Nalle, 1912. (Listed as Mary L. Bonney Rambaut)

McHenry, Robert, ed. *Famous American Women: A Biographical Dictionary from Colonial Times to the Present.* New York: Dover, 1980.

Malone, Dumas, ed. *Dictionary of American Biography.* New York: Charles Scribner's Sons, 1935.

National Cyclopaedia of American Biography. New York: James T. White, 1929. (Listed as Rambaut, Mary L. Bonney)

Ohles, John F., ed. *Biographical Dictionary of American Educators.* Westport, CT: Greenwood, 1978. (Listed as Rambaut, Mary Lucinda Bonney)

Whitman, Alden, ed. *American Reformers: An H. W. Wilson Biographical Dictionary*. New York: H. W. Wilson Company, 1985.
Willard, Frances E., and Mary A. Livermore, eds. *A Woman of the Century*. Buffalo, NY: Charles Wells Moulton, 1893. (Listed as Rambaut, Mrs. Mary L. Bonney)
_____, and _____, eds. *American Women Fifteen Hundred Biographies*. New York: Mast, Crowell & Kirkpatrick, 1897. (Listed as Rambaut, Mrs. Mary L. Bonney)

Shorter Works About Mary L. Bonney

Bonney, Charles L. *The Bonney Family*. Chicago: Chicago Legal News, 1898.
"Death List of a Day." *New York Times* (July 26, 1900): 7.
Dewey, Mary Elizabeth. *Historical Sketch of the Formation and Achievements of the Women's National Indian Association of the United States*. [Philadelphia: The Association], December 1900.
Fox, Norman. *Preacher and Teacher: A Sketch of the Life of Thomas Rambaut*. New York: Fords, Howard & Hulbert, 1892.
Keen, William Williams, ed. *The Bi-Centennial Celebration of the Founding of the First Baptist Church of the City of Philadelphia, 1898*. Philadelphia: American Baptist Publication Society, 1899.
"Obituary." *Hamilton Republican* (July 26, 1900).
"Obituary." *Indian's Friend* (August 1900).
"Obituary." *Ogontz Mosaic* (October 1900).
"Obituary." *Public Ledger* (July 25, 1900).

Other Works About Mary L. Bonney

Theses

Wanken, Helen M. "'Woman's Sphere' and Indian Reform: The Women's National Indian Association, 1879–1901." Ph.D. diss., Marquette University, 1981.

Primary Source Material Relating to Mary L. Bonney

First Baptist Church of Philadelphia. Records. Extent of collection: Not listed. Finding aids: Not listed. Location: American Baptist Archives Center, P.O. Box 851, Valley Forge, Pennsylvania 19482-0851. Scope of collection: Annual reports of Woman's Home Missionary Society 1886 to 1896; manuscript minutes of Society from May 1877 to January 6, 1897; one folder of materials on WNIA.

Mary Lucinda Bonney Rambaut. Extent of collection: 4 items. Finding aids: Not listed. Location: American Baptist Historical Society, 1106 South Goodman St., Rochester, New York 14620-2532. Scope of collection: Ledger of Female

Seminary, 1878–1888; autobiographical sketch of Mrs. Rambaut; history of Chestnut St. Seminary, written in 1894; 1869 catalog of Chestnut St. Female Academy.

12. Gertrude Simmons Bonnin
(1876?–1938)
Advocate for Native American rights; author; and lecturer

BIOGRAPHICAL INFORMATION

Chronological Biography

Born February 22, 1876?, at Yankton Sioux Agency in South Dakota to Ellen Tate' Iyohiwin Simmons, full-blood Sioux. Details regarding her father are sketchy, but it is possible that he was a Caucasian named Felker who deserted Ellen before Gertrude's birth. Mother named her Simmons after second husband; Gertrude took name Zitkala-Sa (Red Bird) later. Mother had two other children; David Simmons, almost ten years older than Gertrude; and Peter St. Pierre, by her first marriage, about three years older.

1884?: At age eight or so, against mother's wishes and despite mother's teachings of distrust of and resentment toward whites, left reservation to obtain education at White's Indiana Manual Institute, Quaker missionary school for Native Americans in Wabash, Indiana. Unhappy and torn between two cultures, left White's after first or third year and returned to reservation where she remained for four years, when she once again attended the Institute, graduating at age 19.   **1895–1897:** Again defying mother, continued education at Earlham College in Richmond, Indiana, studying to become teacher. Won prizes in debating and published poetry and essays in school newspaper before graduation.   **1896:** Took second place in Indiana State Oratorical Contest for essay explaining both resentment felt by Native Americans as their lives were disrupted by whites, as well as desire of some to learn some of ways of whites. Some in audience mocked her and shouted racial slurs. This set tone for her life's work, fighting for recognition of importance of preserving Native American culture yet encouraging acculturation in some respects. Believed equality of races could be obtained through equal educational opportunities. Fought for Native American self-determination, and she dedicated life to improving social and educational awareness of Native Americans.   **1897–1900:** Taught at Carlisle (Pennsylvania) Indian School which emphasized total assimilation, with which she did not agree; felt college education rather than vocational training was important. Left to study at Boston or New England Conservatory of Music. Accompanied

Carlisle Indian School Band to Paris Exposition as violin soloist in 1900, receiving outstanding reviews for her performances. Probably met Carlos Montezuma, Native American physician, at Carlisle. They planned to marry, but she broke off relationship due to ideological differences regarding Native American issues; they maintained friendship for many years, however. **Early 1900s:** Autobiographical essays and short stories published in *Atlantic Monthly, Harper's Magazine, Everybody's Magazine*, etc.; many were reprinted in 1921 collection, *American Indian Stories*. One of first Native Americans to bring traditions and problems to attention of white audience. **1901:** First book, *Old Indian Legends*, published; contained art work by Angel De Cora, also Native American, who was art teacher at Carlisle. **May 10, 1902:** Married Raymond Talesfase Bonnin, Sioux co-worker she met while working as issue clerk for Bureau of Indian Affairs at Standing Rock Sioux Reservation in North Dakota. They transferred same year to Uintah and Ouray Reservation in Utah where they lived for 14 years, until 1916. Worked as clerk for most part, while husband was agent. For short time she was teacher and organized brass band for children. Also worked with women of reservation, showing them how to cook, clean and raise children like whites did. **1903:** Only child, Raymond O. (Ohiya?), born. **1911:** Began corresponding with Society of American Indians which had been formed in 1911. It was first pan–Native American group and required active members to be of Native American blood. Organization's purposes were mixed—governmental reforms, employment of Native Americans, and preservation of history and culture of race, but also citizenship, abolition of Bureau of Indian Affairs, termination of communal property holdings, and assimilation. Not all Native Americans were in agreement with these controversial goals. Ran community center in Fort Duchesne, Utah, under auspices of Society. **1913:** Coauthored and collaborated with William F. Hanson on composition and production of Native American opera, *Sun Dance Land*. Premiered in Vernal, Utah, February 20–21, 1913, at Orpheus Hall, and was very successful among both Native Americans and whites. Played in Provo, Utah, at Brigham Young University shortly after, and again in 1935. Selected in late 1937 as American Opera of year by New York Light Opera Guild, which produced it in 1938 with large cast and full orchestra at Broadway Theater. Ohiya, hero of opera, may have been named for her son. **1916–1920:** Moved to Washington, D. C., with husband after being elected secretary of Society of American Indians. Duties included national lecturing, corresponding with Bureau of Indian Affairs, and lobbying congress on behalf of Native American legislation. Acting editor from 1918 to 1919 of *American Indian Magazine* (also called *Quarterly Journal of the Society of American Indians*), published by Society. Used magazine to express views on reform measures, gaining much public recognition. Encouraged education, learning of English language, improvement and establishment of schools on reservations and increasing salaries of Native Americans working for Bureau. **February 1918:** Testified before House committee regarding peyote use, advocating restrictive legislation. **1920–?:** Society of American Indians having dissolved, began to work with General Federation of Women's Clubs to enlist support for betterment of education, health care, etc., and expose corruption at Bureau of Indian Affairs. Organization established Indian Welfare Committee in 1921. General Federation, in cooperation with other groups such as Indian Rights Association, sponsored investigation into government treatment of Oklahoma Native Americans. Subsequent report, *Oklahoma's Poor Rich Indians*, published in 1924 by Indian Rights Association, written by Bonnin, Charles F. Fabens, and Matthew K. Sniffen, described corruption and brutality of Bureau of Indian Affairs. This led to Meriam Commission report in 1928 which surveyed conditions among Native Americans, and also led to appointment by President Hoover in 1929 of members of Indian Rights Association to top two positions in Bureau of Indian Affairs. Husband began to work as law clerk in Washington legal office. **1921:** *American Indian Stories*, published; depicted her childhood, etc. **1924:** Native Americans granted U.S. citizenship; she had urged Native Americans to support action. **February 1926:** Founded National Council of American Indians, remaining as president until organization foundered in about 1936. Husband served as secretary-treasurer of group in 1930. Published *Indian Newsletter* to continue drive for self-determination and reforms. **1926– 1938:** With assistance of husband, continued efforts as progressive assimilationist to improve conditions for Native Americans, lecturing, lobbying, representing individual claims and testifying as witness at congressional committee hearings numerous times regarding land claims, education, poverty, housing, etc. Also continued to defend and lecture on Native American culture, often in traditional dress. **February 23, 1927, and January 1928:** Congressional witness representing National Council of Indians concerning conditions of Native Americans. **February/March 1930:** Testified at House hearings regarding creation of Native American trust estates. **January 26, 1938:** Died in Washington, D. C., at age of 61 of cardiac dilatation and kidney disease. Buried in Arlington National Cemetery after services in Church of Latter Day Saints. Remained controversial to some Native Americans because she advocated some aspects of acculturation and assimilation, even though she also defended Native American culture and strove to establish sense of tribalism which would provide common heritage for those who remained on reservation as well as those who did not. Never wavered in fight for abolition of Bureau of Indian Affairs and for self-determination so that Native Americans could manage own lives. She herself never fully succeeded in living in both worlds. Son predeceased her and husband died a few years after her death.

Background Information

Parents: Ellen Tate' Iyohiwin Simmons. **Siblings:** Two (David Simmons, Peter St. Pierre). **Children:** One (Raymond O. [Ohiya?]). **Influences:** Raymond Talesfase Bonnin. **Ethnicity:** Native American (Sioux). **Also known as:** Zitkala-Sa; Red Bird; Zitkala-Sha. **Historical sites, landmarks, etc.:** Tombstone and grave, Arlington National Cemetery, Arlington, Virginia.

BIBLIOGRAPHICAL INFORMATION

Biographical Sketches About Gertrude Simmons Bonnin

Dockstader, Frederick J. *Great North American Indians: Profiles in Life and Leadership*. New York: Van Nostrand Reinhold, 1977.
James, Edward T., ed. *Notable American Women 1607–1950: A Biographical Dictionary*. Cambridge, MA: Belknap Press of Harvard University Press, 1971.
Whitman, Alden, ed. *American Reformers: An H. W. Wilson Biographical Dictionary*. New York: H. W. Wilson Company, 1985.
Zophy, Angela Howard, ed. *Handbook of American Women's History*. New York: Garland, 1990.

Books by Gertrude Simmons Bonnin

American Indian Stories. Washington: Hayworth Publishing House, 1921. Reprint. Lincoln: University of Nebraska Press, 1985. (Written under the name of Zitkala-Sa.)
Oklahoma's Poor Rich Indians, an Orgy of Graft and Exploitation of the Five Civilized Tribes, Legalized Robbery; a Report by Gertrude Bonnin, et al. Philadelphia, PA: Office of the Indian Rights Association, 1924.
Old Indian Legends. Boston: Ginn & Company, 1901. Reprint. Lincoln: University of Nebraska Press, 1985. (Written under the name of Zitkala-Sa.)

Shorter Works by Gertrude Simmons Bonnin

Bonnin was a regular contributor to *American Indian Magazine* and the *Quarterly Journal of the Society of American Indians.*
"America, Home of the Red Man." *American Indian Magazine* 6 (Winter 1919): 165–67.
"America's Indian Problem." *Edict* 2 (December 1921): 1–2.

"Impressions of an Indian Childhood." *Atlantic Monthly* 85 (January 1900): 37–47. (Written under the name of Zitkala-Sa.)

"Impressions of an Indian Childhood." In *Fragments of Autobiography*, compiled by Leon Stein. New York: Arno, 1974.

"The Indian Dance." *Red Man and Helper* (August 22, 1902).

"Indian Gifts to Civilized Man." *American Indian Magazine* 6 (July–September 1918): 115–16.

"Indian Teacher Among Indians." *Atlantic Monthly* 85 (March 1900): 381–86. (Written under the name of Zitkala-Sa.)

"Indian Teacher Among Indians." In *Fragments of Autobiography*, compiled by Leon Stein. New York: Arno, 1974.

"The Indian's Awakening." *American Indian Magazine* 4 (January–March 1916): 57–59.

"Letter to the Chiefs and Head Men of the Tribes." *American Indian Magazine* 6 (Winter 1919): 196–97.

"School Days of an Indian Girl." *Atlantic Monthly* 85 (February 1900): 185–94. (Written under the name of Zitkala-Sa.)

"School Days of an Indian Girl." In *Fragments of Autobiography*, compiled by Leon Stein. New York: Arno, 1974.

"Side by Side." *Earlhamite* 2 (March 16, 1896): 177–79. (Written under the name of Gertrude Simmons.)

"Soft-Hearted Sioux." *Harper's Monthly Magazine* 102 (March 1901): 505–08. (Written under the name of Zitkala-Sa.)

"Trial Path: An Indian Romance." *Harper's Monthly Magazine* 103 (October 1901): 741–74. (Written under the name of Zitkala-Sa.)

"Warrior's Daughter." *Everybody's Magazine* 6 (April 1902): 346.

"Why I am a Pagan." *Atlantic Monthly* 90 (December 1902): 801–03. (Written under the name of Zitkala-Sa.)

"Why I am a Pagan." In *Fragments of Autobiography*, compiled by Leon Stein. New York: Arno, 1974.

"A Year's Experience in Community Service Work Among the Ute Tribe of Indians." *American Indian Magazine* 4 (October–December 1916): 307–10.

Shorter Works About Gertrude Simmons Bonnin

Bernstein, Alison. "A Mixed Record: The Political Enfranchisement of American Indian Women During the Indian New Deal." *Journal of the West* 23 (July 1984): 13–20.

Cary, E. L. "Career." *Book Buyer* 24 (February 1902): 20, 23–25.

Debo, Angie. *And Still the Waters Run*. Princeton: Princeton University Press, 1950.

Fisher, Dexter. "The Evolution of a Writer." *American Indian Quarterly* 5 (1979): 229–38.

———. "The Transformation of Tradition: A Study of Zitkala Sa and Mourning Dove, Two Transitional American Indian Writers." In *Critical Essays on American Literature*, edited by Andrew Wiget. Boston: G. K. Hall, 1985.

Gridley, Marion E. *American Indian Women*. New York: Hawthorne, 1974.

_____. *Indians of Today*. Chicago: Lakeside, 1936.

Hertzberg, Hazel. *The Search for an American Indian Identity: Modern Pan-Indian Movements*. Syracuse: Syracuse University Press, 1971.

Hoople, Cheryl G., comp. *As I Saw It: Women Who Lived the American Adventure*. New York: Dial, 1978.

Houghton, Louise Seymour. *Our Debt to the Red Man*. Boston: Stratford, 1918.

Johnson, David L., and Raymond Wilson. "Gertrude Simmons Bonnin, 1876-1938: 'Americanize the First American.'" *American Indian Quarterly* 12 (1988): 27–40.

"Portrait." *Harper's Bazaar* 33 (April 14, 1900): 330.

"Portrait." *Outlook* 65 (May 5, 1900): 81.

"Portrait." *Outlook* 127 (March 9, 1921): 375.

"Portrait." *Survey* 63 (February 1, 1930): 523.

Wells, Mildred White. *Unity in Diversity: The History of the General Federation of Women's Clubs*. Washington: General Federation of Women's Clubs, 1953.

Willard, William. "Gertrude Bonnin and Indian Policy Reform, 1911-1938." In *Indian Leadership*, edited by Walter Williams. Manhattan, KS: Sunflower University Press, 1984.

_____. "Zitkala Sa: A Woman Who Would Be Heard!" *Wicazo Sa Review* 1 (1985): 11–16.

Other Works by Gertrude Simmons Bonnin

Opera

Hanson, William F. *Sun Dance Land*. Provo, UT: J. Grant Stevenson, 1967. (Bonnin collaborated with Hanson on this opera.)

Other Works About Gertrude Simmons Bonnin

Theses

Fisher, Alice Poindexter. "The Transformation of Tradition: A Study of Zitkala Sa and Mourning Dove, Two Transitional American Indian Writers." Ph.D. diss., City University of New York, 1979.

Welch, Deborah Sue. "Zitkala-Sa: An American Indian Leader, 1876-1938." Ph.D. diss., University of Wyoming, 1985.

Primary Source Materials Relating to Gertrude Simmons Bonnin

Carlos Montezuma. Papers. ca. 1892-1937. Extent of collection: 4.5 cu. ft. Finding aids: Available in repository. Location: State Historical Society of Wisconsin, Archives Division, 816 State Street, Madison, Wisconsin 53706. Scope of collection: Many letters from Bonnin to Montezuma.

United States. Bureau of Indian Affairs. Records. Records Group 75. Extent of collection: 16,329 cu. ft. Finding aids: Not listed. Location: National Archives and Records Administration, Seventh St. & Pennsylvania Ave. N.W., Washington, D. C. 20408. Scope of collection: Contains hundreds of pages of correspondence from and about Bonnin.

13. *Mariana Bracetti*
(ca. 1840–1904?)
Puerto Rican revolutionary/patriot

BIOGRAPHICAL INFORMATION

Chronological Biography

Probably born in town of Mayaguez, Puerto Rico, around 1840, but may have been born in Anasco. Enjoyed carefree youth in well-to-do family.

?: Married Miguel Rojas, second husband. He was brother of Manual Rojas who became one of leaders of El Grito de Lares (The Cry of Lares) revolution for Puerto Rican Independence from Spain and to abolish slavery. **November 12, 1867:** Government had decreed two-thirds of property tax be paid in advance; many landowners were heavily in debt, as was the government. Wrote letter to governor requesting permission to keep her slave; hurricanes previous month had caused much destruction on her farm, and since husband was sickly and only son crippled, she needed income the slave brought from working at bakery to supplement money she earned by sewing. **1867–68:** Named Brazo de Oro (Golden Arm) by fellow rebels because of her bravery and dedication to independence, equal to that of men in movement. Source of inspiration and she drew many volunteers to cause, including some of its eventual leaders. In addition, was active in raising consciousness of public. Sewed and embroidered revolutionary flag which served as symbol of revolutionaries; banner was rectangular in shape, red and white with white horizontal cross and white star in upper, lefthand corner. Design of flag has been attributed to various persons. **February 24, 1868:** Politically active, chosen as one of two alternates to eight-member Centro Bravo, revolutionary junta in town of Lares. Played leading role in council. **September 23/24, 1868:** Along with two other council members, decided to launch attack prematurely because list had been found with participant's names, and government was taking steps to stop revolt. Approximately 400 people captured government in Lares, raised flag, and declared independence from Spain, proclaiming Republic of Puerto Rico. Revolt was unsuccessful for number of reasons: rebels were inexperienced, not fully organized and lacked sufficient arms; public was generally not supportive, preferring change by slower means; and officials, having learned of coming attack, were able to repel attempted takeover of Pepino (San Sebastian) following day. Revolutionaries dispersed, but many were later taken prisoner. Jailed in Arecibo prison; may have been pregnant and delivered stillborn son during imprisonment. Eighty others died from illness in prison; rest of participants eventually had sentences commuted in general Spanish amnesty. Although quickly extinguished, rebellion was beginning of nationalism of Puerto Rico and sparked many reforms.   ?: May have been married for third time to Santiago Labiosa.   1869: Spain conferred on Puerto Rico status of province.   1873: Slavery was abolished.   1897: Puerto Rico gained some measure of autonomy from Spain.   1898: Spain surrendered Puerto Rico to United States. 1904?: Died in poverty in small town of Anasco, possibly of pneumonia.

Background Information

Parents: Not known.   **Siblings:** None known.   **Children:** One son (no known name). **Influences:** None known.   **Ethnicity:** Puerto Rican.   **Also known as:** Brazo de Oro; Ana Maria; Braceti; Rojas; Cuevas; Labiosa. **Historical sites, landmarks, etc.:** In 1969, September 24th was proclaimed official holiday in commemoration of uprising, Puerto Rico; Annual celebration is held in Lares, particularly by those who favor independence for Puerto Rico; In plaza of Lares, on column commemorating revolution of Lares, is a sculpture of Bracetti, lifting her banner toward sky; Painting, *El Grito de Lares*, by Augusto Marin.

BIBLIOGRAPHICAL INFORMATION

Biographical Sketches About Mariana Bracetti

Enciclopedia Clásicos de Puerto Rico. Barcelona, Spain: Ediciones Latinoamericanas, 1971.
La Gran Enciclopedia de Puerto Rico. Madrid: Ediciones R., 1976.
Mujeres de Puerto Rico: lecturas suplementarios para estudiantes de escuela elemental. Río Piedras, P. R.: Universadad de Puerto Rico, 1984.
Rosa-Nieves, Cesareo, and Esther M. Melon. *Biografías Puertorriquenas: Perfil Histórico de un Pueblo.* Sharon, CT: Troutman, 1970.
Schmidt, Minna Moscherosch. *400 Outstanding Women of the World and Costumology of Their Time.* Chicago: The Author, 1933. Listed as Braceti, Mariana.

Votaw, Carmen Delgado. *Puerto Rican Women: Some Biographical Profiles.* Washington: National Conference of Puerto Rican Women, 1978.

Shorter Works About Mariana Bracetti

Corretjer, Juan Antonio. *El Lenero: Poema de la Revolución de Lares.* Guaynabo, P. R.: n.p., 1972.
Geigel Polanco, Vicente. *El Grito de Lares: Gesta de Heroísmo y Sacrificio.* Río Piedras, P. R.: Editorial Antillana, 1976.
Lidin, Harold J. *History of the Puerto Rican Independence Movement.* Puerto Rico: Master Typesetting of Puerto Rico, 1981.
Martinez, Luis de la Rosa. *La Periferia del Grito de Lares: Antología de Documentos Históricos (1861–1869).* [Santo Domingo?], República Dominicana: Editora Corripio, 1983.
Peoples Press. Puerto Rico Project. *Puerto Rico: The Flame of Resistance.* San Francisco: Peoples Press, 1977.
Perez Moris, Jose. *Historia de la Insurrección de Lares.* Río Piedras, P. R.: Editorial Edil, 1975. (This account may have been written deliberately to discredit and minimize the importance of the revolution.)
Puerto Rico: A People Challenging Colonialism. Washington: Epica Task Force, 1976.
United States. National Archives and Records Service. *Expediente Sobre la Rebelión de Lares, 1868–1869.* National Archives. Washington, D. C.: National Archives and Records Service, General Services Administration, 1969.
Virella, Federico E. *Honrando.* San Juan, P. R.: Biblioteca de Autores Puertorriquenos, 1979.
Wagenheim, Kal. *Puerto Rico: A Profile.* New York: Praeger, 1975.
_____, and Olga Jimenez de Wagenheim, eds. *The Puerto Ricans: A Documentary History.* New York: Praeger, 1973.
Wagenheim, Olga Jimenez de. *El Grito de Lares: A Socio-historic Interpretation of Puerto Rico's Uprising Against Spain in 1868.* N.p.: n.p., 1981.
_____. *Puerto Rico's Revolt for Independence: el Grito de Lares.* Boulder, CO: Westview, 1985.

Other Works About Mariana Bracetti

Brazo de Oro. Play by Cesareo Rosa-Nieves (1961).
Llorens Torres, Luis. *El Grito de Lares: Drama Histórico-poético.* San Juan, P. R.: Editorial Cordillera, 1973.
Marques, Rene. *Mariana O El Alba.* Edición Centenario del Grito de Lares. Barcelona, Spain: Editorial Antillana, 1968.

Primary Source Materials Relating to Mariana Bracetti

Various Collections. Extent of collection: Not listed. Finding aids: Not listed. Location: Archivo General de Puerto Rico. San Juan, Puerto Rico. Scope of collection: Governmental records, testimony of witnesses and participants, letters, etc.

14. *Donaldina Mackenzie Cameron*
(1869–1968)
Humanitarian; social worker; teacher; and missionary

BIOGRAPHICAL INFORMATION

Chronological Biography

Born July 26, 1869, to Isabella (Mackenzie) and Allan Cameron on sheep station at Clutha River in upper Clydevale area, Otago Land District, on South Island of New Zealand. Youngest of seven children, six girls and one boy.

1871: Family moved to California where father began sheep ranching in San Joaquin Valley near Berenda and Merced, California. 1874: Mother died. Father moved family to The Willows, San Jose suburb. Older daughters, Annie and Helen, kept house and raised Donaldina. Attended Castleman School for Girls. Attended school in Oakland after family moved there. 1885: Father became manager of sheep ranch in San Gabriel Valley; family moved to La Puente near Los Angeles. 1886?: Started teacher training at Los Angeles Normal School. 1887: Dropped out of college after father's death. 1888: Became engaged to George Sargent, friend of brother's; they did not marry. 1895: At 25, encouraged by Mary Ann Frank Brown, president of Occidental Women's Board of Foreign Missions and mother of Oakland schoolmate, began to teach sewing and to assist the director, Margaret Culbertson, of the Chinese Presbyterian Mission Home on Sacramento Street in San Francisco. Home had been established by Women's Occidental Board of Foreign Missions in 1873 to provide haven for Asian women who had been smuggled into United States from China and forced into slavery in hotels and gambling dens. Her campaign against slave trade alerted authorities and hastened the demise of such practices. 1897: Culbertson died. Continued to work at Mission Home under Mary H. Field. 1900: Became superintendent of Mission Home after Field resigned. 1911: Agreed to marry Nathaniel Tooker, well-to-do widower, but he died unexpectedly in July. 1925: Established another home, designed by Julia Morgan, in Oakland as refuge for young children. 1934: Retired from Mission

Home at age 65. Remained in San Francisco to help her successor, Lorna Logan. **1939:** Moved to Oakland to help care for three older unmarried sisters. **June 7, 1942:** Mission Home renamed Donaldina Cameron House. **1942:** Moved to Palo Alto with two remaining sisters. **January 4, 1968:** Died at 99 of pulmonary embolism shortly after breaking her hip. **January 30, 1968:** House Resolution Number 62 presented to Assembly of California State Legislature by Assemblywoman March Fong; resoluton recognized Cameron's lifetime work and contribution to Chinese community in San Francisco.

Background Information

Parents: Isabella (Mackenzie) and Allan Cameron. Parents were Scottish descendants of Highland sheep ranchers and devout Presbyterians. **Siblings:** Six (Annie [her "second mother"], Helen, Catharine, Jessie, Isabella and Allan). **Children:** None. **Influences:** None. **Ethnicity:** Not known. **Also known as:** Fahn Quai (white devil); Lo Mo (old mama). **Historical sites, landmarks, etc.:** Cameron House, 920 Sacramento Street, San Francisco, California, now a community center.

BIBLIOGRAPHICAL INFORMATION

Biographical Sketches About Donaldina Mackenzie Cameron

Kim, Hyung-Chan. *Dictionary of Asian American History.* New York: Greenwood, 1986.
Sicherman, Barbara, and Carol Hurd Green, eds. *Notable American Women: The Modern Period: A Biographical Dictionary.* Cambridge, MA: Belknap Press of Harvard University Press, 1980.

Books About Donaldina Mackenzie Cameron

Logan, Lorna E. *Ventures in Mission: The Cameron House Story.* Wilson Creek, WA: Crawford Hobby Print Shop, 1976.
Martin, Mildred Crowl. *Chinatown's Angry Angel: The Story of Donaldina Cameron.* Palo Alto, CA: Pacific Books, 1977.
Wilson, Carol Green. *Chinatown Quest: One Hundred Years of Donaldina Cameron House, 1874–1974.* San Francisco: California Historical Society, 1974. Reissue of *Chinatown Quest: The Life Adventures of Donaldina Cameron.* Stanford, CA: Stanford University Press, 1931.

_____. *Chinatown Quest: The Life Adventures of Donaldina Cameron.* Stanford, CA: Stanford University Press, 1931.

Shorter Works by Donaldina Mackenzie Cameron

"For the Guild of Intercessors." *Outreach* (May 1952).
"Rescue Work of the Occidental Board." *Women's Work* (January 1911).

Shorter Works About Donaldina Mackenzie Cameron

"Cameron House — Lo Mo's Legacy: Love, Service." *East-West* (January 17, 1968).
Chen, Jack. *The Chinese of America.* New York: Harper and Row, 1980.
Dewitt, Jack. "Smashing the Slave Girl Traffic." *Real Detective* (June 1936).
"Donaldina Cameron and the San Francisco Chinese Slave Trade." *Everybody's Magazine* 11 (1904): 40.
Dosch, Arno. "The Uplift in San Francisco." *Pacific Monthly* (September 1907).
Gray, Dorothy. *Women of the West.* Millbrae, CA: Les Femmes Publishing, 1976.
Hammack, Valentine C., as told to Dean S. Jennings. "Broken Blossoms." *Famous Detective Cases* (October 1935).
Jennings, Dean. "Smashing California's Yellow Slave Traffic." *True Magazine* (January 1936).
Lacy, Suzanne, and Linda Palumbi. "Life and Times of Donaldina Cameron." *Chrysalis* 7 (1979–1980): 29.
Lee, Rose Hum. *The Chinese in the United States of America.* Hong Kong: Hong Kong University Press, 1960.
Martin, Mildred Crowl. "Cameron House." *San Francisco Magazine* (June 1969).
McClain, Laurene Wu. "Donaldina Cameron: A Reappraisal." *Pacific History* 27 (1983): 24–35.
_____. "Donaldina Cameron: Rescuer of Girl Slaves." *American West* 18 (March–April 1981): 22.
Strother, E. French. "Setting Chinese Slave Girls Free." *California Weekly* (February 26, 1909).

Other Works About Donaldina Mackenzie Cameron

Theses

Durham, Carolyn Ross. "Educational Evangelism in Operation: A Description of the Program of the Donaldina Cameron House." Master's thesis, San Francisco Theological Seminary, 1956.

Primary Source Materials Relating to Donaldina Mackenzie Cameron

Women's Occidental Board of Foreign Missions of the Presbyterian Church. 1873–1920. Extent of collection: 4 vols. Finding aids: Not listed. Location:

San Francisco Theological Seminary Library, San Anselmo, California 94960. Scope of collection: Includes information on establishment of Occidental Mission School and Home, later Donaldina Cameron House. Contains 1903 report by Cameron, letters from pupils at home and report of house to House Visitation Committee intended to help seclusion of Chinatown women.

(THE ABOVE ENTRY WAS CONTRIBUTED BY DOROTHY S. TAO)

15. *Shirley Chisholm*
(1924–)

U.S. congresswoman; New York state legislator; educator;
and advocate for women's rights and African American rights

BIOGRAPHICAL INFORMATION

Chronological Biography

Born November 30, 1924, in Bedford-Stuyvesant section of Brooklyn, New York. Oldest of four girls born to Ruby (Seale) and Charles Christopher St. Hill.
1927: At about three years old, sent with three younger sisters to live with grandmother, Emmeline Seale, on farm in Barbados so that parents could save money for children's education; grandmother was a strong influence who taught her pride, courage and faith. Stayed for about eight years. Received British elementary school education and acquired West Indian rhythm of speech. **1935:** Returned to United States to live with parents at about 11 years old. **1939:** Graduated from Girls High School in Brooklyn, New York. **1943:** Received B.A. degree cum laude in sociology from Brooklyn College; Professor Warsoff encouraged her to go into politics. **1946–1953:** Nursery school teacher in Metropolitan New York City area. Also director of Friends Day Nursery in Brownsville, New York. **October 8, 1949:** Married Conrad Q. Chisholm, social service investigator. **1952:** Received M.A. in education from Columbia University. **1953–1959:** Director of Hamilton Madison Child Care Center in lower Manhattan. **1957:** Received Alumna of Year Award from Brooklyn College. Outstanding Work in Field of Child Welfare Award received from Women's Council of Brooklyn. **1959–1964:** Educational consultant in Division of Day Care of New York City's Bureau of Child Welfare. **1964–1968:** Entered politics. Ran successfully on Democratic ticket to become first black woman from Brooklyn to serve in New York State Assembly. Represented the

55th Assembly District. **1965:** Received Certificate of Honor for Outstanding Service to Youth from Junior High School 271 in Brooklyn. Received award for Outstanding Service in Early Childhood and Welfare from Sisterhood of Concordia. Recipient of Woman of Achievement Award from Key Women, Inc. **Summer 1968:** Chosen State National Committeewoman at Democratic National Convention in Chicago. **November 1968:** First black woman to be elected to U.S. House of Representatives. Won seat for Representative to Congress for court-ordered 12th New York Congressional District. Defeated well-known Republican-Liberal candidate, James Farmer, nationally prominent civil rights leader. **January 1969:** As member of 91st congress, protested serving on forest and rural villages subcommittees of Agriculture Committee, requesting committee appointments concerned with urban affairs. In unprecedented move, Ways and Means Committee reassigned her to Veterans Affairs Committee which had more relevance to her constituency. **May 1969:** Declined Doctorate of Humane Letters from Pratt Institute because its Brooklyn Campus had shortly before been scene of demonstrations by black students and she had agreed with their demands. **Summer 1969:** Joined other visiting lecturers in special Great Scholars program at Southampton College. **June 1969:** Addressed graduating class of Douglas College. **July 1969:** Spoke at annual conference of Urban League in New York. **August 1969:** Spoke at forum of New School for Social Research. Said she "encountered harsher criticism in fighting for rights of women than in fighting for Negro rights." **November– December 1969:** Testified before House committees regarding social security and welfare proposals. Witness at Senate Family Planning and Population Research hearing, and House Comprehensive Preschool Education and Child Day-Care Act of 1969. **1969:** Received Sojourner Truth Award from Association for the Study of Negro Life and History, achievement award from Albert Einstein College of Medicine, Deborah Gannett Award from National Media Women, Russwurm Award from Newspaper Publishers Association, Youth in Action Humanitarian Award of Family Counseling, and honorary LL.D. from North Carolina Central University and from Talladega College. **March–December 1970:** Appeared as congressional witness numerous times regarding various subjects including Comprehensive Preschool Education and Child Day-Care Act, Manpower Development and Training Legislation, Equal Rights Amendment, educational and professional discrimination against women, migrant and seasonal farm workers, Repeal of Emergency Detention Act of 1950, and family planning and population research (in opposition to "compulsory pregnancy under present abortion laws"). **May 11, 1970:** Gave commencement address at Metropolitan State College in Denver, Colorado. **1970:** Received honorary LL.D from Hampton Institute and Wilmington College. **March–May 1971:** Gave testimony before House and Senate committees concerning operation of

Public Health Service hospitals, nonvoting delegates in Guam and Virgin Islands, Emergency Employment Act of 1971, Equal Employment Opportunity Enforcement Procedure, veterans affairs, Comprehensive Child Development Act and operation and funding of VA medical programs. **1971:** One of founders of National Women's Political Caucus, formed to increase participation of women in public and political life. Received honorary LL.D. from Capitol University, LaSalle College, University of Maine, William Patterson College and Coppin State College. **1972:** First black woman candidate for United States presidency. Ran unsuccessfully in Democratic presidential primary. Introduced major women's rights issues into campaign and emerged as dynamic speaker and nationally known spokesperson for women and blacks. Received honorary LL.D. from Pratt Institute. **May 17, 1973:** Testified before Senate Continuation Hearing on Social Security regulations. **1973:** Received honorary LL.D. from Kenyon College. Named Clairol's "Woman of the Year" for outstanding achievement in public affairs. **December 4, 1974:** Submitted statements to House in support of Nelson A. Rockefeller for vice president of United States. **February 7, 1975:** Witness before Senate committee on depressed condition of U.S. for tanker industry. **February 1977:** Divorced Conrad Chisholm. **November 26, 1977:** Married businessman Arthur Hardwick, Jr. **1977–1982:** Testified at least 37 times before congressional committees concerning wide range of issues including consumer affairs, Youth Employment and Training Act, education, welfare reform, school safety, medical issues, Head Start Program, juvenile delinquency prevention, housing, endowments for arts, humanities and libraries, farmworker housing, job training for handicapped, student loans, enterprise zones and immigration. **1980:** Received award from Metropolitan State College in Denver. **1980?:** Received honorary LL.D from Aquinas College, North Carolina College, Reed College, Smith College and University of Cincinnati. **September 17, 1981:** Served as chairperson of House Task Force on Refugees of Congressional Black Caucus. **February 10, 1982:** Announced she would not seek reelection to Congress because of desire to return to private life. **1983–1987:** Purington professor of political science at Mount Holyoke College in South Hadley, Massachusetts. **1985:** Visiting scholar at Spelman College. **1986:** Husband died. **1987:** Retired from teaching. **January 1991:** Named chair of protocol for World University Games to be held in 1993 at State University of New York at Buffalo. Serves as national chair of National Political Congress of Women. **April 25, 1991:** Keynote speaker at conference entitled "Affirmative Action: History, Myths & the Crystal Ball," at State University of New York at Buffalo.

Background Information

Parents: Ruby (Seale) and Charles Christopher St. Hill. Mother born in Barbados; employed as seamstress and domestic. Father born in British

Guiana (now Guyana); worked as unskilled laborer in burlap factory. **Siblings:** Three (Known names: Odessa, Muriel). **Children:** None. **Influences:** Emmeline Seale; Professor Warsoff. **Ethnicity:** African American. **Also known as:** None known. **Historical sites, landmarks, etc.:** None known.

BIBLIOGRAPHICAL INFORMATION

Biographical Sketches About Shirley Chisholm

Evory, Ann, ed. *Contemporary Authors: A Bio-Bibliographical Guide to Current Authors and Their Works.* Detroit: Gale Research, 1978.

Low, W. Augustus, ed. *Encyclopedia of Black America.* New York: McGraw-Hill, 1981.

Moritz, Charles, ed. *Current Biography, 1969.* New York: H. W. Wilson Company, 1969.

Ploski, Harry A., and James Williams, comps. and eds. *The Negro Almanac: A Reference Work on the Afro-American.* New York: Wiley, 1982.

Smith, Jessie Carney, ed. *Notable Black American Women.* Detroit: Gale Research, 1992.

Zophy, Angela Howard, ed. *Handbook of American Women's History.* New York: Garland, 1990.

Books by Shirley Chisholm

The Good Fight. New York: Harper & Row, 1973.

Unbought and Unbossed. Boston: Houghton Mifflin, 1970.

Books About Shirley Chisholm

Brownmiller, Susan. *Shirley Chisholm: A Biography.* Garden City, NY: Doubleday, 1970. Reprint. Garden City, NY: Doubleday, 1971.

Duffy, Susan. *Shirley Chisholm: A Bibliography of Writings by and About Her.* Metuchen, NJ: Scarecrow, 1988.

Haskins, James. *Fighting Shirley Chisholm.* New York: Dial, 1975.

Hicks, Nancy. *The Honorable Shirley Chisholm: Congresswoman from Brooklyn.* New York: Lion Books, 1971.

Scheader, Catherine. *Shirley Chisholm, Teacher and Congresswoman.* Hillsdale, NJ: Enslow, 1990.

Williamson-Ige, Dorothy K. *Shirley Chisholm and Women's Rights Rhetoric.* 1982. [ED247625].

Shorter Works by Shirley Chisholm

"'All We Are Saying Is'—." *Freedomways* 12 (Second Quarter 1972): 118–23.

"The Black as a Colonized Man." In *The Rape of the Powerless: A Symposium at the Atlanta University Center,* edited by William Osborne. New York: Gordon and Breach, 1971.

"Black Politicians and the American Electorate." *Black Scholar* 7 (October 1975): 40–42.

"Career Education and Minorities." *New Generation* 55 (Winter 1973): 26–28.

"The Culturally Disadvantaged Gifted Youth." *G/C/T* no. 5 (November / December 1978): 2 + .

"Desegregation and National Policy." *Integrated Education* 13 (May–June 1975): 122–26.

"Excerpt from Debate: Should Congress Limit the Present Scope of the Federal Food Stamp Program?" *Congressional Digest* 54 (May 1975): 151 + .

"Excerpt from Statement: Is Proposed Conversion of U.S. Armed Forces to an All-Volunteer Basis a Sound National Policy?" *Congressional Digest* 50 (May 1971): 154 + .

"Excerpt from Testimony: Should Congress Approve the 'Equal Rights Amendment'?" *Congressional Digest* 50 (January 1971): 20 + .

"Excerpt from Testimony: Should Congress Establish a Separate Cabinet-Level U.S. Department of Education?" *Congressional Digest* 57 (November 1978): 277 + .

"Literacy: Democracy's Basic Ingredient." *Adult Literacy and Basic Education* 12 (1988): 57–65.

"Love Is Not Enough." *Parents' Magazine & Better Family Living* 46 (December 1971): 52 + .

"Needed: Equal Educational Opportunity for All." *School and Society* 100 (April 1972): 223–24.

"Number One Method." *Nation* 210 (January 26, 1970): 69–70.

"Political Concerns for Women." *Journal of the National Association of Women Deans and Counselors* 36 (1972): 13–18.

"Race, Revolution and Women." *Contact* 3 (July 1972): 27–29.

"Racism and Anti-Feminism." *Black Scholar* 14 (September–October 1983): 2–7.

"The Role of the Black University." *Black Politician* 3 (1971): 40–42.

Rubin, Louis, ed. *Educational Reform for a Changing Society: Anticipating Tomorrow's Schools.* Boston: Allyn and Bacon, Longwood Division, 1978. [ED169671]

"The Search for a Quality Life." *Hospital Progress* 53 (October 1972): 58 + .

"Sexism and Racism: One Battle to Fight." *Personnel and Guidance Journal* 51 (October 1972): 123–26.

"Shirley Chisholm on Community Control." *Clearing House* 48 (October 1973): 72.

"Shirley Speaks Her Mind." *Ebony* 33 (October 1978): 134–36 + .

"A Time for Strong Alliances." *Journal of Integroup Relations* 4 (1975): 7–13.

"United States Presidential Candidates' Views on Education: Old Ivy Needs to Go." *Journal of Continuing Education and Training* 1 (1972): 246–49.

"Visiting Feminine Eye." *McCalls* 97 (August 1970): 6.
"Vote for the Individual, Not the Political Party." *Vital Speeches of the Day* 44 (August 15, 1978): 670–71.
"We Have Become Too Plastic. We Have Become Too Theoretical. We Need People in Politics Who Are Compassionate, Concerned, Committed." *Glamour* 80 (November 1982): 98 + .
"When 'Free Speech' Becomes a Weapon." *Encore* 5 (January 5, 1976): 38.
"The White Press: Racist and Sexist. Notes." *Black Scholar* 5 (September 1973): 20–22.
"Women in Elective Office." In *Women's Role in Contemporary Society: The Report of the New York City Commission on Human Rights, Sept. 21-25, 1970.* New York: Avon, 1972.

Shorter Works About Shirley Chisholm

Ainsworth, M. "Black Political Activists." *Black Law Journal* 2 (Summer 1972): 149–53.
"Black and Proud." *Newsweek* 79 (February 7, 1972): 26.
"Black Congresswoman Fights Detention Act." *Jet* 38 (April 16, 1970): 20–26.
Blount, James M. "Congresswoman Shirley Chisholm: Senior Woman in the U.S. House of Representatives." *About Time* 9 (December 1981): 8–11 + .
Boneparth, Ellen, ed. *Women, Power, and Policy.* New York: Pergamon Press, 1982.
Brown, Warren. "Women Challenge System in Bids for Congress Seats." *Jet* 43 (September 28, 1972): 12–16.
Cadden, Vivian. "Mrs. Chisholm . . . Are You Really Running for President?" *Redbook* 139 (July 1972): 47 + .
Career Education, Comments by Plato (And Others). U.S. Department of Health, Education and Welfare, Office of Education, Washington, D.C., 1973. [ED080753]
"Chisholm Nixes Bid, Hits Racism, Sexism." *Jet* 42 (March 3, 1972): 48–49.
"Chisholm Says Inner Cities Should Be 'Disaster Areas'." *Jet* 42 (June 29, 1972): 5.
"Chisholm Speaks Out." *Encore* 4 (September 22, 1975): 15.
"Chisholm Tells Retirees She Still Boogies At 61." *Jet* 70 (June 16, 1986): 27.
"Clear It with Shirley." *Newsweek* 78 (October 18, 1971): 35–36.
"Congresswoman Shirley Chisholm." *Vogue* 153 (May 1969): 170–71.
The Ebony Success Library. Vol. 2. Chicago: Johnson Publishing, 1973.
Engelbarts, Rudolf. *Women in the United States Congress, 1917-1972; Their Accomplishments; with Bibliographies.* Littleton, CO: Libraries Unlimited, 1974.
"First Black Woman in the U.S. House of Representatives." *Negro History Bulletin* 33 (May 1970): 128.
"First Congresswoman." *Ebony* 30 (August 1975): 6.
Gant, Liz. "Black Women Organized for Action – They Collect Political IOU's." *Essence* 7 (October 1976): 46 + .

Gillespie, Marcia Ann. "Ever Since I've Emerged in Politics, Controversy Has Swirled About My Head." *Essence* 3 (November 1972): 40–43 +.

Howard, Jane. "A Shaker-upper Wants to be Madame President Chisholm" *Life* 71 (November 5, 1971): 81.

"In Search of a Black Strategy." *Time* 98 (December 20, 1971): 9–10.

"An Interview on Title IX with Shirley Chisholm, Holly Knox, Leslie R. Wolfe, Cynthia G. Brown, and Mary Kaaren Jolly." *Harvard Educational Review* 49 (November 1979): 504–26.

Jackson, George F. *Black Women Makers of History: A Portrait.* Oakland, CA: GRT Book Printing, 1985.

Jaquith, Cindy. "Where Is the Women's Political Caucus Going?" *International Socialist Review* 33 (May 1972): 4 +.

Keeter, Larry. "Minority Students at Risk: An Interview with Professor Shirley Chisholm." *Journal of Developmental Education* 10 (January 1987): 14–17.

Kilson, Martin. "Black Politics: A New Power." *Dissent* 18 (August 1971): 333–45.

Kuriansky, Joan, and Catherine Smith. "Shirley Chisholm, Democratic Representative from New York." In *Citizens Look at Congress,* by Ralph Nader Congress Project. Washington, D. C.: Grossman, 1972–1974.

"The Lady Wants to be President." *Sepia* 21 (January 1972): 24–31.

Lanker, Brian. *I Dream a World: Portraits of Black Women Who Changed America.* New York: Stewart, Tabori & Chang, 1989.

Lay, Ben. "Fiesty Congresswoman Shirley Chisholm: Is Her Will to Fight Against Conservatism Diminishing?" *Sepia* 30 (October 1981): 51–52.

Lerner, Gerda, ed. *Black Women in White America.* New York: Vintage, 1973.

Levitt, David M. "Shirley Chisholm in South Africa: Congresswoman Sees Apartheid Firsthand." *Encore American & Worldwide News* 10 (January 1982): 14–15.

Lofton, John D., Jr. "Shirley Chisholm vs. the GAO." *Human Events* 33 (December 22, 1973): 21.

Martin, Wendy, comp. *The American Sisterhood: Writings of the Feminist Movement from Colonial Times to the Present.* New York: Harper and Row, 1972.

Metzger, Linda, ed. *Black Writers: A Selection of Sketches from Contemporary Authors.* Detroit: Gale Research, 1989.

"New Kind of Candidate: She's Black." *Newsweek* 79 (February 24, 1972): 24–26.

"Number 1 Method." *Nation* 210 (January 26, 1970): 69–70.

Payne, Les. "Mrs. Chisholm Calls It Quits." *Essence* 13 (August 1982): 72–74 +.

Pinderhughes, Diane. "Black Women and National Educational Policy." *Journal of Negro Education* 51 (Summer 1982): 301–08.

Poole, Isaiah J. "Chisholm Opts for Love." *Black Enterprise* 12 (June 1982): 52.

"Race, Revolution and Women." *Black Scholar* 3 (December 1971): 17–21.

Redding, Saunders, ed. *Black Americans in Government.* Jamaica, NY: Buckingham Learning Corporation, 1969.

"Rep. Shirley Chisholm Ties Nuptial Knot Near Buffalo." *Jet* 53 (December 15, 1977): 13.

Ross, Pat, comp. *Young and Female: Turning Points in the Lives of Eight American Women, Personal Accounts.* New York: Random House, 1972.

"Shirley Chisholm Eyes Tyson to Portray Her." *Jet* 67 (October 88, 1984): 62.

"Shirley Chisholm of Brooklyn Is First Black Woman on Capitol Hill." *Ebony* 24 (February 1969): 58 + .

"Shirley Chisholm Slams Foes on Spending Charges." *Jet* 45 (December 6, 1973): 12–13.

"Shirley Chisholm to Address Black Women Lawyers." *Jet* 69 (January 27, 1986): 8.

"Shirley Chisholm to Head Black Women's Congress." *Jet* 68 (June 24, 1985): 6.

Steinem, Gloria. "The Ticket That Might Have Been . . . President Chisholm." *Ms.* 1 (January 1973): 73 + .

Stimpson, Catherine R., ed. *Discrimination Against Women: Congressional Hearings on Equal Rights in Education and Employment.* New York: Bowker, 1973.

Tanner, Leslie Barbara, comp. *Voices from Women's Liberation.* New York: New American Library, 1971.

Taylor, Tim. "Shirley Chisholm." *Black Law Journal* 9 (Winter 1985): 213–14.

Weiss, Ted. "National Truth-in-Testing Legislation." *Journal of Negro Education* 49 (1980): 233–37.

White, Joyce. "Women in Politics: In Spite of Many Obstacles, Black Women Are Adding 'Color' to the Political Scene." *Essence* 6 (October 1976): 56 + .

Wieck, Paul R. "On the Chisholm Campaign Trail." *New Republic* 165 (December 4, 1971): 16 + .

"Women in Government: A Slim Past, But a Strong Future." *Ebony* 32 (August 1977): 89–92.

"Women Unite to Form a New Political Caucus; Name Chisholm Leader." *Jet* 66 (August 27, 1984): 26.

Other Works by Shirley Chisholm

Speeches

"Address Before the Second Annual Youth Workers Conference, Georgetown University, June 8, 1978." (ED156785]

Other Works About Shirley Chisholm

Theses

Williamson, Dorothy Kay. "Rhetorical Analysis of Selected Modern Black American Spokespersons on the Women's Liberation Movement." Ph.D. diss., Ohio State University, 1980.

Media Materials by Shirley Chisholm

Film

Black Views on Race. Time-Life Films, [197–]. 80 min; sound; color; 16mm.

Sound Recordings

James Farmer – Shirley Chisholm Debate. New York: Schomburg Center Oral

History Collection, Schomburg Center for Research in Black Culture, New York Public Library, 1968. Cassette.

Shirley Chisholm: Representative Chisholm Urges Women to Run for Office. Center for Cassette Studies, 1974. One cassette; 2 track; mono; 35 min.

Media Materials About Shirley Chisholm

Films

Accomplished Women. Braverman Productions. Released by Films Incorporated, 1974. 25 min.; sound; color; 16mm.

Chisholm: Pursuing the Dream. Freedonia Films. Released by New Line Cinema, 1974. 42 min.; sound; color; 16mm.

Conversations in Black Higher Education Series. New York: Holt, Rinehart and Winston. 16 mm.; 30 min.; optical sound; black and white.

Koplin, Mert, and Charles Grinker. *Shirley Chisholm.* Released by Time-Life Films, 1970. 4 min.; sound; color; 16mm.

Werner, Tom. *Chisholm Pursuing the Dream.* Distributor, New Line Cinema, New York City. 48 mm.

Filmstrips

Black Americans in Government. Buckingham Learning Corp., 1969. Released by McGraw-Hill, 1970. 5 filmstrips; color; 35mm.; 5 phonodiscs; 2 sides each (1 side for manual projector, 1 side for automatic projector); approximately 23 min. each.

Five Black Americans and Their Fight for Freedom. Westminster, MD: Random House Educational Enrichment Materials, 1974. 6 filmstrips; color; 35mm.; 6 sound cassettes; about 8 min. each.; analog; 1 teaching guide.

Shirley Chisholm: Political Representation. Paideia. Released by BFA Educational Media, 1974. 57 frames; color; 35mm.; phonodisc; 2 sides; 12 in.; 33⅓ rpm; approximately 8 min.

Sound Recordings

Interview with Shirley Chisholm. Part III. New York: Schomburg Center Oral History Collection, Schomburg Center for Research in Black Culture, New York Public Library, 1968. Cassette.

Interview with Shirley Chisholm. Part VIII. New York: Schomburg Center Oral History Collection, Schomburg Center for Research in Black Culture, New York Public Library, 1968. Cassette.

Interview with Shirley Chisholm. Part XIII. New York: Schomburg Center Oral History Collection, Schomburg Center for Research in Black Culture, New York Public Library, 1968. Cassette.

Interview with Shirley Chisholm. Part XXI. New York: Schomburg Center Oral History Collection, Schomburg Center for Research in Black Culture, New York Public Library, 1968. Cassette.

Urban Environment: Racism and the Urban Crisis. Los Angeles: Pacific Tape Library. Cassette; 1 ⅞ ips; 51 min.

Young and Female. New York: Caedmon. Audio tape cassette: 1 ⅞ ips.

Video Recordings

Accomplished Women. Distributed by Films, Inc. of Chicago, IL. Santa Monica, CA: Braveman Productions, 1974. 25 min.; ¾ or ½ inch.

Primary Source Materials Relating to Shirley Chisholm

Diana Mara Henry. Photographs. 1969–1976 (inclusive). Extent of collection: 49 folders, 1 oversize folder. Finding aids: Published and unpublished indexes. Location: Schlesinger Library, Radcliffe College, Cambridge, Massachusetts 02138. Scope of collection: Includes photographs of Chisholm.

National Organization for Women. New York Chapter. Records. 1966–1973, 1970–1972 (bulk). Extent of collection: 3.5 lin. ft. Finding aids: Unpublished guide. Location: Tamiment Institute Library, New York University Libraries, 70 Washington Square South, New York, New York 10012. Scope of collection: Correspondence, clippings, newsletters, etc.

New Democratic Coalition of New York. Records. 1960–1978. Extent of collection: 49 cu. ft. Finding aids: In repository. Location: Rutgers University Libraries, New Brunswick, New Jersey 08903. Scope of collection: Includes materials concerning Chisholm.

People for Chishom (Madison, WI). Records. 1960–1978. Extent of collection: 0.1 cu. ft. Finding aids: Not listed. Location: State Historical Society of Wisconsin, Archives Division, 816 State Street, Madison, Wisconsin 53706. Scope of collection: Collection is unprocessed.

Western Kentucky University. Audiotapes. 1963–1980. Extent of collection: 500 audiotapes. Finding aids: Unpublished inventory/register. Location: Western Kentucky University, Department of Library Special Collections, University Archives, Helm Library 100, Western Kentucky University, Bowling Green, Kentucky 42101. Scope of collection: Includes guest lecturer tapes of Chisholm.

(THE ABOVE ENTRY WAS CONTRIBUTED BY LEVIRN HILL)

16. Harriet Maxwell Converse
(1836–1903)

Advocate for Native American rights; author

BIOGRAPHICAL INFORMATION

Chronological Biography

Born January 11, 1836, in Elmira, New York, last of seven children of Maria (Marie) (Purdy) and Thomas Maxwell. Grandfather and father had been concerned about Native Americans; both had been adopted by Seneca

Indians in 1794 and 1804 respectively. Mother, father's second wife, died when she was nine. Sent to live in Milan, Ohio, with aunt where she was educated. Met and married George B. Clarke in Ohio.

1861: First husband having died, married childhood friend, Franklin Buchanan Converse, Westfield, Massachusetts, musician, writer, and inventor. Travelled in Europe, United States, Asia and Africa for five years while husband gathered material for book on unusual native musical instruments. He had previously lived with Native Americans in western part of United States. Contributed articles and poetry, some in Old Scottish language, to Scottish and American periodicals under pseudonyms "Musidora" and "Salome." **1864:** Inherited considerable amount of money when father died. First husband's death had also left her financially secure. **1866:** Returned to America and lived in New York City. In later years, home became center for visiting Native Americans from all over North America. Also, assisted many of city's community of about 100 Native Americans in legal, financial and other difficulties. **1881:** Met General Ely S. Parker, Seneca Indian chief, engineer and army aide to General Ulysses S. Grant; he later served as Commissioner of Indian Affairs when Grant was president. Through Parker, visited reservations in Canada and New York State and became informed and greatly interested in preserving Native American culture, festivals, folklore and artifacts. Began to use own name in print. **1882:** Well-received first book of poetry, *Sheaves*, published; it had several subsequent editions. **1884: Poem,** *The Ho-de'-no-sau nee* published. **June 15, 1885:** Formally adopted by Seneca Indians, becoming great-granddaughter of Red Jacket. Received into Snipe clan and given name of Ga-ya-nes-ha-oh, "Bearer of the Law." **1886?:** Admitted to secret Little Water Medicine Society, probably the first white woman to receive this honor. Also honored by membership in Society of Mystic Animals. **Spring 1891:** Lobbying efforts and testimony extremely important in preventing passage of New York state's Whipple Bill which would have ended tribal ownership of land in favor of individual allotment. Bill was defeated in committee. Before Native Americans spoke at hearing, was invited to sit in Six Nation council in Albany, probably the first white woman to receive such an honor. In appreciation of actions, was unanimously made legal member of Senecas and given name of "Ya-ie-wa-noh" meaning "she who watches over us" or "ambassador"; name had previously belonged to wife of famous chief. Husband was adoped into clan at this time. **March 25, 1892:** Held in such high esteem and affection, confirmed a chief of Six Nations, honor never before conferred upon white woman. Had been unanimously elected and installed September 18, 1891, but was unaware of this as ceremony had not been in English language. **1902:** Continued efforts to save Native American lands. Letters to Washington and New York newspapers instrumental in defeat of federal legislation that would have cost Senecas $200,000 to defend land claim. **September 1903?:** Husband died. **November 18,**

1903: Died in New York City of kidney failure due to nephritis at age 67. Funeral included Iroquois as well as Protestant Episcopal Church services with representatives of Six Nations in attendance. Buried in Elmira's Woodlawn Cemetery next to husband. Not trained as an ethnographer, writings were frequently too sentimental. Main contributions were defense of Native American lands and significant contributions and efforts to preserve relics and artifacts for future scholars and general public. Used grants to purchase items and gave father's 100-year-old collection to New York State Museum. Persuaded Onondagas to donate wampum belts of Five Nations to state museum. Spent much of own money acquiring items for American Museum of Natural History and Museum of the American Indian in New York City, as well as to Peabody Museum at Harvard University. **1908:** *Myths and Legends of the New York State Iroquois* published. Edited after her death by Seneca anthropologist Arthur C. Parker, grandnephew of Ely S. Parker.

Background Information

Parents: Maria (Marie) (Purdy) and Thomas Maxwell. Father was attorney, county clerk, assemblyman, congressman and vice president of Erie Railroad; also wrote for *Knickerbocker Magazine*. Grandfather had been respected, honest trader with Native Americans. **Siblings:** Six (No known names). **Children:** None. **Influences:** Franklin Buchanan Converse. **Ethnicity:** Scottish American. **Also known as:** "Musidora" and "Salome" (pseudonyms). **Historical sites, landmarks, etc.:** Grave, Woodlawn Cemetery, Elmira, New York.

BIBLIOGRAPHICAL INFORMATION

Biographical Sketches About Harriet Maxwell Converse

James, Edward T., ed. *Notable American Women 1607–1950: A Biographical Dictionary.* Cambridge, MA: Belknap Press of Harvard University Press, 1971.

Johnson, Rossiter, ed. *The Twentieth Century Biographical Dictionary of Notable Americans.* Boston: The Biographical Society, 1904.

Whitman, Alden, ed. *American Reformers: An H. W. Wilson Biographical Dictionary.* New York: H. W. Wilson Company, 1985.

Willard, Frances E., and Mary A. Livermore, eds. *A Woman of the Century.* Buffalo, NY: Charles Wells Moulton, 1893.

Books by Harriet Maxwell Converse

The Ho-de'-no-sau-nee: The Confederacy of the Iroquois [the Six Nations]: A Poem. New York: G. P. Putnam's Sons, 1884.

Iroquois Masks. Grotesque Workmanship, but Full of Symbolism, Ancient Work the Best. Modern Indians Cannot Make Good Masks — How They Were Used and What They Signified — Usages Still Kept Up on the Reservations. [Buffalo, 1899].
The Iroquois Silver Brooches. Albany: University of the State of New York, 1902.
Jones, Hettie. *Longhouse Winter: Iroquois Transformation Tales.* New York: Holt Rinehart and Winston, [1972]. (Adapted from *Myths and Legends of the New York State Iroquois.*)
Myths and Legends of the New York State Iroquois. Albany: University of the State of New York, 1908. Reprint. Albany: University of the State of New York, State Education Department, 1974.
Sheaves: A Collection of Poems. New York: G. P. Putnam's Sons, 1882. Reprint. New York: G. P. Putnam's Sons, 1885.

Books About Harriet Maxwell Converse

Kunz, George Frederick. *Harriet Maxwell Converse.* New York: Albany, 1905.

Shorter Works by Harriet Maxwell Converse

"Gau-wi-di-ne and Go-hay, Winter and Spring." *Kindergarten Primary Magazine* 21 (March 1909): 209–11.
"Induction of Women into Iroquois Tribes." *Journal of American Folk-Lore* 6 (April 1893): 147–48.
"The Last Rite of Adoption into the Confederacy of the Iroquois." In *Rites of Adoption by the Seneca Indians on the Cattaraugus Reservation, June 15th, 1885.* Geneva, NY: n.p., 1885.
"Nya-gwa-ih, How the Bear Lost Its Tail." *Kindergarten Primary Magazine* 21 (February 1909): 175.
"The Seneca New-Year Ceremony and Other Customs." *Indian Notes* 7 (January 1930): 69–89.
"Wampum Records of Iroquois Indians." *Monthly Illustrator* 4 (1895): 342.

Shorter Works About Harriet Maxwell Converse

Eyres, Lawrence E. "Ya-ie-wa-noh (She Who Watches Over Us) Harriet Maxwell Converse." *Chemung Historical Journal* (December 1957): 379–83.
Fenton, William Nelson. *The Iroquois Eagle Dance: An Offshoot of the Calumet Dance.* Washington, D. C.: U.S. GPO, 1953.
"Indians' Love for Harriet M. Converse." *New York Times Magazine* (September 12, 1897): 7.
"Indians Mourn at Mrs. Converse's Bier." *New York Times* (November 23, 1903): 12.
"Mrs. H. M. Converse Dead." *New York Times* (November 20, 1903): 16.
Parker, Arthur Caswell. *The Life of General Ely S. Parker, Last Grand Sachem of the Iroquois and General Grant's Military Secretary.* Buffalo, NY: Buffalo Historical Society, 1919.

Primary Source Materials
Relating to Harriet Maxwell Converse

Arthur Caswell Parker. Papers. 1860–1952. Extent of collection: 12 ft. Finding aids: Partial card index to letters. Inventory sheet of Parker's materials in library. Location: University of Rochester, Rush Rhees Library, Rochester, New York 14627. Scope of collection: Includes material relating to Native Americans, particularly of New York state, Converse, etc.

Ely S. Parker. Papers. 1794–1946. Extent of collection: ca. 600 items. Finding aids: Not listed. Location: American Philosophical Society Library, Independence Square, Philadelphia, Pennsylvania 19106. Scope of collection: Contains letters to Converse.

Joseph Keppler. Papers. 1882–1944, 1899–1944 (bulk). Extent of collection: 4.4 cu. ft. Finding aids: Summary of each letter, arranged chronologically. Location Museum of the American Indian, Heye Foundation, Library, Annex Bruckner Blvd. & Middletown Road, Bronx, New York 10454. Scope of collection: Includes news clipping referring to death of Converse and many of her letters.

17. Angela Davis
(1944–   )

Political activist; Communist; advocate for political rights and African American rights; and African American scholar

BIOGRAPHICAL INFORMATION

Chronological Biography

Born January 26, 1944, in Birmingham, Alabama, in Children's Home Hospital. Oldest of four children, two girls and two boys, of Sallye E. and B. Frank Davis. Raised in public housing until age four. Both parents were teachers; father then left teaching and purchased small business in downtown Birmingham. Parents were activists and members of National Association for the Advancement of Colored People (NAACP) which was declared an illegal organization in Alabama and dissolved. The NAACP replaced by Alabama Christian Movement for Human Rights. Parents also members of Southern Negro Youth Congress.

1948: Family moved from public housing to home purchased on Center Street, first African American family to integrate area. Became acutely aware of racism and hostility of whites toward blacks. Sister Fania born. 1949: Neighboring house where African American family lived was bombed. Neighborhood became known as Dynamite Hill. Began reading at age four;

attended Carrie A. Tuggle Elementary School. Early education included "Negro History" beginning in first grade. Segregation was law and it forced African Americans to look to themselves for validation and spiritual nourishment. Avid reader. Encouraged by parents at early age to be independent thinker and person of integrity. Important always to do what felt "right." **1952–1953:** Entire neighborhood of Dynamite Hill populated by African Americans. **December 4, 1955:** Rosa Parks (see entry 48) refused to move to back of Montgomery, Alabama, bus and civil rights movement was begun. African Americans in South were beginning to awaken, although civil rights movement was not yet organized in Birmingham. She and small group of classmates demonstrated solidarity with bus boycott by riding in front of buses and refusing to move to back. As young girl, became angered by inaction or silence in presence of wrongdoing. **1956:** Paternal grandmother, who was symbol of strength, age, wisdom and suffering, died. **1958:** In junior high school felt restless, limited, and generally dissatisfied. Could not tolerate provincialism of Birmingham and decided to leave. Early career aspiration was to attend medical school and become pediatrician. Two opportunities were presented—early entrance to Fisk University in Nashville, Tennessee, or participation in experimental, integrated, academic program in North developed by American Friends Service Committee. Decided to participate in American Friends Service Committee academic program. Moved to New York City where she lived in home of the Reverend and Mrs. William Howard Melish and attended Elisabeth Irwin private high school in Greenwich Village. Mother had serious misgivings about danger she might be confronted with in New York City at young age of 15, but consented. The Reverend and Mrs. Melish, Episcopalians, were sympathetic to Communists and members of Soviet-American Friendship Organization. Both were active in civil rights movement and the Reverend Melish was winner of 1956 Stockholm Peace Prize. Introduced to ADVANCE, Marxist-Leninist youth organization with fraternal ties to communist party. Met Herbert Aptheker, much respected communist historian, and his daughter Bettina, who played major role in ADVANCE. Felt very much like outsider during two years spent at Elisabeth Irwin High School because of family-like, clannish atmosphere. Unlike her, most students entered when they were four and stayed through grade 12, receiving entire education there. **1961:** Graduated from high school. Wanted to return South to join civil rights movement but parents insisted she continue education. Attended Brandeis University in Waltham, Massachusetts, on full scholarship. One of only two African Americans attending the then all-female institution. Felt alone, alienated and angry. Drawn to foreign students. Unofficially called herself a Communist. **Summer 1962:** During summer attended Eighth World Festival for Youth and Students in Helsinki, Finland. Travelled in London, Paris and Switzerland en route to two-week conference. Under observation by Central Intelligence Agency

(CIA) while in Finland and questioned by Federal Bureau of Investigation (FBI) agent upon return as to reasons for attending Communist youth festival. **1963:** Spent third year of college in France at Sorbonne. Greatly impressed professors and peers alike.   **September 16, 1963:** While in France, learned of bombing of Sixteenth Street Baptist Church in Birmingham, Alabama, and death of four childhood friends. Grief was deep and personal. Felt peers did not share any understanding of violence of racism.   **November 22, 1963:** Learned of assassination of President John Fitzgerald Kennedy. Contrasted uncontrollable grief expressed by her peers and other Americans for President Kennedy with lack of grief they expressed for four African Amercian girls killed earlier in Birmingham.   **1964–1965:** Upon completion of junior year, realized strong desire to study philosophy in spite of being on verge of receiving degree in French literature. Had strong interest in Marx, his predecessors and successors. Returned to Brandeis for senior year and audited course taught by Herbert Marcuse, "European Political Thought Since the French Revolution." Began studying philosophy under Professor Marcuse's tutelage; considered best student he had had in over 30 years of teaching. Graduated from Brandeis University, Magna Cum Laude, Phi Beta Kappa.   **1965–1967:** Studied philosophy on full scholarship at Johann Wolfgang von Goethe University in Frankfurt, Germany, under Oskar Negt and Theodore Adorno. Again considered outstanding student; learned German quickly and proficiently. Intention was to complete doctorate in Frankfurt.   **1967:** Left Germany feeling need to become part of African Americans' struggle for civil rights. Arranged to continue studies by working with Herbert Marcuse at University of California at San Diego. Became activist and organizer on campus. Arrested for participation in Vietnam War protests. Became involved in organizing black student union. Attended black youth conference in November in Los Angeles. Introduced to Black Panther political party. Interested in working within black community to organize masses to protest inequities of "the system."   **1968:** Worked in Black Panther political party and Black Panther Party for Self-Defense as well as Student Non-Violent Coordinating Committee (SNCC) to develop mass movement of blacks in Los Angeles. Given responsibility of planning "Liberation School" and becoming its director. Groups under constant police surveillance and harassment. Dr. Martin Luther King, Jr., was shot on April 4, 1968, and tensions approached breaking point between various community activist groups and Los Angeles Police Department. Police harassment increased. On June 22, 1968, became full-fledged member of Communist Party of U.S.A. Passed Ph.D. qualifying exam and became teaching assistant in philosophy department. Remained active in campus and community politics. Helped establish Lumumba Zapata College on University of California at San Diego campus. College dedicated to serving students of oppressed social groups—blacks, chicanos, and working class whites.   **1969:** In July, travelled with delegation of Communists who were invited to spend month in Cuba. Trip represented milestone signalling political maturity. Upon return, joined philosophy faculty of University of California at Los Angeles (UCLA). Governor Ronald Reagan instructed chancellors to fire her upon learning she was a Communist; UCLA's regents charter did not allow hiring of Communists. Court injunction prohibited regents from firing individual because of political beliefs and ordered UCLA to reinstate her. Racists and anticommunists made threats on her life; protection was required around clock. Campus Che-Lumumba Club, Communist club of which she was member, assigned 24-hour protection. All autonomy was lost and overnight she was transformed into celebrity. Family members were arrested and constantly harassed. Open admission to being Communist marked launching of systematic plan to discredit her and black liberation struggle she was committed to and involved with.   1970: In February, Soledad Brothers case was brought to her attention. George Jackson, Fleeta Drumgo and John Clutchette were unjustly indicted for murder of a prison guard and she was deeply affected by plight of these black men. Using her visibility, she spearheaded successful effort to generate attention to case. Spoke on their behalf at college campuses and coordinated community efforts to bring national attention to case. Fired second time in June by UCLA because of extreme revolutionary views. Once Soledad Brothers campaign received national attention, it was escalated to "free all political prisoners." Became close friends of Jackson family, particularly younger brother Jonathan Jackson. On August 7th, Jonathan Jackson took a judge, district attorney and several prisoners hostage from Marin County courtroom. Party fled to van where they were attacked by police. Judge Haley and prisoner James McClain were killed; District Attorney Garry Thomas, a woman juror, and prisoner Ruchell McGhee were wounded. Jonathan Jackson was killed at age 17. Guns used in shoot-out were registered to her and police were immediately in pursuit. She fled, feeling it impossible to receive fair trial due to her Communist affiliation and activism. FBI agents were swarming around friends preventing access to them so she hid in West Adams area of Los Angeles with sympathetic family until nightfall. Escaped to Chicago and safety of friend David Poindexter. Fear of identification by friend of Poindexter forced both to flee. Adopted disguise to hide identity. Travelled to New York by car with stop in Detroit. From New York City took train to Miami where she rented apartment and remained in seclusion; Poindexter travelled back to Chicago. Pursuit became more intense; FBI contacted Poindexter's mother who lived near Miami. Unable to contact friends, as all were still under surveillance, and low on money, contemplated leaving country but could not bear thought of being in exile. Left Miami, returned to New York City. Added to FBI's "Ten Most Wanted" list of fugitives. On October 13th, captured by FBI agents in New York City at Howard Johnson Motor Lodge. Held at New York

Women's House of Detention (near Elisabeth Irwin High School) in Greenwich Village. Jail conditions sub-human. Charged with murder, kidnapping, conspiracy to commit murder and free prisoners. Charged with interstate flight to avoid prosecution. At first court appearance, arraigned on federal charges of interstate flight to avoid prosecution. Bail set at $250,000. Second court appearance, bail rescinded and released on own recognizance. Immediately arrested again by New York City police as prisoner of New York state on charges of murder, kidnapping and conspiracy. By December, momentum gathered in national "Free Angela Davis" movement. Eyes of world were on case. Extradited to California on December 21, 1970. Booked, jailed, and arraigned on charges of kidnapping, murder and conspiracy. Prison conditions slightly improved, though still sub-human. Racist treatment by prison guards and administrators continued. **1971:** Arraigned in court in January and officially charged with kidnapping, murder and conspiracy. Convinced by Bettina Aptheker to coauthor anthology, *If They Come in the Morning,* as fundraiser for Angela Davis Defense Committee. Book's objective was to deepen public's knowledge of repression, prison, political prisoners and injustice in America. In July, had eight-hour meeting with Soledad Brother George Jackson to plan trial strategy. In August, George Jackson was murdered by police; shot in back at San Quentin Prison on first anniversary of brother Jonathan Jackson's death. Marin County jury selection began; served as co-defense attorney for self. Won change of venue to San Jose as fair trial not possible in Marin County due to deep seated racism and anticommunist prejudice. Rebooked and jailed in San Jose in December. Sub-human prison conditions continued as she was confined to filthy, cold, water-filled cell. **1972:** In February, state of California abolished death penalty thereby providing legal basis for request of bail trial. Bail, finally granted by Judge Arnason and set at $102,500, posted by Rodger McAffee, California farmer and Communist party member. Reunited with parents. Began attending Soledad Brothers trial; Soledad Brothers acquitted on March 27th, opening day of her trial. Delivered opening and closing statement for own defense. On June 4th, after 13 hours of deliberation, jury of 11 whites and one Mexican American returned verdict of acquittal on all counts. Now free, embarked on three-week tour of United States to raise money to pay legal expenses. Tour concluded at Madison Square Garden in New York City. The UCLA philosophy department asked California Board of Regents to reconsider hiring her — they still refused. Toured Soviet Union. **1973:** One of the founders of National Alliance Against Racist and Political Repression, organization dedicated to protection of peoples' right to organize and elimination of repression. **1974:** Published *Angela Davis—An Autobiography.* **1978:** Hired as professor of women's and ethnic studies at San Francisco State University. **1979:** Awarded Lenin Peace Prize by Soviet Union. **1980:** Ran as Communist party candidate for U.S. vice president.

Married Hilton Braithwaite, photographer and faculty colleague at San Francisco State University. Marriage ended in divorce several years later.   **1981:** Published *Women, Race & Class.*   **1984:** Ran again as Communist party candidate for vice president of United States.   **1989:** Published *Women, Culture & Politics.*   **1990–:** Lives in Oakland, California. Continues to teach in ethnic and women's studies department at San Francisco State University; also is professor in department of history of consciousness at University of California at Santa Cruz, and instructor at San Francisco County Jail Education Program. Co-chairs National Alliance Against Racist and Political Repression. Promotes multi-cultural coalitions and global strategies to achieve equality and end racism and oppression. Active in National Black Women's Health Project and Communist party. Lectures on college campuses throughout the United States and world. Forthcoming book is entitled *Ma Rainey, Bessie Smith and Billie Holiday: Black Women's Music in the Shaping of Social Consciousness.*

Background Information

Parents: Sallye E. and B. Frank Davis.   **Siblings:** Three (Fania [Jordan], Benjamin, Reginald).   **Children:** None.   **Influences:** None.   **Ethnicity:** African American.   **Also known as:** None known.   **Historical sites, landmarks, etc.:** None known.

BIBLIOGRAPHICAL INFORMATION

Biographical Sketches About Angela Davis

Evory, Ann, and Linda Metzger, eds. *Contemporary Authors: New Revision Series.* Detroit: Gale Research, 1983.

Johnpoll, Bernard K., and Harvey Klehr, eds. *Biographical Dictionary of the American Left.* Westport, CT: Greenwood, 1986.

Metzger, Linda, ed. *Black Writers: A Selection of Sketches from Contemporary Authors.* Detroit: Gale Research, 1988.

Moritz, Charles, ed. *Current Biography.* New York: H. W. Wilson Company, 1972.

Ploski, Harry A., and James Williams, comps. and eds. *The Negro Almanac: A Reference Work on the African American.* Detroit: Gale Research, 1989.

Smith, Jessie Carney, ed. *Notable Black American Women.* Detroit: Gale Research, 1992.

Zophy, Angela Howard, ed. *Handbook of American Women's History.* New York: Garland, 1990.

Books by Angela Davis

Angela Davis—An Autobiography. New York: Random House, 1974. Reprint. London: Women's Press, 1990.

The Angela Davis Trial. Dobbs Ferry, NY: Trans-Media, 1974.

Frame-Up: The Opening Defense Statement Made by Angela Y. Davis, March 29, 1972. San Francisco: National United Committee to Free Angela Davis, 1972.

Lectures on Liberation. New York: New York Committee to Free Angela Davis, 1971?.

Violence Against Women and the Ongoing Challenge to Racism. Latham, NY: Women of Color Press, 1985.

Women, Culture, & Politics. New York: Random House, 1989.

Women, Race & Class. New York: Random House, 1981. Reprint. New York: Vintage, 1983.

Books About Angela Davis

Abt, John J. On the Defense of Angela Davis . . . Los Angeles: National United Committee to Free Angela Davis, 1970?.

Aptheker, Bettina. The Morning Breaks: The Trial of Angela Davis. New York: International, 1975.

Ashman, Charles R. The People vs. Angela Davis. New York: Pinnacle, 1972.

Conway, Bill. From Joan to Angela: A Bitter Ballad of Oppression and Martyrs. Los Angeles: FAD Publishers, 1971.

Finke, Blythe Foote. Angela Davis: Traitor or Martyr of the Freedom of Expression. Charlotteville, NY: SamHar Press, 1972. Reprint. Charlotteville, NY: SamHar Press, 1975.

Giovanni, Nikki. Poems of Angela Yvonne Davis. New York: Afro Arts, 1970.

Major, Reginald. Justice in the Round: The Trial of Angela Davis. New York: Third Press, 1973.

Meiklejohn Civil Liberties Institute. Angela Davis Case Collection: Annotated Procedural Guide and Index. Dobbs Ferry, NY: Trans-Media, 1974.

Mitchell, Charlene. The Fight to Free Angela Davis: Its Importance for the Working Class. New York: New Outlook, 1972.

Mwandishe, Kuweka Amiri. The Nigger Cycle: For Angela Davis Kidnapped by the FBI on Oct. 13, 1970. Detroit: Broadside, 1971.

Nadelson, Regina. Who Is Angela Davis? The Biography of a Revolutionary. New York: Peter H. Wyden, 1972.

National United Committee to Free Angela Davis. Bail for Angela: Right Without Remedy. San Francisco: The Committee, 1971.

_____. Closing Defense Statement Made in the Angela Davis Case, June 1, 1972. San Francisco: The Committee, 1972?.

New York Committee to Free Angela Davis. A Political Biography of Angela Davis. New York: The Committee, 1971.

Parker, J. A. Angela Davis: The Making of a Revolutionary. New Rochelle, NY: Arlington House, 1973.

The Professor. Angela: Portrait of a Revolutionary. London: Sphere, 1971.

Timothy, Mary. *Jury Woman*. Palo Alto, CA: Emty Press, 1974.
————. *Jury Woman: The Story of the Trial of Angela Y. Davis*. San Francisco: Glide, 1975.

Shorter Works by Angela Davis

"Angela Davis on Women." *Off Our Backs* 4 (June 1974): 10.
Aptheker, Bettina. *The Academic Rebellion in the United States*. Secaucus, NJ: Citadel, 1972. (Introduction by Davis.)
"Billie Holiday's 'Strange Fruit'." *Political Affairs* 2 (February 1988): 5.
"The Black Family and the Crisis of Capitalism." *Black Scholar* 17 (September–October 1986): 33–40.
"Black Writers: Views of America." *Freedomways* 19 (1979): 151–62.
"For a People's Culture." *Political Affairs* 64 (March 1985): 17–27.
"In the Mirror of the Press." *World Marxist Review* 25 (February 1982): 38–39.
"Joanne Little: The Dialectics of Rape." *Ms.* 3 (June 1975): 74–77.
"Lifting As We Climb" *Peace and Freedom* 48 (September 1988): 6.
"The Myth of the Black Matriarch." In *The First Ms. Reader,* edited by Francine Klagsbrun. New York: Warner, 1973.
"NWSA: Weaving Women's Colors." *Off Our Backs* 17 (August–September 1987): 1–3 +.
"Racism and Contemporary Literature on Rape." *Freedomways* 16 (First Quarter 1976): 25–33.
"Rape, Racism and the Capitalist Setting." *Black Scholar* 9 (April 1978): 24–30.
"Rape, Racism and the Capitalist Setting." *Black Scholar* 12 (November–December 1981): 39–45.
"Reflections on the Black Woman's Role in the Community of Slaves." *Black Scholar* 3 (December 1971): 2–15.
"Reflections on the Black Woman's Role in the Community of Slaves." *Black Scholar* 12 (November–December 1981): 2–15.
"Reflections on the Black Woman's Role in the Community of Slaves." *Massachusetts Review* 13 (Winter–Spring 1972): 81–100.
"Rhetoric vs. Reality." *Ebony* 26 (July 1971): 115–20.
"The Soledad Brothers." *Black Scholar* 2 (April–May 1971): 2–7.
"Struggle of Ben Chavis and the Wilmington 10." *Black Scholar* 6 (April 1975): 27–31.
"To Save Our Nation." *Freedomways* 20 (Second Quarter 1980): 82–86.
Davis, Angela Yvonne, and Fania Davis. *The Black Family: The Ties that Bind.* New York: Communist Party of the United States of America, 1987.
————, [and others]. *If They Come in the Morning: Voices of Resistance.* New York: Third Press, 1971.

Shorter Works About Angela Davis

"AAUP Censures California Regents Over Angela Davis Case." *Intellect* 101 (October 1972): 9–10.

Abbott, D. "Revolution by Other Means [interview]." *New Statesman* 114 (August 14, 1987): 16–17.

"Academic Freedom Again." *National Review* 21 (November 4, 1969): 1103.

Aikins, Lenton. "Lessons of Angela Davis' Case." *Black World* 20 (March 1971): 79–83.

"Alibi." *Newsweek* 79 (June 5, 1972): 40.

Alston, C., and L. Branton. "In Defense of Angela: Profile of the Davis Defense Team." *Black Law Journal* 2 (Spring 1972): 45–53.

"Angela." *Off Our Backs* 2 (April 1972): 20.

"Angela and the Presbyterians." *Christian Century* 88 (July 7, 1971): 823.

"Angela and the Presbyterians: Discussion." *Christian Century* 88 (August 18, 1971): 979–80.

"The Angela Davis Case." *Newsweek* (October 26, 1970): 18–24.

"Angela Davis: Controversy." *Atlas* 21 (January 1972): 21–23.

"Angela Davis Day Is Proclaimed in Berkeley." *Jet* (August 19, 1971): 6–7.

"Angela Davis Gets Warm Welcome From Russians." *Jet* 42 (September 14, 1972): 5.

"Angela Davis Goes Free." *Progressive* 36 (July 1972): 8.

"Angela Davis Subject of Soviet Sculptor." *Jet* 41 (April 15, 1971): 25.

"Angela Davis, Sweetheart of the Far Left Finds Her Mr. Right." *People* 14 (July 21, 1980): 52.

"Angela Davis Talks About Her Fortune and Her Freedom." *Jet* 42 (July 27, 1972): 54–57.

"Angela Davis Tells Blacks to Defy Campus Racism." *Jet* 78 (April 30, 1990): 29.

"Angela Freed." *National Review* 24 (June 23, 1972): 680.

"Angela Gets Black Lawyer Who Is No Stranger to Struggle." *Jet* 39 (January 21, 1971): 5.

"Angela Liberata." *National Review* 24 (September 29, 1972): 1053.

"Angela's Return." *Time* 97 (January 4, 1971): 27.

"Angela's Triumphant Acquittal." *Time* 99 (June 12, 1972): 18.

Baldwin, James. *An Open Letter to My Sister, Miss Angela Davis.* New York: New York Committee to Free Angela Davis, 1970?.

————, and Shlomo Katz. "Of Angela Davis and 'The Jewish Housewife Headed for Dachau'." *Midstream* 17 (1971): 3–7.

Beals, M. "Still Planning for Revolution." *People* 9 (January 23, 1978): 22–23.

"Behind the Verdict." *Newsweek* 79 (June 19, 1972): 30.

Bennett, R. K. "Angela Davis: The Making of a Martyr." *Reader's Digest* 98 (March 1971): 108–12.

Benson, Chris. "Angela Davis and New Husband Tell How They Met and Married." *Jet* 58 (July 24, 1980): 14–16.

"Bernard Geis and Bantam Books Sign Angela Davis." *Publishers' Weekly* 202 (October 30, 1972): 36.

"Black Community Angered by Soviet Propaganda." *Jet* 39 (February 18, 1971): 15.

"Black Panthers Plead 'Come Home Angela'." *Jet* 43 (September 28, 1972): 9.

Blackwell, Earl, ed. *Celebrity Register.* New York: Simon and Schuster, 1973.

"Brothers and Angela." *Time* 99 (April 10, 1972): 16–17.

Browne, John. "Soporific Evening with Angela Davis." *National Review* 24 (July 21, 1972): 791.

Bryfonski, Dedria, ed. *Contemporary Issues Criticism.* Detroit: Gale Research, 1982.

Buckley, W. F., Jr. "Angela Davis and the Regents." *National Review* 22 (July 14, 1970): 748–49.

————. "The Indian at Dartmouth." *National Review* 40 (November 25, 1988): 61.

————. "Miss Davis and Steinem." *National Review* 23 (December 31, 1971): 1486.

"California Points the Way." *Progressive* 36 (April 1972): 7.

Campbell, W. "Envisioned Coalitions Connect Struggle." *New Womens' Times* 9 (January 1983): 5.

"Case of Angela the Red." *Time* 94 (October 17, 1969): 64.

Cassese, Sid. "Angela Davis: Ten Years Later." *Essence* 12 (August 1981): 60.

Chandler, R. "Up the Down Roller Coaster: Presbyterians Protest Angela." *Christianity Today* 15 (July 2, 1971): 35–36.

"Changing Times." *Nation* 209 (November 3, 1969): 460.

Clark, C. M. "Race, Class, Gender and Sexuality—On Davis, Angela Y., Women, Culture and Politics." *Social Justice* 17 (1990): 195–202.

"Clift Balks at Davis Gift Voted by SRRT Council." *Library Journal* 96 (May 1, 1971): 1553.

Cole, Harriet. "Angela Davis: Good-Health Advocate." *Essence* 18 (January 1988): 67.

Cole, Johnetta. "Affirmation to Resistance: A Response to Angela Davis." *Massachusetts Review* 13 (Winter–Spring 1972): 100–03.

"Come to Our Trial." *Economist* 238 (January 16, 1971): 44.

Coombs, Orde. "Angela Davis Keeps the Faith." *New York* 11 (April 17, 1978): 43–47.

"Davis Affair." *Newsweek* 75 (June 22, 1970): 78.

"Day in Court: Arraignment." *Newsweek* 77 (January 18, 1971): 20.

"Death in the Van." *Newsweek* 79 (April 17, 1972): 33–34.

DeLeon, Robert A. "Angela Davis Eyes Future After 13 Week Trial." *Jet* 42 (June 22, 1972): 22–25.

————. "Angela Davis Freed on $102,500 Bail." *Jet* 41 (March 9, 1972): 5–7.

————. "Angela Davis Works to Bring Change in Prison System." *Jet* 46 (May 16, 1974): 12–18.

————. "A Look at Angela Davis From Another Angle: Her Jail Cell." *Jet* 41 (February 24, 1972): 8–14.

————. "A New Look at Angela Davis." *Ebony* 27 (April 1972): 53–60.

————. "A Revealing Report on Angela Davis' Fight for Freedom." *Jet* 41 (November 18, 1971): 12–17.

Dicks, Vivian I. "Courtroom Rhetorical Strategies: Forensic and Deliberate Perspectives." *Quarterly Journal of Speech* 67 (May 1981): 178–92.

Dobbin, M. "Causes for Hope." *Briarpatch* 15 (November 1986): 12.

"Enigmatic Angela." *Time* 96 (October 26, 1970): 28.

Fowlkes, Diane L., and others. "Jury Selection as Political Action." *Annual Meeting of the American Political Science Association (Washington, D. C.: September 1–4, 1977).* [ED146107]

"Free Angela Like Lt. Calley, Cry Supporters." *Jet* 39 (February 18, 1971): 15.

"Free Angela with Love; With Excerpts from Letters to George Jackson." *Newsweek* 79 (May 8, 1972): 37–38.

"Freed Angela." *Time* 99 (March 6, 1972): 26.

Frook, J. "Communist Dairy Farmer Who Bailed Out Angela Davis." *Life* 72 (March 10, 1972): 73.

"Fugitive." *Time* 96 (August 31, 1970): 14.

Gardner, Marilyn. "Angela Davis Packs Life of Adventure into 30 Years." *Biography News* 1 (December 1974): 1375–76.

Gillespie, Marcia, and Ronald Van Downing. "Angela Davis: Black Woman on the Run." *Essence* (November 1970): 50.

"Girl Who Has Everything." *National Review* 22 (November 3, 1970): 1144.

Greene, Cheryll Y. "Angela Davis: Talking Tough." *Essence* 17 (August 1986): 63.

_____. "Woman Talk (Interview with J. Jordan and A. Davis)." *Essence* 21 (May 1990): 92–94 + .

Hall, Gus. *Out of Indo-China! Freedom for Angela Davis! Our Goals for 1971 and How to Win Them; The Sharpening Crisis of U.S. Imperialism and the Tasks of the Communist Party.* New York: New Outlook, 1971.

"Hard on Communism." *Newsweek* 74 (October 6, 1969): 101.

"Hardly the Last Word." *Time* 95 (June 29, 1970): 45.

"Interview with Angela Davis." *Crime and Social Justice* 3 (Summer 1975): 30.

"Is Dartmouth Joining the Eastern Bloc?" *National Review* 40 (October 14, 1988): 16. (Angela Davis invited to give keynote address).

Jackson, James. "Lessons of the Battle for Angela Davis." *World Marxist Review* 15 (1972): 123–25.

"Jails Rob Prisoners of Humanity." *Jet* 41 (January 13, 1972): 6.

Jones, J. "Three Strands of History." *Nation* 34 (July 20, 1982): 213.

Katz, Shlomo. "An Open Letter to James Baldwin." *Midstream* 17 (1971): 3–5.

Kaufman, A. S. "Communist and the Governor." *New Republic* 162 (January 3, 1970): 21–24.

Keerdoja, E., and M. Reese. "Davis: Campaigning as a Communist." *Newsweek* 95 (June 9, 1990): 12.

Lanker, Brian. "I Dream a World." *National Geographic* 176 (August 1989): 206.

Larner, J. "To Speak of Black Violence." *Dissent* 20 (Winter 1973): 67.

"Leaders Applaud Angela Davis' Acquittal; 'Case Against Her Was Flimsy'." *Jet* 42 (June 22, 1972): 25.

Levin, B. "Angela Davis: Heads, She Wins, Tails They Lose, English View of the Verdict." *National Review* 24 (July 7, 1972): 728.

Lewis, Alice A. "Angela Davis in Port Gibson, Mississippi." *Freedomways* 15 (1975): 114–17.

"Love Story." *Newsweek* 79 (April 10, 1972): 19.

"Making of a Revolutionary." *Sepia* 19 (December 1970): 8–11.

"Man Seized with Angela Free, Calls for Outcry." *Jet* (April 29, 1971): 15.

Marcuse, H. "Dear Angela; Letter." *Ramparts Magazine* 9 (July 1971): 22.

"Maureen Reagan Blasted at UN Confab by Angela Davis." *Jet* 68 (July 29, 1985): 10.

Maynard, S. "Angela Davis Defends Our Rights." *Rites* 4 (April 1988): 6.

Miller, Judy Ann. "The State of California vs. Angela Y. Davis and Ruchell Magee." *Black Politician* 2 (1971): 8–15, 52–57.

"Motive in a Diary." *Time* 99 (May 15, 1972): 50.

Myerson, M. "Angela Davis in Prison; Interview." *Ramparts Magazine* 9 (February 1971): 20.

Nero, C. "Sex in Frontenac County." *Rites* 4 (April 1988): 6.

Noble, Jeanne. *Beautiful Also Are the Souls of My Black Sisters.* Englewood Cliffs, NJ: Prentice-Hall, 1978.

"The Obsequious Treatment of Angela Davis." *Human Events* 42 (October 9, 1982): 6.

Pachter, H. M. "Private Lives of Rebels." *Harper* 251 (August 1975): 83.

"Path of Angela Davis." *Life* 69 (September 11, 1970): 20–27.

"People Rest." *Newsweek* 79 (May 29, 1972): 32.

Pitman, J. "She Was Hated and Feared." *World Marxist Review* 19 (January 1976): 133–37.

"Professor's Guns." *Time* 96 (August 24, 1970): 13.

"Public Finally to See Documentary on Angela Davis." *Jet* 41 (November 25, 1971): 47.

"Questions and Answers." *Political Affairs* 59 (September 1980): 19.

"Right Out." *Newsweek* 79 (March 6, 1972): 40.

Roberts, S. V. "Russians Are Coming at UCLA." *Commonweal* 91 (November 7, 1969): 174–75.

Robinson, L. "How Psychology Helped Free Angela; Unique Methods in Selecting Fair Davis Jury." *Ebony* 28 (February 1973): 44.

Rosenbaum, R. "Whither Thou Goest." *Esquire* 78 (July 1972): 77–92.

"Ruchell Magee: Slave Rebel." *Black Scholar* 4 (October 1972): 41–45.

"Saint Angela." *Time* 99 (April 3, 1972): 32.

Sanders, C. L. "Radicalization of Angela Davis." *Ebony* 26 (July 1971): 114–20.

"Says Angela 'One of Most Nonviolent Persons'." *Jet* 39 (March 25, 1971): 23.

Scheider, Sue. "Angela Davis: Keynote on Economics." *Off Our Backs* 14 (June 1984): 1–4.

Scobie, W. L. "Selling of Angela." *National Review* 24 (March 17, 1972): 280.

Shils, Edward. "The Political University and Academic Freedom." *Minerva* (October 1970): 479–91.

Simon, Rita J., and Norma Pecora. "Coverage of the Davis, Harris and Hearst Trials by Major American Magazines." *Studies in Communications* 3 (1986): 111–34.

Skolnick, J. H., and S. A. Brick. "Fair Trial for Angela Davis?" *Nation* 213 (July 19, 1971): 46–50.

———, and ———. "The Angela Davis Trial." *New Society* 18 (July 15, 1971): 100–03.

Smith, R. H. "Story Behind the Book: If They Come in the Morning." *Publishers' Weekly* 200 (November 15, 1971): 52–53.

Snell, M. B. "Child Care or Workfare [interview]." *New Perspectives Quarterly* 7 (Winter 1990): 19–22.

"Soledad Story." *Newsweek* 76 (August 24, 1970): 21.

"Soledad Verdict Brightens Angela's Hopes in Trial." *Jet* 42 (April 13, 1972): 7.

"Soviet Scientists Appeal for Angela's Safety; Confinement Driving Bobby Seale Nuts." *Jet* 39 (January 14, 1971): 7.

"SRRT $200 for Angela Davis Approved by ALA Executive Board." *Library Journal* 96 (June 1, 1971): 1913.

"Still on the Front Line: Angela Davis." *Ebony* 65 (July 1990): 56–58.

Storey, Jill. "Is There Life After Notoriety?" *Ms.* 10 (October 1981): 110.

"Student Told Angela Is Lowest Kind; Blacks in New York Explode." *Jet* 42 (July 2, 1972): 12.

"Support for Angela Davis." *Library Journal* 96 (March 15, 1971): 903.

Thomas, M., Sr. "Poem to Angela Davis From Black Political Prisoners." *Black Scholar* 2 (April–May 1971): 5.

Thompson, C. S. "Angela's Case Puts Justice on Trial." *Jet* (May 6, 1971): 44–49.

Thompson, M. C. "Politics Key Topic at SCLC Convention in Dallas: Angela Davis Speaks to Group." *Jet* 42 (August 31, 1972): 8.

"Thousands March to Protest Prisons in North Carolina." *Jet* 46 (July 25, 1974): 30–31.

"TV, Radio Announcers Name Angela Davis 'Woman of Year,' Fletcher 'Man of Year' at Convention." *Jet* (September 2, 1971): 61–63.

"University Censored for Dismissing Angela Davis." *Jet* 42 (May 1972): 8.

"Uproar Over the Angela Davis Case: The Facts, The Issues." *U.S. News & World Report* 71 (October 11, 1971): 39.

"Verdict on Poindexter." *Newsweek* 77 (April 26, 1971): 31.

Watts, Sarah, and Elizabeth Higginbotham. "The New Scholarship on Afro-American Women." *Women's Studies Quarterly* 16 (September 1988): 12–21.

"Whither Angela Davis." *Christianity Today* 14 (July 17, 1970): 22.

Williams, C. "A Conversation With Angela." *Black Scholar* 3 (March 1972): 36.

Williams, Irene. "Women in Dark Times: Three Views of the Angela Davis Trial." *San Jose Studies* 4 (February 1978): 34–43.

Zack, G. "For Angela, a Poem." *Black World* 2 (June 1971): 69.

Other Works About Angela Davis

Theses

Dicks, Vivian Irene. "A Rhetorical Analysis of the Forensic and Deliberative Issues and Strategies of the Angela Davis Trial." Ph.D. Diss., Ohio State University, 1976.

Huntley, Richard Thomas. "Events and Issues of the Angela Davis Dismissal." Ed.D. diss., University of Southern California, 1976.

Media Materials About Angela Davis

Films

Angela Davis: Portrait of a Revolutionary. New York: Released by New Yorker Films, 1972. 16mm.; 60 min.; sound; color.

Angela: Like It Is. New York: WABC-TV. Released by American Documentary Films, 1970. 16mm.; 60 min.; sound; black and white.

Sound Recordings

Angela Davis. Alabama: University of Alabama in Birmingham, 1970, 1979. Sound recording.

Angela Davis and Charlene Mitchell. Los Angeles: Pacifica Radio Archive, 1971. Phonotape; 25 min.
Angela Davis on Black Women in America. Los Angeles: Pacifica Tape Library, 1974. Sound recording; 46 min.
Angela Davis Speaks. New York: Folkways Records, 1971. Stereophono; 33 ⅓ rpm.
Angela Davis Speaks: The Controversial Marxist Leader in the Black Movement. North Hollywood, CA: Center for Cassette Studies, 1973. 24 min.
Interviews with Angela Davis. Radio Free People. 3 ¾ ips; 5 in.
Soul and Soledad. New York: Flying Dutchman Productions: Atco Records. Stereo; FD 10141.

Video Recordings

Assignment America. Angela Davis: A Closer Look. New York: WNET/13. Educational Broadcasting Corporation, 1975. 1 cassette; 26 min.; ¾ in; sound; color.

Primary Source Materials Relating to Angela Davis

Angela Davis Case Collection. Extent of collection: Not listed. Finding aids: Published guide. Location: Meiklejohn Civil Liberties Institute Library, 1715 Francisco Street, Box 673, Berkeley, California 94701. Scope of collection: Complete file of Davis case, material filed in court, attorneys' work products, public relations materials, petitions, newsclippings, etc. Microfilm available.
Angela Davis Defense Committee Records. ca. 1971–1972. Extent of collection: Not listed. Finding aids: Not listed. Location: Stanford University Libraries, Manuscript Divison, Stanford, California 94305-6004. Scope of collection: Fan mail from Europe while in jail.
Angela Yvonne Davis. Papers. 1969–1972. Extent of collection: 2 boxes. Finding aids: Published guide. Location: Smith College Library, Sophia Smith Collection, Northampton, Massachusetts 01063. Scope of collection: Articles, statements, cartoons, flyers, posters, etc.
Black Oral History Interviews. 1970–1973. Extent of collection: 35 items. Finding aids: Available in library. Location: Fisk University Library and Media Center, 17th Avenue N., Nashville, Tennessee 37208-3051. Scope of collection: Transcripts of tape recorded interview with Davis.
California. Department of Education. Superintendent of Public Instruction. Correspondence. 1963–1965, 1967–1970. Extent of collection: 85 file folders. Finding aids: Unpublished inventory. Location: California State Archives, 1020 O Street, Sacramento, California 95814. Scope of collection: Contains materials regarding controversy surrounding Davis.
California. Lieutenant Governor. Reinecke, Edwin A. Subject Files. 1969–1974. Extent of collection: 9 cu. ft. Finding aids: Unpublished inventory. Location: California State Archives, 1020 O Street, Sacramento, California 95814. Scope of collection: Materials relating to Davis' teaching, public outcry, speeches, etc.
Elizabeth Catlett. Papers. 1902–1984. Extent of collection: ca. 2 ft. (ca. 2200 items). Finding aids: Available in repository. Location: Amistad Research

Center, Tulane University, Tilton Hall, New Orleans, Louisana 70118. Scope
of collection: Includes material relating to organizations seeking release of
Davis.

Eugene Gordon. Papers. 1941–1969. Extent of collection: .4 lin. ft. Finding aids:
Partial inventory. Location: Schomburg Center for Research in Black Culture, Rare Books, Manuscript and Archives Section, 515 Lenox Avenue,
New York, New York 10037. Scope of collection: Manuscripts by Gordon,
communist party leader. Includes sketch books concerning Davis.

Mary Timothy. Angela Davis Trial. 1972–1974. Extent of collection: 4 lin. ft. Finding aids: Unpublished guide. Location: Department of Special Collections,
Stanford University Libraries, Stanford, California 94305-6004. Scope of collection: Timothy was foreperson of Davis' trial jury. Includes trial transcripts,
tape-recordings, news clippings, etc.

Meiklejohn Civil Liberties Institute Library. Angela Davis Book Collection. Extent of collection: Not listed. Finding aids: Special catalog. Location: Meiklejohn Civil Liberties Institute Library, 1715 Francisco Street, Box 673, Berkeley, California 94701. Scope of collection: Book collection. Open to public.

National Alliance Against Racist and Political Repression (U.S.). Angela Davis
Defense Committee Collection. 1970–1976. Extent of collection: 1.4 lin. ft.
Finding aids: Not listed. Location: Schomburg Center for Research in Black
Culture, Rare Books, Manuscripts and Archives Section, 515 Lenox Avenue,
New York, New York 10037. Scope of collection: Records of Davis Defense
Committee, postcards, etc.

National United Committee to Free Angela Davis. Records. ca. 1970–1972. Extent of collection: Not listed. Finding aids: Not listed. Location: Department
of Special Collections, Stanford University Libraries, Stanford, California
94305-6004. Scope of collection: Letters of support, clippings, personal correspondence, etc.

(THE ABOVE ENTRY WAS CONTRIBUTED BY GLENDORA JOHNSON-COOPER)

18. Dorothy Day
(1897–1980)
Social activist; journalist; pacifist; and
advocate for civil rights and political rights

BIOGRAPHICAL INFORMATION

Chronological Biography

Born November 8, 1897, in Brooklyn Heights, New York, to Grace (Slatterlee) and John Day, third of five children.

1904–1907: Journalist father found employment in California in 1904 and family moved to Oakland. Although family was not injured during 1906 earthquake, newspaper's printing plant was destroyed. Days relocated to Chicago in hopes of finding employment. Father was unable to find work and family settled in tenement flat. It was her first experience with poverty. Began to attend Episcopal Church. When she was ten, father was appointed sport editor of *The Inter Ocean* and family moved to Chicago's North Side, having regained middle class status.   **1913–1914:** Oldest brother, Donald, found employment with *The Day Book* newspaper, which exposed working conditions in Chicago, and she was introduced to American Left and labor movement. Interest in urban poverty was piqued and involvement in church ceased. Graduated from Waller High School and won scholarship to University of Illinois at Urbana. While at school, father was again unemployed. Joined writing club named Scribblers, and Socialist party, but found it dull. At Urbana, established close friendship with radical Rayna Simmons. Through Simmons, a Jew, first became aware of anti–Semitism. (Simmons died in 1927 in Moscow, where she had gone to celebrate anniversary of Revolution and enter Lenin Institute.)   **1916:** Left college and returned to parents' home in New York City, where father was employed as sportswriter by *New York Telegraph*. Against father's wishes, sought employment as reporter. Found work with Socialist paper *The Call*; moved out of parents' home and rented tenement room. Covered strikes, protests and speeches by leading radicals, including Elizabeth Gurley Flynn (see entry 25) future leader of American Communist Party. Conducted numerous interviews, including one with Leon Trotsky. Became close friend of Mike Gold, writer of *Jews Without Money* and later editor of the Communist party organ, *Daily Worker*. Befriended playwright, Eugene O'Neill.   **1917:** In April, after seven months with *The Call*, resigned position and went to work with Anti-Conscription League. Several weeks later, joined staff of *The Masses*, which included Max Eastman, Floyd Dell and John Reed. Authorities increasingly harassed radical newspaper and it went out of business in late 1917.   **November 1917:** Went to Washington to support actions of protesting suffragists. Arrested and sentenced to 30 days in jail. Joined suffragists in their hunger strike while imprisoned. On November 28th, President Wilson pardoned the women and they were set free.   **1918–1919:** In spring of 1918, began nurse's training at King's County Hospital in Brooklyn. While employed there, met and fell in love with Lionel Moise, who was working as an orderly. He later became journalist with *Chicago Tribune* and *San Francisco Examiner*. Affair with Moise was tumultous one; he demanded that she be "his woman" and renounce her work and writing. He was also given to fits of jealous rage. Discovered in summer that she was pregnant by Moise who had earlier warned her that he would leave her if she had a child. Chose to have abortion in the fall. Moise, who had promised to meet her after operation, failed to show up.   **1920:** In spring, married Barkeley Tobey, well-to-do man, 20 years her senior, and founder of Literary Guild. They left for year in Europe that summer. While there, she wrote autobiographical novel, *The Eleventh Virgin*, published in 1924, in which she detailed her love life and abortion.   **1921–1922:** Upon returning from Europe, left Tobey, knowing that her love for Moise was far from over. Moved to Chicago in order to be close to him, working number of menial jobs there. Eventually found work as secretary to Robert Minor, editor of Communist paper, *The Liberator*.   **July 1922:** Chicago's police "Red Squad" raided Industrial Workers of the World (IWW) house where she was temporarily residing. Arrested and jailed for two days. Rented room in Catholic household; experience rekindled childhood interest in religion. **1923:** By early 1923, obsession with Moise was over and she and friend Mary Gordon left for New Orleans. In New Orleans, became reporter for *New Orleans Item*. Began to pray regularly at St. Louis Cathedral.   **Spring 1923:** *The Eleventh Virgin* was published but received poor reviews. Hollywood movie studio bought rights to work for $5,000, but no film was ever made. Received half of this settlement.   **1924–1927:** Returned to New York and bought beach cottage on Staten Island in early 1925. Met Forster Batterham, in her words "an anarchist, an Englishman by descent, and a biologist." They fell in love and entered into common-law marriage. Considered these years her happiest. Her interest in religion grew stronger; began to attend Mass on Sundays. Discovered she was pregnant in June of 1926; she was overjoyed but Batterham was not, believing world was too cruel to bring children into it. **March 3, 1927:** Daughter, Tamar Theresa, born.   **July 1927:** Daughter baptized Catholic.   **December 28, 1927:** Baptized into Catholic Church ending relationship with Batterham, avowed atheist.   **1932:** Covered Hunger March to Washington for *Commonweal* and *America* in late fall. Experience had profound affect on her. She prayed "that some way would open up for me to use what talents I possessed for my fellow workers, for the poor." Returned to New York and met Peter Maurin, eccentric French peasant philosopher, who wanted to enlist her in working for "Green Revolution," his new Christian social order. He was instrumental in founding *Catholic Worker* and defining its vision of social justice.   **May 1, 1933:** Along with Maurin, published first issue of *Catholic Worker* out of her tenement flat. It proclaimed establishment of houses of hospitality to help homeless and called for eventual creation of communitarian society. It cost one penny. With initial printing of 2,500, its popularity soared, and by December, 100,000 copies were being published monthly.   **1936–1938:** Over 30 *Catholic Worker* houses provided assistance for poor throughout country. At same time "farms" were established as part of Maurin's Green Revolution. First agrarian community was in Easton, Pennsylvania. With outbreak of Spanish Civil War, took unpopular stance by refusing to support either side, thus incurring wrath of both pro–Franco Catholics and those who supported Republican cause.   **1938:** Autobiography, *From Union Square to Rome*, published.

1939: War broke out in Europe and her steadfast belief in pacifism was heavily criticized by those who supported war effort. While she actively opposed Hitler and Third Reich, she refused to compromise her views.   **May 1939:** Helped found Committee of Catholics to Fight Anti-Semitism in attempt to counter Father Charles Coughlin's anti–Jewish movement. *House of Hospitality* published.   **1940–1945:** Pacifistic stance had serious consequences for *Catholic Worker* movement; by 1942, half of satellite houses were lost as *Catholic Worker* groups in Chicago, Los Angeles, and elsewhere rejected pacifism. By end of war, *Catholic Worker* publication declined to barely 50,000, from pre–World War II circulation high of 160,000.   **April 1945:** At age 18, daughter Tamar married David Hennessy. They would have nine children.   **1948:** Catholic Worker Books published *On Pilgrimage*.   **May 15, 1949:** Peter Maurin, spiritual founder of *Catholic Worker* movement, died.   **1949:** Gravediggers' union went on strike against Archdiocese of New York; Cardinal Francis Spellman believed action to be Communist inspired. She disagreed publically in her writings and chose to march in picket line behind St. Patrick's Cathedral. At height of "Red Scare," she refused to condemn Communists or ignore workers' demands.   **1951:** Cardinal Spellman ordered that name of *Catholic Worker* be changed or cease publication. She politely refused, appealing for discourse and not suppression; Archdiocese rescinded order.   **1952:** Harper & Row published autobiography, *The Long Loneliness*.   **1955–1960:** Under Ammon Hennacy's guidance, *Catholic Worker* became involved in direct action against United States military build-up. When New York state ordered participation in civil defense drills in 1955, she and handful of others refused, hoping to publicize futility of surviving nuclear war. They were arrested that year and again in 1956 and 1957. In 1957, sentenced to 30 days in jail. Struggle for civil rights in South occupied time and concerns. In 1956, visited community in rural Georgia, founded in 1942 to promote racial harmony. At height of racial tensions, while on guard duty, segregationists shot at her; she was not injured.   **1960:** Study of Saint Theresa, *Therese*, published.   **September 8, 1962:** Travelled to Cuba to cover revolution for *Catholic Worker*. Her reports offered alternative view of Cuba's social and economic conditions.   **1963:** Visited Rome as one of 50 "Mothers of Peace." Attended public audience with Pope John XXIII, where he thanked "pilgrims of peace" and directed his remarks to them.   **September 1965:** Returned to Rome and took part in ten day fast during third and final session of Vatican Council II. She and 20 other women hoped Council would strongly support nonviolent activism, condemn proliferation of nuclear weapons and encourage conscientious objectors everywhere. Much of what women had prayed for was adopted when Council passed *Constitution on the Church in the Modern World*.   **Fall 1965:** Catholic workers vigorously protested escalation of Vietnam War. Two young men gained national attention because of their actions: David Miller burned his draft card, defying federal law and initiating new form of protest. On November 9th, in front of United Nations building, Roger LaPorte poured gasoline on his body and set it aflame. His self-immolation caused her much anguish, as did many other events of war. **1967–1969:** *Catholic Worker* continued longtime commitment to agricultural workers by supporting Cesar Chavez and United Farm Workers in 1960s. Chavez first visited her and *Catholic Worker* community in April 1967. They established close friendship. **May 1969:** Visited Chavez in San Joaquin Valley while on speaking tour and participated in picketing of grape fields. **1970:** Despite heart failure, travelled to Utah, Georgia, Florida and Boston. Later in year, visited Australia, Hong Kong, Tanzania, Rome, England and India, where she met Mother Teresa. **1971:** During summer, travelled to Poland, Bulgaria, Hungary and Soviet Union. Later in year, visited Chavez in California. **April 1972:** Internal Revenue Service investigated *Catholic Worker* and found that group had not paid $296,359 in taxes. *Catholic Worker* had refused to incorporate as nonprofit agency and also refused to pay "war taxes." After much publicity and public outcry, IRS withdrew its charges in July. **November 1972:** Celebrated 75th birthday. *America* devoted special issue to her. Notre Dame University bestowed Laetare Medal, its highest award, on her. **Summer 1973:** Invited by Joan Baez to attend Institute for Study of Nonviolence in California. State judge forbade farm worker picket lines. Immediately chose to join picketers; arrested and sent to "industrial farm," euphemism for prison. After two weeks charges were dropped and "industrial farmers" released. **Winter 1973:** At Mother Teresa's behest, travelled to England and Northern Ireland to visit houses of hospitality. **1974:** Paulists presented her with Isaac Heckler Award. Aided by Trappist community, able to start house for homeless women in New York City close to *Catholic Worker* headquarters. **March 1975:** Retired from day-to-day activities of *Catholic Worker*. **Spring 1976:** Maryhouse, home for homeless women begun in 1974, was finally opened on East 3rd Street. Spent her last days there. **August 6, 1976:** Invited, along with Mother Teresa, to speak to Eucharistic Congress in Philadelphia; received standing ovation. **September 1976–1979:** Suffered heart attack in September 1976. Too weak to leave room at Maryhouse from October 1977 to February 1978. Cesar Chavez visited at Easter, 1979, and Mother Teresa in summer. **November 29, 1980:** Died at Maryhouse. Buried wearing simple dress in pine coffin. Huge, diverse crowd attended funeral. Cardinal Terence Cooke blessed her body and she was buried in donated grave.

Background Information

Parents: Grace (Slatterlee) and John Day. Father was journalist. **Siblings:** Four (Donald [1895]; Sam Houston [1896]; Della [1899]; John [1912].

Three brothers became journalists.)   **Children:** One (Tamar Theresa).   **Influences:** Peter Maurin.   **Ethnicity:** Irish American, Scottish American. **Also known as:** None known.   **Historical sites, landmarks, etc.:** None known.

BIBLIOGRAPHICAL INFORMATION

Biographical Sketches About Dorothy Day

Eliade, Mircea, ed. *Encyclopedia of Religion.* New York: Macmillan, 1987.

Moritz, Charles, ed. *Current Biography Yearbook: 1962.* New York: H. W. Wilson Company, 1963.

Van Doren, Charles, and Robert McHenry, eds. *Webster's American Biographies.* Springfield, MA: G. & C. Merrian, 1974.

Whitman, Alden, ed. *American Reformers: An H. W. Wilson Biographical Dictionary.* New York: H. W. Wilson Company, 1985.

Zophy, Angela Howard, ed. *Handbook of American Women's History.* New York: Garland, 1990.

Books by Dorothy Day

By Little and By Little: The Selected Writings of Dorothy Day. Edited by Robert Ellsberg. New York: Alfred A. Knopf, 1983.

The Eleventh Virgin. New York: Boni, 1924.

From Union Square to Rome. Silver Spring, MD: Preservation of the Faith Press, 1938.

House of Hospitality. New York: Sheed and Ward, 1939.

Loaves and Fishes. New York: Harper & Row, 1963.

The Long Loneliness: The Autobiography of Dorothy Day. New York: Harper & Row, 1952.

Mediation. Edited by Stanley Vishnewski. New York: Newman, 1970.

On Pilgrimage. New York: Catholic Worker Books, 1948.

On Pilgrimage: The Sixties. New York: Curtis, 1972.

A Penny a Copy: Readings from the Catholic Worker. Edited by Thomas C. Cornell and James H. Forest. New York: Macmillan, 1968.

Therese. Notre Dame, IN: Fides Publishers Association, 1960. Reprint. Springfield, IL: Templegate, 1985.

Books About Dorothy Day

Church, Carol Bauer. *Dorothy Day, Friend of the Poor.* Minneapolis: Greenhaven, 1976.

Coles, Robert. *Dorothy Day: A Radical Devotion*. Reading, MA: Addison-Wesley, 1987.

Egan, Eileen Mary. *Dorothy Day and the Permanent Revolution*. Erie, PA: Benet, 1983.

Ellis, Marc H. *A Year at the Catholic Worker*. New York: Paulist, 1978.

Forest, Jim. *Love Is the Measure: A Biography of Dorothy Day*. New York: Paulist Press, 1986. Reprint, Basingstoke: Marshall Pickering, 1987.

Klejment, Anne, and Alice Klejment. *Dorothy Day and the Catholic Worker: A Bibliography and Index*. New York: Garland, 1984. Reprint. New York: Garland, 1986. (Extensive listing of Dorothy Day's writings.)

Miller, William D. *All Is Grace: The Spirituality of Dorothy Day*. Garden City, NY: Doubleday, 1987.

_____. *Dorothy Day: A Biography*. San Francisco: Harper & Row, 1982.

_____. *A Harsh and Dreadful Love: Dorothy Day and the Catholic Worker Movement*. New York: Liveright, 1972. Reprint. New York: Image, 1974.

Roberts, Nancy L. *Dorothy Day and the Catholic Worker*. Albany: State University of New York Press, 1984.

Shorter Works by Dorothy Day

Dorothy Day wrote extensively in *The Masses* and *The Call*, as well as in many newspapers.

"A. J., Death of a Peacemaker." *Commonweal* 86 (March 24, 1967): 14–16.

"Abbé Pierre and the Poor." *Commonweal* 71 (October 30, 1959): 146–48.

"About Mary." *Commonweal* 39 (November 5, 1943): 62–63.

"All in the Same Boat." *Newsday* (March 16, 1975): 1, 10–11.

"Another Letter to an Agnostic." *America* 51 (September 1, 1934): 491–92.

"Bed." *Commonweal* 14 (May 27, 1931): 100–01.

"Brother and the Rooster: Story." *Commonweal* 10 (September 18, 1929): 501–03.

"A Catholic Speaks His Mind." *Commonweal* 55 (April 4, 1952): 640–41.

Catholic Worker, 1933–1980 (monthly articles).

"Communism and the Intellectuals." *America* 48 (January 28, 1933): 401–02.

"Conscience and Civil Defense." *New Republic* 133 (August 6, 1922): 6.

"Decent Poverty the Social Ideal." In *American Catholic Thought on Social Questions*, edited by Aaron I. Abell. Indianapolis: Bobbs-Merrill, 1968.

"Defense Against the Bombs." *Commonweal* 72 (May 20, 1960): 197–98.

"Diabolic Plot." *America* 49 (April 29, 1933): 82–83.

"Dorothy Day Describes the Launching of the *Catholic Worker* and the Movement Behind It." In *Documents of American Catholic History*, edited by John Tracy Ellis. Milwaukee: Bruce, 1956.

"Dorothy Day on Hope." *Commonweal* 91 (November 14, 1969): 217–18.

"Dorothy Day Remembers." *Sign* 51 (July 1972): 1.

"East Twelfth Street." *Commonweal* 17 (November 30, 1932): 128–29.

"For the Truly Poor." *Commonweal* 17 (March 15, 1933): 544–45.

"From Dorothy Day." *Commonweal* 68 (June 13, 1958): 282–83.
"Guadaluape." *Commonweal* 11 (February 26, 1930): 477–78.
"Helping Each Other in the Great Depression." *Newsday* (March 16, 1975): 1, 10–11.
"House on Mott Street." *Commonweal* 28 (May 6, 1938): 37–39.
"House on Mott Street : Reprint from May 6, 1938." *Commonweal* 99 (November 16, 1973): 163–64.
"Houses of Hospitality." *Commonweal* 27 (April 15, 1938): 683–84.
"A Human Document." *Sign* 50 (June 1971): 13.
"Hunger Marchers in Washington." *America* 48 (December 24, 1932): 277–79.
"Imagination Please." *Commonweal* 96 (June 16, 1972): 332.
"In Memory of Ed Willock." *Commonweal* 73 (February 24, 1961): 549–51.
"It Was a Good Dinner." *Commonweal* 32 (August 23, 1940): 364–65.
"King, Ramsay and Connor." *Commonweal* 31 (April 19, 1940): 551–52.
"Letter from Mexico City." *Commonweal* 11 (April 16, 1930): 683–84.
"Letter to an Agnostic." *America* 51 (August 4, 1934): 390–91.
"Money and the Middle-Class Christian: Interview." *National Catholic Reporter* (February 18, 1970): 1, 5–6.
"New Revolt in the NMU." *New Republic* 122 (January 9, 1950): 15–16.
"Notes from Florida." *Commonweal* 16 (June 22, 1932): 212–13.
"Now We Are Home Again." *Commonweal* 14 (August 19, 1931): 382–83.
"Pacifists in Prison." *Commonweal* 70 (May 1, 1959): 116.
"Pacifists in Prison: Crime of Pacifism." *Commonweal* 71 (October 30, 1959): 149–50.
"Peter and Women." *Commonweal* 45 (December 6, 1946): 188–91.
"Picketing the White House." In *Young and Female: Turning Points in the Lives of Eight American Women*, edited by Pat Ross. New York: Random House, 1972.
"Pilgrimage to Mexico." *Commonweal* 69 (December 26, 1958): 336–38.
"Priest of the Immediate." *Commonweal* 65 (December 28, 1956): 331–33.
"Real Revolutionists." *Commonweal* 17 (January 11, 1933): 293–94.
"Real Revolutionists." *Commonweal* 17 (February 22, 1933): 467.
"Reminiscence at 75." *Commonweal* 98 (August 10, 1973): 424–25.
"Saint John of the Cross." *Commonweal* 18 (July 14, 1933): 287–88.
"Scandal of the Works of Mercy." *Commonweal* 51 (November 4, 1949): 99–102.
"Sharecroppers." *America* 54 (March 7, 1936): 516–17.
"Southern Pilgrimage." *Commonweal* 74 (March 31, 1961): 10–12.
"Spring Festival in Mexico." *Commonweal* 12 (July 16, 1930): 296–97.
"Story of Steve Hergenbam: Excerpt from 'The Long Loneliness'." *Commonweal* 55 (January 11, 1952): 352–55.
"Tale of Two Capitals." *Commonweal* 30 (July 14, 1939): 288–90.
"Tobacco Road." *Commonweal* 39 (November 26, 1943): 140–41.
"Traveling by Bus." *Commonweal* 51 (March 10, 1950): 577–79.
"We Plead Guilty." *Commonweal* (December 27, 1957): 830–33.

Shorter Works About Dorothy Day

"Arrest of the Pacifists." *Commonweal* 66 (July 26, 1957): 413.
"Aspirations and Realities." *Commonweal* 66 (August 16, 1957): 483–84.

Auden, W. H. "Happy Birthday, Dorothy Day." *New York Review of Books* 19 (December 14, 1972): 3–4.

Berrigan, Daniel. "A Day to Remember." *U.S. Catholic* 46 (May 1981): 30–32.

_____. *Portraits of Those I Love.* New York: Crossroad, 1982.

Bloom, Naomi. *Contributions of Women: Religion.* Minneapolis: Dillon, 1978.

Burns, Jeffrey M. "Catholic Laywomen in the Culture of American Catholicism in the 1950s." *Catholic Historian* 5 (1986): 385–400.

Campion, Donald R. "Of Many Things." *America* 119 (October 19, 1968): Inside Cover.

Caritas, Christi, and Mariell G. Benziger. "Catholic Workers Mission: New York." *Catholic World* 144 (November 1936): 220–28.

Cogley, John. "Catholic Worker." *Commonweal* 68 (May 16, 1958): 180.

_____. "Lonely Protest." *Commonweal* 66 (August 16, 1957): 496.

Coles, Robert. *A Spectacle Unto the World: The Catholic Worker Movement.* New York: Viking, 1973.

Cornell, Tom. "Dorothy Day Recalled." *National Catholic Reporter* 18 (November 27, 1981): 1.

Cort, John C. "Capitalism: Debates and Definitions." *Commonweal* 61 (November 26, 1954): 221–22.

_____. "'Catholic Worker' and the Workers." *Commonweal* 55 (April 4, 1952): 635–37.

_____. "Dorothy Day at 75." *Commonweal* 97 (February 23, 1973): 475–76.

_____. "My Life at the *Catholic Worker.*" *Commonweal* 107 (June 20, 1980): 361–67.

Curran, Charles E. "The Catholic Worker and Paul Hanly Furfey." In *American Catholic Social Ethics: Twentieth-Century Approaches.* Notre Dame, IN: University of Notre Dame Press, 1982.

Deedy, John. "Honoring the Deserving." *Commonweal* 97 (October 27, 1972): 74.

"Dorothy Day." *Commonweal* 96 (March 31, 1972): 76.

"Dorothy Day and the Catholic Worker Movement: Symposium." *America* 127 (November 11, 1972): 378, 380–99.

"Dorothy Day in Jail." *Commonweal* 65 (February 1, 1957): 452.

"Dorothy Day's Diary." *Newsweek* 39 (January 21, 1952): 85.

Ellis, Marc. *Peter Maurin: Prophet in the Twentieth Century.* New York: Paulist Press, 1981.

"Faith, Hope." *Newsweek* 47 (March 12, 1956): 64.

Finn, James. *Protest: Pacifism and Politics; Some Passionate Views on War and Nonviolence.* New York: Random House, 1967.

"Forum: Dorothy Day." In *Catholics in Conversation: 17 Interviews with Leading American Catholics,* edited by Donald McDonald. Philadelphia: Lippencott, 1960.

Fremantle, Anne. "Dorothy Day." *Commonweal* 65 (February 15, 1957): 513.

_____. "Good Like Bread." *Saturday Review* 35 (March 1, 1952): 12–13.

_____. "Work of Dorothy Day in the Slums." *Catholic World* 170 (February 1950): 333–37.

Gregory, Judith. "Remembering Dorothy Day." *America* 144 (April 25, 1981): 344–47.

Grumbach, Doris. "Father Church and the Motherhood of God." *Commonweal* 93 (December 11, 1970): 268–69.

Hillenbrand, R. H. "Catholic Worker: Review of House of Hospitality." *Commonweal* 31 (December 1, 1939): 138–39.

"Interview with Dorothy Day." In *Hard Times*, edited by Studs Terkel. New York: Avon, 1970.

Jordan, Patrick. "Dorothy Day: Still a Radical." *Commonweal* 112 (November 29, 1985): 665–69.

McCarthy, Colman. "Colman McCarthy on Dorothy Day." *New Republic* 168 (February 24, 1973): 30–33.

MacDonald, Dwight. "Profiles: The Foolish Things of the World—I and II." *New Yorker* 28 (October 4, 1952): 37 + ; (October 11, 1952): 37 + .

———. "Revisiting Dorothy Day." *New York Review of Books* 16 (January 28, 1971): 12–13.

McDowell, Barbara, and Hana Umlauf, eds. *Women's Almanac*. (Good Housekeeping). New York: Newspaper Enterprise Association, 1977.

McHenry, Robert. *Liberty's Women*. Springfield, MA: Merriam, 1980.

McMahon, F. E. "Catholic Worker." *New Republic* 127 (August 4, 1952): 20.

Marlow, Joan. *The Great Women*. New York: A & W, 1979.

Merton, Thomas. "Letter to Dorothy Day." In *Seeds of Destruction*. New York: Farrar, Straus and Giroux, 1964.

Miller, William D. "The Church and Dorothy Day." *Critic* 35 (Fall 1976): 62–70.

———. "Dorothy Day, 1897–1980: All Was Grace." *America* 143 (December 13, 1980): 382–86.

Moritz, Charles, ed. *Current Biography Yearbook: 1981*. New York: H. W. Wilson Company, 1982.

Nies, Judith. *Seven Women: Portraits from the American Radical Tradition*. New York: Viking, 1977.

O'Brien, David J. "The Pilgrimage of Dorothy Day." *Commonweal* 107 (December 19, 1980): 711–15.

O'Neill, Lois Decker, ed. *The Women's Book of World Records and Achievements*. Garden City, NY: Anchor Books / Doubleday, 1979.

Piehl, Mel. *Breaking Bread: The Catholic Worker and the Origin of Catholic Radicalism in America*. Philadelphia: Temple University Press, 1982.

"A Pilgrimage Achieved." *America* 143 (December 13, 1980): 381.

Purden, Carolyn. "Six Women: Images of Christ." *U.S. Catholic* 44 (April 1979): 24–29.

Reinhold, H. A. "Long Loneliness of Dorothy Day." *Commonweal* 55 (February 29, 1952): 521–22.

"Rights of Non-Conformity: Violators of New York State Defense Emergency Act During Mock Air Attack." *Commonweal* 62 (July 15, 1955): 363–64.

Roberts, Nancy L. "Journalism for Justice: Dorothy Day and the Catholic Worker." *Journalism History* 10 (1983): 2–9.

Ross, Pat, comp. *Young and Female: Turning Points in the Lives of Eight American Women: Personal Accounts with Introductory Notes*. New York: Random House, 1972.

"Saint and the Poet and the House of Hospitality." *Time* 67 (March 12, 1956): 89.

Schroth, Raymond A. "Dorothy Day." *America* 119 (October 19, 1968): 357.
Significant American Women. Chicago: Children's Press, 1975.
"Silence and Sham." *Commonweal* 66 (September 20, 1957): 615.
Trese, Leo J. "Not to Us, O Lord." *Commonweal* 49 (January 28, 1949): 400–01.
Umlauf Lane, Hana, ed. *World Almanac of Who.* New York: World Almanac, 1980.
Vishnewski, Stanley. "Dorothy Day: A Sign of Contradiction." *Catholic World* 209 (August 1969): 203–06.
Vree, Dale. "A Radical Holiness: On the Catholic Worker's Fiftieth Anniversary." *Commonweal* 110 (May 6, 1983): 266–69.
Wakefield, Dan. "Miracle in the Bowery." *Nation* 182 (February 4, 1956): 91–92.
Wills, Garry. "Dorothy Day at the Barricades." *Esquire* 100 (December 1983): 228–33.

Other Works About Dorothy Day
Theses

Anderson, Ruth Diana. "The Character and Communication of a Modern-Day Prophet: A Rhetorical Analysis of Dorothy Day and the Catholic Worker Movement." Ph.D. diss., University of Oregon, 1979.
Aronica, Michele Teresa. "The New York Catholic Worker Movement's Development: A Case Study of Adaptation Beyond Charismatic Leadership." Ph.D. diss., Boston College, 1985.
Fisher, James Terence. "The Sign of Contradiction: Catholic Personalism in American Culture, 1933–1962." Ph.D. diss., Rutgers University, the State University of New Jersey (New Brunswick), 1967.
Frary, Thomas D. "The Ecclesiology of Dorothy Day." Ph.D. diss., Marquette University, 1972.
Groutt, Kathleen Eleanor McKenna. "A Metahealth Analysis of the Lives of Gwendolyn Brooks, Dorothy Day, Ruth Gordon, Anais Nin, Georgia O'Keefe." Ph.D. diss., University of Maryland-College Park, 1986.
LeBrun, John Leo. "The Role of the Catholic Worker Movement in American Pacifism, 1933–1973." Ph.D. diss., Case Western University, 1973.
O'Shea, Daniel Joseph. "The Peacemaking Ministry of Dorothy Day and the Catholic Worker Movement." Ph.D. diss., Colgate Rochester Divinity School, Crozer Theology Seminary, 1985.
Roberts, Nancy Lee. "Dorothy Day and 'The Catholic Worker,' 1933–1982." Ph.D. diss., University of Minnesota, 1982.
Statnick, Roger Andrew. "Dorothy Day's Religious Conversion: A Study in Biographical Theology." Ph.D. diss., University of Notre Dame, 1983.
Voss, Norine Kay. "'Saying the Unsayable': A Study of Selected American Women's Autobiographies." Ph.D. diss., Indiana University, 1983.

Media Materials About Dorothy Day
Sound Recordings

John Cogley. Center for the Study of Democratic Institutions, [196?]. Sound tape reel; 80 min.; 3 ¾ ips; 2 track audio tape.

Pacifism and the Catholic Church. Guilford, CT: Jeffrey Norton, 1960. Cassette; 50 min.; 1 ⅞ ips audio tape.

Young and Female, edited by Pat Ross, Donna Barkman; performance by Sandy Dennis, Eileen Heckart, Claudia McNeil. New York: Caedmon Records, 1974. Cassette; 60 min.; ⅞ ips audio tape.

Video Recordings

Dorothy Day: A Retrospective: Still a Rebel. Bill Moyer's Journal Series. New York: WNET, 1973. 30 mins.; ¾ or ½ inch video cassette.

Primary Source Materials Relating to Dorothy Day

Dorothy Day and *The Catholic Worker*. Papers. 1897–1980. Extent of collection: ca. 100 cu. ft. Finding aids: Unpublished register in depository. Location: Department of Special Collections, University Archives, Marquette University Libraries, 1415 West Wisconsin Ave., Milwaukee, Wisconsin 53233. Scope of collection: Correspondence, diaries, speeches, manuscripts, photos and other papers.

Jeannine Dobbs. Class Essays. 1977. Extent of collection: 2 folders. Finding aids: Unpublished finding aid. Location: Schlesinger Library, Radcliffe College, Cambridge, Massachusetts 02138. Scope of collection: Class essays on notable American Women including Day.

(THE ABOVE ENTRY WAS CONTRIBUTED BY JANE E. ASHWILL)

19. *Ada Deer*
(1935–)

Social worker; advocate for Native American rights and women's rights

BIOGRAPHICAL INFORMATION

Chronological Biography

Born August 7, 1935, in Keshena, Wisconsin, to Constance Stockton (Wood) and Joseph Deer. Oldest of nine children, four of whom died in infancy. Lived most of first 18 years on Menominee reservation in one-room log cabin near Wolf River without electricity or running water.

1941–1953: Educated in Shawano and Milwaukee public schools; was in top ten of high school class. Early in life felt strongly that education was crucial. **1957:** Graduated with B.A. in Social Work from University of Wisconsin in Madison, one of two Native Americans among 19,000 students. Scholarships included Menominee Tribal Scholarship and King Christian

Brotherhood Award from University of Wisconsin, Madison. **1961:** Received MSW from Columbia University School of Social Work in New York City. Recipient of John Hay Whitney Foundation Opportunity Scholarship and Delta Gamma Foundation Memorial Fellowship. Worked as community organizer in Bedford-Stuyvesant, low income district of New York City. **1966:** Outstanding Young Woman of America honor. **1967–1968:** Served on Joint Commission on Mental Health of Children, Inc. Later worked as social worker in Minneapolis schools, coordinator of Native American affairs in University of Minnesota's Training Center for Community Development, and social worker for private organizations. **1969–1975:** Member of national board of Girl Scouts of U.S.A. **1970:** Co-founder of DRUMS (Determination of Rights and Unity for Menominee Shareholders), militant grass roots organization. In 1961, federal government had terminated reservation status as part of a policy that encouraged Native Americans to meld into larger society. Menominees' forest land was transformed into county with governmental responsibilities but lacking finances to meet needs. Native Americans would no longer receive government services like health and education. Menominees lost existence as tribe and membership rolls were closed, denying membership to all Menominee children born after 1954. Menominee Common Stock and Voting Trust was formed to manage tribe's assets. Some land had to be sold due to newly imposed financial burdens. Tribal hospital could not be kept up to state standards and was closed, as was school. **1970–1971:** Acting Director of Program for Recognizing Individual Determination through Education (PRIDE) at University of Wisconsin, Stevens Point. **1970–1983:** Member of national board of Americans for Indian Opportunity. **June 1971–September 1971:** Studied during summer at American Indian Law Program at University of New Mexico in Albuquerque. **July 21, 1971:** Testified before Senate committee regarding Native American and Alaska Natives Policy. **September 1971–January 1972:** Attended University of Wisconsin Law School in Madison. Left after one semester to work on federal legislation to halt destruction of tribe. Felt it important to restore reservation status because government is the main resource in most reservation areas as few, if any, corporations will assist Native Americans, and reservation is place where transmission of Native American culture takes place. **1971–1973:** Chair of Menominee Common Stock and Voting Trust which administered tribal property. **1972–1973:** Became vice president and Washington, D. C., lobbyist of National Committee to Save Menominee People and Forest, Inc., which she had established. Spent six months influencing congressmen and mobilizing support of people throughout country, resulting in much national publicity. Worked with tribal members unsure of public speaking abilities but who were in positions requiring such actions. Staged 150 mile march from reservation to Madison to present goals for restoration to congressman. Although the congressman did not think legislation would succeed, agreed to introduce it. Restoration act was signed into law December 22, 1973, restoring federal recognition and protection to tribe, and return of its land. House of Representatives passed measure by vote of 404-3 and Senate vote was unanimous; this was an historic reversal of Native American policy. Majority of credit for passage, and speed with which it occurred, is attributed directly to her almost single-handed efforts. **May–June 1973:** Witness before House committee regarding Menominee Restoration Act. **September 17, 1973:** Gave testimony before Senate committee concerning Menominee Restoration Act. **1973–:** Ex-officio member of American Indian Scholarships, Inc. **1973–1976:** Elected chair (chief) of Menominee tribe, highly unusual for woman to gain such position. As chair of Menominee Restoration Committee (interim tribal government), supervised successful creation of tribal government for 5,200 member tribe. **1974:** Received honorary Doctor of Humane Letters from University of Wisconsin; Doctor of Public Service, Northland College; and White Buffalo Council Achievement Award, Denver, Colorado. **1974–1978:** National board member of Common Cause. **June 12, 1975:** Spoke before North American Indian Women's Association at Northern Michigan University regarding "The Roles and Rights of Native Indian Women." **1975:** Recipient of award from Ethical Culture Society of New York. **1975–1976:** Member of Special Committee on Minority Presence of Girl Scouts of U.S.A. **1975–1977:** Appointed to American Indian Policy Review Commission in Washington, D. C. As part of U.S. Senate Select Committee on Indian Affairs, group was charged to conduct full review of U.S. historical and legal relationship with Native Americans to provide framework for future policy. Spoke for Native American self-determination and federal protection of land. **Late 1976:** Resigned after constitution was adopted, feeling group had accomplished goals and that it was time for new leadership. **January 1977–:** Moved to Madison and accepted position of lecturer with joint appointment in School of Social Work and Native American Studies Program at University of Wisconsin, Madison. **September 1977–January 1978:** Studied under fellowship at Harvard Institute of Politics, JFK School of Government, in Cambridge, Massachusetts. **1977–1981:** Member of Committee on Minorities of National Association of Social Workers. **1977–1983:** Served on President's Commission on White House Fellowships. Member of national board of Council on Foundations. **1978:** Delegate to Democratic Party National Party Mid-term Conference. **1978–:** National board member of Rural America. **1978–1980:** President of Association of American Indian and Alaska Native Social Workers. **1978 and 1982:** Unsuccessful in bid for Democratic nomination for Wisconsin secretary of state. First Native American to run for statewide office in Wisconsin. **June 25, 1980:** Appeared before Senate committee entitled "To Make the Select Committee on Indian Affairs a Permanent Committee of the Senate." 1980: Member of advisory board to 1980 Platform Committee of Democratic Party. Member of advisory board and speaker for OHOYO, Native American women's leadership network. 1980– 1984: National board member of Independent Sector. 1981–1982: Member of Hunt Commission of Democratic National Committee. 1982: One of first 18 women, and one of two Native American women, honored by newly established national Wonder Woman Foundation. Received $7,500 prize in "Women Taking Risks" category for having risked own finances and safety. 1982–: National board member of Housing Assistance Council. **March 1984:** Testified at hearing held by Alaska Native Review Commission in Anchorage regarding claims settlement act and effect on Alaska natives. Cautioned that act would cut federal ties as well as federal recognition of natives as distinct cultural group, and that act imposes corporate model on tribal people. Possible takeover of native assets by outsiders could occur when restrictions on sale of stock is lifted in 1991. 1984: Delegate-at-Large to Democratic National Convention. National vice president of Mondale-Ferraro Campaign. 1984–: Member of Advisory Panel to Office of Technology Assessment for National Indian Health Study. Native American Rights Fund member. **August 1985:** Invited participant in national Gallery of Women in Denver, Colorado. **November 1985:** November Woman on Heroine Calendar. 1992: Ran unsuccesfully for U.S. Congress from Wisconsin. **Present–:** Senior lecturer in School of Social Work and in American Indian Studies Program at University of Wisconsin-Madison. Known as tenacious activist who prefers to work within the system. Strong advocate of Native American self-determination. Believes that in order to succeed, Native Americans must obtain good education and develop pride in heritage to develop dignity and self-worth. Has served as consultant to various organizations and groups, including television series on Native American affairs, as well as on boards of many organizations including Girl Scouts to encourage involvement of minority girls in scouting. Served in Peace Corps, and Bureau of Indian Affairs, has been director of Upward Bound Project involving Native Americans at University of Wisconsin at Stevens Point, and legislative liaison for Native American Rights Fund in Washington, D. C.

Background Information

Parents: Constance Stockton (Wood) and Joseph Deer. Mother was white public health nurse working on reservation for Bureau of Indian Affairs. Father was full-blooded Menominee Indian. **Siblings:** Eight (No known names). **Children:** None. **Influences:** None. **Ethnicity:** Native American (Menominee). **Also known as:** None known. **Historical sites, landmarks etc.:** None known.

BIBLIOGRAPHICAL INFORMATION

Biographical Sketches About Ada Deer

Gridley, Marion E., ed. and comp. *Indians of Today.* N.p.: I.C.F.P., 1971.
Klein, Barry T. *Reference Encyclopedia of the American Indian.* New York: Todd Publications, 1986.
O'Neill, Lois Decker, ed. *The Women's Book of World Records and Achievements.* Garden City, NY: Anchor Press/Doubleday, 1979.
Wood, Theodore E. B. *A Portfolio of Outstanding Contemporary American Indians.* Menlo Park, CA: Educational Consortium of America, 1974.

Books by Ada Deer

Speaking Out. Chicago: Childrens Press, 1970.

Shorter Works by Ada Deer

"The Effects of Termination on the Menominee." *American Indian Culture Center Journal* 4 (1973): 6–14.
"The Menominee Restoration Act." *American Indian Culture Center Journal* 5 (1973): 29–30.
"Menominee Restoration: How the Good Guys Won." *Journal of Intergroup Relations* 3 (1974): 41–50.
"The Power Came from the People." In *I Am the Fire of Time: The Voices of Native American Women,* edited by Jane B. Katz. New York: E. P. Dutton, 1977.

Shorter Works About Ada Deer

Fanlund, Lari. "Indians in Wisconsin." *Wisconsin Trails* (March–April 1983): 18–21.
"Found Women: Two Who Are Making a Difference." *Ms.* 1 (April 1973): 120.
Halverson, John. "Our Town." *Shawano Evening Leader* 101 (November 27, 1982).
McClanahan, A. J. "Indian Leader Says Keep Tribal Ties." *Anchorage Times* (March 9, 1984): B-6.
Meetings of the American Indian Policy Review Commission (March 5, May 2, June 13, July 11, and September 12, 1975). Washington, D. C.: Congress of the U.S., Senate Select Committee on Indian Affairs, 1977. [ED190306]
Para, Madeleine. "Ada Deer—A Leader of All People." *National NOW Times* 24 (April 1992): 8.
"'Running Deer' and the Florida Avenue Muggers." *Washington Star* (February 17, 1981).
"Self-portrait at 200." *Newsweek* 88 (July 4, 1976): 62.
Wisconsin Women, a Gifted Heritage: A Project of the American Association of University Women, Wisconsin State Division. [Milwaukee]: The Division, 1982.

Other Works by Ada Deer

Paper Presented

Olson, Mary B., and Ada E. Deer. "Through the 'Safety Net': The Reagan Budget
   Cuts and the American Indian with a Focus on the Menominee Tribe."
   Paper presented at the conference of the Rural Sociological Society, 1982.

Media Materials by Ada Deer

Sound Recordings

American Indians and Natural Resources. Racine, WI: Johnson Foundation, 1975.
   1 side of sound cassette; 28 min.; 3 sec.; 1 ⅞ ips; 2-track; mono; NAB 3 ⅞ × 2
   ½ in.; ⅛ in. tape.

Making a Difference. [University Lecture Series, Iowa State University: 1987].
   Sound cassette; analog.

Restoration Is a Long Road. Rooseveltown, NY: Akwesasne Notes, Mohawk Nation, [1975?]. Sound cassette; 90 min.; 1 ⅞ ips; 2-track; mono.

What Do Indians Want? Waverly, IA: Wartburg College, 1983. Sound cassette; 1
   ⅞ ips; mono; 3 ⅞ × 2 ½ in.; ⅛ in. tape.

Video Recordings

The American Indian: A Quiet Revolution. Washington, D. C.: Public Television
   Library, 1976. Cassette; 29 min.; sound; color; ¾ in.

Indian Action in the 80's. Tahlequah, OK: John Vaughan Library, Audio Visual
   Service, 1980. Videocassette; 35 min.; sound; color; ¾ in.

The New Federalism: Severing the Life-line to American Indians. Waukesha, WI:
   Carroll College, 1984. Videocassette; VHS; 50 min.; sound; color; ½ in.

Media Materials About Ada Deer

Sound Recordings

Ada Deer Interview. St. Paul: Minnesota Public Radio, [1972]. Cassette; 2-track;
   mono.

Video Recordings

Vita Stone Working with Indians. Madison: University of Wisconsin, Bureau of
   Audio Visual Instruction, 1978. Videocassette; ¾ or ½ in.; 60 min.; black and
   white.

Primary Source Materials Relating to Ada Deer

Ada Deer. Newsclippings. 1969–1974. Extent of collection: 0.1 cu. ft. (1 folder);
   plus 0.4 cu. ft. of unprocessed additions. Finding aids: Not listed. Location:
   State Historical Society of Wisconsin, Archives Division, 816 State Street,
   Madison, Wisconsin 53706. Scope of collection: Photocopied newsclippings

concerning efforts of Menominee Indian leader to restore federal aid and reservation status to Menominee tribe in Wisconsin.

20. *Alice Dunbar-Nelson*
(1875–1935)

Author; teacher; social worker; public speaker; and
advocate for African American rights and women's rights and suffrage

BIOGRAPHICAL INFORMATION

Chronological Biography

Born Alice Ruth Moore, July 19, 1875, in New Orleans, Louisiana, second of two daughters, into middle-class family of Patricia (Wright) and Joseph Moore. Fair complexion and reddish-blond hair reflected Creole ancestry of black, white, and Native American; as adult occasionally would use appearance to visit museums, attend operas, etc., which were closed to her due to racial discrimination. Attended public schools; creativity and intelligence apparent early as she excelled scholastically.

1889–1892: Graduated from high school and entered Straight College in New Orleans at 15, enrolling in two-year teacher-training program. Took courses in nursing, stenography and law, as well as literature and classics. Played violin, cello and mandolin in classical and popular groups. Served as editor of woman's page of *New Orleans Journal of the Lodge,* official organ of black fraternal order. Graduated in 1892. In later years, earned M.A. from Cornell University, attended Pennsylvania School of Industrial Art, Columbia University and studied psychology and educational testing at University of Pennsylvania.   **1892:** Began teaching public school at Old Marigny Elementary School in New Orleans shortly after turning 17.   **1895:** First book of poetry and short stories, *Violets and Other Tales,* published. Her photograph and a poem were published in *Boston Monthly Review* attracting attention of newly prominent black poet and author Paul Laurence Dunbar who initiated correspondence which continued for two years.   **1896:** Moved with family to West Medford, Massachusetts.   **February 1897–March 1898:** Finally met Dunbar on February 5th, night before he left for reading tour in England, and became engaged. Teacher at public schools 66 and 83 in Brooklyn. At same time, taught evening and Sunday classes at White Rose Mission (later called White Rose Home for Girls in Harlem), which she helped to establish. Often used own money to buy supplies and games for children. Continued activities with black women's club movement which worked to combat negative stereotypes about black women and aid betterment of blacks materially and spiritually. Joined Woman's Era Club of Boston, served as recording secretary for National Association of Colored Women, planned conventions, etc.   **March 6, 1898:** Despite family's objections, secretly (since women teachers could not be married) wed Dunbar in New York City. Moved to Washington, D. C., shortly after.   **1899:** Second book published, *The Goodness of St. Rocque and Other Stories.* Generally well-received.   **1902–1920:** Separated from husband in 1902 after quite stormy marriage. Unable to find work in Washington, moved to Delaware with mother, sister and sister's four children. Taught English and drawing at Howard High School in Wilmington (as did sister), eventually serving as head of English department. Continued writing poetry, novels and articles. Edited anthologies for students. Wrote for black newspapers. Worked for black and women's rights. Worked with Delaware State Colored Teachers Association to help equalize salaries of black and white teachers outside Wilmington. Held office in Delaware chapter of Federation of Colored Women's Clubs. Wrote Cornell master's thesis on influence of Milton on Wordsworth.   **1903–1904:** Employed as teacher at Hampton Institute in Virginia during summer school sessions.   **February 9, 1906:** Husband died at age 34 of tuberculosis in Dayton, Ohio.   **1908–1914:** With exception of 1912, directed summer sessions for in-service teachers at State College for Colored Students in Dover, Delaware.   **January 19, 1910:** Secretly married teacher Henry Arthur Callis in Wilmington. He left to attend medical school in Chicago the following year and they were divorced.   **1912:** Taught summer school at National Religious Training School in Durham, North Carolina.   **1913–1915:** Associate editor of *A. M. E. Church Review,* publication of African Methodist Episcopal Church.   **1914:** *Masterpieces of Negro Eloquence: The Best Speeches Delivered by the Negro from the Days of Slavery to the Present Time,* which she edited, was published.   **1915:** Served as field organizer in Middle Atlantic States in women's suffrage movement.   **April 20, 1916:** Married widower newspaper publisher and journalist Robert John Nelson. Helped raise his two children until they died in 1918 and 1924.   **1918:** Founded local chapter of Circle of Negro War Relief and served as volunteer to demonstrate that women could contribute during World War I; racial discrimination generally prevented black women's involvement. Organization helped black soldiers and their families. Toured South as only known black field representative of Woman's Committee of United States Council of National Defense to gather information and assist nine states in organizing black women for war relief effort. Organized Flag Day parade-demonstration June 14th in which 6,000 blacks participated.   **1920:** After being threatened with dismissal from teaching position if she did not abstain from political activity, was fired after attendance at Social Justice Conference held at home of Republican presidential candidate Warren G. Harding in Marion, Ohio, to decide party's campaign position regarding racial problems. First black woman to serve on State Republican Committee of Delaware. Directed political activities of black women members while chair of League of Colored Republican Women. Worked with women from State Federation of Colored Women to found Industrial School for Colored Girls in Marshalltown, Delaware. Facility housed delinquent and homeless female juveniles. Met at Tuskegee Institute in July with members of National Association of Colored Women including Mary Eliza Church Terrell (see entry 61). Helped draft "Platform of the Colored Women of America," political document encouraging black women to vote, recommending racially relevant educational improvements, protesting mob violence, etc. **1920–1922:** With husband, founded and co-edited *Wilmington Advocate*, weekly progressive newspaper committed to achievement of equal rights for blacks. **1921:** Chaired publicity committee of National League of Colored Republican Women. In September, was member of delegation of prominent black citizens who presented racial concerns to President Harding at White House and sought clemency for black soldiers involved in Houston race riot. **November 1921:** Addressed Delaware State Colored Teachers Association annual conference, speaking on "English in the Elementary Schools." **1922:** Headed Anti-Lynching Crusaders in Delaware fighting for Dyer Anti-Lynching Bill. **1924:** Directed activities of black women in New York Democratic campaign. Had left Republican party because Delaware Republicans failed to back anti-lynching legislation in congress. **1924–1928:** Headed Industrial School for Colored Girls' public school department; taught classes; directed musical and dramatic presentations; counseled regarding education; served as parole office, etc. **1926 and 1930:** Wrote column "From a Woman's Point of View" (later called "Une Femme Dit") for black newspaper, *Pittsburgh Courier*. **1926–1930:** Wrote "As in a Looking Glass," column in *Washington Eagle*. Gave speeches in support of Al Smith for president. **June 1, 1928–April 1, 1931:** Commuted daily to Philadelphia to work as executive secretary of American Interracial Peace Committee, set up by American Friends Service Committee (Quakers), to foster peace work among blacks, equality and understanding between races, and international peace. Attended meetings, spoke at conferences, called on people, etc. Gained national attention during her speaking tours and programs. Full time paying position helped to ease financial burdens which plagued her nearly entire life. **January–May 1930:** Wrote column, "So It Seems to Alice Dunbar-Nelson," in *Pittsburgh Courier*. **January 1932:** Moved to Philadelphia when husband was appointed to Pennsylvania State Athletic Commission. They became prosperous and owned comfortable home. She continued community activities in Mercy Hospital Service Club, Board of Trustees of Douglass Hospital and others. **April**

1933: Spoke at mass demonstration protesting unjust sentencing of "Scottsboro Boys," case concerning alleged rape of two white girls by nine black youths. **January 1934:** Served on committee to distribute relief among unemployed Philadelphia blacks. **October 18, 1934:** Delivered speech, "Point of View of Women," attacking New Deal policies. **September 18, 1935:** Died of heart trouble at age 60 in University of Pennsylvania hospital. Cremated in Wilmington because no establishment in Philadelphia would perform cremation for black person. In accordance with her wishes, husband scattered her ashes by the waters of the Delaware River. **1984:** Autobiographical *Give Us Each Day: The Diary of Alice Dunbar-Nelson* published; covers last half of 1921 and 1926–1931.

Background Information

Parents: Patricia (Wright) and Joseph Moore. Mother was seamstress, father was seaman. **Sibling:** One (Mary Leila). **Children:** None. **Influences:** None. **Ethnicity:** African American. **Also known as:** Moore; Dunbar; Nelson. **Historical sites, landmarks, etc.:** None known.

BIBLIOGRAPHICAL INFORMATION

Biographical Sketches About Alice Dunbar-Nelson

James, Edward T., ed. *Notable American Women 1607–1950: A Biographical Dictionary.* Cambridge, MA: Belknap Press of Harvard University Pres, 1971. (Listed as Nelson, Alice Dunbar.)
Low, Augustus W., ed. *Encyclopedia of Black America.* New York: McGraw-Hill, 1981. (Listed as Nelson, Alice Ruth Moore Dunbar.)
Mainiero, Lina, ed. *American Women Writers.* New York: Frederick Ungar, 1981. (Listed as Alice Ruth Moore Dunbar Nelson.)
May, Hal, and Susan M. Trosky, eds. *Contemporary Authors.* Detroit: Gale Research, 1988. (Listed as Nelson, Alice Ruth Moore Dunbar.)
Smith, Jessie Carney, ed. *Notable Black American Women.* Detroit: Gale Research, 1992.

Books by Alice Dunbar-Nelson

An Alice Dunbar-Nelson Reader. Edited by R. Ora Williams. Washington: University Press of America, 1979.

Give Us Each Day: The Diary of Alice Dunbar-Nelson. Edited by Gloria T. Hull. New York: W. W. Norton, 1984.
The Goodness of St. Rocque and Other Stories. New York: Dodd, 1899. Reprint. New York: AMS Press, 1975. (Written under the name of Alice Dunbar.)
Violets and Other Tales. [Boston]: Monthly Review, 1895. (Written under the name of Alice Ruth Moore.)
The Works of Alice Dunbar-Nelson. Edited by Gloria T. Hull. New York: Oxford University Press, 1988.
Works of Alice Ruth Moore Dunbar [Nelson]. [N.p.]: 3M Co., International Microfilm Press (IMPRESS), 1969.
Dunbar, Alice Moore, ed. *Masterpieces of Negro Eloquence: The Best Speeches Delivered by the Negro from the Days of Slavery to the Present Time.* New York: Bookery Publishing, 1914. Reprint. New York: Johnson Reprint Corporation, 1970.
Dunbar, Mrs. Paul Laurence, William Saunders Scarborough, and Reverdy C. Ransom. *Paul Laurence Dunbar, Poet Laureate of the Negro Race.* Philadelphia: Reverdy C. Ransom, [1914].
Dunbar, Paul Laurence. *The Life and Works of Paul L. Dunbar.* St. Paul, MN: 3 M, 1969. (Contains the works of Alice Ruth Moore Dunbar.)
Dunbar-Nelson, Alice Moore, ed. *The Dunbar Speaker and Entertainer, Containing the Best Prose and Poetic Selections by and About the Negro Race, with Programs Arranged for Special Entertainments.* Naperville, IL: J. L. Nichols, [1920].

Shorter Works by Alice Dunbar-Nelson

"Appointed. Some Points of View." *Daily Crusader* (July 2, 1894).
"April Is on the Way." In *Ebony and Topaz.* New York: National Urban League, 1927.
"The Author's Evening at Home." *Smart Set* (September 1900): 105–06.
"The Ball Dress." *Leslie's Weekly* 93 (December 12, 1901): 552.
"The Big Quarterly in Wilmington." *Journal Every Evening* (August 27, 1932): 8, 9.
"The Boys of Howard High." In *The Dunbar Speaker and Entertainer.* Naperville, IL: J. L. Nichols, 1920.
"Canto — I Sing." *American Interracial Peace Committee Bulletin* (October 1929).
"Chalmette." In *The Dunbar Speaker and Entertainer.* Naperville, IL: J. L. Nichols, 1920.
"Communion." *Opportunity* 3 (July 1925): 216.
"Compensations of a Teacher of English." *Education* 34 (June 1914): 646–52. (Written under the name of Alice Dunbar.)
"Delta Sigma Theta, National Hymn." In *The Official Ritual of Delta Sigma Theta Grand Chapter.* Washington, D. C.: Delta Sigma Theta Sorority, 1950.
"Facing Life Squarely." *Messenger* 9 (July 1927): 219.
"Forest Fire." *Harlem: A Forum of Negro Life* 1 (November 1928): 22.
"Harlem John Henry Views the Airmada." *Crisis* 41 (January 1932): 458 + .
"Hope Deferred." *Crisis* 8 (September 1914): 238–42.

"'Hysteria': The Old Time Mass Meeting Is Dead." *Competitor* 1 (February 1920): 32–33.

"I Sit and Sew." In *Negro Poets and Their Poems,* edited by Robert Kerlin. Washington, D. C.: Associated Publishers, 1923.

"Is It Time for the Negro Colleges in the South to Be Put in the Hands of Negro Teachers?" In *The American Negro, His History and Literature,* edited by D. W. Culp. New York: Arno, 1969.

Johnson, Grace Nail, and others. Untitled anti-lynching statement. In *Black Women in White America,* edited by Gerda Lerner. New York: Vintage, 1973.

"The Life of Social Service as Exemplified in David Livingstone." In *Masterpieces of Negro Eloquence.* New York: Bookery Publishing, 1914. Reprint. New York: Johnson Reprint Corporation, 1970.

"The Lights at Carney's Point." In *The Dunbar Speaker and Entertainer.* Naperville, IL: J. L. Nichols, 1920.

"Lincoln and Douglass; Excerpt from Lives of Lincoln and Douglass." *Negro History Bulletin* 23 (February 1960): 98 +.

"The Little Mother." *Standard Union* (Brooklyn) (March 7, 1900).

"Music." *Opportunity* 3 (July 1925): 216.

"Negro Literature for Negro Pupils." *Southern Workman* 51 (February 1922): 59–63.

"The Negro Looks at an Outworn Tradition." *Southern Workman* 57 (May 1928): 195–200.

"Negro Women in War Work." In *Scott's Official History of the American Negro in the World War,* by Emmet J. Scott. N.p.: n.p., 1919.

"Of Old St. Augustine." *Opportunity* 3 (July 1925): 216.

"People of Color in Louisiana." Parts 1, 2. *Journal of Negro History* 1, 2 (October 1916, January 1917): 361–76; 51–78.

"The Poet and His Song." In *Paul Laurence Dunbar: Poet Laureate of the Negro Race,* special issue of *A. M. E. Church Review* 21 (October 1914): 5–19.

"Politics in Delaware." *Opportunity* (November 1924): 339–40.

"The Problem of Personal Service." *Opportunity* (November 1924): 184.

"The Proletariat Speaks." *Crisis* 36 (November 1929): 378.

"Rainy Day." *Advertiser* (Elmira, NY). (September 18, 1898).

"Science in Frenchtown—A Short Story." *Saturday Evening Mail* (December 7, 1912): 8–9, 26–27.

"Snow in October." In *Caroling Dusk,* edited by Countee Cullen. New York: Harper, 1927.

"Some of the Work of the National Association of Colored Women." *Long Island Review* 7 (November 1899): 338–39.

"Song of Love; Poem." *Munsey* 27 (July 1902): 603. (Written under the name of Alice Dunbar.)

"Sonnet." In *The Book of American Negro Poetry,* edited by James Weldon Johnson. New York: Harcourt, Brace and Company, 1931.

"Sonnet; Poem." *Crisis* 18 (August 1917): 193.

"Sonnet; Poem." *Crisis* 77 (November 1970): 365.

"Summit and Vale." *Lippincott's Magazine* 60 (December 1902): 175.

"Textbooks in Public Schools: A Job for the Negro Woman." *Messenger* 9 (May 1927): 149.
"These 'Colored' United States." Parts 1, 2. *Messenger* 6 (August, September 1924): 244–46, 276–79.
"To Madame Curie." *Public Ledger* (August 21, 1921).
"To the Negro Farmers of the United States." In *The Dunbar Speaker and Entertainer*, Naperville, IL: J. L. Nichols, 1920.
"Training of Teachers of English." *Education* 29 (October 1908): 97–103. (Written under the name of Alice M. Dunbar.)
"Violets; Poem." *Literary Digest* 69 (June 4, 1921): 38. (Written under the name of Alice Dunbar Nelson.)
"What Has the Church to Offer the Men of Today?" *A. M. E. Church Review* 30 (July 1913): 5–13.
"Woman's Most Serious Problem." *Messenger* 9 (March 1927): 73, 86.
"Wordsworth's Use of Milton's Description of Pandemonium." *Modern Language Notes* 24 (April 1909): 124–25.

Shorter Works About Alice Dunbar-Nelson

"Biographical Sketch." *Negro History Bulletin* 31 (April 1968): 4–5.
Brawley, Benjamin Griffith. *Paul Laurence Dunbar, Poet of His People*. Chapel Hill: University of North Carolina Press, 1936.
Breen, William J. "Black Women and the Great War: Mobilization and Reform in the South." *Journal of Southern History* 44 (1978): 421–40.
_____. "Southern Women in the War: The North Carolina Woman's Committee, 1917–1919." *North Carolina Historical Review* 55 (Summer 1978): 251–83.
Bryan, Violet Harrington. "Creating and Re-creating the Myth of New Orleans: Grace King and Alice Dunbar-Nelson." In *Publications of the Mississippi Philological Association* (1987): 185–96.
Centenary Conference on Paul Laurence Dunbar, University of California, Irvine, 1972. *A Singer in the Dawn: Reinterpretations of Paul Laurence Dunbar*. Edited by Jay Martin. New York: Dodd, Mead, [1975].
Hull, Gloria T. "Alice Dunbar-Nelson: Delaware Writer and Woman of Affairs." *Delaware History* 17 (1976): 87–103.
_____. *Color, Sex, & Poetry: Three Women Writers of the Harlem Renaissance*. Bloomington: Indiana University Press, 1987.
_____. "Researching Alice Dunbar-Nelson: A Personal and Literary Perspective." *Feminist Studies* 6 (Summer 1980): 314–20.
_____. "Researching Alice Dunbar-Nelson: A Personal and Literary Perspective." In *All the Women Are White, All the Blacks Are Men, but Some of Us Are Brave: Black Women's Studies*, edited by Gloria T. Hull, Patricia Bell Scott, and Barbara Smith. Old Westbury, NY: Feminist Press, 1982.
_____. "Shaping Contradictions: Alice Dunbar-Nelson and the Black Creole Experience." *New Orleans Review* 15 (Spring 1988): 34–37.
_____. "'Two-Facing Life': The Duality of Alice Dunbar-Nelson." *Collections* 4 (1989): 19–35.

"Obituary." *Journal of Negro History* 21 (January 1936): 95–96.

"Protest and Vindication." In *The Negro Genius: A New Appraisal of the Achievement of the American Negro in Literature and the Fine Arts*, by Benjamin Griffith Brawley. New York: Dodd, Mead & Company, 1937.

Rush, Theressa Gunnels, Carol Fairbanks Myers, and Esther Spring Arata. *Black American Writers Past and Present: A Biographical and Bibliographical Dictionary*. Metuchen, NJ: Scarecrow, 1975.

Simson, Renate. "The Unsung Past: Afro-American Women Writers of 19th Century." Paper presented at the Annual Meeting of the National Council of Teachers of English (69th, San Francisco, CA, November 22–24, 1980). [ED182764]

Staples, Brent. "She Was Hard to Impress." *New York Times Book Review* (April 14, 1985): 20.

Whitlow, Roger. "Alice Dunbar-Nelson: New Orleans Writer." In *Regionalism and the Female Imagination: A Collection of Essays*, edited by Emily Toth. New York: Human Sciences Press, 1985.

Williams, Ora. "Alice Moore Dunbar Nelson." In *Dictionary of Literary Biography*, edited by Trudier Harris. Detroit: Gale Research, 1986.

————. "Works by and About Alice Ruth (Moore) Dunbar-Nelson: A Bibliography." *College Language Association Journal* 19 (March 1976): 322–26.

Young, P. A. "Paul Laurence Dunbar: An Intimate Glimpse." *Freedomways* 12 (1972): 319–29.

Other Works by Alice Dunbar-Nelson

Play

"Mine Eyes Have Seen." In *Black Theater, U.S.A.: Forty-five Plays by Black Americans, 1847–1974*, edited by James V. Hatch. New York: Free Press, 1974. (Written under the name of Alice Dunbar Nelson.)

Other Works About Alice Dunbar-Nelson

Theses

Metcalf, Eugene Wesley, Jr. "The Letters of Paul and Alice Dunbar: A Private History." Ph.D. diss., University of California, Irvine, 1973.

Williams, Ruby Ora. "An In-depth Portrait of Alice Dunbar-Nelson." Ph.D. diss., University of California, Irvine, 1974.

Young, Patricia Alzatia. "Female Pioneers in Afro-American Drama: Angelina Weld Grimke, Georgia Douglas Johnson, Alice Dunbar-Nelson, and Mary Powell Burrill." Ph.D. diss., Bowling Green State University, 1986.

Primary Source Materials Relating to Alice Dunbar-Nelson

Alice Dunbar-Nelson. Papers. ca. 1890–1942. Extent of collection: 8 ft. Finding aids: Unpublished inventory in repository. Location: University of Delaware

Library, Newark, Delaware 19717-5267. Scope of collection: Extensive files of correspondence; diaries and scrapbooks; manuscripts of stories, novels, poems, plays and essays; photographs; clippings and ephemera; family papers; and miscellaneous material.

Culleen-Jackman Memorial Collection: Dunbar, Paul Lawrence. Papers. No Date. Extent of collection: No size given. Finding aids: Unpublished guide. Location: Atlanta University, Trevor Arnett Library, Negro Collection, Atlanta, Georgia 30314. Scope of collection: Correspondence and other papers of Paul Dunbar including a poem accompanied by an explanatory letter from Dunbar's wife, Alice N. Dunbar.

Paul Laurence Dunbar. Papers. 1873–1936. Extent of collection: 4.5 cu. ft. Finding aids: Not listed. Location: Archives-Library Division, Ohio Historical Society, 1985 Velma Avenue, Columbus, Ohio 43211. Scope of collection: Correspondence, scrapbooks, and financial records of Paul L. Dunbar. Also contains correspondence, diaries, and scrapbooks of Alice Ruth Dunbar Nelson, including correspondence between her and Paul L. Dunbar. Microfilm available.

21. *Sarah Elizabeth Van De Vort Emery*
(1838–1895)

Greenback and Populist party leader; political journalist; and advocate for women's suffrage and temperance

BIOGRAPHICAL INFORMATION

Chronological Biography

Born May 12, 1838, to Ellen (Horton) and Thomas Van De Vort in Phelps, Ontario County, New York, seventh among nine children.

1856: At 18, after local schooling, began teaching in district school. **1859–1863:** Alternated teaching with study at Clinton (New York) Liberal Institute, Universalist school. **1866:** Moved to Midland, Michigan, at 28 where she taught and superintended school. **1869:** Married fellow teacher, Wesley Emery. Settled in Lansing and soon became active in reform politics. **1874:** Joined woman suffrage movement. Daughter Effie born; died in childhood. **1880:** Attended Michigan state convention of Greenback party with husband. Began career as public speaker. Played prominent role as lecturer in Northwestern Farmers' Alliance throughout 1880s. **1881:** Elected delegate-at-large to state Greenback Convention of Michigan, first woman so honored from state. **1884:** One of Michigan's delegates to Greenback Labor party's national convention. Became member of Women's Christian Temperance Union. **1886:** As representative of Woman Suffrage Association, persuaded Prohibitionist (but not Democratic) state convention to adopt woman suffrage plank. **1887:** Attended Union Labor party's first national convention. Published *Seven Financial Conspiracies Which Have Enslaved the American People*, her most notable contribution to Farmers' Alliance cause. Book sold over 400,000 copies, was translated into several languages, and was used extensively in Populist presidential and congressional campaigns. **1891:** One of state leaders who addressed legislative committee on behalf of municipal suffrage. Joined People's (Populist) party as speaker, writer and associate editor of party's national magazine, *New Forum*, published in St. Louis. **1891–1893:** Campaigned strenuously throughout Midwest and West for People's party. **1892:** Delegate to St. Louis Conference of Industrial Organizations, which rallied labor and other reform groups to Populist banner. Published *Imperialism in America, Its Rise and Fall*, powerful antimonopoly work. **1894:** Forced to retire from active politics due to illness. **October 10, 1895:** Died of cancer in Lansing, Michigan, at age 57. Buried in Van De Vort family plot at Phelps, New York.

Background Information

Parents: Ellen (Horton) and Thomas Van De Vort. Father operated brandy and peppermint distillery and was devout Universalist and well-educated man. **Siblings:** Eight (No known names). **Children:** One (Effie). **Influences:** Wesley Emery. **Ethnicity:** Dutch American. **Also known as:** None known. **Historical sites, landmarks, etc.:** Gravesite, Phelps, New York.

BIBLIOGRAPHICAL INFORMATION

Biographical Sketches About
Sarah Elizabeth Van De Vort Emery

James, Edward T., ed. *Notable American Women, 1607–1950: A Biographical Dictionary*. Cambridge, MA: Belknap Press of Harvard University Press, 1971.
Whitman, Alden, ed. *American Reformers: An. H. W. Wilson Biographical Dictionary*. New York: H. W. Wilson, 1985.
Zophy, Angela Howard, ed. *Handbook of American Women's History*. New York: Garland, 1990.

Books by Sarah Elizabeth Van De Vort Emery

Imperialism in America: Its Rise and Progress. Lansing, MI: n.p., 1892. Reprint.
Lansing, MI: Emery & Emery, 1893.
Seven Financial Conspiracies Which Have Enslaved the American People. Lansing,
MI: L. Thompson, 1888. Reprint. Westport, CT: Hyperion, 1975.

Books About Sarah Elizabeth Van De Vort Emery

Adams, Pauline, and Emma S. Thornton. *A Populist Assault: Sarah E. Van De
Vort Emery on American Democracy, 1862–1895.* Bowling Green, OH: Bowling Green State University Popular Press, 1982.

Shorter Works About Sarah Elizabeth Van De Vort Emery

Bliss, William Dwight Porter, ed. *The Encyclopedia of Social Reform: Including
Political Economy, Political Science, Sociology and Statistics.* New York:
Funk & Wagnalls, 1898.
Buhle, Mari Jo. *Women and American Socialism, 1870–1920.* Urbana: University
of Illinois Press, 1981.
Diggs, Annie L. "The Women in the Alliance Movement." *Arena* 6 (July 1892):
161–79.
————. "The Women in the Alliance Movement." In *Lives to Remember,*
edited by Leon Stein. New York: Arno, 1974.
Thornton, Emma S., and Pauline Adams. "Speaking to the People: 19th Century
Populist Rhetoric." *Journal of Popular Culture* 13 (Spring 1980): 654–58.

(THE ABOVE ENTRY WAS CONTRIBUTED BY AMY DIBARTOLO ROCKWELL)

22. Crystal Dreda Bird Fauset
(1893?–1965)

*Race relations specialist; state legislator; civic leader;
and advocate for African American rights*

BIOGRAPHICAL INFORMATION

Chronological Biography

Born June 27, 1893?, to Portia E. (Lovett) and Benjamin Oliver Bird in
Princess Anne, Maryland, youngest of nine children.

1897: Father died; mother took over his position as principal of Princess Anne Academy. **1900:** Mother died. Afterwards brought up in Boston, Massachusetts, by aunt, her mother's sister. Attended integrated public schools. **1914:** Graduated from Boston Normal School. **1915–1918:** Taught for three years in Boston. **1918:** Left teaching position in 1918 to join National Board of Young Women's Christian Association (YWCA). Travelled nationally as field secretary responsible for Girl Reserves programs directed toward black students and working girls. **September 15, 1927–1928:** Field representative staff member for Interracial Section of American Friends Service Committee (Quakers) in Philadelphia; made 210 speeches in schools and clubs, at conferences and religious meetings, to about 50,000 people. Exceptional public speaker, hoped to further interracial understanding by discussing needs and achievements of blacks, and ways in which blacks and whites could help each other. **1928:** Visited Europe to study and rest. **1931:** Graduated with B.S. from Teachers College, Columbia University. Married Philadelphia school principal, Arthur Huff Fauset. They later separated. **1933:** Instrumental in creation of Swarthmore (Pennsylvania) College Institute of Race Relations, and joint executive secretary of its summer seminars for two years. Met Eleanor Roosevelt during this time. **1934?:** Named special assistant to director of Philadelphia Works Progress Administration (WPA). Founded Philadelphia Democratic Women's League, first venture into arena of party politics. **1936:** Democratic National Committee's Director of Colored Women's Activities. **1938:** Due to involvement in civic activities and politics, and public speaking excellence, tapped by Democratic Party in Philadelphia to run for state legislature. Elected after bitter primary to Pennsylvania House of Representatives on November 8th, in two-thirds white district, winning by more than 7,000 votes; enjoyed much support from women voters. Resulted in national recognition as she was country's first black woman elected to any state legislature. Campaign issues included fair employment legislation, slum clearance and low-cost housing. **1939:** Awarded Meritorious Service Medal of Pennsylvania. Resigned from State Assembly to accept position of assistant state director of Pennsylvania Works Progress Administration's Education and Recreation Program with additional responsibility as race relations adviser in all sectors of state WPA. **1941:** Named race relations advisor to New York City mayor, Fiorello La Guardia. On October 21st, joined national Office of Civilian Defense as special racial relations advisor to director in an attempt to involve blacks in civil defense programs. Became member of influential "Black Cabinet," group of blacks holding key positions in Washington which advised President Franklin D. Roosevelt, worked to end discrimination and to further causes of blacks. Close friend and adviser of Eleanor Roosevelt. **January 3, 1944:** Left Office of Civilian Defense to work for Democratic National Committee in upcoming presidential election. **September 1944:** Joined Republican party and supported their presidential candidate because she felt Democratic leadership did not welcome involvement of black women in campaign. **1944:** Husband began divorce proceedings. **1945:** Instrumental in establishment of United Nations Council of Philadelphia, later called World Affairs Council. Travelled extensively in India, Middle East and Africa. Worked with Council's inter-cultural committee. Attended inaugural session of United Nations in San Francisco as observer. **1945–1950:** Served as officer of World Affairs Council in Philadelphia. **1950:** Attended independence ceremonies of country of India as guest of Madame Pandit. **1955:** Awarded Meritorious Service Medal of Pennsylvania for her educational work as board member of American Korean Foundation. **1957:** Sent telegram to White House protesting lack of black woman in delegation to mark independence of Ghana. **March 28, 1965:** At age 71, died in her sleep in Philadelphia while on visit from home at National YWCA in New York City. Her body was cremated. **May 23, 1965:** Memorial service held in her honor by Lincoln Dames organization.

Background Information

Parents: Portia E. (Lovett) and Benjamin Oliver Bird. Mother born in Virginia. Father born in Gettysburg, Pennsylvania, in 1853 and graduated from Centenary Biblical Institute. He was first principal of Princess Anne Academy for black youth, later absorbed into Maryland State College, and currently University of Maryland. **Siblings:** Eight (Known names: Portia [Mrs. A. Mercer Daniel], Ira Bud). **Children:** None. **Influences:** None. **Ethnicity:** African American. **Also known as:** Faucet; Crystal Byrd. **Historical sites, landmarks, etc.:** None known.

BIBLIOGRAPHICAL INFORMATION

Biographical Sketches About Crystal Dreda Bird Fauset

O'Neill, Lois Decker, ed. *The Women's Book of World Records and Achievements.* Garden City, NY: Anchor Press/Doubleday, 1979.

Ploski, Harry A., and James Williams, eds. *The Negro Almanac: A Reference Work on the African American.* Detroit: Gale Research, 1989.

Sicherman, Barbara, and Carol Hurd Green, eds. *Notable American Women: The Modern Period: A Biographical Dictionary.* Cambridge, MA: Belknap Press of Harvard University Press, 1980.

Smith, Jessie Carney, ed. *Notable Black American Women*. Detroit: Gale Research, 1992.

Shorter Works by Crystal Dreda Bird Fauset

"Colored Girl Reserves." *Southern Workman* 50 (August 1921): 353–56. (Written under the name of Crystal Bird.)

Shorter Works About Crystal Dreda Bird Fauset

"The Cover." *Crisis* 45 (December 1938): Cover.
"Crystal B. Fauset, Former Legislator." *New York Times* (March 30, 1965): 47.
"Crystal Fauset Dies, Set Mark in Legislature." *Philadelphia Inquirer* (March 30, 1965): 14.
"Distaff Politicos Hold 17 State Legislature Posts." *Ebony* 22 (September 1967): 27 + .
"First Ladies of Colored America—no. 11." *Crisis* 50 (July 1943): 207.
Jones, Mary Hoxie. *Swords into Ploughshares*. New York: Macmillan, 1937.
"Legislator." *Aframerican Woman's Journal* (Summer 1940): 26.
"Mrs. Crystal Bird Fauset Is Dead." *New York Amsterdam News* (April 3, 1965): 1 + .
"Mrs. Crystal Bird Fauset Tells Her Chief Interest." *New York Amsterdam News* (December 3, 1938): 15.
Ottley, Roi. *New World A-Coming*. New York: Arno Press and the New York Times, 1968.
"Portrait." *Time* 32 (November 21, 1938): 13.
"Women." *Ebony* 37 (March 1982): 131.
"Women in Politics." *Ebony* 11 (August 1956): 81 + .

Primary Source Materials Relating to Crystal Dreda Bird Fauset

Adelaide Fish Hawley Cumming. Papers. 1922–1967 (inclusive). Extent of collection: 1.23 lin. ft. Finding aids: Unpublished guide. Location: Schlesinger Library, Radcliffe College, Cambridge, Massachusetts 02138. Scope of collection: Contains some materials on Fauset.
American Friends Service Committee Archives. Interracial Section. Letters. Extent of collection: 1 folder. Finding aids: Not listed. Location: American Friends Service Committee, 1501 Cherry St., Philadelphia, Pennsylvania 19102-1479. Scope of collection: Contains letters about Fauset's work with AFSC and two letters by her. Also some materials relating to Institute of Race Relations at Swarthmore College in 1930s.
Crystal Bird Fauset. Papers. 1946–1965. Extent of collection: 3 ft. Finding aids:

Register in the repository. Location: Howard University, Moorland-Spingarn Research Center Library, Washington, D. C. 20059-0001. Scope of collection: Papers from Fauset's work with United Nations Council of Philadelphia; letters of condolence at her death, photos and other materials documenting her career.

Philadelphia Yearly Meeting. Committee on Race Relations. 1929–1969. Extent of collection: Not listed. Finding aids: Checklist available in library. Location: Friends Historical Library, Swarthmore College, Swarthmore, Pennsylvania 19081. Scope of collection: Correspondence from Fauset regarding the Institute of Race Relations.

Swarthmore College Archives. Presidential Papers. Frank Aydelotte. 1864 to present. Extent of collection: Not listed. Finding aids: Checklist available in library. Location: Friends Historical Library, Swarthmore College, Swarthmore, Pennsylvania 19081. Scope of collection: Correspondence from Fauset regarding the Institute of Race Relations.

YWCA of the U.S.A. National Board Archives. Records Files Collection. 1886 to present. Extent of collection: Not listed. Finding aids: Unpublished guide. Location: YWCA of the U.S.A. National Board, 726 Broadway, New York, New York 10003. Scope of collection: Reports relating to Fauset's work as staff member of National Board.

23. *Rebecca Ann Latimer Felton*
(1835–1930)

Author; advocate for women's rights and suffrage and temperance; orator; penal reform; educator; and first woman to be seated in U.S. Senate

BIOGRAPHICAL INFORMATION

Chronological Biography

Born June 10, 1835, in DaKalb County, near Decatur, Georgia, to Eleanor Ann (Swift) and Charles Latimer, oldest of three children. Enjoyed carefree childhood in prosperous, intellectually stimulating circumstances where a love of books and music was encouraged. Mother was feminist and temperance worker. Father was liberal farmer and postmaster; also ran inn (Latimer's Tavern) and general store at stagecoach stop on family property. Educated in one-room schoolhouse on family property; after it was destroyed by fire when she was about nine, she boarded in clergyman's home to attend school at Miss Hayes in Oxford. After family moved to Decatur, continued to receive best private education available to girls in Georgia.

1852: After receiving instruction in drawing, music, French, etc., graduated with honors from Methodist institution, Madison (Georgia) Female College, youngest in class. Served on committee that selected commencement speaker, Dr. William Harrell Felton. **October 11, 1853:** At age 18, wed Dr. Felton, 30-year-old widower with young daughter, in her parents home. Husband was Methodist preacher, physician, liberal politician and strong supporter of women's education, who had served a term in Georgia legislature. Moved to his large farm near Cartersville where he had retired due to poor health. Had five children, only one of whom, Howard Erwin, survived childhood. **1854:** First child, John Latimer, born. **1856:** Daughter, Mary Eleanor, born. Died within a year. **1859:** Birth of son William Harrell, Jr. **Civil War Years:** Supported Confederates; opposed secession, while husband favored it. Worked with husband caring for wounded soldiers. Fled to refugee area near Clinton in spring 1864 when fighting was within 50 miles of their home. **1864:** Son Willie died of measles. **1865:** Eldest child, John, died of malaria. **Post War Period:** After death of two sons and many hardships, returned with sons' caskets containing their bodies to devastated farm in late summer 1865, despising war with firm belief that when men who she characterized as stupid and cruel governed, it was women and children who suffered most. During Reconstruction years they rebuilt farm. She taught music and mathematics in school they ran in Cartersville Methodist church for 80 children. Began involvement in local temperance and charitable organizations. **1869:** Fourth child born, Howard Erwin. While only child to survive childhood, he, too, predeceased her. **1871:** Last child born, son Paul Aiken. Died in infancy, in 1872 or 1873. **1874–1882:** With husband's encouragement, played dominant role in his successful campaigns for Congress as independent Democrat, drawing on strong support of small businessmen and farmers from their Seventh District in northwest Georgia, opposing conservative faction of party run by big business. At first, conducted efforts as campaign manager and press secretary out of public eye, writing letters, drafting speeches, speaking privately with people, compiling negative information regarding opponents; husband took no step without her assistance and guidance. By second run in 1876, she was accomplished public speaker, openly running his campaigns, conducting his affairs in Washington, drafting bills, helping to make constituents' needs known to various departments, travelling with him as he became nationally known. At his defeat in 1880 by the Bourban Democratic machine, wrote to press charging his supporters had been prevented from voting. He ran unsuccessfully again in 1882. **1881:** Feltons returned to Cartersville where they founded local newspaper, the *Courant* (first named *Cartersville Free Press*), to air their views; she edited weekly for a year. Conducted personal investigation of convict camps to publicize terrible conditions including housing of women and children together with men. **1884–1890:** Husband served three terms in

Georgia state legislature; deeply involved on all levels, she was by now popular public figure. He worked for a number of causes; temperance, public education and prison reform, all particular interests of hers.   **1886:** Became a member of the Woman's Christian Temperance Union, enlisting their help in furthering prison reform until convict camps were eliminated in Georgia in 1908.   **1890:** Dr. Felton defeated in Congressional bid.   **1890–1894:** Temporary president, then member of Georgia's board of lady managers of Chicago World's Fair (Columbian Exposition).   **1891:** During visit to Georgia House of Representatives, became first woman honored by all rising as she was seated beside Speaker of the House.   **1894:** Husband retired after unsuccessful Populist party run for Congress. Increased her involvement in local and state issues, becoming even more prominent. Became first woman in Georgia to deliver school and college commencement addresses.   **1894–1895:** Chaired the woman's executive board of the Cotton States and International Exposition in Atlanta.   **1894 and 1895:** General agricultural juror at Louisiana Purchase Exposition.   **February 1897:** Addressed National Mothers' Congress in Washington, D. C.   **1897:** Advocated lynching as punishment for rape of white women. Served as state representative to Tennessee Centennial Exposition.   **1899–1927:** Hoping to increase circulation and small farmer support, Hoke Smith, publisher of *Atlanta Journal*, requested that she write column for rural edition of multi-weekly publication. (Smith later became governor of Georgia and U.S. Senator from that state.) Through "Mrs. Felton's Timely Talks," gave advice on running of farm and home and strongly influenced public opinion on important issues. Used column, skills as eloquent lecturer and legislative appearances to continue efforts toward prohibition, penal reform, farmer's concerns and compulsory education; to lobby for women's rights (including suffrage to assist in maintenance of white supremacy and prohibition), vocational education, and admission to the state university; and to air her negative views toward blacks, Catholics, Jews, evolution, etc.   **1900:** Joined suffrage movement, led in Georgia for many years by her sister, Mary Latimer McLendon.   **April 1901:** Addressed Atlanta Woman's Club.   **November 1901:** Spoke before joint session of Georgia General Assembly in Atlanta regarding public school system.   **June 1902:** Gave speech about motherhood and marriage to Georgia Sociological Society.   **1902:** Addressed joint session of Georgia legislature regarding public schools.   **1904:** Served as juror on general agriculture at Louisiana Purchase Exposition in St. Louis.   **1907:** Liquor outlawed in Georgia.   **1909:** Husband died. Managed farms they had acquired to provide steady income.   **1911:** *My Memoirs of Georgia Politics* published.   **1912:** Delegate to the Progressive Republican national convention in Chicago.   **1914 and 1915:** Debated Mildred Lewis Rutherford regarding woman's suffrage before state legislative committee.   **World War I:** Vehemently opposed war, draft and League of Nations.   **1915:** Responsible in large measure for establishment in Atlanta of Georgia Training School for Girls to provide vocational training for poor white girls.   **1919:** *Country Life in Georgia in the Days of My Youth* published.   **1920:** Heavily involved in successful campaigns of isolationists Thomas E. Watson, an old friend, for U.S. Senate, and Thomas Hardwick for Georgia governor.   **1921:** Sister Mary died.   **September 26, 1922:** Democratic Senator Watson died.   **October 3, 1922:** In effort to win female support, Governor Hardwick, who had opposed suffrage movement, appointed her to serve remainder of term; Congress was not in session and a successor would be elected before it reconvened. **November 21–22, 1922:** Attracting much national attention, sworn in, at age 87 becoming first woman to be seated in U.S. Senate. Served until next day when elected Senator Walter F. George, whom she had persuaded to delay appearing, took oath of office. Left after short speech in which she said women were now no longer limited in their ambitions.   **1922:** Awarded honorary degree by University of Georgia.   **1922–1930:** Returned to Cartersville; remained outspoken and active in public affairs.   **1930:** Third book, *The Romantic Story of Georgia Women*, published.   **January 24, 1930:** While in Atlanta for a meeting of the trustees of the Georgia Training School for Girls, died of bronchial pneumonia in a hospital at age 94. Buried in a marble mausoleum in Cartersville near husband's grave.   **January 25, 1930:** United States Senate adjourned early out of respect for only woman to have been one of its members.

Background Information

Parents: Eleanor Ann (Swift) and Charles Latimer. Parents' families had previously lived in upper South, father's in Maryland, moving to Georgia after Revolution when father was seven years old.   **Siblings:** Two (Known names: Mary Latimer McLendon [1840–1921]).   **Children:** Five (John Latimer, Mary Eleanor, William Harrell, Jr., Howard Erwin, and Paul Aiken). **Influences:** William Harrell Felton.   **Ethnicity:** English American, Irish American, Scottish American.   **Also known as:** None known.   **Historical sites, landmarks, etc.:** Marker at site of Felton home; had been listed in National Register, now burned down, US 411, Cartersville, Georgia; Marker near place of her birth, Welburne Road, US 278, Decatur, Georgia.

BIBLIOGRAPHICAL INFORMATION

Biographical Sketches About Rebecca Ann Latimer Felton

James, Edward T. *Notable American Women 1607–1950: A Biographical Dictionary.* Cambridge, MA: Belknap Press of Harvard University Press, 1971.

Johnson, Allen, and Dumas Malone, eds. *Dictionary of American Biography.* New York: Scribner's, 1959.
McHenry, Robert, ed. *Famous American Women.* New York: Dover, 1980.
Whitman, Alden, ed. *American Reformers: An H. W. Wilson Biographical Dictionary.* New York: The H. W. Wilson Company, 1985.
Williard, Frances E., and Mary A. Livermore, eds. *A Woman of the Century.* Buffalo, NY: Charles Wells Moulton, 1893.

Books by Rebecca Ann Latimer Felton

Country Life in Georgia in the Days of My Youth. New York: Arno, 1980.
Country Life in Georgia in the Days of My Youth, Also Addresses Before Georgia Legislature Woman's Clubs, Women's Organizations and Other Noted Occasions. Atlanta, GA: Printed by Index Printing, 1919.
In Memory of Charnell Hightower: Who Died November 19th, 1887. [Atlanta: n.p., 1887].
My Memoirs of Georgia Politics. Atlanta, GA: Index Printing, 1911. (Written under the name of Mrs. William H. Felton.)
The Romantic Story of Georgia's Women. By Rebecca Latimer Felton, as told to Carter Brook Jones in the *Atlanta Georgian.* [Atlanta]: Atlanta Georgian and Sunday American, 1930.
Sermon and Address by Hon. W. H. Felton and His Wife, Mrs. W. H. Felton on the Life and Character of General Robert E. Lee. [N.p.: n.p., 1915].
The Subjection of Women and the Enfranchisement of Women. [Cartersville, GA: n.p., 1915]. (Written under the name of Mrs. William H. Felton.)

Books About Rebecca Ann Latimer Felton

Talmadge, John Erwin. *Rebecca Latimer Felton: Nine Stormy Decades.* Athens: University of Georgia Press, [1960].

Shorter Works by Rebecca Ann Latimer Felton

"Convict System of Georgia." *Forum* 2 (1887?): 484–90.
"Country Life in Georgia in the Days of My Youth." In *The Heritage of America: Readings in American History,* edited by Henry Steele Commager and Allan Nevins. Boston: Little, Brown and Company, 1939.

Shorter Works About Rebecca Ann Latimer Felton

Atlanta Journal (January 26, 1930). (Contains many columns devoted to Felton's life.)
Chamberlin, Hope. *A Minority of Members: Women in the U. S. Congress.* New York: Praeger, 1973.

Eaton, C. "Breaking a Path for the Liberation of Women in the South. *Georgia Review* 28 (Summer 1974): 190–91.

Ethridge, W. S. "Lady from Georgia." *Good Housekeeping* 76 (January 1923): 27.

"First Woman Senator." *Literary Digest* 75 (October 21, 1922): 14–15.

"First Woman Senator." *Outlook* 132 (October 18, 1922): 272–74.

Floyd, Josephine Bone. "Rebecca Latimer Felton, Champion of Women's Rights." *Georgia Historical Quarterly* 30 (June 1946): 81–104.

————. "Rebecca Latimer Felton, Political Independent." *Georgia Historical Quarterly* 30 (March 1946): 14–34.

Hirsch, Eleanor G. "Grandma Felton and the U.S. Senate." *Mankind* 4 (1974): 52–57.

"Life as a Brave Adventure." *Senior Scholastic* 89 (September 30, 1966): 7.

Montgomery, Horace. *Georgians in Profile.* Athens: University of Georgia Press, 1958.

"Obituary." *Woman's Journal* 15 (March 1930): 28.

"Portrait." *Current History Magazine of the New York Times* 17 (November 1922): 326.

"Portrait." *Current Opinion* 73 (December 1922): 732.

"Portrait." *Review of Reviews, American* 66 (November 1922): 471.

Rogers, Evelyna Keadle. "Famous Georgia Women: Rebecca Latimer Felton." *Georgia Life* 5 (1978): 34–35.

Talmadge, John. "The Seating of the First Woman in the United States Senate." *Georgia Review* 10 (Summer 1956): 168–73.

Warnock, Henry Y. "Andrew Sledd, Southern Methodists, and the Negro: A Case History. *Journal of Southern History* 31 (1965): 252–71.

Primary Source Materials Relating to Rebecca Ann Latimer Felton

Atlanta League of Women Voters. Records. 1894–1972. Extent of collection: 18 cu. ft. and 1 folder. Finding aids: Partial inventory. Location: Georgia Department of Archives and History, Public Services Division Library, 330 Capitol Ave. S.E., Atlanta, Georgia 30334. Scope of collection: Atlanta League of Women Voters and early Georgia suffrage records. Includes speech by Felton, "The Subjection of Women and the Enfranchisement of Women."

John Laffitteau Sutline. Papers. 1959–71. Extent of collection: 9 items. Finding aids: Unpublished guide. Location: Georgia Historical Society Library, 501 Whitaker Street, Savannah, Georgia 31499. Scope of collection: Includes reports concerning Savannah society from 1916 to 1927.

Rebecca (Latimer) Felton. Papers. 1851–1930. Extent of collection: 4812 items. Finding aids: Unpublished lists in library. Location: University of Georgia Libraries, Athens, Georgia 30602. Scope of collection: Items dealing with Felton's work in Georgia politics, temperance movement, women's rights, penal reform, education, religion and banking laws.

Rebecca Latimer Felton and William Harrell Felton. Papers. 1835–1930. Extent of collection: 570 items. Finding aids: Unpublished list in library. Location: University of Georgia Libraries, Athens, Georgia 30602. Scope of collection: papers of Felton and her husband.

24. *Eunice Fiorito*
(1930–   )
Social worker; advocate for rights of the differently abled

BIOGRAPHICAL INFORMATION

Chronological Biography

Born October 1, 1930, in Chicago, Illinois, second daughter of Anna (Root) and Joseph Frelly. Parents were determined to succeed; pushed children to work hard and keep trying. Credits father especially with building her self-confidence.

1931: At eight months of age, diagnosed as blind; had been given overdose of silver nitrate in eyes at birth. Parents resolved to raise her as if she could see, fostering independence. Cataract removed from one eye at one year of age. **1933?:** Second cataract removed at age three, resulting in nearly normal vision for first time in life. **December 8, 1946:** Became totally blind at 16 when sight in left eye failed. Had lost vision in right eye previously due to a severe blow and glaucoma. **Late 1940s:** Graduated from Good Counsel High School. Exceptional ability to travel alone enabled her to negotiate 100 blocks to school. Nun separated her from closest friend so that she would be as independent as possible. Strong sense of responsibility from Catholic upbringing and encouragement of parents contributed to her protecting those being treated unfairly, in neighborhood or school. Began singing to county jail prisoners from age nine and professionally at 12. **?:** Learned about vocational rehabilitation from radio advertisement, raising expectations that she could find employment quickly; hopes dimmed as agency took 18 months to process application. Successfully gained job at Chicago Lighthouse for the Blind, but earned only five cents per hour assembling wires for telephones. Organized dispirited co-workers to sing union songs at lunch time. Employers urged her to leave to attend college because, in her opinion, they saw her as troublemaker. Taught independent living skills by blind social worker, Ethel Heeren; learned to read and write

Braille in only two weeks.   1954: Graduated cum laude in three years from Loyola University in Chicago with bachelor's degree in education.   1954–1958?: Covering Chicago area, worked as counseling and rehabilitation teacher for Illinois State Department of Public Welfare in Special Services for Visually Handicapped Persons Division. Responsibilities included provision of home instruction in mobility skills to newly blinded persons, individual and family counseling, and developing community resources for aging and multiple handicapped blind individuals. Pursued master's degree by taking evening classes at Loyola's School of Social Work.   1958–19??: Received scholarship to School of Social Work at Columbia University. Interned at Roosevelt Hospital and Jewish Guild for Blind working in new field providing psychiatric social work services to blind children with emotional disturbances. Granted M.A. in Social Work from Columbia.   19??: Remained in New York City, employed as a social worker for Family Service Division and Psychiatric Children's Clinic of Guild. Instituted country's first psychiatric social work program for blind persons; services included counseling, school and vocational planning, and interagency program coordination. Also gave numerous public speeches regarding the agency and its services. Crucial aspect of program was home visitation as she believed it important to know how individuals viewed themselves and each other within the family before she could assist them.   ?: Married James Fiorito, sighted printer. Although union ended few years later due, she felt, to her devotion to career and to not giving marriage enough time to work out, couple remained close friends.   January 6, 1964: Feeling it important to broaden experience to include sighted individuals and to avoid typecasting, began working with autistic children and their families at Bellevue Hospital Center of New York University as Senior Psychiatric Social Worker. Co-workers had varying degrees of difficulty accepting her blindness. Outraged at treatment of patients and terrible facilities, organized medical students and patients to clean area and paint it in bright colors.   196?: Promoted to Psychiatric Social Work Supervisor and Assistant Administrator for Out-Patient Psychiatric Clinic by Bellevue administrators. Charged with reorganizing clinic, one of largest of its kind in world; responsible for staff, programs and supervision of graduate social work students. Worked to relicense facility by making personnel changes, initiating new services and beginning in-service training to keep staff current regarding their field.   196?–1970: Agreed to become Bellevue's acting director of Social Work and Rehabilitation Services on condition that she would return to former duties if not given job permanently in three months time. Hearing of no decision, social work staff organized successful demonstration of all of the hospital's professional staff to demand she be made permanent director. As director, strove to improve relationships between various professionals working on the wards; brighten surroundings; help patients by allowing them to wear own clothes, perform meaningful work, participate in community activities out of hospital, and obtain career planning; also continued treating individual patients. **?:** Organized successful lobby to change New York state law which had provided for mental retardation programs to be operated only by private associations. City-sponsored program established in Manhattan as result. Began to seek political solutions because of belief that political actions caused many of the problems of disabled. **1970:** Appointed acting director of New York City Mayor's Advisory Committee on Handicapped, forerunner of Office of Handicapped. Resigned from Bellevue to accept position. **April 9, 1973:** Spoke before U.S. Senate Subcommittee on Handicapped regarding education for handicapped children. **May 21, 1973:** Sworn in by New York City Mayor Lindsay as first director of Office of Handicapped. Had headed office since its creation in December 1972. Saw her role as advocate for disabled; tried to keep various groups advised and to present their views to city. Duties included administering advisory referral service to provide disabled with counseling regarding medical services, equipment, educational programs, etc. Also coordinated efforts of government and voluntary agencies to improve employment opportunities and special services. **May 1973:** Gave testimony at budget hearings regarding appropriations for departments of Labor and Health, Education and Welfare. **1973:** Extremely important Federal law passed protecting rights of disabled in federally sponsored programs and activities, Section 504 of 1973 Rehabilitation Act. Had lobbied extensively for law which calls for removal of physical barriers, prevents discrimination in programs and activities funded in any part by federal government, etc., and provides disabled with explicit legal rights for first time. **1973–198?:** Envisioned coalition to unite disparate groups of disabled to fight for their rights, seeing it as disability movement's counterpart to National Association for Advancement of Colored People (NAACP) and National Organization for Women (NOW). Travelled nationwide to recruit volunteers to establish foundation for organization and to overcome doubts that it could succeed. Founded and served as first president of American Coalition of Citizens with Disabilities (ACCD) to represent 36 million disabled persons in country, bringing immense political power to cause. Formed League of Disabled Voters to consolidate voting strength of differently abled. **January 1974:** Visited Federal Fuel Office in Washington, D. C., in continuing attempt to gain exemption from gas rationing for disabled who could not use public transportation. **September 1974:** Spoke at National Conference on Housing and Handicapped in Houston. **June 1975:** Witness regarding Supplemental Security Income (SSI) before federal House Subcommittee on Public Assistance, representing Office of Handicapped. **February 26, 1976:** Testified as President of ACCD at hearing before federal Senate Subcommittee on Handicapped regarding rehabilitation programs. **Mid–1976:** Appointed co-chair of presidential candidate Jimmy Carter's Disability Policy

Committee. **1976:** Having failed, despite three years of effort, to force federal government to carry out 1973 law, demanded to meet with Secretary of Health, Education and Welfare, one person who could end delay. After meeting in which he spoke to her in condescending manner, and patted her on head, she threatened to hold demonstration at Republican National Convention and expose situation to press. Secretary promised implementation before November election, so demonstration did not take place, but he failed to do so.   **March 1977:** Informed new administration of ACCD's intent to hold sit-ins in each of HEW's ten regional city offices if enforcement did not take place by April 4th. Regulations were not published, so demonstration took place. Led critical sit-in in Washington headquarters of HEW where several hundred disabled people sang "We Shall Overcome" and other songs of protest. Secretary promised publication of new regulations by May, but compromise was rejected by group. Administration cut off communications as well as food and medical supplies, cordoned off building, and tried "divide and conquer" tactics, but group prevailed. San Francisco demonstration lasted more than 25 days. Secretary finally signed regulations in advance of his own deadline.   **April 1977:** As president of American Council of the Blind in New York state and ACCD, spoke out about possible dangerous affect on differently-abled of new law permitting right turns at red stoplights. **October 1977:** Spoke at New York City ceremony marking Handicapped Citizens Opportunity Week.   **1977:** Delegate to International Women's Year Conference in Houston. Coauthored section on rights of disabled women included in U.S. Women's Plan for Action.   **1978?–:** Appointed special assistant to the commissioner of Rehabilitation Services Administration in U.S. Department of Education. Washington, D. C., office sets policy and provides guidance, supervision and funding to rehabilitation programs throughout country. Stresses consumer involvement in governmental decision making, in-service training to sensitize workers to needs of disabled, etc. Resigned as ACCD president to accept special assistant position to avoid possible conflict of interest.   **1979:** Loudly complained that disabled people were not being permitted equal access to papal masses when Pope visited United States.   **June 1980:** Presented paper concerning disability rights at World Congress of Rehabilitation International in Winnipeg, Canada.   **1980:** Delegate to World Conference of United Nations Decade for Women. Attended conference in Copenhagen, Denmark; only disabled person out of 2,300 delegates. Succeeded in passage of resolution and inclusion of disabled women in text of plan of action.   **1984:** Coauthored paper presented at National Conference of Howard University Model to Improve Rehabilitation Services to Minority Populations with Handicapping Conditions.   **June 1985:** Appointed North American Representative to Committee on Status of Blind Women of World Blind Union. Also associated with World Council of Disabled People's International; serves on Affairs of Women committee.

Present–: Continues as special assistant to the commissioner of Rehabilitation Services Administration in U.S. Department of Education. Believes past experience shows it is imperative for organizations and people with disabilities to join efforts and coordinate actions, as only through such efforts will needs and rights of differently-abled be met. Self-determination can only be achieved as the disabled demand and gain greater control over decisions and conditions affecting their lives.

Background Information

Parents: Anna (Root) and Joseph Frelly, manager (later a vice president) at International Harvester company. Mother immigrated from Germany; educated through third grade. Father came from Poland and completed eighth grade. **Siblings:** Number not known (No known names). **Children:** None. **Influences:** None. **Ethnicity:** German American, Polish American. **Also known as:** None known. **Historical sites, landmarks, etc.:** None known.

BIBLIOGRAPHICAL INFORMATION

Biographical Sketches About Eunice Fiorito

Bhalerao, Usha. *Eminent Blind Women of the World: Their Contribution and Achievements.* New Delhi: Sterling Publishers, 1988.

Books About Eunice Fiorito

Blind People and Air Travel: A Conversation with Eunice Fiorito. New York: Ninnescah International Service, [1983].

Shorter Works by Eunice Fiorito

"Choices and Chances in the 80s." *Journal of Visual Impairment and Blindness* 77 (June 1983): 286–87.
"Disability Rights Issues: The Role of Advocacy in Government." In *Participation of People with Disabilities: An International Perspective, Selected Papers from the 1980 World Congress of Rehabilitation International (Winnipeg, Canada, June 22–27, 1980),* edited by Kathleen S. Miller, and others. East Lansing, MI: Michigan State University, University Center for International Rehabilitation, 1981. [ED2345526]

Doherty, Jim, and Eunice Fiorito. "Most Disabled People Accept Their Disabilities. It's Other People Who Have Trouble Accepting Them. That Has to Change." *Glamour* 80 (May 1982): 162.

Fiorito, Eunice, and Jim Doherty. "Overcoming." In *Equal to the Challenge: Perspectives, Problems, and Strategies in the Rehabilitation of the Nonwhite Disabled. Proceedings of the National Conference of the Howard University Model to Improve Rehabilitation Services to Minority Populations with Handicapping Conditions (1984)*, edited by Sylvia Walker, and others. 1986. [ED276200]

Lavine, Eileen M., ed. *Proceedings of National Conference on Housing and the Handicapped (September 10-12, 1974), Houston, Texas).* Bethesda, MD: Health and Education Resources, Incorporated, 1974. [ED112592]

Spiegel, Allen D., and Simon Podair. *Rehabilitating People with Disabilities into the Mainstream of Society.* Park Ridge, NJ: Noyes Medical Publications, 1981. (Preface by Fiorito.)

"Severely Disabled Women in the Federal Work Force." *Programs for the Handicapped* (January–February 1982): 4 + .

Shorter Works About Eunice Fiorito

"City Forms Office of Handicapped." *New York Times* (December 21, 1972): 39.

"Disabled Honored at City Hall Plaza." *New York Times* (October 4, 1977): 40.

"Eunice Fiorito." In *Comeback: Six Remarkable People Who Triumphed Over Disability*, by Frank Bowe. New York: Harper & Row, 1981.

Hudson, Edward. "Right Turns on Red Lights: Many Finding System 'Go'." *New York Times* (April 11, 1977): 31.

Johnston, Laurie. "Gasoline Crisis Hard on Handicapped." *New York Times* (January 20, 1974): 34.

"List of Delegates to Conference." *New York Times* (June 17, 1980): 16.

"No Fuel Tax for Handicapped Urged." *New York Times* (January 3, 1974): 25.

"Notes on People." *New York Times* (May 22, 1973): 37.

"'Y' Scored on Turning Away Blind Man." *New York Times* (July 13, 1974): 27.

25. Elizabeth Gurley Flynn
(1890–1964)
Social activist; labor organizer; and Communist

BIOGRAPHICAL INFORMATION

Chronological Biography

Born August 7, 1890, in Concord, New Hampshire, oldest of four children of Annie (Gurley) and Thomas Flynn, Irish immigrants and socialists.

Father was quarry laborer who became civil engineer; mother was custom tailor and suffragette.

1897–1900: Growing up amidst poverty of working-class families in textile towns of Manchester, New Hampshire, and Adams, Massachusetts, made lasting impression on her. **1900:** Flynns moved to South Bronx, New York. **1904:** Won gold medals in debating and English upon graduation from grammar school. **1906:** Joined International Workers of the World (IWW) which was founded in Chicago in 1905 with purpose of organizing all workers regardless of industry or political party. Delivered first public speech entitled "What Socialism Will Do for Women" at Harlem Socialist Club. **1907:** Left high school to work full-time for IWW as labor organizer. **January 1908:** Married John Archibald Jones, ore miner active in labor movement. They separated before birth of their son in 1910. **1908–1910:** Took part in IWW battles for freedom of speech and assembly in Montana, Washington, and other western states. **May 19, 1910:** Birth of son, Fred. **1912:** Helped organize and participated in textile strikes in Lawrence, Massachusetts. **1913:** Helped organize and participated in silk strike in Paterson, New Jersey. **1913–1925:** Lived and worked with Carlo Tresca, Italian-born anarchist. **1916:** Raised relief and legal defense funds for Mesaba Range ironworker's strike in Minnesota. **1918:** Instrumental in founding of Worker's Liberty Defense Union (WLDU) whose mission was to help immigrants threatened with deportation in post-war purge of radicals. **1918–1922:** Served as secretary for, and worked with, WLDU to free all industrial and political prisoners who were arrested and threatened with deportation in "Palmer Raids" of Attorney General A. Mitchell Palmer during 1919–1920. **1920:** Divorced John Jones. Founding member of National Committee of American Civil Liberties Union (ACLU). **1920–1927:** Worked to free Sacco and Vanzetti, Italian-born anarchists who were accused of murder in Massachusetts. Helped engage lawyers, publicize case and raise money up until their execution. **1927–1930:** Served as chair of International Labor Defense Committee, organization formed by merger of International Labor Defense and WLDU. **1927–1937:** Inactive for ten years as result of serious heart condition. Lived with and was cared for by Dr. Marie Equi in Portland, Oregon. **1937:** Resumed political activities and joined Communist Party USA (CPUSA). **1937–1951:** Tireless organizer, writer and speaker on behalf of CPUSA. **1940:** Expelled from National Committee of ACLU for her membership in CPUSA. Son Fred died of lung cancer. **1941:** Elected to CPUSA's Central Committee. **1942:** Ran unsuccessfully for United States Congress on CPUSA ticket. **1950:** Led resistance to Internal Security Act which required all Communist groups to register with U.S. Attorney General. One of 135 plaintiffs who unsuccessfully brought suit to declare act unconstitutional. **1951:** Among 21 CPUSA members indicted for criminal conspiracy under Smith Act of 1940. **1952:** Headed Self-

Defense Committee of 17 Victims (those individuals who went to trial); served 30 days on contempt of court charges. **1953:** Among 13 who were finally convicted. **1955–1957:** Served two years, four months of three year prison term in Women's Federal Reformatory in Aldese, West Virginia. **1955:** *I Speak My Own Piece: Autobiography of the "Rebel Girl"* was published. *The Rebel Girl* was song written by IWW minstrel Joe Hill and inspired by a young Flynn. **March 1961:** First woman elected chair of National Committee of CPUSA to succeed Eugene Debs, who died January 31, 1961. **1964:** Suit (Aptheker v. Secretary of State) that challenged Subversive Activities Control Act 1950 was brought by Flynn and Herbert Aptheker, editor of Party's theoretical journal, *Political Affairs.* After suit was won, she secured passport to visit Soviet Union. **September 5, 1964:** Died of gastro-entercolitis in Moscow at age 74. Received full-scale state funeral in Red Square headed by Mrs. Nikita Khrushchev and was buried in Waldheim Cemetery in Chicago.

Background Information

Parents: Annie (Gurley) and Thomas Flynn. **Siblings:** 3 (Kathy [1892]; Thomas, Jr. [1894]; Bina [1897]). **Children:** 1 (Fred). **Influences:** John Archibald Jones, Carlo Tresca. **Ethnicity:** Irish American. **Also known as:** None known. **Historical sites, landmarks, etc.:** Gravesite, Waldheim Cemetery, Chicago, Illinois.

BIBLIOGRAPHICAL INFORMATION

Biographical Sketches About Elizabeth Gurley Flynn

Faust, Langdon Lynne, ed. *Women Writers: A Critical Reference Guide From Colonial Times to the Present.* New York: Ungar, 1988.

Fink, Gary M., ed. *Biographical Dictionary of American Labor Leaders.* Westport, CT: Greenwood, 1974.

Garrity, John, ed. *Dictionary of American Biography.* New York: Charles Scribner's Sons, 1981.

Johnpoll, Bernard, and Harvey Klehr, eds. *Biographical Dictionary of the American Left.* Westport,CT: Greenwood, 1986.

Sicherman, Barbara, and Carol Hurd Green, eds. *Notable American Women: The Modern Period: A Biographical Dictionary.* Cambridge, MA: Belknap Press of Harvard University Press, 1980.

Whitman, Alden, ed. *American Reformers: An H. W. Wilson Biographical Dictionary.* New York: H. W. Wilson Co., 1985.

Books by Elizabeth Gurley Flynn

The Alderson Story: My Life as a Political Prisoner. New York: International, 1963.
An Appeal to Women. New York: National Women's Commission, Communist Pary, USA, 1950.
Coal Miners and the War. New York: Workers Library, 1942.
Daughters of America: Ella Reeve Bloor and Anita Whitney. New York: Workers Library 1942.
Debs and Dennis, Fighters for Peace. New York: New Century, 1950.
Debs, Haywood, Ruthenberg. New York: Workers Library, 1939.
Earl Browder, the Man from Kansas. New York: Workers Library, 1941.
Elizabeth Gurley Flynn Speaks to the Court. New York: New Century, 1952.
Freedom Begins at Home. New York: New Century, 1961.
Horizons of the Future for a Socialist America. New York: Communist Party, USA, 1959.
I Didn't Raise My Boy to Be a Soldier for Wall Street. New York: Workers Library, 1940.
I Speak My Own Piece: Autobiography of the "Rebel Girl." New York: Masses and Mainstream, 1955.
Labor's Own William Z. Foster: A Communist's Fifty Years of Working-Class Leadership and Struggle. New York: New Century, 1949.
The McCarran Act: Fact and Fancy. New York: Gus Hall-Benjamin Davis Defense Committee, 1963.
Meet the Communists. New York: Communist Party, USA, 1946.
Memories of the Industrial Workers of the World. New York: American Institute for Marxist Studies, 1977.
The Plot to Gag America. New York: New Century, 1950.
The Rebel Girl: An Autobiography, My First Life (1906–1926). New York: International, 1973.
Sabotage, the Conscious Withdrawal of the Workers' Industrial Efficiency. Cleveland: IWW Publishing Bureau, 1915.
Stool-pigeon. New York: New Century, 1949.
Thirteen Communists Speak to the Court. New York: New Century, 1953.
The Twelve and You: What Happens to Democracy Is Your Business Too. New York: New Century, 1948.
Women Have a Date with Destiny. New York: Workers Library, 1944.
Women in the War. New York: Workers Library, 1942.
Women's Place in the Fight for a Better World. New York: New Century, 1947.

Books About Elizabeth Gurley Flynn

Baxandall, Rosalyn Fraad. *Words on Fire: The Life and Writing of Elizabeth Gurley Flynn.* New Brunswick: Rutgers University Press, 1987.
Lamont, Corliss, ed. *The Trial of Elizabeth Gurley Flynn by the American Civil Liberties Union.* New York: Horizon, 1968.

Shorter Works About Elizabeth Gurley Flynn

Aptheker, Herbert. "The Rebel Girl Passes On." *Political Affairs* 43 (1964): 40–44.
Banner, Lois. *Women in America: A Brief History.* New York: Harcourt Brace Jovanovich, 1974.
Baxandall, Rosalynn Fraad. "Elizabeth Gurley Flynn: The Early Years." *Radical America* 9 (1975): 97–115.
Buhle, Mari Jo. *Women and American Socialism, 1870–1920.* Urbana: University of Illinois Press, 1981.
Dubofsky, Melvyn. *We Shall Be All: A History of the IWW.* Chicago: Quadrangle, 1969.
Holbrook, Stewart. *Dreamers of the American Dream.* New York: Doubleday, 1957.
Hymowitz, Carol. *A History of Women in America.* New York: Bantam, 1978.
Irwin, Inez. *Angels and Amazons: A Hundred Years of American Women.* Garden City, NY: Doubleday, 1933.
Kizer, Benjamin H. "Elizabeth Gurley Flynn." *Pacific Northwest Quarterly* 57 (1966): 110–12.
Lane, Hana Umlauf. *The World Almanac Book of Who.* New York: World Almanac, 1980.
Lumer, Hyman. "EGF: A Tribute." *Political Affairs* 43 (1964): 15–19.
Marpin, Joyce. *Labor Heroines: Ten Women Who Led the Struggle.* Berkeley, CA: Union Wage Educational Committee, 1974.
O'Neill, Lois Decker, ed. *The Women's Book of World Records and Achievements.* Garden City, NY: Anchor Press/Doubleday, 1979.
Sochen, June. *Herstory: A Woman's View of American History.* New York: Alfred Publishing, 1974.
————. *Movers and Shakers: American Women Thinkers and Activists, 1900–1970.* New York: Quadrangle, 1973.
Venn, George W. "The Wobblies and Montana's Garden City." *Montana: Magazine of Western History* 21 (1971): 18–30.
Vorse, Mary (Heaton). "Elizabeth Gurley Flynn." *Nation* 122 (1926): 175–76.
Winston, Fern. "The 'Rebel Girl's' 90th Birthday." *Political Affairs* 59 (September 1980): 24–28.

Other Works About Elizabeth Gurley Flynn

Song

Hill, Joe. "The Rebel Girl." In *Folk Song Encyclopedia,* edited by Jerry Silverman. New York: Chappell Music Company, 1975. (Written in February 1915 by Joe Hill while in jail and dedicated to Elizabeth Gurley Flynn.)
————. "The Rebel Girl." In *Here's to the Women: 100 Songs For and About American Women,* by Hilda E. Wenner and Elizabeth Freilicher. Syracuse, NY: Syracuse University Press, 1987.

Theses

Camp, Helen Collier. "Gurley: A Biography of Elizabeth Gurley Flynn, 1890–1964." Ph.D. diss., Columbia University, 1980.

Gorteis, Margaret. "Coming of Age with the Industrial Workers of the World: The Early Career of Elizabeth Gurley Flynn." Master's thesis, Tufts Univ., 1975.

Olmstead, Audrey. "Agitator on the Left: The Speechmaking of Elizabeth Gurley Flynn, 1904–1964." Ph.D. diss., Indiana University, 1971.

Scholten, Pat Lee. "Militant Women for Economic Justice: The Persuasion of Mary Harris Jones, Ella Reeve Bloor and Elizabeth Gurley Flynn." Ph.D. diss., Indiana University, 1979.

Primary Source Materials Relating to Elizabeth Gurley Flynn

Elizabeth Gurley Flynn. Papers. 1903–1964. Extent of collection: 8 ft. Finding aids: Unpublished guide. Location: Tamiment Institute Library, New York University, 70 Washington Square South, New York, New York 10012. Scope of collection: Correspondence, biographical sketches, autobiographical notes, telegrams, published and unpublished articles, clippings, programs, invitations, course materials, broadsides, handbills, posters, annotated books, pamphlets and articles, as well as over 200 photographs.

Elizabeth Gurley Flynn. Papers. 1917–1923. Extent of collection: 1 box. Finding aids: Published and unpublished guides. Location: State Historical Society of Wisconsin, 816 State Street, Madison, Wisconsin 53706. Scope of collection: Papers relating to efforts during years 1917–1923 to secure justice for political prisoners, anarchists and labor agitators. Microfilm available.

Elizabeth Gurley Flynn. Papers. 1920–1964. Extent of collection: 1 box. Finding aids: Unpublished guides. Location: Dartmouth College Library, Special Collections, Hanover, New Hampshire 03755. Scope of collection: Copies of clippings, essays, and correspondence concerning her activities as a Communist.

Elizabeth Gurley Flynn. 1962. Extent of collection: 1 box. Finding aids: None listed. Location: Wayne State University, Archives of Labor and Urban Affairs, 5401 Cass Street, Detroit, Michigan 48202. Scope of collection: Tapes, photographs and items relating to Flynn's involvement with International Workers of the World.

(THE ABOVE ENTRY WAS CONTRIBUTED BY BARBARA L. MORGAN)

26. *Emma Goldman*
(1869–1940)
Anarchist; feminist; agitator for free speech and birth control; lecturer; and author

BIOGRAPHICAL INFORMATION

Chronological Biography

Born June 27, 1869, in Kovno (Kaunas) in Lithuania (then part of Russian Empire) of Orthodox Jewish parents; family moved several times while father pursued employment as innkeeper, stagecoach manager, etc. First child of Taube (Bienowitz/Bienowitch) and Abraham Goldman; strongly felt father would have preferred it if she had been a boy. Couple also had two or three sons, eldest of whom died while a child. Mother had been widowed previously and had two girls.

1882: Denied admission to high school because she failed to conform to school rules; began working in factory in St. Petersburg. **December 1885:** At 17, to avoid father's plans for her marriage, fled to United States with half-sister Helena, where she again worked in factory. Lived in Rochester, New York, where another half-sister lived. 1886: After Chicago Haymarket Square riot, became avowed anarchist. Believed in replacement of political and authoritarian social structure by free association of strong, independent individuals. **February 1887:** Married Jacob Kersner, naturalized citizen. 1889: Divorced Kersner and moved to New York City. Became student of Johann Most, leading anarchist orator in United States, who encouraged her to speak before union meetings and groups of workers. By day earned living as garment worker; by night organized, attended and often addressed anarchist meetings and demonstrations. 1892: Her radicalism led her to espouse acts of violence; she was accomplice of lover Alexander Berkman in attempted murder of Henry Clay Frick (steel magnate and chair of Carnegie's company) during Homestead steel strike. Berkman spent 14 years in penitentiary for crime. **August 1, 1893:** Arrested for inciting to riot in Union Square, New York City. In speech to unemployed, urged them to "take bread" if they were starving. Incarcerated at Blackwell's Island for one year. While in prison, became acquainted with nursing and received training as practical nurse. Served fellow prisoners as nurse and counselor and was eventually given charge of hospital ward. 1895: Went to Europe to acquire further nurse's training. Received certificates in nursing and in midwifery after year's study in Vienna. Attended lectures by Freud and discovered Nietzsche. Upon return to New York City, worked as midwife and nurse among poor immigrant women on New York City's Lower East Side. 1897: First cross-country lecture tour. **September 6, 1901:** Anarchist Leon Czolgosz shot President William McKinley in Buffalo, New York. Jailed in Chicago for two weeks before being released for lack of evidence linking her with assassination. 1906: Began to publish monthly anarchist magazine, *Mother Earth*, which was eventually suppressed by U.S. government in 1917. In May, toured United States with Berkman, who had been released from prison. 1908: Met Ben Reitman, who became manager, co-worker, and great love of her life. 1915: Joined Margaret Sanger in deliberately disobeying laws prohibiting dissemination of birth control information. Jailed for two weeks in 1916. 1916: One of earliest defenders of Tom Mooney and other labor leaders accused of Preparedness Day bombing in San Francisco. 1917: Arrested with Berkman for opposing draft and thereby violating Selective

Service Act. They had organized No-Conscription League during World War I to aid draft resisters. **1919:** During Red Scare, deported on December 21st along with Berkman and 247 others. Returned to Russia, staying two years; disillusioned, left to travel and speak in Europe and Canada. **1920:** Arrived in Russia in January, but along with Berkman soon became disillusioned with increasing centralization, bureaucratization and militarization of revolution. **1923:** Permitted to make her home in England; married James Colton for convenience of British citizenship. Her work, *My Disillusionment in Russia*, was published. **1924:** Published *My Further Disillusionment in Russia*. **1931:** While residing in England, Canada and in the south of France, wrote autobiography *Living My Life*. **1934:** Tour through Germany convinced her of threat of fascism. Lectures on topic gained her 90 day visit to United States, where she made political speeches. **1936:** Devoted herself to Loyalist cause of Spanish Civil War and traveled to Canada to raise money. **1940:** After death at 70 in Toronto on May 14, 1940, authorities allowed her body to be brought back to Illinois to be buried near her Haymarket idols. There is a monument to four labor leaders who were hanged as result of Haymarket riot of 1886; many socialists, labor activists and civil rights leaders have chosen to be buried near it in Dissenters Row, some in unmarked graves, others with monuments.

Background Information

Parents: Taube (Bienowitz / Bienowitch) and Abraham Goldman. **Siblings:** Four or five (Known names: half-sisters Helena Zodokoff and Lena). **Children:** None. **Influences:** Alexander Berkman, Johann Most, Ben Reitman. **Ethnicity:** Lithuanian/Jewish. **Also known as:** None known. **Historical sites, landmarks, etc.:** Gravesite, Forest Home Cemetery (then called Waldheim), Dissenters Row, 863 S. Desplaines Avenue, Forest Park, Illinois. Goldman's monument bears bas-relief of her face by Jo Davison, dates of her birth and death and quotation: "Liberty will not descend to a people, a people must raise themselves to liberty."

BIBLIOGRAPHICAL INFORMATION

Biographical Sketches About Emma Goldman

Bullough, Vern L., Olga Maranjian Church, and Alice P. Stein, eds. *American Nursing: A Biographical Dictionary*. New York: Garland, 1988.

Harris, Frank. *Contemporary Portraits*. Fourth Series. New York: Brentano's, 1923.
James, Edward T., ed. *Notable American Women 1607–1950: A Biographical Dictionary*. Cambridge, MA: Belknap Press of Harvard University Press, 1971.
Schuyler, Robert Livingston, ed. *Dictionary of American Biography*. Supplement 2. New York: Charles Scribner's Sons, 1958.
Stein, Gordon, ed. *Encyclopedia of Unbelief*. Buffalo, NY: Prometheus, 1985.
Whitman, Alden R., ed. *American Reformers: An H. W. Wilson Biographical Dictionary*. New York: H. W. Wilson, 1985.
Zophy, Angela Howard, ed. *Handbook of American Women's History*. New York: Garland, 1990.

Books by Emma Goldman

Anarchism and Other Essays. New York: Mother Earth Publishing Association, 1910. Reprint. Port Washington, NY: Kennikat, 1969.
Anarchism: What It Really Stands For. New York: Mother Earth Publishing Association, 1911.
The Crushing of the Russian Revolution. London: Freedom, 1922.
Emma Goldman Papers: A Microfilm Edition. Edited by Candace Falk, Ronald J. Zboray, and Daniel Cornford. Alexandria, VA: Chadwyck-Healey, 1990.
Emma Goldman Papers: Sample Reel List and Indices for the International Institute of Social History. Edited by Candace Falk. [Amsterdam]: International Institute of Social History, [1989?].
A Fragment of the Prison Experiences of Emma Goldman and Alexander Berkman in the State Prison at Jefferson City, Mo., and the U.S. Penitentiary at Atlanta, Ga., February, 1918–October, 1919. New York: S. Comyn, 1919?
Glimpses of Emma Goldman. Edited by Lydia Gans. Pasadena, CA: Tabula Rasa, 1979.
Leon Malmed ... Emma Goldman ... Papers, 1899–1940, 1956. Guide to the Microfilm, prepared by Bert Hartry. Cambridge, MA: Schlesinger Library, 1983.
Living My Life. New York: A. A. Knopf, 1931. Reprint. London: Pluto, 1987.
Love Among the Free. Buffalo, NY: Friends of Malatesta, 1970.
Marriage and Love. New York: Mother Earth Publishing Association, 1911. Reprint. New York: Mother Earth Publishing Association, 1916.
My Disillusionment in Russia. Garden City, NY: Doubleday, Page, & Company, 1923. Reprint. London: Pluto, 1989.
My Further Disillusionment in Russia. Garden City, NY: Doubleday, 1924.
Patriotism: A Menace to Liberty. New York: Mother Earth Publishing Association, 1908?
Philosophy of Atheism and the Failure of Christianity: Two Lectures. New York: Mother Earth Publishing Association, 1916.
The Place of the Individual in Society. Chicago: Sponsored by the Free Society Forum, 1940.
Preparedness, the Road to Universal Slaughter. New York: Mother Earth Publishing Association, 1915.

Psychology of Political Violence. New York: Mother Earth Publishing Association, 1911. Reprint. New York: Gordon, 1974.

Rebel. Mt. View, CA: I. W. W., n.d.

Red Emma Speaks: An Emma Goldman Reader. Compiled and edited by Alix Kates Shulman. New York: Schocken Books, 1983.

Red Emma Speaks: Selected Writings and Speeches. Compiled and edited by Alix Kates Shulman. New York: Random House, 1972.

The Social Significance of the Modern Drama. Boston: R. G. Badger, 1914. Reprint. New York: Applause Theatre Book Publishers, 1987.

The Suppression of Free Speech in New York and in New Jersey. East Orange, NJ: East Orange Record, 1909?

Syndicalism: The Modern Menace to Capitalism. New York: Mother Earth Publishing Association, 1913.

The Traffic in Women and Other Essays on Feminism. With a Biography by Alix Kates Shulman. New York: Times Change Press, 1970.

The Tragedy of Woman's Emancipation. New York: Mother Earth Publishing Association. [1910?]. Reprint. [s.l.: s.n., 197?].

Trotsky Protests Too Much. Glasgow: Anarchist Communist Federation, [1939?].

The Truth About the Bolsheviki. New York: Mother Earth Publishing Association, 1918.

Vision on Fire: Emma Goldman on the Spanish Revolution. Edited with introductions by David Porter. New Paltz, NY: Commonground, 1983.

Voltairine de Cleyre. Berkeley Heights, NJ: Published privately by the Oriole Press, 1932.

What I Believe. New York: Mother Earth Publishing Association, 1908.

White Slave Traffic. New York: Mother Earth Publishing Association, 1909.

A Woman Without a Country. Sanday, Scotland: Cienfuegos, 1979.

Goldman, Emma, and Alexander Berkman. *Deportation, Its Meaning and Menace: Last Message to the People of America.* New York: M. E. Fitzgerald, 1919.

_____, and _____. *Nowhere at Home: Letters from Exile of Emma Goldman and Alexander Berkman.* Edited by Richard Drinnon and Anna Maria Drinnon. New York: Schocken Books, 1975.

Books About Emma Goldman

Calvert, Bruce. *Emma Goldman and the Police.* Griffith, IN: Open Road, [194?].

Doctorow, E. L. *Ragtime.* New York: Random House, 1975. Reprint. New York: Vintage International, 1991. (Fictional treatment.)

Drinnon, Richard. *Rebel in Paradise: A Biography of Emma Goldman.* Chicago: University of Chicago Press, 1961. Reprint. Chicago: University of Chicago Press, 1982.

Emma Goldman: A Life of Anarchy. [Toronto]: Canadian Broadcasting, 1983.

Emma Goldman Will Speak in San Francisco for One Week at the Victory Theater. [San Francisco: Social Science League, 1909.]

Falk, Candace. *Love, Anarchy, and Emma Goldman.* New York: Holt, Rinehart, and Winston, 1984. Reprint. New Brunswick, NJ: Rutgers University Press, 1990.

Frazer, Winifred L. *E. G. and E. G. O.: Emma Goldman and the Iceman Cometh.* Gainesville: University Presses of Florida, 1974.

Ganguli, Birendranath N. *Emma Goldman: Portrait of a Rebel Woman.* New Delhi: Allied, 1979.

Goldman, Emma, Defendant. *Anarchism on Trial: Speeches of Alexander Berkman and Emma Goldman Before the United States District Court in the City of New York, July, 1917.* New York: Mother Earth Publishing Association, 1917.

Goldman, Emma, Plaintiff-in-error. *Supreme Court of the United States, October Term, 1917, No. 702.* New York: H. Weinberger, 1918.

Ishill, Joseph. *Emma Goldman, A Challenging Rebel.* Berkeley Heights, NJ: Oriole, 1957.

Lord, Ann. *Emma Goldman's 1934 Lecture Tour in the United States.* N.P.; 1934.

Madison, Charles Allan. *Emma Goldman: A Biographical Sketch.* New York: Libertarian Book Club, 1960.

Mannin, Ethel Edith. *Red Rose: A Novel Based on the Life of Emma Goldman ('Red Emma').* London: Jarrolds, 1941. (Fictional treatment.)

Shulman, Alix Kates. *To the Barricades: The Anarchist Life of Emma Goldman.* New York: Crowell, 1971.

Solomon, Martha. *Emma Goldman.* Boston: Twayne, 1987.

United States. Dept. of Justice. *Investigation Activities of the Department of Justice.* Washington, D. C.: GPO, 1919.

Waldstreicher, David. *Emma Goldman.* New York: Chelsea House, 1990.

Weinberger, Harry. *Emma Goldman: Speech Delivered at Her Funeral, Chicago, May 17th, 1940.* Berkeley Heights, NJ: Published privately by the Oriole Press, 1940.

Wexler, Alice. *Emma Goldman: An Intimate Life.* New York: Pantheon, 1984.

————. *Emma Goldman in America.* Boston: Beacon Press, 1984.

————. *Emma Goldman in Exile: From the Russian Revolution to the Spanish Civil War.* Boston: Beacon Press, 1989.

Shorter Works by Emma Goldman

"Assassination of McKinley." *American Mercury* 24 (September 1931): 53–67.

"Emma Goldman on Palestine and Socialist Politics." *Genesis Two* 19 (Summer 1988): 16.

"Johann Most." *American Mercury* 8 (June 1926): 158–66.

"Leon Trotsky Protests Too Much." *Vanguard* 4 (July 1938): 5–8.

Malpede, Karen, ed. *Women in Theatre: Compassion & Hope.* New York: Drama Book Publishers, 1983.

"Marriage and Love." In *Women's Liberation in the Twentieth Century,* edited by Mary C. Lynn. New York: Wiley, 1975.

Mazow, Julia Wolf, ed. and comp. *The Woman Who Lost Her Names: Selected Writings of American Jewish Women.* San Francisco: Harper & Row, 1980.

"Red Emma Speaks." *Madness Network* 2 (February 1975): 19.
"There Is No Communism in Russia." *American Mercury* 34 (April 1935): 393–401.
"Tragedy of Emancipation." *Takeover* 4 (March 21, 1974): 9.
"Tragedy of the Political Exiles." *Nation* 139 (October 10, 1934): 401–02.
"Voyage of the Buford." *American Mercury* 23 (July 1931): 276–86.
"Was My Life Worth Living?" *Harper's Magazine* 170 (December 1934): 52–58.

Shorter Works About Emma Goldman

Acott, T. "How Stupid Got His Voice." *Industrial Worker* 77 (January 15, 1980): 5.
Baritz, Loren, ed. *The American Left: Radical Political Thought in the Twentieth Century*. New York: Basic Books, 1971.
Barko, N. "The Emma Goldman You'll Never See in the Movies." *Ms.* 10 (March 1982): 27–31.
Benton, Sarah. "The Passion and the Life." *New Statesman* 115 (May 13, 1988): 28–29.
Berkman, Alexander. *Prison Memoirs of an Anarchist*. New York: Mother Earth Publishing Association, 1912. Reprint. New York: Schocken Books, 1970.
"Berkman and Goldman." *Outlook* 123 (December 24, 1919): 529–30.
Berneri/Ravachol. "Goldman Papers Seized." *Fifth Estate* 20 (Summer 1986): 18.
Borden, L. "Women and Anarchy." *Heresies* 1 (May 1977): 71.
Bromlez, M. "Freedoms Bible." *Peacemaker* 24 (October 9, 1971): 6.
Brooks, Van Wyck. *The Confident Years: 1885–1915*. New York: Dutton, 1955.
Bruns, Roger A. *The Damndest Radical: The Life and World of Ben Reitman, Chicago's Celebrated Social Reformer, Hobo King, and Whorehouse Physician*. Urbana: University of Illinois, 1987.
Cassidy, Keith. "The American Left and the Problem of Leadership, 1900–1920." *South Atlantic Quarterly* 82 (1983): 386–97.
Cobbs, L. "Kollontai/Goldman/Women and Labor." *Longest Revolution* 1 (June 1977): 12.
Cook, Blanche Wiesen. "Female Support Networks and Political Activism: Lillian Wald, Crystal Eastman, Emma Goldman." In *A Heritage of Her Own: Toward a New Social History of American Women*, edited by Nancy F. Cott and Elizabeth H. Pleck. New York: Simon & Schuster, 1979.
————. "Female Support Networks and Political Activism: Lillian Wald, Crystal Eastman, Emma Goldman." In *Women's America: Refocusing the Past*, edited by Linda Kerber and Jane DeHart-Matthews. New York: Oxford University Press, 1987.
————. *Women and Support Networks*. Brooklyn, NY: Out and Out Books, 1979.
Danab, M. "Labor Liberation and Minnie Liberti." *Majority Report* 4 (March 8, 1975): 11.
Dell, Floyd. *Women as World Builders: Studies in Modern Feminism*. Chicago: Forbes, 1913.

Deutelbaum, Wendy. "Epistolary Politics: The Correspondence of Emma Gold-man and Alexander Berkman." *Prose Studies* [Great Britain] 9 (1986): 30–46.

Devon, A. "Visioning the Future—An Editorial." *Kick It Over* no. 17 (Winter 1986): 3.

Duggleby, J. "IEDS/Ten Days Shook World/Living Life." *Our Generation* (Fall 1982): 60.

"Emma Goldman." *Nation* 138 (March 21, 1934): 320.

"Emma Goldman." *Ramparts* 10 (February 1972): 10 + .

"Emma Goldman." *Rising Up Angry* 2 (January 1, 1971): 12.

"Emma Goldman: A Misfit in Russia." *Literary Digest* 70 (September 10, 1921): 49.

"Emma Goldman and Hearst." *Nation* 140 (May 8, 1935): 541.

"Emma Goldman: Elderly Red Here to Pay Us 90-day Visit." *Newsweek* 3 (January 20, 1934): 20.

"Emma Goldman Names Her Magazine." *Open Road* no. 1 (Summer 1976): 2.

"Emma Goldman's Blue Days in Red Russia." *Literary Digest* 79 (December 15, 1923): 34–36.

"Emma Goldman's Faith." *Current Literature* 50 (February 1911): 176–78.

Falk, Candace. "Amorous Anarchists." *Mother Jones* 9 (August/September 1984): 14 + .

Forster, Margaret. *Significant Sisters: The Grassroots of Active Feminism, 1839–1939.* New York: Knopf, 1985.

Fravis, B. "The Battle of Red Emma." *Worker's Power* no. 15 (July 25, 1977): 11.

Giffin, Frederick C. "The Radical Vision of Helen Keller." *International Social Science Review* 59 (1984): 27–32.

————. *Woman as Revolutionary.* New York: New American Library, 1973.

Glasgow, C. "Emma Goldman in London." *Contemporary Review* 126 (December 1924): 782–83.

Goldsmith, Margaret. *Seven Women Against the World.* London: Methuen, 1935.

Hapgood, H. "Emma Goldman's Anarchism." *Bookman* 32 (February 1911): 639–40.

Hayley, R. "A Herstory of Anarcha-Feminism." *Kick It Over* no. 18 (Spring 1987): 12.

Heiple, P. "Emma Goldman." *Insurgent Sociologist* 3 (Spring 1973): 74.

Hewitt, M. "Emma Goldman: Case for Anarcho-Feminism." *Our Generation* 17 (Fall 1985): 167.

Jacobs, William Jay. *Great Lives: Human Rights.* New York: Scribner, 1990.

Jensen, Oliver Ormerod. *The Revolt of American Women: A Pictoral History of the Century of Change from Bloomers to Bikinis, from Feminism to Freud.* New York: Harcourt, Brace, 1952. Reprint. New York: Harcourt Brace Jovanovich, 1971.

Jones, L."Vision on Fire." *Strike* (June 1984): 12.

Leeder, E. "Let Our Mothers Show the Way." *Social Anarchism* 6 (1986): 13.

Lester, D. "Education Memo." *FPS: Magazine of Youth Liberation* no. 44 (May 1975): 1.

Lynn, K. S. "Living My Life." *New Republic* 165 (November 27, 1971): 26–28.

McKinley, Blaine. "The Quagmires of Necessity: American Anarchists and Dilemmas of Vocation." *American Quarterly* 34 (1982): 503–23.

Madison, Charles Allan. *Critics & Crusaders: A Century of American Protest.* New York: H. Holt, 1947.

————. *Leaders and Liberals in 20th Century America.* New York: F. Ungar, 1961.

Mannin, Ethel Edith. *Women and the Revolution.* New York: E. P. Dutton, 1939.

Marriner, Gerald L. "Feminist Revolt: The Emergence of the New Woman in the Early 20th Century." *Humboldt Journal of Social Relations* 1 (Spring–Summer 1974): 127–34.

Marsh, Margaret S. *Anarchist Women: 1870–1920.* Philadelphia: Temple University Press, 1981.

Massa, Ann. "Chicago's Martyrs: A Parable for the People." *Chicago History* 15 (1986): 54–63.

Meschan, et al. "Women in History." *Portland Scribe* 4 (July 5, 1975): 8.

"Notes from the Capital: Emma Goldman." *Nation* 104 (June 28, 1917): 766–77.

"Obituary." *Current Biography.* New York: H. W. Wilson, 1940.

"Obituary." *New Republic* 102 (June 3, 1940): 747.

"Obituary." *Newsweek* 15 (May 20, 1940): 8.

Pachter, H. M. "Private Lives of Rebels." *Harper's Magazine* 251 (August 1975): 83 +.

Perlin, Terry M. "Anarchism and Idealism: Voltairine De Cleyre (1866–1912)." *Labor History* 14 (1973): 506–20.

Poirier, Suzanne. "Emma Goldman, Ben Reitman, and Reitman's Wives: A Study in Relationships." *Women's Studies* 14 (1988): 277–97.

"Portrait." *American Magazine* 69 (March 1910): 608.

"Portrait." *Independent* 116 (March 13, 1926): 291.

"Portrait." *Literary Digest* 84 (January 31, 1925): 36.

Postal, Bernard, and Lionel Koppman. *Guess Who's Jewish in American History.* New York: Shapolsky, 1989.

Rich, Andrea L. *Rhetoric of Revolution: Samuel Adams, Emma Goldman, Malcolm X.* Durham, NC: Moore, 1970?

Rocker, Rudolf. *Pioneers of American Freedom: Origin of Liberal and Radical Thought in America.* Los Angeles: Rocker Publications Committee, 1949.

Rosenberg, Karen. "An Autumnal Love of Emma Goldman." *Dissent* 30 (Summer 1983): 380–83.

————. "Red Emma." *In These Times* 7 (May 4, 1983): 24.

Sacks, K. "Class Roots of Feminism." *Monthly Review* 27 (February 1976): 28.

Salerno, S. "Candace Falk on Emma Goldman." *Black Rose* no. 11 (Winter 1985): 40.

Salleh, A. "Emma Goldman." *Social Alternatives* 7 (September 1988): 72.

Schuster, Eunice M. *Native American Anarchism: A Study of Left-Wing American Individualism.* Northampton, MA: Department of History, Smith College, 1932.

Shulman, A. "Emma Goldman Feminism." *Socialist Review* no. 62 (March 1982): 31.

Shulman, Alix Kates. "Emma Goldman: Anarchist Queen." In *Feminist Theorists: Three Centuries of Key Women Thinkers,* edited by Dale Spender. New York: Pantheon, 1983.

Simonhoff, Harry. *Saga of American Jewry, 1865–1914: Links of an Endless Chain.* New York: Arco, 1959.

"Sketch." *American Magazine* 69 (March 1910): 605.
Sochen, June. "Feminism First in the Village." *In These Times* 6 (February 10, 1982): 19.
————. *Movers and Shakers: American Women Thinkers and Activists, 1900–1970.* New York: Quadrangle, 1973.
Solomon, Martha. "Ideology as Rhetorical Constraint: The Anarchist Agitation of 'Red Emma' Goldman." *Quarterly Journal of Speech* 74 (May 1988): 184– 200.
Stansell, C. "Nowhere at Home." *Liberation* 20 (January 1977): 29.
"They Stand Out From the Crowd." *Literary Digest* 117 (January 27, 1934): 13.
"Two Women Who Wouldn't: Emma Goldman and Rose Pastor Stokes." In *America's Immigrant Women,* by Cecyle S. Neidle. Boston: Twayne, 1975.
"Uncle Sam's Obstreperous Niece." *Literary Digest* 55 (August 18, 1917): 54 +.
Wexler, Alice R. "The Early Life of Emma Goldman." *Psychohistory Review* 8 (1980): 7–21.
————. "Emma Goldman and Women." *Our Generation* 17 (Fall 1985): 167.
————. "Emma Goldman on Mary Wollstonecraft." *Feminist Studies* 7 (Spring 1981): 113–33.

Other Works by Emma Goldman

The Blast. Volume 1, no. 1 (January 15, 1916); ceased with Volume 2, no. 5 (June 1, 1917). San Francisco: [Alexander Berkman]. (Goldman was co-editor.)
Mother Earth, A Montly Magazine Devoted to the Social Science and Literature. Volume 1, no. 1 (March 1906)—Volume 12, no. 6 (August 1917). New York: Emma Goldman, publisher, 1906–1917. (Goldman was editor from April 1915 to August 1917.)
Mother Earth Bulletin. Volume 1, no. 1 (October 1917)—Volume 1, no. 7 (April 1918). New York: Emma Goldman, publisher and editor, 1917–1918. (Final issue carries letter by Goldman from prison.)

Other Works About Emma Goldman

Plays

Bolt, Carol. *Buffalo Jump; Gabe; Red Emma.* Toronto: Playwrights Co-op, 1976.
————. *Red Emma, Queen of the Anarchists.* Toronto: Playwrights Co-op, 1973.
Litwak, Jessica. "Emma Goldman: Love, Anarchy and Other Affairs." In *Women Heroes: Six Short Plays from the Women's Project,* edited by Julia Miles. New York: Applause Theatre Book Publishers, 1987.
Zinn, Howard. "Emma." In *Playbook,* by Maxine Klein, Lydia Sargent, and Howard Zinn. Boston: South End, 1986.

Song

Hirschhorn, Linda. "Dance a Revolution (for Emma Goldman)." In *Here's to the Women: 100 Songs For and About American Women,* by Hilda E. Wenner and Elizabeth Freilicher. Syracuse, NY: Syracuse University Press, 1987.

Theses

Berry, Elizabeth Wehde. "Rhetoric for the Cause: The Analysis and Criticism of the Persuasive Discourse of Emma Goldman, Anarchist Agitator, 1906–1919." Ph.D. diss., University of California, Los Angeles, 1969.

Burch, Connie Beth Saulmon. "Women's Voices, Women's Visions: Contemporary American-Jewish Women Writers." Ph.D. diss., Purdue University, 1987.

Drimmer, Melvin. "Nietzsche in American Thought, 1895–1925." Ph.D. diss., University of Rochester, 1965.

Drinnon, Richard. "Emma Goldman: A Study in American Radicalism." Ph.D. diss., University of Minnesota, 1957.

Leeder, Elaine J. "The Gentle Warrior: Rose Pesotta, Anarchist and Labor Organizer." Ph.D. diss., Cornell University, 1985.

Levine, Ira Alan. "Theatre in Revolt: Left-Wing Dramatic Theory in the United States (1911–1939)." Ph.D. diss., University of Toronto, 1980.

Luter, Gary Sheldon. "Sexual Reform on the American Stage in the Progressive Era, 1900–1915." Ph.D. diss., University of Florida, 1981.

Morton, Keith William. "Community as Metaphor: Anarchy and Structure in American Culture, 1830–1920." Ph.D. diss., University of Minnesota, 1986.

Nowlin, William Gerard, Jr. "The Political Thought of Alexander Berkman." Ph.D. diss., Tufts University, 1980.

Reisman, Gail Landau. "Life Themes in the Lives of Two Exceptional Women as Revealed in Their Personal Documents." Ph.D. diss., University of Toronto, 1984.

Sargent, Patricia McGinnis. "A Spokesman for the Disillusioned: Emma Goldman as a Threat to the American Way of Life." Master's thesis, University of Minnesota, 1969.

Stevenson, Billie Jeanne H. "The Ideology of American Anarchism, 1880–1910." Ph.D. diss., University of Iowa, 1972.

Weiner, Jill R. "Agitation for the Ideal: The Feminist Rhetoric of Emma Goldman, 1906–1911." Master's thesis, State University of New York at Buffalo, 1976.

Wesely, Rebecca Jeanne. "The Triumph of the System: Alexander Berkman, Anarchism, and America." Ph.D. diss., Saint Louis University, 1981.

Media Materials About Emma Goldman

Computer Game

Martian Dreams. Austin, TX: Origin Systems, 1991. Three computer disks; sound; color; 5 ¼ in. plus two guides, two booklets and one map.

Films

Emma Goldman. Toronto: Avco Embassy Pictures, 1975. One reel; 25 min.; sound; color; 16mm.

Sound Recordings

Emma Goldman. Deland, FL: Everett/Edwards, Inc., n.d. Cassette; 30 min.; 1 ⅞ ips; mono.

Emma Goldman, 1869-1940. BC 2149. Los Angeles: Pacifica Tape Library, [197-?]. Cassette; 57 min.; 2.5 × 4 in.

Out of the Kitchen and Into the Sweat Shop — The Story of Working Women in America. Los Angeles: Pacifica Tape Library, n.d. Cassette; 62 min.; 1 ⅞ ips; mono.

Socio-Political Literature. Washington, D. C.: National Public Radio, 1981. Cassette; 1 ⅞ ips; mono.

Primary Source Materials Relating to Emma Goldman

Emma Goldman. Papers. 1906-1940. Extent of collection: 2 boxes. Finding aids: Not listed. Location: New York Public Library, Manuscripts and Archives, Fifth Avenue and 42nd Street, New York, New York 10018. Scope of collection: Correspondence, address books, and other papers relate to anarchism, labor, war, and militarism, conditions in Germany and Russia after World War I, Spanish Civil War and other topics. Microfilm available.

Emma Goldman. Papers. 1907-1939. Extent of collection: 4 boxes. Finding aids: Inventory. Location: Boston University, Mugar Memorial Library, Special Collections, Boston, Massachusetts 02215. Scope of collection: Correspondence of Goldman with Berkman, Reitman and Sperry.

Emma Goldman. Papers. 1909-1939. Extent of collection: 28 items. Finding aids: Card catalog. Location: Northwestern University, Special Collections, 633 Clark Street, Evanston, Illinois 60208. Scope of collection: Includes letters to James B. Pond, manager of Goldman's 1934 speaking tour of United States.

Emma Goldman. Papers. 1909-1940. Extent of collection: 104 items. Finding aids: Not listed. Location: Labadie Collection, University of Michigan, Ann Arbor, Michigan 48109. Scope of collection: Correspondence, circular letters, particularly concerning *Mother Earth* and Mother Earth Publishing Association. Also papers relating to lecture tours, activities in support of anarchists and revolutionaries, particularly in Russia, England, and Spain, her response to reviews of *Living My Life*, last illness and death of Berkman, etc.

Emma Goldman. Papers. 1911-1940. Extent of collection: 1 box. Finding aids: Published guide. Location: Smith College, Sophia Smith Collection, Northampton, Massachusetts 01063. Scope of collection: Correspondence, biographical material, reprints of articles on anarchism, prison experiences, her philosophy of atheism, white slave traffic and deportation.

Emma Goldman. Papers. 1924-1940. Extent of collection: 2.5 lin. ft. Finding aids: Unpublished guide available in library. Location: New York University, Tamiment Institute Library, 70 Washington Square South, New York, New York 10012. Scope of collection: Includes 1934 tour of United States, Jeanette Levey's unpublished manuscript "Emma Goldman Speaks," correspondence, addresses, etc.

Emma Goldman. Papers of Leon Malmed and Emma Goldman. 1899-1982 (inclusive), 1899–1940 (bulk). Extent of collection: 2.5 lin. ft. Finding aids: Un-published finding aid. Location: Schlesinger Library, Radcliffe College, Cambridge, Massachusetts 02138. Scope of collection: Almost entirely cor-respondence, with over 450 letters, postcards and telegrams from Goldman to Malmed, 1900–1939.

(THE ABOVE ENTRY WAS CONTRIBUTED BY RENEE D. CHAPMAN)

27. *Fannie Lou Townsend Hamer*
(1917–1977)
Advocate for African American rights

BIOGRAPHICAL INFORMATION

Chronological Biography

Born October 6, 1917, in Ruleville, Mississippi, to Lou Ella and Jim Townsend, youngest of 20 children. Parents were sharecroppers on Mont-gomery County plantation.

1919: Family moved to Sunflower County, Mississippi. 1923: At age of six, began picking cotton. 1923–1929: Attended classes for only four months each year because children were needed to work in fields. 1941: Married Perry (Pap) Hamer and went to work on neighboring plantation as sharecropper and timekeeper. 1962: After hearing James Forman of Stu-dent Non-Violent Coordinating Committee (SNCC) speak at rally in Rule-ville, decided to exercise her right to vote. August 31, 1962: Along with 17 others, attempted unsuccessfully to vote in Ruleville, county seat. She was jailed, beaten and her family was evicted from farm where she had worked for 18 years and where Pap had worked for 30 years. 1962: Hamers moved to Ruleville and Fannie Lou began working full-time with SNCC voter regis-tration drive. 1962–1964: Constantly harassed and threatened for her work in helping blacks register to vote. In addition, husband was repeatedly dis-charged from jobs as result of her activism. June 9, 1963: Badly beaten, almost losing sight in left eye and suffering permanent kidney damage after registration activities near Winowa, Mississippi. 1963: Joined James Mere-dith in his march on University of Mississippi. 1964: Helped organize Mis-sissippi Freedom Summer, massive voter registration drive spearheaded by SNCC. Taught course at training school in Oxford, Ohio, for college student volunteers who wished to go to Mississippi to help blacks register to vote. Hamer and group of co-workers founded Mississippi Freedom Democratic Party (MFDP) to challenge right of regular Democratic party delegates to be seated at presidential nominating convention. She electrified convention and national television audience with story of her beatings after attempting to register to vote. **1965:** Joined in Selma march with Dr. Martin Luther King, Jr. **1968:** The MFDP joined with integrationist and white liberal groups to form faction called Loyal Democrats which successfully challenged regular Mississippi Democrats for recognition at party's National Convention. One of 22 blacks seated as delegates in Chicago. **1969:** Received honorary degree from Morehead College in Atlanta along with Dr. Martin Luther King, Sr., and Vice President Hubert Humphrey. **1969–1970:** Formed Freedom Farm Cooperative, agricultural venture based on acquisition of 51 acres of Mississippi Delta land, with intention of creating individual homesteads for its members and garment factory to provide jobs for local blacks. **1970:** Received Doctor of Humane Letters from Columbia College. **1971:** Helped found and was elected to Central Committee of National Women's Political Caucus. **March 14, 1977:** Died of cancer at age of 59.

Background Information

Parents: Lou Ella and Jim Townsend. **Siblings:** 19 (No known names). **Children:** Two (Jean and Virgie Ree, both adopted. Jean died of cerebral hemorrhage in 1967.) **Influences:** Perry (Pap) Hamer. **Ethnicity:** African American. **Also known as:** None known. **Historical sites, landmarks, etc.:** None known.

BIBLIOGRAPHICAL INFORMATION

Biographical Sketches About Fannie Lou Townsend Hamer

D'Emilio, John. *Civil Rights Struggle: Leaders in Profile.* New York: Facts on File, 1979.

Fax, Elton. *Contemporary Black Leaders.* New York: Dodd, 1970.

Lichtenstein, Nelson, ed. *Political Profiles: The Johnson Years.* New York: Facts on File, 1976.

Saunder, Charles, ed. *Ebony Success Library.* Chicago: Johnson Publishing, 1973.

Smith, Jessie Carney, ed. *Notable Black American Women.* Detroit: Gale Research, 1992.

Uglow, Jennifer, comp. and ed. *International Dictionary of Women's Biography.* New York: Continuum, 1982.

Whitman, Alden, ed. *American Reformers: An H. W. Wilson Biographical Dictionary.* New York: H. W. Wilson, 1985.

Books About Fannie Lou Townsend Hamer

Hagen, Susan Deaton. *Fannie Lou Hamer and SNCC's Mississippi Campaign for Civil Rights, 1962–1964.* Ottawa: National Library of Canada, 1990.

Jordan, June. *Fannie Lou Hamer*. New York: Crowell, 1972.

Kling, Susan. *Fannie Lou Hamer: A Biography*. Chicago: Women for Racial and Economic Equality, 1979.

Rubel, David. *Fannie Lou Hamer: From Sharecropping to Politics*. Englewood Cliffs, NJ: Silver Burdett, 1990. (Introduction written by Andrew Young.)

Shorter Works by Fannie Lou Townsend Hamer

Sugarman, Tracy. *Stranger at the Gates: A Summer in Mississippi*. New York: Hill and Wang, 1967. (Forward written by Fannie Lou Hamer.)

Shorter Works About Fannie Lou Townsend Hamer

Brisbane, Robert. *Black Activism: Racial Revolution in the United States, 1954–1970*. Valley Forge, PA: Judsen Press, 1974.

Burke, Joan Martin. *Civil Rights*. New York: Bowker, 1974.

DeMuth, John. "Tired of Being Sick and Tired." *Nation* 198 (June 1, 1964): 548–51.

Diamonstein, Barbara. *Open Secrets*. New York: Viking, 1972.

Egerton, John. *A Mind to Stay Here: Profiles from the South*. New York: Macmillan, 1970.

Forman, James. *The Making of Black Revolutionaries*. Washington, D. C.: Openhand Publishers, 1985.

Garland, P. "Builders of a New South." *Ebony* 21 (August 1966): 27–30.

Gozemba, Patricia A., and Marilyn L. Humphries. "Women in the Anti–Ku Klux Klan Movement, 1865–1984." *Women's Studies International Forum* 12 (1989): 35–40.

Grant, Jacquelyn. "Civil Rights Women: A Source for Doing Womanist Theology." In *Women in the Civil Rights Movement: Trailblazers and Torchbearers, 1941–1965*, edited by Vicki L. Crawford, Jacqueline Anne Rouse, and Barbara Woods. Brooklyn: Carlson, 1990.

Ladner, Joyce. "Fannie Lou Hamer: In Memoriam." *Black Enterprise* 7 (May 1977): 56.

Lerner, Gerda. *Black Women in White America: A Documentary History*. New York: Pantheon, 1972.

————. *Majority Finds Its Past: Placing Women in History*. New York: Oxford University Press, 1979. Reprint. Oxford: Oxford University Press, 1981.

Locke, Mamie E. "Is This America? Fannie Lou Hamer and the Mississippi Freedom Democratic Party." In *Women in the Civil Rights Movement: Trailblazers and Torchbearers, 1941–1965*, edited by Vicki L. Crawford, Jacqueline Anne Rouse, and Barbara Woods. Brooklyn: Carlson, 1990.

McCord, William. *Mississippi: The Long Hot Summer*. New York: W. W. Norton, 1965.

Norton, E. H. "Woman Who Changed the South." *Ms.* 6 (July 1977): 51 + .

O'Dell, J. H. "Life in Mississippi: An Interview with Fannie Lou Hamer." *Freedomways* (Spring 1965): 231–42.

Peterson, Franklynn. "Fannie Lou Hamer: Mother of Black Women's Lib." *Sepia* 21 (December 1972): 16–24.

—————. "Sunflowers Don't Grow in Sunflower County." *Sepia* 19 (February 1970): 8–18.

Reagon, Bernice Johnson. "Women as Culture Carriers in the Civil Rights Movement: Fannie Lou Hamer." In *Women in the Civil Rights Movement: Trailblazers and Torchbearers, 1941–1965*, edited by Vicki L. Crawford, Jacqueline Anne Rouse, and Barbara Woods. Brooklyn: Carlson, 1990.

Selby, Earl. *Odyssey: Journey Through Black America.* New York: Putnam, 1971.

Sewell, George. "Fannie Lou Hamer." *Black Collegian* 8 (May / June 1978): 18–20.

Silver, James. *Mississippi: The Closed Society.* New York: Harcourt, Brace and World, 1966.

Wiley, Jean. "On the Front Lines." *Essence* 20 (February 1990): 45 + .

X, Malcom. "With Mrs. Fannie Lou Hamer." In *Malcolm X Speaks: Selected Speeches and Statements*, edited with prefatory notes by George Breitman. New York: Pathfinder, 1989.

Media Materials About Fannie Lou Townsend Hamer

Films

Fannie Lou Hamer. Produced by Rediscovery Productions and distributed by Sterling Educational Films. 16mm.; 10 min.; color.

Never Turn Back: The Life of Fannie Lou Hamer. Westport, CT: Rediscovery Productions, 1983. 16mm.; 60 min.; sound; color.

Sound Recordings

B'lieve I'll Run On . . . See What the End's Gonna Be. Written by Bernice Johnson Reagon in 1978. Album released by Redwood Records. LP.

Video Recordings

Eyes on the Prize: America's Civil Rights Years. Mississippi, Is This America? Alexandria, VA: PBS Video, 1986. ½ in. video, 1 videocassette of 6 (VHS); 60 min.; sound; color with black and white segments.

Fannie Lou Hamer. Produced by Rediscovery Productions and distributed by Sterling Educational Films. ¾ in. or ½ in. video; 10 min.; color.

Missing Pages, a Moment in Black History. Women in the Movement. ¾ in. videocassette; 60 sec.; sound; color with black and white sequences.

Never Turn Back: The Life of Fannie Lou Hamer. Westport, CT: Rediscovery Productions, 1983. 1 videocassette; 60 min.; sound; color.

Primary Source Materials Relating to
Fannie Lou Townsend Hamer

Fannie Lou Hamer. 1964-1977. Extent of collection: 8 items. Finding aids: Published and unpublished guides. Location: Mississippi Department of Archives and History, P.O. Box 571, Jackson, Mississippi 39205. Scope of collection: Videocassette of funeral services in 1977, scattered references in newsfile collection, and sound recordings of speech delivered by Hamer at Mary Holmes Junior College in 1967.

Fannie Lou Hamer. Papers. 1966-1978. Extent of collection: 16 lin. ft. Finding aids: Unpublished guide and published register. Location: Amistad Research Center, Tulane University, New Orleans, Louisiana 70118. Scope of collection: Contains more than 3000 items of correspondence. Also programs, financial records, photographs, newspaper articles, invitations and other printed items. Microfilm available.

(THE ABOVE ENTRY WAS CONTRIBUTED BY BARBARA L. MORGAN)

28. *Iola M. Pohocsucut Hayden*
(1934–   )
Advocate for Native American rights; educator

BIOGRAPHICAL INFORMATION

Chronological Biography

Born September 5, 1934, in Lawton, Oklahoma.

1952: Graduated from Fort Sill Indian High School. **1956:** Received B.S. in education from Oklahoma State University in Stillwater. Studied at Oklahoma University in Norman for Masters in Public Administration. **1956-1959:** Taught at Intermountain School, government school in Brigham City, Utah. Pupils included special students from Navaho tribe and programs to meet needs of older individuals to prepare them for employment. **1959-1965:** Employed by Oklahoma State University under Bureau of Indian Affairs contract as Associate Home Demonstration Agent to work with Native American families in areas of child care, food and nutrition, management and clothing. Helped identify resources for families to utilize. **1965-1970:** Co-founder and executive director of Oklahomans for Indian Opportunity (OIO), funded by U.S. Office of Economic Opportunity. Developed and implemented newly organized unique statewide program to use federal programs in non-reservation setting. Headed Talent Search project funded by U.S. Office of Education to work with young people in public schools to help alleviate dropout problems. Program grew from staff of three to large multi-funded organization. **February 19, 1968:** As executive director of OIO, testified regarding Native American education at Senate hearing. **April 1968:** Witness before Senate Subcommittee on Government Research, Human Resources Development, part 1. **Early 1970s:** Appointed member of Oklahoma State Advisory Committee to U.S. Commission on Civil Rights. **September 1970–July 1972:** Asked to serve as Executive Director of Americans for Indian Opportunity (AIO), newly formed national Native American organization. Major focus was to provide training and technical assistance to Native American groups in program planning and funding. Generated funding from multiple private sources and managed financial and personnel functions. Developed Native American Legal Defense and Education Fund (NALDEF), funded by Ford Foundation and Rockefeller Brothers fund. NALDEF was legal advocacy program set up to serve as federal agencies "watchdog." Obtained grant to develop direct mail program to make AIO self-sufficient. Created only Native American Small Business Investment Company in country. **October 1972–October 1973:** Director of Minority Studies Program in federal Office of Research Development in Social and Rehabilitation Services in Department of Health, Education and Welfare. Program was designed to build research capacity of minority groups. **1973:** Earned Certificate in Civil Service Management in Washington, D. C. **1973–:** Executive director of Oklahomans for Indian Opportunity, educational and self-help project. Programs for Native American clientele include Native American Credit Union, curriculum for entrepreneurial training, Youth Entrepreneurial training, Native American-owned tour company to highlight Native American experience in Oklahoma, business and economic development, working with tribes to assist in breaking dependency syndrome, and improvement of human resources delivery systems. **October 8, 1976:** Testified before Senate committee concerning problems of Native Americans attempting to finance new businesses, and proposed solutions. **Present–:** Serves as Executive Director of Oklahoma Institute of Indian Heritage, coalition of 28 tribes to develop Native American tourism in state. Career activities include: instrumental in establishment of Indian Education Center in Oklahoma and Community Action Program in Lawton; elected Committeeperson for Comanche Tribe for six years; member of policy-making board of National Committee of Household Employment; member of Executive Committee of Oklahoma Governor's Task Force on Small Business; chair of school board of Fort Sill Indian School; representative for Task Force on Indian Education for Bureau of Indian Affairs; chair of Comanche Tribal Private Industry Council; and teacher in Indian Economic Development at University of Arts and Science of Oklahoma.

Background Information

Parents: Not known. **Siblings:** None known. **Children:** Three (John, Marcia, Sarah). **Influences:** None. **Ethnicity:** Native American (Comanche). **Also known as:** None known. **Historical sites, landmarks, etc.:** None known.

BIBLIOGRAPHICAL INFORMATION

Biographical Sketches About Iola M. Pohocsucut Hayden

Gridley, Marion E., ed. and comp. *Indians of Today.* [N.p.]: I.C.F.P., Inc., 1971.

29. *Dorothy I. Height*
(1912–   )

Advocate for African American rights and women's rights; social worker

BIOGRAPHICAL INFORMATION

Chronological Biography

Born March 24, 1912, in Richmond, Virginia, to Fannie (Burroughs) and James Edward Height, oldest of two daughters. When she was four, family moved to Rankin, Pennsylvania, where she attended integrated schools. Excellent student, won spelling bees, debates, and essay and oratorical contests. Graduated from Rankin High School with four-year college scholarship for winning national oratorical contest sponsored by Elks. Her essay concerned 13th, 14th and 15th Amendments of U.S. Constitution. Parents were active church workers, mother working with missionary society, and father choirmaster and Sunday school superintendent. Much of early life spent in church and related organizations' activities. **1934:** Applied to Barnard College but was told school already had two black students so she would have to wait one term or more for admission. Readily accepted by New York University. Helped organize all-black Rameses Club. Graduated in three years, earned master's degree year later, and subsequently did further postgraduate work at New York School of Social Work. First job was as caseworker for New York City Welfare Department where she worked for two years. **1937:** Chosen as one of 10 youth delegates, only black in group, to represent United States at Universal Christian Council, first international ecumenical council of Protestant churches, held in Oxford, England. Quit caseworker position and joined staff of Harlem branch of Young Women's Christian Association (YWCA) upon return from conference. **1938:** Testified before New York City Council regarding domestic workers. About this time, as officer of Harlem Christian Youth Council, experienced first civil rights activity, speaking to merchants on 125th Street. **1944–?:** Member of National Board of YWCA. **1947–1958:** President of Delta Sigma Theta Sorority, public service sorority of African American women. **Fall 1952:** Visiting professor at Delhi School of Social Work in New Delhi, India. **1952–1955:** Appointed by General George C. Marshall to Advisory Committee on Women in the Services of U.S. Department of Defense. **1957–:** Became fourth president of National Council of Negro Women, Inc. (NCNW), organization begun by Mary McLeod Bethune (see entry 8) in 1935 to unite black women in humanitarian causes and social-action programs, stressing inter-race and inter-class cooperation, and to advance interests of black women, their families and communities. Had previously served on board of directors and as executive director. **1958–1974:** Member of New York State Board of Social Welfare. **1959:** Under sponsorship of International Seminars, toured South America with 29 other leaders of private organizations, studying social conditions and attitudes, especially as they affected family life and children. **1960:** Sent by Committee on Correspondence to study women's organizations in five African countries. **1963–:** Chosen to lead intensive integration drive within YWCA to desegregate local swimming pools, club residences and leadership hiring and training programs. **Summer 1964:** Participated in project called "Wednesdays in Mississippi" which involved visits to Mississippi by teams of black and white women from cities in East, Midwest and West. Purpose was to open channels of communication between races, to improve conditions within state, and to create better image of state in eyes of United States and world. **Fall 1964:** Directed voter registration drive sponsored by NCNW and radio station in New York City. **1964–1970:** Served on board of governors of American Red Cross. **1965:** Director of YWCA Center for Racial Justice, which she had helped develop. **March and June 1966:** Representing NCNW testified regarding Economic Opportunity Act of 1964. **1966:** Recipient of John F. Kennedy Memorial Award for distinguished service in humanitarian causes. Awarded Ernest O. Melby Award of Alumni Association of New York University's School of Education. **1967:** As director of training for New York City YWCA and head of NCNW, was witness in May at hearings concerning Juvenile Delinquency Prevention Act of 1967. Also testified at June hearings for Examination of War on Poverty, and in July at House committee proceedings for Economic Opportunity Act Amendments of 1967 and Senate witness for Housing Legislation of 1967. **1969:** Testified in spring before Senate committee regarding extension of programs authorized under Economic Opportunity Act, and in November about Social Security and Welfare Proposals. **1960s:** NCNW contributed money and staff to voter registration drives in South and financial aid for students who interrupted their education to work in civil rights movement. She worked to establish communication between black and white women in several Alabama communities and reported on evidence of harassment of registrars or intimidation of prospective voters. **1970:** Announced that YWCA was beginning national effort to form bold assault on racial injustice. Very instrumental in changing YWCA convention from focusing solely on women's liberation to stressing overriding problem of racism. **July 1971:** One of founders and member of ruling council of National Women's Political Caucus. Goal of organization is equal representation of women with men at all levels of political system. **1971:** Received Distinguished Service Award from National Conference on Social Welfare. **January 27, 1972:** As vice president of National Council of Churches of Christ, spoke at Senate proceedings concerning welfare recipients. **May 1973:** Elected president of Women in Community Services, Inc. Named to National News Council, organization formed to monitor fairness and accuracy of news reporting. Honored at birthday celebration attended by more than 200 leaders from major businesses and corporations throughout country; $185,000 was raised for NCNW Opportunity Scholarship Fund to provide financial assistance to students who showed promise, aptitude and desire to return to black community with skills that could readily be used by community. **1974:** Named one of eight "Women of the Year, 1974" by *Ladies' Home Journal* magazine. **1974–1975:** Chief designer of International Women's Year program. **September 23, 1977:** Testified at Labor Reform Act of 1977 hearings regarding unions. **December 16, 1977:** As president of NCNW, gave testimony before joint committee in support of White House Conference on Humanities in 1979. **1977:** Retired from YWCA. **February 9, 1978:** As president of Alliance for Volunteerism, appeared before Senate committee on Domestic Volunteer Service Act. **March 8, 1978:** Spoke at hearings regarding UN Decade for Women programs. **August 4, 1978:** Testified in support of extension of ratification period for proposed Equal Rights Amendment. **1979:** Representing Alliance for Volunteerism and NCNW, appeared before House and Senate committees in April and May regarding volunteer programs. **March 13, 1980:** Testified in support of proposed Presidential Commission on National Service and National Commission on Volunteerism. **April 1982:** Guest of honor at restaurant opening in Washington, D. C., which also served as benefit for NCNW. **May 20, 1982:** Discussed achievements of Mary McLeod Bethune and NCNW at hearings considering designation of Bethune Council House as national historic site and for assistance to NCNW from Interior Department for preservation of site. **June 10, 1982:** Spoke at House hearing examining racial discrimination in National Football League field management recruitment and hiring practices. **July 2, 1982:** Again testified regarding Bethune Council House. **May 7, 1985:** Discussed impact of teenage pregnancy on black families at House committee hearings. **October 10, 1985:** Witness regarding appropriations for Bethune Museum and Archives. **November 1985:** The NCNW celebrated 50th anniversary, representing 30 organizations with 4 million members. Under Height's leadership, NCNW had vastly expanded and developed extensive array of programs throughout United States and Africa, focusing on youth, employment, civil rights, and development. It had established Bethune Museum and Archives for Black Women's History and spearheaded erection of Bethune statue, first memorial to black American in Washington, D. C. **April 1986:** Served as national general chair for *Dollars and Sense* magazine's second annual salute to America's top 100 black business and professional women. **October 3, 1986:** Testified at House hearing on "Plight of the Black Elderly: A Major Crisis in America." **1986?:** Began holding "Black Family Reunion" celebrations, sponsored by NCNW, to affirm need to strengthen black families to reverse poverty and underachievement. **September 30, 1987:** Spoke at House hearing entitled "Infants at Risk: Is the Federal Government Assuring Prenatal Care for Poor Women?" **November 1987:** The NCNW held teleconference workshop at Howard University to focus on parent as child's first teacher and offer examples from programs that help parents become more involved in their children's education. **September 13, 1988:** As executive director of NCNW, testified at hearing concerning minorities in higher education. **September 1988:** Third Black Family Reunion drew more than 90,000 people to Washington Mall. **April 1989:** Honored at National Urban Coalition awards dinner. **November 17, 1989:** Along with other members of Black Leadership Forum, met with President George Bush at White House to discuss racism in United States, housing, education, etc. **1989–:** Continues as president and chief executive officer of NCNW. Chair of Black Leadership Forum, group of heads of 14 national predominantly black organizations who meet to exchange information, discuss mutual concerns and plan appropriate joint strategies. Recipient of numerous awards and honorary degrees, has served on countless commissions and committees including National Council of Women of the United States, Commission on the Status of Women, and President's Committee for Employment of the Handicapped, as well as many executive positions in YWCA.

Background Information

Parents: Fannie (Burroughs) and James Edward Height. Mother was nurse; father building contractor. **Siblings:** One (No known names). **Children:** None. **Influences:** None. **Ethnicity:** African American. **Also known as:** None known. **Historical sites, landmarks, etc.:** None known.

BIBLIOGRAPHICAL INFORMATION

Biographical Sketches About Dorothy I. Height

Jackson, George F. *Black Women, Makers of History: A Portrait.* Oakland, CA: GRT Book Printing, 1985.

Low, W. Augustus, ed. *Encyclopedia of Black America.* New York: McGraw-Hill, 1981.

Moritz, Charles, ed. *Current Biography Yearbook 1972.* New York: H. W. Wilson Company, 1973.

O'Neill, Lois Decker, ed. *The Women's Book of World Records and Achievements.* Garden City, NY: Anchor Press/Doubleday, 1979.

Ploski, Harry A., and James Williams, comps. and eds. *The Negro Almanac: A Reference Work on the African American.* Detroit: Gale Research, 1989.

Smith, Jessie Carney, ed. *Notable Black American Women.* Detroit: Gale Research, 1992.

Books by Dorothy I. Height

America's Promise—The Integration of Minorities. New York: Woman's Press, 1946.

The Core of America's Race Problem. New York: n.p., [1945].

Job of the Program Director. New York: Publications Services, National Board, YWCA, [1951].

Step by Step with Interracial Groups. New York: Woman's Press, 1946. Reprint. [N.p.]: Publications Services, National Board, YMCA, [1955].

Taking a Hand in Race Relations. New York: Publications Services, 1951.

Chalmers, Frances K., and Dorothy I. Height. *Fair Practice in Employment.* New York: Woman's Press, 1948.

Books About Dorothy I. Height

Interview with Dorothy I. Height: February 11, April 10, May 29, October 6, November 10, 1974, February 2, March 28, May 25, October 5, 1975, February 1, May 31, November 6, 1976; [conducted by Polly Cowan]. [Cambridge, MA]: Schlesinger Library, Radcliffe College, 1982.

Shorter Works by Dorothy I. Height

"Capital Monument Honors Mrs. Mary McLeod Bethune." *Pennsylvania Black Observer* (April/May 1974): 37.

"Changing the Pattern of Children Having Children." *Journal of Community Health* 11 (Spring 1986): 41–44.

Dowling, Ann, ed. *Twenty-Five Years Since Brown. A Commemorative Booklet.* New York: National Association for the Advancement of Colored People Legal Defense and Educational Fund, 1978. [ED191924]

"Family and Community: Self-Help—A Black Tradition." *Nation* 224 (July 24, 1989): 136–38.

Height, Dorothy, and John Jacob. "Re: April 7 Editorial Page Column by Paul Gigol 'More Bloodletting in the Name of Civil Rights'." *Wall Street Journal* (May 2, 1989): A19.

"National Council of Negro Women Bethune Memorial Dedication." *Negro Heritage* 13 (1974): 122–28.

"The New Black Woman." *Journal of Ecumenical Studies* 16 (1979): 166–69.

"A Time to Listen: Civil Rights and the Mass Media." *Southwest Review* 53 (1968): 221–35.

"To Be Black and a Woman." In *Women's Role in Contemporary Society*, by New York City Commission on Civil Rights. New York: Avon, 1972.

"What Martin Luther King, Jr. Means to Me." *Ebony* 41 (January 1986): 74.

"What Must Be Done About Children Having Children." *Ebony* 40 (March 1985): 76+.

Shorter Works About Dorothy I. Height

"Afro-American or Black: What's in a Name? Prominent Blacks and-or African Americans Express Their Views." *Ebony* 44 (July 1989): 76.

"Biography." *Current Biography* 33 (September 1972): 27–30.

"Birthday Party Produces Scholarship Funds." *Jet* 44 (May 3, 1973): 10.

Booker, Lorri Denise. "Black Group [at Hungry Club luncheon] told [Jesse] Jackson 'winning spirit of young' [by Dorothy Height, of National Council of Negro Women]." *Atlanta Constitution* (April 21, 1988): B4.

Booker, Simeon. "Washington Notebook." *Ebony* 33 (May 1978): 29.

————. "Washington Notebook." *Ebony* 36 (January 1981): 25.

"'Children Having Children'." *America* 152 (March 30, 1985): 245.

"Dorothy Height Honored at D. C. Restaurant Opening." *Jet* 62 (April 19, 1982): 8.

Downey, Maureen. "Dorothy Height Has Shifted Focus Toward Fighting Economic Inequity." *Atlanta Constitution* (June 12, 1987): C1.

Dupree, Adolph. "Dr. Dorothy Irene Height: Motivating the Strengths of Black Women." *About Time* 14 (June 1986): 8–23.

"EBONY Article Aids in Bill to Help Welfare Families." *Jet* 68 (August 12, 1985): 5.

Faber, Harold. "Justice Brennan Joins Ranks of Roosevelt Award Winners." *New York Times* (October 15, 1989): 44.

"Family Affair." *Wall Street Journal* (September 20, 1988): 38.

Farmer, James. "Secret Meetings of the Six Who Shaped the Movement." *Ebony* 40 (April 1985): 108+.

Gilbert, Lynn, and Gaylen Moore. *Particular Passions.* New York: Clarkson N. Potter, 1981.

Gilliam, Dorothy. "Carrying on the Good Work." *Washington Post* (November 18, 1985): C3.

"Height Urges Black Women to Vote." *Jet* 59 (November 6, 1980): 14.

"Help Along the Way." *Essence* 10 (January 1980): 13.

Hoffman, Marilyn. "Dorothy Height — An Optimist With No Illusions." *Christian Science Monitor* (March 26, 1980): 19.

Hornsby, Alton, Jr. *Chronology of African-American History.* Detroit: Gale Research, 1991.

Hunter, Charlayne. "Many Blacks Wary of 'Women's Liberation' Movement in U.S." *New York Times* (November 17, 1970): 47 + .

Hunter, Marjorie. "Caucus to Look at Women's Needs." *New York Times* (May 6, 1979): 72.

"Interest in Contributions of Black Women to the American Heritage Continues to Grow." *Chicago Tribune* (March 20, 1985): Sec. 5, 1.

Kantrowitz, Barbara, and Lynda Wright. "A Show of Strength; Celebrating the Black Family with 'Reunions'." *Newsweek* 110 (August 17, 1987): 73.

"Ladies' Home Journal Women of the Year 1974." *Ladies' Home Journal* 91 (April 1974): 82.

Lanker, Brian. *I Dream a World: Portraits of Black Women Who Changed America.* New York: Stewart, Tabori & Chang, 1989.

Lee, Amy. "Dorothy Height Gets Out Votes." *Christian Science Monitor* (October 23, 1964): 4.

Lewis, Carolyn. "Her Job: Leading Negro Women." *Washington Post* (January 8, 1967): F8.

Overbea, Luix. "Civil Rights Leaders Focus on Strengthening the Black Family." *Christian Science Monitor* (November 20, 1986): 35.

"Rheingold Salutes a Good Neighbor . . . Dorothy I. Height." *Ebony* 16 (February 1961): 8.

Rowan, Carl T. "Crusade of Hope." *Washington Post.* (September 1, 1987): A23.

Rule, Sheila. "A Quiet Crusader for Civil Rights, Still Active at 67." *New York Times* (August 13, 1979): C15.

Toner, Robin. "Black Women's Group Urged to Assist the Poor." *New York Times* (November 17, 1985): 34.

"Two Blacks Are Named to News Media Council." *Jet* 44 (May 24, 1973): 16.

Warren, Ruth. *Pictorial History of Women in America.* New York: Crown, [1975].

"Women at the Top." *Ebony* 37 (August 1982): 146–48.

"Women's Clubs." *Ebony* 32 (July 1977): 71 + .

Media Materials by Dorothy I. Height

Filmstrips

U.P.W. Regional Meeting 1972. [N.p.]: United Presbyterian Church in the U.S.A., 1972. 2 filmstrips; color; 35mm.; 1 sound cassette; 1 ⅞ ips; mono; 2 scripts and 1 guide.

Media Materials About Dorothy I. Height

Video Recordings

Another Voice. [25 Years After Brown vs. Board of Education]. Philadelphia: WHYY-TV, 1979. Videocassette; 29 min.; sound; color; ¾ in.; U-matic.

Black Journal. What Is a Black Leader? New York: Educational Broadcasting Corp., 1977. Cassette; 29 min.; sound; color; ¾ in.

Black Perspective on the News. Series 1. Philadelphia: WHYY-TV, PBSV, 1975-76. Video; 29 min.; color.

Primary Source Materials Relating to Dorothy I. Height

Dorothy Irene Height. Transcript of Oral History. 1976. Extent of collection: 97 pages. Finding aids: Not listed. Location: Schlesinger Library, Radcliffe College, Cambridge, Massachusetts 02138. Scope of collection: Part of Black Women Oral History Project. Interview with Height.

Edith Spurlock Sampson. Papers. 1927-1979 (inclusive), 1934-1979 (bulk). Extent of collection: 7 lin. ft. Finding aids: Unpublished finding aid. Location: Schlesinger Library, Radcliffe College, Cambridge, Massachusetts 02138. Scope of collection: Height is one of correspondents.

30. *Aileen Clarke Hernandez*
(1926–)

Feminist; labor educator; urban and public affairs consultant; and advocate for women's rights and African American rights

BIOGRAPHICAL INFORMATION

Chronological Biography

Born May 23, 1926, in New York City, only daughter and middle child of three of Ethel and Charles Clarke. Grew up in Bay Ridge area of Brooklyn; family was only black family in neighborhood. Raised in household where she, as well as two brothers, learned to cook, care for own room and sew. Class valedictorian from Public School 176.

1943: Graduated from Bay Ridge High School as salutatorian; encouraged by advisor to continue education.   **1943–1947:** Won scholarship to Howard University in Washington, D. C.; experienced discrimination having to wait for last taxi, unable to use downtown hotels, restaurants or movie houses, etc. Joined campus branch of National Association for the Advancement of Colored People (NAACP). Active in civil rights issues, participated in picketing National Theatre, Lisner Auditorium and Thompson restaurant chain to protest segregation, and supported World War II veterans in efforts to desegregate Washington. Became convinced of need to participate in government processes to effect change, but opposed ideas of black bloc voting and unified party affiliation; instead stressed individuality. Extracurricular activities included Howard Players, campus choir, modern dance group and School of Religion's little theater troupe. During last two years of school, wrote university affairs column for *Washington Tribune* and edited school newspaper, *The Hilltop*. Elected in junior year to honor society that was equivalent of Phi Beta Kappa in black colleges. Earned B.A. magna cum laude in political science and sociology. **Summer 1947:** Attended University of Oslo in Norway for graduate work in comparative government through International Student Exchange program. **1947–1949?:** Worked at Macy's as saleswoman in toy department for short time. Research assistant in political science department at Howard University for two years; left due to illness. **1949–1961:** Took classes at New York University in public administration and worked as volunteer in several political campaigns. Attended University of California at Los Angeles and University of Southern California, taking graduate courses in nursery and adult education. Majored in government at Los Angeles State College, earning M.S. with straight A average in 1961; elected to Pi Sigma Alpha honor society. **1950–1951:** Attended International Ladies' Garment Workers' Union (ILGWU) labor college which trained labor leaders; graduated in 1951. **1951–1959:** Assigned to ILGWU Pacific Coast Regional Office in Los Angeles as organizational assistant and assistant educational director. **1957:** Married Mexican American garment cutter from Los Angeles. **1958–1960:** Adult education instructor at University of California's extension at Los Angeles; taught unionism principles and prenaturalization classes in English and citizenship to foreign-born union members. **1959–1961:** Director of Public Relations and Education at ILGWU. **Summer 1960:** As result of extensive experience through her union work with problems of Mexican Americans, toured six Latin American countries as labor education specialist for U.S. State Department, lecturing in English and Spanish on conditions in American trade unions, minority groups, women's status and American political system. **1961:** Selected as Woman of Year by Community Relations Conference of Southern California. Divorced from husband. **1961–1962:** Left ILGWU to serve as campaign coordinator for Alan Cranston running on Democratic party ticket for California State Controller; he was elected in November 1962. **1962–1965:** Appointed assistant chief of California Fair Employment Practices Commission. Supervised 50 member staff in field offices in Los Angeles, San Francisco, San Diego and Fresno, working on personnel issues, affirmative action programs, etc. Established technical advisory committee on testing to conduct comprehensive analysis of industrial testing as it affects hiring of minorities. **May 1965–November 1966:** After recommendation by California Governor Edmund Brown, appointed by President Lyndon Johnson as only woman commissioner on U.S. Equal Employment Opportunity Commission (EEOC). Influential in getting airlines to reverse policy of firing stewardesses when they married. Resigned after 18 months, frustrated by bureaucratic lack of progress in enforcing federal laws against employment discrimination due to race, color, religion, sex or national origin. Felt commission work should not only be concerned with employment but should also be related to housing and school environment. **1966–:** Founded Hernandez and Associates, public relations and management consulting firm in San Francisco which advises business, labor, and government on programs relating to women and minority groups. **1967:** Received Bay Area Alumni Club Distinguished Postgraduate Achievement Award from Howard University. **February 1967–1970:** Western vice president of National Organization for Women (NOW). **1968:** Recipient of Howard University's Charter Day Alumni Postgraduate Achievement in Labor and Public Service Award. Named by San Francisco *Examiner* as one of ten most distinguished women in Bay Area. **1968–1969:** Lecturer and instructor in political science at San Francisco State College; course entitled "Government For and Against the People." **1969–1974:** Western representative, consultant and member of Board of Directors of National Committee Against Discrimination in Housing, a national citizens' group working to achieve open housing and communities throughout country. **March 1970–1971:** One of founding members of NOW, elected its second president in March 1970, succeeding founder Betty Friedan and becoming first black woman to hold that office. Worked to make organization relevant to needs of working class women, especially those of racial or ethnic minority groups. **May 5, 1970:** Representing NOW, testified regarding Equal Rights Amendment before subcommittee on constitutional amendments. **March 31, 1971:** Appeared as NOW president before House committee concerning equal rights for women and men. Questioned validity of state protective laws for women and whether union leadership opposing equal rights amendments truly represented women workers. **September 1971:** Elected chair of national advisory committee of NOW following her term as president. **October 27, 1971:** Witness as western representative of National Committee Against Discrimination in Housing regarding federal government's role in achieving equal opportunity in housing. Charged that there was a lack of administration commitment to creating equal opportunity in housing; discussed local area practice of barring low and moderate-income housing developments, as well as the need for and recommendations for national housing growth policy. **July 11, 1973:** Gave testimony as former EEOC member concerning economic problems of women. **1973:** Co-founder of Black Women Organized for Action in San Francisco. Organization's focus is discrimination in employment; offers employment opportunity clinics; assisted in forming feminist credit union; urges black women to seek political office. **February 11, 1975:** As president of National Committee Against Discrimination in Housing, appeared before Senate committee regarding national budget priorities and effect on state of California. **1977:** Member of California Federal Judiciary Selection Committee. **1978–1979:** Instructor in department of urban and regional planning at University of California, Berkeley. **1979:** Received honorary Doctor of Humane Letters from Southern Vermont College. **1981:** Chosen for Equal Rights Advocates award. **July 1982:** Joined 15 other ex-government officials to form panel to monitor civil rights records of U.S. Congress and administration. Goal of privately financed bipartisan group is to oversee enforcement of laws barring discrimination. **1984:** Honored with Friends of Commission on Status of Women Award. **1985:** Received San Francisco League of Women Voters Award, and Parren J. Mitchell Award from San Francisco Black Chamber of Commerce. **1987:** Presented with Service Award from National Urban Coalition. **1988–:** Public affairs/urban consultant. Member of many organizations, boards, and commissions including Institute for Civil Justice, National Institute for Women of Color, Commission to Study U.S. Policy toward South Africa, etc. **January 8, 1992:** Honored as one of former NOW presidents at President's Dinner at French Embassy in Washington, D. C.

> I think one of the problems is that all too many men in personnel view every woman who comes before them as an image of their wife and therefore they look at that person and say, "What would I like my wife to be doing?" And if this woman is applying for something they would not like their wife to be doing, they automatically decide that she shouldn't be doing it either.
> — Aileen Clarke Hernandez, "Current Report on Equal Employment Opportunities," unpublished keynote address to Equal Employment Opportunities in the '70s Meeting, University of California, 1972.

McPhee, Carol, and Ann FitzGerald, comps. *Feminist Quotations.* New York: Crowell, 1979.

Background Information

Parents: Ethel and Charles Clarke. Emigrated from Jamaica. Mother worked in garment industry during Depression; father employed in art supply house. **Siblings:** Two (No known names). **Children:** None. **Influences:** None. **Ethnicity:** African American. **Also known as:** None known. **Historical sites, landmarks, etc.:** None known.

BIBLIOGRAPHICAL INFORMATION

Biographical Sketches About Aileen Clarke Hernandez

Christmas, Walter, ed. *Negroes in Public Affairs and Government*. Yonkers, NY: Educational Heritage, 1966.

Moritz, Charles, ed. *Current Biography Yearbook*. New York: H. W. Wilson Company, 1971.

O'Neill, Lois Decker, ed. *The Women's Book of World Records and Achievements*. Garden City,NY: Anchor Press / Doubleday, 1979.

Ploski, Harry A., and James Williams, comps. and eds. *The Negro Almanac: A Reference Work on the African American*. Detroit: Gale Research, 1989.

Smith, Jessie Carney, ed. *Notable Black American Women*. Detroit: Gale Research, 1992.

Tuttle, Lisa. *Encyclopedia of Feminism*. New York: Facts On File, 1986.

Books by Aileen Clarke Hernandez

Hernandez, Aileen, and Letitia P. Sommers. *The First Five Years, 1966-1971*. Chicago: National Organization for Women, [1971?].

Shorter Works by Aileen Clarke Hernandez

"Editorial." In *The New Feminism in Twentieth-Century America*, edited by June Sochen. Lexington, MA: D. C. Heath, 1971.

"Equal Employment Opportunities for Women: Problems, Facts & Answers." *Contact* 4 (February 1973): 9 + .

"Exerting Leverage on the Cities." *Center Magazine* 9 (March/April 1976): 76–77.

"How Different Is the World of 1984 from the World of 1964 — Comment." *Rutgers Law Review* 37 (1985): 755–57.

"How to File a Job Complaint with the EEOC." *Crisis* 72 (November 1965): 57–76.

"Money: Small Change for Black Women." *Ms.* 3 (August 1974): 16–18.

Shorter Works About Aileen Clarke Hernandez

Bradley, Valerie J. "Black Woman Heads Drive to Liberate All Women." *Jet* 38 (June 4, 1970): 46–50.

"Conversation — Ida Lewis & Aileen Hernandez, Interview." *Essence* 1 (February 1971): 20–25 + .

Dreyfuss, Joel. "Civil Rights and the Women's Movement." *Black Enterprise* 8 (September 1977): 35 + .

King, Helen H. "The Black Woman and Women's Lib." *Ebony* 26 (March 1971) 68–70 + .

"Many Blacks Wary of 'Women's Liberation' Movement in U.S." *New York Times* (November 17, 1970): 47.

"The Negro Woman in Politics." *Ebony* 21 (August 1966): 96–100.

"16 Ex-U.S. Officials Join Group to Study Civil Rights Records." *New York Times* (July 25, 1982): 13.

Sochen, June. *Movers and Shakers: American Women Thinkers and Activists 1900–1970*. New York: Quadrangle/The New York Times Book Company, 1973.

Media Materials by Aileen Clarke Hernandez

Sound Recordings

All Issues Are Women's Issues. Pacifica Tape Library, 1972. Cassette; 39 min.; 2-track; mono.

Feminism — Its History and Purpose: Aileen Hernandez on the Growth and Status of Women's Liberation. North Hollywood, CA: Center for Cassette Studies, [197?]. Cassette; 59 min.; ½ track; mono.

Women's Liberation: Its History, Philosophy and Purpose. San Rafael, CA: Big Sur, 1971. Cassette; 60 min. 1 ⅞ ips.

Media Materials About Aileen Clarke Hernandez

Video Recordings

Going Past Go — An Essay on Sexism. Washington, D. C. : PBS Video, 1977. Video cassette; 59 min.; ¾ or ½ inch; color.

31. *Grace Hutchins*
(1885–1969)

*Advocate for political rights; author;
labor researcher; and economist*

BIOGRAPHICAL INFORMATION

Chronological Biography

Born August 19, 1885, in Boston, Massachusetts, into affluent family of Susan Barnes (Hurd) and Edward Webster Hutchins. Third of five children and third daughter; both sisters died in childhood. Parents were part of social elite; father successful lawyer, mother active in community. Educated at private elementary and secondary schools.

1898–1899: Toured world with parents.   1907: Earned B.A. from Bryn Mawr College. Developed interest in woman suffrage while in college, but parents objected.   1912–1916: As missionary in China, taught at St. Hilda's Episcopal School for Chinese Girls in Wuchang; served as principal from 1915 to 1916.   1916–19?: Returned to Boston due to poor health and parental insistence. Began involvement in labor movement. As result of joining Socialist party to protest American participation in World War I, was almost fired from teaching position at social training school in New York City. 1920–1923: Attended New York School of Philanthropy (New York School of Social Work), studying labor problems. Worked for number of months in Seidenbery cigar factory in New York City, in conjunction with courses, to study working conditions of women. During 1922–23 academic year, pursued graduate work at Teachers College of Columbia University. Became close friends with, and later co-worker of Anna Rochester, Marxist economist and historian who had worked in settlement house and who was active in seeking improvement of working conditions for women and children, etc.; she became strong influence on Hutchins. Joined Christian pacifist group Fellowship of Reconciliation (FOR) and lectured, travelled and wrote for organization. 1922: *Jesus Christ and the World Today*, written by both women, was published; concerned social problems Christians must confront.   1922–1924: Contributing editor to FOR's monthly newspaper *World Tomorrow*, of which Rochester was editor-in-chief from 1922 to 1926.   1923: Travelled with Rochester to FOR international conference in Denmark, and then to Hellerau, Germany, to German Youth Movement meeting.   1924: Moved into Greenwich Village apartment with Rochester, which they shared for rest of their lives. Took part in textile strike in Paterson, New Jersey.   1924–1926: Press secretary of FOR.   1925–1926: FOR's business executive.   1926–1927: Both women travelled to Far East, India, Europe and Soviet Union; met with social reformers including Gandhi, visited factories, and wrote of their experiences in number of American publications. Became correspondent for Federated Press after return to United States. 1927: Along with Rochester, left church and became active member of Communist party due to increasing conservatism of *The World Tomorrow*, as well as a result of her observations of Soviet Union's reforms. Arrested in August during pro–Sacco and Vanzetti demonstration in Boston. Although parents were greatly upset, they did not discontinue their substantial financial support; she remained close to family and inherited portion of estate. Founded Labor Research Association (LRA) with Rochester and Robert W. Dunn (co-founder of American Civil Liberties Union), to serve as economic consultant and to furnish economic information and labor analyses in form of books, reports and statistics to trade unions, labor organizations and publications.   1927–1928: Appointed investigator for Bureau of Women in Industry of New York State Department of Labor but resigned after only five months due to poor health.

1928: Participated in New Bedford, Massachusetts, textile strike.   **1929:** *Labor and Silk*, description of industrial conditions, published.   **1929–1967:** Served on staff of LRA. Wrote number of pamphlets for organization regarding labor, children and women's issues. Was one of editors of seventeen volumes of biennial *Labor Facts Book*.   **1933:** First edition of *Women Who Work* published. Describes struggle to organize women workers, importance of women in strikes since 1820s and fight to improve working conditions; was used effectively by organizers to unionize women workers.   **1935:** Ran unsuccessfully on Communist party ticket for city alderman in New York.   **1936:** Failed in attempt to become New York State controller as Communist party nominee. Elected treasurer of Communist National Election Campaign Committee.   **1937–1962:** Edited *Railroad Notes*, publication of LRA.   **1940:** Ran for New York state lieutenant governor, again without success, on Communist party ticket.   **1940–1956:** Frequently wrote for Communist newspaper, *Daily Worker* (predecessor of *Daily World*), of which she was one of major stockholders and owners.   **1948:** Accused by Alger Hiss witness Whittaker Chambers, during Congressional hearings and in his 1952 autobiography, of threatening him if he did not return to Communist party; vehemently denied charges.   **1951:** As trustee of Bail Bond Fund of Civil Rights Congress, posted $10,000 bail for Communist leader Elizabeth Gurley Flynn (see entry 25), and $5,000 for Alexander Trachtenberg, both of whom had been indicted under Smith Act.   **1951–1956:** Involved in litigation concerning Bail Bond Fund's liquidation.   **1964:** Secretary of Elizabeth Gurley Flynn Memorial Committee.   **May 11, 1966:** Anna Rochester died of pneumonia at age 86 in New York City.   **July 15, 1969:** After long illness, died at home on Bedford St. in New York City at age 83 of arteriosclerosis. There was no funeral service. Had remained active in various organizations including International Labor Defense, American Committee for Protection of Foreign Born and Civil Rights Congress, despite becoming target of anti-communist crusaders.

Background Information

Parents: Susan Barnes (Hurd) and Edward Webster Hutchins. Members of Trinity Episcopal Church. Mother active in charitable work in number of institutions including Home for Aged Women, Baldwinsville Hospital for Crippled Children and Society of Colonial Dames. Father prominent attorney, founder of Legal Aid Society, one of original incorporators of Boston Bar Association. **Siblings:** Four (Known names: Henry). **Children:** None. **Influences:** Anna Rochester. **Ethnicity:** English American. **Also known as:** None known. **Historical sites, landmarks, etc.:** None known.

BIBLIOGRAPHICAL INFORMATION

Biographical Sketches About Grace Hutchins

Fink, Gary M., ed. *Biographical Dictionary of American Labor*. Westport, CT: Greenwood, 1984.

Sicherman, Barbara, and Carol Hurd Green, eds. *Notable American Women: The Modern Period: A Biographical Dictionary*. Cambridge, MA: Belknap Press of Harvard University Press, 1980.

Whitman, Alden, ed. *American Reformers: An H. W. Wilson Biographical Dictionary*. New York: H. W. Wilson Company, 1985.

Books by Grace Hutchins

Children Under Capitalism. [New York: International Pamphlets, 1933].
From Bantu Jungle to Church College. Hartford, CT: Church Missions, 1936.
Japan Wars on the U.S.A. New York: International, 1941.
Japan's Drive for Conquest. New York: Labor Research Association, 1935.
Labor and Silk. New York: International, [1929].
The Truth About the Liberty League. [New York: International Pamphlets, 1936].
What Every Working Woman Wants. New York: Workers Library, 1935.
Women and War. [New York: Central Committee, Communist Party of the U.S.A., 1932].
Women Who Work. New York: International Pamphlets, [1932]. Reprint. New York: International, [1952].
Youth in Industry. New York: International Pamphlets, [1932].
Hutchins, Grace, and Anna Rochester. *Jesus Christ and the World Today*. New York: George H. Doran, [1922].
Sturgis, Lucy C., and Grace Hutchins. *Pickaninnies' Progress*. Hartford, CT: Church Missions, 1910.

Shorter Works by Grace Hutchins

"5,000,000 Women Workers Eligible for Trade Unions." *AFL Rank and File Federationist* (June 1948): 8.
"1001 Laws Discriminating Against Women." *Woman Today* (April 1937): 20-1.
"Rose Pastor Stokes." *Working Woman* 4 (August 1933): 4.
"Seeing Red in Canton." *Survey* 57 (March 15, 1927): 775 + .

Shorter Works About Grace Hutchins

Feldman, Betty. "Grace Hutchins Tells About 'Women Who Work'." *Worker* (March 1, 1953).

"Grace Hutchins, Labor Economist." *New York Times* (July 16, 1969): 45.

Kihss, Peter. "Red Bail Jumpers Wreck Fund; State Takes Over to Liquidate It." *New York Times* (April 15, 1952): 1+.

"Obituary." *Daily World* (July 17, 1969).

Streat, Sidney. "Grace Hutchins—Revolutionary." *Daily Worker* (September 16, 1935).

Zeligs, Meyer A. *Friendship and Fratricide: An Analysis of Whittaker Chambers and Alger Hiss.* New York: Viking, 1967.

Primary Source Materials Relating to Grace Hutchins

Anna Rochester. Papers. 1880–1965. Extent of collection: 2 ft. Finding aids: Inventory and supplement to published guide. Location: University of Oregon Library, Special Collections, Eugene, Oregon 97403-1299. Scope of collection: Correspondence, journal about her life that was kept from 1880 to 1918 by her mother, records of Community House, book reviews, and printed works.

Grace Hutchins. Papers. 1898–1954. Extent of collection: 1.5 ft. Finding aids: Inventory and supplement to published guide. Location: University of Oregon Library, Special Collections, Eugene, Oregon 97403-1299. Scope of collection: Letters and correspondence of Hutchins and material on St. Hilda's School in Wuchang, China.

Lewis Mumford. Papers. ca. 1905–1987. Extent of collection: 1 item. Folder 5468. Finding aids: Not listed. Location: Special Collections Department, Van Pelt Library, University of Pennsylvania, Philadelphia, Pennsylvania 19104–6206. Scope of collection: 1926 letter to Lewis Mumford from Hutchins, secretary of *World Tomorrow.*

Robert Williams Dunn. Labor papers. 1926, 1948–1960. Extent of collection: ca. 2 ft. Finding aids: Unpublished inventory with the collection. Location: University of Oregon Library, Special Collections, Eugene, Oregon 97403-1299. Scope of collection: Persons represented include Hutchins.

Ruth Erickson. Letters of Ruth Erickson and Eleanor Stevenson. 1924–1970. Extent of collection: 3 ft. Finding aids: Unpublished finding aid in the repository. Location: University of Oregon Library, Special Collections, Eugene, Oregon 97403-1299. Scope of collection: Correspondents include Hutchins.

32. *Helen Maria Fiske Hunt Jackson*
(1830?–1885)

Advocate for Native American rights; poet; and author

BIOGRAPHICAL INFORMATION

Chronological Biography

Born October 15?, 1830?, in Amherst, Massachusetts, first of four children, two girls and two boys; both brothers died in infancy. Mother, Deborah (Vinal) and father, Nathan Welby Fiske, were Calvinists and home was strict and pious. Spirited child, rebelled against puritanical upbringing and did not affiliate with any church as adult. Poet Emily Dickinson was neighbor and good friend from childhood. **February 19, 1844:** Mother died of tuberculosis when she was 13. She and sister were cared for by aunt in Falmouth, Massachusetts. Educated first at home by mother, then at Falmouth Female Seminary, Ipswich Female Seminary, and Abbott School in New York City. **May 27, 1847:** Father died in Jerusalem of dysentery; had gone there to search for cure for tuberculosis which he, too, had contracted. Maternal grandfather then cared for sisters. **1849:** Lived in New York at home of father's clergyman friend, John Abbott. Attended Springler Institute run by Abbott's brother. **1851:** Met Lt. Edward Bissell Hunt while visiting in Albany, New York. He was army engineer and brother of New York Governor Washington Hunt. **October 28, 1852:** Married to Edward Hunt. Lived in number of locations due to husband's career. **1853:** First of two sons, Murray, born. **August 1854:** Murray died of brain tumor at 11 months of age in Tarrytown, New York. **1855:** Last child, Warren Horsford, nicknamed Rennie, born. **October 2, 1863:** Husband killed in New York harbor by suffocation while experimenting with submarine gun he had invented. **April 13, 1865:** Rennie died at nine years of age of diphtheria at aunt's home in West Roxbury, Massachusetts. **1865:** Began to publish poetry. **February 10, 1866:** At about age 34, moved to Newport, Rhode Island, where she and husband had once lived. Devastated and alone, turned to writing, with critic/writer Thomas Wentworth Higginson as literary mentor. Prolific writer, but intensely disliking publicity, wrote under several pseudonyms, as well as frequently submitting unsigned poems, book reviews and articles to *New York Evening Post, The Nation, Independent, Hearth and Home,* etc. Achieved rapid success and, handling her money wisely, was financially comfortable. **November 1868–February 1870:** Travelled abroad gathering material for *Bits of Travel.* **1870:** *Verses,* first book, published. **May 1872:** Journeyed to California for first time. **1873–1874:** Lived at Colorado Springs Hotel during part of this time. Met William Sharpless Jackson, prosperous businessman and banker. **October 22, 1875:** Married William Jackson in Quaker ceremony at her sister's home in Wolfboro, New Hampshire; he was 39 and she 45. Lived in Colorado Springs from that time on, although she travelled extensively. Continued to write large volume of literature, including stories for children. **December 1879:** Gradually became aware of problems of Native Americans. While in Boston for celebration of Oliver Wendell Holmes' birthday, heard Chief Standing Bear and Bright Eyes (Susette La Flesche) (see entry 37) speak about injustices inflicted by U.S. government and others on Native Americans. Although up to this time had not espoused any causes, such as suffrage or abolition, plight of Native Americans aroused her concern and she embarked on campaign to help them. Sent letters to newspapers, ministers, Army officers, college presidents, legislators, etc. Waged effort through published letters with Secretary of Interior Carl Schurz, gaining national attention. **January–May 1880:** Spent several months at Astor Library in New York City, combing government records to document charges. Wrote report of findings and left for Europe. **January 1881:** *A Century of Dishonor*, history of Native American wars and indictment of government dealings with Native Americans based on her research, published. Every member of Congress, as well as federal government officials involved in Native American affairs, was sent copy of bloodred bound book at her expense in hope reparations would be made. **March 1881:** Some changes resulted as Congress ruled that Ponca Indians be reimbursed for losses and granted land and financial assistance. **May 1881:** Returned to Colorado Springs after spending winter in East. **Winter 1881–1882:** In California to write articles for *Century Magazine*, began study of Mission Native Americans. Visited all missions from San Diego to San Francisco; went to ranches, Native American villages and remote areas to gather information; interviewed people and researched in libraries: all too familiar story of Native Americans being forced from land granted to them emerged. **July 1882:** Received appointment as special commissioner from Department of Indian Affairs, signed by President Arthur, to investigate and prepare report on condition and needs of Mission Native Americans. Had initiated correspondence to get appointment months before and had stated she herself would pay any expenses she incurred beyond amount funded by government. **March 1883:** Returned to California with three others to help her gather more material. **July 13, 1883:** Submitted report to Commissioner of Indian Affairs Hiram Price. It contained facts, statistics and recommendations, but government still made no significant changes. **Fall 1883:** Frustrated by government inaction despite her efforts, decided to write novel in belief that public would read novel rather than nonfiction, and might be moved to demand government rectify injustices, much as *Uncle Tom's Cabin* had helped to do. **December 1, 1883–March 1884:** Wrote *Ramona*, historical romance which originally was to be published in serial form in *The Christian Union*. Obsessed, worked compulsively, hating to be away, but often forced to stop due to illness. Worked part of time in New York City. Classic novel, emphasizing land grabbing and mistreatment of Native Americans and Mexican Americans, was published late in year. Depicts mistreatment of Native Americans, which did raise some public consciousness, but its popularity comes more from its setting in picturesque old California. It has been made into stage play and at least three movies and has remained in print ever since, having gone through over 300 printings. Although she usually did not sign her works with real name because she did not like publicity, she felt so strongly about issue that she signed both *Ramona* and *A Century of Dishonor* with real name. **June 1884:** Suffered compound fracture of hip or leg and never was able to walk again. Went to Los Angeles and then San Francisco, hoping health would improve, but she became worse, possibly from cancer of the stomach. **August 2, 1885:** Husband arrived in California to be with her. **August 8, 1885:** Wrote to President Grover Cleveland thanking him for his efforts to help Native Americans and asking him to read *A Century of Dishonor* and continue to right the wrongs. **August 12, 1885:** Died in San Francisco at age 54. Temporarily buried in San Francisco, then moved to near top of Cheyenne Mountain in spot overlooking Colorado Springs, which she had picked out herself. Husband moved her body to Evergreen Cemetery in Colorado Springs in 1891 after owners of site began charging to visit her grave. Brilliant and impetuous, she had remained prolific writer until her death.

Background Information

Parents: Deborah (Vinal) and Nathan Welby Fiske. Mother was born in Boston and attended Adams Academy. Father's ancestors had emigrated from Suffolk, England, in 1642. He had studied for ministry, graduated from Dartmouth, and taught Latin and Greek, among other subjects, at Amherst College. **Siblings:** Three (Known names: Ann[e]). **Children:** Two (Murray, Warren Horsford). **Influences:** None. **Ethnicity:** English American. **Also known as:** Helen Hunt; Helen Hunt Jackson; Helen Jackson; "H. H.," "Saxe Holm," "Marah," "Rip Van Winkle," and "No Name" (pseudonyms). **Historical sites, landmarks, etc.:** Childhood Home, 249 S. Pleasant Street, Amherst, Massachusetts; Grave, Evergreen Cemetery, Colorado Springs, Colorado; Memorial Rooms, Pioneer Museum, 215 S. Tejon, Colorado Springs, Colorado; Ramona Bowl, Hemet, California, Ramona Pageant Association has produced story as outdoor festival every spring since 1923; Helen Hunt Falls, North Cheyenne Canyon, Colorado.

BIBLIOGRAPHICAL INFORMATION

Biographical Sketches About Helen Maria Fiske Hunt Jackson

James, Edward T., ed. *Notable American Women 1607–1950: A Biographical Dictionary.* Cambridge, MA: Belknap Press of Harvard University Press, 1971.
McHenry, Robert, ed. *Famous American Women.* New York: Dover, 1980.
Mainiero, Lina, ed. *American Women Writers.* New York: Frederick Ungar, 1980.

Malone, Dumas, ed. *Dictionary of American Biography.* New York: Charles Scribner's Sons, 1961.
Whitman, Alden, ed. *American Reformers: An H. W. Wilson Biographical Dictionary.* New York: H. W. Wilson Company, 1985.

Books by Helen Maria Fiske Hunt Jackson

Ah-wah-ne Days: A Visit to the Yosemite Valley in 1872. San Francisco: Book Club of California, 1971. (Written under the name of H. H.)
Between Whiles. Boston: Roberts Brothers, 1887.
Bits of Talk About Home Matters. Boston: Roberts Brothers, 1873. Reprint. Boston: Little, Brown and Company, 1904.
Bits of Talk, in Verse and Prose, for Young Folks. Boston: Roberts Brothers, 1876. (Written under the name of H. H.)
Bits of Travel. Boston: J. R. Osgood, 1872. Reprint. Boston: Roberts Brothers, 1881.
Bits of Travel at Home. Boston: Roberts, 1878. Reprint. Boston: Roberts Brothers, 1890. (Written under the name of H. H.)
A Calendar of Sonnets. Boston: Roberts Brothers, [1886]. Reprint. Boston: Roberts Brothers, 1891.
Cat Stories. Boston: Roberts Brothers, 1886. Reprint. Boston: Little, Brown and Company, 1907.
A Century of Dishonor: A Sketch of the United States Government's Dealings with Some of the Indian Tribes. New York: Harper & Brothers, 1881. Reprint. Williamstown, MA: Corner House, 1979.
A Century of Dishonor: A Sketch of the United States Government's Dealings with Some of the Indian Tribes. New Ed., Enl. by the Addition of the Report of the Needs of the Mission Indians of California. Boston: Roberts Brothers, 1885. Reprint. St. Clair Shores, MI: Scholarly Press, 1972.
Easter Bells: An Original Poem. New York: White, Stokes, & Allen, 1884. Reprint. New York: Frederick A. Stokes, 1891. (Written under the name of H. H.)
Father Junipero and His Work: A Sketch of the Foundation, Prosperity, and Ruin of the Franciscan Missions in California. El Cajon, CA: Frontier, [1966].
Father Junipero and the Mission Indians of California. Boston: Little, Brown and Company, 1902.
Glimpses of California and the Missions. Boston: Little, Brown and Company, 1902. Reprint. Boston: Little, Brown and Company, 1927.
Glimpses of Three Coasts. Boston: Roberts Brothers, 1886. Reprint. Boston: Roberts Brothers, 1898.
The Helen Jackson Yearbook: Selections by Harriet T. Perry. Boston: Roberts Brothers, 1895.
Hetty's Strange History. Boston: Roberts Brothers, 1886. Reprint. Boston: Roberts Brothers, 1877.
The Hunter Cats of Connorloa. Boston: Roberts Brothers, 1884. Reprint. Boston: Little, Brown and Company, 1899.
Letters from a Cat: Pub. by Her Mistress for the Benefit of all Cats and the Amusement of Little Children. Boston: Roberts Brothers, 1879. Reprint. Boston: Little, Brown and Company, 1902. (Written under the name of H. H.)

Mammy Tittleback and Her Family: A True Story of Seventeen Cats. Boston: Roberts Brothers, 1881. (Written under the name of H. H.)

Mercy Philbrick's Choice. Boston: Roberts, 1876. Reprint. New York: AMS, 1970.

My Day in the Wilderness. [San Francisco]: Published for its members by the Book Club of California, 1939.

My Legacy. Boston: H. H. Carter & Karrick, 1888.

Nelly's Silver Mine: A Story of Colorado Life. Boston: Roberts Brothers, 1878. Reprint. New York: Garland, 1976. (Written under the name of H. H.)

Pansy Billings and Popsy. Boston: Lothrop, 1898. (Written under the name of H. H.)

Poems. Boston: Roberts Brothers, 1892. Reprint. New York: Arno, 1972.

[Poems. Selections]. Verses. Sonnets and Lyrics. Boston: Roberts Brothers, 1888. Reprint. Boston, Roberts Brothers, 1890. (Written under the name of H. H.)

The Procession of Flowers in Colorado. Boston: Roberts Brothers, 1897.

Puget Sound. [N.p.: n.p., 1883?].

Ramona: A Story. Boston: Roberts Brothers, 1884. Reprint. New York: Avon, 1970.

Ramona: Adapted by Olive Eckerson. New York: Globe Book Company, [1952].

Saxe Holm's Stories. New York: Scribner, Armstrong & Company, 1874–78. Reprint. New York: Garrett, [1969].

Saxe Holm's Stories. First Series. New York: Scribner, Armstrong, 1874. Reprint. Freeport, NY: Books for Libraries Press, [1970].

Saxe Holm's Stories, Second Series. New York: Scribner, 1878. (Authorship uncertain; has been attributed to Helen Hunt Jackson.)

Sonnets and Lyrics. Boston: Roberts Brothers, 1886. Reprint. Boston: Roberts Brothers, 1895.

Spinning. Cliftondale, MA: Coates Brothers, [ca. 1880]. (Written under the name of H. H.)

The Story of Boon. Boston: Roberts Brothers, 1874. (Written under the name of H. H.)

The Training of Children. New York: New York & Brooklyn Publishing, 1882. (Written under the name of H. H.)

Verses. Boston: Field, Osgood, 1870. Reprint. Boston: Roberts Brothers, 1893. (Written under the name of H. H.)

Zeph. A Posthumous Story. Boston: Roberts Brothers, [1885]. Reprint. Freeport, NY: Books for Libraries Press, 1971.

Florian. *Bathmendi: A Persian Tale, Translated for the Children, from the French of Florian.* Boston: Loring, 1867. (Translated under the name of H. H.)

Jackson, Helen Hunt, and Abbot Kinney. *Report on the Condition and Needs of the Mission Indians of California.* Washington, D. C.: GPO, 1883.

Jackson, Helen Maria Fiske Hunt, and Abbot Kinney. *Report of Mrs. Helen Hunt Jackson and Abbot Kinney on the Mission Indians in 1883.* Boston: Press of Stanley and Usher, 1887.

M. H., and H. H. *Old Times: With Other Familiar Sketches in Prose and Verse: For Young People.* Lowell, [MA]: Daniel Bixby, 1846. (Sometimes attributed to Helen Hunt Jackson.)

Books About Helen Maria Fiske Hunt Jackson

Allen, Margaret V. *Ramona's Homeland.* Chula Vista, CA: Denrich, 1914.

Banning, Evelyn I. *Helen Hunt Jackson.* New York: Vanguard, [1973].

Brigandi, Phillip, ed. *Looking Back — On the Ramona Pageant.* Orange, CA: Wrangler, 1985.

Clough, Edwin H. *'Ramona's Marriage Place,' the House of Estudillo.* Chula Vista, CA: Denrich, 1910.

Davis, Carlyle Channing. *The True Story of "Romona," Its Facts and Fictions, Inspiration and Purpose.* New York: Dodge, [1914].

Getz, Thomas P. *The Story of Ramona's Marriage Place, Old San Diego, California.* North San Diego: T. P. Getz, n.d.

Gover, Mary Edith. *Sketches in the Country of H. H. Jackson's "Ramona."* N.p.: n.p., 1891.

Hufford, David Andrew. *The Real Ramona of Helen Hunt Jackson's Famous Novel.* Los Angeles: D. A. Hufford, 1900.

In Memoriam Helen Hunt Jackson (H. H.). [Denver, CO]: n.p., 1886.

James, George Wharton. *Through Ramona's Country.* Boston: Little, Brown and Company, 1909. Reprint. Boston: Little, Brown and Company, 1913.

Jearie. Arthur. *Ramona, a Dramatization of Helen Jackson's Immortal Romance.* Minneapolis: Northwestern Press, 1940.

Lummis, Charles Fletcher. *The Home of Ramona: Photographs of Camulos, the Fine Old Spanish Estate Described by Mrs. Helen Hunt Jackson, as the Home of "Ramona."* Los Angeles: Lummis, 1888.

Martin, Minerva L. *Helen Hunt Jackson in Relation to Her Times.* N.p.: University of Louisiana Press, [1939].

May, Antoniette. *The Annotated Ramona.* San Carlos, CA: Wide World/Tetra, 1988.

————. *Helen Hunt Jackson: A Lonely Voice of Conscience.* San Francisco: Chronicle Books, 1987.

Odell, Ruth. *Helen Hunt Jackson and Her Times.* New York: Appleton-Century, 1939.

————. *Helen Hunt Jackson H. H.* New York: D. Appleton-Century, 1939. Reprint. [Lincoln, NE]: University of Nebraska, 1942.

Randall, A. [Frank]. *Mrs. Helen Hunt Jackson and Ramona.* N.p.: n.p., 1888.

Stark, Dolores. *The Story of the Historic Jackson House.* [N.p.: n.p.], 1979. (Colorado Springs, CO: Reprinted by O'Brien Typesetting and Printing).

Vroman, A. C., and T. F. Barnes. *The Genesis of the Story of Ramona: Why the Book Was Written, Explanatory Text of Points of Interest Mentioned in the Story.* Los Angeles: Kingsley-Barnes & Neuner, 1899.

Whitaker, Rosemary. *Helen Hunt Jackson.* Boise, ID: Boise State University, 1987.

Shorter Works by Helen Maria Fiske Hunt Jackson

"April; poem." *Nature Study Review* 15 (April 1919): 134.

Bernikow, Louise, ed. *The World Split Open: Four Centuries of Women Poets in England and America, 1552–1950.* New York: Vintage Books, 1974.

"Down to Sleep; poem." *Normal Instructor and Primary Plans* 34 (November 1924): 54.
"Echoes in the City of the Angels." *Century Magazine* 27 (December 1883): 194–210. (Written under the name of H. H.)
"Echoes in the City of the Angels." *Journal of the West* 7 (July 1968): 381–96.
"Georgetown and the Terrible Mine." In *Chronicles of Colorado*, selected and introduced by Frederick R. Rinehart, Boulder, CO: Roberts Rhinehart, 1984.
"How Ramona Was Written." *Atlantic Monthly* 86 (November 1900): 712–14.
"The Last Words." In *A Memorial of Josiah Gilbert Holland: Discourses and Tributes Called Forth by His Death, October 12, 1881.* [United States]: Printed, not published, [1882?].
"October's Bright Blue Weather; poem." *Primary Education-Popular Educator* 46 (October 1928): 150.
Rays of Light: Selections for Every Day in the Month, Arranged by Helen P. Strong. New York: American Tract Society, 1888.
"September; song." *Normal Instructor and Primary Plans* 36 (September 1927): 70.
"Slavery Among the Indians of Northwest America." *Pacific Northwest Quarterly* 9 (1918): 277–82.

Shorter Works About Helen Maria Fiske Hunt Jackson

Abbot, Willis John. *Women of History, the Lives of Women Who in All Ages, All Lands and in All Womanly Occupations Have Won Fame and Put Their Imprint on the World's History.* Philadelphia: J. C. Winston, 1913.
Banning, Evelyn I. "A Boarder in Sleepy Hollow." *Newport History* 48 (1975): 247–54.
———. "Helen Hunt Jackson in San Diego." *Journal of San Diego History* 24 (Fall 1978): 457–67.
Beck, Nicholas. "The Vanishing Californians: the Education of Indians in the Nineteenth Century." *Southern California Quarterly* 69 (1987): 33–50.
Bienstock, Barry W. "Helen Hunt Jackson." In *Dictionary of Literary Biography*, edited by Clyde N. Wilson. Detroit: Gale Research, 1986.
Bolton, Sarah. *Lives of Girls Who Became Famous.* [New York?]: T. Y. Crowell, 1865.
Byers, John R., Jr. "The Matter of Helen Hunt Jackson's Ramona: From Fact to Fiction." *American Indian Quarterly* 2 (1975): 331–46.
"The Calling of Helen Hunt Jackson." In *Kit Carson's Long Walk: and Other True Tales of San Diego*, by Henry Schwartz. La Mesa, CA: Associated Creative Writers, 1980.
Capelle, Owen. "Ramona." *Land of Sunshine* 1 (1894): 49.
Carr, Jeanne C. "Helen Hunt Jackson." *Woman's Journal* (September 5, 1885): 283.
Chamberlin, J. E. "Homeland and Frontier." *Queen's Quarterly* 89 (1982): 325–37.
Clark, Harry. "Their Pride, Their Manners, and Their Voices: Sources of the Traditional Portrait of the Early Californians." *California Historical Quarterly* 53 (1974): 71–82.
"Colorado Cairn." *American Heritage* 32 (1980): 109.

Cook, Lenora. "NCTE Goes to LA: The Literature of California." *English Journal* 76 (November 1987): 74–78.

Davison, Kenneth E. "President Hayes and the Reform of American Indian Policy." *Ohio History* 82 (1973): 205–14.

del Rio, Juan. "Ramona." *Land of Sunshine* 14 (1901): 4.

DeSantis, V. P. "Helen Hunt Jackson." In *Heritage of '76*, edited by Jay P. Dolan. Notre Dame, IN: University of Notre Dame Press, 1976.

Dillon, Richard. *Humbugs and Heroes; A Gallery of California Pioneers*. Garden City, NY: Doubleday, 1970.

Edselas, F. M. "Visit to Ramona's Home." *Catholic World* 57 (September 1893): 789–802.

Ellis, Millen. "Recommended: Helen Hunt Jackson." *English Journal* 71 (December 1982): 55–56.

Fuller, Theodore W. *San Diego Originals*. Pleasant Hill, CA: California Profiles, 1987.

Gould, E. P. "Author of Ramona." *Education* 21 (November 1900): 182–84.

"Growth of a Legend." In *Southern California Country: An Island on the Land*, by Carey McWilliams. New York: Duell, Sloan & Pearce, 1946.

"H. H. and Saxe Holm." *Critic* 17 (n.s. 14) (November 22, 1890): 263.

"'H. H.' in Southern California." In *Fashions in Literature, and Other Literary and Social Essays & Addresses*, by Charles Dudley Warner. New York: Dodd, Mead, 1902. Reprint. New York: AMS Press, [1969].

Halaas, David Fridtjof. "America's Blurred Vision: A Review Essay on Indian-White Histories." *Colorado Heritage* (1983): 42–47.

Harsha, W. J. "How 'Ramona' Wrote Itself." *Southern Workman* (August 1930): 370–75.

Hawthorne, H. "Summer Day with Ramona." *Delineator* 88 (March 1916): 9 + .

"Helen Fiske Jackson: 'H. H.'" In *The Warner Library*, edited by John W. Cunliffe and Ashley H. Thorndike. New York: Printed at the Knickerbocker Press for the Warner Library Co., 1917.

"Helen Hunt Jackson and 'Ramona'." In *Prefaces*, by James Frank Dobie. Boston: Little, 1975.

"Helen Hunt Jackson: Ramona." In *California Classics: The Creative Literature of the Golden State*, by Lawrence Clark Powell. Los Angeles: W. Ritchie, 1971.

"Helen Hunt Jackson: Ramona." In *Nine American Women of the Nineteenth Century*, by Moira Davison Reynolds. Jefferson, NC: McFarland, 1988.

Higginson, Thomas Wentworth. *Contemporaries*. Boston: Houghton Mifflin, 1899. Reprint. Upper Saddle River, NJ: Literature House, 1970.

_____. *Short Studies of American Authors*. Boston: Lee & Shepard, 1880. Reprint. Enl. Ed. Pottstown, PA: Philadelphia, PA reprinted for the Americanist Press by the Rozov Press, 1967.

"House of Ramona; pictures." *Chautauquan* 31 (June 1900): 297–98.

Howard, R. Palmer. "A Historiography of the Five Civilized Tribes: A Chronological Approach." *Chronicles of Oklahoma* 47 (1969): 312–31.

Hunt, Rockwell Dennis. *California's Stately Hall of Fame*. Stockton: College of the Pacific, 1950.

James, George Wharton. *Old Missions and Mission Indians of California.* Los Angeles: B. R. Baumgardt, 1895.

Jordan, M. B. "Ramona's Home." *Catholic World* 69 (April 1899): 10–16.

Keller, Karl. "Helen Hunt Jackson: Pioneer Activist of Southern California." *Seacoast* 2 (March 1981): 60–65.

Kelly, E. A. "Grandma Varner and Tommy." *Overland Monthly* n.s. 50 (September 1907): 255–59.

Kennedy, Don H. "Ramona's People." *Californians* 4 (1986): 46–49.

McConnell, Virginia. "'H. H.,' Colorado, and the Indian Problem." *Journal of the West* 12 (April 1973): 272–80.

McWilliams, C. "Southern California: Ersatz Mythology." *Common Ground* 6 (Winter 1946): 29–38.

Marsden, Michael T. "A Dedication to the Memory of Helen Hunt Jackson, 1830–1885." *Arizona and the West* 21 (Summer 1979): 108–12.

———. "Helen Hunt Jackson—Docudramatist of the American-Indian." *Markham Review* 10 (Fall 1981): 15–19.

Mathes, Valerie Sherer. "Helen Hunt Jackson." *Masterkey* 55 (1981): 18–21.

———. "Helen Hunt Jackson and the Campaign for Ponca Restitution, 1800–1881." *South Dakota History* 17 (1987): 23–41.

———. "Helen Hunt Jackson and the Ponca Controversy." *Montana—The Magazine of Western History* 39 (1989): 42–53.

———. "Helen Hunt Jackson: Official Agent to the California Mission Indians." *Southern California Quarterly* 63 (1981): 63–82.

Meyer, A. N. "H. H.'s Grave on Cheyenne Mountain." *Critic* 19 (n.s. 16) (September 19, 1891): 142–43.

———. "Removal to Colorado Springs." *Critic* 19 (n.s. 16) (November 21, 1891): 288.

Mirande, Alfredo, and Evangelina Enriquez. *La Chicana: The Mexican-American Woman.* Chicago: University of Chicago Press, 1979.

"Mrs. Helen Hunt Jackson (H. H.)." *Century Magazine* 31 (December 1885): 251–57.

Munger, L. A. "Collector of Other Days." *Hobbies* 46 (August 1941): 102.

Nevins, Allan. "Helen Hunt Jackson, Sentimentalist vs. Realist." *American Scholar* 10 (Summer 1941): 269–85.

Oandasan, William. "Ramona: Reflected Through Indigenous Eyes." *California Courier* (February–March 1986): 7.

Pollitt, Josephine. *Emily Dickinson: The Human Background of Her Poetry.* New York: Harper and Brothers, 1930.

"Portrait." *Mentor* 7 (August 15, 1919): 2.

Pound, L. "Biographical Accuracy and H. H." *American Literature* 2 (January 1931): 418–21.

"Ramona and Helen Hunt Jackson's Centenary." *Publisher's Weekly* 120 (October 10, 1931): 1701–02.

Ranta, Taimi. "Helen Hunt Jackson." In *Dictionary of Literary Biography,* edited by Glenn E. Estes. Detroit: Gale Research, 1985.

Smith, Michael T. "The History of Indian Citizenship." *Great Plains Journal* 10 (1970): 25–35.

Staub, Michael E. "White Moth and Ox: The Friendship of ED with H. H. Jackson." *Dickinson Studies* 68 (1988): 17–25.

Steckmesser, Kent L. "Custer in Fiction." *American West* 1 (1964): 47–52, 63–64.

Stellmann, L. J. "Man Who Inspired Ramona." *Overland Monthly* n.s. 50 (September 1907): 252–55.

Stern, Norton B. "The King of Temecula: Louis Wolf." *Southern California Quarterly* 58 (1976): 63–74.

Thayer, S. H. "Grave of Helen Hunt Jackson." *Overland Monthly* 28 series 2 (August 1896): 198.

"Tradition and the Individual Talent: Helen Hunt Jackson and Emily Dickinson." In *The Nightingale's Burden: Women Poets and American Culture Before 1900*, by Cheryl Walker. Bloomington: Indiana University Press, 1982.

Treleaven, O. C. "Why Ramona Was Not Written in San Juan." *Overland Monthly* n.s. 73 (June 1919): 490–91.

Turner, Frederick W., III. "The Century After a Century of Dishonor: American Conscience and Consciousness." *Massachusetts Review* 16 (Fall 1975): 715–31.

Warner, Charles Dudley. "'H. H.' in Southern California." *Critic* 176 (n.s. 10) (May 14, 1887): 237–38.

Warren, A. "Ramona Tradition." *Saturday Review of Literature* 26 (October 30, 1943): 15.

Watts, Emily Stipes. *The Poetry of American Women from 1632 to 1945.* Austin: University of Texas Press, 1977.

Wey, Auguste. "Sidelights on H. H. Jackson." *Land of Sunshine* 3 (1895): 17.

Whitaker, Rosemary. "Helen Hunt Jackson, (1830–1885)." *Legacy* 3 (September 1986): 56–62.

Wilkman, Nancy. "Ramona Lives!: How a Tale of Love and Death in Old California Changed History and Became One of Our Most Enduring Myths (The Person Behind the H. H. J. Novel *Ramona*)." *Los Angeles* 33 (April 1988): 33 + .

Wiseman, E. F. "Hacienda de Ramona." *Overland Monthly* 33 series 2 (February 1899): 112–21.

Media Materials About Helen Maria Fiske Hunt Jackson

Sound Recordings

Helen Hunt Jackson Fights for the Rights of American Indians. South Holland, IL: Wilcom, Inc. Audio tape cassette; 1 ⅞ ips; stereo.

Ramona. New York: Center for Cassette Studies, Inc. Audio tape cassette; 1 ⅞ ips; 52 min.; mono.

Other Works by Helen Maria Fiske Hunt Jackson

Score

Whelpley, Benjamin. *October's Bright Blue Weather*. Boston: Boston Music Co., 1916. (Words by Helen Hunt Jackson.)

Other Works About Helen Maria Fiske Hunt Jackson

Play

Dillaye, Ina. *Ramona: A Play in Five Acts, Adapted from Helen Hunt Jackson's Indian Novel*. Syracuse, NY: F. Le C. Dillaye, 1887.

Theses

Ellicott, Karen Sue. "The Portrayal of the American Indian Woman in a Select Group of American Novels." Ph.D. diss., University of Minnesota, 1979.

Friend, Ruth Ellen. "Helen Hunt Jackson: A Critical Study." Ph.D. diss., Kent State University, 1985.

Martin, Minerva L. "Helen Hunt in Relation to Her Time." Ph.D. diss., Louisiana State University and Agricultural and Mechanical College, 1940.

Matis, Marilyn Elaine. "'We Demand the Flame': The Assembly of Emily Dickinson's Female Audience (Massachusetts)." Ph.D. diss., State University of New York at Buffalo, 1983.

Maynard, David Eugene. "The Complete Production of a Documentary Film Called 'A Visit with Helen Jackson'." Ed.D diss., University of Northern Colorado, 1980.

Odell, Ruth. "Helen Hunt Jackson and Her Times." Ph.D. diss., University of Nebraska-Lincoln, 1937.

Snider, John Michael. "The Treatment of American Indians in Selected American Literature: A Radical Critique." Ph.D. diss., University of Illinois at Urbana-Champaign, 1983.

Walker, Cheryl Lawson. "The Women's Tradition in American Poetry." Ph.D. diss., Brandeis University, 1973.

Primary Source Materials Relating to Helen Maria Fiske Hunt Jackson

Helen Hunt Jackson. Papers. 1837–1884. Extent of collection: 280 items. Finding aids: Not listed. Location: Jones Library, 43 Amity St., Amherst, Massachusetts 01002. Scope of collection: Letters, manuscripts, biographical, bibliographical and critical studies and most of Jackson's published works.

Helen Maria (Fiske) Hunt Jackson. Papers. 1828–1886. Extent of collection: 7 ft.

Finding aids: Unpublished finding aid in repository. Location: Colorado College Library, 1021 N. Cascade Avenue, Colorado Springs, Colorado 80903. Scope of collection: Correspondence, notes, drafts, writings, printed material, photos and other papers, relating to Jackson's early years, family life, writing career and role as special commissioner on Native American affairs. Includes partial manuscript of novel *Ramona*.

Helen Maria (Fiske) Hunt Jackson. Papers. 1852–1887. Extent: 169 items. Finding aids: Item cards in manuscript catalog. Location: Huntington Library, 1151 Oxford Rd., San Marino, California 91108. Scope of collection: Correspondence from Jackson to other literary figures, generally discussing her writing and opinions, and 24 of her literary manuscripts.

Helen Maria Fiske Hunt Jackson. Papers. 1873. Extent of collection: 1 folder. Finding aids: Unpublished finding aid. Location: Schlesinger Library, Radcliffe College, Cambridge, Massachusetts 02138. Scope of collection: Photograph of Jackson, unsigned sonnet entitled "Ariadne's Farewell," and note by Thomas Wentworth Higginson, her friend and tutor, dating photograph at 1873.

Helen Maria (Fiske) Hunt Jackson. Papers. No date. Extent of collection: 2 folders. Finding aids: No guide. Location: New York Public Library, Manuscripts and Archives, Fifth Avenue and 42nd St., New York, New York 10018. Scope of collection: Incomplete manuscript of unpublished novel *Elspeth Dynor*; clippings, primarily of book reviews from *New York Times* concerning biographical work about Jackson; and sales catalogs, including some of her works and work in which she was interested.

Helen Maria (Fiske) Hunt Jackson. Papers. No date. Extent of collection: 1 portfolio. Finding aids: No guide. Location: University of California, Berkeley, Bancroft Library, Berkeley, California 94720. Scope of collection: Correspondence and other material.

33. *Barbara Jordan*
(1936–   )

Legislator; educator; orator; lawyer; and advocate for civil rights

BIOGRAPHICAL INFORMATION

Chronological Biography

Born February 21, 1936, in Houston, Texas, last of three daughters of Arlyne (Patten) and the Reverend Benjamin M. Jordan. Family lived with paternal grandfather, Charles Jordan, and his wife in fifth ward of Houston.

Church activities were extremely important to Jordan family and all attended Good Hope Missionary Baptist Church.

1938-1939?: Father became Baptist minister; initial church, First Greater Pleasant Hill Baptist Church, was in Houston Heights. Congregation was small and all Jordan children were expected to participate in all church activities. With older sister Bennie, sang with Count Sisters at church and often recited passages; favorite was James Weldon Johnson's "The Creation." **1941-1948?:** Attended Houston Public Schools. **1948-1952:** Attended Phillis Wheatley High School, named after first slave and second woman to publish book of poetry in America. On "Career Day," 1949-1950, Edith Spurlock Sampson was guest speaker at school. Ms. Sampson, a Chicago lawyer, was first black woman to receive Masters of Law degree at Loyola University; she later became a judge. Because of presentation, Jordan decided to become lawyer. Member of various school clubs and president of Honor Society. **June 1952:** Chosen as "Girl of the Year" of Phillis Wheatley High School by national black sorority Zeta Phi Beta. Organization chose most outstanding black senior girl from each of participating schools. Graduated in top five percent of class. **July 3, 1952:** Won first prize in Ushers Oratorical State Contest in Waco, Texas. Before winning state competition, had won at local, regional and district levels of contest. **July 25, 1952:** In Chicago, representing state of Texas, won first prize in National Ushers Convention Oratorical Contest. Winning speech, entitled "Is the Necessity for a Higher Education More in Demand Today than a Decade Ago?," was same one that won her state competition. Received $200 scholarship to school of choice and literary medal to add to her collection of other oratorical contest medals. **1952:** Won Julius Levy Oratorical Contest Award. **September 1952-June 1956:** Entered Texas Southern University, all-black institution in Houston. Ran for freshman class president, but it was essentially a popularity contest and she lost to male opponent. After losing election decided that class politics was not to her liking; she returned to familiarity of oratorical contests. Joined Sigma Pi Alpha Forensic and Dialectical Symposium and university debating team. Team won series of championships. **1954:** Awarded "The Most Valuable Participant" in Southern Intercollegiate Forensic Conference at Baylor University, first integrated university debating contest. Joined Delta Sigma Theta Sorority and later became dean of pledges. Was elected member-at-large to student council. Served as editor of university yearbook in senior year; graduated magna cum laude with Bachelor of Arts in political science and history. **September 1956-August 1959:** With encouragement and financial support of family, applied and was accepted to Boston University Law School. Being one of only two black women in program, had to work twice as hard to achieve recognition because of race and lack of connections. Organized study group with other black law students. **June 1959:** Received LL.B. from Boston University. Stayed on in

Boston for summer and passed Massachusetts Bar. Feeling she did not "fit in" in Boston, returned home to Houston at end of summer. **Late 1959:** Passed Texas Bar and was able to practice law in home state. Ran law practice from family's dining room table. Dealt with real estate to domestic affairs to business matters. Many of clients were church members and neighbors. Became member of American Bar Association and Houston Lawyers Association, an all-black organization. **1960:** Since she was not getting great deal of business as lawyer, during free time she aided in Harris County Democrats' local campaign for John F. Kennedy/Lyndon B. Johnson presidential ticket. Did volunteer work addressing envelopes, etc., until one evening speaker for campaign cancelled and she volunteered to speak at rally. Realizing her talents had previously been wasted, she was given directorship of enlisting vote in Houston's black community. Launched person-per-block precinct drive and was very successful, her precincts having highest voting record during election. Continued to speak on behalf of Harris County Democrats and was swept up by excitment of politics. She was becoming a phenomenon in Houston — an articulate black woman lawyer. **Spring 1961:** Opened law office at 4100 Lyons Avenue in Houston with Asbury Butler. Continued to work for Harris County Democrats and was encouraged by them to seek political career. **February 3, 1962:** Announced candidacy for Democratic nomination for state representative, position ten. Thrust of campaign was on social issues, especially welfare and reform. **1962:** Elected president of Houston Lawyers Association, only woman member and one of youngest at the age of 26. Elected second vice president of the Harris County Democrats. Became board member of Houston Council on Human Rights. Lost race for state representative to Willis Whatley. **January 25, 1964:** Announced candidacy for Texas legislature, position ten. **1964:** Appointed administrative assistant to Harris County Judge Bill Elliott, first black to be appointed to such a high level county position. **1965:** With Supreme Court "One-Man-One-Vote" decision, reapportionment was mandated in state of Texas. She was now living in new state senatorial district 11. **February 4, 1966:** With no encumbent in new 11th district, decided to file as candidate for state senate, opposing another Democrat, J. C. Whitfield. **November 1966:** Elected to state senate with 80 percent of vote. **1966:** Crescent Foundation, private, non-profit corporation, selected her as coordinator of special project to aid unemployed. **January 10, 1967:** Sworn in as state senator, first black to sit in Texas state senate since 1883. During lottery at senate session, received only two-year term. **February 1967:** Invited to White House by President Johnson to preview civil rights message and proposed fair housing legislation. Chosen to attend over other prominent black leaders of day since she already had reputation as level-headed politician. **May 27, 1967:** Voted outstanding freshman senator of Texas state senate. **Fall 1967:** Appointed vice chair of Democratic Voter Registration Drive in Texas. **1967:** Chaired

Labor and Management Relations Committee in state senate; held position throughout her two terms.   **January 1968:** Appointed by President Johnson to Presidential Commission on Income Maintenance Problems.   **November 1968:** Ran unopposed in 11th district; re-elected to four-year term in state senate.   **1968:** Became member of Environmental Health Committee of Council of State Governments.   **1968–1972:** During two terms as Texas state senator, one-half of her bills were enacted into law. Aided in establishment of Texas Fair Employment Practice Commission, chaired Urban Affairs Study Committee, served as vice chair of Legislature, Congressional and Judicial Committee and member of several committees ranging from education to state affairs.   **September 1970:** Named convention secretary of Texas State Democratic Convention, first black ever appointed to position; eventually named permanent secretary.   **December 1970:** Cited by *Harper's Bazaar* as one of "One Hundred Women in Touch with Our Time."   **February 1971:** Cosponsored bill to add amendment to state constitution to guarantee equal rights for women; passed unanimously by Texas senate.   **April 1971:** Successfully sponsored bill to create State Department of Community Affairs in Texas.   **May 1971:** Due to 1970 Census, redistricting of U.S. Congressional districts in Texas was mandated. Named vice chair of Redistricting Subcommittee.   **June 1971:** Redistricting measures suggested by committee were passed; she was now living in new 18th congressional district.   **October 1, 1971:** Mayor Louie Welch of Houston proclaimed October 1st as "Barbara Jordan Appreciation Day."   **October 1971:** President Johnson attended fundraiser dinner for her campaign for U.S. House of Representatives.   **March 28, 1972:** Elected president pro-tempore of Texas senate. Served as assistant to lieutenant governor and presiding officer of state senate, first black woman in U.S. history to preside over legislative body.   **May 6, 1972:** Won 80 percent of vote in Democratic primary for seat in U.S. House of Representatives.   **June 10, 1972:** Traditionally, president pro-tempore of Texas senate becomes "Governor for a Day" when both governor and lieutenant governor are out of state. She was given this honor and was therefore first black woman "governor" in United States. "Governor Barbara Jordan Day" declared by Houston's Mayor Louie Welch.   **June 11, 1972:** Father, who had been ill with heart problems, dried of stroke suffered minutes after seeing his daughter sworn in as "governor" of Texas. Family established Reverend Benjamin M. Jordan Memorial Scholarship Fund.   **September 1972:** Appointed vice-chair of State Democratic Executive Committee.   **November 1972:** Won 18th district of U.S. House of Representatives seat by landslide, winning with 81 percent of vote. She and Andrew Young of Georgia were first black representatives from South since 1901; she was first black woman from deep South to sit in House. As freshman Congresswoman, named fellow of Institute of Politics in John F. Kennedy School of Government at Harvard University. Attended classes at Institute with other freshmen representatives to orientate themselves to Congress and to prepare for up-coming congressional session. **1972–1978:** During her two terms in Congress, held one of highest voting records and sponsored or cosponsored more than 30 bills that were eventually enacted into law. **January 3, 1973:** Sworn into U.S. House of Representatives from 18th district of Texas. Elected secretary of Texas delegation. **January 1973:** With aid of President Johnson, selected to become member of House Committee on the Judiciary. **October 1973:** After resignation of Vice President Agnew, Judiciary Committee had to approve appointment of Gerald R. Ford as vice president. She was against nomination based on his poor civil rights record, and believed he was insensitive to poor, was too "pro–Pentagon" and would be unable to provide leadership. **October 31, 1973:** Testified at House hearing on Special Prosecutor and Watergate Grand Jury Legislation in support of creating permanent system for special judicial prosecutor. **July 25, 1974:** At House Judiciary Committee Hearings on impeachment of President Nixon, each member of committee was to give 15 minute statement. Spoke on second day of televised hearings. After culling notes on study of constitutional history and judicial opinion, prepared statement that began with now-famous line, "My faith in the Constitution is whole, it is complete, it is total. I am not going to sit here and be an idle spectator . . ." Gave most electrifying and memorable speech of all participants and became national figure overnight. Her photo was featured in *Time* and *Newsweek*; *Washington Post* printed complete text of her speech following day, and she was inundated with invitations to speak at all kinds of events. **August 21, 1974:** Invited to White House by President Ford as member of Black Congressional Caucus. **September 1974:** Visited Mainland China with Congressional delegation, only freshman member on trip. **November 1974:** Won second Congressional race with almost 85 percent of vote. **December 1974:** Assigned to 94th Congress Government Operations Committee and to Democratic Compliance Review Commission. Appointed first black woman "at-large" member of Steering and Policy Committee of Democratic Caucus; also appointed to Special Task Force of 94th Congress. **1974:** Selected by *World Almanac* as "One of the 25 Most Influential Women in America." Remained on list for 12 consecutive years. **February 26, 1975:** Witness at House hearing on extension of Voting Rights Act. Supported extension of act to expand protection of minorities' rights, particularly Spanish-speaking Americans; amendment was enacted into law. **February 1975:** Specially commissioned portrait of her was unveiled in Texas Senate Chambers. **May 1975:** Received honorary degree from alma mater, Texas Southern University. Voted one of "Women of the Year" by *Ladies' Home Journal.* Introduced bill to abolish fair-trade laws; bill was enacted into law in December. **November 10, 1975:** Addressed conference at Lyndon B. Johnson School of Public Affairs at University of Texas at Austin in honor of International Women's Year; summarized her thoughts on injustices done to women. **November 1975:** Named one of "Six Women Who Could Be President" in *Redbook.* **1975:** Selected "Democratic Woman of the Year" by Women's National Democratic Club. *Time* selected her as one of "Ten Women of the Year," only black on list. Received Faith in Humanity Award from National Council of Jewish Women. **March 11, 1976:** Testified at House hearing of Law Enforcement Assistance Administration; suggested improvements and reorganization for administration and encouraged strengthening of civil rights enforcement provisions. Amendment was enacted into law. **July 12, 1976:** Keynote speaker at Democratic National Convention held at Madison Square Garden in New York City, first black woman keynoter ever to address convention. Again, like Watergate hearing statement of two years previous, mesmerized audience and challenged party to reevaluate and to prove itself to American public. **November 1976:** Re-elected to third term in Congress. **May 11, 1977:** Witness at House hearing on President's hospital cost containment proposal. Requested that truth in hospital billing act be included in proposal. **November 19, 1977:** Keynote speaker at National Women's Conference. **December 10, 1977:** Announced she would not seek re-election to Congress. **January 1978:** *Good Housekeeping* named her one of "10 Most Admired Women." **March 1978:** Rated number one in performance of Congresswomen by *Redbook.* **April 1978:** Donated personal and career papers to Texas Southern University. **May 18, 1978:** Supported Equal Rights Admendment extension to March 22, 1986. **October 1979:** Selected as first choice in poll conducted by *Redbook* on "Women Who Could Be Appointed to the Supreme Court." **November 1979:** *Ladies' Home Journal* voted her as one of "Women of the Decade." **1979:** Accepted LBJ Public Service Professorship at Lyndon B. Johnson School of Public Affairs, University of Texas at Austin. With Shelby Hearon, wrote *Barbara Jordan: A Self-Portrait.* Passed District of Columbia Bar. Became member of Presidential Advisory Board on Ambassadorial Appointments and remained so until 1981. Member of board of directors of Mead Corporation and of Texas Commerce Bancshares Inc. **1980:** Named to Board of Directors of *Washington Post.* **Early 1980s:** Began experiencing mobility problems, but continued all activities. **July 1981:** Hearings officer for National Institute of Education Hearings on Minimum Competency Testing. Member of executive committee of National Democratic Party Council. **July 1982:** Public Broadcasting System premiered television series entitled "Crisis to Crisis with Barbara Jordan" which she hosted. **1982–:** LBJ Centennial Chair in National Policy in Lyndon B. Johnson School of Public Affairs at University of Texas at Austin. **September 13, 1984:** Inducted into Texas Women's Hall of Fame at Lyndon B. Johnson Presidential Library at Austin, sponsored by Governor's Commission for Women. **1984:** Recipient of Eleanor Roosevelt Humanities Award. Voted "Best Living Orator" by International Platform

Association. Given distinguished Alumnus Award by Association of State Colleges and Universities. Shared podium with President Reagan at National Prayer Breakfast. Member of U.S. Trilateral Commission. Coauthored *Local Government Election Systems* with Terrell Blodgett. **September 1985:** Appointed by secretary-general of United Nations to serve on 11 member panel to conduct hearings on role of transnational corporations in South Africa and Namibia. **1985:** Asked to attend Democratic Party Retreat. Party had suffered from 1984 elections and wanted her guidance and wisdom to help re-evaluate party and ponder its future. Member of Board of Directors of Public Broadcasting System. **1986:** Coedited *The Great Society: A Twenty-Year Critique* with Elspeth Rostow. **March 5, 1987:** Recipient of twenty-first Charles Evans Hughes Gold Medal of National Conference of Christians and Jews. **September 21, 1987:** Testified at Senate hearings on nomination of Robert H. Bork to be associate justice of U.S. Supreme Court; presented opposition to nomination based on his interpretation of constitutional protections. **May 1989:** Awarded Hubert H. Humphrey Civil Rights Award at Leadership Conference on Civil Rights. Supported bill sponsored by Senator Edward M. Kennedy to make states remove barriers to voter registration by assessing registration rules in each state. **August 26, 1990:** Inducted into National Women's Hall of Fame in Seneca Falls, NY. **July 13, 1992:** Spoke at Democratic party's national convention in Madison Square Garden, New York, New York. Received many honors and awards throughout her career. Fund for Gifted Students was established in her name at Lyndon B. Johnson School of Public Affairs at University of Texas at Austin. Received more than 29 honorary doctorate degrees from Harvard, Princeton, Notre Dame, William and Mary, and others. Member of National Association for the Advancement of Colored People (NAACP), Southern Regional Council, Texas Trial Lawyers Association, Houston Bar Association and American Management Association. One of founders and member of board of directors of People for the American Way. Member of board of directors of Federal Home Mortgage Loan Corporation and board of trustees of Henry J. Kaiser Family Foundation. Appointed by Texas Governor Ann Richards as her advisor on ethics in government.

Background Information

Parents: Arlyne (Patten) and the Reverend Benjamin M. Jordan. Mother was volunteer worker at family church. Father, in addition to being minister, was warehouse clerk at Houston Terminal Warehouse and Cold Storage. **Siblings:** Two (Bennie [Jordan] Creswell, Rose Mary [Jordan] McGowan). **Children:** None. **Influences:** None. **Ethnicity:** African American. **Also known as:** None known. **Historical sites, landmarks, etc.:** Governor's

Commission for Women, State Capitol, P.O. Box 12428, Austin, Texas. Jordan is honoree in Hall of Fame in Public Service Category; High School named in her honor: Barbara Jordan High School for Careers, 5800 Eastex Freeway, Houston, Texas; Barbara Jordan Campus is evening campus for Minority Transfer Opportunities Program: Houston Community College System, 800 Eastex Freeway; National Women's Hall of Fame, 76 Fall Street, Seneca Falls, New York. Jordan is honoree in Hall of Fame; Orator's Hall of Fame, International Platform Association, P.O. Box 250, Winnetka, Illinois. Jordan is honoree in Hall of Fame.

BIBLIOGRAPHICAL INFORMATION

Biographical Sketches About Barbara Jordan

Crawford, Ann Fears, and Crystal Sasse Ragsdale. *Women in Texas: Their Lives, Their Experiences, Their Accomplishments.* Burnet, Texas: Eakin, 1982.

Greenbaum, Louise G. *Contributions of Women: Politics and Government.* Minneapolis: Dillon, 1977.

May, Hal, and Susan M. Trosky, eds. *Contemporary Authors.* Detroit: Gale Research, 1988.

Moritz, Charles, ed. *Current Biography Yearbook 1974.* New York: H. W. Wilson Company, 1974.

Ragsdale, Bruce A., and Joel D. Trease. *Black Americans in Congress 1870–1989.* Washington, D. C.: GPO, 1990.

Skjervold, Christian K., et al. *Minneapolis Multi-Ethnic Curriculum Project— Power Unit.* Minneapolis: Minneapolis Public Schools Department of Intergroup Education, 1975. [ED183482]

Smith, Jessie Carney, ed. *Notable Black American Women.* Detroit: Gale Research, 1992.

Books by Barbara Jordan

Jordan, Barbara, and Shelby Hearon. *Barbara Jordan: A Self-Portrait.* Garden City, NY: Doubleday, 1979.

————, and Elspeth Rostow, eds. *The Great Society: A Twenty-Year Critique.* Austin: Lyndon B. Johnson Library and Lyndon B. Johnson School of Public Affairs, University of Texas at Austin, 1986.

Blodgett, Terrell, and Barbara Jordan. *Local Government Election Systems.* Policy Research Project Series #62. Austin: Lyndon B. Johnson School of Public Affairs, University of Texas at Austin, 1984.

Books About Barbara Jordan

Bryant, Ira Babington. *Barbara Charline Jordan: From the Ghetto to the Capitol.*
Houston: D. Armstrong Company, 1977.
Haskins, James S. *Barbara Jordan.* New York: Dial, 1977.
Jacobs, Linda. *Barbara Jordan: Keeping Faith.* St. Paul, MN: EMC Corporation, 1978.
Roberts, Naurice. *Barbara Jordan: The Great Lady From Texas.* Chicago: Children's Press, 1984.

Shorter Works by Barbara Jordan

"Black Voices of the South." *Ebony* 26 (August 1971): 50–54.
"How I Got There: Staying Power." *Atlantic* 235 (March 1975): 38–39.
"If Comprehensive Freedom Is Mandated, Will It Stifle Talent?" *Center Magazine* 12 (March–April 1979): 9.
"Impact of Emerging Public Policy on Educational Planning." In *Impact of Emerging Public Policy on Educational Planning.* New York: New York College Entrance Examination Board, 1975. [ED126600]
"Individual Rights, Social Responsibility." *Rights & Responsibilities* (November 1978): 9–17.
"An Overview of Federal Concerns in Health Care and Preventive Medicine." *Journal of School Health* 48 (January 1978): 643–45.
"Reducing American Cynicism: Excerpts from Address." *USA Today* 108 (October 1979): 2–3.
"Reflections on the Constitution." *Houston Lawyer* 25 (September–October 1987): 8–10.
"Role of the Black Press." *Ebony* 6 (July 5, 1977): 25–26.
"Still Two Nations—One Black, One White." *Human Rights* 13 (Fall 1985): 21.
"Texts of Keynote Addresses [at the Democratic National Convention, New York, New York July 12–15, 1976] John Glenn and Barbara Jordan." *Congressional Quarterly Weekly Report* 34 (July 17, 1976): 1930–32.
"Who Then Will Speak for the Common Good?" *Vital Speeches* 42 (August 15, 1976): 645–46.

Shorter Works About Barbara Jordan

Alpern, D. M., and E. Cleft. "After the Fall." *Newsweek* 88 (November 15, 1976): 34–35.
"Barbara Jordan: Another Texas First." *Sepia* 15 (August 1966): 8–11.
"Barbara Jordan, Congresswoman; Interview." *Newsweek* 88 (July 4, 1976): 70.
"Barbara Jordan, 52: 3-Term Texas Congresswoman and Professor." *Life* 11 (April 4, 1988): 63.
"Barbara Jordan—Political Rising Star." *U.S. News & World Report* 80 (February 9, 1976): 43–44.
"Barbara Jordan Receives Outstanding Alumnus Award." *Jet* 67 (December 24, 1984): 23.

"Barbara Jordan's Vision of America." *Ebony* 31 (September 1976): 150–51.

Bennett, Lerone. *Before the Mayflower: A History of Black America.* New York: Penguin, 1984.

————. "Black Firsts in Politics, Entertainment, Sports and Other Fields." *Ebony* 37 (March 1982): 128–33.

"Blacks Score Well in Democratic Primary Elections." *Jet* 42 (May 25, 1972): 6–7.

Booker, S. "Washington Notebook." *Ebony* 33 (March 1978): 22.

Bowman, Kathleen. "New Women in Politics." *Creative Education* (1976): 26–33.

Brown, Warren. "U.S. Congress Gets Three New Black Lawmakers." *Jet* 43 (November 3, 1972): 2–26.

————. "Women Challenge System in Bids for Congress Seats." *Jet* 43 (September 28, 1972): 12–16.

Browne, Ray B., ed. *Contemporary Heroes and Heroines.* Detroit: Gale Research, 1990.

Broyles, William. "Making of Barbara Jordan." *Texas Monthly* 4 (October 1976): 127.

Brubaker, Robert L., ed. *Contemporary Issues Criticism.* Detroit: Gale Research, 1984.

Burke, Joan Martin. *Civil Rights: A Current Guide to the People, Organizations and Events.* New York: R. R. Bowker, 1974.

Carpenter, Liz. "Isn't It Time to Have a Woman on the Supreme Court?" *Redbook* 153 (October 1979): 27, 178–85.

————. "On My Mind — Barbara Jordan Talks About Ethics, Optimism and Hard Choices in Government." *Ms.* 13 (April 1985): 75–76 + .

————. "Six Women Who Could be President." *Redbook* 146 (November 1975): 93 + .

Chamberlin, Hope. *A Minority of Members: Women in the U.S. Congress.* New York: Praeger, 1973.

Diamonstein, Barbaralee D. *Open Secrets: Ninety-Four Women in Touch with Our Time.* New York: Viking, 1970.

Dowling, E., ed. "Barbara Jordan: Brains + Voice = Power: Interview." *Senior Scholastic* 110 (October 6, 1977): 8–10.

"Dozen Who Made a Difference." *Time* 107 (January 5, 1976): 19.

Emerson, Frank E. "Jordan's Rising Tide." *Encore* 4 (January 20, 1975): 32–33.

"Five Prominent Americans Reflect on the Constitution." In *The Constitution: Perspectives on Contemporary American Democracy.* Arlington, VA: Close Up Foundation, 1986. [ED275619]

Frye, Jerry K., and Franklin B. Krohn. "An Analysis of Barbara Jordan's 1976 Keynote Address." *Journal of Applied Communications Research* 5 (November 1977): 73–82.

Gant, Liz. "Barbara Jordan: Who Is She and What Is She to You?" *Essence* 8 (September 1977): 62–63 + .

Gates, D., et al. "Jordan Is Immune to the Political Bug." *Newsweek* 102 (December 19, 1983): 17 + .

"Gay Northeasterns Honor Congresswoman Jordan in Confab in Philadelphia." *Jet* 44 (May 31, 1973): 17.

Giddings, Paula. "Barbara Jordan: When the Applause Dies Down." *Encore* 8 (May 7, 1979): 50–51.

———. "Will the Real Barbara Jordan Please Stand." *Encore* 6 (May 9, 1977): 14–19.

Greenfield, M. "New Lone Star of Texas." *Newsweek* 85 (March 3, 1975): 31.

Henry, David. "Barbara Jordan: (1936–), Member of Congress from Texas, Public Advocate." In *American Orators of the Twentieth Century: Critical Studies and Sources,* edited by Bernard K. Duffy and Halford R. Ryan. New York: Greenwood, 1987.

"Interview with Barbara Jordan." *Educational Evaluation and Policy Analysis* 3 (November–December 1981): 79–82.

Jackson, George F. *Black Women, Makers of History: A Portrait.* Oakland, CA: GRT Book Printing, 1975.

"Jimmy's Talent File." *Time* 108 (December 20, 1976): 13.

"Jordan Elected into Orator's Hall of Fame." *Jet* 66 (July 30, 1984): 22.

"Jordan Reads Her Compass." *Newsweek* 90 (December 19, 1977): 23.

"Jordan: Seeking the Power Points." *Newsweek* 84 (November 4, 1974): 22.

Keerdoja, E., and G. Henry. "Barbara Jordan, College Teacher." *Newsweek* 98 (August 3, 1981): 5 +.

"Keynoters: Glenn and Jordan." *National Review* 28 (August 6, 1976): 830–31.

Kotz, M. L. "Meet the Real Barbara Jordan." *Good Housekeeping* 186 (January 1978): 44 +.

"Ladies' Home Journal Women of the Year." *Ladies' Home Journal* 92 (May 1975): 39.

Larkins, Kathy, Al Coombes, and Stephen Decatur, comps. "Women in the '80s." *Ladies' Home Journal* 96 (November 1979): 187–94.

Lasher, Patricia. *Texas Women: Interviews and Images.* Austin, TX: Shoal Creek, 1980.

Lee, Essie E. *Women in Congress.* New York: Messner, 1979.

Lerner, Gerda. *Black Women in White America: A Documentary History.* New York: Vintage, 1973.

McReynolds, Ginny. *Women in Power.* Milwaukee: Raintree, 1979.

Manning, Marable. "The Post-Movement Reaction: Thoughts on Black Politics." *Southern Exposure* 7 (1979): 60–64.

Martin, Donald R., and Vicky Gordon Martin. "Barbara Jordan's Symbolic Use of Language in the Keynote Address to the National Women's Conference. [November 19, 1977]." *Southern Speech Communication Journal* 49 (1984): 319–30.

Minimum Competency Testing Clarification Hearing (July 8–10, 1981). Washington, D. C.: National Institute of Education, 1981. [ED215000- 215002]

Murchland, Bernard. "The Union 200 Years Later." In *Reflections on America,* edited by Robert Lehman. Dayton: Charles F. Kettering Foundation, 1987. [ED282808]

Nocera, Joseph. "Failure of Barbara Jordan's Success." *Washington Monthly* 11 (March 1979): 36–43.

Parramore, Barbara, ed. "Why Should There be Social Studies in the Elementary School?" *Social Education* 45 (October 1981): 430–35.

Pederson, Lucille M. *Pedagogical Methods of Teaching "Women in Public Speaking."* 1979. [ED188272]

Phillips, B. J., ed. "Recognizing the Gentleladies of the Judiciary Committee." *Ms.* 3 (November 1974): 70–73.

Pincus, Ann. "How the Women in Congress Use Their Power." *Redbook* 150 (March 1978): 114–15, 178–88.

Preece, H. "Two New Black 'First' Ladies in Congress." *Sepia* 21 (October 1972): 47–48 + .

Radin, Beryl A., and Hoyt H. Purvis, eds. *Women in Public Life: Report of a Conference.* Austin: Lyndon B. Johnson School of Public Affairs, University of Texas at Austin, 1976. [ED164641]

Remarkable American Women, 1776–1976. New York: Time, Inc., 1976.

"Representative Barbara Jordan Named to Special House Task Force." *Jet* 47 (January 2, 1975): 6.

"Representative Jordan Regarded with Immense Respect." *Biography News* 1 (August 1974): 910.

"Representative Jordan Stuns Many with Her 'Retirement' Plan." *Jet* 53 (December 29, 1977): 14.

Robinson, Louie. "Woman Lawmakers on the Move." *Ebony* 27 (October 1972): 48–56.

Romero, Patricia W. *In Black America.* New York: Books Inc., 1969.

Ross, I. "Barbara Jordan—New Voice in Washington." *Reader's Digest* 110 (February 1977): 148–52.

Ryan, Halford Ross. *American Rhetoric from Roosevelt to Reagan: A Collection of Speeches and Critical Essays.* Prospect Heights, IL: Waveland, 1983.

Sanders, Charles L. "Barbara Jordan: Texan Is a New Power on Capitol Hill." *Ebony* 30 (February 1975): 136–42.

Schoenebaum, Eleanora W., ed. *Political Profiles: The Nixon/Ford Years.* New York: Facts on File, 1979.

"A Second Surprising Reader's Poll." *People Weekly* 13 (March 24, 1980): 27–38.

"Self-Portrait at 200." *Newsweek* 88 (July 4, 1976): 70.

Shapiro, Walter. "What Does This Woman Want?" *Texas Monthly* 4 (October 1976): 134.

"Sight for the Eyes of Texas." *Newsweek* 79 (May 22, 1972): 34–35.

Stevens, W. K. "Commanding Presence, Political Past." *New York Times Biography Service* 10 (February 1979): 202–03.

Stineman, Esther F. *American Political Women: Contemporary and Historical Profiles.* Englewood, CO: Libraries Unlimited, 1980.

Styer, Sandra. "Exploring Women's Political Careers Through Biographies." *Social Studies* 73 (July/August 1982): 175–77.

"10 Most Admired Women." *Good Housekeeping* 186 (January 1978): 28–30.

Thompson, Wayne N. "Barbara Jordan's Keynote Address: Fulfilling Dual and Conflicting Purposes." *Central States Speech Journal* 30 (August 1979): 272–77.

_____. "Barbara Jordan's Keynote Address: The Juxtaposition of Contradictory Values." *Southern Speech Communication Journal* 44 (Spring 1979): 223–32.
"Two Blacks to Help Choose U.S. Diplomats." *Jet* 56 (April 19, 1979): 12.
"200 Faces for the Future." *Time* 104 (July 15, 1974): 52.
"Veep Jordan." *People Weekly* 5 (June 28, 1976): 46.
"Women in Government: A Slim Past, But a Strong Future." *Ebony* 32 (August 1977): 89–92.
"Women Who Make State Laws." *Ebony* 21 (September 1967): 27–29.
"Words of the Week." *Jet* 55 (March 8, 1979): 30.
Young, Margaret B. *Black American Leaders*. New York: Watts, 1969.
"Young Builders of America." *U.S. News & World Report* 80 (February 9, 1976): 43.

Other Works About Barbara Jordan

Theses

House, Robert Gerald. "An Analysis of Richard M. Weaver's Philosophy and Methodology as Applied to Two of Barbara Jordan's Speeches." Master's thesis, University of North Texas, 1979.

Media Materials About Barbara Jordan

Films

Meet the Negro Texan. San Antonio: Institute of Texan Cultures, 1968. 16mm film; 5 min.; optical sound; color.

Sound Recordings

Barbara Jordan [in Headliner II Series]. St. Paul, MN: EMC Corporation. Audio tape cassette.
Barbara Jordan: A Self Portrait. Washington, D. C.: Library of Congress, Division for the Blind and Physically Handicapped. 4-track audio tape; stereo.
A Profile of Barbara Jordan. Danbury, CT: Encyclopedia Americana/CBS News Audio Resource Library, 1979. Vital History cassette. June 1979, no. 1. 4-track audio tape; stereo.

Video Recordings

Crisis to Crisis with Barbara Jordan. PBS Television Series. Debuted July 1982.
The Dick Cavett Show: Barbara Jordan. New York: Daphne Productions, 1979. Videocassette; 29 min.; ¾ inch; U-Matic; color.
Interview with Barbara Jordan. Washington, D. C.: PBS Video, 1980. Videocassette; 30 min.; ¾ inch; color.
The MacNeil/Lehrer Report: Interview with Barbara Jordan. New York: Educational Broadcasting Corporation, 1978. Videocassette; 29 min.; ¾ inch; color.
Tribute from Texas. Austin: Department of Radio-Television-Film, College of Communication, University of Texas at Austin, 1983. Videocassette; 50 min.; ¾ inch; U-Matic; stereo; color.

Who's Keeping Score Day 1-3. Washington, D. C.: National Institute of Education, 1981. Videocassette; 59 min.; ¾ or ½ inch; color.

Primary Source Materials Relating to Barbara Jordan

Barbara Jordan Archives Collection. Extent of collection: Not listed. Finding aids: Not listed. Location: Texas Southern University Library, 3201 Wheeler, Houston, Texas 77004. Scope of collection: Letters, speeches, films, video segments and memorabilia.

Candidates for Public Office. Campaign Materials. 1966–1979 (inclusive). Extent of collection: .5 lin. ft. Finding aids: Unpublished finding aid. Location: Schlesinger Library, Radcliffe College, Cambridge, Massachusetts 02138. Scope of collection: Flyers, leaflets, bumper stickers, photographs, buttons, and other campaign materials of women running for political office in United States.

Edith Spurlock Sampson. Papers. 1927–1979 (inclusive), 1934–1979 (bulk). Extent of collection: 7 lin. ft. Finding aids: Unpublished finding aid. Location: Schlesinger Library, Radcliffe College, Cambridge, Massachusetts 02138. Scope of collection: Bulk of collection pertains to Sampson's activities as judge.

Houston Public Library. Houston Metropolitan Research Center. Newspaper Clippings. Extent of collection: ca. 15 ft. Finding aids: Not listed. Location: Houston Public Library, Houston Metropolitan Research Center, 500 McKinney, Houston, Texas 77002. Scope of collection: Includes newspaper clippings on Jordan.

Jeannine Dobbs. Class Essays. 1977. Extent of collection: 2 folders. Finding aids: Unpublished finding aid. Location: Schlesinger Library, Radcliffe College, Cambridge, Massachusetts 02138. Scope of collection: Class essays on notable American women including Jordan.

Oral History Collection. Extent of collection: 1 item. Finding aids: Oral History Program 25th Anniversary Catalog, 1964–1989. Location: University of North Texas, Box 5188, North Texas Station, Denton, Texas 76203. Scope of collection: Interview with Jordan is a part of collection.

(THE ABOVE ENTRY WAS CONTRIBUTED BY CYNTHIA L. SEITZ)

34. *Coretta Scott King*
(1927–   )
Civil rights leader; lecturer; and concert singer

BIOGRAPHICAL INFORMATION

Chronological Biography

Second of three children born April 27, 1927, to Bernice (McMurray) and Obidiah (Obie) Scott in Marion, Alabama.

1945: Graduated first in high school class of 17 from Lincoln School, private missionary school in Marion. 1948: Made concert debut singing at Second Baptist Church in Springfield, Ohio. 1951: Graduated from Antioch College in Ohio with A.B. in Education/Music. Entered New England Conservatory of Music in Boston with Jesse Smith Noyes Fellowship. 1952: Gave premier performance at conservatory of Motivos de Son, song cycle by Cuban composer Amadeo Roldan. Met Martin Luther King, Jr., Atlanta minister working on Ph.D in philosophy at Boston University. June 18, 1953: Married Martin Luther King, Jr.; the Rev. Martin Luther King, Sr., married them in Scott home in Marion, Alabama. 1954: Graduated from New England Conservatory of Music. Moved to Montgomery, Alabama, where husband had first pastorate at Dexter Avenue Baptist Church. 1955: First child, daughter Yolanda Denise, born on November 17th. Assisted husband in leading Montgomery bus boycott which gave birth to new era in civil rights movement. January 30, 1956: Bomb exploded on front porch of King home while husband was away; occupants were not injured. 1957: Unexploded bomb found on front porch of King's home. Second child, Martin Luther III, born on October 23rd. Received Annual Brotherhood Award from National Council of Negro Women. Along with husband, helped found Southern Christian Leadership Conference (SCLC). Couple attended Ghana's independence celebration. 1959: Toured Europe and Asia with husband and performed singing concerts in India. Couple spent month in India studying Gandhi's techniques of nonviolence, as guests of Prime Minister Nehru. Received Outstanding Citizenship Award from Montgomery Improvement Association. 1960: Moved to Atlanta in January to devote full time and effort to civil rights struggle; husband and his father copastored Ebenezer Baptist Church. Delegate to White House Conference on Children and Youth. Recipient of Merit Award from St. Louis Argus. January 30, 1961: Third child, Dexter Scott, born. 1962: Taught voice in music department of Morris Brown College in Atlanta, Georgia. Delegate to Women's Strike for Peace at 17th international conference in Geneva, Switzerland. Received Distinguished Achievement Award from National Organization of Colored Women's Clubs. Named Woman of the Year by Utility Club of New York City. March 28, 1963: Fourth child, Bernice Albertine, born. August 28, 1963: Participated in rally of 250,000 people in Washington, D. C., to dramatize need for new federal legislation to integrate blacks completely into American society. Awarded Louise Waterman Wise Award by American Jewish Congress Women's Auxiliary. Received citation for work in peace and freedom from Women's Strike for Peace. 1964: Recipient of Human Dignity and Human Rights award from Norfolk chapter of Links. In November, began performing "freedom concerts" at Town Hall in New York City, singing, reciting poetry and lecturing. Has performed over 30 of these concerts to benefit Southern Christian Leadership Conference. In December, accompanied husband to Oslo, Norway, where he received Nobel Peace Prize. **1965:** Received Myrtle Wreath Award from Cleveland Hadassah. Participated in march from Selma to Montgomery in March. **April 4, 1968:** Husband assassinated at age 39 in Memphis, Tennessee. **April 1968:** Day before husband's funeral, took his place at head of march of striking Memphis garbage collectors whose grievances had brought husband to city where he met his death. Attended peace rally in New York City speaking in husband's behalf. **June 19, 1968:** Fulfilled husband's last appointment by speaking before Poor People's Campaign at Lincoln Memorial in Washington, D. C., on Solidarity Day. Gave speech calling upon American women to "unite and form a solid block of woman power" to fight three great evils of racism, poverty and war. **1968:** Received Wateler Peace Prize, Award for Excellence in Field of Human Relations, and Universal Love Award from Premio San Valentine Committee. Narrator of Aaron Copeland's "A Lincoln Portrait" at concerts performed by Washington National Symphony Orchestra in Washington and New York City. Named Woman of Year by National Association of Radio and Television Announcers. **1968 and 1969:** Selected in National College Student Poll of Most Admired Women. **January 1969:** Announced plans for creation of Martin Luther King, Jr. Memorial in Atlanta. Accepted Nehru award for international understanding presented posthumously to husband in India. Accepted Saint Valentine award in husband's behalf in Italy. Had special audience with Pope Paul VI. Sponsored Harijan (untouchable) student from India at King Memorial Institute in Atlanta. **February 1969:** Appointed to boards of directors of National Organization for Women and Southern Christian Leadership Conference. **March 1969:** After husband's killer was convicted, stated her belief that assassination was result of conspiracy and expressed hope that search for conspirators would continue. First woman to speak from pulpit of St. Paul's Cathedral in London. Received Dag Hammarskjold award, and diploma as academician from World Organization of Diplomatic Press-Académie Diplomatique de la Paix. Received Pacem in Terris Award of International Overseas Service Foundation. Received honorary doctorates from Boston University, Marymount Manhattan College and Brandeis University. Member of YWCA Board of Directors. Assisted in founding Martin Luther King, Jr. Foundation in Great Britain. Trustee of Robert F. Kennedy Memorial. **1970:** Narrated Aaron Copeland's "A Lincoln Portrait" performed by San Francisco Symphony. Received honorary doctorates from University of Bridgeport, Wilberforce University, Bethune-Cookman College, Morgan State College, Morehouse College, Princeton University and Keuka College. **1971:** Earned Mus.D. from New England Conservatory of Music. Received honorary doctorates from Northeastern University and Bates College, as well as Leadership for Freedom Award from Roosevelt University, Martin Luther King, Jr. Memorial Medal from College of City of New York and International Viareggio Award. **1974:** Served on National Commission for Full Employment. Member of board of directors of Southern Christian Leadership Conference. **1974–1989:** President of Martin Luther King, Jr. Center for Nonviolent Social Change in Atlanta. **January 1975:** Named one of 40 most highly respected women in U.S. in *Good Housekeeping* magazine poll. **April 4, 1975:** Witness during House hearing on Equal Opportunity and Full Employment. **December 1975:** Witness during joint hearings held in Atlanta on Jobs and Prices in Atlanta. **March 1976:** Witness during House hearings on approval of legislation regarding Equal Opportunity and Full Employment. **May 19, 1976:** Provided additional testimony during Senate hearings on Full Employment and Balanced Growth Act, 1976. **January 18, 1978:** Witness during House hearings on Full Employment and Balanced Growth Act. **February 2, 1978:** Testified during Senate hearings on Full Employment and Balanced Growth Act. **August 9, 1978:** Witness during House hearings on Striking of National Medals in commemoration of late husband. **1980–:** Commentator for CNN (Cable News Network). **March 4, 1983:** Awarded Franklin D. Roosevelt Freedom Medal at Hyde Park, New York. **June 7, 1983:** Testified during House hearings on Martin Luther King, Jr. Holiday Bill. **November 2, 1983:** Participated in White House ceremonies establishing federal holiday in honor of husband. **March 27, 1987:** Witness during Senate hearings on Guaranteed Opportunity Act. **January 14, 1989:** Resigned as president of Martin Luther King, Jr. Center for Nonviolent Social Change; remained as chief executive officer and spokesperson for Center. **November 17, 1989:** As member of Black Leadership Forum (BLF), met with President George Bush to discuss rising racism in United States. **Present:** Continues working for civil rights.

Background Information

Parents: Bernice (McMurray) and Obidiah (Obie) Scott. Mother drove school bus; Father owned country store and also hauled lumber. **Siblings:** Two (Edythe [Mrs. Arthur Bagley], older sister; Obie Leonard, younger brother). **Children:** Four (Yolanda Denise ["Yoki"]; Martin Luther III; Dexter Scott, Bernice Albertine). **Influences:** Martin Luther King, Jr. **Ethnicity:** African American. **Also known as:** None known. **Historical sites, landmarks, etc.:** SRRT Coretta Scott King Award, Social Responsibilities Round Table, American Library Association. Annual awards presented to African American authors and illustrators whose distinguished books promote an understanding and appreciation of the culture and contribution of all people to the realization of the "American Dream."

BIBLIOGRAPHICAL INFORMATION

Biographical Sketches About Coretta Scott King

Evory, Ann, ed. *Contemporary Authors: A Bio-Bibliographical Guide to Current Authors and Their Works*. Detroit: Gale Research, 1978.

Jackson, George F. *Black Women, Makers of History: A Portrait*. Oakland, CA: GRT Book Printing, 1985.

Moritz, Charles, ed. *Current Biography, 1969*. New York: H. W. Wilson Company, 1969.

Ploski, Harry A., and James Williams, eds. *The Negro Almanac: A Reference Work on the Afro-American*. New York: Wiley, 1982.

Smith, Jessie Carney, ed. *Notable Black American Women*. Detroit: Gale Research, 1992.

Zophy, Angela Howard. *Handbook of American Women's History*. New York: Garland, 1990.

Books by Coretta Scott King

My Life with Martin Luther King, Jr. New York: Holt, Rinehart and Winston, 1969. Reprint. London: Hodder and Stoughton, 1970.

Books About Coretta Scott King

Patrick, Diane. *Coretta Scott King*. New York: F. Watts, 1991.

Patterson, Lillie. *Coretta Scott King*. Champaign, IL: Garrad, 1977.

Taylor, Paula. *Coretta King, a Woman of Peace*. Mankato, MI: Creative Education, Chicago, 1974.

Vivian, Octavia. *Coretta: The Story of Mrs. Martin Luther King, Jr*. Philadelphia: Fortress, 1970.

Shorter Works by Coretta Scott King

"Coretta King: Keeping the Dream Alive." *Ebony* 35 (January 1980): 60–62.

"Excerpts from CNN Commentaries on South Africa ... Delivered by Coretta Scott King." In *Four Decades of Concern: Martin Luther King, Jr., The Martin Luther King, Jr. Center for Nonviolent Social Change, Inc. and South Africa*, by Martin Luther King, Jr. Center for Nonviolent Social change. Atlanta: The Center, 1986.

"He Had a Dream; Excerpts from My Life with Martin Luther King, Jr." *Life* 67 (September 12, 1969): 54–54B +; (September 19, 1969): 82–86 +.

"How Many Men Must Die?" *Life* 64 (April 19, 1968): 34–35.

"Keeper of the Dream." *Newsweek* 73 (March 24, 1969): 38.

"Martin's Legacy." *Ebony* 41 (January 1986): 105–06 + .
"More on the Responsibility of the Educated Woman." *AAUW Journal* 63 (October 1969):5–7.
"Needed: A National Academy of Peace and Conflict Resolution." *National Forum; The Phi Kappa Phi Journal* 63 (Fall 1983): 6 + .
"Remarks of the President and Mrs. Coretta Scott King at the Signing Ceremony for Martin Luther King, Jr. Holiday Legislation [November 2, 1983]." *Ebony* 41 (January 1986): 36–38.
"Role of Nonviolence." *Current* 208 (December 1978): 3–7.
"South Africa: Selected Quotes of Coretta Scott King, 1973–1986." In *Four Decades of Concern: Martin Luther King, Jr., The Martin Luther King, Jr. Center for Nonviolent Social Change, Inc. and South Africa*, by Martin Luther King, Jr. Center for Nonviolent Social Change. Atlanta: The Center, 1986.
"Special Christmas Message." *Good Housekeeping* 167 (December 1968): 84–85 + .
"Today's Student." *International Education* 2 (1972): 24–30.
"We Need a National Coalition Against Age Discrimination." *50 Plus* 24 (July 1984): 10–11.
"We Were Sharing Him with All Americans, Black and White: Making of TV Film Rekindles Memories of Martin Luther King's Widow." *TV Guide* 26 (February 1978): 4 + .
"Why We Still Can't Wait." *Newsweek* 88 (August 16, 1976): 13.
Davis, Angela Yvonne. *If They Come in the Morning; Voices of Resistance.* New York: Third Press, 1971. (Letter of support from Coretta Scott King.)
King, Martin Luther, Jr. *The Trumpet of Conscience.* New York: Harper & Row, 1968. (Forward written by Coretta Scott King.)
_____. *Where Do We Go from Here: Chaos or Community?* New York: Bantam, 1968. (Special introduction by Coretta Scott King.)
_____. *The Words of Martin Luther King, Jr.* New York: Newmarket Press, 1983. Reprint. New York: Newmarket Press, 1987. (Introduction by Coretta Scott King.)
Rummel, Jack. *Langston Hughes.* New York: Chelsea House, 1988. (Introductory essay by Coretta Scott King.)
Washington, Harold. *Climbing a Great Mountain: Selected Speeches of Mayor Harold Washington.* Chicago: Bonus Books, 1988. (Forward by Coretta Scott King.)
Weissberg, Ted. *Arthur Ashe — Tennis Great.* New York: Chelsea House, 1991. (Introductory essay by Coretta Scott King.)

Shorter Works About Coretta Scott King

Asante, Molefi K. "Spotlight on Kariamu Company." *Essence* 8 (March 1978): 16.
Blount, Carolyne S. "Coretta Scott King: On Leadership Development." *About Time* 17 (December 1989): 21.
"Coretta King Calls for Rally to Honor 25th Anniversary of March on Washington." *Jet* 74 (May 9, 1988): 12.

"Coretta King Endorses McGovern for President." *Jet* 42 (June 8, 1972): 16.

"Coretta King Pushes Reagan to OK South African Sanctions After Recent Visit There." *Jet* 71 (October 6, 1986): 16.

"Coretta King Upset by Holiday Date Chosen for MLK in Georgia." *Jet* 67 (December 10, 1984): 7.

"Coretta King Urges World Peace on King's Birthday." *Jet* 69 (October 7, 1985): 4.

"Coretta Scott King's Dedication to 'Dream' Rekindles Rights Drive." *Jet* 65 (September 19, 1983): 4–8 + .

Crawford, Vicki L., Jacqueline Anne Rouse, and Barbara Woods, eds. *Women in the Civil Rights Movement.* Brooklyn: Carlson, 1990.

Evers, Mrs. Medgar W. "Mrs. King and Mrs. Kennedy." *Ladies' Home Journal* 85 (June 1968): 32.

"FBI Spied on Mrs. King, Abernathy and Others, Top Columnist Testifies." *Jet* 42 (July 13, 1972): 20–22.

Fitch, Robert Beck. *My Eyes Have Seen.* San Francisco: Glide Publications, 1972.

Garland, P."Coretta King: In Her Husband's Footsteps." *Ebony* 23 (September 1968): 154–58 + .

Goodwin, J. "South African Journal." *Ladies' Home Journal* 104 (January 1987): 74 + .

Greenwald, J. "Into the Racial Maelstrom." *Time* 128 (September 22, 1986): 45.

"History Proves Error of Nixon Snub of M. L. King at Memorial: Mrs. King." *Jet* 71 (December 22, 1986): 5.

Johnson, R. E. "King's Children Tell How They Remember Him." *Jet* 41 (February 3, 1972): 18–20.

"King Family Arrested and Jailed for Embassy Protest." *Jet* 68 (July 15, 1985): 5.

"King Institute Holds 1st Meeting on Non-Violence." *Jet* 50 (August 19, 1976): 8.

"King Left No Will; Widow Sues Boston University to Return His Papers." *Jet* 73 (January 18, 1988): 26 + .

Lanker, Brian. *I Dream a World: Portraits of Black Women Who Changed America.* New York: Stewart, Tabori & Chang, 1989.

Leviton, J. "Bio." *People* 9 (February 20, 1978): 72–74 + .

Long, Marion. "Paradise Tossed." *Omni* 10 (April 1988): 14 + .

"Martin Luther King, Jr. Center for Social Change: A Monument to a Martyr." *Ebony* 29 (April 1974): 126–28 + .

"Martin Luther King, Jr.: His Widow Keeps His Dream Alive." *Jet* 69 (January 20, 1986): 10 + .

"Martin Luther King III Says Bodyguard Saved Mother from 'Crazy Man'." *Jet* 74 (September 26, 1988): 30.

"Moral Leadership, from the Young People, Is Our Real Hope; Interview, edited by H. Gulliver." *Today's Health* 51 (November 1973): 12–13.

"Mrs. King Approves Release of Official MLK Sculpture." *Jet* 71 (February 9, 1987): 57.

"Mrs. Martin Luther King, Jr.; Classic Nobility." *Vogue* 153 (May 1969): 168–69.

"NEA President Don Morrison Interviews Mrs. Martin Luther King, Jr." *Today's Education* 61 (January 1972): 14–17 + .

Norment, Lynn. "Coretta Scott King: The Woman Behind the King Anniversary." *Ebony* 45 (January 1990): 116–18 + .

_____. "The King Family: Keepers of the Dream." *Ebony* 42 (January 1987): 25–26 + .

Osborne, J. "Doctor King's Memorial." *New Republic* 161 (October 11, 1969): 9–10.

Paul, Angus. "Scholars Tend to Favor the Martin Luther King, Jr. Center Over Boston University as the Home for All of King's Papers." *Chronicle of Higher Education* 34 (July 20, 1988): A4–5 + .

Perry, Harmon. "Mrs. Coretta King's Dream Is Becoming a Reality." *Jet* 53 (January 19, 1978): 6–9.

"Queen Is with Us." *Newsweek* 73 (May 12, 1969): 37.

"Reveal Progress at MLK Center: March for Full Employment." *Jet* 49 (February 5, 1976): 6–8.

Sanders, C. L., ed. "Finally, I've Begun to Live Again." *Ebony* 26 (November 1970): 172–76 + .

Walker, A. "Growing Strength of Coretta King." *Redbook* 137 (September 1971): 96–97 + .

"Woman Behind Martin Luther King." *Ebony* 14 (January 1959): 33–38.

"Women at the Top." *Ebony* 37 (August 1982): 146–48.

Women's History Research Center. *Women and Law. Section VI: Black and Third World Women and Law*. Berkeley: Women's History Research Center, 1975.

"You're Such a Brave Lady." *Newsweek* 71 (April 1968): 32.

Other Works About Coretta Scott King
Theses

Holland, Endesha Ida Mae. "The Autobiography of a Parader Without a Permit." Ph.D. diss., University of Minnesota, 1986.

Media Materials About Coretta Scott King
Films

Koplin, Mert, and Charles Drinker. *Black Views on Race*. Time-Life Films, [197–]. 16 mm; 80 min.; sound; color.

_____, and _____. *Coretta King*. Time-Life Films, 1976. 16 mm; 80 min.; sound; color.

Sound Recordings

A Conversation with Coretta Scott King. Racine, WI: Johnson Foundation, 1983. 1 side of cassette; 28 min., 15 sec; 1 ⅞ ips; 2 track; mono.

Coretta Scott King at the National Press Club. Washington, D. C.: National Public Radio, 1985. Cassette; 60 min.; 1 ⅞ ips; mono.

Dr. Martin Luther King, Jr. — Speeches and Sermons. New York: Martin Luther King Foundation, 1968. Cassette; 39 min. (Introduction by Coretta Scott King.)

Free at Last, Free at Last: His Truth Is Marching On. Caedmon, 1972. Phonodisc; 2 sides; 12 in.; 33 ⅓ rpm; stereophonic.

Free at Last, Free at Last: His Truth Is Marching On. Caedmon, 1972. Cassette; 62 min., 6 secs.; 2 track; mono.

The Freedom Movement. Caedmon, 1972. Cassette; 2 track; 49 min., 42 secs.; mono.
Human Rights: The Challenge of the Future. Iowa State University, 1979. Cassette;
    36 min.; 2 track; mono.
I, Too, Have a Dream: Mrs. Coretta King Discusses Her Life and Optimistic Hopes.
    Iowa State University.
The Movement. Caedmon, 1972. Phonodisc; 2 sides; 12 in.; 33 ⅓ rpm; stereophonic.
My Life with Martin Luther King, Jr. Caedmon, 1969. 3 cassettes; 164 min.; 1 ⅞
    ips; 2 track; mono.
My Life with Martin Luther King, Jr. Caedmon, 1972. Phonodisc; 6 sides; 12 in.;
    33 ⅓ rpm; stereophonic.

Video Recordings

Black Leadership: A New Direction. Chicago: WBBM-TV, 1981. Videocassette; U-
    matic; 23 min.; ¾ in.; sound; color.
Eyes on the Prize: America's Civil Rights Years. Awakenings 1954–1956. Alexan-
    dria, VA: PBS Video, 1986. Episode 1 of 6. Videocassette; 60 min; ½ in.;
    VHS; sound; color with black and white segments.
Martin Luther King, Jr. Chicago: Encyclopaedia Britannica Educational Corpora-
    tion, 1981. Video; 24 min.; ¾ in.; U-matic, or ½ in. Beta, or ½ in. VHS; sound;
    color.
Martin Luther King, Jr.: The Making of a Holiday. Washington, D. C.: On the Poto-
    mac Productions, Inc.; Princeton, NJ: Films for the Humanities [distributor],
    1988. Videocassette; 25 min.; ½ in.; sound; color with black and white se-
    quences.

Primary Source Materials Relating to Coretta Scott King

Frank McCallister. Papers. 1923–1971. Extent of collection: 20 ft. Finding aids:
    Unpublished guide. Location: University of Chicago at Chicago Circle,
    Library, Manuscript Collection, Chicago, Illinois 60615. Scope of collection:
    Includes correspondence from King.
Leadership Conference on Civil Rights. Records. 1963–1974. Extent of collec-
    tion: 95 containers. Finding aids: Container List. Location: Library of Con-
    gress, Manuscript Division, Washington, D. C. 20540. Scope of collection:
    Includes correspondence with King and others.
Montgomery Bus Boycott Collection. 1955–1957. Extent of collection: 4 vols.
    Finding aids: Not listed. Location: Alabama State University Archives,
    Montgomery, Alabama 36195. Scope of collection: Includes clippings and
    other papers on King and other persons involved in boycott.
National Peace Action Coalition. Records. 1970–1973. Extent of collection: 10 reels
    of microfilm. Finding aids: Register. Location: State Historical Society of
    Wisconsin, Archives Division, 816 State Street, Madison, Wisconsin 53706.
    Scope of collection: Includes information regarding involvement of King.
National Union of Hospital and Health Care Employees. Records. 1937–1980. Ex-
    tent of collection: 240.3 lin. ft. Finding aids: File folder listing available in

repository and on interlibrary loan. Location: Labor-Management Documentation Center, M. P. Catherwood Library, Cornell University, Ithaca, New York 14853. Scope of collection: Speeches and other information regarding participation of King in organizing campaigns, etc.

Rosa Parks. Papers. 1955–1976. Extent of collection: 2 ft. and 2 boxes. Finding aids: Unpublished finding aid in repository. Location: Wayne State University, Walter P. Reuther Library, Archives of Labor and Urban Affairs, Detroit, Michigan 48202. Scope of collection: Includes clippings and correspondence from King.

Sarah Patton Boyle. Papers. 1949–1970. Extent of collection: 12,000 items. Finding aids: Unpublished list in library. Location: University of Virginia Library, Charlottesville, Virginia 22906. Scope of collection: Includes correspondence from King.

Whitney M. Young. Papers. 1960–1977. Extent of collection: ca. 109,300 items. Finding aids: Register and contents list. Location: Columbia University, Rare Book and Manuscript Library, New York, New York 10027. Scope of collection: Includes correspondence with King.

Women Mobilized for Change. Records. 1966–1971. Extent of collection: 2.5 ft. Finding aids: Unpublished guide. Location: University of Illinois at Chicago Circle, Library, Chicago, Illinois 60615. Scope of collection: Collection grew out of meeting with King.

(THE ABOVE ENTRY WAS CONTRIBUTED BY LEVIRN HILL)

35. *Elizabeth Duncan Koontz*
(1919–1989)

Educator; president of National Education Association;
advocate for civil rights; and director of U.S. Women's Bureau

BIOGRAPHICAL INFORMATION

Chronological Biography

Born June 3, 1919, to Lena Bell (Jordan) and Samuel Edward Duncan in Salisbury, North Carolina, youngest of seven children. Parents were well-educated, mother was teacher and father high school principal. Mother taught illiterate adults to read at home in evenings; by third grade "Libby" helped with their lessons and became aware that not everyone had opportunity to attend school. Brought up with understanding that education was very important and with it came obligation to use it on behalf of others. Throughout years, family helped others attend college. Wanted to become teacher, but also interested in women's and children's health issues. Pursued education despite segregated schools.

1923?: Began school at age four, already able to read and write.   1928?: Father died when she was nine years old. Became junior church secretary at A. M. E. Zion Church.   1935: Salutatorian at graduation from Price High School in Salisbury.   1938: Received bachelor's degree, with honors, in English and elementary education from Livingstone College in Salisbury. 1938–1940: Taught at Harnett County Training School in small lumber town of Dunn, North Carolina. Fired because of instigating protest against high boarding charges teachers had to pay to school.   1941: Awarded M.A. in elementary education from Atlanta University. Later did further graduate work at Columbia University and Indiana University; also received certificate in special education for mentally retarded at North Carolina State College in Durham.   1941–1942: Teacher in Landis, North Carolina, at Aggrey Memorial School.   1942–1945: Taught at 14th Street School in Winston-Salem, North Carolina.   1945–1968: Taught in Salisbury at Price High School and Monroe School; became special education teacher at Price Junior-Senior High School in 1957. Also taught summer sessions at Livingstone College. Developed lifelong interest in teaching children classified as retarded; believed many were simply slow learners and showed that patience and understanding would help them learn and achieve.   **November 26, 1947:** Married Harry Lee Koontz, mathematics teacher; later athletic director and teacher at Rowan County (North Carolina) Dunbar High School.   1950–1989: Clerk and member of St. Philip's Episcopal Church in Salisbury.   1951–1963: Secretary-treasurer of St. Philip's Churchwomen. 1952: Began activity in National Education Association when North Carolina Negro Teachers Association was admitted to NEA as affiliate of all-white North Carolina Education Association. Held various positions in local association.   1954–1959: Chair of Interracial Committee of North Carolina Diocese of Episcopal Churchwomen.   1955: Delegate to Triennial Convention of Episcopal Churchwomen.   1955–1957: Member of Youth Commission of Rowan County.   1958–1962: President of North Carolina Association of Classroom Teachers for two terms. Goal of work with educational organizations was to change system to help teachers succeed and stay in profession, so that children would be afforded education they needed and deserved.   1962: Member of North Carolina's Governor's Commission on Status of Women. Represented National Education Association (NEA) in West Berlin.   1964: Attended World Confederation of Organizations of the Teaching Profession Conference in Seoul, Korea, as NEA representative. Spent six weeks as member of American delegation to fourth Dartmouth Conference in Soviet Union; represented American public school teachers. 1965–1989: Member of Education Committee of National Urban League and of Editorial Board of *Education USA*.   1965–1966: President of Department of Classroom Teachers (later renamed Association of Classroom Teachers), largest division of National Education Association (NEA). Had previously served as secretary and vice president. Took year's leave of absence as job entailed national travel, etc. **1965–1968:** Member of President Johnson's National Advisory Council on Education of Disadvantaged Children. **1966 and 1967:** Received Honorary Doctor of Humane Letters and Distinguished Alumni Award from Livingstone College. **March 1967:** As president of Department of Classroom Teachers, testified regarding elementary and secondary education amendments of 1967. **April 18, 1867:** Designated "Libby Koontz Day" in Salisbury. **1967:** Mother died. **1967– 1968:** National vice president of NEA. **1967–1970:** Member of editorial board of *Education Digest*. **July 6, 1968–January 1969:** First black president of over million member National Education Association (NEA), country's largest organization of teachers. Elected in July 1967; took office one year later. Spoke out for "teacher power" and changing of passive attitudes of teachers. Supported teacher's organizing efforts, agitation and strikes (as last resort) for improved conditions and higher pay. Advised communities to support teachers and make profession more lucrative so as to attract and keep high calibre of teachers as children deserved dedicated, caring teachers. Began Center for Human Relations in NEA which undertook such issues as desegregation of schools and bilingual education. Also fought for children's civil rights regarding native languages and representation of their cultures in their classrooms. Initiated conference on Critical Issues in Education which sought to eliminate discrimination against women, minorities and handicapped. Resigned to accept federal position of Director of Women's Bureau. **1968:** Received Civitan Distinguished Teacher Award from Civitan Club in Salisbury. Eldest brother, Samuel, died in July. **January 30, 1969–1973:** Appointed U.S. Delegate to United Nations Commission on Status of Women, first black woman in position. **February 6, 1969:** Nomination hearing regarding appointment by President Nixon as Director of Women's Bureau of U.S. Labor Department. **1969:** Gave testimony at hearings regarding departmental appropriations, and comprehensive preschool education and child day care act. **1969–1973:** As director, became first major black appointee in Nixon administration and first black woman to head Bureau. Accepted position because she believed she could change things and would have support of Secretary of Labor George Schultz. Championed equal rights and opportunities for women; fought for equal pay, enforcement of protective labor laws, and Equal Rights Amendment. Worked to improve skills of household workers and raise their pay by having them covered under minimum wage laws. Coalition of Labor Union Women formed from group of union women she encouraged to meet to discuss their common responsibilities; group was strongly supportive of her efforts as director. Accomplishments may have contributed to her not being reappointed as some may have felt she was not really expected to effect much change. **May 6, 1970:** Witness regarding problems associated with economic security of elderly Americans.   **May 1970:** Presented budget request and discussed increased scope for Women's Bureau at Congressional hearings.   **July 30, 1970:** Senate budget hearings and discussion of advancement of women's opportunities and status.   **July 31, 1970:** Gave statement before House committee investigating discrimination against women.   **1972:** Named Deputy Assistant Secretary of Labor and special counselor to Secretary for Women's Affairs.   **July 11, 1973:** Testified as former Director of Women's Bureau at hearings to investigate discrimination against women in employment, earnings, credit, and insurance.   **1973–1975:** Returned to North Carolina where she coordinated nutrition programs of State Department of Human Resources in Raleigh.   **June 21, 1974:** Spoke at hearing concerning national nutrition policy.   **1975–1982:** Assistant State Superintendent for Teacher Education in State Department of Public Instruction in North Carolina.   **1976:** Awarded College Entrance Exam Board Medal for distinguished service to education.   **1982:** Retired.   **July 26, 1984:** As chair of National Commission on Working Women, testified at hearing examining Women's Bureau management and operations.   **1986:** Husband died.   **January 6, 1989:** Died of heart attack at her home in Salisbury, North Carolina, at age 69. Known as both tactful and blunt, depending upon situation; unafraid of tackling difficult issues. Recipient of numerous honorary degrees, awards and citations; member of and consultant to many organizations and national commissions.

Background Information

Parents: Lena Bell (Jordan) and Samuel Edward Duncan. Mother was teacher in Dunbar Elementary School. Father was principal of Dunbar High School in East Spencer, North Carolina, about two miles from Salisbury. **Siblings:** Six (Known names: John B., lawyer and first black city commissioner of District of Columbia; Samuel, eldest brother, who was president of Livingstone College for ten years until his death in July 1968; Julia, registrar-treasurer of Livingstone College). **Children:** None. **Influences:** None. **Ethnicity:** African American. **Also known as:** None known. **Historical sites, landmarks, etc.:** None known.

BIBLIOGRAPHICAL INFORMATION

Biographical Sketches About Elizabeth Duncan Koontz

Jackson, George F. *Black Women, Makers of History: A Portrait.* Oakland, CA: GRT Printing, 1985.

Moritz, Charles, ed. *Current Biography Yearbook*. New York: The H. W. Wilson Company, 1969.
O'Neill, Lois Decker, ed. *The Women's Book of World Records and Achievements*. Garden City, NY: Anchor Press/Doubleday, 1979.
Ploski, Harry A., and James Williams, eds. *The Negro Almanac: A Reference Work on the African American*. Detroit: Gale Research, 1989.
Smith, Jessie Carney, ed. *Notable Black American Women*. Detroit: Gale Research, 1992.

Books by Elizabeth Duncan Koontz

The Best Kept Secret of the Past 5,000 Years: Women Are Ready for Leadership in Education. Bloomington, IN: Phi Delta Kappa Educational Foundation, [1972]. [ED062725]
A Consumer's Hopes and Dreams for Teacher Education. Presented at the Twenty-First Annual Meeting of the American Association of Colleges for Teacher Education, Chicago, Illinois, February 26, 1969. [Washington: American Association of Colleges for Teacher Education, 1969].
Household Employment: The Quiet Revolution. Washington, D. C.: U.S. Department of Labor, 1969.
New Horizons: Household Employment and the Home-Related Arts. Washington, D. C.: U.S. Women's Bureau, 1970.
Koontz, Elizabeth D., Charles F. Deubel, and Ruth Trigg. *Handbook for Presidents of State Departments of Classroom Teachers*. Washington: National Education Association of the United States. Department of Classroom Teachers, [1965].

Books About Elizabeth Duncan Koontz

United States Congress. *Hearing Before the Committee on Labor and Public Welfare. United States Senate. Ninety-First Congress, First Session*. Washington, D. C.: U.S. GPO, 1969. [US Y4.L11/2: N72 5 969-3].

Shorter Works by Elizabeth Duncan Koontz

"Career Potential in Home Economics." *Journal of Home Economics* 62 (December 1970): 739–40.
"Changing Role of Women." *Journal of Home Economics* 63 (November 1971): 588–90.
"Childbirth and Child Rearing Leave: Job Related Benefits." *New York Law Forum* 17 (1971): 480–502.
"Complete Integration Must be the Goal." *Ebony* 25 (August 1970): 138–41.
"A Consumer's Hopes and Dreams for Teacher Education." *American Association of Colleges for Teacher Education. Yearbook. 1969.* (1969): 13–21.

"Counseling Women for Responsibilities." *Journal of the National Association of Women Deans and Counselors* 34 (1970): 13–17.

"Education and Leisure: New Workers." *Change* 11 (July–August 1979): 35.

"Fighting Stereotypes: Women Want Up the Career Ladder." *American Vocational Journal* 48 (1973): 35–36.

"Home Economists: Beware of Professional Detachment." *Journal of Home Economics* 64 (September 1972): 22–23.

"How in the World Can We Do All of This." In *Higher Education: New Directions for Leadership, Spring Workshop*, edited by Arthur F. Terry and Wanda M. Martin. Salem, OR: Interinstitutional Consortium for Career Education, 1978. [ED168398]

"NEA Views on Teacher Strikes." *Childhood Education* 45 (April 1969): 435–37.

"Needed: Better Teaching for Slow Learners." *Parents' Magazine & Better Family Living* 44 (February 1969): 24.

"A New Look at Education for Girls." *Contemporary Education* 43 (1972): 195–97.

"New Priorities and Old Prejudices." *Education Digest* 36 (May 1971): 32–33.

"New Priorities and Old Prejudices." *Today's Education* 60 (March 1971): 25–26.

"One o'Clock, Two o'Clock, Three o'Clock Rock!" *High School Journal* 59 (1975): 27–30.

"Plans for Widening Women's Educational Opportunities." Paper presented at Wingspread Conference on Women's Higher Education: Some Unanswered Questions. Racine, Wisconsin, March 13, 1972. [ED067990]

"Profession and the Media." *Today's Education* 58 (February 1969): 17.

"The Progress of the Women Workers: An Unfinished Story." *Issues in Industrial Society* 2 (1971): 29–31.

"See How They Learn!" *Today's Education* 58 (February 1969): 15–30.

"Service and Strength Take Members and Money." *NEA Journal* 57 (May 1968): 45.

"Somebody Needs You." *Ladies' Home Journal* 86 (October 1969): 74.

"Teen-agers Speak Out About Sex: A Symposium of High School Students and a Reaction by Elizabeth Koontz." *Today's Education* 58 (March 1969): 23–26.

"Volunteerism: A Vital Contribution." *AAUW Journal* 63 (January 1970): 66–68.

"What's Right in American Education?" *Educational Horizons* 54 (Spring 1976): 144–45.

"Why Teachers Are Militant." *Education Digest* 33 (January 1968): 12–14.

"Women and Jobs in a Changing World." *American Vocational Journal* 45 (1970): 13–15.

"Women as a Minority Group." In *Voices of the New Feminism*, edited by Mary Lou Thompson. Boston: Beacon, 1970.

"Women as a Wasted Resource." *Compact* 4 (1970): 10–11.

"Women in the Labor Force." In *Women's Role in Contemporary Society*, by New York City Commission on Human Rights. New York: Avon Books, 1972.

"Women's Bureau Looks to Future." *Monthly Labor Review* 93 (1970): 3–9.

Shorter Works About Elizabeth Duncan Koontz

"Appointed Head of the Women's Dept. in the Dept. of Labor." *Negro History Bulletin* 32 (April 1969): 20.

35. Elizabeth Duncan Koontz   [238]

"Black Women; Double Discrimination." *Sepia* 18 (September 1969): 18–19.
"Born Teacher, a Tested Leader." *Michigan Education Journal* 46 (October 1968): 33.
"Education's Lady on the Go." *Ebony* 21 (December 1965): 29–32 +.
"Elizabeth D. Koontz, President-elect 1968, of the National Education Association." *Negro History Bulletin* 30 (December 1967): 4–5.
"Elizabeth Duncan Koontz." In *Open Secrets*, by Barbaralee Diamonstein. New York: Viking, 1972.
"Elizabeth Duncan Koontz." In *Particular Passions*, by Lynn Gilbert and Gaylen Moore. New York: Clarkson N. Potter, 1981.
"Fighting Lady for N.E.A." *Time* 92 (July 12, 1968): 39.
"Filling More Jobs." *Time* 93 (January 17, 1969): 15.
"Group Requests More Minority Women on TV." *Jet* 59 (March 12, 1981): 26.
Harding, A. C. "Libby Koontz, NEA President." *Today's Education* 57 (September 1968): 18–20.
"It's a Matter of Relationships; interview." *Illinois Education* 57 (September 1968): 10–13 +.
"It's a Matter of Relationships; interview." *Kentucky School Journal* 47 (September 1968): 16–19 +.
"It's a Matter of Relationships; interview." *Michigan Education Journal* 46 (October 1968): 32–35.
"It's a Matter of Relationships; interview." *Minnesota Journal of Education* 49 (September 1968): 30–34.
"It's a Matter of Relationships; interview." *New York State Education* (October 1968): 12–14 +.
"It's a Matter of Relationships; interview." *Pennsylvania School Journal* 117 (January 1969): 318–19.
"It's a Matter of Relationships; interview." *Virginia Journal of Education* 62 (September 1968): 35–38.
"It's a Matter of Relationships; interview." *Wisconsin Journal of Education* 101 (October 1968): 9–10 +.
Kenneally, James J. *Women and American Trade Unions*. St. Albans, VT: Eden Press Women's Publications, 1978.
"Leader in Education." *Education* 89 (November 1968): 182.
"Liberated, All Liberated." *Vogue* 155 (June 1970): 120–21.
"NEA Honors Mrs. Koontz for Aiding Women's Rights." *Jet* 43 (January 4, 1973): 12.
"Obituary." *Current Biography* 50 (April 1989): 63.
"Obituary." *Journal of Home Economics* 81 (Summer 1989): 58.
"Obituary." *New York Times Biographical Service* 20 (January 1989): 33.
"President of the National Education Association Given the Carter G. Woodson Award for Distinguished Service at the 53rd Convention of the Association for the Study of Negro Life and History in N.Y. City." *Negro History Bulletin* 31 (December 1968): 19 +.
"Profile with Excerpts from Charlotte, N.C., Observer." *Negro History Bulletin* 28 (December 1964): 55–56.
"Six Weeks in Russia." *NEA Journal* 54 (May 1965): 51.

Media Materials by Elizabeth Duncan Koontz

Sound Recordings

The Political Aspects of Managing the School and Classroom. N.p.: IDEA Fellows Program, 1982. 1 sound cassette.

Media Materials About Elizabeth Duncan Koontz

Sound Recordings

Educating Toward an Open Society. Bloomington, IN: Indiana University, 1968. Sound cassette; 108 min.; analog; 1 ⅞ ips.

How Good Are Our Schools? Washington, D. C.: National Education Association of the U.S., [196?]. Sound tape reel; ca. 60 min.; 3 ¾ ips; 2 track; 7 in.

Leaders on Leadership. Bloomington, IN: Phi Delta Kappa, 1974. 3 cassettes; 1 hr. 50 min.; 2 track; mono.

Pay Equity for Women. WI: Johnson Foundation, 1983. 1 side of sound cassette; 28 min., 17 sec.; 1 ⅞ ips; 2 track; mono; NAB; 3 ⅞ × 2 ½ in.; ⅛ in. tape.

Primary Source Materials Relating to Elizabeth Duncan Koontz

Elizabeth Duncan Koontz. Papers. Extent of collection: Not listed. Finding aids: Not listed. Location: Livingstone College, Andrew Carnegie Library, Afro-American Studies, Salisbury, North Carolina 28144. Scope of collection: Not listed.

Friends of the Schlesinger Library. Records. 1970–1975. Extent of collection: 7 tapes. Finding aids: Unpublished guide. Location: Schlesinger Library, Radcliffe College, Cambridge, Massachusetts 02138. Scope of collection: Collection consists of recordings of talks given before group's annual meetings with address by Koontz in May 1970.

36. Margaret E. Kuhn
(1905–)

Gray Panthers founder and national convener;
advocate for human rights, social justice and peace; and author

BIOGRAPHICAL INFORMATION

Chronological Biography

Maggie (Margaret Eliza) Kuhn was born August 3, 1905, in her grandmother's house in Buffalo, New York. Parents, Minnie Louise (Kooman) and

Samuel Frederick Kuhn, had been living in Memphis, but had returned to native city for daughter's birth because her mother refused to have her child in South, as protest against racial segregation. One younger brother, Samuel Kooman Kuhn. Greatly influenced by maternal grandmother's warm, caring manner, father's social conscience and strength, mother's activist community spirit, and a suffrage leader aunt. Moved to Cleveland at early age when father was transferred; may have also lived in Memphis. Joined local chapter of Audubon Society at age eight.

1922: Graduated from West High School in Cleveland.   1926: Earned B.A. from Flora Stone Mather College at Case Western University majoring in English and sociology, with minor in French. Wrote for college magazine and was one of organizers of college chapter of League of Women Voters. Started practice teaching at Fairmount Junior High in Cleveland, but scuffle among students in her class at end of game was witnessed by supervisor, ending hopes for educational career. Acting on father's suggestion to take some time to decide on career, worked as volunteer at Young Women's Christian Association (YWCA).   1928–1939?: Friend of mother's who was YWCA board member secured for her a position on board of Committee of Management of central branch in Cleveland. Turning point in her life as she realized she wanted to make social action her life's work. Introduced YWCA's programs to young undereducated women working under deplorable conditions — long hours, poor pay, lack of unions. Programs enabled them to come together to discuss their lives as well as interest them in political areas. Continued organizing efforts in Philadelphia, becoming radicalized as she saw women unionizing, building reputation as "women's libber." Late 1930s–1970: Accepted publications editor position with YWCA national staff in New York City; later employed with General Alliance of Unitarian Women in Boston. Returned to New York City where she took job with social action group for United Presbyterian Church, serving as associate secretary in Office of Church and Society, as editor and writer for church magazine, *Social Progress* (later named *Church and Society*), as alternate observer at United Nations, and as program coordinator in Division of Church and Race to improve relations between races. Duties included inserting socially responsible point of view into teaching materials as well as recommending social action policy of church. Instrumental in gaining support in controversial areas such as organized labor and study of medical care, and was just barely defeated in suggestion that church take absolute pacifist stand against war. Wrote *You Can't Be Human Alone; Handbook on Group Procedures for the Local Church.*   1970: Forced by Church's mandatory policy to retire on 65th birthday. Had been commuting from Philadelphia, where she lived and cared for ill mother and brother, to New York City. Father had died few years earlier and mother died just before she retired. In June, depressed at thought of vegetating at home, joined with five women friends who were also unwilling to give up activities. Free from restrictions caused by institutional policies, decided to use energies for social change, beginning with protesting Vietnam War. Used networking to notify other retirees, and organization grew tremendously. Underlying principle was, and continues to be, intergenerational approach to problems. Young and old are equally discriminated against and need to work together on issues of concern to effect systematic social change and create public policy to eradicate ageism, sexism, racism and economic imperialism. 1971: Organization, named Consultation of Older and Younger Adults for Social Change, numbered about 100. Realizing importance of participation in decision-making process regarding issues affecting them all, joined with older adults of black and Puerto Rican groups to testify at White House Conference on Aging, arguing that funds spent in Vietnam War should be used instead for human services. First referred to as "Gray Panthers" by New York City television station WPIX reporter; name officially adopted in 1971. Feels "gray" is appropriate due to many older members but also because organization seeks participation by people of all ages and all colors, and if all colors of rainbow are mixed, gray is result. 1972: First office set up in church basement in Philadelphia with help of college students. National headquarters remains in Philadelphia but regional groups have great deal of autonomy to encourage many leaders, rather than reliance and deference to founder, which she feels would handicap its existence after her death. Author of *Get Out There and Do Something About Injustice*. July 12, 1973: Testified on behalf of organization before Senate subcommittee on Health of Elderly regarding home health care. December 1, 1973: Merged with one of Ralph Nader's Public Citizen Groups, Retired Professional Action Group, with which it had been co-operating in training older persons to use skills in public-interest work. Gray Panther Project Fund incorporated to receive donations and allocate funds. Continued promotion of legislation concerning hearing aid industry and nursing homes, begun by merged group. Organized citizen-action groups into National Coalition for Nursing Home Reform and initiated three-year study. Demonstrated at American Medical Association meetings and presented position papers to organization; believes national health care program and elimination of profit motive are crucial to quality care. Said "socialized medicine" works well for armed forces, Congress, and President and his family, so it should be extended to all. 1974: Received first annual Award for Justice and Human Development of Witherspoon Society. October 1975: First Gray Panthers general convention attracted delegates from over 30 states and District of Columbia. 1975: Honored with Distinguished Service Award in Consumer Advocacy of American Speech and Hearing Association. 1976: Delivered Alumni Address at 50th college class reunion. Selected as one of first people to visit People's Republic of China in October. Received Freedom Award of Women's Scholarship Association of Roosevelt

University, and Annual Award of Philadelphia Society of Clinical Psychologists.   **April 4, 1977:** Appeared before House committee regarding fragmentation of health care services and lack of involvement in planning and development of programs.   **September 1977:** Testified regarding findings of Panther's Media Watch concerning negative stereotyping of elderly on TV stating it contributes to alienation between young and old.   **October 1977:** Attendance at second convention in Chevy Chase, Maryland, was 350 delegates representing 8,000 affiliate members of about 70 network groups. **November 7, 1977:** Witness before House committee regarding nutrition education.   **1977:** *Nursing Homes: A Citizen's Action Guide,* published as result of study begun in 1973. Recipient of annual Peaceseeker Award of United Presbyterian Peace Fellowship. *Maggie Kuhn on Aging: A Dialogue,* published.   **1978:** Chosen by U.S.-China People's Friendship Association to serve as tour leader for visit to China. Named one of 25 most influential women in United States by *World Almanac.* Selected as Humanist of Year by American Humanist Association; received honorary doctorates from Swarthmore College and Moravian College. Testified before House committee recommending funding priorities for programs for the elderly.   **1978–1980:** Member of Commission on Mental Health.   **1979:** Four hundred people from 30 states attended Gray Panther's biennial meeting. Recipient of honorary degree from Antioch College. As Gray Panther convener, and co-chair of National Committee for Responsive Philanthropy, gave statement before House committee regarding distribution of charitable contributions of federal employees.   **June 1980:** Testified before House committee concerning living arrangements of elderly and effects of age segregation.   **1980:** Received honorary degree from Simmons College and Albright College. **February 4, 1981:** Witness before House committee regarding inequities of social security system treatment of women.   **November 1981:** Honored by alma mater, Case Western Reserve, with Distinguished Alumni Award. **1981:** Recipient of honorary degrees from Marycrest College and State University of New York at Fredonia.   **March 1982:** Chosen as delegate observer at United Nations Forum on Aging in Vienna, Austria.   **May 1982:** Received Gimbel Award.   **November 1982:** Awarded Presidential Citation of American Public Health Association.   **February 1983:** Testified before House committee predicting adverse impact of proposals on elderly beneficiaries and younger workers.   **October 1983:** Selected as one of 100 most important women in America in October issue of *Ladies' Home Journal.* **1983:** Led Gray Panther delegation to World Assembly for Peace and Life, Against Nuclear War, in Prague, Czechoslovakia. Received honorary degree from Grinnell College. Appointed Distinguished Senior Scholar to work in Aging Health Policy Center at University of California, San Francisco. **1985:** Addressed Society of British Gerontologists and other groups in Manchester and London. Received honorary degrees from New Hampshire College,

Cedar Crest College and Antioch College. **July 1986:** Member of Philadelphia delegation to Soviet Union, sponsored by Philadelphia/Leningrad Sister Cities Project. **1986:** Gray Panthers membership stood at about 60,000 in United States. Recipient of honorary doctorate from Beaver College. **1987:** Honorary degree received from Russell Sage College. **February 1988:** Addressed conference of American Physical Therapy Association, crediting treatment of therapists in hometown for quick recovery from November, 1987, Philadelphia mugging. **May 1988:** Received honorary degree from Pennsylvania College of Optometry. **March 1989:** Participant at Villanova University conference exploring women and poverty. **June 1989:** Received honorary degree and spoke at commencement exercises at University of Massachusetts, Boston Gerontology Institute about children with AIDS, stating elderly have obligation to be advocates for children. **1989–:** Presented awards to outstanding women and men chosen by local group as representing ideals of Gray Panthers. Resides in racially mixed section of Germantown in Philadelphia in home that she purchased in late 1950s; shares home with others of varying ages, another idea she has promoted. Has studied at graduate level in social group work at Temple University, sociology and ethics at University of Southern California, University of Hawaii, San Francisco Theological Seminary and LaSalle College. Fiery, straightforward speaker, continues to lecture nationwide, and to serve on many boards and committees. Has made numerous television appearances. Feels that elderly have nothing to lose by being radical and militant, and they thrive when they have a goal that bears on common good. Gray Panther organization of 70,000 members continues to bring historical perspective of elderly to ideas of the young; concerns include universal free health care, special problems of older women, patient advocacy, mental health, sexuality of elderly, public ownership of utilities, opposition to mandatory retirement, hospice and home health care, rights of disabled, housing, all the while reiterating need for fundamental social change in goal to obliterate ageism, racism and sexism. **April 16, 1991:** Gave speech entitled "New Roles for Older Persons" at Central Presbyterian Church in Buffalo, New York.

BACKGROUND INFORMATION

Parents: Minnie Louise (Kooman) and Samuel Frederick Kuhn. Father was credit manager of German extraction. **Siblings:** One (Samuel Kooman). **Children:** None. **Influences:** None. **Ethnicity:** German American. **Also known as:** Maggie. **Historical sites, landmarks, etc.:** None known.

BIBLIOGRAPHICAL INFORMATION

Biographical Sketches About Margaret E. Kuhn

Gilbert, Lynn, and Gaylen Moore. *Particular Passions*. New York: Clarkson N. Potter, 1981.

May, Hal, ed. *Contemporary Authors*. Detroit: Gale Research, 1983.

Moritz, Charles, ed. *Current Biography Yearbook 1978*. New York: H. W. Wilson Company, 1978.

O'Neill, Lois Decker, ed. *The Women's Book of World Records and Achievements*. Garden City, NY: Anchor Press/Doubleday, 1979.

Books by Margaret E. Kuhn

Get Out There and Do Something About Injustice. New York: Friendship, [1972].

You Can't Be Human Alone: Handbook on Group Procedures for the Local Church. [New York: Published for the Division of Christian Life and Work and the Division of Christian Education by] National Council of the Churches of Christ in the U.S.A., [1956].

Hessel, Dieter, ed. *Maggie Kuhn on Aging: A Dialogue*. Philadelphia: Westminster, 1977.

Shorter Works by Margaret E. Kuhn

"Advocacy in This New Age." *Aging* 297 (July 1979):2–5.

"Editorial." *Gray Panther Network* (Fall 1987): 15.

"Editorial." *Gray Panther Network* (November 1988): 13.

"Excerpt from Testimony on Proposed Welfare Reform, November 1, 1977." *Congressional Digest* 57 (May 1978): 147 + .

"Gray Is Beautiful." *Lutheran Women* 11 (Fall 1973): 13–17.

"Gray Panther Thoughts on Ageism, Health Care and Worklife." *Journal of the Institute for Socioeconomic Studies* 2 (Autumn 1977): 33–42.

"Gray Panthers." In *The Encyclopedia of Aging*, edited by George L. Maddox. New York: Springer, 1987.

"Health Care: Basic Human Right." *Gray Panther Network* (May 1983): 13.

"Insights on Aging." *Journal of Home Economics* 70 (1978): 18–20.

"Kuhn Defends Legal Services." *Gray Panther Network* (May 1981): 16.

"Learning by Living." *International Journal of Aging and Human Development* 8 (1978): 359–65.

"Looking Down the Road." *Gray Panther Network* (September 1982): 7.

"Open Letter [With Reply by G. L. Maddox]." *Gerontologist* 18 (October 1978): 422–27.

"Ten Steps to Prepare You for New Advocacy Role." *Gray Panther Network* (Summer 1984): 5.

"What Old People Want for Themselves and Others in Society." In *Advocacy and Age: Issues, Experiences, Strategies,* edited by Paul A. Kerschner. Los Angeles: Ethel Percy Andrus Gerontology Center, University of Southern California, 1976.
"Why Old and Young Should Live Together." *50 Plus* 18 (October 1978): 18–20.
Horn, Linda, and Elma Griesel. *Nursing Homes: A Citizens' Action Guide.* Boston: Beacon, 1977. (Introduction written by Kuhn.)

Shorter Works About Margaret E. Kuhn

Benedict, Helen. "My Side (interview)." *Working Woman* 7 (May 1982): 169–71.
Blalock, R. "Gray Power." *Saturday Evening Post* 215 (March 1979): 32 +.
Daugherty, Jane. "Whatever Happened to the Gray Panthers?" *50 Plus* 23 (October 1983): 25.
Fisher, Jan. "Maggie Kuhn's Vision: Young and Old Together." *50 Plus* 26 (July 1986): 22 +.
"Gray Panther Power: An Interview." *Center Magazine* 8 (March 1975): 21–25.
Halamandaris, Val J. "Compassionate Revolutionary: A Tribute to Maggie Kuhn." *Caring* (February 1986): 34–39.
Halligan, T. "Social Security Reform Package." *Gray Panther Network* (January 1983): 1.
"How to Fight Age Bias." *Ms.* 3 (June 1975): 91.
Jantzen, E. "Maryland Proposal to Privatize Medicare." *Gray Panther Network* (Spring 1986): 4.
Kanin, Garson. *It Takes a Long Time to Become Young.* Garden City, NY: Doubleday, 1978.
————. "To Rest Is to Rust: Forced to Retire at 65, Maggie Kuhn Angrily Founded the Gray Panthers." *Quest* 3 (June 1979): 64 +.
"Legions of the Old." *Newsweek* 101 (January 24, 1983): 23.
Long, C. "Maggie Kuhn: Around the World." *Gray Panther Network* (Summer 1985): 4.
Lyman, Francesca. "Maggie Kuhn: A Wrinkled Radical's Crusade." *Progressive* 52 (January 1988): 29–31.
"Kuhn, Maggie." *Current Biography* 39 (July 1978): 13–16.
McDonald, Donald. "Gray Panther Power: An Interview with Maggie Kuhn." *Center Magazine* 8 (March–April 1975): 21 +.
Mallowe, Mike. "Forty Over Eighty: These 40 People Have Left the Biggest Footprints Over the Last 80 Years": *Philadelphia Magazine* 79 (September 1988): 146 +.
Mandel, Bill. "Maggie Kuhn: What Makes Maggie Kuhn Gallop at 69?" *Biography News* 2 (May–June 1975): 576–77.
Mehren, E. "Gray Panther Convention." *Gray Panther Network* (January 1982): 1.
Oesch, M. "Activist, Maggie Kuhn." *Congress Watcher* (September 1983): 13.
Offen, C., ed. "Profile of a Gray Panther: Interview." *Retirement Living* 12 (December 1972): 32–37.
"Open Letter (with Reply by G. L. Maddox)." *Gerontologist* 18 (1978): 422–27.

Rosser, P. "Shared Housing, Creative Work Plans, and Other Alternatives for a Sane and Secure Long Life." *Ms.* 10 (January 1982): 83–84.
Seskin, Jane. *More Than Mere Survival: Conversations with Women Over 65.* New York: Newsweek Books, 1980.
Shapiro, Bruce. "Maggie, You Can Speak Your Mind." *In These Times* 6 (August 25–September 7, 1982): 12.
Stoenner, Herb. "Gray Panther Chief Fights to Keep Elderly from Getting Clawed." *Biography News* 1 (May 1974): 556.
Streinick, H. "Maggie Kuhn: All of Us Are in This Together." *Health PAC Bulletin* 14 (January 1983): 19.
Tannehauser, Carol. "Passion with a Purpose, Women with a Cause." *Woman's Day* (January 20, 1987): 96 + .
Wandres, J., ed. "Retirees Should Be Recycled for Public-Interest Work: Interview." *Retirement Living* 15 (December 1975): 40–42 + .

Other Works About Margaret E. Kuhn
Song
Freilicher, Elizabeth. "Maggie Kuhn." In *Here's to the Women: 100 Songs For and About American Women,* by Hilda E. Wenner and Elizabeth Freilicher. Syracuse, NY: Syracuse University Press, 1987.

Media Materials by Margaret E. Kuhn
Sound Recordings
Maggie Kuhn Speaks. Los Angeles: Pacifica Tape Library, [1983?]. Sound cassette; 43 min.; 1 ⅞ ips; mono.
"Surviving and Thriving in a New Age." In *Practical Interventions in Geriatrics: Enhancing Quality of Life Through Quality of Care.* Pittsburgh, PA: Media Production Series, 1987. 7 cassettes; 630 min.; 1 ⅞ ips; 2 track; mono; ⅛ in. tape.
Women in a Changing World. Ames: Media Resources Center, Iowa State University, 1980. Cassette; 55 min.; 2 track; mono.

Video Recordings
Age and Outrage. Madison: School of Social Work, University of Wisconsin, 1977. 2 videocassettes; 80 min.; black and white; sound; ¾ in.
New Roles For the Elders of the Tribe. Portland, ME: n.p., 1975. Videocassette; black and white; sound; VHS; ½ in.
Wellness and Aging. Chicago: Augustana Hospital School of Nursing, 1981. Videocassette; 15 min.; color; sound; ¾ in.

Media Materials About Margaret E. Kuhn
Films
Maggie Kuhn—Wrinkled Radical. Bloomington, IN: Indiana University Audio-Visual Center, 1977. 16 mm.; 27 min.; color.

A Matter of Indifference. New York: Phoenix /BFA Films and Video, Inc., 1974. 16 mm.; 48 min.; black and white.

Sound Recordings

"The Church in Ministry with Older Adults." In *Thesis Theological Cassettes.* Pittsburgh: Thesis, 1973. Cassette; 2 track; mono.

Cohen, Stephen Z. *The Other Generation Gap.* Washington, D. C.: National Public Radio, 1978. Sound cassette; 59 min.; analog.

Health Care of Older Americans: Money and Attitudes. New York: National Nursing Network, [1988]. Sound cassette; 75 min.; 1 7⁄8 ips.

[Maggie Kuhn and Claude Pepper Talk About Gain and Setbacks for Senior Citizens in the Past Decade]. PBS (Over Easy), April 28, 1981. Sound tape reel; 25 min.; 7 ½ ips.; mono; 7 in.

A Wrinkled Radical: The Founder of the Grey Panthers Talks with Studs Terkel. Audio-text 38865. [19?]. Tape cassette.

Video Recordings

Aging—A Human Experience. Baltimore, MD: College of Notre Dame of Maryland, 1979. 2 video cassettes; sound; black and white; ¾ in.

Maggie Kuhn— Wrinkled Radical. Bloomington, IN: Indiana University Audio-Visual Center, 1977, made 1975. Cassette; 27 min.; sound; color; ¾ or ½ in.

A Matter of Indifference. New York: Phoenix/BFA Films and Video, Inc., 1974. Video; 48 min.; black and white; ¾ or ½ in.

Portrait—Maggie Kuhn. Ann Arbor: University of Michigan TV Center, 1979. Video cassette; 30 min.; color; ¾ in.

Primary Source Materials Relating to Margaret E. Kuhn

United Presbyterian Church in the U.S.A. Board of Christian Education. Office of Church and Society. Records. 1945–66 and 1949–69. Extent of collection: 19 ft. (ca. 5,100 items) and 17 ft. (ca. 31,500 items). Finding aids: Not listed. Location: Presbyterian Church USA, Presbyterian Office of History Library, Department of History, 425 Lombard St., Philadelphia, Pennsylvania 19147. Scope of collection: Correspondents include Kuhn.

37. *Susette La Flesche*
(1854–1903)
Advocate for Native American rights; lecturer

BIOGRAPHICAL INFORMATION

Chronological Biography

Born in 1854 near what is now Bellevue, Nebraska, in Omaha Indian village. Second of five children and oldest daughter of Mary (Gale) and

Joseph La Flesche (Iron Eye). Father was chief of Omaha tribe, but had had much contact with whites and felt strongly that Native Americans must learn white ways in order to survive. Encouraged children to learn English and become educated. Native American name was Inshta Theumba (various spellings), "Bright Eyes." Raised first in earth lodge, later in two-story log and frame house on reservation bordering Missouri River. Educated at Presbyterian mission school beginning at age eight.

1873?: First of her tribe to attend school in East, graduated from Elizabeth Institute, private girls' seminary in New Jersey. Returned to reservation; after some months of difficulty in gaining position (despite promises that Native Americans would be given first preference for agency jobs), began teaching in government school.   **Early 1879:** Through government mistake in 1877, Ponca Indians' homeland in Nebraska was given to Sioux tribe; Poncas were then forced to move to Oklahoma Indian Territory where about one third died within few years. Standing Bear, Ponca chief, tried to lead small group back to original home; Army arrested them, intending to send them back to Indian Territory. During this time, accompanied her father on visit to Poncas.   **April 1879:** Thomas Henry Tibbles, *Omaha Herald* newspaperman, began legal action which resulted in Poncas' release and legal ruling that Native Americans were to be recognized as persons before the law.   1879–1880: Wishing to publicize case and raise public sympathy to plight of Native Americans, Tibbles began lecture tour in the East. Standing Bear accompanied him, with Susette acting as interpreter. Brother Francis was also part of group. Articulate and eloquent speaker, became most widely known Native American woman of her time and first woman to speak for rights of Native Americans. Wore Native American dress and used Native American name, drawing large crowds in Boston, Philadelphia, and Washington, D. C. As result of lectures, during which she spoke of injustice to Native Americans and consequent suffering, Boston Indian Committee (Indian Citizenship Committee) was formed by well-known people who worked for change in government policies and actions. Helen Maria Fiske Hunt Jackson (see entry 32) was so moved that she began campaign to secure Native American rights. Mary L. Bonney (see entry 11) also heard her speak and began her work. Other organizations were formed and people contributed financially as she stirred consciences. Continued to lecture with Standing Bear, and then with Tibbles. Favored education and assimilation but also retention of some traditional cultural values. Testified before several Senate committees.   **Spring 1880:** Witness at Senate hearing relating to removal of Ponca Indians.   **July 23, 1881:** Married Tibbles.   1881: Edited *Ploughed Under: The Story of an Indian Chief.* Presented paper before Association for Advancement of Women entitled, "The Position, Occupation and Culture of Indian Women."   1886: Couple travelled to England and Scotland for ten-month lecture tour on Native American affairs, culture and women; again, she was well received.   1887: Clear, forceful speaker, made strong impression on audiences; lectures greatly influenced passage of Dawes Act which authorized allotment of land and citizenship rights to Native Americans. 1895: Husband edited weekly *Independent*, Populist paper, in Lincoln, Nebraska; previously they had lived briefly in Washington, D. C., writing and lecturing.   1898: Illustrated *Oo-Mah-Ha Ta-Wa-Tha (Omaha City)*; may have been first book illustrated by Native American Indian.   1902: In ill health, moved with husband near Bancroft, Nebraska, to land given to her as allotment as tribe member. Continued to edit *Independent*, published in Lincoln, which she had begun to do some time before.   May 26, 1903: Died at about age 49 and was buried in Bancroft. Had contributed stories to newspapers and magazines, among them *St. Nicholas* magazine; probably also wrote number of articles for husband's papers, but did not sign them.

Background Information

Parents: Mary (Gale) and Joseph La Flesche (Iron Eye). Mother's parents were Native American woman and white Army surgeon. Father was son of French fur trader and Native American woman and had grown up among Native Americans as well as living in St. Louis for some time. Father had more than one wife and had children by one other wife.   **Siblings:** Five (Rosalie, Marguerite, Susan, Francis, Lucy [half-sister].   **Children:** None. **Influences:** Thomas H. Tibbles.   **Ethnicity:** Native American (Omaha), French American.   **Also known as:** Tibbles; Bright Eyes; Inshta Theumba. **Historical sites, landmarks, etc.:** None known.

BIBLIOGRAPHICAL INFORMATION

Biographical Sketches About Susette La Flesche

Dockstader, Frederick J. *Great North American Indians*. New York: Van Nostrand Reinhold, 1977.
Encyclopedia Americana. Danbury, CT: Grolier, 1990. (Listed under Bright Eyes.)
James, Edward T., ed. *Notable American Women 1607–1950: A Biographical Dictionary*. Cambridge, MA: Belknap Press of Harvard University Press, 1971. (Listed under Tibbles, Susette La Flesche.)
Johnson, Allen, and Dumas Malone, eds. *Dictionary of American Biography*. New York: Charles Scribner's Sons, 1958. (Listed under Bright Eyes.)
McHenry, Robert, ed. *Famous American Women*. New York: Dover, 1980.

Books About Susette La Flesche

Crary, Margaret. *Susette La Flesche: Voice of the Omaha Indians.* New York: Hawthorn, [1973].
Wilson, Dorothy Clarke. *Bright Eyes: The Story of Susette La Flesche, an Omaha Indian.* New York: McGraw-Hill, [1974].

Shorter Works by Susette La Flesche

"The Indian Question." *Christian Union* (March 10, 1880).
"An Indian Woman's Letter." *Southern Workman* 8 (April 1879): 44.
"Nedawi." *St. Nicholas* (January 1881).
"Omaha Legends and Tent-Stories." *Wide Awake* (June 1883).
Harsha, William Justin. *Ploughed Under: The Story of an Indian Chief, Told by Himself, with an Introduction by Inshta Theamba (Bright Eyes).* New York: Fords, Howard & Hulbert, 1881. (La Flesche edited and wrote introduction to this work.)
Tibbles, Thomas Henry. *The Ponca Chiefs.* Boston: Lockwood, Brooks & Co., 1880. Reprint. Lincoln: University of Nebraska Press, [1972]. (Introduction was written by La Flesche.)

Shorter Works About Susette La Flesche

Bolton, Herbert Eugene. *[Articles from] Handbook of American Indians North of Mexico.* Edited by Frederick Webb Hodge. Washington, D. C.: GPO, 1907.
"Bright Eyes." *Council Fire* (December 1881): 187–88.
Cutter, Irving S. "Dr. John Gale, a Pioneer Army Surgeon." *Journal of the Illinois State Historical Society* 23 (January 1931): 630–41.
Eastman, Elaine Goodale. *Pratt, the Red Man's Moses.* Norman: University of Oklahoma Press, 1935.
Gray, Dorothy. *Women of the West.* Millbrae, CA: Les Femmes, 1976.
Green, Norma Kidd. "Four Sisters: Daughters of Joseph La Flesche." In *Lives to Remember,* edited by Leon Stein. New York: Arno Press, 1974.
————. "Four Sisters: Daughters of Joseph La Flesche." *Nebraska History* 45 (June 1964): 165–76.
————. *Iron Eye's Family: The Children of Joseph La Flesche.* Lincoln: Johnsen, [1969].
Herzog, Kristin. "The La Flesche Family: Native American Spirituality, Calvinism, and Presbyterian Missions." *American Presbyterians* 65 (1987): 222–32.
Miller, J. D. "'Bright Eyes,' Emancipator of the Indian." *National Magazine* 12 (1900): 394.
Odell, Ruth. *Helen Hunt Jackson.* New York: D. Appleton-Century Company, 1939.
Scholten, Pat Creech. "Exploitation of Ethos: Sarah Winnemuca and Bright Eyes on the Lecture Tour." *Western Journal of Speech Communication* 41 (1977): 233–44.

Seymour, Flora Warren. *Indian Agents of the Old Frontier*. New York: D. Appleton-Century Company, 1941.
Street, Douglas. "La Flesche Sisters Write to St. Nicholas Magazine." *Nebraska History* 62 (1981): 515–23.
Tibbles, Thomas Henry. *Buckskin and Blanket Days: Memoirs of a Friend of the Indians Written in 1905*. Garden City, NY: Doubleday, 1957. Reprint. Chicago: R. R. Donnelley & Sons, 1985.

Other Works by Susette La Flesche

Giffen, Fannie Reed. *Oo-Mah-Ha Ta-Wa-Tha (Omaha City)*. Lincoln, Nebraska: Published by the Authors, 1898. (With illustrations by Susette La Flesche Tibbles.)

Other Works About Susette La Flesche
Theses

Haupt, Carol Magdalene. "The Image of the American Indian Female in the Biographical Literature and Social Studies Textbooks of the Elementary Schools." EDD diss., Rutgers the State University of New Jersey-New Brunswick, 1984.

Primary Source Materials Relating to Susette La Flesche

La Flesche Family. Papers. 1859–1933. Extent of collection: ca. 800 items. Finding aids: Not listed. Location: Nebraska State Historical Society, 1500 R St., P.O. Box 82554, Lincoln, Nebraska 68501. Scope of collecton: Family papers including La Flesche's autograph album, books and correspondence.
Museum of the American Indian, Heye Foundation. Records. 1860–1983, 1890–1980 (bulk). Extent of collection: 160 cu. ft. Finding aids: Folder inventory. Location: Museum of the American Indian, Heye Foundation, Archives, Annex Bruckner Blvd. & Middletown Rd., New York, New York 10454. Scope of collection: Major component of collection is correspondence, including La Flesche Tibbles.

38. *Roberta Campbell Lawson*
(1878–1940)
Clubwoman; Native American leader

BIOGRAPHICAL INFORMATION

Chronological Biography

Daughter of Emeline (Emma, Emmaline) (Journeycake), Delaware Indian, and John Edward Campbell. Born October 31, 1878, at Alluwe, Cherokee

Nation, Indian Territory, later Oklahoma. Eldest of three children, one of two brothers died in infancy. Brought up in hospitable home in remote rural area; comfortable surroundings included books, musical instruments, fine paintings and horses. Devoted to Native American grandfather from whom she learned Native American legends and chants as well as lifelong spiritual values from his sermons. Became life-long friends with Cherokee humorist Will Rogers who lived on adjoining ranch. Educated at home by private tutors and attended girls' seminary in Independence, Missouri. Studied music at Hardin College in Mexico, Missouri. Upon return from college, formed club with three others which travelled locally to promote friendship and culture, and share benefits of their education.

October 31, 1901: On twenty-third birthday, in Alluwe, married Eugene Beauharnais Lawson. Originally from Kentucky, he practiced law in nearby town of Nowata where they made their home. They soon became leaders in community civic and financial areas as Indian Territory expanded prior to becoming state. President and one of organizers of town's first woman's club in 1903; first federated club in territory. Helped establish public library and park, and was active in YWCA. Husband was one of founders of First National Bank and established interests in oil field which later grew into Lawson Petroleum Company. Financial security enabled her to actively participate in civic and educational organizations, and pursue personal concerns including improvement of women's role in politics. Another enduring interest was preservation and composition of Native American music. Gave lecture-concerts and participated in national radio program to bring chants learned as child to public's attention. Also included chants, songs, and poems of own creation in programs. Translated number of Native American chants and transcribed old Delaware melodies that would likely have been lost. **1905:** Only child, Edward Campbell Lawson, born. **World War I:** Chaired women's division of Council of National Defense. **1916–1929:** One of directors of First National Bank. **1917–1919:** President of Oklahoma State Federation of Women's Clubs; previously served as president of district association. **1918–1922:** One of directors of General Federation of Women's Clubs. **1918–1940:** Member of board of regents of Oklahoma College for Women in Chickasha. **1926:** *Indian Music Programs for Clubs and Special Music Days* published. **1926–1928:** Chair of music division of General Federation of Women's Clubs. Moved to Tulsa about this time due to husband's increasing oil business. Served as director of Oklahoma Historical Society. **1928–1932:** Second vice president of General Federation of Women's Clubs. **1930–1938:** Only woman trustee of University of Tulsa. **1931:** Asked by Will Rogers to become executive chair of committee to administer sizeable fund he had collected through benefit appearances for drought relief in various states, especially Oklahoma. Husband died. **1932–1935:** First vice president of General Federation of Women's Clubs. **1933:**

Member of first General Federation's World Friendship Tour; presented several programs of Native American music in Czechoslovakia. **1933–1934:** Member of Eleanor Roosevelt's committee for mobilization of human needs. **1934:** Delegate to Woman's Pan-Pacific Association convention in Honolulu. **1935–1938:** President of General Federation of Women's Clubs, largest organization of women in world, bringing her national prominence. Women's clubs provided one of few avenues available to women interested in public life and frequently were important force for social and political change. Theme of her administration was "Education for Living." Very instrumental in establishment of national Academy of Public Service, similar to West Point and Annapolis, to prepare students for government service. Championed causes of Native Americans, using considerable leadership and speaking skills to enlist others to work in their behalf. Particularly concerned with improvement of Native American education. **1937:** Spoke at memorial dedication of building at Bacone State College named for her great-grandmother, Sally Journeycake. **1937–1940:** Vice president of Pan-Pacific Women's Association. **1938:** Retired from presidency of General Federation of Women's Clubs. **July 1940:** One of four prominent Democrats opposed to New Deal who were named by Wendell Willkie to committee to organize support for his presidential candidacy. **December 31, 1940:** Died at age 62 of leukemia in hospital in Tulsa, Oklahoma. Buried in city's Memorial Park Cemetery. Had continued active involvement in many organizations including American Pen Women's Association, National Council of Women and Indian Council Fires of Chicago. **1947:** Important collection of art and objects given by son and wife to Philbrook Art Center in Tulsa where it resides in Indian Room. Long a student of Native American culture and music, she and husband had assembled collection of artifacts, as well as a library on Native American history, including many rare and out-of-print books, in effort to preserve traditions and culture of Native Americans. Collected over period of many years, had originally been kept in her home in Tulsa.

Background Information

Parents: Emeline (Emma, Emmaline) (Journeycake) and John Edward Campbell. Mother had come to territory from Kansas and was daughter of the Rev. Charles Journeycake, last chief of Delaware Indians; he had been ordained Baptist minister at 52 years of age, had helped establish Bacone College, only college in United States for Native Americans for many years, and founded Native American church at Alluwe. Father came from pioneer Virginia family; built up prosperous mercantile and cattle business. **Siblings:** Two (No known names). **Children:** One (Edward Campbell). **Influences:** None.

Ethnicity: Native American (Delaware), Scottish American. **Also known as:** None known. **Historical sites, landmarks, etc.:** Bronze bust in Outdoor Memorial, National Hall of Fame for Famous American Indians, US Route 62, Anadarko, Oklahoma; Grave, Memorial Park Cemetery, Tulsa, Oklahoma; Indian Room, Philbrook Art Center, 2727 S. Rockford Road, Tulsa, Oklahoma.

BIBLIOGRAPHICAL INFORMATION

Biographical Sketches About Roberta Campbell Lawson

Dockstader, Frederick J. *Great North American Indians.* New York: Van Nostrand Reinhold, 1977.

James, Edward T., ed. *Notable American Women 1607–1950: A Biographical Dictionary.* Cambridge, MA: Belknap Press of Harvard University Press, 1971.

National Cyclopaedia of American Biography. Ann Arbor, MI: University Microfilms, 1967.

O'Neill, Lois Decker, ed. *The Women's Book of World Records and Achievements.* Garden City, NY: Anchor Press/Doubleday, 1979.

Books by Roberta Campbell Lawson

Indian Music Programs for Clubs and Special Music Days. Nowata, OK: n.p., 1926.

Shorter Works by Roberta Campbell Lawson

"The Evolution of Indian Music." *Community Arts & Crafts* (May 1929): 15 + .

"What Democracy Means to Me – IV." *Senior Scholastic* 31 (January 22, 1938): 7.

Shorter Works About Roberta Campbell Lawson

Drennen, M. "In the Service of Others; interview." *Christian Science Monitor Weekly Magazine Section* (January 8, 1936): 3.

Hagerty, James C. "Douglas and Hanes Join Willkie Ranks." *New York Times* (July 23, 1940): 1.

———. "Willkie Counts on Wilson Democrats and Those of 1932." *New York Times* (July 30, 1940): 1.

———. "Willkie Hails Aid of Smith, Seabury." *New York Times* (July 31, 1940): 12.

"Love of Life." In *Thoroughbred Hearts,* by Marguerite Drennen. New York: Comet Press Books, 1957.

Marable, Mary Hayes, and Elaine Boylan. *A Handbook of Oklahoma Writers.* Norman: University of Oklahoma Press, 1939.
"Portrait." *Woman's Home Companion* 62 (March 1935): 92.
"Prominant Club Woman." *Indian Leader* 39 (October 25, 1935): 1.
Rainey, Luretta Gilbert. *History of Oklahoma State Federation of Women's Clubs.* Guthrie, OK: Co-operative Publishing Company, [1939].
"Roberta Campbell Lawson: Leader of Three Million Women." In *American Indian Women,* by Marion E. Gridley. New York: Hawthorn, 1974.
"Roberta Lawson, Led Clubwomen." *New York Times* (January 1, 1941): 23.
Scouller, Mildred Marshall. *Women Who Man Our Clubs.* Philadelphia: John C. Winston, [1934].
Wells, Mildred White. *Unity in Diversity; The History of the General Federation of Women's Clubs.* [Washington]: General Federation of Women's Clubs, 1953.
"The William Penn Elm Tree." *Chronicles of Oklahoma* (June 1933): 755–57.

Primary Source Materials Relating to Roberta Campbell Lawson

Democrats-for-Willkie. Records. 1940. Extent of collection: 18.0 cu. ft. Finding aids: Register. Location: University of Rochester, Rush Rhees Library, Department of Rare Books, Manuscripts and Archives, Rochester, New York 14627. Scope of collection: Records include correspondence, telegrams, printed material, memoranda, photographs, press releases, news clippings, treasurer's records and a guest book. Prominent people in movement include Lawson.

39. *Mary Elizabeth Clyens Lease*
(1850?–1933)

Populist party lecturer; advocate for
birth control and women's rights and suffrage

BIOGRAPHICAL INFORMATION

Chronological Biography

Daughter of Mary Elizabeth (Murray) and Joseph P. Clyens. Born September 11, 1850?, probably in Ridgway, Elk County, Pennsylvania, sixth of eight or ten children, third of four daughters, but may have been born before parents came to United States. Raised in Ceres Township, McKean County, on farm near New York state border. Attended Catholic schools. **August 17, 1864:** Father died during Civil War in Confederate Andersonville prison, leaving family impoverished. **1865–1868:** At age 15, graduated with teaching certificate from St. Elizabeth's Academy in Allegany, New York, by the generosity of family friends who financed her education. **1865/8–1870:** Taught school in local area near Ceres, Pennsylvania. Unsuccessful in efforts to organize colleagues to fight for wage increase. **Fall 1871:** Moved to Osage Mission, Neosho County, Kansas, for higher paying teaching job. Taught at St. Anne's Academy, Catholic girls' boarding school run by Mother Mary Bridget Hayden. Taught one term at nearby grade school. **January 20, 1873:** Married local pharmacist Charles L. Lease; gave up Catholicism. **1873–1883:** In Osage Mission, gave well-received performance in play, *The Coming Woman; or the Spirit of '76*, portraying life if country were run by women. Wrote verse for Osage Mission *Transcript*. Husband was elected mayor of Osage Mission in April 1884, but couple moved in summer of that year, most likely to Denison, Texas, where husband may have considered opening own pharmacy; may have first farmed, unsuccesfully, in Kingman County, Kansas. Husband found job in local pharmacy. Took in laundry to supplement family finances. Charles Henry (November 1874), Evelyn Louise (1880) and Grace Lena (1883) born in Denison. Became involved in Woman's Christian Temperance Union and began giving speeches. **Mid 1880s:** Returned to Kansas, living first in small town of Kingman where she wrote series of newspaper articles entitled "Are Women Inferior to Men?"; moved to Wichita in 1884. Three more children born, two of whom died in infancy. Ben Hur, last child, born in 1885. Husband worked as pharmacist. Thrived on urban life. In January 1886, founded Hypatia Society, women's current issues discussion group and was elected president. Poetry was published in *Wichita Eagle*. Elected president of Wichita Equal Suffrage Association. Joined Knights of Labor and Kansas Farmers' Alliance. **1885:** Charismatic, emotional speaker who captured and held audiences with strong, resonant voice and dignified appearance but may have occasionally stretched truth to make a point. Agitator, publicist and advocate for causes, rather than political theorist or original thinker. Began appearing as paid lecturer. Conducted statewide fund-raising tour for Irish National League. Spoke in support of woman suffrage in Wichita at state convention of Union Labor Party; had helped to found group which supported small farmers. **1888:** Made speeches for Labor Party throughout state during campaign. Refused nomination for county superintendent of schools in order to edit party paper *Union Labor Press* for six months, renaming it *Wichita Independent*. **April 1889:** Admitted to Wichita bar after studying law at home. May have been admitted to state bar in mid 1880s. Opened law office with woman partner. **1889:** Severe drought, high shipping costs, mortgage foreclosures, etc. combined with political system that neglected their concerns, spurred discontented Kansas farmers to form People's party, later called Populist party. On visit to Colorado for her health, helped found labor paper, *Colorado Workman*. **1890:** Toured state giving over 160 speeches for Populist party campaign. Fiery speeches in which she may have urged them to "raise less corn and more hell" made her controversial figure, farmers calling her "Our Queen Mary," detractors "Kansas Pythoness," and "Mary Yellin," which accounts for her periodically being incorrectly referred to as "Mary Ellen." **August 1891:** First woman to address Georgia state legislature. **September 1891:** Populist women founded National Woman's Alliance. Signed charter along with Marion Marsh Todd (see entry 62), Sarah Elizabeth Van De Vort Emery (see entry 21), and others. **1891:** Extended party's campaign into Missouri and the South, as well as far West, becoming national leader. Elected president of large local Knights of Labor. **February 1892?:** Spoke at first Washington Convention of National Council of Women regarding women in Farmers' Alliance movement. At St. Louis convention, appointed to Populist committee that moved party to national level. **June 1892:** Delegate to Kansas state convention. Initiated equal suffrage amendment which was endorsed. **July 1892:** At convention in Omaha, Nebraska, seconded nomination of General James B. Weaver as Populist party presidential candidate. Only woman delegate from Kansas. Campaigned with Weaver in mountain and midwest states, on West Coast and in South in fall of that year. Inability to make political compromises, competitive and erratic temperament, however, made it difficult for others in party, strategist Annie L. Diggs included, to work with her. **1892:** Author Hamlin Garland patterned heroine Ida Wilbur after Lease in novel *A Spoil of Office*, published in 1892. **1893:** Party achieved major victories in Kansas, and Lease became first woman appointed president of State Board of Charities as reward for her efforts. Spoke at World's Columbian Exposition in Chicago on Kansas Day. Elected national vice president at World Peace Congress in Chicago. Unsuccessfully ran for U.S. Senate. **December 1893–1894:** Removed from Board of Charities by Governor Lorenzo D. Lewelling after refusal to accede to his request to select some allied Democrats for appointed positions under her control. Lease had deep hatred of Democrats, holding them responsible for Civil War related deaths of father and two older brothers. State Supreme Court ruled action illegal after her 30-year fight. **1895:** Only book, *The Problem of Civilization Solved,* published. Wide-ranging discussion of reforms including nationalization of railroads, free trade, colonization, etc. **1896:** Continued favor of party regulars overcame estrangement from leadership, allowing her to be delegate at presidential nomination convention in St. Louis. Despite great effort, was unable to prevent nomination of Democratic candidate William Jennings Bryan as Populist choice; nevertheless participated in campaign referring to him as "God's Great Messiah." **1896–**

1933: With party popularity waning, relocated with her children to New York City and worked as political reporter for Joseph Pulitzer publication *New York World*. Lectured in support of birth control, woman suffrage and prohibition. Supported William McKinley for president and worked in Theodore Roosevelt campaign. May have served as president of National Society for Birth Control. Religious interests ranged from Campbellite to Theosophist to Christian Scientist. Had small law practice on Lower East Side of New York City. Offered free legal advice to poor. 1899: Lectured for Socialist Labor party for six months. Participated in Spiritualist debate. 1901: Filed for divorce and bankruptcy, but managed to put children through college despite limited financial circumstances. 1902: Returned to Kansas very briefly to obtain divorce; at children's request had previously attempted to reconcile with husband in 1901. Grounds cited as non-support although husband had previously supported activities by caring for children, etc. Lived for short time with daughter Evelyn Louise, but primarily with son Ben in Brooklyn. 1908–1918: Gave occasional adult education lectures for New York City Board of Education covering topics from federal price fixing to Einstein's theories to the Soviet Union's five-year plan. 1918: Retired from public life. Sometime later, bought small farm in Delaware Valley near Callicoon, New York. October 29, 1933: Death due to leg infection and chronic nephritis at Callicoon. Buried in Cedar Grove Cemetery in Flushing, Long Island, New York.

Background Information

Parents: Mary Elizabeth (Murray) and Joseph P. Clyens, Irish Catholics married in 1842. Came to United States from Ireland in late 1840s to escape British rule. Mother may have been niece of Bishop of Dublin. **Siblings:** Seven or nine (No known names). **Children:** Four (Charles Henry, Evelyn Louise, Grace Lena, Ben Hur). **Influences:** None. **Ethnicity:** Irish American. **Also known as:** Leese; Mary Ellen. **Historical sites, landmarks, etc.:** Grave, Cedar Grove Cemetery, Flushing, Long Island, New York.

BIBLIGRAPHICAL INFORMATION

Biographical Sketches About Mary Elizabeth Clyens Lease

James, Edward T., ed. *Notable American Women 1607–1950: A Biographical Dictonary*. Cambridge, MA: Belknap Press of Harvard University Press, 1971.

McHenry, Robert, ed. *Famous American Women*. New York: Dover, 1980.
Starr, Harris E., ed. *Dictionary of American Biography*. New York: Charles Scribner's Sons, 1958.
Whitman, Alden, ed. *American Reformers: An H. W. Wilson Biographical Dictionary*. New York: H. W. Wilson Company, 1985.
Uglow, Jennifer S., comp. and ed. *The Continuum Dictionary of Women's Biography*. New York: Continuum, 1989.
Zophy, Angela Howard, ed. *Handbook of American Women's History*. New York: Garland, 1990.

Books by Mary Elizabeth Clyens Lease

The Problem of Civilization Solved. Chicago: Laird & Lee, 1895.

Books About Mary Elizabeth Clyens Lease

Garland, Hamlin. *A Spoil of Office; A Story of the Modern West*. Boston: Arena, 1892. (Fictional treatment.)
Stiller, Richard. *Queen of Populists; The Story of Mary Elizabeth Lease*. New York: T. Y. Crowell, [1970].

Shorter Works by Mary Elizabeth Clyens Lease

Great Quadrangular Debate at Salina, Kansas, December 1893: Question, "Which of the Political Parties Is the Best Qualified to Solve the Social Problems of the Day?" Salina: Open Church, 1894.
"Synopsis of Peace." In *The Congress of Women*, edited by Mary Kavanaugh Oldham Eagle. Chicago: n.p., 1893. Reprint. New York: Arno, 1974.
"Women in the Farmers' Alliance." In *Transactions of the National Council of Women of the United States, Assembled in Washington, D. C., February 22 to 25 , 1891*, edited by Rachel Foster Avery. Philadelphia: J. B. Lippincott, 1891.

Shorter Works About Mary Elizabeth Clyens Lease

Bachtold, Louise M. *Gifted Women in Politics and the Arts and Sciences*. Saratoga, CA: Century Twenty One, 1981.
Blumberg, Dorothy Rose. "Mary Elizabeth Lease, Populist Orator: A Profile." *Kansas History* 1 (Spring 1978): 1–15.
Brown, Dee Alexander. *The Gentle Tamers; Women of the Old Wild West*. New York: Putnam, [1958].
Buhle, Mari Jo. *Women and American Socialism, 1870–1920*. Urbana: University of Illinois Press, 1981.

Clanton, O. Gene. "Intolerant Populist? The Disaffection of Mary Elizabeth Lease." *Kansas Historical Quarterly* 34 (Summer 1968): 189–200.

_____. *Kansas Populism: Ideas and Men.* Lawrence: University Press of Kansas, [1969].

Diggs, Annie L. "The Women in the Alliance Movement." *Arena* (July 1892): 161–79.

_____. "The Women in the Alliance Movement." In *Lives to Remember,* edited by Leon Stein. New York: Arno, 1974.

Goodwyn, Lawrence. *Democratic Promise: The Populist Movement in America.* New York: Oxford University Press, 1976.

Gray, Dorothy. *Women of the West.* Millbrae, CA: Les Femmes, 1976.

Hicks, John D. *The Populist Revolt.* Minneapolis: University of Minnesota Press, 1931.

James, Edward T. "More Corn, Less Hell? A Knights of Labor Glimpse of Mary Elizabeth Lease." *Labor History* 16 (1975): 408 + .

Johnson, Gerald White. *The Lunatic Fringe.* Westport, CT: Greenwood, [1973].

Levinson, Harry. "Mary Elizabeth Lease: Prairie Radical." *Kansas Magazine* (1948): 18–24.

Livermore, A. L. "Mary Elizabeth Lease: The Foremost Woman Politician of the Times." *Metropolitan Magazine* 14 (November 1896): 163–66.

Mayfield, L. "Mary Elizabeth Lease or Yellin' Ellen, the Kansas Tornado." *Texas Quarterly* 18 (Summer 1975): 13–20.

Nugent, Walter T. K. *The Tolerant Populists: Kansas Populism and Nativism.* Chicago: University of Chicago Press, 1963.

[Populism]. *Kansas Quarterly* 1 (Fall 1969): 7–124. (Entire issue is devoted to populism.)

"Portrait." *Bookman* 22 (November 1905): 249.

Wagner, Maryjo. "Prairie Populists: Luna Kellie and Mary Elizabeth Lease." In *Northwest Women's Heritage,* edited by Karen Blair. Seattle: Northwest Center for Research on Women, 1984.

Warren, Ruth. *A Pictorial History of Women in America.* New York: Crown, 1975.

White, William Allen. *The Autobiography of William Allen White.* New York: Macmillan, 1946.

Other Works About Mary Elizabeth Clyens Lease

Theses

Ecroyd, Donald H. "An Analysis and Evaluation of Populist Political Campaign Speech Making in Kansas 1890–1894." Ph.D. diss., University of Iowa, 1950.

Primary Source Materials Relating to Mary Elizabeth Clyens Lease

Families and Individuals. Collection. No Date. Extent of collection: No size given. Finding aids: Partial inventory. Location: Wichita Public Library,

223 South Main, Wichita, Kansas 67202. Scope of collection: Occasional correspondence, biographical material, articles, clippings and photos concerning persons prominent in Wichita's history.

Ignatius Donnelly. Papers. 1856–1972. Extent of collection: 53 ft. and 77 vols. Finding aids: Published guide. Location: Minnesota Historical Society, Library and Archives, 1500 Mississippi Street, Saint Paul, Minnesota 55101. Scope of collection: Candidate of Populist party for vice president of the United States in 1900. Correspondents include Lease.

Kansas State Historical Society Collections Department. Extent of collection: Not listed. Finding aids: Unpublished guides. Location: Kansas State Historical Society, Center for Historical Research, 120 West Tenth, Topeka, Kansas 66612. Scope of collection: Photographs, articles and manuscripts.

40. Betty Jean Lifton
(1926–   )
Advocate for adoptee rights; author; and playwright

BIOGRAPHICAL INFORMATION

Chronological Biography

Born June 11, 1926, in Staten Island, New York. Mother, who was 17 when she was born, worked and kept her in Home for Hebrew Infants, visiting her on weekends, because family would not allow her to bring daughter home as she and father were not married. Afraid that child would die if she stayed in institution, mother gave her up for adoption after about two years. Spent four months in foster home and was then adopted as only child of Hilda and Oscar Kirschner at about age two and one half. Lived in comfortable home in Cincinnati, Ohio.

1931–1935: Family forced to move to small apartment in Chicago due to losses suffered as result of Depression. Attended public school. Shy, docile and withdrawn child.   **1933:** Told by adoptive mother at age seven that she had been adopted after biological parents' deaths; cautioned not to tell father that she knew.   **1935–1944:** Family moved back to Cincinnati and financial circumstances improved. Increasingly felt incomplete because she did not know anything about her blood relatives, circumstances of her birth, etc. Popular in high school, took part in school plays and other activities, but told no one she was adopted, being ashamed and afraid to do so. Relationship with mother deteriorated due to mother's demanding nature; father was quiet, unassuming man. **1944:** Attended University of Illinois. Worked on college paper, was good student, popular with young men. Joined Jewish sorority, but did not immerse herself in their activities, feeling different, like she did not quite fit in. **1945–1948:** Transferred to Barnard College in New York City; graduated with B.A. in literature. Would have attended graduate school in literature or drama, but parents were unwilling for her to do so. **1948–1952:** Stayed in New York rather than return home. Studied typing and speedwriting. Held series of jobs in media, i.e. secretarial assistant to blind TV writer, scriptwriter for "Beat the Clock" television show, copywriter at *Journal American,* production assistant for weekly TV drama. Felt immense guilt for not wishing to return home, feeling "real daughter" would have done so. Had been dating multimillionaire from Indiana while in college whom parents had hoped she would marry and return to Ohio to be near them, but she wanted different life. Unable to eat, lost weight, etc. An uncle to whom she felt close told her that her feelings of insecurity about background might be cause of distress and make her incapable of loving anyone; suggested she seek help of psychiatrist. Also advised her to stay in New York and make own life. Saw psychologist for short time who helped her to stop feeling guilty about wishing to pursue career. Maintained relationship with adoptive parents but still felt distress at not being able to do what they wanted. Met future husband on double blind date. He was date of other woman and was scheduled to enter military service for two years. She was leaving following month for long-planned trip to Europe. He got orders to report to Japan and met her in Europe. She felt unsure about readiness for marriage, with strong feelings of not wanting to be trapped and need for freedom pulling against need to belong; feels this is common feeling among adoptees. **March 1, 1952:** Married psychiatrist and author, Robert Jay Lifton, at large wedding parents gave in Ohio and moved to Japan. **1952–1954:** Lived in Tokyo. Felt at home at once. Time spent in Far East had great influence on future writings with themes of nonviolence and of the gentle spirit of Buddha. **1954–1956:** Lived in Hong Kong. Travelled in Vietnam and Southeast Asia as journalist for *Tokyo Evening News* and American magazines. **1955:** Adoptive father died. **1956:** Returned to United States after three and one half years abroad and bought hundred year old colonial house in Cambridge, Massachusetts. At age 30, began search for biological mother after cousin told her that she had heard her biological parents had died in car crash, which was not what she had been told by adoptive mother. Felt intense guilt and disloyalty toward adoptive parents but the need to know her background was stronger. Wanted to rid herself of confusion, to "be real." Obtained some information from adoption agency and after much searching of public records for birth certificates, etc., located biological mother. Unfairness of the difficulty involved in obtaining knowledge of own background reinforced convictions that adoption process which seals birth records and withholds knowledge of origins is extremely unfair and harmful to adoptees who live a life feeling unreal, secretive and transplanted. It also punishes women who give up children by refusing to ever let them know what happened to child. Met mother and found out she had half-brother from mother's first marriage. Mother refused to tell brother of her existence. Years later was able to meet him by pretending to interview him but without revealing her identity. Did not tell adoptive mother that she had searched for and found biological mother.   1960: Received *New York Herald Tribune* award for book, *Kap the Kappa*.   1960–1962: Resided in Tokyo, Kyoto and Hiroshima.   **June 19, 1961**: First child, Kenneth Jay, born in Japan.   1965: Second and last child, Karen, born in New Haven.   **November 1970**: Children's play, *Moonwalk*, produced on Broadway at City Center in New York.   1970: Won *New York Herald Tribune* award for book, *Return to Hiroshima*.   1970s: Saw television show and contacted Florence Fisher who was forming adoptee organization called ALMA (Spanish for soul), Adoptees' Liberty Movement Association. Attended meeting intending only to observe but experienced sense of camaraderie and love as people spoke of their lives and searches to find lost relatives. Fisher expressed view that sealing of records was violation of Constitutional rights and that mother has no right to privacy from her child because result is sense of anonymity of adoptee. Discovered other organizations; began corresponding and meeting with other adoptees. Still having feeling of incompleteness, recontacted biological mother, to whom she had not spoken for some time, to obtain information about father. Mother again stressed she did not want half-brother to know of her existence. After some time mother finally told her her father's name but tried to make her promise not to contact him. Again, after much searching, located father's relatives and found he had died seven months previously of heart attack.   1973: Book, *Children of Vietnam*, nominated for National Book Award.   1975: *Twice Born: Memoirs of an Adopted Daughter* published. Tells story of her life and struggle to learn about origins in attempt to inform public of pain, guilt and ambivalence experienced by adoptees. Advocates open adoptions and rights of adopted to learn about roots so that they can integrate two lives and advocates that mother has right to know what happened to her child.   **Late 1970s**: Adoptive mother died.   **1979**: After much research into adoption process and communication with those involved, *Lost and Found: The Adoption Experience* published.   **1981**: *I'm Still Me*, fictional account of high school student's search for biological parents, published. 1982–: Continues to research and write about adoption as well as other subjects. Affiliated with American Adoption Congress, Adoption Circle and PEN Club.   1988: Awarded SHALOM Center Brit HaDorot Peace Award.   1989: Received Present Tense Joel H. Cavior Literary Award and International Janusz Korczak Society Literary Award (Warsaw, Poland) for *The King of Children*. Also nominated for Jewish Book Council Award.

Background Information

Parents: Hilda and Oscar Kirschner, adoptive parents. **Siblings:** One (half-brother). **Children:** Two (Kenneth Jay, Karen). **Influences:** Robert Jay Lifton. **Ethnicity:** Jewish American. **Also known as:** None known. **Historic sites, landmarks, etc.:** None known.

BIBLIOGRAPHICAL INFORMATION

Biographical Sketches About Betty Jean Lifton

Commire, Anne. *Something About the Author*. Detroit: Gale Research, 1974.
De Montreville, Doris, and Donna Hill, eds. *Third Book of Junior Authors*. New York: H. W. Wilson Company, 1972.
Kirkpatrick, D. L., ed. *Twentieth-Century Children's Writers*. New York: St. Martin's, 1978.
Metzger, Linda, ed. *Contemporary Authors*. Detroit: Gale Research, 1984.

Books by Betty Jean Lifton

Chirps from a Bamboo Cage. Tokyo: Tokyo News Service, 1954.
The Cock and the Ghost Cat. New York: Atheneum, 1965. Reprint. New York: Atheneum, 1967.
A Dog's Guide to Tokyo. New York: Norton, [1969].
The Dwarf Pine Tree. New York: Atheneum, 1963.
Good Night, Orange Monster. New York: Atheneum, 1972.
I'm Still Me. New York: Knopf, 1981. Reprint. New York: Bantam, 1982.
Jaguar, My Twin. New York: Atheneum, 1976.
Joji and the Amanojaku. New York: Norton, 1965.
Joji and the Dragon. New York: Morrow, 1957. Reprint. Hamden, CT: Linnet, 1989.
Joji and the Fog. New York: Morrow, 1959.
Kap and the Wicked Monkey. New York: Norton, 1968.
Kap the Kappa. New York: Morrow, 1960.
The King of Children: A Biography of Janusz Korczak. New York: Farrar, Straus and Giroux, 1988. Reprint. New York: Schocken Books, 1989.
Lost and Found: The Adoption Experience. New York: Dial, 1979. Updated edition with new afterword. New York: Perennial Library, 1988.
The Many Lives of Chio and Goro. New York: Norton, 1968.
Mogo the Mynah. New York: Morrow, 1958.
The Mud Snail Son. New York: Atheneum, 1971.
The One-legged Ghost. New York: Atheneum, 1968.

A Place Called Hiroshima. Tokyo: Kodansha International; New York: distributed in the U.S. through Harper & Row, 1985.

Return to Hiroshima. New York: Atheneum, 1970.

The Rice-cake Rabbit. New York: Norton, 1966.

The Secret Seller. New York: Norton, [1968].

The Silver Crane. New York: Seabury, [1971].

Taka-chan and I: A Dog's Journey to Japan, by Runcible as Told to Betty Jean Lifton. New York: Norton, [1967].

Twice Born: Memoirs of an Adopted Daughter. New York: McGraw-Hill, [1975]. Reprint. New York: Penguin, 1977.

Lifton, Betty Jean, and Thomas C. Fox. *Children of Vietnam.* New York: Atheneum, 1972.

Lifton, Betty Jean, ed. *Contemporary Children's Theater.* New York: Equinox, 1974.

Shorter Works by Betty Jean Lifton

"Adopted Daughter Meets Her Natural Mother; Excerpt from 'Twice Born: Memoirs of an Adopted Daughter'." *Ms.* 4 (December 1975): 23 + .

"Cruel Legacy: The Children of Our GIs Left Behind in Asia." *Saturday Review* 3 (November 29, 1975): 10 + .

"Girl of the Paper Cranes." *New York Times Magazine* (August 1, 1965): 35.

"How the Adoption System Ignites a Fire." *New York Times* (March 1, 1986): 27.

"In Search of Kappas." *Horn Book Magazine* 37 (February 1961): 34–41.

"Let a Thousand Paper Cranes Fly." *New York Times Magazine* (July 27, 1975): 29 + .

"Memories of the Pony Chorus." *Cincinnati Arts* (Summer 1989): 22.

"My Search for My Roots." *Seventeen* 36 (March 1977): 132–33 + .

"New Japanese Woman." *Mademoiselle* 48 (December 1958): 58–59 + .

"On Children's Literature: A Runcible Symposium." *Horn Book Magazine* 46 (June 1970): 255–63.

"Orphans in Limbo." *Saturday Review* 3 (May 1, 1976): 20–22.

"Putting the Dog Down." *Seventeen* 35 (April 1976): 94 + .

"Report on a Thousand Cranes." *Horn Book Magazine* 45 (April 1969): 148–52.

"The Search." *New York Times Magazine* (January 25, 1976): 15 + .

"Shepherd of the Ghetto Orphans." *New York Times Magazine* (April 20, 1980): 93 + .

"Thousand Cranes." *Horn Book Magazine* 39 (April 1963): 211–16.

"Why Adoptees Search for Their Parents." *Seventeen* 36 (October 1977): 145.

"Will I Ever Find My Real Parents?" *Seventeen* 43 (May 1984): 177–78 + .

"Young Women of Indochina." *Mademoiselle* 41 (July 1955): 50–55 + .

Shorter Works About Betty Jean Lifton

"Conversation with Betty Jean Lifton." *Cincinnati Arts* (Summer 1989): 24.

Media Materials by Betty Jean Lifton

Films

A *Thousand Cranes*. 1969. 24 min.; sound; black and white; 16 mm.

Sharon, Muriel, producer and director. *The Unborn*. New York: 92nd Street Young Men's & Young Women's Hebrew Association, 1965. 26 min.; sound. (Based on story idea by Lifton who worked closely with Sharon during making of film. Original of film resides in archives of Association at 1395 Lexington Avenue, New York, New York 10128.)

Video Recordings

To Die, to Live: The Survivors of Hiroshima: A BBC TV Production. Chicago, IL: Films Incorporated, 1982. 60 min.; sound; color with black and white sequences; videocassette; ½ in. VHS. Also issued as motion picture. (Lifton assisted in research for production.)

Other Works by Betty Jean Lifton

Plays

"Kap the Kappa." In *Contemporary Children's Theater*, edited by Betty Jean Lifton. New York: Equinox, 1975.

Moon Walk. Produced on Broadway at City Center in New York, November 26, 1970.

41. *Belva Ann Bennett McNall Lockwood*
(1830–1917)

Lawyer; pacifist; and advocate for women's rights and suffrage

BIOGRAPHICAL INFORMATION

Chronological Biography

Born October 24, 1830, to Hannah (Green) and Lewis Johnson Bennett at Royalton Township, New York, second of five children.

1835–45: Attended country schools near Royalton, New York. **1845–48:** Attended Royalton Academy during winter months and taught in district school during summer months. **November 8, 1848:** Married Uriah H. McNall, farmer and sawmill operator. **July 31, 1849:** Daughter, Lura, born. **Spring 1853:** McNall died. **Fall 1853–54:** Attended Gasport Academy.

1855: Entered Genesee Wesleyan Seminary, Lima, New York. **1857:** Received B.S. from Genesee College, Lima, New York. **1857–1861:** Preceptress at Lockport Union School; started classes in gymnastics and public speaking for girls. **About 1860:** Met Susan B. Anthony. **1861–1862:** Preceptress at Gainesville Female Seminary, Gainesville, New York. **1862:** Taught in Hornellsville, New York. **1863–1865:** Preceptress at Owego Female Seminary, Owego, New York. **1866:** Moved to Washington, D. C. Taught at Miss M. J. Harrover's Young Ladies Seminary for five months. Opened McNall's Academy, in Union Hall. Begun as school for women, but changed to coeducational following year. **1867:** Helped found Universal Suffrage Association, first suffrage group in Washington, D. C. **March 11, 1868:** Married Ezekiel Lockwood, retired dentist and Baptist minister. **1869:** Daughter, Jesse Belva, born. **1870–72:** Worked for passage of bill to give women government workers equal pay for equal employment (Arnell Bill). **July 1871:** Jesse Belva died. **1871:** Admitted to National University Law School. Graduated after completing curriculum, but denied diploma because male graduates did not want to graduate with women. **1872:** Spoke at Cooper Union in New York City on behalf of Victoria Woodhull's candidacy for president of United States. Later campaigned for Horace Greeley in South. **September 1873:** Received law degree after appealing to President Ulysses S. Grant. **September 24, 1873:** Admitted to practice before Supreme Court of District of Columbia. **December 1873:** Refused right to practice before U.S. Court of Claims because she was a woman. **1876:** Refused right to practice before U.S. Supreme Court because she was a woman. **April 23, 1877:** Husband died. **February 1879:** Secured passage of bill to allow women to practice before U.S. Supreme Court. **March 3, 1879:** First woman admitted to practice before U.S. Supreme Court. Three days later, admitted to U.S. Court of Claims. **1870s and early 1880s:** Active in Washington conventions of National Woman Suffrage Association. Addressed Congressional committees and wrote resolutions and bills. **1880:** Sponsored Samuel R. Lowery, first southern African American admitted to practice before U.S. Supreme Court. Addressed Platform Committee of National Republican convention in Chicago, asking for woman's suffrage. **1880s–1890s:** Served on executive committee of Universal Peace Union and on editorial board of its paper, *Peacemaker*. One of its chief lobbyists. **August 23, 1884:** Nominated for president of United States by National Equal Rights party. Campaigned for equal rights for all, prohibition, uniform marriage and divorce laws and universal suffrage. Received 4,149 votes. **1884–1892?:** Lectured on tour. **1888:** Nominated for president of United States by Equal Rights party. **1889:** Delegate of Universal Peace Union to International Peace Conference in Paris. **1890:** Took course of university extension lectures at Oxford, England, and received certificate. **1891:** American secretary of International Bureau of Peace founded in Berne, Switzerland.

1894: Daughter Lura died. First woman granted license to practice law in Virginia. **1896:** Helped secure married women's property rights legislation in District of Columbia. Appointed by State Department to represent United States at the Convention of Charities and Corrections held in Geneva, Switzerland. Presented paper at Woman's Congress in Berlin on "Legal and Political Status of the Women of the United States." **1901:** Elected president of National Women's Press Club. **1903:** Urged inclusion of woman suffrage clauses in statehood bills for Oklahoma, Arizona and New Mexico. **1906:** One of attorneys for Eastern Cherokee Indians in case against United States. Argued case before U.S. Supreme Court and won settlement of 5 million dollars. **1909:** Received honorary LL.D. degree from Syracuse University. **May 19, 1917:** Died in Washington, D. C., at age of 86.

Background Information

Parents: Hannah (Green) and Lewis Johnson Bennett. **Siblings:** Four (Rachel, Warren, Cyrene, Inverno). **Children:** Two (Lura, Jesse Belva). **Influences:** None. **Ethnicity:** Not known. **Also known as:** None known. **Historical sites, landmarks, etc.:** Royalton, New York, Plaque commemorates birthplace; Lockwood is honoree in National Women's Hall of Fame, 76 Fall Street, Seneca Falls, New York; U.S. Postage Stamp, 17 cent stamp.

BIBLIOGRAPHICAL INFORMATION

Biographical Sketches About
Belva Ann Bennett McNall Lockwood

James, Edward T., ed. *Notable American Women 1607–1950: A Biographical Dictionary.* Cambridge, MA: Belknap Press of Harvard University Press, 1971.
Malone, Dumas, ed. *Dictionary of American Biography.* New York: Charles Scribner's Sons, 1933.
Whitman, Alden, ed. *American Reformers: An H. W. Wilson Biographical Dictionary.* New York: H. W. Wilson Company, 1985.
Willard, Frances E., and Mary A. Livermore, eds. *A Woman of the Century.* Buffalo, NY: C. W. Moulton, 1893.
Zophy, Angela Howard, ed. *Handbook of American Women's History.* New York: Garland, 1990.

Books by Belva Ann Bennett McNall Lockwood

An Appeal for Woman Suffrage, Made by Mrs. James Bennett, in the Legislative Hall, Frankfort, Kentucky, January, 1884. Lafayette, IN: Our Herald, 1884.

Arbitration and the Treaties. [Washington, D. C.: n.p., 1897].

The Central American Peace Congress and an International Arbitration Court for the Five Central American Republics. Paper Presented by Belva A. Lockwood of Washington, D. C. to the 17th International Peace Congress, in Caxton Hall, London, England, July 31, 1908. [Washington?: n.p.], 1908.

A Complete List of All the Treaties Entered into by the United States with the Various Nations of the World from the Foundation of the Republic Until July 15, 1893. Compiled for the Universal Peace Union by Belva A. Lockwood. Washington, D. C., July 15, 1893. Philadelphia: Office of the Universal Peace Union, 1893.

The Growth of Peace Principles and Methods of Propagating Them. Washington, D. C.: n.p., 1895.

The Hague Arbitration Court, a Supplement to 'Peace and the Outlook.' Washington, D. C.: [M. Tibbetts, printer], 1901.

International Arbitration Court and a Congress of Nations. Washington, D. C.: n.p., 1893.

Peace and the Outlook: An American View. Washington, D. C.: [T. W. Cadick, printer], 1899.

A Résumé of International Arbitration and the National Conference at Washington April 22d and 23d, 1896. Parkesburg, PA: n.p., 1896.

The Right of Women to Vote Guaranteed by the Constitution: Memorial of Belva A. Lockwood and Others, with the Moral and Constitutional Argument in Support of the Same. Washington, D. C.: Universal Franchise Association, 1871.

Books About Belva Ann Bennett McNall Lockwood

Brown, Drollene P. *Belva Lockwood Wins Her Case.* Niles, IL: A Whitman, 1987.

Dunnahoo, Terry. *Before the Supreme Court: The Story of Belva Ann Lockwood.* Boston: Houghton Mifflin, 1974.

Fox, Mary Virginia. *Lady for the Defense: A Biography of Belva Lockwood.* New York: Harcourt Brace Jovanovich, 1975.

Holmes, Bea. *Before the Supreme Court: The Story of Belva Ann Lockwood.* Boston: Houghton Mifflin, 1974.

Kerr, Laura Nowak. *Girl Who Ran for President.* New York: T. Nelson, [1947].

Winner, Julia Hall. *Belva A. Lockwood.* Lockport, NY: Niagara Country Historical Society, 1969.

Shorter Works by Belva Ann Bennett McNall Lockwood

"How I Ran for the Presidency." *National Magazine* 16 (March 1903): 728–733.

"My Efforts to Become a Lawyer." *Lippincott's Monthly Magazine* 41 (February 1888): 215–229.

Shorter Works About Belva Ann Bennett McNall Lockwood

Boynick, David K. *Women Who Led the Way: Eight Pioneers for Equal Rights.* New York: Crowell, 1972.

Davis, Julia. "Belva Ann Lockwood: Remover of Mountains." *American Bar Association Journal* 65 (July 1979): 924–28.

————. "A Feisty Schoolmarm Made the Lawyers Sit Up and Take Notice." *Smithsonian* 11 (March 1981): 133–34 + .

Grupp, George W. "First Woman Presidential Nominee." *National Republic* 42 (January 1955): 17–18 + .

McGinty, Brian. "Belva Lockwood: Woman in a Man's World." *American History Illustrated* 20 (March 1985): 36–37.

O'Donnell, Alice L. "A Long Way, Baby: Women and Other Strangers Before the Bar." *Supreme Court Historical Society Yearbook* (1977): 59–62 + .

Records of the Columbia Historical Society. Vol. 35–36. Washington, D. C.: The Society, 1935.

Reed, Helena Ducie. "Belva Ann Lockwood First of Our Great Women Lawyers." *Kappa Beta Pi Quarterly* 38 (June 1954).

Remarkable American Women, 1776–1976. [New York: Time, Inc., 1976].

Riegel, Robert Edgar. *American Feminists.* Lawrence: University of Kansas Press, 1963.

Salmon, Jacqui. "A Woman's Place." *Magazine of the Buffalo News* (April 3, 1983): 14–15 + .

Stern, Madeleine B. "Notable Women of 19th Century America." *Manuscripts* 34 (1982): 7–20, 169–84.

————. "Two Unpublished Letters from Belva Lockwood." *Signs: The Journal of Women in Culture and Society* 1 (Autumn 1975): 269–72.

————. *We the Women: Career Firsts of Nineteenth-Century America.* New York: Schulte, 1963.

Winner, Julia H. "Belva A. Lockwood — That Extraordinary Woman." *New York History* 56 (October 1958): 321–40.

Media Materials About Belva Ann Bennett McNall Lockwood
Films

She Also Ran. (As It Happened Series). N.p.: ABC TV, n.d. 16 mm. film; 26 min.; black and white.

Sound Recordings

Women Work for Reconstruction, Reform and the Vote. N.p.: Educational Development Corporation, n.d. Cassette.

Primary Source Materials Relating to Belva Ann Bennett McNall Lockwood

Belva A. Lockwood. Papers. 1878–1917. Extent of collection: 2 ½ in. Finding aids: Checklist. Location: Swarthmore College Peace Collection, Friends

Historical Library of Swarthmore College, Swarthmore, Pennsylvania 19081. Scope of collection: Small amount of Lockwood's personal correspondence with family members, several briefs and legal memoranda, miscellaneous speeches, writings, memorabilia and photographs. Also articles and newspaper clippings about Lockwood.

Belva Ann (Bennett) Lockwood. Papers. 1881–1916. Extent of collection: 77 items. Finding aids: Unpublished finding aid in repository. Location: Smithsonian Institution, National Museum of American History, Division of Political History, Washington, D. C. 20560. Scope of collection: Correspondence, chiefly relating to feminist movement; speeches, brochures, and pamphlets, relating to feminism and world peace; and newspaper clippings (1886–88) relating to Lockwood's activities, including her presidential campaign (1888).

Belva Lockwood Collection. ca. 1879–ca. 1889. Extent of collection: .3 cu. ft. Finding aids: Narrative description. Location: New York State Historical Association, Library, Cooperstown, New York 13326. Scope of collection: Diploma (1879), passport (1889), biographical material including clippings and pictures, and about 500 manuscript pages of lecture notes.

Woman Suffrage Collection. ca. 1871–1910. Extent of collection: ca. 25 items. Finding aids: Card catalog. Location: Chicago Historical Society, Clark St. at North Ave., Chicago, Illinois 60614-6099. Scope of collection: Letters.

(THE ABOVE ENTRY WAS CONTRIBUTED BY KATHRYN M. KERNS)

42. *Carmen Rosa Maymi*
(1938–)

*Advocate for civil rights, women's rights
and labor; director of U.S. Women's Bureau*

BIOGRAPHICAL INFORMATION

Chronological Biography

Born March 17, 1938, in Santurce, Puerto Rico, suburb of San Juan, only child of Socorro (Sierra) and Luis Maymi-Garcia.

1941: Moved to Toa Alta where father became city auditor and continued practice as accountant. Very happy childhood. **1946:** Relocated back to Santurce to further father's profession. Attended Castelar Elementary School, where mother taught fourth grade and then junior high school. Sang on radio, excelled at studies, voracious reader; lived in comfortable circumstances. Education was encouraged, there never being any doubt that she would attend college; independence also valued. **1951–1955:** Wanting daughter to further education on U.S. mainland, father moved family to Chicago, giving up comfortable existence and taking job as foot-press machine operator for $1.25 per hour, minimum wage. Lived in impoverished, ethnically diverse area in northwest side of city. Family active in Spanish-speaking community. Attended Wells High School despite great difficulty in speaking English. Being black, Spanish-speaking and one of best students often put her in position of mediator between school factions split along similar lines. **1955–1963:** In 1959, graduated from DePaul University in Chicago with a B.A. in Spanish, where she also earned an M.A. in education in 1961. Additional graduate work at University of Illinois. Had applied for scholarship while junior in college; despite recognized financial need and grades among highest in class, denied assistance due to gender, Chancellor stating money would be wasted as she was pretty and likely to marry soon after completing school. **1959–1965:** Wanting to assist people in all aspects from civil rights to welfare, began career as employment counselor in Chicago with Migration Division of the Commonwealth of Puerto Rico; promoted to regional supervisor of Education and Community Organization. Organized community action groups, developed Spanish-language curriculum for use by police, social workers and teachers working with new arrivals to United States from Puerto Rico. **1963:** Only child, daughter Rosa, born. Marriage was short-lived. **February 1965–June 1966:** Assistant director of Montrose Urban Progress Center of Chicago Committee on Urban Opportunity; also served as Urban Program Unit director in Cabrini-Green Area. **June 1966–July 1968:** Began federal career as community services specialist directing programs for Native Americans and migrants in Great Lakes Regional office in Chicago Office of Equal Opportunity (OEO). **1967:** Named Outstanding Puerto Rican Woman by Council of Puerto Rican Organizations of the Midwest. **July 1968–June 1969:** Moved to Washington, D. C., to work as community action program specialist on OEO projects related to model housing and service to Native American reservations and migrant programs. **June 1969–January 1972:** Project director of Model Cities Integrated Social Service Delivery System at Volt Information Sciences, Inc., consulting firm providing assistance to model cities program. **February 1972–May 1972:** In Washington, appointed to President's Cabinet Committee on Opportunities for Spanish Speaking People; evaluated effectiveness of ten major federal agencies regarding opportunities for Hispanic population; also developed Affirmative Action plans. **1972–1977:** Joined Women's Bureau of U.S. Labor Department as consultant in May 1972. Conducted major analysis of Women's Bureau's goals and activities. Served as associate director for program development of Bureau beginning in November 1972. Her appointment hearing for director was June 4, 1973. With appointment as director in June 1973, became highest-ranking Puerto Rican in government and only Hispanic woman in top administration; at age 35, youngest woman ever named to position and one of youngest to head major government agency. Duties subsequently increased to include position as deputy assistant secretary of Employment Standards Division, and advisor to Secretary of Labor on women's affairs. Supervised staff of 90 and 10 regional offices. Viewed being chief advocate of women workers as primary responsibility and Bureau's most important goal to elevate economic status of women. Felt that sex was common aspect of discrimination against women, more so than race or color. Served as liaison with unions, women's and minority organizations, government agencies; formulated policies and standards; directed outreach programs, travelled extensively, making speeches, etc., all the while mediating between frequently differing points of view of groups served. Helped minority women form own groups including assisting Native American women in starting National Association of North American Women. Succeeded in having amendment passed to ensure domestic workers are covered by minimum wage law; organized program to assist women on welfare in learning nontraditional trades such as carpentry and electrical repair and installation. Daughter often travelled with her, maintaining excellent grades despite school absences. **July 11, 1973:** As director, was witness at federal hearings entitled Economic Problems of Women, Part 1. **October 24, 1973:** Testified before House Subcommittee on International Organizations and Movements. **March 6, 1974 and April 25, 1974:** Participated in House and Senate hearings regarding appropriations for Bureau. **1974:** Member of Republican Women's Forum advisory board. **1974–1975:** Member of board of advisors to Special Services Center for Correctional Programs at Lewis University. **February 20, 1975:** Testified at joint Senate and House hearing concerning Child and Family Services Act, 1975, Part 1, supporting child care programs for working families of all economic levels. **September 27, 1975:** Spoke before Puerto Rican Women's Conference Observing International Women's Year in New York City. **1975:** Appointed by President Gerald Ford as alternate delegate to U.S. Delegation to United Nations General Assembly. One of U.S. delegates to International Labor Organization Conference in Geneva. Member of U.S. delegation to World Conference of International Women's Year in Mexico City. Awarded honorary degree from Lewis University. **May 16, 1978:** As project director of Arlington, Virginia's Center for Multicultural Awareness, was witness at House hearings regarding prevention of drug abuse. **1980–1986:** Headed Office of Equal Opportunity in the federal Office of Personnel Management. **April 1986–:** Director of federal Office for Equal Opportunity in Interior Department in Washington, D. C. Career has included service on Board of Directors of U.S. Department of Agriculture Graduate School, consultant on problems of women to International Labor Organization, advisory committee for Adult Career Education in Corrections Program, American Council of Education's Commission on Women in Higher Education, and many others. She is a member of the National Conference of Puerto Rican Women.

Background Information

Parents: Socorro (Sierra) and Luis Maymi-Garcia. Mother was teacher; father city auditor, accountant and machine operator. **Siblings:** None. **Children:** One (Rosa). **Influences:** None. **Ethnicity:** Puerto Rican, African American, Hispanic American. **Also known as:** None known. **Historical sites, landmarks, etc.:** None known.

BIBLIOGRAPHICAL INFORMATION

Biographical Sketches About Carmen Rosa Maymi

O'Neill, Lois Decker, ed. *Women's Book of World Records and Achievements.* Garden City, NY: Anchor, 1979.
Telgen, Diane, and Jim Kamp, eds. *Notable Hispanic American Women.* Detroit: Gale Research, 1993.
Votaw, Carmen Delgado. *Puerto Rican Women: Some Biographical Profiles.* Washington, D. C.: National Conference of Puerto Rican Women, 1978.

Books by Carmen Rosa Maymi

Career Education: Projecting Into the 21st Century. Washington, D. C.: 1976. [ED124236]
The Protection of Human Rights of Women in the Inter-American System. Washington, D. C.: United States Women's Bureau, 1974.

Books About Carmen Rosa Maymi

United States. Congress. Senate. Committee on Labor and Public Welfare. *Nomination: Hearing Before the Committee on Labor and Public Welfare, United States Senate, Ninety-third Congress, First Session, on Carmen R. Maymi, of the District of Columbia, to be Director of the Women's Bureau. Department of Labor. June 4, 1973.* Washington, D. C.: U.S. GPO, 1973.

Shorter Works by Carmen Rosa Maymi

"Fighting to Open the Doors to Opportunity." *Agenda: A Journal of Hispanic Issues,* no. 4 (Spring 1974): 8–10.

"New Careers, New Opportunities." *APGA Guidepost* 16 (March 22, 1974): 1–2.

"Puerto Rican Women Working Together." In *Puerto Rican Women in the United States: Organizing for Change*. Washington, D. C.: National Conference of Puerto Rican Women, 1977.

"Symposium on Minorities and Primary Prevention." In *Drug Dependence and Alcoholism, Volume 2: Social and Behavioral Issues*, edited by Arnold J. Schecter. New York: Plenum, 1981.

"United States Discusses Fulfillment of Goals of International Women's Year in the U.N.: Statements, December 3 and 5, 1975." *Department of State Bulletin* 74 (January 26, 1976): 110–15.

"U.S. Rejects Call by Cuba in U.N. for Puerto Rican Independence: Statement, October 8, 1975." *Department of State Bulletin* 73 (November 10, 1975): 678.

"U.S. Welcomes Adoption by U.N. of Declaration on Torture: Statement, November 28, 1975." *Department of State Bulletin* 74 (January 19, 1976): 86–88.

"Using Existing Individual and Collective Resources." In *Puerto Rican Women in the United States: Organizing for Change*. Washington, D. C.: National Conference of Puerto Rican Women, 1977.

"Women and Work — Rights, Realities, and Prospects." *Journal of Employment Counseling* 3 (1976): 122–25.

"Women in the Labor Force." In *Women: A Developmental Perspective. Proceedings of a Research Conference Sponsored by the National Institute of Child Health and Human Development in Cooperation with the National Institute of Mental Health and the National Institute on Aging (Bethesda, Maryland, November 20–21, 1980)*, edited by Phyllis W. Berman and Estelle R. Rameg. Bethesda, MD: National Institute of Mental Health and the National Institute of Aging, 1982 [ED223862]

Shorter Works About Carmen Rosa Maymi

Brookmire, Paula. "Bias Against Women Still Includes Wages." *Biography News* 2 (December 30, 1974): 149.

Martinez Board, Dolores. "Carmen Rosa Maymi: Long Time Champion of Women's Rights." *La Luz* 2 (June–July 1973): 38–40.

"Mrs. Maymi Confirmed as Head of Women's Unit." *Labor* 55 (July 14, 1974): 5.

"New Director Named for Women's Bureau." *AFL-CIO News* 18 (May 26, 1973): 2.

Newlon, Clarke. "Carmen Maymi: Activist." In *Famous Puerto Ricans*. New York: Dodd, Mead & Company, 1975.

Wheelock, Warren, and J. O. "Rocky" Maynes, Jr. *Carmen Rosa Maymi, to Serve American Women; Roberto Clemente, Death of a Proud Man; Jose Feliciano, One Voice, One Guitar*. St. Paul: EMC Corp., 1976.

Media Materials by Carmen Rosa Maymi
Sound Recordings

Equal Employment for Women. Ithaca, NY: Cornell University Uris Undergraduate Library Media Room, 1973. 40 min.; reel; 3 ¾ ips; mono; 2 tracks.

43. Luisa Moreno
(1907–1990?)

Advocate for civil rights; labor leader and organizer

BIOGRAPHICAL INFORMATION

Chronological Biography

Born in 1907 into wealthy family in Guatemala. Educated at Convent of the Holy Names, fashionable boarding school in Oakland, California. Rebellious teenager, renounced family's privileged social position while lobbying for expanded educational opportunities for Guatemalan women. Moved to Mexico City where she worked as correspondent for Guatemalan newspaper and married.

1928–mid 1930s: She and Mexican artist husband emigrated to United States. Began working in garment factory in New York City when depression began, operating sewing machine in sweatshop to support infant daughter and unemployed husband. Joined International Ladies' Garment Workers' Union (ILGWU). Member of original caucus at 1936 American Federation of Labor (AFL) convention. Became professional labor organizer as result of work experiences. Began union organizing activities for AFL. Sensitive person with talent for rallying different people around goal, worked to improve conditions for all working-class people, not only union members. Led protest in New York City against police murder of Mexican man as he picketed film *Under a Texas Moon*, was was considered to be racist. When daughter was about six, she and husband were divorced. Daughter accompanied her on union and civil rights campaigns for ten years.   **1937:** Became member of Congress of Industrial Organizations (CIO). Organizer and newspaper editor for United Cannery, Agricultural, Packing and Allied Workers of America (UCAPAWA), CIO affiliate. During career, travelled extensively from Texas to Colorado to Michigan, helping to organize cotton, beet, canning and pecan shelling workers. Later organized cigar plant workers in Florida and Pennsylvania and over 60,000 cannery workers in California. Recruited many women to become organizers and union professionals. Established study groups to instruct workers in reading and writing, civil and political rights, organization and Marxist theory.   **1938:** Participated in pecan shellers' strike in San Antonio. One of primary founders of El Congreso de los Pueblos de Habla Español (National Congress of the Spanish Speaking People) to fight discrimination and poor working conditions. One of first national organizations for political and civil rights activities on behalf of Chicanos in country. Consisted of students, educators, workers, youths, and politicians from many parts of United States, about 6,000 members from 1938 to 1940. First meeting was originally slated to take place in Albuquerque but U.S. House of Representatives Un-American Activities Committee came to city, called organization Communist-inspired and placed pressure on local Chicano leaders to oppose conference. It was moved to Los Angeles where it was well-attended, with number of resolutions being passed.   **Early 1940s:** Consolidated and revitalized Local 75 at Cal San company in California. Worked to ensure that government regulations and contract stipulations were met. Encouraged workers to air grievances. Used her fluency in Spanish and English to resolve misunderstandings between workers and supervisors. Through her efforts union was strong and united. Placed in charge of organizing other UCAPAWA locals in food processing plants in southern California. Employed innovative and effective technique of using rank-and-file union members to assist in convincing workers of benefits of unionization. Local 3 was formed and permanent alliance between workers forged. By 1942, Local 3 was second-largest UCAPAWA union. Due to her leadership many gains were made. Her emphasis on local leadership made unions vital and active with great deal of worker involvement.   **1941–1947:** Elected one of international vice presidents of UCAPAWA. Highly intelligent and greatly respected for her organizing abilities. Elected state vice president of CIO and chaired California committee against discrimination in labor movement during '40s. Member of Committee to Aid Mexican Workers established by Los Angeles CIO Council in November 1941, to improve conditions of Mexican workers. Scheduled as one of two principal speakers for large, important conference to be held December 7, 1941, to consider discrimination in employment, need for workers to learn English, ways in which Mexicans could increase union participation, etc. Due to bombing of Pearl Harbor, it is not known if conference took place as media did not report on local activities that day. She and other members met several days later with chief of California State Division of Housing and Immigration and others. One of results was reaffirmation that existing non-discrimination in hiring laws would be enforced as well as President Roosevelt's Executive Order 8802 forbidding racial discrimination in hiring by firms with war defense contracts.   **1942:** Elected vice president of Los Angeles Industrial Council and of California CIO Executive Board. Led bitter, hard-fought organizing campaign at Val Vita plant in Fullerton, California. Working conditions were deplorable, supervisors exploited personnel and women were paid substandard wages. Despite much violence and intimidation, won resoundingly. Strong local leadership won significant wage increases, improved working conditions and established company nursery.   **1942–1943:** Organized Sleepy Lagoon Defense Committee in Los Angeles with assistance from Mrs. Will Rogers, actors Rita Hayworth, Orson Welles and Joseph Cotten, and other Chicano leaders in response to Chicano youths' conviction of murder. Succeeded in enlisting support of California CIO. Group gathered evidence to prove constitutional rights of defendants had been violated and youths were finally freed in late 1944. Worked to organize Chicano workers in agriculture and related industries. Spoke out against denial of civil rights to Mexican workers when southern California officials were making plans to obliterate barrios and deport all inhabitants. The FBI, along with U.S. congressional and state committees, accused El Congreso of subversive activities. Limited access to media, and start of World War II contributed to end of organization by mid '40s. **1943:** Instrumental in bringing attention to servicemen attacking Mexican youths in barrios—called "zoot-suit" riots. Subsequent publicity forced U.S. government to act to end beatings. Along with two other union women, founded Citrus Workers Organizing Committee which was immensely successful in unionizing workers. Appointed member of California CIO Committee on Minorities. **1945–1946:** Due to outstanding success in southern California, placed in charge of effort to organize food processing workers in northern part of state in direct competition with Teamsters union. Assembled largest group of organizers ever for single campaign, many of them women, drawing support from other locals and unions. Many workers organized on their own time. In two months more than 14,000 signed pledge cards to enable application to be made for representative election; 25 locals were established, and union won right to represent workers in October 1945 election. National Labor Relations Board (NLRB) bent to pressure of powerful Teamsters, nullified results of vote and ordered new election. It also prohibited either union from negotiating closed-shop agreement with canneries, but Teamsters did so in open defiance. Using tactics of severe intimidation and violence, as well as access to media and employees, Teamsters won vote to represent workers by small margin in August 1946. **1947:** Retired from union activities to private life. **1948:** Immigration and Naturalization Service (INS) began formal proceedings against her. **Early 1950s:** Activism and prominent, radical position made her target for McCarthyism. Deported to homeland of Guatemala under terms of McCarren-Walter Immigration Act on grounds of alleged affiliation with Communist party although she and other UCAPAWA leaders denied party's influence or financial support. Went to Mexico. Later participated in Castro revolution in Cuba. Returned to Guadalajara, Mexico; also spent some time in Guatemala. Died destitute, probably in 1990.

Background Information

Parents: Not known. **Siblings:** None known. **Children:** One (No known names). **Influences:** None. **Ethnicity:** Guatemalan. **Also known as:** None known. **Historical sites, landmarks, etc.:** None known.

BIBLIOGRAPHICAL INFORMATION

Biographical Sketches About Luisa Moreno

Meier, Matt S. *Mexican American Biographies: A Historical Dictionary, 1836–1987.* New York: Greenwood, 1988.

————, and Feliciano Rivera. *Dictionary of Mexican American History.* Westport, CT: Greenwood, 1981.

Telgen, Diane, and Jim Kamp, eds. *Notable Hispanic American Women.* Detroit: Gale Research, 1993.

Zophy, Angela Howard. *Handbook of American Women's History.* New York: Garland, 1990.

Shorter Works About Luisa Moreno

Acuna, Rodolfo. *Occupied America: A History of Chicanos.* New York: Harper & Row, 1981. Reprint. New York: Harper & Row, 1988.

Arroyo, Luis Leobardo. "Chicano Participation in Organized Labor: The CIO in Los Angeles, 1938–1950, An Extended Research Note." *Aztlan* 6 (Summer 1975): 277–303.

Camarillo, Albert. *Chicanos in California: A History of Mexican Americans in California.* San Francisco: Boyd & Fraser, 1984.

Evans, Sara M. *Born for Liberty: A History of Women in America.* New York: Free Press, 1989.

Larralde, Carlos. *Mexican American Movements and Leaders.* Los Alamitos, CA: Hwong Publishing, 1976.

Mirande, Alfredo, and Evangelina Enriquez. *La Chicana: The Mexican-American Woman.* Chicago: University of Chicago Press, 1979.

Nelson-Cisneros, Victor. "UCAPAWA in California: The Farm Worker Period." *Aztlan* 7 (Fall 1976): 453–77.

Ruiz, Vicki L. *Cannery Women/Cannery Lives: Mexican Women, Unionization, and the California Food Processing Industry, 1930–1950.* Albuquerque: University of New Mexico Press, 1987.

San Francisco Labor Herald. See issues from the 1940s.

Scharf, Lois, and Joan M. Jensen, eds. *Decades of Discontent: The Women's Movement, 1920–1940.* Westport, CT: Greenwood, 1983.

Other Works About Luisa Moreno

Theses

Ruiz, Vicki Lynn. "UCAPAWA, Chicanas, and the California Food Processing Industry, 1937–1950." Ph.D. diss., Stanford University, 1982.

44. Constance Baker Motley
(1921-)

Federal judge; lawyer; and advocate for African American rights

BIOGRAPHICAL INFORMATION

Chronological Biography

Ninth of 12 children of West Indian parents, born September 14, 1921, in New Haven, Connecticut, to Rachel (Huggins) and Willoughby Alva Baker. Attended good New Haven public grammar and high schools and biracial Sunday school at Episcopal church; felt relatively little overt discrimination but aware of its existence. Grew up in secure, but poor family, living near Yale University. Had frequent contact with educated people, including black lawyers.

1935–1939: Voracious reader, especially books regarding American black history; used public library as financial circumstances limited number of books at home. Parents valued education but did not encourage pursuit of career, believing it impossible for her to achieve because of gender and race. Early ambition was to be interior decorator. Interest in civil rights sparked by 1938 Supreme Court decision regarding equal educational opportunities for blacks and by having experienced some incidents of discrimination. Served as president of New Haven National Association for the Advancement of Colored People (NAACP) Youth Council and secretary of adult New Haven Community Council; both groups worked to promote civil rights. Graduated from New Haven High School with honors.   **1939–1940:** Denied employment as dental assistant due to race. Found job with National Youth Administration in New Haven. Spoke at Dixwell Community House, an establishment begun for blacks, but little used by blacks; cited reason for low participation as lack of involvement of blacks on board of directors and in planning programs. White businessman Clarence Blakeslee, who had financed center, heard her and next day offered to pay for whatever education she wished to pursue.   **February 1941–1946:** Attended Fisk University in Nashville, Tennessee, transferring to New York University's Washington Square College, where she received B.A. in economics in October 1943. Had studied government, been honor student and been elected to Justinian Society, undergraduate pre-law club. Earned LL.B. from Columbia University School of Law in June 1946. Established law practice and served as legal assistant for NAACP.   **October 1945:** While in last year of law school, began working as law clerk for NAACP Legal Defense and Educational

Fund at national office in New York City. Clerked for chief counsel, and later Supreme Court Justice, Thurgood Marshall. Believes that without this opportunity she would not have advanced as a lawyer because women were not being hired as attorneys at that time. **August 18, 1946:** Married Joel Wilson Motley, student at New York University Law School from Decatur, Illinois; honeymooned in Montreal, Canada. **1948:** Admitted to bar in New York State. **1948–1965:** Continued to work as staff member of NAACP as it began to focus on educational segregation; significant participant in almost every major school integration case. Cases paved way for 1954 *Brown v. Board of Education* Supreme Court ruling which legally ended desegregated schools in U.S. Promoted to assistant counsel in 1949. Argued crucial cases in Alabama, Florida, Georgia, Ohio, New York, etc. With October 1961 appointment as associate counsel with NAACP Legal Defense and Educational Fund, its second highest position, became first woman to hold position. Worked with discrimination cases regarding housing, transportation, recreation and civil disobedience. Defended Martin Luther King, Jr., on number of occasions. Superb attorney and tactician, commanding presence in court, achieved fame as defender of civil rights. Despite much travelling, maintained family life by flying home weekends or having husband and son join her. **1949:** Participated in first trial. She and colleague were first black lawyers to try case in Mississippi in 20th century. Local newspapers refused to call her "Mrs.," instead referring to her as "the Motley woman." **May 13, 1952:** Only child, son Joel Wilson III, born. **1958–1964:** Served as public member of New York State Advisory Council on Employment and Unemployment Insurance. **1961:** Was probably first black woman to argue case before Supreme Court. **1961–1962:** Brilliantly represented James Meredith in effort to gain admission to all-white University of Mississippi. He was finally admitted in September 1962 under protection of federal troops, breaking barriers of segregation in universities. **1962:** Presented with Distinguished Service Award from Harlem Lawyers Association. Received Award of Merit from Barristers Club of Philadelphia. **May 1963:** Successfully fought suspension of over 1,000 black public school students in Birmingham, Alabama, for participating in demonstrations. **September 1963:** Directed NAACP Fund's legal effort to prevent Governor George C. Wallace from blocking school desegregation in four Alabama counties. **November 1963:** Won federal court case to declare unconstitutional the insurrection law which carried the dealth penalty under which four civil rights workers in Americus, Georgia, had been convicted. **1963:** Won Lawyer of Year Award from Frontiers Club of Newark, New Jersey. **February 4, 1964:** First black woman elected to New York state senate. Had won special election to fill unexpired term of senator who had been appointed Civil Court judge. **November 3, 1964:** Supported by Democratic party, defeated Republican opponent, black lawyer Cora T. Walker, for New York state senate seat.

February 23, 1965–August 30, 1966: First woman to be elected by City Council as Borough President of Manhattan, and first woman to sit on New York City Board of Estimate; resigned senate seat. Worked to obtain federal funds to rehabilitate housing and increase employment in Harlem, to improve educational facilities and to increase local community participation on city planning boards. **March 1965:** Represented New York City in march from Selma to Montgomery, Alabama. **April 18, 1965?:** Received Alumni Achievement Award from Washington Square College for work with NAACP Legal Defense and Educational Fund and for being first black woman elected to New York state senate. **1965:** Left position at NAACP Legal Defense and Educational Fund. Had successfully argued nine of ten cases before U.S. Supreme Court covering desegregation of buses in Jackson, Mississippi, Memphis airport restaurant, and Birmingham lunch counters, among others; tenth case had been decided without argument. Received Elizabeth Blackwell Award (see entry 9) from Hobart and William Smith College, and honorary degrees from Smith College, Western College for Women and Morehouse College. **1966:** Recipient of honorary degrees from Virginia State College, Howard University and Morgan State College. **1966–1982:** Appointed Federal Judge of Southern District of New York state by President Lyndon Johnson upon recommendation of senator from New York State, Robert F. Kennedy, becoming first black woman to be named federal judge. Confirmed August 30th and sworn in September 9th; confirmation had been delayed by Senator James O. Eastland of Mississippi since January 25th nomination. Had originally been named to become Appeals Court judge but opposition from southern Democrats forced compromise to district court position. Among major decisions was ruling that New York City public school students were entitled to representation by attorney at hearings on their possible suspension or expulsion. **1968:** Appointed trustee of New York University. **1969–1987:** Awarded many honorary degrees including: Iowa Wesleyan College 1969; Fordham University 1970; Brown University, Atlanta University and University of Hartford 1973; Alberta Magnus College 1976; John Jay Institute of Criminology, Spelman College and Trinity College 1979; University of Puget Sound 1980; New York Law School 1982; University of Bridgeport Law School 1984; New York University School of Law, 1985; Colgate University and Yale University, 1987. **1982–1986:** Appointed chief judge of Federal District Court covering Manhattan, Bronx, and six counties north of New York City. **1986–:** Named senior federal District Court judge, continuing illustrious career. Respected by attorneys on both sides of cases, maintains sense of humor even while presiding over difficult cases. Believes it crucial that those who are interested in civil rights enter politics, that state legislatures have responsibility to address underlying barriers to civil rights such as unemployment, job training, etc. Urges women, particularly black women, to increase activity and run for public office.   **1987:** Recipient of Columbia Law School Medal for Excellence.   **1988:** Guided five month long Wedtech racketeering trial which she felt was most complex of her career. Received New York State Bar Association Gold Medal Award.   **1989:** Georgetown University School of Law and Princeton University conferred honorary degrees.   **1990:** Received honorary degrees from Tulane University and University of Connecticut.

Background Information

Parents: Rachel (Huggins) and Willoughby Alva Baker. Emigrated to United States from island of Nevis, West Indies, under sponsorship of mother's older brother. Father arrived in 1906 and worked as cobbler and chef. Mother came in 1907 at age 18, and parents were married. Both had completed eight years of school and were third-generation Anglicans.   **Siblings:** 11 (No known names).   **Children:** One (Joel Wilson III).   **Influences:** None.   **Ethnicity:** African American.   **Also known as:** None known.   **Historical sites, landmarks, etc.:** None known.

BIBLIOGRAPHICAL INFORMATION

Biographical Sketches About Constance Baker Motley

Jackson, George F. *Black Women, Makers of History: A Portrait.* Oakland, CA: GRT Book Printing, 1985.

Leavitt, Judith A. *American Women Managers and Administrators: A Selective Biographical Dictionary of Twentieth-Century Leaders in Business, Education, and Government.* Westport, CT: Greenwood, 1985.

Lichtenstein, Nelson, ed. *Political Profiles: The Johnson Years.* New York: Facts on File, 1976.

Moritz, Charles, ed. *Current Biography Yearbook.* New York: H. W. Wilson Company, 1964.

Ploski, Harry A., and James Williams, comps. and eds. *The Negro Almanac: A Reference Work on the African American.* Detroit: Gale Research, 1989.

Smith, Jessie Carney, ed. *Notable Black American Women.* Detroit: Gale Research, 1992.

Books by Constance Baker Motley

Address by the Honorable Constance Baker Motley at the Graduation Ceremony at the University of North Dakota, School of Law, May 9, 1987. Grand Forks, ND: University of North Dakota, School of Law, 1987.

Taylor, Telford, Constance Baker Motley, and James K. Feibleman. *Perspectives on Justice.* Evanston, IL: Northwestern University Press, 1975.

Shorter Works by Constance Baker Motley

"Anomalies in Prison Sentences." *Center Magazine* 11 (January 1978): 17–18.
"Civil Rights: Our Legacy and Our Responsibility." *North Dakota Law Review* 64 (1988): 121–33.
"Constitution – Key to Freedom." *Ebony* 18 (September 1963): 221–22 + .
"The Continuing American Revolution." *Journal of Negro History* 6 (1976): 7–15.
"Continuing American Revolution; Excerpts from Address, October 1975." *Negro History Bulletin* 39 (February 1976): 522–23.
"Desegregation and Education." *Mississippi Law Journal* 58 (Fall 1988): 221–369.
"From Brown to Bakke: The Long Road to Equality." *Harvard Civil Rights Civil Liberties Law Review* 14 (Spring 1979): 315–27.
"James Meredith in Perspective." *Crisis* 70 (January 1963): 5–11.
"'Law and Order' and the Criminal Justice System." *Journal of Law & Criminology* 64 (September 1973): 259–69.
"The Legal Aspects of the Amistad Case." *Journal of the New Haven Colony Historical Society* 36 (Spring 1990): 23–31.
"The Legal Status of the Black American." In *The Black American Reference Book*, edited by Mabel M. Smythe. Englewood Cliffs, NJ: Prentice-Hall, 1976.
"The Legal Status of the Negro in the United States." In *The American Negro Reference Book*, edited by John P. Davis. Englewood Cliffs, NJ: Prentice-Hall, 1966.
"A Letter Taken from Oyster River Quarter Records 1666–1775: Wills of Margaret Willis and George Willard (Both dated 1780)." *Journal of Negro History* 61 (1976): 309, 312.
"Massive Resistance: America's Second Civil War." *Arkansas Law Review* 41 (1988): 123–40.
"Prisoners' Rights." *Brooklyn Law Review* 62 (Spring 1976): 887–94.
"Race Discrimination Cases: The Legacy of Justice Lewis F. Powell." *Suffolk University Law Review* 21 (Winter 1987): 971–87.
"The Role of Law in Effecting Social Change." *Crisis* 85 (January 1978): 24–28.
"Some Recollections of My Career." *Law & Inequality* 6 (May 1988): 35–40.
"Standing on His Shoulders: Thurgood Marshall's Early Career." *The Harvard Blackletter Journal* (Spring 1989): 9–17.
"Twenty Years Later." In *The Continuing Challenge: The Past and the Future of Brown v. Board of Education.* Evanston, IL: Integrated Education Associates, 1975. [ED111064]
"Wanted: A Compulsory Federal FEPC." *Crisis* 59 (November 1952): 569–71.

Shorter Works About Constance Baker Motley

"American Women: The Changers." *Vogue* 149 (May 1967): 184.
Bennett, Lerone, Jr. "Black Firsts." *Ebony* 37 (March 1982): 128–33.

Berry, Bill. "Behind Every Successful Woman There Is . . ." *Ebony* 32 (April 1978): 154–58.
Berry, Mary F. "Twentieth Century Black Women in Education." *Journal of Negro Education* 51 (Summer 1982): 288–300.
"Biography." *Current Biography* 25 (May 1964): 36–38.
"Civil Rights Lawyers Revisited." *Ebony* 42 (December 1986): 76 + .
"Constance Baker Motley Becomes First Woman Borough President of Manhattan." *Sepia* 14 (May 1965): 71.
Dannett, Sylvia G. L. *Profiles of Negro Womanhood.* Yonkers: Educational Heritage, 1966.
Flynn, James J. *Negroes of Achievement in Modern America.* New York: Dodd, Mead, 1970.
"4 Who Blazed New Career Trails." *U.S. News & World Report* 86 (May 14, 1979): 61–63.
French, Howard W. "Guiding Wedtech Trial, a Sure Hand." *New York Times* (August 8, 1988): 32.
Gilbert, Lynn, and Gaylen Moore. *Particular Passions.* New York: Clarkson N. Potter, 1981.
Harris, Ron. "The Turning Point That Changed Their Lives." *Ebony* 34 (January 1979): 75 + .
Jensen, Beverly. "Alexander, Harris, Kennedy, Motley and Murray: Attorneys-At-Law." *Black Enterprise* 8 (August 1977): 19–24.
Lamson, Peggy. *Few Are Chosen.* Boston: Houghton Mifflin, 1968.
Lanker, Brian. *I Dream a World: Portraits of Black Women Who Changed America.* New York: Stewart, Tabori & Chang, 1989.
Lewis, Shawn D. "Professional Woman: Her Fields Have Widened." *Ebony* 32 (August 1977): 114–16 + .
"Mme. Borough President: Constance Baker Motley." *Crisis* 72 (April 1965): 224–25.
Morrison, A. "Top Woman Civil Rights Lawyer." *Ebony* 18 (January 1963): 50–52 + .
"Mrs. Constance Baker Motley." *Sepia* 15 (November 1966): 70.
"The Negro Woman in Politics." *Ebony* 21 (August 1966): 96–100.
"New York's New Lady Senator." *Sepia* 13 (May 1964): 35–39.
"People of the Week." *U.S. News & World Report* 60 (February 7, 1966): 16.
"People of the Week." *U.S. News & World Report* 61 (September 12, 1966): 22.
Quindlen, A. "Judge Motley Versus Life." *New York Times Biographical Service* 8 (August 1977): 1137–39.
Rayner, William P. *Wise Women: Singular Lives That Helped Shape Our Century.* New York: St. Martin's, 1983.
Reasons, George, and Sam Patrick. *They Had a Dream.* Los Angeles: Los Angeles Times Syndicate, 1970.
"Soul Sisters in Politics: Fannie Lou Hamer, Anna Langford, Constance Baker Motley, Myrlie Evers." In *Changing of the Guard: The New Breed of Black Politicians,* by Alfred Duckett. New York: Coward, McCann & Geoghegan, [1972].
Stoddard, Hope. *Famous American Women.* New York: Crowell, 1970.
"Unlimited Visibility; interview." *New Yorker* 42 (September 17, 1966): 48–50.

Williams, Barbara J. "Black Women in Law." *Black Law Journal* 1 (Summer 1971): 171–83.

Media Materials by Constance Baker Motley

Sound Recordings

Weathervane: the Fifth Amendment. Santa Barbara, CA: Center for the Study of Democratic Institutions, [1971]. Sides 1 and 2 of tape cassette; duration of program: 59′ 44″.

Media Materials About Constance Baker Motley

Video Recordings

Vecchione, Judith, producer and director. *Eyes on the Prize: America's Civil Rights Years. Fighting Back 1957–1962.* Alexandria, VA: PBS Video, 1986. Videocassette; 60 min.; sound; color with black and white segments; ½ in.; VHS.

Other Works About Constance Baker Motley

Andrew, Jean Douglas. "Constance Baker Motley: Black, Female and Successful: Assets and Liabilities." Paper presented at the annual meeting of the American Political Science Association, 1974.

Primary Source Materials Relating to Constance Baker Motley

Constance Baker Motley. Papers. No date. Extent of collection: ca. 8 document boxes. Finding aids: Published guide. Location: Smith College, Sophia Smith Collection, Northampton, Massachusetts 01063. Scope of collection: Papers include correspondence relating to Motley's appointment as federal judge and addresses on such subjects as urban renewal, antipoverty programs, school integration, NAACP, day-care centers and careers for women in law.

Constance Baker Motley. Reminiscences of Constance Baker Motley: Oral History, 1978. Extent of collection: Transcript: 801 leaves. Tape: 8 reels. Finding aids: Name index available. Location: Columbia University, Oral History Research Office, Box 20, Room 801 Butler Library, New York, New York 10027. Scope of collection: Interview concerns family background, education, impact of various cases, etc.

Peggy Lamson. Papers. ca. 1967. Extent of collection: .5 lin. ft. Finding aids: Unpublished finding aid. Location: Schlesinger Library, Radcliffe College, Cambridge, Massachusetts 02138. Scope of collection: Phonotapes and transcripts of interviews which Lamson conducted for her book, *Few Are Chosen.* Included is interview with Motley.

45. *Eleanor Holmes Norton*
(1937-)

Equal Employment Opportunity Commission chair;
lawyer; feminist; educator; and advocate for civil rights

BIOGRAPHICAL INFORMATION

Chronological Biography

Born June 13, 1937, in Washington, D. C., oldest of three daughters of
Vela (Lynch) and Coleman Holmes. Attended segregated schools as only
buses were integrated in city at that time. Values formed amid family discussions of politics and social problems. High expectations of parents and grandmother inspired confidence in own abilities. It was assumed she would attend
college.

1955: Graduated from Dunbar High School; other graduates of the
preparatory school for blacks had been Ralph Bunche, Edward Brooke, and
William Hastie, first black to become federal judge.   **1957:** Participated in
early Martin Luther King Washington prayer pilgrimage.   **1960:** One of few
black students, received B.A. from Antioch College majoring in history.
Science-oriented at first, decided to become civil rights lawyer in sophomore year due to convergence of many factors — civil rights movement
was just beginning, social consciousness of family, and desire and ability to
advocate.   **1960–1964:** Chose Yale due to emphasis on social aspects of law.
Few blacks or women in attendance. President of school chapter of National
Association for Advancement of Colored People (NAACP). Earned M.A. in
American Studies in 1963 and LL.B. in 1964.   **Summer 1963:** Despite family's concern, participated in civil rights actions in Mississippi. The FBI stated
they could not protect civil rights workers, maintaining there was no federal
basis for it. Student Nonviolent Coordinating Committee (SNCC), of which
she was member, planned strategy carefully, but situation was very dangerous.
Many people were beaten during sit-ins, etc. Medgar Evers was killed hours
after they met and she had departed for nearby city. Fannie Lou Townsend
Hamer (see entry 27) and Lawrence Guyot had been arrested, but she was
able to get them released, without being arrested herself, using quick thinking and clever tactics.   **1963:** Member of national staff for "March on Washington."   **1964:** Assisted in preparation of legal brief to enable Mississippi
Freedom Democratic party to successfully challenge all-white state delegation to Democratic national convention. As direct result, both major political
parties now employ affirmative action to ensure minority and women

representation. **1964–1965:** Law clerk in Philadelphia for Judge Leon Higgenbotham, presiding justice of Federal District Court. **1965:** Married Edward W. Norton when he was in last year of Columbia Law School. **1965–1970:** Assistant legal director at American Civil Liberties Union (ACLU) in New York City. Specializing in freedom of speech cases, defended First Amendment rights of individuals as well as groups, often meeting opposition and protest. Helped write brief for Julian Bond action, won promotions for 60 women employees of *Newsweek* magazine and represented first soldier arrested for Vietnam War activities. Also defended American Nazi party, Ku Klux Klan and George Wallace. Believes free speech is critical for social change and that best way to emphasize its importance is to represent someone with whom you disagree. **1968–1985:** Received honorary degrees from: Cedar Crest College 1969; Bard College 1971; Princeton University 1973; Marymount College 1974; City College of New York 1975; New York University, Howard University, Brown University and Wilberforce University 1978; Wayne State University 1980; Syracuse University, Yeshiva University, Lawrence University and Emanuel College 1981; Spelman College 1982; University of Massachusetts, Smith College and Medical College of Pennsylvania 1983; Tufts University 1984; and Bowdoin University 1985. **1970–1977:** First woman to head New York City Commission on Human Rights. Appointed by Mayor John V. Lindsay, and renewed by Mayor Abraham D. Beame in 1974. Extremely successful in converting laws into actual gains for women and minorities. Instituted new procedures and streamlined existing ones to expedite cases and fostered revision of outmoded federal and state laws regarding worker's compensation, minimum wages, abortion and day care centers. Numerous important victories overcame discriminatory practices resulting in improved conditions in housing, jobs, hiring, maternity benefits, opening of former men-only bars, etc. Cohosted Sunday morning television program. **1970:** First of two children, daughter Katherine, born shortly after assuming Human Rights position. **1971:** Received Louise Waterman Wise award from American Jewish Congress. **1973:** One of founders and member of board of National Black Feminist Organization. **1974:** As chair of New York City Commission, testified before federal committees regarding economic problems of women on June 17th, and Equal Employment Opportunity Commission on September 18th. **November 10, 1975:** Federal witness concerning impact of New York City's economic crisis on national economy. **1976:** Harper Fellow at Yale Law School. **May 24, 1977:** Testified before Senate committee on May 24th regarding own nomination to Equal Employment Opportunity Commission (EEOC). **1977–1981:** Appointed first woman chair of federal Equal Employment Opportunity Commission (EEOC) by President Jimmy Carter. Agency was in very poor condition, had been without head for over a year and was severely criticized for huge backlog. Responsible for enforcing Title VII of Civil Rights

Act of 1964 and Equal Employment Act of 1972. Built on experience and successful methods of previous position, completely revamping organization, clearing accumulation of 70,000 cases. Highly praised for accomplishments. Agency's budget, staff, and responsibilities increased as direct result of her efforts. **1977:** Named "One of 25 Most Influential Women in America" by Newspaper Enterprise Association. On July 27th, as EEOC commissioner, gave testimony before House subcommittee on equal employment opportunities which was examining EEOC's operations. **1978:** Appeared before House and Senate committees at least eight times between March and November, concerning EEOC budgets, reforms, reorganization, etc. **1979:** Gave testimony, as head of EEOC, to federal committees regarding budgets, sexual harrassment, equal employment opportunity for differently-abled, religious discrimination in employment, academic institution attempts to block affirmative action for women and others. **1980:** Continued appearances before Senate and House bodies concerning age discrimination, additional representation of minorities and women in federal work force, unemployment benefits, and sexual harrassment definition and employer liability. Published far-reaching regulations in April explicitly forbidding sexual harrassment of employees by supervisors, declaring it a violation of Civil Rights Act of 1964. Said comparable worth was the issue of the eighties. Worked to gather documentation, develop enforcement policies, file suits, etc. **1981:** Representing 48 women's organizations, testified on April 21st regarding sexual discrimination in workplace, and on July 15th in opposition to proposed revisions reducing affirmative action requirements in Office of Federal Contract Compliance Programs. **1981–1982:** Senior Fellow at Urban Institute. **1982–1990:** Professor of Law, Georgetown University School of Law, Washington, D. C. Testified December 2nd regarding pay equity. **1983:** Appeared before House committee on October 27th, representing Joint Center for Political Studies and Tarrytown Group (later named Committee on Policy for Racial Justice), discussing welfare system inadequacy for black, female-headed households and adverse effect of administration's social policies on black families. **1984:** Representing National Council on the Future of Women in the Workplace, gave testimony before House subcommittee on economic stabilization on January 25th regarding development of national industrial policy. Council, chaired by her, had been created by National Federation of Business and Professional Women's Clubs, Inc., to explore implications for women of new patterns in work place regarding pay equity, child care and technological change. Chair of National Advisory Council of ACLU. **1985:** Visiting Phi Beta Kappa Scholar. **1986:** Continued appearances before federal committees concerning economics and criticizing current EEOC enforcement policies. **1987:** Representing National Committee for Full Employment, appeared March 26th before Senate committee regarding worker dislocation, and on April 2nd, representing

Amalgamated Clothing and Textile Workers Union and 30 other organizations, discussed family and medical leave act of 1987 before House committees. **May 1988:** Chosen by the Rev. Jesse Jackson to handle platform discussions during his presidential campaign. **1989:** One of 100 scholars who produced study entitled "A Common Destiny: Blacks and American Society" by National Research Council. **October 1990–:** Elected delegate to House of Representatives representing District of Columbia. **1991:** One of three chief sponsors of bill to extend full statehood to District of Columbia. **Present:** Continues civil rights advocacy efforts, especially regarding sex discrimination and equal opportunity.

Background Information

Parents: Vela (Lynch) and Coleman Holmes. Mother was schoolteacher with degree from Howard University; father was attorney and government housing expert. **Siblings:** Two (No known names). **Children:** Two (Katherine, John H.). **Influences:** None. **Ethnicity:** African American. **Also known as:** None known. **Historical sites, landmarks, etc.:** None known.

BIBLIOGRAPHICAL INFORMATION

Biographical Sketches About Eleanor Holmes Norton

The Good Housekeeping Woman's Almanac. New York: Newspaper Enterprise Association, 1977.

Leavitt, Judith A. *American Women Managers and Administrators.* Westport, CT: Greenwood, 1985.

Moritz, Charles, ed. *Current Biography Yearbook 1976.* New York: H. W. Wilson Company, 1976.

O'Neill, Lois Decker, ed. *The Women's Book of World Records and Achievements.* Garden City, NY: Anchor Press/Doubleday, 1979.

Ploski, Harry A., and James Williams, eds. *The Negro Almanac: A Reference Work on the African American.* Detroit: Gale Research, 1989.

Smith, Jessie Carney, ed. *Notable Black American Women.* Detroit: Gale Research, 1992.

Books by Eleanor Holmes Norton

Babcock, Barbara Allen, Ann E. Freedman, Eleanor Holmes Norton, and Susan C. Ross. *Sex Discrimination and the Law: Causes and Remedies.* Boston: Little, Brown, 1975.

The Constitutional Stimulus and the New Equality. New York: Dept. of Political
Science, Hunter College of the City University of New York, 1988.
Feminist Pluralism. New York: Ford Foundation, [1987].
New York City Commission on Human Rights. *The Challenge of Equality: The
Work of the New York City Commission on Human Rights 1970–1977; Eleanor
Holmes Norton, Chair.* New York: The Commission, 1977.
New York City Commission on Human Rights, Eleanor Holmes Norton, Chair-
person. *After Integration: Problems of Race Relations in the High School To-
day.* New York: The Commission, 1974.
*Remarks of Eleanor Holmes Norton at "The Law School Curriculum and the Legal
Rights of Women," A Symposium Presented by the Association of American
Law Schools and New York University School of Law on Friday, October 20
and Saturday, October 21, 1972.* N.p.: n.p., 1972.
United States. Equal Employment Opportunity Commission. Eleanor Holmes
Norton, Chair. *Guidelines for the Development of a Federal Recruitment Pro-
gram to Implement U.S. Section 7201, as Amended.* Washington, D. C.: U.S.
EEOC, 1978.
*Who Are the Poor?: A Profile of the Changing Faces of Poverty in the United States
in 1987.* Prepared for Justice for All by Michael Harrington; with the
assistance of Robert Greenstein and Eleanor Holmes Norton. Washington,
D. C.: Justice for All, 1987.

Books About Eleanor Holmes Norton

*A Conversation with Commissioner Eleanor Holmes Norton: Held on June 29, 1979
at the American Enterprise Institute for Public Policy Research, Washington,
D. C.* Washington, D. C.: The Institute, 1980.
United States. Congress. Senate. Committee on Human Resources. *Nomination:
Hearing before the Committee on Human Resources, United States Senate,
Ninety-Fifth Congress, First Session, on Eleanor Holmes Norton, of New York,
to be a Member of the Equal Employment Opportunity Commission, May 24,
1977.* Washington: U.S. GPO, 1977.

Shorter Works by Eleanor Holmes Norton

"An Assessment from an Enforcement Perspective." In *Consultations on the Af-
firmative Action Statement of the U.S. Commission on Civil Rights.* Vol. 1.
Washington, D. C.: The Commission, 1982.
The Black Experience. Proceedings of the Symposium on Racial Justice and Educa-
tion Toward Excellence: Education, Race and Justice (Albany, New York,
February 1, 1984). Albany: New York State Education Dept., Cultural Educa-
tion Center, 1984. [ED247368]
"Black Women as Women." *Social Policy* 3 (1972): 2–3.
"Comment on the Bakke Decision." *Personnel Administrator* 23 (1978): 26–28.
"A Critical Year for Equal Employment." *Journal of Intergroup Relations* 6
(December 1978): 3–10.

"The Democrats: Fitting the Pieces Together." *Atlanta Journal/Atlanta Constitution* (July 17, 1988): P7.

"Eleanor Holmes Norton, Lawyer." *Ms.* 10 (October 1981): 92–93.

"Employment of Black Males Declines." *Crisis* 88 (October 1981): 400 + .

"End of a Period." *Nation* 202 (May 2, 1966): 529–30.

"Fair Housing and Neighborhood Stabilization." *St. Louis University Public Law Forum* 3 (1983): 55–68.

"Goodbye ERA . . . Hello Equality." *Human Rights* 12 (1984): 24–25.

"How to Select Good Teachers: Some Old Ways and Some New Ones." *Social Policy* 2 (1971): 29–31.

Jaynes, Gerald D., and Robin M. Williams, Jr., eds. *A Common Destiny: Blacks and American Society*. Washington, D. C.: National Academy Press, 1989.

Morgan, Robin, comp. *Sisterhood Is Powerful: An Anthology of Writings from the Women's Liberation Movement*. New York: Random House, 1970.

"The Most Irresponsible Industry in New York City." *Integrated Education* 10 (1972): 8–12.

"Overhauling EEOC." *Labor Law Journal* 28 (1977): 683–95.

"Population Growth and the Future of Black Folk." *Crisis* 80 (May 1973): 151–53.

"Public-Assistance, Post-New Deal Bureaucracy, and the Law — Learning from Negative Models." *Yale Law Journal* 92 (1983): 1287–99.

"Quote in Context." *American Bar Association Journal* 70 (1984): 10.

"Race-Relations and New York City Commission on Human Rights." *Political Science Quarterly* 90 (1975): 348–50.

"Reform at the EEOC." *Personnel Administrator* 23 (1978): 21–25.

"Restoring the Traditional Black Family." *New York Times Magazine* (June 2, 1985): 42–43 + .

"The Role of Black Presidential Appointees." *Urban League Review* 9 (1985): 106–11.

"Statement of Eleanor Holmes Norton, Former Chair, Equal Employment Opportunity Commission." In *Consultations on the Affirmative Action Statement of the U.S. Commission on Civil Rights*. Vol. 2. Washington, D. C.: The Commission, 1982.

"A Strategy for Change." In *Women's Role in Contemporary Society; The Report of the New York City Commission on Human Rights, September 21–25, 1970*. New York: Avon Books, 1972. (Norton also wrote introduction.)

"What the Democratic Party Needs Is Hard Facts." *Atlanta Constitution* (January 4, 1989): A15.

"Woman Who Changed the South: A Memory of Fannie Lou Hamer." *Ms.* 6 (July 1977): 51 + .

"Womens Rights — An End, A Beginning." *Human Rights* 13 (1986): 44 + .

"You and Me Brother: 'The Urban Ghettos Are Crueler than the Countryside from Which We Came'." *Essence* 7 (July 1976): 53–55.

Shorter Works About Eleanor Holmes Norton

Avery, P. "Top Women Bureaucrats Talk About Jobs, Bias and Their Changing Roles." *U.S. News and World Report* 83 (September 5, 1977): 38–39.

"Biography." *Current Biography* 37 (November 1976): 15–17.

Bird, Caroline. *Enterprising Women.* New York: Norton, 1976.

"Bright Future?" *Wall Street Journal* (July 1, 1988): 1.

"A Conversation With Commissioner Eleanor Holmes Norton — American Enterprise Institute." *Education* 101 (1981): 300.

Curran, A. "Job Bias; interview." *Working Woman* 5 (March 1980): 43–46.

"Defender of Unpopular Causes." *Ebony* 24 (January 1969): 37 +.

Dionne, E. J., Jr. "Two Party Insiders to Lead Jackson's Convention Drive." *New York Times* (May 14, 1988): A10.

Dreifus, C. "I Hope I'm Not a Token." *McCall's* 99 (October 1971): 51.

"Eager New Team Tackles Job Discrimination." *Business Week* (July 25, 1977): 116 +.

"EEOC Unfair, Says Former Appointee of Carter." *Jet* 70 (June 2, 1986): 6.

"Eleanor Holmes Norton." *New Woman* 1 (September 1971): 86–87.

"Eleanor Holmes Norton." In *Open Secrets,* by Barbaralee Diamonstein. New York: Viking, 1972.

"Eleanor Holmes Norton." In *Particular Passions,* by Lynn Gilbert and Gaylen Moore. New York: Clarkson N. Potter, 1981.

"Firing Up the Attack on Job Bias." *Business Week* (June 25, 1979): 64 +.

Golden, Bernette. "Black Women's Liberation." *Essence* 5 (February 1974): 36–37 +.

Goodman, W. "Return of the Quota System." *New York Times Magazine* (September 10, 1972): 28–29 +.

Gubbins, Barbara Kashian. "Eleanor Holmes Norton: Human Rights Commissioner." *Biography News* 2 (January–February 1975): 163–64.

"Head of EEOC Tells Bankers What to Expect: Age-Discrimination Complaints Are Growing Fast; Comparable-Worth Issue Expected to Move Slowly." *ABA Banking Journal* 72 (September 1980): 68 +.

Hershman, Arlene. "The Big Change at EEOC." *Dun's Review* 111 (February 1978): 65.

Hunter-Gault, C. "Fiery Passion and Concern." *New York Times Biographical Service* 8 (May 1977): 733.

Jackson, George F. *Black Women, Makers of History: A Portrait.* Oakland, CA: GRT Book Printing, 1985.

"Job Opportunities Deemed Unequal." *Washington Post* (July 3, 1978): A4.

Kelly, Janis, Carol Anne Douglas and Alice Henry. "Women's Agenda." *Off Our Backs* 6 (November 1976): 8 +.

Kevles, B., ed. "When I Was Seventeen; interview." *Seventeen* 30 (October 1971): 130 +.

Lamson, Peggy. *In the Vanguard: Six American Women in Public Life.* Boston: Houghton Mifflin, 1979.

Lanker, Brian. *I Dream A World: Portraits of Black Women Who Changed America.* New York: Stewart, Tabori & Chang, 1989.

Levy, Elizabeth. *Lawyers for the People: A New Breed of Defenders and Their Work.* New York: Knopf, 1974.

"On the Job; Fair Employment." *Economist* 266 (January 14, 1978): 26 +.

Pyatt, Richard I. "Eleanor Holmes Norton: From Human Rights to Equal Opportunity." *Encore* 6 (June 20, 1977): 48.

"Reagan's '85 Budget Unfair to Women, Norton Charges." *Jet* 66 (April 16, 1984): 7.
Stone, Chuck. "Eleanor Holmes Norton: A Tough New Sister at EEOC." *Black Collegian* 8 (March–April 1978): 124–26 +.
"Task for Eleanor Norton." *Nation* 224 (May 28, 1977): 645.
"Troubled Drive for Efficiency at the EEOC." *Business Week* (December 19, 1977): 90–91 +.
Walker, Greta. *Women Today: Ten Profiles.* New York: Hawthorn, 1975.
Williams, D. A., and others. "Cleaning Up a Mess." *Newsweek* 91 (January 16, 1978): 26.
"Women in Government: A Slim Past, But a Strong Future." *Ebony* 32 (August 1977): 89–92 +.
Wortham, Jacob. "EEOC: Has It Really Worked." *Black Enterprise* 8 (September 1977): 21–24.

Media Materials by Eleanor Holmes Norton
Sound Recordings

National Women and the Law Conference. *Keynote Address.* Washington, D. C.: National Women and the Law Conference, 1976. Sound cassette; 1 ⅞ ips; 2 track.

Teenage Pregnancy: Children Caring for Children. Irwindale, CA: Cassette Productions Unlimited, Chautauqua Institute, 1986. Sound cassette; 30 min.; 1 ⅞ ips; mono.

Unity, Reaching In, Reaching Out. Ames: Media Resources Center, Iowa State University, 1981. Sound cassette; 1 ⅞ ips.

Media Materials About Eleanor Holmes Norton
Sound Recordings

The Black American Family. Racine, WI: Johnson Foundation, 1983. One side of sound cassette; 28 min., 4 sec.; 1 ⅞ ips; 2 track; mono; NAB; 3 ⅞ × 2 ½ in.; ⅛ in. tape.

The Bork Nomination. [Atlanta, GA]: CNN, [1987]. Sound tape reel; 26 min.; 3 ¾ ips.; mono.; 7 in. × ¼ in.; tape.

The Duke Did It! [Atlanta, GA]: CNN, [1988]. Sound tape reel; 26 min.; 3 ¾ ips; mono; 7 in. × ¼ in.; tape.

Employment and the Black Community. Racine, WI: Johnson Foundation, [1984]. Sound cassette; 28 min., 13 sec.; 1 ⅞ ips; mono; 3 ⅞ × 2 ½ in.

Just What Does a Librarian Do? Chicago: American Library Association, 1982. 2 sound cassettes; 1 ⅞ ips; mono.

Race or Economics, Which Is the Bigger Barrier? St. Paul: Minnesota Public Radio, [1981]. Sound cassette; 59 min.; 1 ⅞ ips.

Single Black Mothers on Welfare as Examined by Social Worker Eleanor Holmes Norton, Former President Johnson, Presidential Candidate Jesse Jackson, Wanda Stokes, Cynthia Jones, Hortense Canady and Others. CBS-TV, 1984. Sound tape reel; 20 min.; 3 ¾ ips; mono.; 7 in. × ¼ in.; tape.

Video Recordings

Agenda For the 90's: Women, Education, and Equal Opportunity. Flint: University of Michigan-Flint, 1989. Videocassette; VHS; 75 min.; sound; color; ½ in.
Black Perspective on the News, Series 41. WHYY-TV; PBSV, 1975–76. Video; 29 min.; color.
MacNeil/Lehrer Report: Bakke Decision. New York: Educational Broadcasting Corp., 1978. Cassette; 29 min.; sound; color; ¾ in.; U-matic.

46. *Kate Richards O'Hare*
(1877–1948)

Advocate for prison reform; socialist; and organizer

BIOGRAPHICAL INFORMATION

Chronological Biography

Born March 26, 1877, to Lucy (Thompson) and Andrew Richards in Ottawa County, Kansas, fourth of five children (second of two daughters).
1883–1893: Attended grammar school in Ottawa County and Kansas City and high school in Burchard, Nebraska. **1887:** Family's prosperous stock ranch ruined by drought, moved to Kansas City, Missouri, where father worked as machinist. **1894:** Began work as apprentice in father's machine shop. **1899:** After hearing speech by Mary Harris "Mother" Jones, joined Socialist Labor party. **1901:** Attended International School of Social Economy conducted under auspices of socialist newspaper *Appeal to Reason;* met Francis P. O'Hare, student-teacher at school. **1901:** Followed majority faction of Socialist Labor party to form more moderate Socialist Party of America. **January 1902:** Married Francis (Frank) P. O'Hare. **1902:** Crisscrossed Great Plains states with husband and lectured as far away as Great Britain, Canada and Mexico. **1904:** Published socialist novel *What Happened to Dan?* (later revised and enlarged in 1908 as *Sorrows of Cupid*). Son, Francis Richards, born. **1906:** Daughter, Kathleen, born. **1908:** Twins, Eugene Robert and Victor Edwin, born. **1910:** Ran for Kansas Congressional seat on Socialist ballot. **1910–1912:** Elected to Socialist Party's National Women's Commission. **1912:** With husband, copublished and co-edited weekly *National Rip-Saw* published in St. Louis (renamed *Social Revolution* in 1917). **1912–1914:** Served as international secretary for Socialist party. **1913:** Represented Socialist party at Second International in London. **July 1917:** Following speech in Bowman, North Dakota, indicted under

new Federal Espionage Act for interfering with national war effort, specifically conscription.   1917: As chair of Socialist Party's Committee on War and Militarism, spoke coast-to-coast against U.S. entry into World War I.   April 13, 1919: Entered Missouri State Penitentiary to begin serving five year term. One of fellow prisoners was Emma Goldman (see entry 26).   1919: Published *Kate O'Hare's Prison Letters*.   May 29, 1920: Sentence commuted by U.S. Justice Department.   1920: Published *In Prison*. Campaigned for Eugene V. Debs for president.   1922: Organized Children's Crusade, a march on Washington, D. C., by children of antiwar agitators still in prison, to demand amnesty for all.   1923: With husband, joined Llano Co-operative Colony, settlement near Leesville, Louisiana, modeled on 19th century utopian communities. Helped found and taught at Commonwealth College, school for socialist workers. Resumed publication of *Social Revolution*.   1924–1926: Conducted national survey of contract labor practices of prisons.   1926–1928: Moved to Mena, Arkansas, with Commonwealth College and served as teacher and dean of women.   June 1928: Obtained divorce.   November 28, 1928: Married Charles C. Cunningham, San Francisco attorney and mining engineer, and thereafter lived in California.   1934: Campaigned actively in Upton Sinclair's "End Poverty in California" (EPIC) movement and in his gubernatorial campaign.   1939: Appointed assistant director of California Department of Penology by Governor Culbert Olsen; helped introduce substantial prison reform program.   January 10, 1948: At age of 71, died of coronary thrombosis in Benecia, California. Her remains were cremated.

Background Information

Parents: Lucy (Thompson) and Andrew Richards. Mother was Campbellite Protestant early in life. Father was partially disabled Civil War veteran who operated prosperous stock ranch until drought of 1887. After that, worked as machinist in shop in Kansas City and later became part owner. **Siblings:** Four (No known names). **Children:** Four (Francis Richards, Kathleen, Eugene Robert, Victor Edwin). **Influences:** Francis (Frank) P. O'Hare, Charles C. Cunningham. **Ethnicity:** Not known.   Also known as: Cunningham. **Historical sites, landmarks, etc.:** None known.

BIBLIOGRAPHICAL INFORMATION

Biographical Sketches About Kate Richards O'Hare

Fink, Gary, ed. *Biographical Dictionary of American Labor*. Westport, CT: Greenwood, 1984.

Garraty, John A., ed. *Dictionary of American Biography*. New York: Charles Scribner's Sons, 1974.
James, Edward T., ed. *Notable American Women 1607–1950: A Biographical Dictionary*. Cambridge, MA: Belknap Press of Harvard University Press, 1971. (Listed as Cunningham, Kate Richards O'Hare.)
Johnpoll, Bernard, and Harvey Klehr, eds. *Biographical Dictionary of the American Left*. New York: Greenwood, 1986.
Whitman, Alden, ed. *American Reformers: An H. W. Wilson Biographical Dictionary*. New York: H. W. Wilson, 1985.

Books by Kate Richards O'Hare

Americanism and Bolshevism. St. Louis: Frank P. O'Hare, 1919.
America's Prison-Hell. Girard, KS: Appeal to Reason, [19??].
Common Sense and the Liquor Traffic. St. Louis: National Rip-Saw Publishing Co., 1911.
Crime and Criminals. Girard, KS: Frank P. O'Hare, [192?].
In Prison. New York: Knopf, 1923. Reprint with new introduction. Seattle: University of Washington Press, 1976.
In Prison; Being a Report to the President of the United States as to the Conditions Under Which Women Federal Prisoners Are Confined in the Missouri State Penitentiary. St. Louis: Frank P. O'Hare, 1920.
Kate O'Hare's Prison Letters. Girard, KS: Appeal to Reason, 1919.
Kate Richards O'Hare: Selected Writings and Speeches. Edited by Philip Foner and Sally Miller. Baton Rouge: Louisiana State University Press, 1982.
Law and the White Slaver. St. Louis: National Rip-Saw Publishing, 1911.
Letters from Kate Richards O'Hare to Her Family From April 20, 1919–May 27, 1920. Girard, KS: Frank P. O'Hare, 1921.
O'Hare, Kate Richards, and Frank P. O'Hare. *World Peace; A Spectacular Drama in Three Acts*. St. Louis: National Rip-Saw Press, 1915.
Socialism and the World War. St. Louis: Frank P. O'Hare, 1919.
Sorrows of Cupid. Vinita, OK: K. R. O'Hare, 1908. Reprint. St. Louis: National Rip-Saw Publishing, 1912.
What Happened to Dan? Kansas City: Press of the Burd and Fletcher Printing Co., 1904.
Zench, William, and Kate Richards O'Hare. *The Truth About the O'Hare Case*. St. Louis: Frank P. O'Hare, 1919.

Shorter Works About Kate Richards O'Hare

Basen, Neil K. "Kate Richards O'Hare: The First Lady of American Socialism, 1901–1917." *Labor History* 21 (Spring 1980): 165–99.
Brommel, Bernard J. "Kate Richards O'Hare: A Midwestern Pacifist's Fight for Free Speech." *North Dakota Quarterly* 44 (1976): 5–19.
Buhle, Mari Jo. *Women and American Socialism, 1870–1920*. Urbana: University of Illinois, 1981.

Conviction of Mrs. Kate Richards O'Hare and North Dakota Politics. New York: National Civil Liberties Bureau, 1918.

Fried, Albert. *Socialism in America: From the Shakers to the Third International: A Documentary History*. Garden City, NY: Doubleday, 1970.

Ginger, Ray. *The Bending Cross*. New Brunswick: Rutgers University Press, 1949.

Mallach, Stanley. "Red Kate O'Hare Comes to Madison: The Politics of Free Speech." *Wisconsin Magazine of History* 53 (1970): 204–22.

Shannon, David. *The Socialist Party of America: A History*. Chicago: Quadrangle, 1967.

Sickels, Eleanor. *Twelve Daughters of Democracy*. Freeport, NY: Books for Libraries Press, 1968.

Sochen, June. *Herstory: A Record of the American Woman's Past*. Sherman Oaks, CA: Alfred Publishing, 1981.

————. *Movers and Shakers: American Women Thinkers and Activists, 1900–1970*. NY: Quadrangle, New York Times Book Co., 1973.

Other Works by Kate Richards O'Hare

National Rip-Saw. St. Louis, MO: National Rip-Saw Publishing Company (1903?–1917). (With husband, copublished and coedited weekly *National Rip-Saw* [renamed *Social Revolution*].)

Social Revolution. St. Louis, MO: Phil Wagner (1917–?).

Primary Source Materials Relating to Kate Richards O'Hare

Kate Richards O'Hare. Papers. 1919. Extent of collection: 31 items. Finding aids: Published guide. Location: Special Collections, University of Oregon, Eugene, Oregon 97403. Scope of collection: 31 letters written by O'Hare to her husband from Missouri State Penitentiary in 1919.

Kate Richards O'Hare. Papers. 1919–1920. Extent of collection: 10 cm. Finding aids: Unpublished guide. Location: State Historical Society of Missouri, Thomas Jefferson Library, 8001 Natural Bridge Road, Kansas City, Missouri 63121. Scope of collection: One volume of letters O'Hare wrote to her family during 14 months she spent in Missouri State Penitentiary; articles and bibliography on her, and Socialist Party of St. Louis and Missouri records, 1909–1964.

Kate Richards O'Hare. Papers. 1919–1920. Extent of collection: 1 item. Finding aids: Unpublished guide. Location: Radcliffe College, Schlesinger Library, 10 Garden Street, Cambridge, Massachusetts 02138. Scope of collection: Contains signed volume, entitled "Dear Sweethearts," which is collection of mimeographed letters from O'Hare to her family written during her incarceration from April 1919 to May 1920.

Swarthmore College Peace Collection. Extent of collection: 5 cm. Finding aids: Collection is listed in general guide to Peace Collection and guide to sources on women. Location: Swarthmore College Peace Collection, Swarthmore, Pennsylvania 19081. Scope of collection: Includes copy of O'Hare's *Prison Letters* (1918), booklet on O'Hare published by National Civil Liberties Bureau, newspaper clippings from *New York Call*, 1919 and 1925, typed copies of prison letters, copies of Frank O'Hare's Bulletin concerning O'Hare's prison term, and one photograph of O'Hare family.

(THE ABOVE ENTRY WAS CONTRIBUTED BY BARBARA L. MORGAN)

47. Graciela (Grace) Olivarez
(1928–1987)

Lawyer; Community Services Administration director;
and advocate for civil rights

BIOGRAPHICAL INFORMATION

Chronological Biography

One of five children born March 9, 1928, in Sonora, small mining town near Phoenix, Arizona, to Eloisa (Solis) and Damian Gil Valero. Partially raised by grandmother, Matilda Solis, who was chief influence on her. Attended grammar school and entered high school. Caught between cultures as white teachers patrolled playground giving "tickets" to children who were speaking Spanish; principal would then hold "court" to determine appropriate punishment. Rationale was that children would be unable to learn English if they spoke Spanish. Spanish, however, was encouraged at home so that rich Mexican heritage would be learned.

1944?: Dropped out of high school at age 16 or 18 when family moved to Phoenix. Later studied at business school but did not graduate; found employment at local radio station. Worked as bilingual secretary in advertising agency which sold time for Spanish language program. Earned high school equivalency diploma about 1950.   **1949:** Travelled to Mexico as interpreter for group of young Americans on exchange visit.   **1952–1962:** First woman disc jockey in Phoenix. Women's program director at Spanish language radio station KIFN in Phoenix. Wrote, produced and broadcast daily programs ranging from cooking to social development; interviewed people prominent in diverse areas, from sports to international politics. One program involved responding to personal problems and she became increasingly aware of problems of Mexican Americans regarding jobs, health issues, social security, etc. Son, Victor, born about 1959. Divorced in 1961.   **1960s:** Active in civil rights movement. Met Father Theodore M. Hesburgh, president of University of Notre Dame during this time. **1960:** Recipient of Outstanding Leadership Award from American Cancer Society. **1962–1966:** At invitation of philanthropist Robert Choate, joined Choate Foundation in Phoenix as staff specialist; worked on programs affecting poverty, juvenile delinquency and education of Mexican American and black children. Received grant from Ford Foundation to survey and study living conditions of Mexican Americans in five southwestern states. **1963:** Planned and conducted first national conference on educational and bilingual problems of Mexican American children, funded by grant from President's Committee on Juvenile Delinquency and Youth Control. **1965:** Executive secretary of National Conference on Poverty in Southwest, which was held in Tucson in January and funded by labor union, Office of Economic Opportunity and Choate Foundation. Wrote proposals for funding of three interethnic, interstate conferences to discuss problems and design solutions to juvenile delinquency. **1966–1967:** Director of Arizona State Office of Economic Opportunity (OEO) in Phoenix. Responsible for organizing all counties in Arizona into Community Action Agencies meeting all OEO requirements; wrote proposals for funds, trained staff, formed state coordinating committee for all federally funded social welfare programs, gave lectures and speeches, and advised governor on regulations of OEO. **1967:** Office of Economic Opportunity project representative to work with departments of Labor, and Health, Education and Welfare in Los Angeles on six-month project to guide development of Concentrated Employment Project (CEP). Worked closely with leaders of principal Mexican American organizations in area. Member of U.S. Department of Labor's task force chaired by Secretary of Treasury George Shultz; group worked on problems of chronically unemployed in ten major urban centers and presented report to President Johnson. Participated in civil rights seminar in England as guest of Ditchley Foundation. **1968:** Field surveyor with U.S. Civil Rights Commission; worked in five southwestern states and Lake County, Indiana. **1968–1969:** Consultant on municipal law at Urban Development Institute at Purdue University. Conducted study of problems of Latin Americans living in Gary, Indiana, and obtained funding for special program assistance. Designed and administered study of Gary city departments to increase efficiency and upgrade departments. **1969:** Worked for Volt Information Sciences on variety of OEO programs in Great Lakes Region and Southwest, evaluating programs, and training staff. Employed with Bureau of Census. Wrote bilingual brochures and contributed to writing of radio and television announcements to promote and explain 1970 census. Served on panel of White House Conference on Food, Nutrition and Health. **June 1970–October 1970:** Consultant on Mexican American affairs to National Urban Coalition to serve needs of Chicano community. Appointed by President Nixon to Commission on

Population Growth and the American Future. **November 1970–June 1972:** Director of OEO-funded program, Food for All, to improve federal food programs in all states and trust territories. **1970:** At age 42, became first woman to graduate from University of Notre Dame Law School. Had been invited to study by Father Hesburgh and provided scholarship despite fact that she had not finished high school or attended college. Also received John Hay Whitney Fellowship. **May 25, 1971:** As vice chair of Presidential Commission on Population Growth and the American Future, testified before Senate committee regarding budget request. **September 15, 1971:** Witness at Senate hearing, as executive director of Food For All, Inc., regarding food problems of elderly and poor, and federal food distribution deficiencies. **June 1972–February 1975:** Professor of law and director of Institute for Social Research and Development at University of New Mexico. Headed program dealing with over $2.75 million in contracts and appropriations. Institute was concerned with programs dealing with education, management, social and economic development, technology, leisure, recreation and criminal justice. **May 10, 1973:** As director of Institute for Social Research and Development, and executive committee member of Citizens Committee on Population and the American Future, gave statement at Congressional hearing regarding Senate approach to family planning services and research on reproduction. **1973:** Received honorary Doctor of Humane Letters degree from Amherst College. **1974:** Performed study of demographics of Mexico funded by Ford Foundation. **February 1975–1977:** Director of State Planning Office of New Mexico, responsible for long- and short-range planning for all state agencies. Also served as advisor to governor and conducted research and maintained agenda for cabinet meetings. **1975:** Named one of "44 Women Who Could Save America" by *Redbook* magazine in April issue. **August 20, 1976:** Appeared before House committee, as New Mexico State Planning Officer, regarding problems, conditions and programs affecting New Mexico elderly. **1976:** Recipient of honorary doctor of laws degree from Michigan State University for her continuous devotion to educational and cultural advancement of nation's Mexican American population. Invited to Mexican President Jose Lopez Portillo's inauguration. **January 24, 1977:** Testified as New Mexico State Planning Officer before Subcommittee on Inter-American Economic Relationships regarding economic implications on United States of developments in Mexico. **April 1977:** Testified on April 22nd at hearings regarding her nomination as Director of Community Services Administration (formerly Office of Economic Opportunity); confirmed as head of this federal antipoverty program on April 28th. Appointed CSA director by President Jimmy Carter, highest-ranking Hispano in his administration, and third highest ranking woman official in federal government. Strove to centralize, streamline and eliminate waste and fraud in federal poverty programs. Stressed needs of rural poor, feeling comprehensive approach involving federal departments as well as other groups was critical to success. **July 15, 1977:** Part of group of about 40 top-level women in Carter Administration to meet with White House aide to protest President's opposition to use of federal funds for elective abortions. 1977: Testified at least six times during year before federal committees as head of CSA, covering issues including energy costs and elderly, strengthening of CSA programs for poor, emergency fuel payment assistance to poor, rural development proposals and economic opportunity amendments. Interviewed on "Today" program on NBC-TV concerning proposed activities as director. 1978: Awarded honorary degree from alma mater, University of Notre Dame. Received Leadership Award from Woodlawn Organization. Appeared before federal committees representing CSA regarding budget appropriations and need for evaluation and assessment of Native American programs and services. Volunteer worker with Fund for Improvement of Post-Secondary Education, Council on Foundations and American Bar Association. Served on national board of American Civil Liberties Union and University of Notre Dame Civil Rights Center Advisory Board. Also chaired Mexican American Legal Defense and Educational Fund. 1979: Honored with Mexican American Opportunity Foundation Aztec Award. Continued federal committee appearances as CSA director to provide information on various subjects including weatherization and food stamp programs, and Home Energy Assistance Act. **February 28, 1980:** Presented budget request for CSA community action and economic development programs to Senate appropriations committee. 1980: Left Community Services directorship to serve as senior consultant with United Way of America, national service organization. Owner of Olivarez Television Company, Inc. **July 1982:** Named to privately financed bipartisan panel to oversee federal government's enforcement of laws barring discrimination on basis of race, sex, religion, ethnic background, age or physical handicap. **1983–1985:** Served on National Catholic Reporter Publishing Company board, resigning due to cancer. **September 19, 1987:** Died at age 59 of cancer from which she had suffered for several years. Felt it was imperative for Hispanos to increase their involvement in policy-making institutions and in regulatory agencies in order to advocate and influence decisions that affect public at large. Had lectured on Mexican American culture, problems and concerns at numerous universities, been appointed to a variety of boards, commissions and committees concerning health, Mexican Americans, education, correctional facilities, etc., and received many honors and awards.

Background Information

Parents: Eloisa (Solis) and Damian Gil Valero. Mother was daughter of naturalized Mexican parents; father was auto mechanic who had immigrated from Spain. **Siblings:** Four (No known names). **Children:** One (Victor Rene). **Influences:** None. **Ethnicity:** Irish American, Hispanic American, Spanish American. **Also known as:** Olivares. **Historical sites, landmarks, etc.:** None known.

BIBLIOGRAPHICAL INFORMATION

Biographical Sketches About Graciela (Grace) Olivarez

Martinez, Al. *Rising Voices: Profiles of Hispano-American Lives.* New York: New American Library, 1974.

Meier, Matt S. *Mexican American Biographies: A Historical Dictionary, 1836–1987.* New York: Greenwood, 1988.

————, and Feliciano Rivera. *Dictionary of Mexican American History.* Westport, CT: Greenwood, 1981.

O'Neill, Lois Decker, ed. *The Women's Book of World Records and Achievements.* Garden City, NY: Anchor Press/Doubleday, 1979.

Telgen, Diane, and Jim Kamp, eds. *Notable Hispanic American Women.* Detroit: Gale Research, 1993.

Wood, Theodore E. B. *Chicanos y Chicanas Prominentes.* Menlo Park, CA: Educational Consortium of America, 1974.

Books by Graciela (Grace) Olivarez

We, the Mexican Americans = Nosotros los Mexico Americanos. Washington, D. C.: U.S. Dept. of Commerce, Bureau of the Census, [1970]. [C3.2: M57]

Books About Graciela (Grace) Olivarez

United States. Congress. Senate. Committee on Human Resources. *Nomination: Hearing Before the Committee on Human Resources, United States Senate, Ninety-fifth Congress, First Session, on Graciela (Grace) Olivarez, of New Mexico, to be Director of the Community Services Administration, April 22, 1977.* Washington: U.S. GPO, 1977. [Y4.H88:N72 977-6]

Shorter Works by Graciela (Grace) Olivarez

"Counteracting Society's Divisiveness." *Origins* 6 (April 28, 1977): 717–18.
"From Style to Substance." *La Luz* 6 (November 1977): 30.

"Keynote Address." In *On Being Hispanic and Disabled: The Special Challenge of an Underserved Population: Report of a Conference. (Chicago, Illinois, June 13–15, 1981).* Springfield: Illinois State Board of Vocational Education and Rehabilitation; Washington, D. C.: Partners of the Americas, 1979. [ED210893]
"The Poor You Shall Always..." *New Catholic World* 227 (July–August 1984): 183.
"Socioeconomic Factors and the Quality of Life." In *Quality of Life Symposium.* Las Cruces: New Mexico State University, New Mexico Environmental Institute, 1973. [ED081596]
"Spanish-speaking Americans." *Public Administration Review* 32 (October 1972): 648–51.

Shorter Works About Graciela (Grace) Olivarez

"Amazing Grace." *Our Sunday Visitor* 65 (May 8, 1977): 4.
Breiter, Toni. "Dr. Olivarez Awarded Honorary Law Degree." *Agenda* 8 (July–August 1978): 45.
"Calls for End of Education Monopoly: Graciela Olivarez." *Our Sunday Visitor* 65 (May 1, 1977): 1.
del Rey, Maria, Sr. "New Mexico's Woman for All Seasons." *Sign* 55 (March 1976): 23–27.
"Esther Peterson Appointed as Special Assistant to President Carter for Consumer Affairs." *New York Times* (April 5, 1977): 19.
Farenthold, F. "44 Women Who Could Save America." *Redbook* 144 (April 1975): 82–83 +.
"Fight Poverty by Fighting Fraud." *New York Times* (August 27, 1977): 20.
Fraser, C. Gerald. "New York City Offers New Plan for Poverty Agencies." *New York Times* (August 7, 1977): 28.
"Graciela Olivares: Depression-Era Child Helps Nation's Poor." *New York Times* (March 26, 1977): 9.
"Graduates Congratulated." *Regeneración* 1 (1970): 5.
Hunter-Gault, Charlayne. "U.S. Directs That Poverty Aides Be Named Rather than Elected." *New York Times* (July 13, 1977): B8.
————. "Washington Bids Beame Dissolve Poverty Council and Assume Role." *New York Times* (July 8, 1977): 1.
"La Raza in the Midwest." *Regeneración* 1 (1970): 1.
Langley, Roger. "An Interview with Graciela Olivarez." *Hispanic Business* 1 (March 1980): 1 +.
"Obituary." *National Catholic Reporter* 24 (November 6, 1987): 2.
"People." *La Luz* 5 (April 1976): 6.
"The Poor Are An 'Easy Target' at Budget-cutting Time; interview." *U.S. News & World Report* 86 (January 22, 1979): 24 +.
Reyes, Domingo Nick. "Hispanic Americans in Politics: The Carter Appointees." *La Luz* 6 (September 1977): 34.
Santiestevan, Henry. "National Chicano Coordinating Committee Statement." *Regeneración* 1 (1970): 17.

"16 Ex-U.S. Officials Join Group to Study Civil Rights Records." *New York Times* (July 25, 1982): 29.

Valdez, Martin L. "Graciela Olivarez Named Director of Community Services Administration." *Somos* 1 (October 1978): 10.

Velez, Larry. "Washington's Top Advocate for the Poor." *Nuestro* 3 (June–July 1979): 33.

Weisman, Steven R. "Beame Compromise on Poverty Council Is Accepted by U.S." *New York Times* (August 17, 1977): B5.

"Who's Who in the Carter Administration." *Washington Monthly* 12 (April 1980): 60.

Winiarski, M. "Olivarez; No Poverty Chic." *National Catholic Reporter* 13 (October 7, 1977): 16.

"Women in Administration Protest Carter Opposition to Abortion Aid." *New York Times* (July 16, 1977): 7.

Other Works About Graciela (Grace) Olivarez

Theses

Zeiger, Jeffrey Brian. "A Rhetorical Analysis of Selected Speeches by Dr. Graciela Olivarez." Master's thesis, Colorado State University, 1978.

48. *Rosa Parks*
(1913–   )

Advocate for civil rights

BIOGRAPHICAL INFORMATION

Chronological Biography

Born February 14, 1913, to Leona (Edwards), teacher, and James McCauley, carpenter, in Tuskegee, Alabama.

1915: With mother and younger brother Sylvester, moved to grandparents' farm in Pine Level, Alabama. **1924:** Enrolled in Montgomery Industrial School for Girls, in Montgomery, Alabama, private school founded by liberal-minded women from northern United States. **1928:** Graduated from Booker T. Washington High School. **1928–1932:** Worked as tailor's assistant, clerk, insurance saleswoman and later as seamstress. Began lifetime campaign against racial segregation and discrimination by never using segregated facilities if possible. **1932:** Married Raymond Parks, barber active in civil rights causes including black voter registration. Attended Alabama State College. **1932–?:** Active in Montgomery Voters League, National Association for the Advancement of Colored People (NAACP) Youth Council and variety of civic and religious organizations. **1943:** Elected secretary of Montgomery branch of NAACP. **December 1, 1955:** Returning home from seamstress job at Montgomery Fair department store, refused to surrender seat on bus to white man because she was tired. Arrested and fined fourteen dollars. Her arrest prompted mass boycott of city buses by black population. **December 2, 1955:** Women's Political Council, group of about 300 middle-class black women, led by president Jo Ann Robinson, produced and distributed 52,000 leaflets throughout Montgomery County announcing one-day bus boycott that would take place on December 5, 1955. **December 5, 1955:** Beginning of bus boycott, which was originally scheduled to last one day. Montgomery Improvement Association (MIA) established with the Rev. Martin Luther King, Jr., named president. The MIA vowed to continue bus boycott until white officials met their demands. **December 8, 1955:** MIA officials met with white city and bus officials, but group's demand for nonsegregated city buses was not given serious consideration. **January 1956:** "Get Tough" policy announced by white city commissioners; MIA car pool drivers harassed by city police. **January 30, 1956:** Bomb blasted Dr. King's home. **February 1, 1956:** MIA filed suit challenging constitutionality of segregation law. **June 5, 1956:** Federal judges voted two to one ruling bus segregation unconstitutional. **November 13, 1956:** United States Supreme Court ruling confirmed decision of federal district court; segregation on public transportation in Alabama was illegal. **December 20, 1956:** Supreme Court order declaring Montgomery's segregated seating laws unconstitutional was served on Montgomery city officials and bus boycott ended. **December 21, 1956:** Rosa Parks rode newly integrated bus and was photographed with James Blake, man who originally arrested her. **August 1957:** Closing of alteration shop in which she worked, coupled with numerous threats and harassments, precipitated move to Detroit, Michigan, to be near her younger brother. **July 1958:** Husband hospitalized with pneumonia. **December 1959:** Hospitalized with stomach ulcers. Moved into two rooms in meeting hall of Progressive Civic League in Detroit. Continued working as seamstress while husband was caretaker of building. **1961:** Couple moved into own apartment. **1963:** Southern Christian Leadership Conference began sponsorship of annual Rosa Parks Freedom award. **March 1965:** Began working in office of U.S. Representative John Conyers, Jr. **1971:** Honored by Women's Missionary Society of A. M. E. Church at Quadrennial Convention in Los Angeles. **1977:** Husband died. **1979:** Received NAACP's Spingarn Medal. Rosa Parks award given annually by Women in Community Service in Virginia to commend the "extraordinary acts of ordinary people." **January 1980:** Presented Martin Luther King, Jr. Peace

Prize, highest award of King Center for Social Change. Received Humanitarian Award at 13th annual Image Awards sponsored by NAACP at Hollywood Palladium. **1980:** Received *Ebony* magazine's 35th service award for contributions to black America. **November 1984:** Received first Eleanor Roosevelt Woman of Courage Award presented by Wonder Woman Foundation. **1985:** Participated in Free South Africa Movement by walking picket lines in Washington, D. C. **1987:** Founded Rosa and Raymond Parks Institute for Self-Development, established to offer guidance to black youth. Received Dr. Martin Luther King, Jr. Leadership award. **January 1988:** Portrait of Parks unveiled at Museum of African-American History in Detroit. **March 1988:** Pacemaker installed. Received honorary degree from Shaw College. **1988:** Presented speeches around country in celebration of her 75th birthday, 25th anniversary of March on Washington, and 125th anniversary of Emancipation Proclamation. **June 30, 1989:** Attended White House celebration of 25th anniversary of Civil Rights Act. **June 1990:** Led march in Washington, D. C., with Jessie Jackson in support of striking Greyhound bus workers. **1990:** *Rosa Parks: My Story* published. **July 2, 1991:** Honored at 22nd Annual Coretta Scott King Award Breakfast during American Library Association Annual Conference in Atlanta, Georgia. **Present:** Continues activist work, encouraging voter registration, giving speeches and overseeing work of Rosa and Raymond Parks Institute. Known as the "Mother of the Modern Civil Rights Movement."

Background Information

Parents: Leona (Edwards) and James McCauley. **Siblings:** One (Sylvester James). **Children:** None. **Influences:** Raymond Parks. **Ethnicity:** African American. **Also known as:** None known. **Historical sites, landmarks, etc.:** Rosa Parks Award, Women in Community Service in Virginia, Alexandria, Virginia; Rosa Parks Freedom Award, Southern Christian Leadership Conference, Atlanta, Georgia; 12th Street renamed Rosa Parks Blvd. in 1969; Rosa Parks Art Center, Detroit, Michigan; Rosa Parks Highway, Toledo, Ohio.

BIBLIOGRAPHICAL INFORMATION

Biographical Sketches About Rosa Parks

Jackson, George F. *Black Women, Makers of History: A Portrait.* Oakland, CA: GRT Book Printing, 1985.

McDowell, Barbara, and Hana Umlauf, eds. *The Good Housekeeping Womens' Almanac.* New York: Newspaper Enterprise Association, 1977.
McHenry, Robert, ed. *Famous American Women.* New York: Dover, 1983.
Moritz, Charles, ed. *Current Biography Yearbook.* New York: H. W. Wilson Company, 1989.
Ploski, Harry A., and James Williams, eds. *The Negro Almanac: A Reference Work on the African American.* Detroit: Gale Research, 1989.
Smith, Jessie Carney, ed. *Notable Black American Women.* Detroit: Gale Research, 1992.
Zophy, Angela Howard. *Handbook of American Women's History.* New York: Garland, 1990.

Books by Rosa Parks

Rosa Parks: My Story. New York: Dial, 1990.

Books About Rosa Parks

Friese, Kai. *Rosa Parks: The Movement Organizes.* Englewood Cliffs, NJ: Silver Burdett, 1990.
Greenfield, Eloise. *Rosa Parks.* New York: Crowell, 1973.
Meriwether, Louise. *Don't Ride the Bus on Monday: The Rosa Parks Story.* Englewood Cliffs, NJ: Prentice-Hall, 1973.

Shorter Works About Rosa Parks

"Activist Rosa Parks Gets Pacemaker at Johns Hopkins." *Jet* 73 (March 28, 1988): 11.
Bennett, Lerone, Jr. "Day the Black Revolution Began." *Ebony* 32 (September 1977): 54 + .
Briley, Michael. "Bus Ride That Changed History." *Modern Maturity* 24 (April–May 1981): 14 + .
Brown, Cynthia. "Rosa Parks: Interview." *Southern Exposure* 9 (Spring 1981): 16–17.
Brown, Roxanne. "Mother of the Movement: Nation Honors Rosa Parks with Birthday Observance." *Ebony* 43 (February 1988): 68–70.
Carter, B. "Reunion in Montgomery." *Newsweek* 86 (December 15, 1975): 12.
Conta, Marcia Maher. *Women for Human Rights.* Milwaukee: Raintree, 1979.
Crawford, Vicki L., Jacqueline Anne Rouse, and Barbara Woods, eds. *Women in the Civil Rights Movement.* Brooklyn: Carlson, 1990.
"The Dream Then and Now." *Life* 11 (Spring 1988): 54–57 + .
Garrow, David. *Bearing the Cross: Martin Luther King, Jr., and the Southern Leadership Conference.* New York: Morrow, 1986.
Holsey, Steve. "Rosa Parks: Mother of the Movement." *Sepia* 23 (June 1974): 23–25.
Hornsby, Alton, Jr. *Chronology of African-American History.* Detroit: Gale Research, 1991.

Lanker, Brian. "For Some, Sexual Equality is as Important as Political Equality in Righting Wrongs." *Life* 11 (April 4,1988): 54.

Mauldin, Ardies. "Voting Rights Pioneer Watches from Shadows." *Jet* 60 (August 27, 1981): 24.

"Memory of a Bus." *Time* 106 (December 15, 1975): 16.

Metcalf, George R. *Black Profiles.* New York: McGraw-Hill, 1968.

"Montgomery Honors Rosa Parks, Who Sparked Bus Boycott." *Jet* 73 (February 29, 1988): 30–31 +.

"Mrs. Leona McCauley, 91, Mother of Rosa Parks, Dies." *Jet* 57 (January 17, 1980): 14.

"NAACP Image Awards Presented to Winners at Hollywood Palladium." *Jet* 59 (January 8, 1981): 44–46 +.

"Parks, Jackson to Receive $5,000 Ebony Service Award for Rights Role." *Jet* 59 (November 27, 1980): 39.

Paul, Mark. "Which Way to Full Equality?" *Senior Scholastic* 114 (March 19, 1982): 14–15.

Robbins, Stacia. "When Rosa Parks Sat Down." *Senior Scholastic* 113 (May 1, 1981): 52 +.

Robinson, Jo Ann Gibson. *The Montgomery Bus Boycott and the Women Who Started It: The Memoir of Jo Ann Gibson Robinson.* Knoxville: University of Tennessee Press, 1987.

"Rosa Parks Honored by Wonder Woman Foundation." *Jet* 67 (December 3, 1984): 19.

"Rosa Parks Receives Long Overdue Peace Prize During King Commemoration." *Jet* 57 (January 31, 1980): 62 +.

Skinner, Don Covill. "A Visit from Rosa Parks: Power of the Ordinary." *Christian Century* 104 (April 1, 1987): 300–01.

Stevenson, Janet. "Rosa Parks Wouldn't Budge." *American Heritage* 23 (1972): 56 +.

"35th Anniversary Service Awards: Ebony Readers Pick Rosa Parks and Jessie Jackson as Most Outstanding Blacks." *Ebony* 36 (November 1980): 142–43.

Thomas, Arthur E. *Like It Is: Arthur E. Thomas Interviews Leaders on Black America.* New York: E. P. Dutton, 1981.

"Tired Feet and Rested Hearts." In *I Have a Dream,* by Emma Gelders Sterne. New York: Alfred A. Knopf, 1965.

"Whatever Happened to Mrs. Rosa Parks." *Ebony* 26 (August 1981): 18.

"Where Are They Now?" *Newsweek* 65 (February 15, 1965): 16.

"Wonder Woman Honor." *Jet* 67 (December 10, 1984): 5.

Media Materials About Rosa Parks

Films

The Long Walk Home. Los Angeles: University of Southern California, School of Cinema-Television, 1987. 1 film reel; 16mm.; sound; color; 20 min.

Filmstrips

Famous Americans of Black Heritage. Chicago: Eye Gate Media, 1989. 8 filmstrips; color; 35mm plus 8 sound cassettes plus 2 guides.

Sound Recordings

Rosa Parks. Los Angeles: Pacifica Tape Library. Audio tape cassette; 1 ⅞ ips; stereo; 17 min.

Yellow Moon. Hollywood, CA: A & M Records, 1989. 1 sound disc; 4 ¾ in.; digital. (Song entitled "Sister Rosa" is included on this Neville Brothers album.)

Video Recordings

Eyes on the Prize: America's Civil Rights Years. Awakenings 1954–1956. Alexandria, VA: PBS Video, 1986. 1 videocassette of 6 (VHS); sound; color with black and white segments; ½ in.; 60 min.

A Walk Through the 20th Century with Bill Moyers Series. Alexandria, VA: Corporation for Entertainment and Learning, 1984. Videocassette; ¾ or ½ in.; sound; color; 58 min.

Primary Source Materials Relating to Rosa Parks

Black Women Oral History Project. Interviews. 1976–1981 (inclusive). Extent of collection: 72 interview transcripts, 353 reels of audiotape. Finding aids: Published and unpublished finding aids. Location: Schlesinger Library, Radcliffe College, Cambridge, Massachusetts 02138. Scope of collection: Tapes and transcripts of oral histories and supporting documentation.

George R. Metcalf. Papers. 1956–1971. Extent of collection: 2 lin. ft. Finding aids: Partial inventory. Location: Schomburg Center for Research in Black Culture, Rare Books, Manuscripts and Archives Section, New York Public Library, 515 Malcolm X Blvd., New York, New York 10037. Scope of collection: Contains material for Metcalf's books including information regarding Parks.

Montgomery Bus Boycott. 1955–1957. Extent of collection: 4 vols. Finding aids: Unpublished catalog. Location: Alabama State University Archives, Montgomery, Alabama 36195. Scope of collection: Papers and clippings from newspapers in Alabama and other states concerning boycott, its aftermath and principals involved.

Montgomery Bus Boycott. Trial Transcript. 1956. Extent of collection: 1 item. Finding aids: Container listing available in repository. Location: Alabama Department of Archives and History, 624 Washington Avenue, Montgomery, Alabama 36130. Scope of collection: Transcript of Circuit Court trial.

Rosa Parks. Papers. 1955–1976. Extent of collection: 2 ft. and 2 boxes. Finding aids: Unpublished guide in repository. Location: Wayne State University, Walter P. Reuther Library, Archives of Labor and Urban Affairs, Detroit, Michigan 48202. Scope of collection: Clippings, correspondence, invitations, awards, programs and organizational material relating to activities in civil rights movement in Alabama and Michigan, and church and community activities in Detroit.

Rosa Parks. Portrait Collection. 1950?–1989? Extent of collection: 5 photoprints. Finding aids: Not listed. Location: Photographs and Prints Division, Schomburg Center for Research in Black Culture, New York Public Library, 515 Malcolm X Blvd., New York, New York 10037. Scope of collection: Photographs of Parks.

Septima Clark. 1973. Extent of collection: 1 tape recording. Finding aids: Not listed. Location: State Historical Society of Wisconsin, Archives Division, 816 State Street, Madison, Wisconsin 53706. Scope of collection: Tape recorded interview with Clark in which she discusses Montgomery bus boycott, role of Parks, etc.

(THE ABOVE ENTRY WAS CONTRIBUTED BY KATHY A. BUROCK)

49. *Mary Ellen Pleasant*
(1812?–1904)

California pioneer; abolitionist; philanthropist;
and advocate for African American rights

BIOGRAPHICAL INFORMATION

Chronological Biography

There are many inconsistencies in reports concerning this controversial woman. Lack of documentation contributes to the mystery surrounding her life. There may also have been a deliberate effort to discredit her.

Born August 19, 1812? in either Virginia, Georgia, Louisiana or Philadelphia. Unclear if free-born or slave. Mother may have been full-blooded black from Louisiana named Mary, and father well-educated merchant from Sandwich (Hawaiian) islands whose name was Louis Alexander Williams. It is also possible mother was fair-skinned mixed blood slave whose ancestors were from Santo Domingo, and father white Virginia planter or Cherokee Indian. Throughout her life, described as brown, very black, or fair enough to pass for white for number of years and for variety of purposes. 1812?–1849: May have been purchased by white planter named Price who sent her to Boston to be educated when she was about ten, after first having enrolled her in New Orleans convent. Also could have been sent by father at age six to Nantucket, Massachusetts, to live with Quaker, Mary Hussey, working in store but gaining little education despite father's instructions. Met number of abolitionists in Boston including William Lloyd Garrison and Alexander (or James W.) Smith, wealthy planter who may have been Cuban; man may have been James Henry Smith, well-to-do black carpenter and contractor, whom she met in Philadelphia. 1839?: Married Smith; couple may have worked with Underground Railroad to smuggle escaped slaves into Canada. 1944?: Husband died, leaving her around $45,000 with instructions to use it for abolitionist work which she may have continued to do for four or five years, possibly at great personal risk.   1848?: Married John James Pleasant (or Pleasants or Pleasance or Plaissance) former slave or overseer on Smith's plantation; may have been cook or seaman.   1848–1852: Arrived in San Francisco during this time, perhaps on April 7, 1852. Reportedly had spent time in New Orleans, became superb cook and continued abolitionist activities by disguising herself so as to move freely among slaves on plantations. Escaped by ship and fled to California via Panama. Reputation as cook either secured her immediate employment with wealthy, or opened own restaurant and boardinghouse at once. Taking advantage of circumstances which allowed her to overhear conversations of influential businessmen, wisely invested money, lent it out at ten percent interest, speculated in stock market and real estate and became very prosperous. May have run prostitution houses as well.   1850s–1860s: Called by some "the mother of civil rights in California" because she greatly assisted blacks in area by providing or finding jobs (she owned a number of laundries by 1855), clothing and feeding them, rescuing slaves, financing transportation of slaves to California, helping them start small businesses. Also protected, educated and helped both black and white women to find suitable husbands; found homes for babies born to single women, etc. Other accounts charge her with performing these acts in an attempt to secure information in order to blackmail those who later rose to powerful or prosperous positions; it was also rumored that she had studied voodoo and intended to control blacks by such methods, thus placing herself in position of great control and influence in San Francisco.   1858: Provided leadership in celebrated Archy Lee fugitive slave case in California. Closed or leased businesses and returned to East; may have lent money to John Brown to finance slave revolt; reportedly returned to use of disguises and worked for some time in South to spread word of coming rebellion. Went into hiding after Brown's capture at Harpers Ferry, and eventually returned to California.   Mid 1860s–1892: Worked as housekeeper for prominent white, affluent banker, Thomas Bell, whose wealth increased after becoming associated with Pleasant. Their relationship is not clear—may have been business partners or lovers or both, but she was able to freely spend his (their?) money as she saw fit. She was instrumental in his marrying one of her protégées, Teresa, in 1879; they all lived in magnificent house (House of Mystery) she built until his mysterious death by a fall October 15, 1892; some say she killed him, but police indicated no suspicions of foul play. He was buried in grave she owned. Continued philanthropic deeds, donating to churches of various denominations, although she herself was Catholic. May have opened more fashionable boarding houses.   1863: Was of major assistance in gaining blacks the right to testify in court.   1865: Gave daughter, Elizabeth (Lizzie) Smith, fashionable wedding at A. M. E. Zion Church.   1866?: Successfully challenged streetcar company's refusal to allow blacks to ride, first suit of its kind in California history.   **1877:** Husband, Pleasant, died.   **1881–1887?:** Involved in nationally famous *Sharon vs. Sharon* case in which woman sued for part of alleged husband's property; he denied marriage and said she was mistress. Local court ruled in favor of woman, but verdict was later overturned by federal court; purported marriage certificate was eventually ruled forgery and during trial it was revealed that Pleasant had given woman more than $5,000 (or $65,000).   **1890–91:** Bought 1,000 acre ranch in Sonoma County.   **1892:** Bell left her nothing in his will, ostensibly at her request. She owned much land, but had little cash and was declared insolvent.   **1895:** While very ill, was showered with flowers, cards and visits from prominent people in recognition of her charity and good works over years.   **April 19, 1899:** Ordered out of house by Teresa Bell, who was probably mentally ill by this time; house was tied up in legal battles regarding deceased Bell's property, which had been going on for some time, and widow was able to evict her. At age 85 forced to move to small apartment, but continued fight to regain property. Bell children left mother to stay in cold apartment with Pleasant but she later sent them back. Teresa Bell, a newspaper reporter whom Teresa confided in, and others, fearing Pleasant would reveal secrets, probably deliberately tried to discredit her. Racism and sexism probably played part as times had changed, influential friends had died or moved, and black woman would not easily be accepted as part of new society in city.   **1902:** Evidence suggests that Teresa Bell bought company that intended to publish Pleasant's memoirs in attempt to suppress them.   **December 20, 1902:** Made will leaving everything to Bell children.   **November 19, 1903:** Found ill by Mrs. L. M. (Olive) Sherwood, white friend from San Francisco, who took her to her home.   **January 4, 1904:** Revised will leaving all property to Sherwoods.   **January 11, 1904:** "Mammy" (she intensely disliked being referred to as such) died in Sherwood residence and was buried in their family plot in Napa, California. Wills were challenged, with courts honoring first document.   **February 12, 1965:** Memorial services held at Tulocay Cemetery in Napa, California. Marker placed on grave by San Francisco Negro Historical and Cultural Society inscribed "She was a Friend of John Brown" and "Mother of Civil Rights in California."   **1976:** Memorial park dedicated by San Francisco African-American Historical and Cultural Society on former site of Pleasant/Bell mansion.

Background Information

Parents: Uncertain.   **Siblings:** None known.   **Children:** One (Elizabeth [Lizzie] Smith).   **Influences:** None.   **Ethnicity:** African American.   **Also known as:** Pleasants; Mammy.   **Historical sites, landmarks, etc.:** Grave and Marker, Tulocay Cemetery, Napa, California; Mary Ellen Pleasant Memorial Park, Octavia and Bush Streets, San Francisco, California.

BIBLIOGRAPHICAL INFORMATION

Biographical Sketches About Mary Ellen Pleasant

James, Edward T., ed. *Notable American Women 1607–1950: A Biographical Dictionary*. Cambridge, MA: Belknap Press of Harvard University Press, 1971.
Logan, Rayford W., and Michael R. Winston. *Dictionary of American Negro Biography*. New York: W. W. Norton, 1982.
Robinson, Wilhelmena S. *Historical Negro Biographies*. New York: Publishers Company, 1969. (Listed as Pleasants, "Mammy" E. [Mrs. Alexander Smith.])
Smith, Jessie Carney, ed. *Notable Black American Women*. Detroit: Gale Research, 1992.

Books About Mary Ellen Pleasant

Holdredge, Helen (O'Donnell). *Mammy Pleasant*. New York: Putnam, [1953]. Reprint. San Carlos, CA: Nourse, 1961.
————. *Mammy Pleasant's Partner*. New York: Putnam, [1954].
————., comp. and ed. *Mammy Pleasant's Cookbook*. San Francisco: 101 Productions, [1970].
Memorial Services in Honor of Mary Ellen Pleasant, 1812–1904, Mother of Civil Rights in California, Friend of John Brown. [San Francisco: San Francisco Negro Historical and Cultural Society, 1965].
Yerby, Frank. *Devilseed*. Garden City, NY: Doubleday, 1984. (Fictional treatment.)

Shorter Works About Mary Ellen Pleasant

Beasley, Delilah Leontium. *The Negro Trail Blazers of California*. Los Angeles: n.p., 1919. Reprint. San Francisco: R and E Research Associates, 1968.
Bennett, Lerone, Jr. "Mystery of Mary Ellen Pleasant." Parts 1, 2. *Ebony* 34 (April–May 1979): 90–92 + , 71–72 + .
Burt, Olive W. *Negroes in the Early West*. New York: Julian Messner, 1969.
"Did You Know?" *Crisis* 60 (April 1953): 250.
Drago, Harry Sinclair. *Notorious Ladies of the Frontier*. New York: Dodd, Mead, [1969].
Goode, Kenneth G. *California's Black Pioneers: A Brief Historical Survey*. Santa Barbara, CA: McNally & Loftin, 1974.
"Historic Recipes from Mammy Pleasant." *Ebony* 26 (February 1971): 108 + .
Horton, J. "The Happy Black Hooker." *Sepia* 21 (December 1972): 26–28 + .
Jackson, George F. *Black Women, Makers of History: A Portrait*. Oakland, CA: GRT Book Printing, 1985.
King, Anita. "Family Tree: Pioneer Vignettes." *Essence* 6 (October 1975): 42.

"A Madam With a Split Personality." In *Remarkable American Women, 1776-1976*. New York: Time, Inc., 1976.

"Mary Ellen Smith (Mammy Pleasant)." In *Legendary Women of the West*, by Brad Williams. New York: D. McKay, 1978.

"A Memorial to Her Dedicated at Napa, California." *Negro History Bulletin* 30 (November 1967): 18-19.

Murdock, Clotye. "America's Most Fabulous Negro Madam." *Ebony* 9 (April 1954): 46-55.

————. "Fabulous Black Madam." *Ebony* 34 (November 1978): 52-54 +.

Pandex of the Press (January, February 1902). Discusses Pleasant's memoirs.

Thurman, Sue Bailey. *Pioneers of Negro Origin in California*. San Francisco: Acme, 1952. Reprint. San Francisco: R and E Research Associates, 1971.

Primary Source Materials Relating to Mary Ellen Pleasant

Manuscripts of Writings. Extent of collection: 13 items. Finding aids: Not listed. Location: California Historical Society, Schubert Hall Library, 2099 Pacific Avenue, San Francisco, California 94109-2235. Scope of collection: Manuscript or typescript of *Mammy Pleasant Legend* by J. Lloyd Conrich.

Mary Ellen "Mammy" Pleasant. Papers. 1860-70. Extent of collection: 427 items. Finding aids: No guide. Location: San Francisco Public Library, Civic Center, San Francisco, California 94102. Scope of collection: Correspondence, daybook, financial papers, address book, cookbooks, grocery book, photos and clippings.

Mary Ellen Pleasant. Papers. 1896. Extent of collection: 1 portfolio. Finding aids: No guide. Location: University of California, Berkeley, The Bancroft Library, Manuscripts Division, Berkeley, California 94720. Scope of collection: Letters to James Grases of San Francisco concerning his niece, Susie.

50. *Amelia Stone Quinton*
(1833-1926)

Advocate for Native American rights and temperance

BIOGRAPHICAL INFORMATION

Chronological Biography

Born July 31, 1833, in Jamesville, New York, near Syracuse to Mary (Bennett) and Jacob Thompson Stone; had at least three brothers. Acquired deep religious beliefs from devout Baptist parents. Grew up in Homer, New York. Educated at Cortland Academy in Homer, showing special aptitude for mathematics and music. Invited to teach at academy near Syracuse. Taught for year in seminary in Madison, Georgia, during which time married the Rev. James Franklin Swanson. Became ill few years later. Shortly after her recovery, husband died. Moved to Philadelphia and taught for year at Chestnut Street Female Seminary headed by Mary L. Bonney (see entry 11), with whom she became close friends. Turned to religious and philanthropic work. Lived in New York City, working as volunteer in prison, almshouse, hospital, etc. Conducted weekly Bible class at shore for sailors.   **1874–1877:** Joined Woman's Christian Temperance Union (WCTU), one of earliest members. Organizational abilities recognized; represented WCTU, setting up new chapters. Elected to serve as state organizer for New York.   **1877:** Exhausted by overwork, took ship to Europe for rest. Met Professor Richard L. Quinton while en route. After short time, began delivering temperance lectures in homes and churches in England.   **February 1878?:** Married Quinton, lecturer in history and astronomy, in London, living there until fall.   **Fall 1878:** Returned to United States, settling in Philadelphia. Joined First Baptist Church where Bonney was also member.   **Spring 1879:** Joined Bonney in efforts to help Native Americans. Bonney had become concerned when she learned of possible Congressional action to open Oklahoma District to white settlers, encroaching on land belonging to Native Americans. This was beginning of Women's National Indian Association (WNIA), although it was not named that until 1883. This was first significant organization of friends of the Native American. Drawing on considerable talents, energy and experience gained in previous volunteer work, became actual leader of WNIA as she planned, organized, and executed efforts, while Bonney provided financial support. Organization advocated end to reservations, division of tribal land into individual plots and assimilation of Native Americans in all respects, believing that only in this way could they survive. Concentrated on practical remedies, including building libraries and homes, teaching health care, cooking, housekeeping, sewing, establishing schools and missions. Efforts directed chiefly at Native American women. Also financed education of promising young Native Americans, loaned money for home-building, provided teachers and developed markets for Native American handicrafts. Intent was to inform and arouse public in order to create pressure and to obtain equitable treatment for Native Americans. **Summer 1879:** Spent long hours in libraries researching issues. Drafted petition and wrote article protesting settlement in Native American Territory. Enlisted members of other philanthropic groups to help circulate petition and pamphlet.   **February 14, 1880:** Prepared 300 foot long petition with 13,000 signatures, which Bonney and two companions presented to President Rutherford B. Hayes and Congress, calling for honoring of land treaties with Native Americans. **1880:** Moved by articles written by Helen Maria Fiske Hunt Jackson (see entry 32) and others, decided to continue campaign. Was inspiration and backbone of WNIA, working diligently to aid cause. Largely due to her efforts, group was enlarged and donations contributed. Prepared second petition and four articles. Assumed responsibility for correspondence. Attended meetings at missionary circles, pastor's conferences, etc., in Pennsylvania as well as other states. Contributed articles to magazines. **1880?–1887:** Served as secretary of WNIA until her election as president. **January 27, 1881:** Henry L. Dawes, senator from Massachusetts, presented Committee's 50,000 signature petition to U.S. Senate urging protection of Native American lands and strict observance of all treaties. **Summer–Fall, 1881:** Travelled throughout Northeast addressing meetings, distributing literature, signing up volunteers and establishing committees. Group was national in scope by year's end as she enlisted workers, successfully sought influence of powerful and prominent people and set up branches in 20 states. Organization was now too large to continue running single-handedly but she remained sustaining force, providing unity and direction. Much admired and greatly respected. **1881:** Suggested that group change name to Indian Treaty-Keeping and Protective Association. Wrote constitution which was adopted in June. Executive board was selected from nominations she had solicited from pastors. **February 1882:** Third petition, which she had written, generated overwhelming response; over 100,000 signatures were gathered. Had instructed workers to approach not only individuals, but to also concentrate on obtaining endorsement of groups. Petition pressed for allotment of tribal lands to individual Native Americans, granting of U.S. citizenship, guaranteed school education, etc. It was presented to President Chester A. Arthur by Quinton and five others and was introduced in Senate by Dawes. This became official policy of United States for next 50 years through Dawes Act of 1887. **1884:** Travelled extensively in Midwest for six months with incredibly heavy schedule to expand organization. Renewed acquaintance with Susette La Flesche (see entry 37). Visited reservations. **1885:** Along with members of Mohonk committee, presented appeal to President Cleveland for Native American land allotment, education and citizenship. Organization's headquarters and branches wrote articles in about 800 periodicals, sent 65 petitions to Congress, held public meetings and motivated countless people to send letters to legislators. Wrote five of headquarter's fifteen new publications and made fifty speeches. Began attending Lake Mohonk annual conferences. **1887:** Husband died; had joined in reform efforts in his later years. **1887–1905:** Unanimously elected president of WNIA; also retained post as organizer. Extended recruitment efforts to southern states. Attended annual Lake Mohonk, New York, conferences and served on its committees; visited reservations; lobbied in Washington to improve conditions on reservations; worked with U.S. Board of Indian Commissioners; continued to write and lecture extensively.   **1888:** Journeyed to England to international missionary convention to focus international attention on Native American reform work.   **1891:** Travelled for seven and one-half months, setting up 34 new WNIA auxiliaries in South and far West, bringing total to over 120. Coordinated efforts of various reform organizations to push for passage of Congressional legislation.   **1901:** WNIA opened membership to men; renamed National Indian Association.   **1902:** Gave up editorship of *Indian's Friend,* WNIA publication.   **1904:** Relocated to New York City when headquarters was moved there.   **1905:** Refusing reelection due to declining health, resigned presidency of WNIA, but continued as head of missionary department as this was her special interest. Had supervised establishment of 50 Native American missions.   **1907:** Moved to California. Worked with state branch for landless California Indians, particularly in Los Angeles and Long Beach.   **1910:** Returning east, settled in Ridgefield Park, New Jersey. Occasionally attended WNIA meetings for number of years.   **June 23, 1926:** Died of cerebral hemorrhage at age 92. Buried in Homer, New York.

Background Information

Parents: Mary (Bennett) and Jacob Thompson Stone.   **Siblings:** Three? (No known names).   **Children:** None known.   **Influences:** Mary L. Bonney.   **Ethnicity:** English American.   **Also known as:** None known.   **Historical sites, landmarks, etc.:** None known.

BIBLIOGRAPHICAL INFORMATION

Biographical Sketches About Amelia Stone Quinton

James, Edward T., ed. *Notable American Women 1607–1950: A Biographical Dictionary.* Cambridge, MA: Belknap Press of Harvard University Press, 1971.
Logan, Mrs. John A. *The Part Taken by Women in American History.* Wilmington: Perry-Nalle, 1912.
Washburn, Wilcomb E. *Handbook of North American Indians.* Washington, D. C.: Smithsonian Institution, 1988.
Whitman, Alden, ed. *American Reformers: An H. W. Wilson Biographical Dictionary.* New York: H. W. Wilson Company, 1985.
Willard, Frances E., and Mary A. Livermore, eds. *American Women.* New York: Mast, Crowell & Kirkpatrick, 1897.

Books by Amelia Stone Quinton

Address of the President, November 30, 1887. [Philadelphia: Women's National Indian Association, 1887].

Annual Address of the President . . . : What the Association Has Done; What It Ought to Do, November 20th, 1889. [Philadelphia: Women's National Indian Association, 1889].

The Fourth Mohonk Indian Conference. [N.p.: n.p., 1886].

Indian Territory Exclusion. [Philadelphia: n.p., n.d.].

Indian Treaty-keeping and Protective Association. *The Petition: to the Senate and House of Representatives in Congress Assembled.* [Philadelphia?: n.p., 1881?]. (Signed at end: Mrs. A. S. Quinton, secretary of Indian-treaty-keeping Committee, Philadelphia, January, 1881 [and 7 others].)

Indians and Their Helpers. [Philadelphia: National Indian Association, 1886?].

A Letter for You From the National Indian Association. [Philadelphia?]: National Indian Association, 1882.

Missionary Work of the Women's National Indian Association. N.p.: Women's National Indian Association, [188?].

Mohonk Indian Conference. [N.p.: Women's National Indian Association, 1885].

Our War Lesson. [Philadelphia: Women's National Indian Association, 1898?].

A Retrospect and Its Lessons. Annual Address [of the President] Dec. 6, 1894. [Philadelphia]: Women's National Indian Association, 1894.

Seven Ways to Help Indians; Annual Address of the President, November 1890. [Philadelphia: Women's National Indian Association], 1890.

Suggestions for the Friends of the Women's National Indian Association. Philadelphia: n.p., 1886.

A Thrilling Record. Philadelphia: n.p., 1880.

The Ute Question. [Philadelphia: Women's National Indian Association, 1892].

Shorter Works by Amelia Stone Quinton

"Abolition of Unnecessary Agencies." In *Lake Mohonk Conference on the Indian and Other Dependent Peoples. Report of the 15th Annual Lake Mohonk Conference on the Indian and Other Dependent Peoples.* Philadelphia: n.p., 1897.

"Care of the Indian." In *Woman's Work in America,* by Annie Nathan Meyer. New York: H. Holt and Company, 1891. Reprint. New York: Arno, 1972.

"The Indian: First Paper." In *The Literature of Philanthropy,* edited by Frances A. Goodale. New York: Harper & Brothers, 1893.

"A Small Request to Pastors." *Council Fire* (December 1881): 186–87.

"The Woman's National Indian Association." In *The Congress of Women Held in the Woman's Building, World's Columbia Exposition, Chicago, USA, 1893,* edited by Mary Kavanaugh Oldham. Cincinnati: E. R. Curtis and Co., 1894. Reprint. New York: Arno, 1974.

"Women's Work for Indians." In *The National Exposition Souvenir. What America Owes to Women,* edited by Lydia Hoyt Farmer, with an introduction by Julia Ward Howe. Buffalo: C. W. Moulton, 1893.

Shorter Works About Amelia Stone Quinton

Dewey, Mary Elizabeth. *Historical Sketch of the Formation and Achievements of the Women's National Indian Association of the United States.* [Philadelphia: The Association], December 1900.

Mardock, Robert Winston. *The Reformers and the American Indian.* [Columbia]: University of Missouri Press, 1971.

Priest, Loring Benson. *Uncle Sam's Stepchildren, the Reformation of United States Indian Policy, 1865–1887.* New Brunswick: Rutgers University Press, 1942.

Other Works About Amelia Stone Quinton

Theses

Bannan, Helen Marie. "Reformers and the 'Indian Problem,' 1878–1887 and 1922–1934." Ph.D. diss., Syracuse University, 1976.

Thompson, Gregory Coyne. "The Origin and Implementation of the American Indian Reform Movement: 1867–1912." Ph.D. diss., University of Utah, 1981.

Wanken, Helen M. "'Woman's Sphere' and Indian Reform: The Women's National Indian Association, 1879–1901." Ph.D. diss., Marquette University, 1981.

Primary Source Materials Relating to Amelia Stone Quinton

Indian Rights Association. Papers. 1864–1973 (inclusive), 1882–1968 (bulk). Extent of collection: 25,000 items. Finding aids: Published finding aid. Location: Historical Society of Pennsylvania, 1300 Locust St., Philadelphia, Pennsylvania 19107-5699. Scope of collection: Contains many letters which WNIA members wrote.

United States. Bureau of Indian Affairs. Records. Records Group 75. Extent of collection: 16,329 cu. ft. Finding aids: Not listed. Location: National Archives and Records Administration, Seventh St. & Pennsylvania Ave. N.W., Washington, D. C. 20408. Scope of collection: Voluminous correspondence of Quinton.

51. *Alice Mary Robertson*
(1854–1931)
Educator of Native Americans; congresswoman

BIOGRAPHICAL INFORMATION

Chronological Biography

Born January 2, 1854, at Tullahassee Mission in Creek Nation, Indian Territory, now Tullahassee, Oklahoma. Second of seven children, six girls and one boy, and second daughter of Ann Eliza (Worcester) and William Schenck Robertson. Christened Mary Alice. Parents were most influential white missionary teachers among Creek Indians. **1861–1866:** Attended school in Wisconsin and Highland, Kansas, when family moved out of Indian Territory during Civil War. **1866–1871:** Educated at home by parents. **1871–1873:** Studied at Elmira College in New York State, while also working to help pay expenses. Withdrew to find employment to enable younger sister to attend college. **1873–1879:** Worked as clerk in Office of Indian Affairs in Washington, first woman to do so. In 1877, authored draft of report and suggestions which successfully overcame plan by Kansas Senator John James Ingalls to foster Creek Indian rebellion which would have resulted in territory being opened to white settlers. **1879–1882:** Taught in mission school at Tullahassee until it was destroyed by fire in December 1880. Secured placement for 25 of her pupils at Carlisle Indian School in Pennsylvania and took job as secretary to school's head, Capt. Richard H. Pratt. **1882:** Returned home due to father's death and mother's poor health. Taught at Okmulgee Indian school. Toured East during 1882 and 1883, successfully lecturing to raise money to help mother rebuild destroyed school, erecting it in Nuyaka instead of Tullahassee. Sister Augusta was first superintendent of school. **1885–1899:** Put in charge of Oklahoma Indian Territory Girls' School, Presbyterian mission boarding institution at Muskogee. First person to teach domestic science to Native American girls. Directed school as it expanded. Very effective in raising money to erect new buildings and create scholarship fund. School chartered in 1894 as coeducational Henry Kendall College. She taught English, history and civics until 1899. In 1907, school moved to Tulsa and in 1920/1921 became University of Tulsa. **1886:** Awarded honorary AM degree from Elmira College. **1889–1900:** Became friends with Theodore Roosevelt during participation in Lake Mohonk Conference of Friends of Indian for several years. Also assisted two Creek students in enlisting in Roosevelt's Rough Rider regiment during Spanish-American War. Granted honorary membership in Spanish-American War Veterans organization for services to soldiers. **1900–1905:** Appointed first federal supervisor of Creek education in Indian Territory after intensive effort on her part. Demanding position due to heavy responsibilities coupled with necessity to travel over rugged territory. **1905–1913:** Appointed by friend President Roosevelt to serve as Muskogee postmistress. **1913–1920:** Retired with adopted Native American daughter, Suzanne Barnett, to her 50-acre Sawokla Dairy Farm near Muskogee. Also operated Sawokla Cafeteria in town. During World War I, "Miss Alice" became famous as she greeted every troop train in her Model-T Ford with coffee and food. As others joined her, canteen expanded into Muskogee Red Cross and served as model for other cities. **1920:** After much urging, ran for U.S. Congress at age 66, despite opposition to woman suffrage; had at one time served as vice president of state antisuffrage league. When Muskogee newspapers refused to support candidacy, bought space in classified columns (want-ads) to publicize position on issues. Campaigned promising farmers, women and soliders she would serve their interests. Slogan was "I cannot be bought, I cannot be sold, I cannot be intimidated." Elected on Republican ticket from Second Congressional District, defeating William W. Hastings, Cherokee incumbent, on principles of "Christianity, Americanism and Standpattism." Impressive victory as Oklahoma had been consistently Democratic. **March 1921–March 1923:** Served as first woman representative from Oklahoma, second woman in House, third woman in Congress. Appointed to Committee on Indian Affairs in recognition of extensive efforts on behalf of Native American education. Submitted reports regarding various Native American concerns to House and Senate hearings on June 30, 1921, June 19, 1922, and January 25, 1923. Generally followed conservative, Republican line in voting except for opposition to Sheppard-Towner Bill which funded clinics for mothers and children, because she felt it opened way to paternalistic legislation. Despite promise to support veterans' benefits, voted against bill to pay bonus to World War I soldiers citing dire state of Treasury, but was successful in obtaining veterans' hospital in Muskogee. Also fought bill to establish federal Department of Education, opposed League of Nations as well as immigration, and denounced League of Women Voters for period of time. **November 7, 1922:** Soundly defeated for reelection by William W. Hastings, largely due to her opposition to veterans' bonus bill. Willingly retired stating that politics was too rough and immoral for women. **1923–1931:** Pittsburgh philanthropist Mrs. Mary C. Thaw, who had been regularly assisting her financially, helped her obtain appointment in April 1923 as social welfare worker at Veterans Hospital in Muskogee. Discharged few months later, probably due to independent disposition or perhaps her vote on the bonus bill. Served as Washington correspondent for *Muskogee News,* and later worked for Oklahoma Historical Society. Testified in January 1929, regarding Child Welfare Extension Service. Selected as "Oklahoma's Most Famous Woman" by Federation of Business and Professional Women's Clubs. Had many admirers; schools were named for her, trees planted in her honor, portraits painted, etc. It was suggested that she be state's representative in National Statuary Hall Collection in Washington, D. C., but Will Rogers, who wrote column about her, was chosen instead. Honorary LL.D. conferred by University of Tulsa. Assisted in later life by contributions from state citizens and other supporters, as tearoom she had opened was destroyed by fire, paper she worked for, *Muskogee Daily News,* closed, and depression cutbacks ended her job at Historical Society. Forced to sell heirlooms and property to support herself. **July 1, 1931:** Died in Muskogee at age 77 of cancer of jaw. Buried in Greenhill Cemetery.

Background Information

Parents: Ann Eliza (Worcester) and William Schenck Robertson. Mother was daughter of noted Congregational missionary to Cherokees, Samuel A. Worcester. Father was graduate of Union College and had come to Tullahassee from Long Island to head boarding school sustained by Creek Indians and Presbyterian missions. Ancestors had been Pilgrim, Puritan and Scotch. **Siblings:** Six (Known names: Augusta, Grace, Sam). **Children:** One (Suzanne Barnett, adopted daughter). **Influences:** None. **Ethnicity:** English American, Scottish American. **Also known as:** Mary Alice; Alice. **Historical sites, landmarks, etc.:** Alice Robertson Junior High School, S Street and Callahan Avenue, Muskogee, Oklahoma; Marker, State Highway 56, nine miles west of town, near site of Nuyaka Mission where ruin of storm cellar remains, Okmulgee, Oklahoma; Dormitory, Robertson Hall, University of Oklahoma, Norman, Oklahoma.

BIBLIOGRAPHICAL INFORMATION

Biographical Sketches About Alice Mary Robertson

Engelbarts, Rudolf. *Women in the United States Congress, 1917–1972: Their Accomplishments; with Bibliographies.* Littleton, CO: Libraries Unlimited, 1974.
James, Edward T., ed. *Notable American Women 1607–1950: A Biographical Dictionary.* Cambridge, MA: Belknap Press of Harvard University Press, 1971.
McHenry, Robert, ed. *Famous American Women: A Biographical Dictionary from Colonial Times to the Present.* New York: Dover, 1980.
Malone, Dumas, ed. *Dictionary of American Biography.* New York: Charles Scribner's Sons, 1935.
Preston, Wheeler. *American Biographies.* New York: Harper & Brothers, 1940.

Books by Alice Mary Robertson

Alice Mary Robertson of Oklahoma. Muskogee, OK: n.p., 1912.
Christmas Time in Indian Territory. Tulsa, OK: University of Tulsa, 1978.

Shorter Works by Alice Mary Robertson

"The Creek Indian Council in Session." *Chronicles of Oklahoma* (September 1933): 895–98.

Shorter Works About Alice Mary Robertson

"A la Cherokee." *Delineator* 98 (April 1921): 68.

"Alice M. Robertson: Republican of Oklahoma." In *A Minority of Members: Women in the U.S. Congress*, by Hope Chamberlin. New York: New American Library, 1974.

"Alice Robertson Dies; Aided Indians." *New York Times* (July 2, 1931): 29.

Bass, Althea. "William Schenck Robertson." *Chronicles of Oklahoma* (Spring 1959): 28–34.

"Congresswoman Elected with Want Ads." *Current Opinion* 70 (January 1921): 41–44.

Debo, Angie. *And Still the Waters Run.* Princeton: Princeton University Press, 1940.

————. *The Road to Disappearance.* Norman: University of Oklahoma Press, 1941.

Foreman, Grant. "The Hon. Alice M. Robertson." *Chronicles of Oklahoma* (March 1932): 13–17.

————. "The Lady from Oklahoma." *Independent* 105 (March 26, 1921): 311 + .

"Highlights: Women in the 65th–77th United States Congresses." In *Women in Congress*, by Annabel Paxton. Richmond, VA: Dietz Press, [1945].

James, Louise B. "Alice Mary Robertson: Anti-Feminist Congresswoman." *Chronicles of Oklahoma* 55 (1977–78): 454–61.

Marshall, M. M. "Woman's Place in Politics." *Woman's Home Companion* 48 (October 1921): 15.

Morgan, T. P. "Miss Alice of Muskogee." *Ladies' Home Journal* 38 (March 1921): 21.

Morris, Cheryl Haun. "Alice M. Robertson: Friend or Foe of the American Soldier." *Journal of the West* 12 (April 1973): 307–16.

"Portrait." *Collier's* 70 (September 2, 1922): 8.

"Portrait." *Collier's* 74 (September 27, 1924): 19.

"Portrait." *Current History Magazine of the New York Times* 14 (April 1921): 41.

"Portrait." *Independent* 104 (November 20, 1920): 263.

"Portrait." *Independent* 115 (December 26, 1925): 726.

"Portrait." *Outlook* 126 (November 17, 1920): 492.

"Portrait." *Outlook* 127 (March 23, 1921): 471.

"Portrait." *Review of Reviews* 62 (December 1920): 571.

"Portrait." *Review of Reviews* 64 (October 1921): 439.

"Portrait." *Woman's Home Companion* 48 (June 1921): 52.

"Portrait." *World's Work* 44 (August 1922): 342.

Stanley, Ruth Moore. "Alice M. Robertson, Oklahoma's First Congresswoman." *Chronicles of Oklahoma* 45 (1967): 259–289.

Wenger, Martin. "Samuel Worcester Robertson." *Chronicles of Oklahoma* (Spring 1959): 45–58.

"Woman Who Got into Congress Through the Want-ad Columns." *Literary Digest* 67 (December 4, 1920): 56–58.

Worcester, Jonathan Fox. *The Descendants of Rev. William Worcester with a Brief Notice of the Connecticut Wooster Family.* Boston: E. F. Worcester, 1914.

Other Works About Alice Mary Robertson

Theses

Spaulding, Joe Powell. "The Life of Alice Mary Robertson." Ph.D. diss., University of Oklahoma, 1959.

Primary Source Materials Relating to Alice Mary Robertson

Alice Mary Robertson. Papers. 1805–1923. Extent of collection: 1 cu. ft. Finding aids: No guide. Location: Oklahoma Historical Society, Historical Building, 2100 N. Lincoln Blvd., Oklahoma City, Oklahoma 73105. Scope of collection: Much of collection is official and personal correspondence related to Robertson's work as postmaster.

Althea Bass. Papers. 1847–1955. Extent of collection: 30 items. Finding aids: Unpublished guide. Location: Western History Collections, University of Oklahoma, 630 Parrington Oval, Room 452, Norman, Oklahoma 73019. Scope of collection: Includes "Inheritance of Alice Robertson," unpublished biography of Oklahoma's first congresswoman.

Edith Cherry Johnson. Photoprints. 1910–1951. Extent of collection: 18 items. Finding aids: Inventory available in repository. Location: Western History Collections, University of Oklahoma, 630 Parrington Oval, Room 452, Norman, Oklahoma 73019. Scope of collection: Black and white original and copy prints of Johnson and others.

Elizabeth Lowell Putnam. Papers. 1887–1935 (inclusive). Extent of collection: 15.5 lin. ft. Finding aids: Unpublished finding aid. Location: Schlesinger Library, Radcliffe College, Cambridge, Massachusetts 02138. Scope of collection: Includes correspondence with Robertson.

Grace Merriman and Ann Eliza (Worcester) Robertson. Papers. 1860–1907. Extent of collection: 2 cu. ft. Finding aids: No guide. Location: Oklahoma Historical Society, Historical Building, 2100 N. Lincoln Blvd., Oklahoma City, Oklahoma 73105. Scope of collection: Family correspondence and miscellaneous papers of Robertson's mother.

Orville Hitchcock Platt. Papers. 1880–1950. Extent of collection: 6 ft. Finding aids: Unpublished guide in repository. Location: Connecticut State Library, 231 Capitol Ave., Hartford, Connecticut 06106. Scope of collection: Correspondents include Robertson.

Robertson Family. Papers of Robertson and Worcester Families. 1815–1932. Extent of collection: 5,000 items. Finding aids: Unpublished inventory in library. Location: University of Tulsa Library, 600 S. College, Tulsa, Oklahoma 74104-3189. Scope of collection: Correspondence, diaries, notebooks, Creek Indian tribal records, scrapbooks, photos, memorabilia and printed matter.

52. Ruby Doris Smith Robinson
(1941?–1967)

Founding member and executive secretary of Student Nonviolent Coordinating Committee; advocate for African American rights

BIOGRAPHICAL INFORMATION

Chronological Biography

Born April 25, 1941 or 1942, in Atlanta, Georgia, second of three girls and four boys. Lived in Summerhill, working-class neighborhood in midst of racial change from white to black. Parents Alice (Banks) and the Rev. John Thomas Smith considered education high priority. Strongly independent child, permitted by parents to begin school at age three when sister was enrolled in church-run kindergarten. Started first grade following year and continued to stay ahead of peers throughout public schooling. Excellent student, graduated from L. J. Price High School at age 16. Participated in activities of church, school and community, but was aware of existing racial discrimination.

1955: At about age 13, deeply impressed by news reports and sight of elderly people walking during the black Montgomery, Alabama, bus boycott. Resolved to join fight to end segregation.   **1959?:** Enrolled in Spelman College in Atlanta, a small, liberal arts college for women. Received half-tuition scholarship as family could not afford college expenses.   **February 1, 1960:** Lunch counter sit-in in Greensboro, North Carolina, took place when she was sophomore. With sister, joined with students from Atlanta University Center (Atlanta Committee on Appeal for Human Rights) and participated in early demonstrations in restaurants connected with government buildings. Sit-ins continued throughout South.   **April 1960:** Attended meeting at Shaw University in Raleigh, North Carolina, which led to formation of Student Nonviolent Coordinating Committee (SNCC).   **February 1961:** Part of SNCC support group who travelled to Rock Hill, South Carolina, where students who sat at segregated lunch counter had been arrested and jailed. Arrested along with three companions for attempting to be served at lunch counter and sentenced to 30 days in jail. The SNCC began to use strategy of "jail, no bail" to further focus attention on issue. First time civil rights workers arrested for this violation chose to serve full sentence rather than post bail. **May 1961:** "Freedom Rides" had been organized by Congress of Racial Equality (CORE) to challenge segregation in interstate travel; Southern states had mandated segregation, while federal laws prohibited it. When riders were jailed in Birmingham, Alabama, she was one of reinforcement group sent by SNCC, although she had difficulty raising money for trip as many Atlanta blacks felt tactics were too dangerous. **May 20, 1961:** Group was attacked by angry white mob when bus travelling from Birmingham arrived in Montgomery. **May 24, 1961:** Arrested for attempted use of white restrooms in Jackson, Mississippi, after ride from Birmingham, and given two-month suspended sentence on charge of breaching the peace, along with $200 fine. Refused to pay fine, choosing to serve term. Confined in four-bunk cell in Hinds County jail with as many as 23 others for two weeks, then spent 45 days in maximum security area of Parchman State Penitentiary under worse conditions as number of jailed Freedom Riders increased. **Summer 1961:** Participated in SNCC voter registration drive in McComb, Mississippi. Attended training seminar for student activists at Fisk University. **Fall 1961:** Re-accepted at Spelman with recommendations written by Dr. Martin Luther King, Jr., among others. Received scholarship assistance from SNCC, National Council of Negro Women and American Baptist Home Mission Societies. As SNCC involvement increased, however, class attendance became sporadic. **December 1961:** Participated in Albany, Georgia, demonstrations. Advocated further demonstrations to increase pressure on city leaders, but view was not supported. **Summer 1962:** Worked with SNCC project in Cairo, Illinois. **Spring 1963:** Withdrew from Spelman. Joined SNCC as full-time administrative assistant to executive secretary, James Forman, becoming one of youngest on staff in Atlanta national headquarters. Responsibilities included organizing student volunteers, assisting field staff and handling emergencies. Understood importance of maintaining harmonious relations between civil rights workers and local community activists and would not tolerate staff acting contrary to instructions or in irresponsible manner, but also strove to respect individual needs of highly individualized staff, often creating stressful situations and criticism from some in SNCC. Felt strongly that committed black students could change conditions under which blacks lived. **April 1963:** Coordinated SNCC's third annual conference in Atlanta. **Summer 1964:** Believing civil rights work in South should be led by blacks, instituted concerted drive to recruit Southern black volunteers to work in major voter registration drive in Mississippi that SNCC was participating in along with CORE, NAACP and Southern Christian Leadership Conference. **Fall 1964:** Assumed larger role in SNCC. During staff retreat to plan SNCC's future efforts, performed daily duties of organization and made policy decisions as need arose, without clear guidelines from its policymaking body. Served in various positions — personnel officer, southern student coordinator and bookkeeper. Participated in sit-in at James Forman's office to protest limited roles available to women in SNCC organization; leadership was male-dominated, she being the exception. **September 1964:** Along with other SNCC staff, visited

Guinea for country's independence day observance, first trip by SNCC to Africa. Group was deeply affected by being in country run by blacks. President Sekou Toure broadened their awareness of discrimination to include economic dimensions, furthering her feeling that civil rights movement had not been of much benefit to poor blacks and adding to her growing commitment to black nationalism. One of first SNCC staff to urge organization to develop association with Africa. **November 1964:** Married fellow Atlantan Clifford Robinson, mail clerk in Atlanta SNCC office. He later became chief mechanic of Sojourner Motor Fleet after she took over its management when SNCC's transportation officer was arrested and jailed in Mississippi. Fleet owned and leased about 100 cars and light trucks crucial to SNCC work in rural areas in south. **May 1965:** Received B.S. from Spelman College, having returned in 1964. **July 1965:** Only child, son Kenneth Toure, named for Guinea president, was born. **May 16, 1966:** Elected to succeed James Forman as executive secretary of SNCC; remained in position until she became ill. Organization's head, John Lewis, was replaced by more radical Stokely Carmichael. Change suggested shift to more militant course for group as well as transition to black nationalism. Some felt founding of all-black political party in South was also possible. **June 1966:** Endorsed call for "Black Power" when first raised during "March Against Fear" in Mississippi after leader James Meredith was wounded by gunshot; some in SNCC voiced strong reservations. Felt that to help poor black people, movement must shift from civil rights legislation to fundamental socioeconomic change. By this time had been affiliated with SNCC longer than any other person in organization and had played major role from beginning. **January 1967:** Became terminally ill. Spent much time in hospital in New York City. **October 7, 1967:** Died at home in Atlanta from lymphoma or leukemia, type of blood cancer. Buried in Atlanta after funeral services at West Mitchell Baptist Church. Active until short time before her death, had been arrested numerous times and served about 100 days in Southern jails for civil rights activities. Cited as "heartbeat" of SNCC and one of its most dedicated administrators, as well as one of its intellectual leaders.

Background Information

Parents: Alice (Banks) and the Rev. John Thomas Smith. Both born in Georgia. Mother was beautician and operated family store; father was mover and Baptist minister. **Siblings:** Six (Known names: Mary Ann). **Children:** One (Kenneth Toure). **Influences:** None. **Ethnicity:** African American. **Also known as:** Smith; Rubye. **Historical sites, landmarks, etc.:** None known.

BIBLIOGRAPHICAL INFORMATION

Biographical Sketches About Ruby Doris Smith Robinson

Garraty, John A., and Mark C. Carnes, eds. *Dictionary of American Biography.* New York: Charles Scribner's Sons, 1988.

Sicherman, Barbara, and Carol Hurd Green, eds. *Notable American Women: The Modern Period: A Biographical Dictionary.* Cambridge, MA: Belknap Press of Harvard University Press, 1980.

Smith, Jessie Carney, ed. *Notable Black American Women.* Detroit: Gale Research, 1992.

Shorter Works About Ruby Doris Smith Robinson

Bennett, Lerone, Jr. "SNCC: Rebels with a Cause." *Ebony* 20 (July 1965): 146–53.

Carson, Clayborne. *In Struggle: SNCC and the Black Awakening of the 1960s.* Cambridge, MA: Harvard University Press, 1981.

Carson, Josephine. *Silent Voices: The Southern Negro Woman Today.* New York: Delacorte, 1969. ("Sarah" is Robinson.)

Evans, Sara. *Personal Politics: The Roots of Women's Liberation in the Civil Rights Movement and the New Left.* New York: Knopf; distributed by Random House, 1979.

Forman, James. *The Making of Black Revolutionaries.* Washington, D. C.: Open Hand, 1985.

Garland, Phyl. "Builders of a New South." *Ebony* (August 1966): 27 + .

Giddings, Paula. *When and Where I Enter: The Impact of Black Women on Race and Sex in America.* New York: Morrow, 1984.

Meier, August, and Elliott Rudwick. *CORE: A Study in the Civil Rights Movement, 1942–1968.* New York: Oxford University Press, 1973.

Mitchell, Susan D. "A Personal Tribute to Ruby Doris Smith Robinson." *SAGE: A Scholarly Journal on Black Women* Student Supplement (1988): 3.

Parms, Deborah, and Jennifer Freeman. "Journeys of a Thousand Miles." *SAGE: A Scholarly Journal on Black Women* Student Supplement (1988): 2.

"Rare Blood Disease Fatal to a Founder of SNCC." *Jet* (October 26, 1967): 28.

Roberts, Gene. "Militants Take Over Student Coordinating Group." *New York Times* (May 17, 1966): 22.

Royster, Jacqueline Jones. "A 'Hearbeat' for Liberation: The Reclamation of Ruby Doris Smith." *SAGE: A Scholarly Journal on Black Women* Student Supplement (1988): 64–66.

"Ruby Robinson, 26, A S.N.C.C. Founder." *New York Times* (October 10, 1967): 47.

Sellers, Cleveland. *The River of No Return; the Autobiography of a Black Militant and the Life and Death of SNCC.* New York: Morrow, 1973.

"SNCC's Ruby Robinson Rites Will Be Saturday." *Atlanta Constitution* (October 11, 1967): 14.

Stoper, Emily. *The Student Nonviolent Coordinating Committee: The Growth of Radicalism in a Civil Rights Organization.* Brooklyn, NY: Carlson, 1989.
Zinn, Howard. *SNCC: The New Abolitionists.* Boston: Beacon, 1964.

Primary Source Materials Relating to Ruby Doris Smith Robinson

Ruby Doris Smith. Extent of collection: See "Scope of collection." Finding aids: See "Scope of collection." Location: Spelman College, Atlanta, Georgia 30314-4399. Scope of collection: College Archives contains her application for admission, etc. and Alumnae Affairs has short write-up.
Student Nonviolent Coordinating Committee. Papers. No Date. Extent of collection: Not listed. Finding aids: Not listed. Location: Martin Luther King, Jr. Center for Nonviolent Social Change, Archives, 449 Auburn Avenue, Atlanta, Georgia 30312. Scope of collection: Not listed.

53. *Josephine St. Pierre Ruffin*
(1842–1924)
Clubwoman; advocate for African American rights and women's suffrage

BIOGRAPHICAL INFORMATION

Chronological Biography

Born August 31, 1842, to Eliza Matilda (Menhenick) and John James St. Pierre in Boston, Massachusetts, last of six children and fifth daughter. Information concerning siblings is minimal; may have died young or entered white world with mixed ancestry of black, French, English, and Native American reflected in their complexion and features as it was in hers. Father was clothes dealer in Boston and one of founders of Zion Baptist Church.
1842–1855: Because Boston schools were segregated, parents sent her to public school in Salem rather than to school for blacks in Boston; may also have attended public school in Charleston and private school in New York.
1855–1858: When Boston's schools were integrated, attended Bowdoin School in city's West End.   1858: Married George Lewis Ruffin at age 16. Husband came from prominent black family which had moved to Boston from Richmond, Virginia, in 1853 to pursue opportunities for their children. Couple left United States shortly thereafter, possibly to escape racial discrimination, residing in Liverpool, England, for several years.   **Civil War**

Years–1894: Returned to Boston during Civil War. Husband first worked as barber, then earned law degree in 1869 and was elected to Massachusetts legislature. Five children born. Husband's career brought her into social prominence in Boston black community; wanting to help people and possessing talent for organizing, became active worker for black rights, women's suffrage, welfare and other causes to further advance black people. Friends included Frederick Douglass and William Lloyd Garrison. War years' projects included working with Sanitary Commission and Home Guard, as well as aiding in effort to recruit soldiers. Later was visitor for Associated Charities of Boston for over ten years. Met Julia Ward Howe, Lucy Stone and others while active in suffrage movement. Served on executive board of Massachusetts Moral Education Association. Charter member of Massachusetts School Suffrage Association. Invited to become member of predominantly white New England Women's Club, founded by Howe. Rights, development and improvement of status and image of black women were her special interests.   **1879:** Helped to establish Boston Kansas Relief Association to supply clothing and money to Southern blacks relocating in Kansas.   **1883:** Husband became first black municipal judge in Charlestown, Massachusetts. Had previously been member of Boston City Council.   **November 19, 1886:** Husband died in Boston, evidently leaving very little money, having given much to charity and welfare causes. By now she was well known in her own right for her work.   **1889:** Offered help of black Northern women to white Southern women in Georgia Educational League who were helping black Southern children. This was one of her many attempts, generally rebuffed, urging white women to unite with black women for benefit of humanity. **Early 1890s:** One of editors and writers of *Boston Courant,* weekly black paper. Joined New England Women's Press Association in 1893, continuing affiliation until early 20th century.   **1894:** Seeing need for black women to organize, as white women had been doing for many years, founded Woman's Era Club (also referred to as Women's Era Club and New Era Club) in Boston with daughter, Florida Ridley, and with Maria Baldwin, Boston school principal. First black women's civic organization in Boston, and one of first in country; aim was furtherance of blacks in general and black women in particular. Group soon included about 60 prominent black women in city. Served as president of club until 1903. Also continued participation in white women's clubs in Massachusetts. Edited organization's monthly periodical, *Woman's Era* (also referred to as *Women's Era*), for several years. Publication was first paper published by black women in country; it began publication in March 1894 and was published for about ten years. About this time, became only black member of Boston's Women's Press Club.   **Summer 1895:** Organized First National Conference of Colored Women at Charles Street AME (African Methodist Episcopal) Church in Boston to create national organization of black women; approximately 20 representatives from other black women's clubs attended. Black women's groups had been excluded from white women's organizations, usually due to Southern women's accusations that black women were immoral and ignorant. In addition, president of Missouri Press Association, James W. Jacks, had criticized black women and Ruffin had seen his statement. She felt that by joining together nationally they could overcome these objections in a way individuals could not, showing that their aims and interests were same as white women, and that they were intelligent, cultured women. National Federation of Afro-American Women, uniting 36 clubs in 12 states, including Woman's Era Club, was formed and Margaret Murray Washington was elected president. 1896: National Federation merged with Colored Women's League of Washington, D. C., rival national organization headed by Mary Eliza Church Terrell (see entry 61) to form National Association of Colored Women. Terrell was first national president and Ruffin one of seven vice presidents. *Woman's Era* became official publication of new association. One of founders of Northeastern Federation of Women's Clubs. 1899–1902: Served on executive board of Massachusetts State Federation of Women's Clubs, which she had helped found and of which the Woman's Era Club was a member. 1900: Executive committee of General Federation of Women's Clubs accepted Woman's Era Club for membership in May. Ruffin was sent to General Federation's convention in Milwaukee as delegate of Woman's Era Club and Massachusetts State Federation, as well as alternate delegate from New England Women's Press Association. When it was discovered that she was representing black Woman's Era Club as well as other two associations which were predominantly white (she was so fair-skinned it is likely she was taken for a white woman), great opposition to acceptance of black club arose, mostly from Southern women; Club was denied admission by board and she was told she could attend convention only as delegate of white groups, which she refused to do. National publicity resulted with most newspapers taking her side; many white clubs and state delegations voiced strong opposition to board's action, among them Catholic Woman's League of Chicago, but General Federation maintained segregationist policy and kept color bar for several decades. Due to Southern clubs' objections, Mary Eliza Church Terrell was also refused permisson to address convention on behalf of National Association of Colored Women; she did speak before other white clubs during early ears of 1900s. 1902: Assisted in establishment, and served as vice president of, American Mount Coffee School Association to enlarge Jennie Davis Sharpe's school in Liberia; Edward Everett Hale was president of organization. November 16, 1921: At age 79, attended Women's Day at Copley Plaza Hotel, heading receiving line of distinguished women of Massachusetts. February 1924: Attended "Founder's Day" reception on February 10th, and on February 28th participated in annual meeting of League of Women for Community Service, which she had previously chaired and had helped to found with Maria Baldwin. Elected to board of management of Sedalia Club of Boston. **March 13, 1924:** Died at home on St. Botolph Street in Boston of nephritis at age 81 after taking to her bed a few days before. League of Women for Community Service held visitation; funeral services were held in Trinity Episcopal Church where she was member; burial took place in Mount Auburn Cemetery in Cambridge. Recognized leader in movement to advance status and condition of black women, had continued club and community activities, assisted in formation of Association for the Promotion of Child Training in the South and of Boston branch of National Association for the Advancement of Colored People (NAACP).

Background Information

Parents: Eliza Matilda (Menhenick) and John James St. Pierre. Mother was born in Cornwall, England. Father was son of early nineteenth century French immigrant from Martinique, Jean Jacques St. Pierre, and Betsey Hill from Taunton, Massachusetts, who was of black, French, and Native American ancestry. One of Hill's forebearers may have been African prince who had escaped from slave ship. **Siblings:** Five (No known names). **Children:** Five (Hubert St. Pierre, lawyer, served in Boston Common Council and state legislature; Florida Yates (Ridley) was Boston public school teacher who was active with mother in many organizations and causes; Stanley, inventor, organist, and manufacturer; George Lewis, organist; and Robert, died in infancy). **Influences:** None. **Ethnicity:** African American. **Also known as:** None known. **Historical sites, landmarks, etc.:** Grave, Mount Auburn Cemetery, Cambridge, Massachusetts.

BIBLIOGRAPHICAL INFORMATION

Biographical Sketches About Josephine St. Pierre Ruffin

Brown, Hallie Q. *Homespun Heroines and Other Women of Distinction.* New York: Oxford University Press, 1988.

Dannett, Sylvia G. L. *Profiles of Negro Womanhood.* Yonkers, NY: Educational Heritage, 1964.

James, Edward T., ed. *Notable American Women 1607–1950: A Biographical Dictionary.* Cambridge, MA: Belknap Press of Harvard University Press, 1971.

Logan, Rayford W., and Michael R. Winston, eds. *Dictionary of American Negro Biography.* New York: W. W. Norton, 1982.

Smith, Jessie Carney, ed. *Notable Black American Women*. Detroit: Gale Research, 1992.

Uglow, Jennifer S., comp. and ed. *The Continuum Dictionary of Women's Biography*. New York: Continuum Publishing Company, 1989.

Zophy, Angela Howard. *Handbook of American Women's History*. New York: Garland, 1990.

Shorter Works by Josephine St. Pierre Ruffin

"The Beginnings of the National Club Movement." In *Black Women in White America*, edited by Gerda Lerner. New York: Vintage, 1973.

Shorter Works About Josephine St. Pierre Ruffin

Aptheker, Bettina. *Woman's Legacy: Essays on Race, Sex, and Class in American History*. Amherst: University of Massachusetts Press, 1982.

"Black Women's Organizations." In *Women Together*, by Judith Papachristou. New York: Alfred A. Knopf, 1976.

Bullock, Penelope L. *The Afro-American Periodical Press, 1838–1909*. Baton Rouge: Louisiana State University Press, 1981.

Coleman, Willie M. "'The Woman's Era,' 1894–1897: Voices from Our 'Womanist' Past." *Sage* 1 (Fall 1984): 36–37.

Davis, Angela Yvonne. *Women, Race, & Class*. New York: Random House, 1981.

Davis, Elizabeth Lindsay. *Lifting as They Climb*. Washington, D. C.: National Association of Colored Women, 1933.

Flexner, Eleanor. *Century of Struggle: The Woman's Rights Movement in the United States*. Cambridge, MA: Harvard University Press, 1959.

Gozemba, Patricia A., and Marilyn L. Humphries. "Women in the Anti–Ku Klux Klan Movement, 1865–1984." *Women's Studies International Forum* 12 (1989): 35–40.

Hopkins, Pauline. "Josephine St. Pierre Ruffin at Milwaukee, 1900." *Colored American Magazine* (July 1902): 210–13.

————. "Some Famous Women." *Colored American Magazine* (August 1902): 273–77.

Howe, Julia Ward, ed. *Sketches of Representative Women of New England*. Boston: New England Historical Publishing, 1904.

Kolmer, Elizabeth. "Nineteenth Century Woman's Rights Movement: Black and White." *Negro History Bulletin* 35 (December 1972): 178–80.

Lerner, Gerda. "Early Community Work of Black Club Women." *Journal of Negro History* 59 (April 1974): 158–67.

Logan, Rayford Whittingham. *The Betrayal of the Negro, from Rutherford B. Hayes to Woodrow Wilson*. Enl. Ed. New York: Collier, [1965].

Major, Geraldyn Hodges. *Black Society*. Chicago: Johnson Publishing, 1976.

National Association of Colored Women (U.S.). *A History of the Club Movement Among the Colored Women of the United States of America: As Contained in* the Minutes of the Conventions, Held in Boston, July 29, 30, 31, 1895, and of the National Federation of Afro-American Women, Held in Washington, D. C., July 20, 21, 22, 1896. [United States: n.p.], 1902.

A New Negro for a New Century. Miami: Mnemosyne Publishing, 1969.

Noble, Jeanne. Beautiful, Also, Are the Souls of My Black Sisters: A History of the Black Woman in America. Englewood Cliffs, NJ: Prentice-Hall, 1978.

Perkins, Linda Marie. Black Feminism and 'Race Uplift,' 1890–1900. Cambridge, MA: Institute for Independent Study, Radcliffe College, 1981. [ED221445]

Scruggs, Lawson Andrew. Women of Distinction: Remarkable in Works and Invincible in Character. Raleigh, NC: L. A. Scruggs, 1893.

Terbor-Penn, Rosalyn. "Nineteenth Century Black Women and Woman Suffrage." Potomac Review 7 (Spring–Summer 1977): 13–24.

Williams, Fannie Barrier. "The Ruffin Incident—1900." In Black Women in White America, edited by Gerda Lerner. New York: Vintage, 1973.

Woman's Journal. Issues for June 16, 23, and 30, 1900, contain accounts of General Federation of Women's Clubs controversy.

Wood, Mary I. The History of the General Federation of Women's Clubs for the First Twenty-Two Years of Its Organization. New York: History Department, General Federation of Women's Clubs, 1912.

Other Works About Josephine St. Pierre Ruffin
Theses

Cash, Floris Loretta Barnett. "Womanhood and Protest: The Club Movement Among Black Women, 1892–1922." Ph.D. diss., State University of New York at Stony Brook, 1986.

Fields, Emma L. "The Women's Club Movement in the U.S., 1877–1900." Master's thesis, Howard University, 1948.

Fuller, Luther M. "The Negro in Boston, 1864–1954." Ph.D. diss., Columbia University, 1956.

Horton, James Oliver. "Black Activism in Boston, 1830–1860." Ph.D. diss., Brandeis University, 1973.

Primary Source Materials Relating to Josephine St. Pierre Ruffin

Heslip-Ruffin Family. Papers. 1833–1943. Extent of collection: 87 items and 5 boxes. Finding aids: Not listed. Location: Amistad Research Center, Tilton Hall, Tulane University, New Orleans, Louisiana 70118-5698. Scope of collection: Correspondence, biographical data, wedding license of Ruffins, letters, etc.

Jeannine Dobbs. Class Essays. 1977. Extent of collection: 2 folders. Finding aids: Unpublished finding aid. Location: Schlesinger Library, Radcliffe College, Cambrige, Massachusetts 02138. Scope of collection: In spring of 1977, Dobbs taught class at Harvard University entitled Expository Writing 12, Women in American History. Photocopies of class essays on notable American women including Ruffin.

54. *Elizabeth Elkins Sanders*

(1762–1851)

Advocate for Native American rights; social critic; and author

BIOGRAPHICAL INFORMATION

Chronological Biography

Second daughter of Elizabeth (White) and Thomas Elkins, born August 12, 1762, in Salem, Massachusetts. Details of early life are unknown. Father died at age 26, before his daughter was two years old.

April 28, 1782: Married Thomas Sanders, son of Gloucester merchant. He initially worked for one of her relatives in East India trade and later became one of most successful and wealthy businessmen in community. Lived in handsome house on Chestnut Street, area in which most other prominent families lived. Known for their hospitality. Raised four daughters and two sons. Attended First Unitarian Church. Contributed generously to various causes to improve conditions of less fortunate.   1783: First child, Charles, born.   1784: Catherine born.   1788: Birth of Mary Elizabeth. 1793: Caroline born.   1793?: Birth of fourth daughter, Lucy.   1804: Last child, George Thomas, born.   1828: First pamphlet, *Conversations, Principally on the Aborigines of North America*, published anonymously in Salem when she was 66. Essay is in form of dialogue between mother and children; discusses atrocities committed by U.S. troops against several tribes, including Creeks of Georgia. Also includes survey of Indian culture emphasizing skills in medicine and agriculture. Extensive reader, had become deeply concerned about conditions and inhumane treatment of Native Americans. Particularly deplored Andrew Jackson's sanctions of confiscation of Native American lands and wrote pamphlet in response to his presidential nomination.   1828?–1844?: Contributed articles, book reviews and letters to New England newspapers expressing views on various social issues. Person of strong and fixed opinions, writing style was direct and frequently sarcastic. Supported prison reform, increased educational opportunities for poor and measures to reclaim delinquents. Concerned also with health reform and protested against doctors who prescribed drugs too freely. Magazine articles, and later pamphlets, declared deep objection to foreign missions. Felt it absurd to expend large sums to maintain missions while injustices in United

States toward Native Americans and African Americans continued. Insisted that missionaries' teachings, especially those of Calvinists, were not beneficial to people whose own religions often compared favorably with ones being taught. Feared natives' way of life would be destroyed.   **1829:** Second Native American rights pamphlet, *The First Settlers of New England,* published. Continued and expanded themes expressed in first publication including suggestion that true Christians would not condone such treatment and that Native Americans were people of superior morality and culture. **1844:** At 82, resumed pamphlet writing with *Tract on Missions.* Some of essays had previously appeared as magazine articles. Husband died.   **1845:** *Second Part of a Tract on Missions* published.   **1848:** *Remarks on the "Tour Around Hawaii," by the Missionaries, Messrs. Ellis, Thurston, Bishop, and Goodrich, in 1823* published.   **February 19, 1851:** Died in Salem at age of 88 of lung problems. Although personally influential and well liked in Salem where she had lived entire life, her values and ideas were not shared by contemporaries who favored expansion and missionary pursuits for many succeeding decades.

Background Information

Parents: Elizabeth (White) and Thomas Elkins.   **Siblings:** Number not known (No known names).   **Children:** Six (Charles, Catherine, Mary Elizabeth, Caroline, Lucy, George Thomas).   **Influences:** None.   **Ethnicity:** Not known.   **Also known as:** "A Lady" (pseudonym).   **Historical sites, landmarks, etc.:** None known.

BIBLIOGRAPHICAL INFORMATION

Biographical Sketches About Elizabeth Elkins Sanders

James, Edward T., ed. *Notable American Women 1607–1950: A Biographical Dictionary.* Cambridge, MA: Belknap Press of Harvard University Press, 1971.
Mainiero, Lina, ed. *American Women Writers.* New York: Frederick Ungar, 1982.
Malone, Dumas, ed. *Dictionary of American Biography.* New York: Charles Scribner's Sons, 1963.
Whitman, Alden, ed. *American Reformers: An H. W. Wilson Biographical Dictionary.* New York: H. W. Wilson Company, 1985.

Books by Elizabeth Elkins Sanders

Circular Addressed to Benevolent Ladies of the United States: The Present Crisis in the Affairs of the Indian Nations in the United States, Demands the

Immediate and Interested Attention of All Who Make Any Claims to Benevolence or Humanity. [Boston: Printed by Crocker and Brewster, 1829]. (Possibly by Sanders.)

Conversations Principally on the Aborigines of North America. Salem, MA: W. & S. B. Ives, 1828.

Remarks on the "Tour Around Hawaii," by the Missionaries, Messrs. Ellis, Thurston, Bishop, and Goodrich, in 1823. Salem, MA: The Author, 1848.

Reviews of a Part of Prescott's "History of Ferdinand and Isabella," and of Campbell's "Lectures on Poetry." Boston: J. H. Francis, 1841.

Second Part of a Tract on Missions. Salem, MA: Gazette Office, 1845.

Tract on Missions. Salem, MA: Printed for the Author, 1844.

Shorter Works About Elizabeth Elkins Sanders

Hurd, Duane Hamilton, comp. *History of Essex County, Massachusetts, with Biographical Sketches of Many of its Pioneers and Prominent Men.* Philadelphia: J. W. Lewis, 1888.

Salem, (MA) *Vital Records of Salem, Massachusetts to the End of the Year 1849.* Salem, MA: Essex Institute, 1916.

Saltonstall, Leverett. *Ancestry and Descendants of Sir Richard Saltonstall: First Associate of the Massachusetts Bay Colony and Patentee of Connecticut.* [Cambridge, MA]: Riverside Press, 1897.

Silsbee, Marianne Cabot Devereux. *A Half Century in Salem.* Boston and New York: Houghton, Mifflin & Co.; Cambridge: Riverside Press, 1887.

55. *Rosika Schwimmer*
(1877–1948)

Feminist; pacifist; journalist; and lecturer

BIOGRAPHICAL INFORMATION

Chronological Biography

Born September 11, 1877, two months prematurely in Budapest, Hungary, to Bertha (Katscher) and Max B. Schwimmer, first of three children. Sickly child, suffered many bouts of illness. Attended convent and public schools in cities of Temesvar and Szabadka and high school in Budapest. Higher education for young women was very limited. Received private tutoring in music and languages and, with chaperon, attended six month commercial course restricted to young men. Had early career as musician and singer. Upper middle class Jewish parents were involved in literary life and often had unconventional views regarding social issues. Mother was freethinker, father agnostic. Decided to work as journalist, having been strongly influenced by maternal uncle, social reformer and writer, Leopold Katscher. **1895 or 6:** Took job as bookkeeper in Szabadka after father's business failure. **1897–1904:** Continued office work after returning with family to Budapest in 1897. Recognizing that women needed social, political and economic independence in order to control their lives, began writing and organizing activities. **1897:** Founded National Association of Women Office Workers and served as president until 1912. **1903:** Organized Hungarian Association of Working Women. **1904:** Formed Hungarian Council of Women. Having achieved international recognition as women's rights advocate due to political articles in German and Hungarian periodicals and newspapers, was invited speaker at International Council of Women and at International Women's Congress in Berlin. Met Carrie Chapman Catt who was heading International Woman Suffrage Alliance. Returned to Budapest and helped found and co-lead Hungarian Feminist Association (Feministák Egyesülete), feminist-pacifist organization which became instrumental in Hungarian suffrage and many other social reforms, including coeducation, admission to all forms of educational and vocation training and equal employment opportunity and wages. Group was unique because of its membership of both women and men. Organization later became Hungarian Section of Women's International League for Peace and Freedom. **1906:** Her Hungarian translation of *Women and Economics* by Charlotte Perkins Gilman, was published. Continued writing pamphlets, short stories, articles and a novel, covering home economics, state child care, marriage, etc. Lectured throughout Europe in several languages on feminist topics. **1907– 1928:** Edited Hungarian pacifist-feminist journal *A Nö és a Társadalom* (*Woman and Society*, later *The Woman*). **March 20, 1909:** Appointed by Count Andrassy to National Board of Child Welfare in recognition of her work toward the passage of legislation for protection of children. **January 16, 1911–January 4, 1913:** Married to Hungarian journalist named Bédy. **1913:** Organized highly acclaimed Seventh Congress of International Woman Suffrage Alliance, held in Budapest; elected corresponding secretary. **1914:** While in London serving as press secretary for International Woman Suffrage Alliance and working as correspondent for several European newspapers, became stranded at outbreak of World War I. Began circulating petitions among European suffrage leaders to urge President Woodrow Wilson to lead United States and other neutral countries to undertake mediation efforts. Sailed to United States in August. She and Catt met with Secretary of State William Jennings Bryan. Delivered petition representing one million suffragists in Europe to Wilson on September 18th. Failing in that approach, toured country speaking in about 60 cities in 22 states in effort to rouse public concern and change Wilson's mind, but he refused to move.   **January 1915:** Several peace groups were organized, largely due to her tour. These were merged and the Woman's Peace party formed with her significant assistance. Served as international secretary with Jane Addams as president.   **February 1915:** Attended national Emergency Peace Conference in Chicago; it had been organized a few months before, largely due to her inspiration.   **April 28–May 1, 1915:** Helped organize and run International Conference of Women, chaired by Addams, at The Hague with over 1,000 women in attendance. International Committee of Women for Permanent Peace (later renamed Women's International League for Peace and Freedom) was formed; Addams was president and Schwimmer vice president. Her plan to promote mediation by world leaders of neutral countries was approved. Headed delegation to neutral countries while Jane Addams visited belligerent nations. Despite evidence that mediation might be possible, President Wilson declined to act on idea.   **November 1915:** Again met unsuccessfully with Wilson.   **November 1915–February 1917:** Persuaded wealthy automobile manufacturer Henry Ford to sponsor expedition of Americans to Europe as unofficial mediation team. Much dissention occurred on ship voyage, many blaming her actions. Reporters ridiculed effort and mission began to disintegrate shortly after first conference in Stockholm in February 1916. Resigned in March after American attacks against her escalated. Effort was disbanded in February 1917.   **June 1916–September 1918:** Organized International Committee for Immediate Mediation. Continued unsuccessful private efforts for peace, hampered by lack of funds.   **October/November 1918:** Returned to Hungary, which had become independent, after being asked to serve on country's governing council. Appointed minister to Switzerland, probably first woman ambassador in modern times.   **March 1919:** Change of government put Communists in power. Refusing to support them, resigned as ambassador and was deprived of her civil rights.   **Early 1920:** Escaped by boat to Vienna as government again changed, becoming anti–Semitic and opposed to her past political activities.   **1920:** Woman suffrage secured in Hungary. Campaign was begun and managed by Hungarian Feminist Association.   **September 1921:** Entered United States, settling in Chicago to live with sister Franciska and take up career as lecturer and journalist (she had previously written primarily for Hungarian and German periodicals and newspapers), but was branded a spy by some groups, seen as part of conspiracy by others, and as a cause of Henry Ford's anti–Semitism because of her Peace Ship involvement. Ford later defended her and in 1929, she won $17,000 in damages from a maligner. Unable to earn living by lecturing and writing, she was supported by sister and close American friend, Lola Maverick Lloyd. Health began to deteriorate; suffered from severe diabetes.   **May 1924–1929:** Request for citizenship became public knowledge, increasing accusations by American Legion, etc. Refusing to state that she would bear arms if United States were attacked, application was denied in 1926 and then reversed. Supreme Court ruled against her on May 27, 1929, six to three; Justice Oliver Wendell Holmes supported her as did many editorials. Although Supreme Court reversed itself in 1946, she refused to reapply and remained a resident alien. **1928:** *Tisza Tales*, children's book of Hungarian legends and folk stories, published. **1929–1948:** Moved to New York City with sister, continued peace efforts and worked toward world citizenship, world government and World Center for Women's Archives. **December 4, 1937:** Presented with World Peace Prize of $8,500 which had been collected by international committee of 200 distinguished women and men from 18 countries who had worked with her for world peace, women's rights and other causes. Committee members included Albert Einstein and Carrie Chapman Catt. Began Campaign for World Government with Lloyd and Lloyd's children to work for establishment of nonmilitary federation of nations. Jointly chaired this first international organization devoted exclusively to this cause. Campaign was based on their 1924 plan which they published as *Chaos, War or a New World Order*. **World War II Years:** Unsuccessful in efforts to convene a world constitutional convention. **1948:** Nominated by several countries for Nobel Peace Prize. Died before recipient was announced. No award was made that year, committee stating it found no suitable living candidate. **August 3, 1948:** Died in New York City, at age 70, of bronchial pneumonia and diabetes at Mount Sinai Hospital. She was cremated and her ashes scattered by Lloyd's children in Lake Michigan near Lloyd's home in Winnetka, Illinois, in memory of their friendship.

Background Information

Parents: Bertha (Katscher) and Max B. Schwimmer. Father was experimental farmer who sold horses, seed corn and produce. **Siblings:** Two (Known names: Franciska). **Children:** None. **Influences:** Lola Maverick Lloyd. **Ethnicity:** Hungarian/Jewish. **Also known as:** Bedy-Schwimmer. **Historical sites, landmarks, etc.:** None known.

BIBLIOGRAPHICAL INFORMATION

Biographical Sketches About Rosika Schwimmer

Garraty, John A., and Edward T. James, eds. *Dictionary of American Biography.* New York: Charles Scribner's Sons, 1974.

James, Edward T., ed. *Notable American Women 1607–1950: A Biographical Dictionary.* Cambridge, MA: Belknap Press of Harvard University Press, 1971.
McHenry, Robert, ed. *Famous American Women.* New York: Dover, 1980.
Uglow, Jennifer S., comp. and ed. *The Continuum Dictionary of Women's Biography.* New York: Continuum, 1989.
Whitman, Alden, ed. *American Reformers: An H. W. Wilson Biographical Dictionary.* New York: H. W. Wilson Company, 1985.

Books by Rosika Schwimmer

Chaos, War or a New World Order? [N.p.]: Campaign for World Government, 1937.
Tisza Tales. Garden City, NY: Doubleday, Doran, 1928.
Union Now: For Peace or War? The Danger in the Plan of Clarence Streit; An Analysis. New York: The Author, 1939.

Books About Rosika Schwimmer

American Civil Liberties Union. *The Case of Rosika Schwimmer: Alien Pacifists Not Wanted!* New York: American Civil Liberties Union, 1929.
Rosika Schwimmer: World Patriot. A Biographical Sketch. N.p.: International Committee for World Peace, 1937. Reprint. Rev. and Enl. Ed. London: Printed by Odhams Press, 1947.

Shorter Works by Rosika Schwimmer

"Cause and Cure of Peace." *World Tommorrow* 16 (February 22, 1933): 181–83.
"Defenceless Victims of War." *Survey* 52 (August 1, 1924): 501.
"Hungarian Literature, July, 1903 to September, 1904." *Athenaeum* 2 (September 3, 1904): 306–07.
"Marianne Hainisch." *Equal Rights* (April 27, 1929): 93–94.
"The Nobel Peace Prize." *World Tomorrow* 15 (January 1932): 20–22.
"Refugees from Oppression." *Nation* 137 (August 9, 1933): 158–59.

Shorter Works About Rosika Schwimmer

"Arms and the Woman." *Outlook* 152 (June 12, 1929): 250.
Bainbridge, J., and R. Maloney. "Where Are They Now? Innocent Voyage; Ford Peace Ship." *New Yorker* 16 (March 9, 1940): 23–29.
"Case of Madame Schwimmer." *Christian Century* 46 (June 12, 1929): 769–71.
Gavit, John Palmer. "A Woman Without a Country." *Survey Graphic* 26 (September 1937): 486–87.
Gibson, J. Timberlake. "Henry Ford's Peace Ship: Not a Better Idea." *Smithsonian* 5 (1974): 92–96.

Hazard, H. B. "Supreme Court Holds Madam Schwimmer, Pacifist, Ineligible to Naturalization." *American Journal of International Law* 23 (July 1929): 626–32.

Holmes, O. W. "Justice Holmes and the Schwimmer Case." *New Republic* 59 (June 12, 1929): 92–93.

McAusland, Elizabeth. "The Citizenship Case of Rosika Schwimmer." *Twice a Year* (1939–1940): 368–81.

"Madame Schwimmer, Without a Country." *Literary Digest* 101 (June 8, 1929): 9.

Morehead, Caroline. *Troublesome People: The Warriors of Pacifism.* Bethesda: Adler & Adler, 1987.

"Obituary." *Nation* 167 (August 14, 1948): 171.

"Obituary." *Newsweek* 32 (August 16, 1948): 58.

"Obituary." *Survey Graphic* 37 (September 1948): 379.

"Obituary." *Time* 52 (August 16, 1948): 76.

Pastor, P. "Diplomatic Fiasco of the Modern World's First Woman Ambassador, Roza Bedy-Schwimmer." *East European Quarterly* 58 (September 1974): 273–82.

"Portrait." *Independent* 81 (January 25, 1915): 124.

"Portrait." *Outlook* 109 (March 24, 1915): 693.

"Portrait." *Survey* 35 (February 12, 1916): 581.

Postal, Bernard. "She Fights—For Peace." *B'nai B'rith Magazine* (December 1937): 132 +.

Rundquist, P. S. "Lost Women." *Ms.* 3 (January 1975): 58–59.

Stockwell, Rebecca S. "Bertha von Suttner and Rosika Schwimmer, Pacifists from the Dual Monarchy." In *Seven Studies in Medieval English History and Other Historical Essays: Presented to Harold S. Snellgrove,* edited by Richard H. Bowers. Jackson: University Press of Mississippi, 1983.

"Treason to Conscience: Mrs. Schwimmer Denied Citizenship." *Nation* 128 (June 12, 1919): 689.

Tuttle, Peter Guertin. *The Ford Peace Ship: Volunteer Diplomacy in the Twentieth Century.* [New Haven]: n.p., 1958.

U.S. Laws, Etc. *A Bill to Amend the Naturalization Law—May 29, 1929—Together With 'Some Material on the Rosika Schwimmer Citizenship Case.'* N.p.: n.p., 1929.

Whitehouse, Vera. *A Year as a Government Agent.* New York: Harper and Brothers, 1920.

"Women and War." *Outlook* 109 (March 24, 1915): 676–77.

Wynner, Edith. "Out of the Trenches by Christmas." *Progressive* (December 1965).

————. *World Federal Government: Why? What? How? In Maximum Terms. Proposals for United Nations Charter Revision.* Afton, NY: Fedonat Press, 1954.

Other Works About Rosika Schwimmer

Theses

Donehower, Weston Gladding. "Conflicting Interpretations of American Patriotism in the 1920's." Ph.D. diss., University of Pennsylvania, 1982.

Kraft, Barbara Sarina. "Some Must Dream: The History of the Ford Peace Expedition and the Neutral Conference for Continuous Mediation." Ph.D. diss., American University, 1976.

Tuttle, Peter Guertin. "The Ford Peace Ship: Volunteer Diplomacy in the Twentieth Century." Ph.D. diss., Yale University, 1958.

Primary Source Materials
Relating to Rosika Schwimmer

Frederick Holford Holt. Peace Papers. 1915–1917. Extent of collection: 509 items. Finding aids: Unpublished finding aid in repository. Location: University of Michigan Library, Department of Rare Books and Special Collections, Ann Arbor, Michigan 48109-1205. Scope of collection: Correspondence, papers, and photos relating to Holt's activities as member of Ford Peace Expedition. Also includes Mrs. Lilian (Silk) Holt's papers as women's suffrage worker and correspondence with Schwimmer.

Rosika Schwimmer. Papers. 1914–1937. Extent of collection: 2 ms. boxes, 1 envelope. Finding aids: Preliminary inventory. Location: Hoover Institution on War, Revolution, and Peace, Stanford University, Stanford, California 94305-1684. Scope of collection: Correspondence, petitions, clippings, printed matter and photographs, relating to pacifist movement during World War I, Henry Ford Peace Expedition, International Congress of Women, and presentation of World Peace Prize to Schwimmer in 1937.

Rosika Schwimmer. Papers. 1930–1948. Extent of collection: 15 items. Finding aids: No guide. Location: Library of Congress, Manuscript Division, Independent Ave. at First St. S. W., Washington, D. C. 20540. Scope of collection: Correspondence of Schwimmer, primarily with Oliver Wendell Holmes about his dissenting opinion to the Supreme Court decision denying her U.S. citizenship.

Schwimmer-Lloyd Collection Relating to Feminism, Pacifism, and World Government. 1852–1980. Extent of collection: 945 ft. Finding aids: Inventory and indexes in repository. Location: New York Public Library, 5th Ave. & 42nd St., New York, New York 10018. Scope of collection: Correspondence, diaries, writings, personal press clippings, morgue files, printed matter, photos and other papers, reflecting work of Schwimmer and Lloyd in Europe and America.

Schwimmer and Lloyd. Papers. ca. 1900–1948. Extent of collection: 4 boxes. Finding aids: Published guide. Location: Smith College, Sophia Smith Collection, Northampton, Massachusetts 01063. Scope of collection: Correspondence, photos, biographical material, articles, clippings, and pamphlets documenting friendships, philosophies and peace crusades of Lola Lloyd, Rosika Schwimmer and Franciska Schwimmer.

56. *Elizabeth Cochrane Seaman*
(1867–1922)
Muckraking journalist "Nellie Bly"; author

BIOGRAPHICAL INFORMATION

Chronological Biography

Born Elizabeth Cochran, May 5, 1867?, in Cochran Mills, Pennsylvania, youngest of three children of Mary Jane (Kennedy), second wife of Michael Cochran. Raised in family of ten which included five half-brothers from father's first marriage.

1879: Educated at home by father until his death when she was 12 years old. 1882: Attended Indiana, Pennsylvania, boarding school for one year. 1883: Family moved to Pittsburgh, Pennsylvania. 1884–1886: Responded anonymously to editorial in *Pittsburgh Dispatch* entitled "What Girls Are Good For," which criticized women who sought careers outside home. Editor George Madden, assuming writer was male, asked to be contacted in subsequent advertisement; her response signed "E. Cochrane" (she had added "e" to surname) set time for appointment. When she arrived at interview with list of story ideas, much abashed Madden offered her job for $5 weekly. He selected name "Nellie Bly" for her byline from popular Stephen Foster song. Began journalism career with daring series entitled "Divorce" and followed with popular articles on factories and workshops of Pittsburgh. Later demoted to writing women's and cultural news when exposé of local sweatshops raised ire of *Dispatch* advertisers. Shortly thereafter quit job to accompany mother on trip to Mexico. Her letters to Madden, printed in *Dispatch* as well as other papers, called for reform in Mexico's agrarian society and caused Mexican government to order her out of country; controversy prompted Madden to ask her to return to *Dispatch* with raise in salary to $15 weekly — she turned him down. 1887:Went to work for Joseph Pulitzer, notorious for sensationalistic style of reporting crime, infidelities, daring escapades and political graft on front pages of *New York World*. Continued to write exposés of underclass exploitation, urban social conditions and corruption in government, using her original undercover approach. Published first book, *Ten Days in a Mad House*. "Subscription series" book, it was collection of three stories written for *World*: sketch of servant girls' experiences at employment agencies, another on shop girls working at paper box factory, and title article on Blackwell's Island Insane Asylum, where Cochrane had admitted herself as patient to conduct research. Latter story caused quite a stir in official circles prompting Grand Jury investigation which sustained her findings and granted three million dollars for improvements to Blackwell's Island Insane Asylum. **1888:** Continued to write first person articles reflecting moral indignation and personal horror at plight of women and children. Penned articles on medical care for city's poor and conditions in old women's homes; also exposed gang of "mashers" who sweet-talked young ladies strolling through park into riding away with them for afternoon. Earned reputation as reformer when officials took note of her findings and acted to relieve conditions; for example, one series of stories on city prisons resulted in matrons being appointed to work with female prisoners. Granted celebrity status by charmed public who eagerly awaited her next escapade. Published *Six Months in Mexico*, personal account of earlier visit. Book examined national "character," exposed corruption and illustrated sensitivity on her part to exploitation of women and native Indian population. Approached Joseph Pulitzer with notion of duplicating journey of Jules Verne's fictional hero, Phileas Fogg, in *Around the World in 80 Days*. At first Pulitzer refused but eventually granted permission for trip. **November 14, 1889–January 25, 1890:** Sailed from Jersey City on trip to London, Paris, Italy, Suez, Ceylon, Singapore, Hong Kong, Yokahama and San Francisco. Wrote regularly of each country's attractions and weaknesses, as perceived by white, middle-class woman of time, while *World* hyped her progress. Arrived home to parade down Broadway in midst of adoring public's mania for Nellie Bly clothes, games and toys; endorsed Pears Soap, was topic of jokes, cartoons and jingles, and had racehorse named for her. **1890:** Published *Nellie Bly's Book: Around the World in Seventy-Two Days*, recounting voyage experiences. **1891–1894:** Continued to write for *World*, often seeking assignments concerning social conditions and child welfare away from New York City area where she was so well known. **April 1, 1895:** Met Robert L. Seaman, millionaire hardware manufacturer, while covering story on midwest drought. **April 5, 1895:** Married Seaman after four-day whirlwind courtship; he was 72, she not yet 30. Retired from journalism at peak of career to become proper wife. **1910?:** Upon husband's death took over and attempted to reform his business, American Steel Barrel Company. **1915–1917:** Fortune diminished by litigation over employee forgeries and various other disputes. Developed into professional litigant; her disposition was reported as contradictory and shrewish. Fled to Vienna where she stayed with friends. Transferred most of property to Austrian ownership to protect it from creditors but lost it all under Alien Custodians' Act when United States entered World War I. **1917–1919:** Detained in Vienna during remainder of World War I. **ca. 1920:** Employed by William Randolph Hearst's *Evening Journal,* but "yellow journalism's" ultra-sensational and sometimes faked approach to news had replaced muckraking style of first-person, undercover accounts she had made famous; "stunt" reporting was dead and finding homes for stray children was no longer newsworthy.   **January 30, 1920:** In final journalistic scoop, interviewed murderer Gordon Hamby shortly before he was executed in electric chair at Sing Sing Prison. Became first woman to witness execution in New York state since 1891. Article ran in *Evening Journal* but drew little notice and less comment.   **January 27, 1922:** Died of pneumonia in New York City hotel room. Funeral services were held at Little Church Around the Corner; buried in Woodlawn Cemetery in unmarked grave.   **January 28, 1922:** *World* ran half-column obituary on inside page.   **1978:** Headstone erected on gravesite by New York Press Club.

Background Information

Parents: Mary Jane (Kennedy) and Michael Cochran. Father worked way up from laborer to mill owner to associate judge of Armstrong County, Pennsylvania.   **Siblings:** Nine (No known names).   **Children:** None.   **Influences:** None.   **Ethnicity:** Not known.   **Also known as:** Cochran; Cochrane; Nelly Bly; "Nellie Bly" (pseudonym).   **Historical sites, landmarks, etc.:** Grave, Woodlawn Cemetery, New York, New York.

BIBLIOGRAPHICAL INFORMATION

Biographical Sketches About Elizabeth Cochrane Seaman

Ashley, Perry J., ed. *American Newspaper Journalists, 1901–1925.* Detroit: Gale Research, 1984. (Listed as Elizabeth [Nellie Bly] Cochrane)

Downs, Robert Bingham, and Jane B. Downs. *Journalists of the United States: Biographical Sketches of Print and Broadcast News Shapers From the Late 17th Century to the Present.* Jefferson, NC: McFarland, 1991. (Listed as Elizabeth [Nellie Bly] Cochrane)

James, Edward T., ed. *Notable American Women 1607–1950: A Biographical Dictionary.* Cambridge, MA: Belknap Press of Harvard University Press, 1971.

McHenry, Robert, ed. *Famous American Women.* New York: Dover, 1980.

McKerns, Joseph P., ed. *Biographical Dictionary of American Journalism.* New York: Greenwood, 1989. (Listed as Elizabeth Cochrane)

Mainiero, Lina, ed. *American Women Writers.* New York: Frederick Ungar, 1979. (Listed as Elizabeth Cochrane)

Malone, Dumas, ed. *Dictionary of American Biography.* New York: Charles Schribner's Sons, 1935.

Willard, Frances Elizabeth, and Mary A. Livermore, eds. *A Woman of the Century.* Detroit: Gale Research, 1967. (Listed as Cochrane, Elizabeth)

Zophy, Angela Howard, ed. *Handbook of American Women's History*. New York: Garland, 1990. (Listed as Bly, Nellie)

Books by Elizabeth Cochrane Seaman

Bly, Nellie. *Nellie Bly's Book: Around the World in Seventy-two Days*. New York: Pictorial Weeklies, 1890. Reprint. Detroit: Omnigraphics, 1991.
————. *Six Months in Mexico*. New York: Munro, 1888. Reprint. New York: J. W. Lovell, 1889.
————. *Ten Days in a Madhouse*. New York: Munro, 1887. Reprint. New York: Lovell, 1889.

Books About Elizabeth Cochrane Seaman

American Flange and Manufacturing Company, Inc. *The Story of Nellie Bly*. New York: n.p., 1951.
Baker, Nina Brown. *Nellie Bly*. New York: Holt, 1956. Reprint. *Nellie Bly, Reporter*. New York: Scholastic Book Services, 1961.
Carlson, Judy. *"Nothing Is Impossible," Said Nellie Bly*. Milwaukee: Raintree, 1989. Reprint. Scarborough, Ontario: Nelson Canada, 1990.
Dunnahoo, Terry. *Nellie Bly, a Portrait*. New York: Reilly & Lee Books, 1970.
Emerson, Kathy Lynn. *Making Headlines: A Biography of Nellie Bly*. Minneapolis: Dillon, 1989.
Erlich, Elizabeth. *Nellie Bly*. New York: Chelsea House, 1989.
Graves, Charles Parlin. *Nellie Bly: Reporter for the World*. Champaign, IL: Garrard, 1971.
Hahn, Emily. *Around the World with Nellie Bly*. New York: Houghton, 1959.
Johnson, Ann Donegan. *The Value of Fairness: The Story of Nellie Bly*. La Jolla, CA: Value Communications, 1977.
Kendall, Martha E. *Nellie Bly: Reporter for the World*. Brookfield, CT: Millbrook, 1992.
Lisker, Tom. *Nellie Bly: First Woman of the News*. New York: CPI, 1978.
Noble, Iris. *Nellie Bly, First Woman Reporter (1867–1922)*. New York: Messner, 1956.
Quackenbush, Robert. *Stop the Presses, Nellie's Got a Scoop!: A Story of Nellie Bly*. New York: Simon & Schuster Books for Young Readers, 1992.
Rittenhouse, Mignon. *The Amazing Nellie Bly*. New York: Dutton, 1956. Reprint. Freeport, NY: Books for Libraries Press, 1971.

Shorter Works by Elizabeth Cochrane Seaman

Nellie Bly wrote for *Pittsburgh Dispatch* (1884–1886), *New York World* (1887–1895), *New York Evening Journal* (1920–1922), and for various other newspapers in a freelance capacity.

"Nellie Bly Visits Spiegel Grove: Mrs. Rutherford B. Hayes' Quiet Home at Freemont, Ohio." *Hayes Historical Journal* 1 (1976): 133–44.

Shorter Works About Elizabeth Cochrane Seaman

Beasley, Maurine Hoffman, and Sheila Silver. *Women in Media: A Documentary Source Book*. Washington: Women's Institute for Freedom of the Press, 1977.

Belford, Barbara. *Brilliant Bylines: A Biographical Anthology of Notable Newspaperwomen in America*. New York: Columbia University Press, 1986.

Bergman, Carol, and Muriel Nussbaum. "Nellie Bly." *American History Illustrated* 22 (March 1987): 22 +.

Davidson, Sue. *Getting the Real Story: Nellie Bly and Ida B. Wells*. Seattle, WA: Seal Press, 1992.

Doyle, Marian I. "Globe-trotting Nellie Bly Inspired the World." *AntiqueWeek* 25 (August 17, 1992): 1 +.

Edwards, Julia. *Women of the World: The Great Foreign Correspondents*. Boston: Houghton Mifflin, 1988.

Greene, Laurence. *America Goes to Press: The News of Yesterday*. Indianapolis: Bobbs-Merrill, 1936.

Jakes, John. *Great Women Reporters*. New York: Putnam, 1969.

Johnston, Johanna. *Women Themselves*. New York: Dodd, 1973.

Kelly, Frank K. *Reporters Around the World*. Boston: Little, Brown, 1957.

Kelly, V. "Oh, My, That Nellie Bly!" *Reader's Digest* 99 (December 1971): 33–34 +.

Longstreet, Stephen. *The Queen Bees: The Women Who Shaped America*. Indianapolis: Bobbs-Merrill, 1979.

Ludlum, D. M. "Nellie Bly's Detour." *Weatherwise* 26 (December 1973): 263–67.

Marzolf, Marion. *Up from the Footnote: A History of Women Journalists*. New York: Hastings House, 1977.

Meals, K. W. "Champions of Freedom." *Instructor* 75 (December 1965): 29 +.

Reifert, Gail, and Eugene M. Dermody. *Women Who Fought*. New York: Reifert and Dermody, 1978.

Rittenhouse, Mignon. "They Called Her the Amazing Nellie Bly." *Good Housekeeping* 140 (February 1955): 48–51 +.

Ross, Ishbel. *Charmers and Cranks: Twelve Famous American Women Who Defied Convention*. New York: Harper, 1965.

———. *Ladies of the Press*. New York: Arno, 1974.

Squire, Elizabeth Daniels. *Heroes of Journalism*. New York: Fleet, 1974.

"The U.S.A.'s First Famous Girl Reporter." In *The Women's Book of World Records and Achievements*, edited by Lois Decker O'Neill. New York: Doubleday, 1979.

Wayne, Bennett, ed. *Women Who Dared to Be Different*. Champaign, IL: Garrard, 1973.

Weisberger, B. A. "Celebrity Journalists." *American Heritage* 40 (March 1989): 20 +.

Wollett, M., and B. Wollett. "Columbian Exposition Satchel." *Antiques & Collecting Hobbies* 92 (August 1987): 39.

Media Materials About Elizabeth Cochrane Seaman
Computer Game

Martian Dreams. Austin, TX: Origin Systems, 1991. 3 computer disks; sound; color 5¼ in. plus 2 guides plus 2 booklets plus 1 map.

Films

Nellie Bly. Lucerne Films, 1979. Color; 97 min.; 16mm.

Scores

Blum, O. R. *Nelly Bly.* Brooklyn, NY: Chas. W. Held, 1890. Scottische for piano.
Wallis, Louis. *Nellie Bly Waltz.* Philadelphia: W. F. Shaw, 1890. Five pages of music for piano.

Sound Recordings

Hinz-Junge, Jeanne. *Nelly Bly.* St. Paul, MI: Dog Days Records, 1984. Stereo; 33 ⅓ rpm; 9 min. 2 sec.
Karson, Danielle (producer). *Nellie Bly.* Washington, D. C.: National Public Radio, 1982. Cassette; 29 min.; analog.

Video Recordings

Conway, James L. (producer). *The Adventures of Nellie Bly.* Los Angeles, CA: Magnum Entertainment, 1985. Color; 101 min.

Primary Source Materials Relating to Elizabeth Cochrane Seaman

Brisbane Family. Papers. 1918–1965. Extent of collection: 5.75 lin. ft. Finding aids: Unpublished guide. Location: George Arents Research Library for Special Collections at Syracuse University, Manuscript Collections, Bird Library, Room 600, Syracuse New York 13244-2010. Scope of collection: Includes over 60 items of correspondence between Seaman and Brisbane, dated 1907–1914.
Frank George Carpenter. Papers. ca. 1845–1917. Extent of collection: 1 document box. Finding aids: Published guide. Location: Smith College, Women's History Sophia Smith Collection, Northampton, Massachusetts 01063. Scope of collection: Includes letters from Seaman.

(THE ABOVE ENTRY WAS CONTRIBUTED BY CAROL A. GLOSS)

57. *Rose Harriet Pastor Stokes*
(1879–1933)

*Socialist; Communist party co-founder;
feminist; labor leader; and author*

BIOGRAPHICAL INFORMATION

Chronological Biography

Born July 18, 1879, to Anna (Lewin) and Jacob Wieslander in small Jewish settlement of Augustow, Suwalki, Russian Poland, about 130 miles from Warsaw. Father died soon after her birth and mother remarried, giving daughter new husband's last name of Pastor.

1882: Family moved to England when she was about three. Very poor, lived in Whitechapel, ghetto area of London. Stepfather employed as cigar maker. She helped mother sew bows on women's slippers beginning at age four to add to family income. Received only two years of formal education, attending Bell Lane Free School, a Jewish school for the poor, between age seven and nine. 1890–1903: Emigrated to United States at age 11 with parents and six younger siblings. Living in slum section of Cleveland, began to work 12 hour days as cigar roller to contribute to family's support. Also employed in shirtwaist factory and as salesperson in department store. Education somewhat augmented as employees were read to as they worked; she also read, studied and wrote poetry in free time, sending poetry to local Jewish paper, *Review and Observer,* and to Yiddish New York City paper, *Jewish Daily News.* When she was fourteen, first collection of poems was published. 1900: At request of *Jewish Daily News,* contributed poems on regular basis earning $2 weekly. 1903: Relocated with family to Bronx, New York, at age 23, joining staff of *Jewish Daily News and Jewish Gazette* as assistant editor of English section, partially as result of letter she had written to the paper in July 1901 regarding conditions of factory workers. Frequently using pen names of "Zelda" and "Observer," wrote poems, advice column for young women and feature articles. Also contributed to *International Socialist Review.* In July, five months after beginning work with paper, interviewed socialist James Graham Phelps Stokes, member of affluent Protestant banking family, who was social worker and resident at University Settlement House on Lower East Side of New York City. Ensuing article was complimentary to Stokes and his views. July 18, 1905: Married Stokes on her 26th birthday and honeymooned for three months in Europe before settling in New York amid a group of radical and artistic friends. Word "obey" was deleted from marriage ceremony at her request. 1905–1917: Millionaires, they worked for various causes including birth control, woman suffrage and free speech. Joining Socialist party in 1906, lectured for its educational branch, Intercollegiate Socialist Society, of which husband was president from 1907 to 1917. Effectiveness as speaker and labor organizer, especially of urban working women, due more to enthusiasm, working-class background and vivaciousness, rather than particular theoretical or organizational skills. Fiery speaker with magnetic personality. Wrote extensively, publishing

poetry, reviews and articles in numerous periodicals. **1909–1910:** Participated in shirtwaist workers' strike. **1912:** One of leaders of New York
restaurant and hotel workers' strike. **1913:** Prominent Socialist party
organizer in garment workers' strike, encouraging huge crowd of strikers to
persevere and not return to work until union won recognition. One signer
of a letter to *International Socialist Review* objecting to removal of Industrial
Workers of the World president from Socialist party's executive board. Action began split between right and left wings of party. **1914:** Co-translator
into English of *Songs of Labor and Other Poems*, written by Yiddish poet
Morris Rosenfeld. **1916:** Author of play *The Woman Who Wouldn't*; had
feminist/socialist theme of woman who becomes labor leader despite ad-
versity. Arrested for attempting to distribute informational leaflets about
birth control at Carnegie Hall rally. **1917:** Couple withdrew from Socialist
party on July 19th because of its condemnation of U.S. entry into World War I.
Assisted in founding of National party, but coalition of pro-war socialists and
progressives lasted only short time. **February 1918:** Rejoined Socialist party
after Russian Bolshevik Revolution, but husband did not, marking beginning
of their estrangement as she moved politically further to left. **March 1918:**
Notoriety drastically increased when convicted and sentenced to 10-year jail
term under Espionage Act. Charges occurred because she had written letter
to *Kansas City Star* accusing U.S. government of alliance with profiteers.
Government later dropped case after reversal in Circuit Court of Appeals in
1920, but case remained symbol of antiradical hysteria of time. **September
1919:** One of several left-wing socialists who left Socialist party and founded
American Communist party. Contributed articles to *Worker* (later named
Daily Worker) and *Pravda*, lectured and picketed. **1921:** Ran unsuccessfully
as Communist for president of borough of Manhattan. **1922:** Escaped
police raid while delegate at Communist party's convention in Bridgeman,
Michigan. During Fourth Congress of Communist International in Moscow,
served as an American delegate and reporter for its Negro Commission. One
of group which favored maintenance of illegal underground nature of
American Communist party, but was overruled by Russian leaders. Elected
to central committee of newly-created Workers' party. In 1925 party name
changed to Workers' (Communist) party and in 1929 became Communist
Party U.S.A. **1925:** Exhibited paintings at Society of Independent Artists
show. On October 17th, divorced by husband who could not accept her
radical views. She disclosed that they had been "friendly enemies" for years.
Refusing all alimony, lived in poverty till her death. **1927:** Married Communist theoretician and language teacher, Isaac Romaine, also known as V. J.
Jerome. **1929:** Arrested while picketing during Needle Trades' Industrial
Union strike. Clubbed by police during pro–Haitian demonstration. **1930:**
Retired to Westport, Connecticut, due to breast cancer which some blamed
on 1929 police clubbing. **June 20, 1933:** Despite medical treatment financed

by friends, died at age 53 in Frankfurt, Germany, in municipal hospital. After cremation, ashes were returned to New York City where memorial service was held at Webster Hall in Greenwich Village, under Communist sponsorship. Estate of less than $2,000 was divided among Communist party friends, as directed in her will.

Background Information

Parents: Anna (Lewin) and Jacob Wieslander. Siblings: Six (No known names: all half-siblings). Children: None. Influences: James Graham Phelps Stokes. Ethnicity: Polish/Jewish. Also known as: Wieslander is often included as part of her name; "Zelda," "Observer" and "Sasha" (pseudonyms). Historical sites, landmarks, etc.: Statement made during Espionage Act trial: "For ten years I have worked and produced things necessary and useful for the people of this country and for all those years I was half starved . . . I worked at doing useful work and never had enough. But the moment I left the useful producing class — the moment I became part of the capitalistic class which did not have to do any productive work in order to exist — I had all the vacations I wanted, all the clothes I wanted. I had all the leisure I wanted — everything I wanted was mine without my having to do any labor in return for all I had received."

BIBLIOGRAPHICAL INFORMATION

Biographical Sketches About Rose Harriet Pastor Stokes

Buhle, Mari Jo, Paul Buhle, and Dan Georgakas, eds. *Encyclopedia of the American Left.* New York: Garland, 1990.

Fink, Gary M., ed. *Biographical Dictionary of American Labor.* Westport, CT: Greenwood, 1984.

James, Edward T., ed. *Notable American Women 1607–1950: A Biographical Dictionary.* Cambridge, MA: Belknap Press of Harvard University Press, 1971.

McHenry, Robert, ed. *Famous American Women.* New York: Dover, 1980.

Malone, Dumas, ed. *Dictionary of American Biography.* New York: Charles Scribner's Sons, 1964.

Whitman, Alden, ed. *American Reformers: An H. W. Wilson Biographical Dictionary.* New York: H. W. Wilson Company, 1985.

Books by Rose Harriet Pastor Stokes

The Woman Who Wouldn't. New York: G. P. Putnam's Sons, 1916.

Books About Rose Harriet Pastor Stokes

In the United States Circuit Court of Appeals, Eighth Circuit: No. 5255, Rose Pastor Stokes, Plaintiff in Error vs. United States of America, Defendant in Error: Brief for Plaintiff in Error. [N.p.: Champlin Law Printing Co., 1918].

Zipser, Arthur, and Pearl Zipser. *Fire and Grace: The Life of Rose Pastor Stokes.* Athens: University of Georgia Press, 1989.

Shorter Works by Rose Harriet Pastor Stokes

"America; poem." *Century* 95 (January 1918): 459.

"Balfour's Device." *Westminster Review* 163 (May 1905): 488–95. (Written under pseudonym of "Observer.")

"Child's Heart; verse." *Forum* 76 (October 1926): 632.

"The Condition of Working Women, From the Working Woman's Viewpoint." *Annals of the American Academy of Political and Social Science* 27 (1906): 165–75.

"Confession." *Century* 95 (January 1918): 457–59.

"Devil May Care; poem." *Forum* 75 (June 1926): 952.

"Face; poem." *Theatre Arts Monthly* 10 (February 1926): 86.

"Is Woman Suffrage Failing?" *Woman Citizen* n.s. 8 (April 5, 1924): 9–10.

"Letter Box." *Socialist Woman* 1 (September 1907).

"Lexicographers Take Notice." *Forum* 79 (May 1928): 797.

"Long Day: A Story of Real Life." *Independent* 59 (November 16, 1905): 1169–70.

"Mysterious Monsieur de Blowitz." *Westminster Review* 159 (May 1903): 569 +. (Written under pseudonym of "Observer.")

"New Democracy; poem." *Everybody's Magazine* 14 (May 1906): 607.

"Possibility of Relieving the Monotony of Factory Work." *Playground* 4 (January 1911): 325–28.

"There Are Few Bad Divorces." *Collier's* 77 (February 13, 1926): 9.

"We Who Stay; poem." *Literary Digest* 69 (June 25, 1921): 32.

"Whither? poem." *Independent* 64 (January 9, 1908): 86.

"Why Race-Suicide with Advancing Civilization?" *Arena* 41 (February 1909): 191–92.

Shorter Works About Rose Harriet Pastor Stokes

Buhle, Mari Jo. *Women and American Socialism, 1870–1920.* Urbana: University of Illinois Press, 1981.

Chafee, Zechariah. *Free Speech in the United States.* Cambridge, MA: Harvard University Press, 1941.

Draper, Theodore. *The Roots of American Communism.* New York: Viking, 1957.

Foner, Philip S. *Women and the American Labor Movement: From Colonial Times to the Eve of World War I.* New York: Free Press, 1979.

_____. *Women and the American Labor Movement: From World War I to the Present.* New York: Free Press, 1980.

Ginger, Ray. *The Bending Cross: A Biography of Eugene Victor Debs.* New Brunswick: Rutgers University Press, 1949.

Gitlow, Benjamin. *I Confess; The Truth About American Communism.* New York: E. P. Dutton & Co., [1940].

Griffin, Lillian Baynes. "Mrs. J. G. Phelps Stokes at Home." *Harper's Bazaar* 40 (September 1906): 794–99.

Hutchins, Grace. "Rose Pastor Stokes." *Working Woman* 4 (August 1933): 4.

McKay, Claude. *A Long Way From Home.* New York: L. Furman, [1937].

"Obituary." *Nation* 137 (July 5, 1933): 3.

"Portrait." *Hampton's Magazine* 27 (January 1912): 758.

"Portrait." *World To-Day* 18 (March 1910): 268.

Renshaw, Patrick. "Rose of the World: The Pastor-Stokes Marriage and the American Left, 1905–1925." *New York History* 62 (1981): 415–38.

"Rose Pastor Stokes." *New Masses* 8 (June 1933): 23.

Shannon, David A. *The Socialist Party of America; A History.* New York: Macmillan, 1955.

"Scott Nearing and Mrs. Stokes Arrested." *Survey* 39 (March 30 , 1918): 711–12.

"Ten Years for Criticism." *Literary Digest* 57 (June 15, 1918): 13.

"Two Women Who Wouldn't: Emma Goldman and Rose Pastor Stokes." In *America's Immigrant Women,* by Cecyle S. Neidle. Boston: Twayne, [1975].

Weinstein, James. *The Decline of Socialism in America 1912–1925.* New York: Monthly Review Press, 1967.

Other Works by Rose Harriet Pastor Stokes
Play

The Woman Who Wouldn't. New York, London: G. P. Putnam's Sons, 1916.

Translation

Rosenfeld, Morris. *Songs of Labor, and Other Poems.* Translated from the Yiddish by Rose Pastor Stokes and Helena Frank. Boston: R. G. Badger, [1914].

Other Works About Rose Harriet Pastor Stokes
Theses

Luter, Gary Sheldon. "Sexual Reform on the American Stage in the Progressive Era, 1900–1915." Ph.D. diss., University of Florida, 1981.

Scholten, Pat Creech. "Militant Women for Economic Justice: The Persuasion of Mary Harris Jones, Ella Reeve Bloor, Rose Pastor Stokes, Rose Schneiderman, and Elizabeth Gurley Flynn." Ph.D. diss., Indiana University, 1978.

Sharp, Kathleen Ann. "Rose Pastor Stokes, Radical Champion of the American Working Class, 1879–1933." Ph.D. diss., Duke University, 1979.

Tamarkin, Stanley Ray. "Rose Pastor Stokes: The Portrait of a Radical Woman, 1905–1919." Ph.D. diss., Yale University, 1983.

Primary Source Materials Relating to Rose Harriet Pastor Stokes

Rose Pastor Stokes. Papers. 1905–1933. Extent of collection: 2.5 lin. ft. (6 boxes).

Finding aids: Guide published in Socialist Collections in Tamiment Library. Location: Tamiment Institute Library, New York University Libraries, 70 Washington Square South, New York, New York 10012. Scope of collection: Contains considerable correspondence, bulk of which was written from 1914 to 1918 concerning Intercollegiate Socialist Society, National Birth Control League, family correspondence, socialist activities and Patrick Quinlan case. Also included are literary manuscripts and articles. Microfilm available.

Rose Pastor Wieslander Stokes. Papers. 1900–1958 (inclusive). Extent of collection: 5 lin. ft. (13 boxes, 1 folio). Finding aids: Unpublished finding aid in repository. Also published index. Location: Manuscripts and Archives, Yale University Library, Box 1603A Yale Station, New Haven, Connecticut 06520. Scope of collection: Correspondence, writings, printed material, clippings, and other papers. Much of material relates to activities and involvement with various radical groups, including American Communist party and Socialist party. Microfilm available.

United States. Dept. of the Army. General Staff. Military Intelligence Division. U.S. Military Intelligence Reports: Surveillance of Radicals in the United States. 1917–1941 (inclusive). Extent of collection: Not listed. Finding aids: Published finding aid. Location: National Archives and Records Administration, Seventh St. & Pennsylvania Ave. N.W., Washington, D. C. 20408. Scope of collection: Selected files relating to U.S. Military Intelligence Division's surveillance of radicals in U.S. Microfilm available.

Victor Jeremy Jerome. Papers. 1923–1967 (inclusive). Extent of collection: 16 lin. ft. (40 boxes). Finding aids: Unpublished finding aid in repository. Location: Manuscripts and Archives, Yale University Library, Box 1603A Yale Station, New Haven, Connecticut 06520. Scope of collection: Correspondence, writings, research notes, biographical material, obituaries and eulogies and other personal and family papers of Jerome, American Communist, writer, editor of *The Communist* and political activist.

58. *Anna Louise Strong*
(1885–1970)
Radical journalist; author; feminist; and pacifist

BIOGRAPHICAL INFORMATION

Chronological Biography

Born November 24, 1885, in two-room parsonage in Friend, Nebraska, eldest of two girls and one boy, to Ruth Maria (Tracy) and Sydney Dix Strong. Both religious and ambitious, mother exerted strong influence on daughter's life; also used contacts as president of Women's Home Missionary Union of Ohio and Illinois to obtain positions for husband. Father, who appeared to favor Anna, was pacifist and had strong sense of social mission.

1887: Family moved to Mount Vernon, Ohio, where father, who was Congregational/Social Gospel minister, became church pastor. Brother Tracy born August 6, 1887.   1891: Father again moved family, this time to Cincinnati. Completed eight years of grammar school in four, finishing at age 11. Attended public and then private school. Able to read by age four, began writing poetry at about age six.   1895–1901: Relocating to Oak Park, Illinois, for father's work, graduated from high school in 1900 at 15. Studied in Europe in 1897 and 1898, acquiring modest fluency in French.   1902: Enrolled at Oberlin College, alma mater of both of her parents. Because of schooling abroad, entered as sophomore.   1903: Pressured by mother, transferred to Bryn Mawr. After contracting typhoid, mother died of heart failure on ship while returning with father from South African missions tour.   1904–1905: Transferred back to Oberlin and graduated at age 19 with A.B., summa or magna cum laude and Phi Beta Kappa.   Fall 1905–March 31, 1906: Journalist in Chicago for weekly, fundamentalist Protestant paper *Advance*; often using various pseudonyms, wrote fairy tales for children, women's page articles, book reviews and feminist column "From a Woman's Window." Continued to write poems, many of which were published. Fired, probably due in part to friction with editor.   April 2, 1906–1908: At urging of father, enrolled at University of Chicago. Received Ph.D. in philosophy; 1908 dissertation entitled *A Consideration of Prayer from the Standpoint of Social Psychology*, published following year as *The Psychology of Prayer*. Youngest person at time to receive Ph.D. from University of Chicago. Wanting to experience life more fully, worked at fruit and vegetable canning plant for $5.50 per week. Also worked at Hull House; met Jane Addams, director and cofounder of the settlement house. Became increasingly concerned about effects American economic system was having on workers.   1909–1910: Preferring to work for social causes, rejected academic life and began working with father who had moved to Seattle. Organized successful civic improvement institute there called "Know Your City," leading to establishment of comparable projects in several other cities in northwest United States. 1911–1914: At invitation of Russell Sage Foundation, filled assistant director of New York Child Welfare Exhibit position for part of 1911. Left Sage but gained international recognition as she continued to direct these popular exhibits in various American cities, as well as in Dublin, Ireland, and Panama. Again worked for Sage in late 1913. Engaged to Roger Baldwin, future director of American Civil Liberties Union, but did not wed because of father's opposition as well as her own judgment that he was not a dedicated Christian. Espoused socialism.   September 1914–Fall 1916: Director of Exhibits for U.S. Children's Bureau in Washington, D. C., under Julia Lathrop, until World War I disrupted efforts, at which time she returned to West Coast. 1916–1918: Worked with Crystal Eastman in Anti-Preparedness League, organizing antiwar demonstrations in midwest. Also active in American

Union Against Militarism and in Emergency Peace Federation. Intended to try for seat in Washington state legislature, but instead was elected in December 1916 to serve on school board of Seattle after several hundred progressives, most of them women, petitioned her to run. First woman member of school board. Covered Everett, Washington, "Massacre" trial of Industrial Workers of the World members in 1917 for *New York Evening Post.* 1918–1921: Authored articles under pseudonym of "Gale" for socialist *Seattle Daily Call* opposing war and capitalism. Removed from school board in March 1918 by small margin of votes because of antidraft activities, although still had support of organized labor. Editor of features department at labor newspaper *Seattle Union Record,* at times using "Anise" as pseudonym. Published February 4, 1919, editorial urging Seattle general strike, increasing her notoriety. On February 6th, Seattle experienced first general strike in history of United States when all industry and most businesses and transportation lines were closed down when members walked over 100 unions. Strike lasted only six days and political power of labor drastically decreased. Published history of Seattle general strike in 1919.   1921–1949: Served for year in Poland and Russia for American Friends Service Committee, assisting famine victims and acting as correspondent. Wanting to experience revolution first-hand, took job as Moscow correspondent with International News Service. Taught English to Russian revolutionary Leon Trotsky, whom she held in high regard. Worked to organize the John Reed Children's Colony for young refugees of Volga famine and the American Working School, a trade school in Moscow, but neither was successful because much of money she had raised for their support was used for other purposes by officials. Became deeply committed to communism although was never allowed to join Russian Communist party. Spent rest of life working principally in Russia and later China, to spread word and report on events, achieving international recognition.   1924: *The First Time in History,* book defending Lenin's New Economic Policy, published.   1925: Lectured in United States to generate interest and spur industrial investment and development in Russia. Travelled to China for first time.   1927: Returned to Hankow, China, seeking involvement in revolution. Travelled to Siberia with group fleeing Chiang Kai-shek, keeping diary of events. Her reports regarding Chinese revolution were especially valuable as few accurate accounts existed at time.   1928: *China's Millions,* partisan account of Chiang Kai-shek's break with Moscow, published.   1930–1935?: Founded *Moscow News,* first English-language newspaper in Moscow; content was directed to Americans working there. Served as managing editor for year, then wrote feature articles. Poor treatment by Russian editors eventually caused her resignation, despite Stalin's intervention.   1932–1942: Maintained relationship with Soviet party member, agronomist and editor of Moscow *Peasant's Gazette,* Joel Shubin; it is unclear whether they were legally married. Because of her travelling, they were frequently separated, but did spend time together in United States in 1939 when he was one of directors of Soviet Pavilion at New York World's Fair and she was writing book about New Deal, *My Native Land,* at suggestion of Eleanor Roosevelt. Shubin died in Soviet Union on March 4, 1942. Strong was in United States at time, unable to travel to Russia due to German invasion. **1935:** Autobiography, *I Change Worlds: The Remaking of an American,* published. **1936–1949:** Reported on war in Spain, World War II events in Russia and actions taking place in China and Poland. **1941–1944:** Lived in United States. Supported Stalin's policies in 1941 book, *The Soviets Expected It.* Worked as technical advisor for *Song of Russia,* film made by MGM. Also wrote novel, *Wild River,* concerning German invasion of Russia. **1944:** Accompanied Red Army through Poland, writing for *Atlantic Monthly* and other periodicals. **1946–1947:** Once again visited China to report on revolution. Interviewed Mao Tse-tung in cave while staying in Yenan Province at Communist Chinese headquarters. Her report of meeting was published in April 1947 issue of *Amerasia.* **1949:** Arrested in Moscow en route to China, branded a spy as result of her turning from Russian to Maoist communism, and deported to Poland. Returned shortly thereafter to United States. **1950–1958:** Lived in California. Despite treatment by Moscow and rejection by party members in United States, remained loyal to cause. **1955:** Absolved by Russia of all charges. **1958:** Visited Moscow briefly. **1959–1970:** Settled permanently in Peking. Respected by Chinese government, enjoyed good relations with Mao Tse-tung and Chou En-Lai. Remained active, writing, lecturing and travelling to Tibet, Laos and North Vietnam. Edited and published English-language newsletter, *Letter from China,* from 1961 until just before her death. Distributed worldwide, it disseminated information about Sino-Soviet debate, etc. **1965:** Honored by Mao Tse-tung on 80th birthday. **1966:** Made honorary member of Red Guard. **1968–1969:** Many close to her arrested during Cultural Revolution. **March 29, 1970:** Active until shortly before her death from heart disease in Peking hospital at age 84. Ashes were buried near grave of Agnes Smedley in Babaoshan Cemetery of Revolutionary Martyrs in outskirts of Peking. Memorial services were held in Peking and at First Unitarian Church in Los Angeles. Headstone reads, "Progressive American Writer and Friend of the Chinese People." Had planned to return to United States to work against Vietnam War, but died before she could carry out her plans.

Background Information

Parents: Ruth Maria (Tracy) and Sydney Dix Strong. Parents' ancestors came to U.S. from England in 1630s. **Siblings:** Two (Ruth Strong Niederhauser, Tracy). **Children:** None. **Influences:** None. **Ethnicity:** English

American. **Also known as:** Shubin; "Anise" and "Gale" (pseudonyms).
Historical sites, landmarks, etc.: None known.

BIBLIOGRAPHICAL INFORMATION

Biographical Sketches About Anna Louise Strong

Garraty, John A., and Mark C. Carnes, eds. *Dictionary of American Biography.*
New York: Charles Scribner's Sons, 1964.
McHenry, Robert, ed. *Famous American Women.* New York: Dover, 1980.
Rothe, Anna, ed. *Current Biography: Who's News and Why 1949.* New York:
H. W. Wilson Company, 1949.
Sicherman, Barbara, and Carol Hurd Green, eds. *Notable American Women: The
Modern Period: A Biographical Dictionary.* Cambridge, MA: Belknap Press of
Harvard University Press, 1980.
Uglow, Jennifer S., ed. *The Continuum Dictionary of Women's Biography.* New
York: Continuum, 1989.

Books by Anna Louise Strong

Boys and Girls of the Bible. Chicago: Howard-Severance Co., 1911.
Cash and Violence in Lao and Viet Nam. New York: Mainstream, 1962.
Child-Welfare Exhibits: Types and Preparation. Washington, D. C.: GPO, 1915.
*Children of Revolution: Story of the John Reed Children's Colony of the Volga,
Which Is as Well a Story of the Whole Great Structure of Russia.* [Seattle:
Pigott Printing Concern, 1926].
China's Fight for Grain; Three Dates from a Diary in Late 1962. Peking: New
World Press, 1963.
China's Millions. New York: Coward-McCann, 1928.
China's Millions; Revolution in Central China, 1927. Peking: New World Press,
1965.
China's Millions: The Revolutionary Struggles from 1927 to 1935. Expanded ed.,
New York: Knight, 1935.
China's New Crisis. [London]: Fore Publications Ltd., [1942?].
The Chinese Conquer China. Garden City, NY: Doubleday, [1949].
Dawn Over China. Bombay: People's Publishing House, 1948.
Dictatorship and Democracy in the Soviet Union. New York: International
Pamphlets, [1934].
*The First Time in History; Two Years of Russia's New Life (August, 1921 to
December, 1923), with a Preface by L. Trotsky.* New York: Boni and Liveright,
[1924].
From Stalingrad to Kuzbas, Sketches of the Socialist Construction in the USSR.
New York: International Pamphlets, [1931].

How the Communists Rule Russia. Girard, KA: Haldeman-Julius Publications, 1927.

The Hungarian Tragedy. [Altadena, CA: National Guardian, 1957].

I Change Worlds: The Remaking of an American. New York: H. Holt and Company, [1935]. Reprint. Seattle: Seal, 1979.

I Saw the New Poland. Boston: Little, Brown and Company, 1946.

In North Korea, First Eye-witness Report. New York: Soviet Russia Today, 1949.

Inside Liberated Poland. New York: National Council of American-Soviet Friendship, [1945?].

Inside North Korea: An Eye-witness Report. Montrose: CA: Strong, [1951?].

King's Palace. Oak Park, IL: Oak Leaves, 1908.

The Kuomintang-Communist Crisis in China. New York: Amerasia, 1941.

Letters from China. Peking: New World Press, [n.d.].

Letters from China. Peking: New World Press, 1963. (Contains letters No. 1–10.)

Lithuania's New Way. London: Lawrence & Wishart Ltd, [1941].

Man's New Crusade. Altadena, CA: Anna Louise Strong, 1957.

Mao, Tse-tung. *Talk with the American Correspondent Anna Louise Strong.* Peking: Foreign Languages Press, 1967.

Modern Farming—Soviet Style. New York: International Pamphlets, [1930].

My Native Land. New York: Viking, 1940.

The New Lithuania. New York: Workers Library Publishers, [1941].

The New Soviet Constitution, a Study in Socialist Democracy. New York: H. Holt and Company, [1937].

One-Fifth of Mankind. New York: Modern Age Books, [1938].

Peoples of USSR. New York: Macmillan, 1944.

The Psychology of Prayer. Chicago: University of Chicago Press, 1909.

Ragged Verse. Seattle, WA: Piggot-Washington Printing Co., 1937 (Written under the name of Anise. Presentation ed.)

Red Star in Samarkand. New York: Coward-McCann, Inc., 1929. Reprint. London: Williams and Norgate, 1930.

Remaking an American. Moscow: Co-operative Publishing Society of Foreign Workers in the U.S.S.R., 1935.

The Rise of the Chinese People's Communes. Ann Arbor, MI: Radical Education Project, [n.d.]. Reprint. Peking: New World Press, 1959.

The Rise of the People's Communes. Detroit: Radical Education Project, n.d.

The Rise of the Chinese People's Communes: And Six Years After. Peking: New World Press, 1964.

The Rise of the People's Communes in China. New York: Marzani and Munsell, 1960.

The Road to the Grey Pamir. Boston: Little, Brown and Company, 1931.

The Russians Are People. London: Cobbett, 1943.

Seattle. General Strike Committee, 1919. History Committee. *The Seattle General Strike; An Account of What Happened in Seattle and Especially in the Seattle Labor Movement, During the General Strike, February 6 to 11, 1919.* Seattle: Seattle Union Record Publishing Co., [1919?]. Reprint. [Charlestown, MA: Printed by the Bum Press, 1972]. (Compiled by Anna Louise Strong.)

The Song of the City. Oak Park, IL: Oak Leaves Press, [1906].

Songs and Fables. Chicago: Langston Press, 1904.

Soviet Farmers. New York: National Council of American-Soviet Friendship, [1944].

The Soviet Union and World Peace: Disarmament, Non-Aggression, the Far-East, League of Nations, Franco-Soviet Pact. . . [New York: International Pamphlets, 1935].

The Soviets Conquer Wheat; the Drama of Collective Farming. New York: H. Holt and Company, [1931].

The Soviets Expected It. New York: Dial, 1941. Reprint. New York: Soviet Russia Today, 1942.

Spain in Arms, 1937. New York: H. Holt and Company, [1937].

The Stalin Era. New York: Mainstream Publishers, 1956. Reprint. [Belfast]: British and Irish Communist Organization, 1976.

Strong, Sydney, and Anna Louise Strong, eds. *The Story of Daniel in Words of the Scripture. (Found in Daniel).* Chicago: Hope Pub. Co., [1906].

_____, and _____, eds. *The Story of David in Words of the Scripture. (Found in I. and II. Samuel).* Chicago: Hope Pub. Co., [1906].

_____, and _____, eds. *The Story of Elijah-Elisha in Words of the Scripture. (Found in I. and II. Kings).* Chicago: Hope Pub. Co., [1906].

_____, and _____, eds. *The Story of Joseph in Words of the Scripture. (Found in Genesis).* Chicago: Hope Pub. Co., [1906].

_____, and _____, eds. *The Story of Joshua in Words of the Scripture. (Found in Joshua).* Chicago: Hope Pub. Co., [1906].

_____, and _____, eds. *The Story of Ruth-Esther in Words of the Scripture.* Chicago: Hope Pub. Co., [1906].

_____, and _____, eds. *The Story of Samson, Deborah, Jephtha, [and] Gideon in Words of the Scripture. (Found in Judges).* Chicago: Hope Pub. Co., [1906].

_____, and _____, eds. *The Story of Samuel in Words of the Scripture. (Found in I. Samuel).* Chicago: Hope Pub. Co., [1906].

_____, and _____, eds. *The Story of Solomon in Words of the Scripture. (Found in I. Kings).* Chicago: Hope Pub. Co., [1906].

This Soviet World. New York: H. Holt and Company, [1936].

Tibetan Interviews. Peking: New World Press, 1959.

Tomorrow's China. New York: Committee for a Democratic Far Eastern Policy, [1948].

When Serfs Stood Up in Tibet. San Francisco: Red Sun, 1976.

When Serfs Stood Up in Tibet; Report. Peking: New World Press, 1960. Reprint. Peking: New World Press, 1965.

Wild River. Boston: Little, Brown, [1943].

Books About Anna Louise Strong

Strong, Tracy B., and Helene Keyssar. *Right in Her Soul: The Life of Anna Louise Strong.* New York: Random House, 1983.

Shorter Works by Anna Louise Strong

"Advises Japanese to Colonize Russia." *Trans-Pacific* 12 (December 5, 1925): 14.

"Airplane from the U.S.S.R." *Asia and the Americas* 42 (January 1942): 28–31.

"American Propaganda in Russia." *American Mercury* 32 (May 1934): 48–55.

"Americans Freed by the Red Army." *Soviet Russia Today* 14 (May 1945): 9.

"Anna Louise Strong Discusses Stalin's 'Heir'." *Nation* 176 (April 18, 1953): inside cover.

"Arctic Sea Route Is Open." *Asia* 36 (February 1936): 94–99.

"The Army That's Defeating Japan." *New Masses* (April 19, 1938): 7–9.

"At the Edge of Civilisation." *Contemporary Review* 140 (October 1931): 504–08.

"Awakened Peasantry of China." *Asia* 28 (January 1928): 32–35.

"Back-Country Bolshevik." *Nation* 121 (October 21, 1925): 460–62.

"Behind the Marching Armies of China." *Christian Century* 44 (September 22, 1927): 1102–03.

"Birobidjan." *Asia* 36 (January 1936): 41–43.

"Bor's Uprising." *Atlantic Monthly* 176 (December 1945): 80–85.

"Bread Rationing Ends in the USSR." *Soviet Russia Today* 3 (January 1935): 11.

"Building Democracy." *Soviet Russia Today* 4 (December 1935): 7.

"Centralia: An Unfinished Story." *Nation* 110 (April 17, 1920): 508–10.

"Challenge to Religion in the Soviet Republic." *Religious Education* 20 (December 1925): 488–93.

"Chang and Feng and Wu." *Asia* (July 1926): 596–601.

"Cheese It — The Cop; poem." *Journal of Education* 71 (June 16, 1910): 694.

"Cheese It — The Cop; poem." *Journal of Education* 73 (June 8, 1911): 650.

"Child Welfare Exhibits." *National Municipal Review* 1 (April 1912): 248–52.

"Children of the Spanish War." *Survey Graphic* 26 (September 1937): 458–62.

"Children's Court; poem." *Journal of Education* 71 (June 9, 1910): 630.

"Children's Court; poem." *Journal of Education* 73 (June 8, 1911): 631.

"Children's Court; poem." *Journal of Education* 77 (June 12, 1913): 654.

"The China-India Border." *New World Review* 27 (November 1959): 46–52.

"China Moves Inland." *Asia* 38 (June 1938): 369–72.

"China's Communes Come of Age." *New World Review* 28 (February 1960): 23–29.

"China's Cromwell." *Outlook* 142 (March 24, 1926): 454–58.

"China's 'Different Way'." *New World Review* 24 (July 1956): 14–18.

"China's Source of Strength." *New World Review* 28 (January 1960): 25–30.

"Chinese Climb Mt. Everest." *New World Review* 28 (September 1960): 28–32.

"Chinese Spirit Goes Up." *Asia* 38 (July 1938): 425–28.

"City Comradeship; poem." *Current Literature* 42 (February 1907): 225.

"City Lights; poem." *Current Literature* 42 (February 1907): 225.

"Civic Institute on Child Life at Seattle." *Pedagogical Seminary* 17 (December 1910): 545–46.

"Communist Regime in Manchuria." *Amerasia* 11 (May 1947): 137–43.

"Country Life Comes to Russia." *Country Life (American)* 49 (February 1926): 68.

"Cubist Theatre of Moscow." *Theatre Arts Monthly* 7 (July 1923): 224–27.

"The Dean Reports on Poland." *Soviet Russia Today* 14 (July 1945): 14.

"The Defense of Moscow." *Soviet Russia Today* 10 (November 1941): 18.
"Disarmament Fails in Moscow." *Nation* 116 (February 7, 1923): 158–59.
"Do Chinese Communes Break Up the Family?" *New World Review* 27 (March 1959): 42–44.
"The Drive That Took Berlin." *Soviet Russia Today* 14 (June 1945): 16.
"Dublin Civic Exhibition." *Survey* 32 (September 12, 1914): 599.
"Economic Paradox in Uzbekistan." *Contemporary Review* 138 (August 1930): 218–24.
"Eighth Route Regions in North China." Parts 1, 2. *China Today* (July, August 1941): 10–12; 8–9.
"Eighth Route Regions in North China." *Pacific Affairs* 14 (June 1941): 154–65.
"Everett's Bloody Sunday." *Survey* 37 (January 27, 1917): 475–76.
"Failure of a Mission." *Nation* 159 (August 19, 1944): 205–06.
"Feng An Old Testament Christian." *Christian Century* 43 (April 15, 1926): 489.
"First Report from North Korea." *Soviet Russia Today* 16 (October 1947): 8.
"Free Women." *Asia* 36 (May 1936): 326–31.
"From Vladivostok to Moscow." *Soviet Russia Today* 4 (June 1935): 6.
"Germans Trade on the Yangtse." *World Tomorow* 10 (October 1927): 416–19.
"Get Rich Quick in Poland." *Nation* 119 (August 13, 1924): 171–72.
"Getting Democracy in Poland." *Atlantic Monthly* 176 (October 1945): 65–70.
"Grabbing an Education in Russia." *Independent* 115 (September 5, 1925): 265–66.
"Grasshoppers, Soldiers, and Silk Weavers." *Atlantic Monthly* 146 (November 1930): 673–81.
"Greatest Man of Our Time." *Forum* 71 (April 1924): 423–28.
"Guatemala: A First Hand Report." *Monthly Review* 5 (March 1954): 556–63.
"'Ham and Eggs to You'." *New Masses* (August 15, 1939): 3–8.
"Haven for Greek Refugees." *Soviet Russia Today* 15 (March 1946): 13.
"Head-High-in-the-Wind." *Harper's Monthly Magazine* 155 (November 1927): 744–49.
"How China Conquered Syphilis." *New World Review* 27 (March 1959): 18–22.
"How China Fights Calamities of Weather." *New World Review* 30 (September 1962): 14.
"How Red Is China Now?" *Asia* 38 (August 1938): 457–60.
"I Watched the Soviets Grow." *Soviet Russia Today* 6 (November 1937): 14.
"Inside China." *New Masses* (March 18, 1941): 3–10.
"Inside Liberated Poland." *Soviet Russia Today* 14 (February 1945): 12.
"Inside Liberated Poland." *Soviet Russia Today* 14 (March 1945): 11 +.
"Is Moscow Out of the World?" *Asia* 39 (May 1939): 272–76.
"Is Soviet Central Asia a Colony?" *New World Review* 24 (February 1956): 8–12.
"Ivan Comes Marching Home." *Soviet Russia Today* 14 (September 1945): 15.
"Jews of Russia Move Back to the Soil." *Current History* 25 (October 1926): 82–88.
"Joseph Stalin on Soviet Democracy and the World Today." *Soviet Russia Today* 5 (April 1936): 14.
"Justice Douglas in Russia." *New World Review* 24 (December 1956): 4–9.
"Karelia Revisited After 13 Years." *Soviet Russia Today* 4 (September 1935): 12.
"Khrushchev Reports on the State of the Union." *New World Review* 24 (April 1956): 7–11.

"Kuomintang-Communist Crisis in China." *Amerasia* 5 (March 1941): 11–23.
"Land of the Living Gods: Excerpts." *Review of Reviews (London)* 84 (August 1933): 46.
"Land Reform in North Korea." *Soviet Russia Today* 16 (November 1947): 20.
"Last Word in the Far East." *Asia* 35 (October 1935): 594–95.
"Letter to the Editor." *Soviet Russia Today* 4 (October 1935): 28.
"Lhalu's Serfs Accuse." *New World Review* 28 (March 1960): 22–28.
"The Local Elections in Yugoslavia." *Soviet Russia Today* 14 (October 1945): 14–15 +.
"Maxim Litvinov Returns." *Soviet Russia Today* 10 (December 1941): 9.
"Making Bolshevists of Central Asians." *Asia* 29 (November 1929): 870–75.
"May Day Around the World." *Soviet Russia Today* 4 (May 1935): 11.
"Medicine Without Microscopes." *Nation* 159 (December 16, 1944): 740.
"Memory of Wonsan." *Eastern Horizon* 7 (March-April 1968): 45–50.
"Modern Farming, Soviet Style." *Atlantic Monthly* 146 (July 1930): 112–20.
"Moscow—and New York." *Soviet Russia Today* 4 (February 1935): 7.
"Moscow Letter." *Soviet Russia Today* 4 (August 1935): 11.
"Moscow Letter." *Soviet Russia Today* 4 (October 1935): 9.
"Moscow Looks at Dumbarton Oaks." *Nation* 159 (September 2, 1944): 261–62.
"Moscow's Peace Drive." *New World Review* 23 (November 1955): 12–15.
"Motoring Out from China." *Asia* 28 (September 1928): 708–13.
"Mrs. Li of Shanghai." *New World Review* 28 (October 1960): 28–33.
"Mrs. Sun Yat-sen Flees from Victory." *China Weekly Review* 46 (October 27, 1928): 287–88.
"Mrs. Sun Yat-sen Flees from Victory." *Survey* 61 (October 1, 1928): 34–35.
"My Automobile in the Soviet Sowing." *Survey Graphic* 23 (April 1934): 190–91.
"The Myth of the 'German-Soviet Alliance'." *New Masses* (November 7, 1939): 5–6.
"A New Charter of Freedom." *Soviet Russia Today* 5 (August 1936): 8.
"New Educational Front in Russia." *Survey* 51 (February 1, 1924): 437–42.
"New Women of Old Canton." *Asia* 26 (June 1926): 493–95.
"A New World in the Caucasus." *Soviet Russia Today* 3 (November 1934): 7.
"A Newspaper Confiscated—and Returned." *Nation* 109 (December 13, 1919): 738–40.
"Night on the Transsiberian; story." *Century* 112 (June 1926): 136–44.
"No More Russian Mystery." *Soviet Russia Today* 10 (October 1941): 12.
"North Korea." *New Statesman and Nation* 35 (January 17, 1948): 47.
"Old and New Gods in Mongolia." *Asia* 28 (July 1928): 564–69.
"100 Million Voters." *Soviet Russia Today* 6 (December 1937): 7.
"Overseas Chinese Come Home." *New World Review* 28 (April 1960): 25–29.
"Party in a Soviet Publishing House." *Soviet Russia Today* 12 (December 1944): 8.
"Peasants and Soldiers in Hunan." *World Tomorrow* 11 (June 1928): 269–71.
"Pioneering on the Roof of the World." *Travel* 54 (April 1930): 7–11.
"Poland's New Leaders." *Soviet Russia Today* 14 (January 1945): 9.
"Poles Take Over." *Nation* 159 (August 12, 1944): 183–84.
"Polish Land Reform." *Nation* 160 (February 3, 1945): 122–23.
"Power of the Press in the USSR." *Soviet Russia Today* 4 (March 1935): 10.

"Preparing for Big Events." *Soviet Russia Today* 14 (December 1945): 13.

"Profane Invasion of Holy Bokhara." *Atlantic Monthly* 144 (July 1929): 103–10.

"The Real Balkans Story." *Soviet Russia Today* 14 (November 1945): 12 +.

"The Red Army in Lithuania." *Soviet Russia Today* (October 1940): 13–14 +.

"The Red Army Marches for Peace." *Soviet Russia Today* (October 1939): 13–15 +.

"Red Holidays in Central Asia." *Travel* 53 (June 1929): 7–12.

"Red Rule in Golden Samarkand." *North American Review* 228 (September 1929): 309–15.

"Religious Aspects of Pragmatism." *American Journal of Theology* 12 (April 1908): 231–40.

"Reply with Rejoinder." *Reporter* 12 (May 19, 1955): 6.

"Report from Moscow." *Soviet Russia Today* 14 (August 1945): 10.

"The Revolution Betrayed—By Whom." *Soviet Russia Today* 6 (May 1937): 36.

"Richest Woman in Town." *Collier's* 76 (September 12, 1925): 26.

"Romance of Radio in Turkestan." *Travel* 53 (September 1929): 24–26.

"Russia Plants Trees, While Abroad . . ." *Soviet Russia Today* (January 1949): 7.

"Russia Rebuilds." *Atlantic Monthly* 174 (December 1944): 92–96.

"Russian Co-operatives Increase in Strength." *Co-operation* 9 (September 1923): 154–55.

"The Russian People at War." *Soviet Russia Today* (April 1942): 10–12 +.

"Russian Program; abstract." *Journal of Criminal Law and Criminology* 26 (September 1935): 469–70.

"Russians Think of Home." *Nation* 159 (September 30, 1944): 378.

"Russia's Post-war Policy." *Nation* 159 (October 21, 1944): 460–61.

"Salaries for Mothers in the U.S.S.R." *Soviet Russia Today* (March 1939): 17 +.

"Samarkand Returns to Power." *Atlantic Monthly* 144 (August 1929): 255–63.

"Searching Out the Soviets." *New Republic* 83 (August 7, 1935): 354–59.

"Security for Farmers." *Soviet Russia Today* (November 1938): 28–29.

"Shanghai Raises Food." *New World Review* 30 (October 1962): 17.

"Small Town Politics." *Asia* 29 (August 1929): 630–35.

"Some Hankow Memories." *Asia* 28 (October 1928): 794–97.

"Soviet Behind the Urals." *Asia and the Americas* 41 (October 1941): 544–48.

"Soviet Democracy." *Soviet Russia Today* 5 (February 1936): 13.

"Soviet Dictatorship." *American Mercury* 33 (October 1934): 169–79.

"Soviet Farms Wage War." *Soviet Russia Today* 12 (March 1944): 12.

"Soviet of the High Pastures." *Atlantic Monthly* 146 (December 1930): 817–27.

"Soviet Outpost in Asia." *Asia* 29 (June 1929): 460–66.

"Soviet People in War." *Asia and the Americas* 42 (March 1942): 161–65.

"The Soviet People Make a Constitution." *Soviet Russia Today* 5 (January 1937): 16.

"The Soviet People's Total Defense." *Soviet Russia Today* 10 (September 1941): 9–11 +.

"Soviet President's Wife." *Asia* 34 (February 1934): 96–99.

"The Soviets Celebrate with Work." *Soviet Russia Today* 12 (November 1944): 10.

"Soviet's Face a Warring World." *Christian Century* 54 (January 20, 1937): 77–79.

"Soviet's Fight Bureaucracy." *American Mercury* 33 (September 1934): 86–89.

"Soviets Pay Their Bills." *Forum and Century* 91 (January 1934): 24–28.
"Spain and the USSR." *Soviet Russia Today* 5 (December 1936): 8.
"Stakhanovism Sweeps the USSR." *Soviet Russia Today* 5 (January 1936): 10.
"Stalin." *Soviet Russia Today* (December 1939): 9–10 + .
"Stalin in Action." *Asia* 34 (January 1934): 19–21.
"Stalingrad Tomorrow." *Nation* 159 (August 5, 1944): 151–52.
"Stalin's Heroic Artists." *Asia* 36 (April 1936): 258–60.
Strong, Anna Louise, and Rufus D. Smith. "Beneath the Surface in Montreal." *Survey* 29 (November 16, 1912): 195–98.
"Tenement Back Yards; poem." *Nation* 84 (February 28, 1907): 199.
"The Terrorists' Trial." *Soviet Russia Today* 5 (October 1936): 9.
"Theatrical Olympiad in Moscow." *Theatre Arts Monthly* 14 (December 1930): 1037–50.
"This Month in Moscow." *Soviet Russia Today* 4 (July 1935): 11.
"Thought of Mao Tse-tung." *Amerasia* 11 (June 1947): 161–74.
"Three Kinds of Transport; poem." *Forum* 69 (February 1923): 1279.
"Three Men of Japan." *Asia* 26 (March 1926): 228–31.
"Tibet: What Happened? What's Ahead?" *New World Review* 27 (June 1959): 8–18.
"Triumph of Lenin." *Nation* 118 (February 13, 1924): 159–60.
"Two Chinese Communes." *New World Review* 30 (April 1962): 16.
"Two Economic Systems." *Soviet Russia Today* 4 (November 1935): 32.
"Verdict at Everett." *Survey* 38 (May 19, 1917): 160–62.
"Village of Wide Bounty." *Atlantic Monthly* 145 (May 1930): 697–705.
"Voice of the Soviet Village." *Current History* 41 (March 1935): 692–97.
"Watch Our Dust: The New Labor Reserve Schools [USSR]." *Soviet Russia Today* 10 (March 1941): 10–11 + .
"Wayside Justice in the Soviet Union." *Survey Graphic* 23 (August 1934): 380–81 + .
"We Get in the Wheat for Peking." *New World Review* 27 (September 1959): 24–30.
"We Soviet Wives." *American Mercury* 32 (August 1934): 415–23.
"Were You Ever a Dictator." *Soviet Russia Today* 4 (April 1935): 10.
"Western Japan Educational Exhibition." *Survey* 31 (October 11, 1913): 44.
"What Canton Learned from Moscow." *Survey* 58 (May 1, 1927): 139–41.
"What Does Moscow Want?" *Asia* 39 (November 1939): 647–49.
"What Soviet Elections Are Like." *Soviet Russia Today* 3 (December 1934): 5.
"When Stalin Spoke." *Soviet Russia Today* 10 (August 1941): 10.
"When the Reds Get Down to Business." *Collier's* 73 (February 16, 1924): 10.
"Where Peace Not War Makes Headlines." *Soviet Russia Today* 10 (May 1941): 10–12.
"Where the Old Year Took the Saloon with It." *Survey* 35 (January 15, 1916): 448.
"Where to, American: Red Adams Is a Fighting Man." Parts 1, 2. *New Masses* (April 23, May 7, 1940): 9–10; 15 + .
"Wireless Reigns in Turkestan." *Discovery* 10 (September 1929): 292–94.
"With the Red Army in Minsk." *Nation* 159 (July 29, 1944): 121–22.
"Woman Citizens of the Soviet Union." *Asia* 28 (April 1928): 294–99.
"Woman Speaks; poem." *Current Opinion* 63 (August 1917): 123.

"Women of Nationalist China." *Woman Citizen* n.s. 12 (November 1927): 18–19.
"The Workers Find a Way." *Soviet Russia Today* 5 (November 1936): 26.
"World's Eye View from a Yenan Cave." *Amerasia* 11 (April 1947): 122–26.
"Young China Tackles the Floods." *China Weekly Review* 45 (July 28, 1928): 291–93.
"Young China Tackles the Floods." *Survey* 60 (July 1, 1928): 377–79.
"Youth Set Free." *Soviet Russia Today* 5 (April 1936): 16.

Shorter Works About Anna Lousie Strong

Alley, Rewi. "Some Memories of Anna Louise Strong." *Eastern Horizon [Hong Kong]* 9 (1970): 45–55.
Alsterlund, B. "Biographical Sketch." *Wilson Library Bulletin* 15 (February 1941): 460.
"Anna Louise Strong." *Nation* 168 (February 26, 1949): 228.
"Anna Louise Strong." *Nation* 168 (April 9, 1949): 402.
"Anna Louise Strong." *New World Review* 23 (May 1955): 7–8.
"Back Home." *Time* 53 (March 7, 1949): 26–27.
"Biography." *Current Biography* 10 (March 1949): 50–52.
Burroughs, J. "I Change Worlds." *Northwest Passage* 20 (January 29, 1980): 19.
"Case of Anna Louise Strong." *New Republic* 120 (March 21, 1949): 21.
Cowley, M. "Fellow Traveler." *New Republic* 82 (May 1, 1935): 345.
Duke, David C. "Anna Louise Strong and the Search for a Good Cause." *Pacific Northwest Quarterly* 66 (July 1975): 123–37.
————. "Spy Scares, Scapegoats, and the Cold War." *South Atlantic Quarterly* 79 (1980): 245–56.
Epstein, Israel. "Smedley, Strong, Snow—Bridge Builders from People to People." *Beijing Review* 28 (July 15, 1985): 15–18+.
"Expelled from Soviet Union." *Publishers' Weekly* 155 (February 26, 1949): 1074.
Foner, Philip S. *Women and the American Labor Movement: From World War I to the Present.* New York: Free Press, 1980.
Gitlow, Benjamin. *Whole of Their Lives.* New York: Charles Scribner's Sons, 1948.
Jaffe, Philip. "The Strange Case of Anna Louise Strong." *Survey [Great Britain]* 53 (October 1964): 129–39.
Klehr, H. "Fellow Traveler Forever." *New Republic* 190 (March 19, 1984): 38–40.
"Lady and the Commissar." *Time* 53 (April 4, 1949): 28–29.
"Lily Red After All." *Newsweek* 45 (March 14, 1955): 52.
Nies, Judith. *Seven Women; Portraits from the American Radical Tradition.* New York: Viking, 1977.
"Obituary." *Britannica Book of the Year 1971* (1971): 568.
"Obituary." *Current Biography* 31 (May 1970): 42.
"Obituary." *Current Biography Yearbook 1970.* (1971): 471.
"Obituary." *New York Times* (March 30, 1970): 1+.
"Obituary." *Newsweek* 75 (April 13, 1970): 81.
"Obituary." *Time* 95 (April 13, 1970): 79.
"Old Friends Part." *New Republic* 120 (March 7, 1949): 6.

"On with the Waltz." *Time* 65 (June 20, 1955): 74 +.

"Portrait." *Christian Science Monitor Weekly Magazine Section* (September 28, 1940): 11.

"Portrait." *News Week* 5 (April 20, 1935): 36.

"Portrait." *News Week* 9 (January 23, 1937): 29.

"Portrait." *Review of Reviews* 83 (April 1931): 6.

"Portrait." *Saturday Review of Literature* 13 (January 18, 1936): 11.

"Portrait." *Saturday Review of Literature* 17 (December 25, 1937): 15.

"Portrait." *Saturday Review of Literature* 24 (December 20, 1941): 7.

"Portrait." *Saturday Review of Literature* 26 (December 4, 1943): 56.

"Portrait." *Time* 27 (May 4, 1936): 81.

"Recreating Strong's Stay in Yanan." *Beijing Review* 28 (December 16, 1985): 31–32.

Scher, M. "Anna Louise Strong." *New China Magazine* 3 (Fall 1977): 43.

"Sentimental Journey." *Time* 53 (February 23, 1949): 28.

"Sins of Miss Strong." *Newsweek* 33 (February 28, 1949): 20.

Snow, E. "Mao and Marx." *Saturday Review of Literature* 32 (November 19, 1949): 18.

"Spy Scare Claims Two New Victims." *Christian Century* 66 (March 2, 1949): 262.

Strong, Tracy B., and Helene Keyssar. "Strong, Anna Louise: Three Interviews with Chairman Mao Zedong." *China Quarterly* 103 (September 1985): 489–509.

"They Stand Out from the Crowd." *Literary Digest* 116 (November 18, 1933): 11.

Thomson, J. C., Jr. "I Kept Silent for the Cause." *New York Times Book Review* (March 11, 1984): 25.

Tinling, Marion. *Women into the Unknown: A Sourcebook on Women Explorers and Travelers.* New York: Greenwood, 1989.

Wales, N. "Anna Louise Strong: the Classic Fellow-traveler." *New Republic* 162 (April 25, 1970): 17–19.

Willen, Paul. "Anna Louise Goes Home Again." *Reporter* 12 (April 7, 1955): 28–31.

Other Works by Anna Louise Strong

Newsletter

Letter from China. Nos. 1–70, published from 1961 to 1970.

Today. Nos. 1–38(?), published from 1951 to 1957.

Score

Songs of Oberlin. Oberlin, Ohio: Oberlin College. (1905 edition edited by Anna Louise Strong and Edna Barrows.)

Thesis

"A Consideration of Prayer from the Standpoint of Social Psychology." Ph.D. diss., University of Chicago, 1908.

Other Works About Anna Louise Strong

Theses

Ogle, Stephanie Francine. "Anna Louise Strong: Progressive and Propagandist." Ph.D. diss., University of Washington, 1981.

_____. "Anna Louise Strong: Seattle Years." Master's thesis, Seattle University, 1973.
Pringle, Robert William, Jr. "Anna Louise Strong: Propagandist of Communism." Ph.D. diss., University of Virginia, 1970.

Primary Source Materials Relating to Anna Louise Strong

Anna Louise Strong. Papers. 1885–1967. Extent of collection: ca. 16 ft. Finding aids: Unpublished finding aids in repository. Location: University of Washington, Suzzallo Library, Archives and Manuscripts Division, 1400 N.E. Campus Pkwy., Seattle, Washington 98195. Scope of collection: Correspondence, diary, manuscripts of published and unpublished works, notebooks and papers.

Philip J. Jaffe. Papers. No Date. Extent of collection: Not listed. Finding aids: In repository. Location: Emory University, Woodruff Library, Atlanta, Georgia 30322. Scope of collection: Includes numerous items of correspondence, clippings, etc., by Strong, as well as items relating to her.

Tracy Strong, Jr. Papers. 1924–1961; (bulk 1924–1931). Extent of collection: 150 items. Finding aids: Not listed. Location: University of Washington, Suzzallo Library, Archives and Manuscripts Division, 1400 N.E. Campus Pkwy., Seattle, Washington 98195. Scope of collection: Diary and writings relating to Tracy Strong's childhood in Geneva, Switzerland, together with letters from his grandfather Sydney Dix Strong, and his aunt Anna Louise Strong.

Survey Associates, Inc. Records. 1891–1952. Extent of collection: 125 ft. Finding aids: Published guide. Location: University of Minnesota, Social Welfare History Archives, 101 Walter Library, 117 Pleasant St. S.E., Minneapolis, Minnesota 55455. Scope of collection: Includes correspondence with Strong.

Sydney Dix Strong. Papers. 1914–1940. Extent of collection: 2 ft. Finding aids: Not listed. Location: Friends Historical Library, Swarthmore College, Peace Collection, Swarthmore, Pennsylvania 19081. Scope of collection: Includes material relating to Sydney Strong's daughter, Anna Louise Strong.

Sydney Strong. Papers. 1876–1938. Extent of collection: 5.5 ft. Finding aids: In repository. Location: University of Washington, Suzzallo Library, Archives and Manuscripts Division, 1400 N.E. Campus Pkwy., Seattle, Washington 98195. Scope of collection: Persons represented include Sydney Strong's wife, Ruth Strong, his daughter, Anna Louise Strong, and his son, Tracy Strong.

59. *Mary Burnett Talbert*
(1866–1923)

Advocate for African American rights, women's rights, children's rights and human rights; educator; and lecturer

BIOGRAPHICAL INFORMATION

Chronological Biography

Born September 17, 1866, in Oberlin, Ohio, youngest of eight surviving children of Caroline (Nicholls) and Cornelius J. Burnett.

1883–1886: Enrolled in literary program at Oberlin College; graduated at 19 and received S.P. degree. Taught algebra, geometry, history and Latin at Bethel University (later became Shorter College) in Little Rock, Arkansas. **1887:** Appointed assistant principal of Bethel University, becoming first woman in state to accede to this position, highest held by woman in state. **1887–1891:** Chosen principal of Union High School in Little Rock and taught until her marriage. **September 8, 1891:** Married William Herbert Hilton Talbert, Buffalo, New York, realtor and municipal clerk. Husband was accountant, but blacks could not hold that title. **1892:** Gave birth to only child, Sarah May, who later graduated from New England Conservatory of Music and became accomplished pianist and composer. **1894:** Received Bachelor of Letters Degree from Oberlin College. **1899:** Charter member of Buffalo Phyllis Wheatley Club. **1901:** Organized Christian Culture Congress at Michigan Avenue Baptist Church, community literary society and forum to address social issues pertaining to African Americans. Group invited such notables as sociologist W. E. B. DuBois, and educators Mary Eliza Church Terrell (see entry 61) and Nannie Helen Burroughs to speak. Protested exclusion of African Americans from Planning Commission of Buffalo Pan-American Exposition. At Biennial Conference of National Association of Colored Women (NACW) in Buffalo, gave lecture and was involved in local arrangements. Meeting re-united her with fellow Oberlin College alumnae Mary Eliza Church Terrell and Anna Julia Cooper, and with Oberlin resident, Hallie Q. Brown. **1909:** Charter member of Empire State Federation of Women's Clubs, association of African American Women's Clubs in New York State. Organization was founded to promote women's education, protect rights of working women and children, advance quality of family and contribute to interracial understanding. **1910:** During her presidential administration, Phyllis Wheatley Club successfully invited National Association for the Advancement of Colored People (NAACP) to organize local chapter in Buffalo. **1910–1912:** Parliamentarian of NACW. **1911–1916:** President of Empire State Federation of Women's Clubs. **1912–1914:** Chair of executive board of National Association of Colored Women's Clubs. **1914–1916:** Vice president-at-large of National Association of Colored Women's Clubs. **1915:** Speaker at "Votes for Women: A Symposium by Leading Thinkers of Colored Women" in Washington, D. C. The NACW president, Margaret Murray Washington, appointed her club representative to board of commissioners for Illinois Exposition celebrating 50 years of freedom of African Americans. **1916:** Attended Amenia Conference at New York estate of NAACP president, Joel Spingarn; organization was interracial group discussing ways of ameliorating racism and economic conditions of African Americans. **1916–1920:** President of NACW. **1918:** Member of Women's Committee on National Defense. Travelled for government in interest of third Liberty Bond Drive to which black women contributed $5 million. Endorsed Children's Year. Organized NAACP branches in Texas and Louisiana (Galveston, Silsbee, Orange, Austin, Corsica, Alexandria, Marshall, Texarkana and Gonzales). Trustee of Frederick Douglass Home. Under her leadership, NACW redeemed mortgage on Douglass home. **1918–1920:** NAACP Board Member. **1919:** Red Cross nurse and YMCA Secretary in Romagne, France. Wrote King Albert of Belgium imploring him to grant colonized Africans their human rights. **1920:** Honorary president of NACW. Travelled to 11 European nations and lectured on conditions of African Americans in United States. American YWCA in Paris refused her accommodations because of her race. Appointed to League of Nations' Women's Committee on International Relations which was reponsible for selecting women nominees for positions in League of Nations. President-for-life of Frederick Douglass Memorial and Historical Association. **September 8, 1920:** As first African American elected delegate (representing NACW) to International Council of Women (ICW) meeting in Christiana, Norway, addressed ICW delegates in Storling House of Parliament. **1920–October 1923:** Vice president of NAACP, position she held until her death. **September 28, 1921:** One of 30 prominent African American delegates who carried petitions to President Warren G. Harding urging him to grant clemency to 24th U.S. Colored Infantry which was convicted falsely of inciting Houston, Texas, riots in 1917. **1922:** Member of Education Committee of International Council of Women of the Darker Races. National Director of NAACP Anti-Lynching Campaign whose task it was to unite one million women against lynching and raise funds to gain support for Congressman Leonidas Dyer's Anti-Lynching Bill. House passed bill but Senate failed to ratify it. Eighth person and first woman to receive Spingarn Medal for efforts on behalf of women and blacks around world and for preservation of Frederick Douglass Home. Medal is highest honor bestowed by NAACP. **October 15, 1923:** Died in Buffalo, New York, of coronary thrombosis; buried in Forest Lawn Cemetery in Buffalo.

Background Information

Parents: Caroline (Nicholls) and Cornelius J. Burnett. Mother was born about 1830 in Raleigh, North Carolina, and reputedly was great granddaughter of Richard Nicholls who captured New Amsterdam in 1644 and renamed it New York. Father was born of free parents in Fayetteville, North

Carolina, June 29, 1813. **Siblings:** Seven (Known names: Clara [Burnett]
Hardy, Henrietta [Burnett] Talbert Perez). **Children:** One (Sarah May
[Talbert] Keelan). **Influences:** William Herbert Hilton Talbert. **Ethnicity:**
African American. **Also known as:** Mary Morris Talbert; Mary Talbert.
Historical sites, landmarks, etc.: Marker, Forest Lawn Cemetery, Buffalo,
York; Talbert Hall, State University of New York at Buffalo, New York;
Talbert Mall Housing Development (renamed Frederick Douglass Towers in
1974), Buffalo, New York; Mary B. Talbert Hospital, Cleveland, Ohio, (merged
with Booth Memorial Hospital and was later taken over by Cleveland
Metropolitan General Hospital); National Association of Colored Women's
Clubs branches are named in her honor in Buffalo, New York; Detroit,
Michigan; Gary, Indiana; and New Haven, Connecticut, as are branches of
City Federation of Women's Clubs in Florida and Texas.

BIBLIOGRAPHICAL INFORMATION

Biographical Sketches About Mary Burnett Talbert

Brown, Hallie Q. *Homespun Heroines and Other Women of Distinction*. Xenia, OH:
    Aldine Publishing, 1926. Reprint. New York: Oxford University Press, 1988.
Dannett, Sylvia G. L. *Profiles of Negro Womanhood*. Yonkers, NY: Educational
    Heritage, 1964.
Davis, Marianna W. *Contributions of Black Women to America*. Columbia, SC:
    Kenday, 1982.
Eggenberger, David, ed. *Encyclopedia of World Biography*. Palatine, IL: McGraw
    Hill/Jack Heraty, 1988.
Hill, John Louis. *When Black Meets White*. Cleveland: Argyle, 1924.
Logan, Rayford W., and Michael R. Winston, eds. *Dictionary of American Negro
    Biography*. New York: Norton, 1982.
Mather, Frank Lincoln. *Who's Who of the Colored Race: A General Biographical Dic-
    tionary of Men and Women of African Descent*. Detroit: Gale Research, 1976.
Robinson, Wilhelmena S. *Historical Negro Biographies*. New York: Publishers
    Company, 1967.
Rywell, Martin. *Afro-American Encyclopedia*. Nashville: Haley and Florida, 1895.
Smith, Jessie Carney, ed. *Notable Black American Women*. Detroit: Gale Re-
    search, 1992. (Listed as Mary Morris Talbert)

Shorter Works by Mary Burnett Talbert

"Concerning the Douglass Memorial." *Crisis* 14 (August 1917): 167–68.
"Did the American Negro Make in the Nineteenth Century, Achievements
    Along the Lines of Wealth, Morality, Education, etc., Commensurate with
    His Opportunities? If So, What Achievements Did He Make?" In *Twentieth
    Century Negro Literature: or, A Cyclopedia of Thought on the Vital Topics*

Relating to the American Negro, by One Hundred of America's Greatest Negroes, edited by Daniel Wallace Culp. Naperville, IL; Toronto, Canada: J. L. Nichols & Co., 1902. Reprint. New York: Arno, 1969.
"The Frederick Douglass Home." *Crisis* 13 (February 1917): 174–76.

Shorter Works About Mary Burnett Talbert

Allison, Madeline G. "Horizon." *Crisis* 22 (July 1921): 130.
_____. "Horizon." *Crisis* 24 (July 1922): 125.
_____. "Horizon." *Crisis* 24 (August 1922): 171 + .
Buchnowski, Joyce. "Mary Talbert Contributed Much to 19th Century Black Progress." *Source (Buffalo, NY)* 5 (Spring 1986): 13 + .
Gozemba, Patricia A., and Marilyn L. Humphries. "Women in the Anti–Ku Klux Klan Movement, 1865–1984." *Women's Studies International Forum* 12 (1989): 35–40.
"A Great Woman." *Crisis* 27 (1923): 77.
"Mrs. Talbert." *Crisis* 27 (December 1923): 56–57.
National Notes 17 (November–December 1914): 2.
National Notes 19 (October 1916): 3.
National Notes 19 (January 1917): 5.
National Notes 23 (October–December 1920): 13.
National Notes 24 (January–March 1922): 5.

Primary Source Materials Relating to Mary Burnett Talbert

Charlotte Hawkins Brown. Papers. 1900–1961 (inclusive). Extent of collection: 2 lin. ft. Finding aids: Unpublished finding aid. Location: Schlesinger Library, Radcliffe College, Cambridge, Massachusetts 02138. Scope of collection: Persons represented include Talbert. Microfilm available.
Empire State Federation of Women's Clubs. Records. 1938–1989. Extent of collection: 2.5 lin. ft. Finding aids: Available in repository. Location: Special Collections and Archives, University Libraries, B-47, State University of New York at Albany, 1400 Washington Avenue, Albany, New York 12222. Scope of collection: Includes minutes of meetings, correspondence, etc.
Mary Church Terrell. Papers. 1851–1962 (inclusive), 1886–1954 (bulk). Extent of collection: Not listed. Finding aids: Unpublished finding aid. Location: Library of Congress, Washington, D. C. 20540. Scope of collection: Major manuscript source on Talbert. Includes correspondence, program notes and miscellaneous material concerning National Association of Colored Women. Microfilm available.
National Association for the Advancement of Colored People. Papers of the NAACP. 1909–1955 (inclusive). Extent of collection: Not listed. Finding aids: Published finding aids. Location: Library of Congress, Washington, D. C. 20540.

Scope of collection: Special correspondence files document Talbert's involvement in organization. Microfilm available.

Oberlin College Archives. Extent of collection: Not listed. Finding aids: Not listed. Location: Oberlin College, Oberlin, Ohio 44074. Scope of collection: Alumnae records and some biographical data.

(THE ABOVE ENTRY WAS CONTRIBUTED BY LILLIAN S. WILLIAMS)

60. Emma Tenayuca
(1916–)
Advocate for Mexican American rights; labor leader

BIOGRAPHICAL INFORMATION

Chronological Biography

Born in 1916 and raised in Mexican barrio section of San Antonio, Texas, in close-knit family. Did not experience discrimination until she began attending school. Serious student, spent much time in public library. By age 14, was reading Charles Darwin, Tom Paine and Karl Marx, and beginning to question American society and Mexican American's inferior position in it. Moved away from Catholicism to more radical materialist position, feeling that Church neglected needs of her people. While still young, about 15, attended political rallies with father. Introduced to socialist thought by grandfather. Consciousness raised by political and economic discussions among family and friends, as well as in community.

February 25, 1931: While still a high school student, helped organize march of unemployed on state capital in Austin, under auspices of Communist-sponsored Trade Union Unity League. Dedicated herself to work for rights of her people, demanding decent wages, working conditions, and reforms for poverty-stricken Mexican Americans, including social, cultural, economic, educational and political demands. Urged people to exercise their right to vote.   **1932 and 1933:** Read about Finck Cigar Company strikes. In 1933, walked picket line with workers and was jailed with them.   **1934:** Graduated from Brackenridge High School. Began organizing neighbors in barrio, speaking out for their civil rights. Found job as elevator operator. Joined Communist party, becoming one of 15 members in San Antonio because she felt they were only ones helping Mexican Americans. Organized San Antonio Mexican American workers into local chapter of Workers Alliance, a militant union; 3,800 workers joined within short time.

Conducted sit-down strikes and demonstrations to demand unemployed be helped. Arrested frequently, twice jailed overnight, continued efforts undeterred. Members were threatened with deportation at one point, simply for being members. Member of executive committee of Workers Alliance of America, national federation of unemployed workers' organizations. Later was general secretary of at least ten chapters of Workers Alliance in San Antonio. **1934 and 1935:** Prominent in formation of two local chapters of International Ladies' Garment Workers Union. **1937:** Police increased surveillance of her activities after she led sit-in of jobless Mexican Americans at city hall to protest discriminatory actions in relief programs. They raided Workers Alliance Hall in July, destroying many records. She was jailed as were other Alliance leaders. Crowd of thousands converged on city jail to demand her release and telegrams came in from all over U.S., thus strengthening union. Resented and feared by many politicians and businessmen who saw her as subversive. Some in labor movement also felt she was too radical and disliked her Communist affiliation. Married Homer Brooks, Houston Communist party organizer, in fall of year but continued to live in San Antonio. **1938:** Workers Alliance began campaign to combat illiteracy. At about the age of 21, became one of primary early leaders of pecan shellers' strike in San Antonio. Fiery speaker with high visibility in Chicano community, she was referred to as "La Pasionaria" and was invited by shellers to organize their strike. Planned strike strategy and recruited more than 6,000 shellers to join union. Strike had began spontaneously in January/February in response to announced wage cut. Workers Alliance dominated bitter struggle until she was jailed and her place taken by less radical member during purge of Communists. Workers, however, elected her honorary strike leader and she remained active in strike despite being singled out for abuse by local police who treated strike as a riot and labelled it a Communist revolutionary movement. Strikers were teargassed at least six times and over 1,000 were jailed. Claiming nervous breakdown due to overwork, left San Antonio and spent number of months in New York City studying Communist methods. **March 1939:** Article entitled "The Mexican Question in the Southwest," published in *The Communist,* monthly magazine of Communist Party of U.S.A. Written with husband while she was state chair, and he was secretary, of Communist party in Texas. **August 1939:** Obtained permit from San Antonio mayor to stage Communist rally on August 26th. Among Communists scheduled to speak was husband. Meeting turned into riot as various "patriotic" groups objected and stormed hall. She escaped but career and influence in city ended. Moved to California and unsuccessfully attempted involvement in Mexican American labor movements in Los Angeles and San Francisco. Met Luisa Moreno (see entry 43) in San Francisco but they did not get along. Moreno felt Tenayuca could have been successful if she had worked to develop her skills; also that she wanted to be center of attention rather than work with others to solve problems. Left San Francisco and dropped out of sight. **19??:** Returned years later to San Antonio as certified teacher and taught until retirement in early 1980s. Active member of COPS (Citizens Organized for Public Service) in San Antonio. **1984:** Honored at annual conference of National Association for Chicano Studies (NACS) along with Manuela Solis Sager, also a labor activist. They were first women to be so honored by NACS since its inception 12 years previously.

Background Information

Parents: Descendent of Spaniards on mother's side and Native Americans on father's side. **Siblings:** None known. **Children:** None known. **Influences:** None. **Ethnicity:** Hispanic American. **Also known as:** Brooks. **Historical sites, landmarks, etc.:** None known.

BIBLIOGRAPHICAL INFORMATION

Biographical Sketches About Emma Tenayuca

Meier, Matt S. *Mexican American Biographies: A Historical Dictionary, 1836–1987.* New York: Greenwood, 1988.
————, and Feliciano Rivera. *Dictionary of Mexican American History.* Westport, CT: Greenwood, 1981.
Telgen, Diane, and Jim Kamp, eds. *Notable Hispanic American Women.* Detroit: Gale Research, 1993.
Zophy, Angela Howard. *Handbook of American Women's History.* New York: Garland, 1990.

Shorter Works by Emma Tenayuca

Tenayuca, Emma, and Homer Brooks. "The Mexican Question in the Southwest." *The Communist* 18 (March 1939): 257–68.

Shorter Works About Emma Tenayuca

Blackwelder, Julia Kirk. *Women of the Depression: Caste and Culture in San Antonio, 1929–1939.* College Station: Texas A & M University Press, 1984.
Calderon, Roberto, and Emilio Zamora. "Manuela Solis Sager and Emma Tenayuca: A Tribute." In *Chicana Voices: Intersections of Class, Race, and Gender.* Austin, TX: CMAS Publications, 1986. (Contains text of Tenayuca's presentation at 1984 conference of National Association for Chicano Studies.)

"Emma Tenayuca." *Fem* no. 48 (October–November 1986): 41.

"Emma Tenayuca: La Pasionaria." In *Mexican American Movements and Leaders*, by Carlos Larralde. Los Alamitos, CA: Hwong Publishing, 1976.

Foner, Philip S. *Women and the American Labor Movement: From World War I to the Present*. New York: Free Press, 1979.

Jamieson, Stuart Marshall. *Labor Unionism in American Agriculture*. New York: Arno, 1976.

Mexican Labor in the United States. New York: Arno, 1974.

Mirande, Alfredo, and Evangelina Enriquez. *La Chicana: The Mexican-American Woman*. Chicago: University of Chicago Press, 1979.

Monroy, Douglas. "Anarquismo y Comunismo: Mexican Radicalism and the Communist Party in Los Angeles During the 1930's." *Labor History* 24 (Winter 1983): 34–59.

"La Pasionaria de Texas." *Time* 31 (February 28, 1938): 17.

San Antonio Express. Various issues in 1938.

San Antonio—The Cradle of Texas Liberty. Austin: Texas Civil Liberties Union, [1938?].

"Working Conditions of Pecan Shellers in San Antonio." *Monthly Labor Review* 48 (March 1939): 549–51.

Primary Source Materials Relating to Emma Tenayuca

United Cannery, Agricultural, Packing, and Allied Workers of America, District 8, CIO. Records. 1938–1947. Extent of collection: 0.5 ft. Finding aid: Unpublished guide. Location: University of Texas at Arlington Library, Division of Special Collections, P.O. Box 19497, UTA Sta., Arlington, Texas 76019. Scope of collection: Records of union's District office include material on pecan workers' strike of 1938 and 1939 led by Tenayuca.

61. Mary Eliza Church Terrell
(1863–1954)

Educator; feminist; lecturer; and advocate for women's suffrage and African American rights

BIOGRAPHICAL INFORMATION

Chronological Biography

Born September 23, 1863, in Memphis, Tennessee, to Louisa (Ayres) and Robert Church, both former slaves. First of two children and only daughter.

ca. 1868: Churches divorced. Mary Eliza (known as Mollie) and younger brother, Thomas, lived with mother. 1870: Enrolled in Model School on campus of Antioch College, Yellow Springs, Ohio. 1875: Moved to Oberlin, Ohio, to attend high school. 1879: Graduated from high school. 1884: Earned B.A. from Oberlin College. Returned to Memphis. 1885–1887: Faculty member at Wilberforce University in Xenia, Ohio. 1887–1888: Moved to Washington, D. C., to teach Latin at M Street High School (known as Preparatory School for Colored Youth), capital's secondary school for blacks. Received M.A. from Oberlin College. 1888–1890: Went abroad to tour western Europe, studying languages. 1890: Returned to United States. Began career as public speaker during this decade. October 28, 1891: Declined appointment to position of registrar at Oberlin College to marry Robert Herberton Terrell who later became judge of Municipal Court in District of Columbia. 1892–1893: Served as first woman president of Bethel Literary and Historical Association. 1892–1898: Had four children; daughter, Phillis, the only one to survive. 1895–1901: Appointed to District of Columbia Board of Education, first black woman on American school board. 1896–1901: Founder and first president of National Association of Colored Women (NACW); served three terms. February 18, 1898: Spoke at biennial session of National American Woman Suffrage Association addressing specific problems of black women during speech entitled "The Progress of Colored Women." 1900: Spoke again at biennial session of National American Woman Suffrage Association addressing issue of "The Justice of Woman Suffrage." 1901: Made honorary president of National Association of Colored Women for life. 1904: Spoke at International Congress of Women in Berlin, addressing meeting in English, French and German. 1905: Adopted niece, Mary Church, daughter of brother Thomas. 1906–1911: Served on reorganized School Board of Washington, D. C. 1909: One of founders of National Association for the Advancement of Colored People (NAACP). 1910: Spoke at Second Annual Conference of National Negro Committee which condemned disfranchisement in South. 1911: Publication of short biography, *Harriet Beecher Stowe: An Appreciation,* honoring abolitionist author on centennial of her birth. 1919: Spoke at second congress of Women's International League for Peace and Freedom in Zurich. 1920: Appointed supervisor of work among black women of Eastern states by National Republican Committee. Early 1920s: Held position of second vice president of International Council of Women of the Darker Races. 1925: Death of husband. 1929: Included in list which recognized Oberlin College's 100 most influential graduates. 1930: Employed by Ruth Hannah McCormick (Simms) in McCormick's 1930 Illinois senatorial campaign to take charge among black women in Illinois. 1932: Reappointed by Republican Committee to supervise work among black women in East. Produced pageant for District of Columbia's public schools in honor of Phillis Wheatley. **1933:** Spoke at 100th anniversary of founding of Oberlin College. **1937:** Addressed International Assembly of World Fellowship of Faiths in London. **1940:** Received honorary degree from Wilberforce University. Autobiography, *A Colored Woman in a White World,* published. **1948:** Received honorary doctorate in humane letters from Howard University and an award for efforts to abolish segregation from Washington branch of Americans for Democratic Action. **1949:** Member of Washington chapter of American Association of University Women (AAUW), bringing end to its policy of excluding blacks. Chair of Coordinating Committee for the Enforcement of the District of Columbia Anti-Discrimination Laws. Chair of national committee to free black Ingram family who were convicted of murdering a white male who had attacked them and sentenced to death. **1950:** One of a group attempting to desegregate John R. Thompson Restaurant in Washington, D. C. **1953:** In October, 700 gathered to honor her in belated birthday celebration. Led delegation to Georgia, seeking Rosa Ingram's parole. Ingrams were freed in 1959. **July 24, 1954:** Died of cancer in Highland Beach, Maryland, at age of 90. Buried in Lincoln Memorial Cemetery, Washington, D. C.

Background Information

Parents: Louisa (Ayres) and Robert Church. Mother was lady's maid in Ayres household and opened hair salon after emancipation. Father was son of Captain Charles B. Church of Holly Springs, Mississippi, and slave maidservant, Emmeline. **Siblings:** Two (Thomas, Annette). **Children:** Five (Known names: Phillis, Mary [adopted niece]). **Influences:** None. **Ethnicity:** African American. **Also known as:** Mollie. **Historical sites, landmarks, etc.:** Gravesite, Lincoln Memorial Cemetery, Washington, D. C.; Mary Church Terrell Elementary School, Washington, D.C.

BIBLIOGRAPHICAL INFORMATION

Bibliographical Sketches About Mary Eliza Church Terrell

Garraty, John A., ed. *Dictionary of American Biography.* New York: Charles Scribner's Sons, 1977.
Logan, Rayford W., and Michael R. Winston, eds. *Dictionary of American Negro Biography.* New York: W. W. Norton & Company, 1982.

Ploski, Harry A., and James Williams, eds. *The Negro Almanac: A Reference Work on the Afro American*. Detroit: Gale Research, 1989.

Sicherman, Barbara, and Carl Hurd Green, eds. *Notable American Women, the Modern Period: A Biographical Dictionary*. Cambridge, MA: Belknap Press of Harvard University Press, 1980.

Smith, Jessie Carney, ed. *Notable Black American Women*. Detroit: Gale Research, 1992.

Toppin, Edgar Allan. *A Biographical History of Blacks in America Since 1528*. New York: David McKay Company, [1971].

Zophy, Angela Howard. *Handbook of American Women's History*. New York: Garland, 1990.

Books by Mary Eliza Church Terrell

A Colored Woman in a White World. Washington, D. C.: Ransdell Inc., 1940. Reprint. Salem, NH: Ayer, 1986.

Colored Women and World Peace. Philadelphia: Women's International League, 1932.

Harriet Beecher Stowe: An Appreciation. Washington, D. C.: Murray Bros. Press, 1911.

The Progress of Colored Women: An Address Delivered Before the National American Women's Suffrage Association, at the Columbia Theater, Washington, D. C., February 18, 1898, on the Occasion of Its Fiftieth Anniversary. Washington, D. C.: Smith Brothers, Printers, [1898].

Books About Mary Eliza Church Terrell

Cooke, Paul P. *Mary Church Terrell: A Tribute*. Washington, D. C.: Cooke, 1980.

Jones, Beverly Washington. *Quest for Equality: The Life and Writings of Mary Eliza Church Terrell, 1863–1954*. Brooklyn, NY: Carlson Publishing, 1990.

Shepperd, Gladys B. *Mary Church Terrell: Respectable Person*. Baltimore: Human Relations Press, 1959.

Shorter Works by Mary Eliza Church Terrell

"A Colored Woman in a White World." In *Living Black in White America*, edited by Bill Adler. New York: W. Morrow, 1971.

"The History of the Club Movement." *Afro-American Women's Journal* 1 (1940): 34.

"The History of the High School for Negroes in Washington." *Journal of Negro History* 2 (July 1917): 252.

"I Remember Frederick Douglass." *Ebony* 8 (October 1953): 73–76 + .

"The Justice of Woman Suffrage." *Crisis* 90 (June–July 1983): 6.

"The Justice of Woman Suffrage." *Woman's Journal* (February 17, 1900): 55.

"Lynching from a Negro's Point of View." *North American Review* 178 (June 1904): 853–68.
"Peonage in the United States: The Convict Lease System and the Chain Gangs." *Nineteenth Century* 62 (August 1907): 306–22.
"A Plea for the White South by a Colored Woman." *Nineteenth Century* 60 (July 1906): 70–84.
"The Progress of Colored Women." *Voice of the Negro* 1 (July 1904): 292.
"Taft and the Negro Soldiers." *Independent* 65 (July 23, 1908): 189–90.
"Woman Suffrage and the Fifteenth Amendment." *Crisis* 10 (August 1915): 191.

Shorter Works About Mary Eliza Church Terrell

Campbell, Karlyn Kohrs. "Style and Content in the Rhetoric of Early Afro-American Feminists." *Quarterly Journal of Speech* 72 (Novemer 1986): 434–45.
Chittenden, Elizabeth F. "As We Climb: Mary Church Terrell." *Negro History Bulletin* 38 (Feburary/March 1975): 350–54.
Dannett, Sylvia G. L. *Profiles of Negro Womanhood.* Chicago: Educational Heritage, 1964.
Gozemba, Patricia A., and Marilyn L. Humphries. "Women in the Anti–Ku Klux Klan Movement, 1865–1984." *Women's Studies International Forum* 12 (1989): 35–40.
Hornsby, Alton, Jr. *Chronology of African-American History.* Detroit: Gale Research, 1991.
Jones, Beverly W. "Before Montgomery and Greensboro: The Desegregation Movement in the District of Columbia, 1950–1953." *Phylon* 43 (June 1982): 144–54.
———. "Mary Church Terrell and the National Association of Colored Women, 1896 to 1901." *Journal of Negro History* 67 (Spring 1982): 20–33.
Marable, Manning. "Groundings with My Sisters: Patriarchy and the Exploitation of Black Women." *Journal of Ethnic Studies* 11 (1983): 1–39.
"Mary Terrell." *Journal of Negro History* 39 (October 1954): 332–37.
Miller, M. Sammy. "Mary Church Terrell's Letters from Europe to Her Father." *Negro History Bulletin* 39 (September/October 1976): 615–18.
"Mrs. Mary Church Terrell Fought Prejudice." *Sepia* 7 (December 1959): 75.
"New Book on Mrs. Terrell by Gladys Shepperd Used as Display Book for Negro Historical Week 1960 by Enoch Pratt Free Library, Baltimore, Md." *Negro History Bulletin* 23 (April 1960): 150.
Render, Sylvia Lyons. "Afro-American Women: The Outstanding and the Obscure." *Quarterly Journal of the Library of Congress* 32 (1975): 306–21.
Sterling, Dorothy. *Black Foremothers: Three Lives.* Old Westbury, NY: Feminist Press, 1979. Reprint. New York: Feminist Press, 1988.
———, and Benjamin Quarles. *Lift Every Voice: The Lives of Booker T. Washington, W. E. B. DuBois, Mary Church Terrell, and James Weldon Johnson.* Garden City, NY: Doubleday, 1965.
White, Gloria M. "The Early Mary Church Terrell, 1863–1910." *Integrated Education* 13 (1975): 39–42.

———. "Mary Church Terrell: Organizer of Black Women." *Integrated Education* 17 (September–December 1979): 2–8.

Other Works About Mary Eliza Church Terrell
Theses

Cash, Floris Loretta Barnett. "Womanhood and Protest: The Club Movement Among Black Women, 1892–1922." Ph.D. diss., State University of New York at Stony Brook, 1986.

Desselle, Frances A. "The Life and Contributions of Mary Church Terrell." Master's thesis, Washington, D. C.: Moorland-Spingarn Research Center, Howard University, 1979.

Holland, Endesha Ida Mae. "The Autobiography of a Parader Without a Permit (The South, African-American Women, Theater, Civil Rights Movement)." Ph.D. diss., University of Minnesota, 1986.

Jones, Beverly Washington. "Quest for Equality: The Life of Mary Eliza Church Terrell, 1863–1954." Ph.D. diss., University of North Carolina at Chapel Hill, 1980.

Media Materials About Mary Eliza Church Terrell
Films

Mary Church Terrell: Meddler with a Mission. Chicago: Society for Visual Education, 1974. 35 mm. plus phonodisc (20 min.) or cassette; teacher's guide and reading scripts; color.

Filmstrips

Mary Church Terrell: Meddler with a Mission. Chicago: Society for Visual Education, 1974. 60 frames; color.

Sound Recordings

Brannon, Jean Marilyn, ed. *The Negro Woman.* Folkways Records FH5523, [1966]. 12 inch; 33 ⅓ rpm; mono; 1 disc.

Destination Freedom: The Long Road. Chicago: WMAQ, 1949. Audiotape.

What If I Am a Woman. Folkways Records FH5537, 1977. 12 inch; 33 ⅓ rpm; 1 disc.

Primary Source Materials Relating to Mary Eliza Church Terrell

Mary (Church) Terrell. Papers. 1884–? Extent of collection: 2 ft. 6 in. Finding aids: Unpublished guide. Location: Howard University, Moorland-Spingarn Research Center, 500 Howard Place N.W., Washington, D. C. 20059. Scope of collection: Correspondence, biographical sketches, manuscripts, articles, clippings, and other papers related to her organizational affiliations. Included are letters from Mrs. Booker T. Washington.

Mary (Church) Terrell. Papers. 1886–1954. Extent of collection: 20 ft. (ca. 11,800 items). Finding aids: Published and unpublished guides. Location: Library of Congress, Manuscript Division, Independent Avenue at First St. S. E., Washington, D. C. 20540. Scope of collection: Correspondence, diaries, manuscripts of autobiography, short stories and poems; speeches, printed matter and memorabilia. Includes information on politics, rights of women and desegregation in District of Columbia. Jane Addams, Mary (McLeod) Bethune, Carrie Chapman Catt, Ruth Hanna McCormick and Booker T. Washington are among correspondents.

Mary (Church) Terrell. Papers. 1895–1953. Extent of collection: 1,310 items. Finding aids: Not listed. Location: Howard University Library, 500 Howard Place N.W., Washington, D. C. 20059. Scope of collection: Correspondence, clippings, newspaper articles, pamphlets, broadsides and other printed matter, as well as other papers chiefly relating to National Association of Colored Women. Articles about Terrell's husband, Judge Robert H. Terrell, copies of minutes (1935–36) of Race Relations Federation of Churches, and letters addressed to Olivia Davidson Washington (Mrs. Booker T. Washington).

Robert R. Church Family. Papers. ca. 1800–1978. Extent of collection: 38 cu. ft. Finding aids: Not listed. Location: Memphis State University Library, Mississippi Valley Collection (Tenn.), Memphis, Tennessee 38152. Scope of collection: Correspondence, receipts, school records, biographical material, estate papers, pamphlets, clippings, printed material, memorabilia, photos and other papers of a black family active in politics and civil rights.

(THE ABOVE ENTRY WAS CONTRIBUTED BY AMY DIBARTOLO ROCKWELL)

62. *Marion Marsh Todd*
(1841–1914?)

Lawyer; author; lecturer; party worker;
and advocate for economic reform

BIOGRAPHICAL INFORMATION

Chronological Biography

One of seven children, born March 1841 in Plymouth, Chenango County, New York, to Dolly Adelia (Wales) and Abner Kneeland Marsh.

1851: Family moved to Eaton Rapids, Michigan, where she attended public school, having previously been educated at home by parents. **1852:** Father was Universalist preacher who died when she was ten years old. He had encouraged her to pursue career. Mother was highly intelligent and model for daughter. **1858?:** Began teaching in public school at age seventeen, having studied at Ypsilanti State Normal School. **1868–late 1870s:** Married

Boston lawyer Benjamin Todd and resigned teaching position. Joined reformer husband in lecturing for greater public opportunities for women including suffrage, political and economic reform and temperance. Made first speech during first year of marriage. Only child, Lula, born during this time. Moved to San Francisco because of husband's health in late 1870s.   **1879:** Began studying at Hastings Law College in San Francisco which had recently begun to admit women. Main area of concentration was finance law.   **1880:** Husband died.   **1881:** Forced to withdraw before completing degree requirements; nonetheless was admitted to California bar and developed successful law practice in San Francisco.**1882:** Having become active in politics and reform, made significant contributions as elected member of Greenback-Labor party platform committee. Received party nomination for state attorney general at September convention, becoming one of first women in country to run for statewide office. Campaigned statewide; lost election, garnering only 1,109 votes, but led all other party nominees in votes.   **1883:** Relinquished practice, turning to lecturing and writing for financial support. Persuasive, knowledgeable and entertaining speaker. One of organizers of Anti-Monopoly party; delegate to its first national convention in Chicago. **1884:** Participated in national convention of Anti-Monopoly party in Chicago, as well as Greenback party's convention in Indianapolis where she served as member of platform committee. Campaigned for Civil War general Ben Butler, presidential nominee of both parties that year; stumped in subsequent campaigns of both parties until about 1886.   **Mid 1880s:** Moved to Michigan.   **1886:** As member of Knights of Labor, was delegate from Michigan to general assembly in Richmond, Virginia. Delegate to labor conference in Indianapolis giving well-received speech. Wrote small book entitled *Protective Tariff Delusion.* Asserted that protective tariffs do not help farmer or laborer and should be abolished. Returned to California for short time to complete important law cases.   **1887:** Along with Sarah Elizabeth Van De Vort Emery (see entry 21), founded national Union Labor party in Cincinnati, speaking brilliantly at convention. Party's aims included railroad and economic reform and representation of farmers' and workers' concerns.   **1890:** Changed residence to Chicago to take over editorship of *Express,* nationally distributed weekly reform magazine. *Professor Goldwin Smith and His Satellites in Congress* published. Originally one of her first series for *Express,* it vehemently attacked Cornell historian's article opposing woman suffrage. Wrote extensively used campaign booklet for People's party, *Honest (?) John Sherman, or a Foul Record.*   **1891:** In May, was delegate to convention in Cincinnati at which People's (Populist) party was formed. Chosen to present the party's chair with flowers; gave memorable speech without preparation. Broadened *Honest (?) John*... pamphlet into book, *Pizarro and John Sherman,* which reflected current major economic concerns. One of signers of charter of National Woman's Alliance, founded in September by leading

Populist Women.   1893: Her major work, *Railways of Europe and America,* published. Extensive analysis of conditions worldwide; contended revamping and nationalization of American system was imperative.   1895–1902: Continued discussions of drawbacks of capitalist system using format of novel, publishing *Rachel's Pitiful History* in 1895, *Phillip: A Romance* in 1900 and *Claudia* in 1902.   1893–1914: Moved from Chicago to Eaton Rapids, Michigan, where she was living in 1893; last known to have lived in Springport. Date and circumstances of death are unrecorded.

Background Information

Parents: Dolly Adelia (Wales) and Abner Kneeland Marsh. Educated New Englanders, mother from Hartford, Connecticut, father native of Shoreham, Vermont.   **Siblings:** Six (No known names).   **Children:** One (Lula).   **Influences:** Benjamin Todd.   **Ethnicity:** Not known.   **Also known as:** None known.   **Historical sites, landmarks, etc.:** None known.

BIBLIOGRAPHICAL INFORMATION

Biographical Sketches About Marion Marsh Todd

James, Edward T., ed. *Notable American Women 1607–1950: A Biographical Dictionary.* Cambridge, MA: Belknap Press of Harvard University Press, 1971.
Mainiero, Lina, ed. *American Women Writers.* New York: Frederick Ungar, 1982.
Whitman, Alden, ed. *American Reformers: An H. W. Wilson Biographical Dictionary.* New York: H. W. Wilson Company, 1985.
Willard, Frances E., and Mary A. Livermore, eds. *American Women.* New York: Mast, Crowell & Kirkpatrick, 1897.
————, and ————, eds. *A Woman of the Century.* Buffalo, NY: Charles Wells Moulton, 1893.
Zophy, Angela Howard. *Handbook of American Women's History.* New York: Garland, 1990.

Books by Marion Marsh Todd

Claudia. Springport, MI: Published by the Author, 1902.
Honest (?) John Sherman, or A Foul Record. Lansing, MI: Reprogle & Co., 1894.
Phillip: A Romance. N.p.: n.p., 1900.
Pizarro and John Sherman. Chicago: F. J. Schulte & Company, [1891].

Prof. Goldwin Smith and His Satellites in Congress. Battle Creek, MI: Wm. C. Gage & Sons, Printers, 1890.

Protective Tariff Delusion. Battle Creek, MI: Gage, 1886. Reprint. Chicago: F. J. Schulte & Co., [1892].

Rachel's Pitiful History. Springport, MI: n.p., 1895.

Railways of Europe and America; or, Government Ownership. With Notes From Official Sources. Boston: Arena Publishing Company, 1893. Reprint. Lansing, MI: W. Emery, 1897.

Shorter Works About Marion Marsh Todd

Adams, Pauline, and Emma S. Thornton. "A Rehabilitation: The Writer and Populist Activist, Marion Marsh Todd." *Society for the Study of Midwestern Literature Newsletter* 11 (Spring 1981): 1–13.

Diggs, Annie L. "The Women in the Alliance Movement." *Arena* 6 (July 1892): 161–79.

—————. "The Women in the Alliance Movement." In *Lives to Remember,* edited by Leon Stein. New York: Arno, 1974.

Michigan State Historical Society. Historical Collections. *Collections and Researches Made by the Michigan Pioneer and Historical Society.* Lansing, MI: Wynkoop, Hallanbeck Crawford, 1892.

Robinson, Leila J. "Women Lawyers in the U.S." Parts 1, 2. *Green Bag* (January, April 1890): 26–27, 181–82.

Winfield, J. Davis. *History of Political Conventions in California 1849–1892.* Sacramento, CA: California State Library, 1893.

Primary Source Materials Relating to Marion Marsh Todd

Joseph Labadie. Papers. 1880–1931. Extent of collection: 3,140 items. Finding aids: Unpublished guide. Location: University of Michigan Library, Department of Rare Books and Special Collections, Ann Arbor, Michigan 48109–1205. Scope of collection: Correspondents include Todd.

63. Harriet Taylor Upton
(1853–1945)
Advocate for child labor reform; author;
feminist; and Republican party leader

BIOGRAPHICAL INFORMATION

Chronological Biography

Only daughter and oldest of two children, born December 17, 1853, in Ravenna, Portage County, Ohio, to Harriet M. (Frazer) and Ezra Booth

Taylor. Attended school in two-room schoolhouse and grew up in warm, happy home. Raised in Presbyterian faith but joined Episcopalian Church in later years. Father was prominent lawyer and later Circuit Court judge; frequently travelled with him on speaking tours and campaigns, learning operation of political system, which fascinated her, first hand.

1861–1879: Family moved to Warren, Ohio. Completed education at local public schools. Contested school regulation at Warren High School prohibiting girls from chemistry laboratory and became first female admitted. Continued touring with father on circuit court route as he did not want her to attend college. Elected secretary of Trumbull County Woman's Christian Temperance Union. Continued association with Temperance Union for many years; at various times also affiliated with Daughters of the American Revolution, Federation of Women's Clubs, Zonta Club, etc. Although not supporter at this time, occasionally attended woman suffrage meetings; in her mid-twenties, heard Susan B. Anthony speak in Warren, but did not yet change opinion as she believed movement implied women were treated unjustly by men, which had not been her experience. **1880–1887:** Her mother died; she moved to Washington, D. C., to serve as father's official hostess when he was elected to House on Republican ticket, filling seat formerly occupied by James A. Garfield who had been elected president. Met national Republican leaders, especially through father's position as chair of House Judiciary Committee. **July 9, 1884:** Married attorney George Whitman Upton who either was father's law partner or became so after their marriage. Lived in Washington when Congress was in session and had main residence in Warren. **1884:** Father was elected president of Ohio Woman Suffrage Association, but was unable to serve, probably due to other responsibilties. **1888:** Again met Susan B. Anthony as well as other leading suffragists including Elizabeth Cady Stanton and Lucy Stone. Although father was active supporter, and she was impressed by Anthony, she still opposed suffrage. About this time, while conducting research for antisuffrage article, changed her view and became ardent and effective champion of cause. **1890:** Became member of National American Woman Suffrage Association (NAWSA). First major work, children's history book, *Our Early Presidents; Their Wives and Children, From Washington to Jackson,* published. Had written to descendants of presidents and done considerable research for book. In addition to books, wrote children's stories, political pieces, fiction and suffrage articles for periodicals, newspapers and magazines for many years. Feeling that historians generally ignored women's role in American history, she emphasized this aspect in her writings and speeches. Also urged humanistic approach to politics. **1893:** Acting chair of NAWSA's congressional committee which discussed suffrage issue with each member of congress to press concerns and solicit views. **1893–1910?:** Treasurer of NAWSA. **1898/9–1908:** President of Ohio Woman Suffrage Association. **1898–1913?:** Elected member of Warren Board of Education; served as president about two years.   **1902–1910:** Edited monthly suffrage newspaper *Progress;* it was expanded in 1907 and became official publication of NAWSA.   **1903–1909:** Administered daily work of NAWSA from national headquarters in Warren assisted only by small staff. Skillful debater, bright and amusing speaker, and down to earth nature won over opposition and contributed to great success as fund-raiser and representative of movement. Combined with good humor and motherly appearance, she was beloved figure among suffrage workers. Worked ceaselessly overseeing literature distribution, travelling, testifying before Congressional hearings, editing convention reports, etc.   **1905:** Along with Ida A. Husted Harper and Susan B. Anthony, met with unsympathetic President Theodore Roosevelt to discuss Congress forbidding Hawaii legislature to extend suffrage to women and to urge him not to allow same action to occur in Philippines.   **March 3, 1908:** Testified at House hearing on woman suffrage.   **1909:** *A Twentieth-Century History of Trumbull County, Ohio,* two-volume work, published.   **April 19, 1910:** Witness before House Committee on Judiciary regarding woman suffrage.   **1910:** Three volume *History of the Western Reserve* published.   **1911–1920:** Again served as president of Ohio Woman Suffrage Association. Although 1912 and 1914 state suffrage referendums which she led failed, 1916 campaign secured municipal suffrage in at least three Ohio cities and presidential vote statewide. Through her efforts, Ohio and Tennessee ratified Nineteenth Amendment; she and Carrie Chapman Catt had conducted intensive campaign in Tennessee.   **December 1913:** Testified before House Committee on woman suffrage.   **1920–1924:** Appointed vice chair of Republican National executive committee, one of highest party positions held by woman up to that time; may have been first woman member of committee, and was probably in highest ranking position a woman had yet held in America. Secured government appointments for qualified women using political contacts and influence gained over the years. Women admitted to diplomatic service and child labor legislation passed due in large measure to her efforts. Instrumental in placing women on advisory committee of Conference for Limitation of Arms.   **1921:** Testified before joint committee on behalf of women in civil service concerning reclassification of civil service salaries. As vice chair of executive committee, again appeared before Senate committee considering issues related to pregnancy, infant mortality, etc. Appeared in July before House committee regarding maternity and infant concerns.   **June 6, 1922:** House committee witness concerning Social Hygiene Board.   **1923:** In January, appeared as vice chair of Republican party executive committee before Senate committee regarding child labor amendment to constitution. Testified in February before Senate committee, "Establishment of a U.S. Industrial Home for Women at Mount Weather, Va." Husband died.   **1924:** Witness before House committee, representing executive committee of Republican party, regarding child labor amendments to constitution. Defeated in primaries as seventy-year-old candidate for father's former Congressional seat. **1928–1931:** Assistant state campaign manager for Ohio Republican party. Served as Governor Cooper's liaison to Department of Public Welfare in Ohio. Accomplishments included reforms at Madison (Ohio) Home for Soldiers' and Sailors' Widows and at Girls' Industrial School in Delaware, Ohio. **1931:** Retired from public life and moved to Pasadena, California. **November 2, 1945:** Died in Pasadena nursing home at age 91 from heart disease.

Background Information

Parents: Harriet M. (Frazer) and Ezra Booth Taylor. Maternal grandmother was first white child born in northeastern Ohio Portage area while it was still part of Connecticut's Western Reserve. **Siblings:** One (No known names). **Children:** None. **Influences:** None. **Ethnicity:** Not known. **Also known as:** None known. **Historical sites, landmarks, etc.:** None known.

BIBLIOGRAPHICAL INFORMATION

Biographical Sketches About Harriet Taylor Upton

James, Edward T., ed. *Notable American Women 1607–1950: A Biographical Dictionary.* Cambridge, MA: Belknap Press of Harvard University Press, 1971.
Mainiero, Lina, ed. *American Women Writers.* New York: Frederick Ungar, 1982.
Whitman, Alden, ed. *American Reformers: An H. W. Wilson Biographical Dictionary.* New York: H. W. Wilson Company, 1985.
Who Was Who Among North American Authors 1921–1939. Detroit: Gale Research, 1976.
Zophy, Angela Howard. *Handbook of American Women's History.* New York: Garland, 1990.

Books by Harriet Taylor Upton

History of the Western Reserve; H. G. Cutler . . . and a Staff of Leading Citizens Collaborated on the Counties and Biographies. Chicago: Lewis Publishing Company, 1910.
Militancy an Excuse. Warren, OH: Ohio Woman Suffrage Association, [1910?].
Our Early Presidents: Their Wives and Children, from Washington to Jackson. Boston: D. Lothrop Co., [c1890].
Random Recollections of Harriet Taylor Upton. N.p.: Committee for Preservation of Ohio Woman Suffrage Records, n.d.

Short Magazine Stories. [Ohio: n.p., 1945?].
A *Twentieth Century History of Trumbull County, Ohio: a Narrative Account of Its Historical Progress, Its People, and Its Principal Interests.* Chicago: Lewis Publishing Company, 1909. Reprint. Evansville, IN: Whipporwill, [1983].

Shorter Works by Harriet Taylor Upton

"Anyone Can Do It." *Woman's Home Companion* 50 (October 1923): 34.
"Heinrich Huff versus Arthur Van Wyck; story." *New England Magazine* n.s. 20 (May 1899): 278–84.
"The Koto and Its Associations." *American Magazine* 9: 93.
"Machine and the Woman." *Ladies' Home Journal* 39 (October 1922): 13.
"What Halts the Child Labor Amendment?" *Woman Citizen* n.s. 9 (February 21, 1925): 9.
"The Woman Suffrage Movement in Ohio." In *History of Ohio,* by Charles Burleigh Galbreath. Chicago: American Historical Society, Inc., 1925.
"Woman's View of Practical Politics." *Woman's Home Companion* 48 (August 1921): 4.

Shorter Works About Harriet Taylor Upton

Allen, Florence Ellinwood, and Mary Welles. *The Ohio Woman Suffrage Movement. 'A Certain Unalienable Right.' What Ohio Women Did to Secure It.* N.p.: Committee for the Preservation of Ohio Woman Suffrage Records, [1952].
Anthony, Susan B., and Ida Husted Harper, eds. *History of Woman Suffrage.* Vol. 4. 1883–1900. [New York:] Source Book Press, 1970.
Drexel, Constance. "Women to Be in Force at Party Conventions." *New York Times* (June 1, 1924): 4.
Evans, Ernestine. "Women in the Washington Scene." *Century* 106 (August 1923): 507–17.
Harper, Ida Husted. *The Life and Work of Susan B. Anthony.* Indianapolis: Hollenbeck Press, 1898.
Hauser, Elizabeth J. "The Woman Suffrage Movement in Ohio." *Ohio Magazine* 4 (February 1908): 83–92.
"Klan Losing Fight in Ohio Primaries." *New York Times* (August 13, 1924): 1.
"Mrs. G. W. Upton, Suffragist, Dead." *New York Times* (November 4, 1945): 44.
"Mrs. Upton Resigns Post." *New York Times* (June 6, 1924): 3.
"Mrs. Upton Sees Coolidge." *New York Times* (June 19, 1924): 2.
Neely, Ruth, ed. *Women of Ohio; A Record of Their Achievements in the History of the State.* Chicago: S. J. Clarke Pub. Co., [193?].
"Portrait." *Ladies' Home Journal* 39 (August 1922): 9.
"Portrait." *Literary Digest* 81 (May 1924): 6.
"Portrait." *Literary Digest* 81 (June 28, 1924): 11.
"Portrait." *Outlook* 136 (January 23, 1924): 149.

"Portrait." *Review of Reviews, American* 69 (April 1924): 419 + .
"Portrait." *Review of Reviews, American* 70 (June–July 1924): 10.
"Portrait." *Woman Citizen* n.s. 9 (June 28, 1924): 8.
"Portrait." *Woman Citizen* n.s. 9 (February 21, 1925): 31.
Savage, C. "Women as Citizens; interview." *Woman Citizen* n.s. 8 (May 31, 1924): 18–19.
Tittle, W. "Portrait." *Century* 106 (August 1923): 510.
Walker, Harvey. *Constructive Government in Ohio.* Columbus: Ohio History Press, 1948.

Other Works by Harriet Taylor Upton

Hand Book of the National American Woman Suffrage Association and Proceedings of the ... Annual Convention. Warren, OH: National American Woman Suffrage Association, 1893–. (Edited by H. T. Upton, 1904–1909.)
Progress. New York: National American Woman Suffrage Association, 1906–1910. (Edited by H. T. Upton, 1906–1910.)

Primary Source Materials Relating to Harriet Taylor Upton

Frances Jennings Casement: Suffrage. Papers. 1840–1928. Extent of collection: 2.5 ft. Finding aids: Inventory. Location: Ohio Historical Society, Archives Library, 1985 Velma Ave., Columbus, Ohio 43211. Scope of collection: Records of Ohio Woman Suffrage Association, National Woman Suffrage Association, Equal Rights Association and copy of *Random Recollections* by Upton.
Harriet Taylor Upton. Letters. Extent of collection: Not listed. Finding aids: Register. Location: University of Rochester, Rush Rhees Library, Department of Rare Books, Manuscripts and Archives, Rochester, New York 14627. Scope of collection: Letters to and from Upton are located in various collections.
Harriet (Taylor) Upton. Papers. 1893–1916. Extent of collection: 1 folder. Finding aids: Published guide. Location: Western Reserve Historical Society, 10825 E Blvd., Cleveland, Ohio 44106-1788. Scope of collection: Correspondence, telegrams, broadsides and other documents.
Harriet Taylor Upton. Papers. 1908. Extent of collection: 1 folder. Finding aids: Unpublished finding aid. Location: Schlesinger Library, Radcliffe College, Cambridge, Massachusetts 02138. Scope of collection: Draft (4 pages) of biographical sketch of Susan B. Anthony, edited by Upton, and letter to publisher of sketch. Also mimeograph copy of *Random Recollections,* her 1927 typewritten autobiography (photocopy available in various libraries).
Samuel Milton Jones. Papers. 1897–1904. Extent of collection: 15 ft. Finding aids: Published guide. Location: Toledo-Lucas County Public Library, 325 Michigan

St., Toledo, Ohio 43624-1614. Scope of collection: Correspondence with local and state suffrage leaders, among them Upton. Microfilm avilable.

Vadae Gwendolyne Meekison. Papers. 1903–1965. Extent of collection: ca. 85 items. Finding aids: Finding aid in repository. Location: Bowling Green State University Library, Center for Archival Collections, Bowling Green, Ohio 43403-0170. Scope of collection: Letters (1912–1916) to Meekison from Upton dealing chiefly with campaign for women's suffrage.

Woman's Rights Collection. Papers. 1897–1925. Extent of collection: 2 folders. Finding aids: Published and unpublished guides. Location: Schlesinger Library, Radcliffe College, Cambridge, Massachusetts 02138. Scope of collection: Correspondence, memorabilia and articles regarding speeches of Upton. Microfilm available.

64. Lillian D. Wald
(1867–1940)

Founder of Henry Street Settlement and
Visiting Nurse Service; public health nurse;
and advocate for child welfare, peace and women's suffrage

BIOGRAPHICAL INFORMATION

Chronological Biography

Born March 10, 1867, in Cincinnati, Ohio, third of four children to Minnie (Schwartz) and Max (Marcus) D. Wald, prosperous businessman in optical goods. "D" in father's name is simply an initial, as it is in her name. Moved to Dayton, Ohio, and eventually to Rochester, New York. Grew up and was educated in Miss Cruttenden's English-French Boarding and Day School for Young Ladies and Little Girls.

1883: Graduated at 16 from Miss Cruttenden's and applied for admission to Vassar; rejected on grounds she was too young.   **1883–1889:** Led active social life, travelled and worked briefly as newspaper correspondent. **August 1889:** At 23, wishing to secure "serious, useful employment," entered Hospital Training School for Nurses in New York City, against parents' wishes.   **March 31, 1891:** Graduated from Hospital Training School. Spent unsatisfactory year at New York Juvenile Asylum.   **1892:** Enrolled at Women's Medical College of New York Infirmary.   **March 1893:** Went to the aid of a sick woman at the urgings of the woman's daughter. Shocked by squalid conditions she found in tenement, quit medical school and began to work in community as public health nurse. Moved to East Side where she and friend Mary Brewster lived and set up office, offering nursing services to community in College Settlement, social settlement house that had been founded in 1891 on Rivington Street. **Fall 1893:** Along with Mary Brewster, moved to top floor of tenement on Jefferson Street and founded Henry Street Settlement and Visiting Nurse Service of New York. **1893:** Organized home nursing classes for lower East Side immigrant families. **1895:** Enlisted financial support of Mrs. Solomon Loeb and her son-in-law, banker Jacob H. Schiff, to establish Nurse's Settlement, later called Henry Street Settlement, at 265 Henry Street. **1896:** Settlement had 11 residents, including nine trained nurses, one of whom was Lavinia Dock. **1899:** Assisted in starting public health lecture series at Teacher's College, Columbia University. **1902:** Arranged to have Henry Street nurses provide nursing services in public school, leading New York City Board of Health to organize world's first public school nursing system. First playground in United States opened in back of Henry Street Settlement. **1903:** Founded and became executive council member of Women's Trade Union League. Henry Street Settlement's tenth anniversary. In 1903, nursing service included 18 centers providing 35,035 home visits, 3,524 convalescent visits and 28,869 first aid treatments. **1904:** Along with Florence Kelley, founded National Child Labor League to limit child labor. **1906:** Served on Mayor's Pushcart Commission of New York City. Founded Vocational Guidance Committee at Henry Street. **1908–1910:** Member of New York State Commission on Aliens. **1909:** Following her suggestion, Metropolitan Life Insurance established nursing service for industrial policy holders. On January 27 and February 1, as head worker of New York City Nurse's Settlement and as trustee of National Child Labor Committee, testified before House Committee on Expenditures for establishment of Children's Bureau in Interior Department. Held National Negro Conference at Henry Street. **1910:** Helped to establish Department of Nursing and Health at Columbia University. Made six-month round-the-world tour visiting China, Japan and Russia. Trip was covered by *New York Times* in front page story. **May 12, 1911:** Testified as head nurse of Henry Street before House Committee on Labor concerning Children's Bureau. **1912:** American Red Cross began rural public health nursing service called Town and Country Nursing Service at her instigation. One of founders and president of National Organization for Public Health Nursing. Supported passage of act creating Federal Children's Bureau. Criticized President Woodrow Wilson for not supporting plank on women's suffrage in Democratic party's platform. Member of Progressive party. Received honorary doctor of laws from Mt. Holyoke College and gold medal from National Institute for Social Sciences. **1913:** Twentieth anniversary of Henry Street Settlement. Settlement had staff of 92 nurses who made 200,000 visits yearly, providing home care, convalescent visits and first aid treatment. Settlement occupied seven houses on Henry Street and had two uptown branches. It was center for civic, educational and philanthropic work in community. **1914:** With Florence Kelley and Jane Addams, founded American Union Against Militarism (AUAM). **1915:** Wrote *House on Henry Street.* Served as first president of AUAM. Henry Street's Neighborhood Playhouse opened. **1916:** In January through February, as chair of Antipreparedness Committee, testified before House Committee on Military Affairs at hearing on increasing military establishment of United States. Also testified before Senate Committee on Military Affairs. On May 8th, led AUAM Peace Delegation with Rabbi Stephen S. Wise of Free Synagogue, Irene Lewisohn, Crystal Eastman and the Reverend John Haynes Holmes to meet with President Wilson. With Henry Street nurses, mounted campaign against polio epidemic in New York City. **1917:** Despite her antiwar sentiments, when United States entered World War I, contributed to war effort by serving as member of Committee on Nursing of General Medical Board of Council of National Defense and on Committee for Vassar (nurse) Training Camp in Poughkeepsie, NY. Also served as head of Committee on Home Nursing of Section on Sanitation of Council of National Defense. On April 14th, testified as chair of AUAM before House Committee on Military Affairs at hearing on Selective Services. AUAM split into Civil Liberties Bureau and Foreign Policy Council, which she cofounded. **1918:** During war, continued to work for peace by coordinating Red Cross drives and compiling more complete training course for visiting nurses. When influenza epidemic swept country, appointed chair of Nurses' Emergency Council, established to recruit nurses to aid in crisis. **1919:** Served as delegate to International Public Health Conference in Cannes, France. Attended Woman's Peace Party's Second International Conference of Women for Peace in Zurich. Appointed advisor to League of Nations Child Welfare Division in Paris. **1920:** Benefactor and mentor, Jacob Schiff, died. **1922:** Served on committee to free Nicola Sacco and Bartolomeo Vanzetti. **1923:** First woman awarded Rotary Club's gold medal in recognition of life-long service as sociologist, organizer and publicist. **1924:** Visited Soviet Union with Elizabeth Farrell to advise on public health nursing and education. **1925:** Travelled to Mexico with Jane Addams. Worked in presidential campaign of Alfred E. Smith. Began to suffer from heart trouble and anemia which continued to afflict her for rest of life. **1926:** Received *Better Times Magazine* medal for "distinguished social service." **1930:** Recipient of honorary doctorate from Smith College. Attended White House Conference on Health and Protection. **1932:** Worked in presidential campaign of Franklin D. Roosevelt. Underwent major surgery from which she never fully recovered. **1933:** Resigned from Henry Street Settlement; moved to "House on the Pond," her home in Westport, Connecticut. **1934:** Published *Windows on Henry Street.* Samuel Dickstein and Emmanuel Cellermade gave speeches praising her in House of

Representatives.   1936: Headed Good Neighbor League. Worked to bring independent voters into Democratic party. Received Lincoln Medallion as outstanding citizen of New York City.   1937: Honored by New York City on seventieth birthday. New York City playground named for her. Resigned as president of Henry Street Settlement and elected president emeritus. **September 1, 1940:** At age 73, died at home in Westport, Connecticut; had suffered cerebral hemorrhage several years earlier. Ashes were buried in family plot in Rochester, New York.   1971: Elected to Hall of Fame for Great Americans at New York University.   1976: Inducted as charter member of American Nurses' Association Hall of Fame in Washington, D.C..

Background Information

Parents: Minnie (Schwartz) and Max (Marcus) D. Wald. Schwartzes and Walds were descended from rabbis, merchants and professional men in Poland and Germany.   **Siblings:** Three (Older sister, Julia [Mrs. Charles P. Barry]; older brother, Alfred; younger brother, Gus).   **Children:** None.   **Influences:** Lavinia Dock; Jacob Schiff.   **Ethnicity:** Jewish American.   **Also known as:** None known.   **Historical sites, landmarks, etc.:** Bronze Bust, Hall of Fame for Great Americans, New York University, Washington Square, New York, New York; Henry Street Settlement, 263-267 Henry Street, New York, New York; Lillian D. Wald Playground, Monroe Street East of Montgomery Street, New York, New York; Plaque, American Nurses' Association Hall of Fame, Washington, D.C.

BIBLIOGRAPHICAL INFORMATION

Biographical Sketches About Lillian D. Wald

Bullough, Vern L., Olga Maranjian Church, and Alice P. Stein, eds. *American Nursing: A Biographical Dictionary*. New York: Garland, 1988.

James, Edward T., ed. *Notable American Women 1607–1950: A Biographical Dictionary*. Cambridge, MA: Belknap Press of Harvard University Press, 1971.

National League of Nursing Education. Publications Committee. *Early Leaders of American Nursing* (Calendar 1923). New York: National League of Nursing Education, 1922.

Roth, C., and Geoffrey Wigoder, eds. *Encyclopedia Judaica*. Jerusalem: Keter, 1970.

Starr, Harris E., ed. *Dictionary of American Biography*. New York: Charles Scribner & Sons, 1958.

Whitman, Alden, ed. *American Reformers: An H. W. Wilson Biographical Dictionary*. New York: H. W. Wilson Company, 1985.

Books by Lillian D. Wald

American Society of Superintendents Training School for Nurses: Annual Report. Baltimore, MD: American Society of Superintendents of Training Schools for Nurses, 1910.

Boarded-Out Babies. New York: Association of Neighborhood Workers of the City of New York, 1907.

House on Henry Street. New York: H. Holt & Co., 1915. Reprint. New Brunswick, NJ: Transaction Publishers, 1991.

Windows on Henry Street. Boston: Little, Brown & Co., 1934.

Books About Lillian D. Wald

Block, Irvin. *Neighbor to the World: The Story of Lillian Wald.* New York: Crowell, 1969.

Coss, Clare, ed. *Lillian Wald, Progressive Activist.* New York: Feminist Press at the City University of New York. Distributed by Talman Co., 1989.

Daniels, Doris. *Always a Sister: The Feminism of Lillian D. Wald.* New York: Feminist Press at the City University of New York. Distributed by Talman Co., 1989.

Duffus, Robert Luther. *Lillian D. Wald, Neighbor and Crusader.* New York: Macmillan, 1938.

Epstein, Beryl. *Lillian Wald, Angel of Henry Street.* New York: J. Messner, 1948.

Rogow, Sally. *Lillian Wald: The Nurse in Blue.* Philadelphia: Jewish Publication Society of America, 1966.

Siegel, Beatrice. *Lillian Wald of Henry Street.* New York: Macmillan, 1983.

Shorter Works by Lillian D. Wald

"Abraham Jacobi. 1830–1919." *Survey* 42 (July 19, 1919): 595.

Addams, Jane. *Forty Years at Hull House.* New York: Macmillan, 1935. (Afterward written by Wald.)

"Address at Mass Meeting in Favor of Disarmament. Armistice Day, New York." *International Conciliation Special Bulletin* (December 1931): 899–904.

"Amelia H. Grant." *Public Health Nurse* 20 (May 1928): 3.

"Best Helps to the Immigrant Through the Nurse." *American Journal of Nursing* 8 (March 1908): 464–67.

"Change Comes to the East Side." *Atlantic* (January 1934): 39–49.

"Child Labor." *American Journal of Nursing* 6 (March 1906): 366–69.

"Child Labor." *American Journal of Nursing* 7 (June 1907): 471–93.

"Development of Public Health Nursing in the United States." *Trained Nurse* 80 (June 1928): 689–92.

"District Nurse's Contribution to the Reduction of Infant Mortality." In *Prevention of Infant Mortality: Being the Papers and Discussion of a Conference*

Held at New Haven, CT, November 11–12, 1909. Easton, PA: American Academy of Medicine, 1909?

"Doctor and the Nurse in Industrial Establishments." *American Journal of Nursing* 12 (February 1912): 403–08.

"Doctor and the Nurse in Industrial Establishments." *Proceedings of the Academy of Political Science* 2 (January 1912): 93–98.

"Feeding of the School Children." *Charities and the Commons* 20 (June 13, 1908): 371–74.

"Fifty Years of Child Welfare." *Survey* 50 (May 1, 1923): 181–83.

"Forty Years of Service to the Sick and Poor." *American Journal of Nursing* 33 (April 1933): 326.

"Forty Years on Henry Street." *Survey* 69 (May 1933): 192.

"Helping the Workers." *Outlook and Independent* 156 (September 24, 1930): 158.

"Henry Street Settlement, New York." *Charities and the Commons* 16 (April 7, 1906): 35–41.

"Honor Where Due." *Commonweal* 15 (February 10, 1932): 396.

"House on Henry Street." *Atlantic* (March 1915): 289–300; (April 1915): 464–73; (May 1915): 649–62; (June 1915): 806–17; (July 1915): 69–83; (August 1915): 240–50.

"Influenza." *Survey* 43 (February 14, 1920): 579–81.

"International Reconciliation." In *Proceedings of Public Mass Meeting in New York City and Washington, D. C. Armistice Day, November 11, 1931, to Prepare for the Disarmament Conference to be Held in Geneva, February, 1932.* New York: Carnegie Endowment, 1931.

"Internationalism in Nursing." *American Journal of Nursing* 25 (October 1925): 866–68.

"Jacob H. Schiff." *Survey* 45 (October 2, 1920): 4.

"Lean Years." *Atlantic* (December 1933): 650–59.

"Medical Inspection of Public Schools." *Annals of the American Academy of Political and Social Science* 25 (March 1905): 290–98.

"Need for a Federal Children's Bureau." *Annals of the American Academy of Political and Social Science* 33 Supplement (March 1909): 23–28.

"Nurse and the Community." *Survey* 30 (July 19, 1913): 516–17.

"Nurses' Settlement." In *Third International Congress of Nurses, Buffalo, NY, September 18–21, 1901.* Cleveland: J. B. Savage, 1901.

"Nurses' Settlement." *American Journal of Nursing* 2 (May 1902): 567–75.

"Nurses' Settlement." *British Journal of Nursing* 29 (August 1902): 135–38.

"Nurses' Social Settlement." *American Journal of Nursing* (June 1901): 682–84.

"Nurses' Social Settlement." *Nursing Record* 26 (January 26, 1901): 69.

"Nursing." *Survey* 31 (December 27, 1913): 355–56.

"Organization Amongst Working Women." *Annals of the American Academy of Political and Social Science* 27 (May 1906): 638–45.

"Our First Birthday Greeting." *Public Health Nursing* 29 (June 1937): 344–46.

"Past, Present, and Future of Nursing." *American Journal of Nursing* 31 (December 1931): 1392–94.

"People Who Have Crossed Our Threshold." *Atlantic* (March 1934): 326–37.

"Prohibition and the Four Million." *Forum* 90 (November 1933): 259–64.

"Public Health in Soviet Russia." *Survey* 53 (December 1, 1924): 270–74.
"Put Responsibility on the Right Shoulders." *Survey* 25 (November 26, 1910): 315–16.
"Red Cross and the Covenant." *Survey* 42 (May–July 1919): 595.
Report for the Years 1928 and 1929 of the Visiting Nurse Service Administered by Henry Street Settlement. New York: Edgar C. Ruwe Co., 1929. (Preface was written by Wald.)
"Report of the Joint Committee Appointed for Consideration of the Standardization of Visiting Nursing." *American Journal of Nursing* 12 (August 1912): 894–98.
"Right Woman in the Right Place." *American City* 6 (June 1912): 847.
"Russia, From Henry Street." *Survey Graphic* 22 (November 1933): 555–57.
"S. Josephine Baker, M.D." *Survey* 48 (April 22, 1922): 108.
"Sanitary Control of an Industry by the Industry Itself." *Public Health Nurse Quarterly* 5 (April 1913): 13–21.
"Shall We Dismember the Child?" *Survey* 63 (January 15, 1930): 458.
"Social Worker's Viewpoint." *Opinion* 6 (October 1930): 16–17.
"Sophiahemmet in Stockholm." *American Journal of Nursing* 1 (December 1900): 180–82.
"State Immigration Bureau." *Survey* 28 (May 25, 1912): 347–49.
Thoms, Adah B. *Pathfinders: A History of the Progress of Colored Graduate Nurses.* New York: Kay Printing House, 1929. Reprint. New York: Garland, 1985. (Preface was written by Wald.)
"Treatment of Families in Which There Is Sickness." *American Journal of Nursing* 4 (March 1904): 427–31; (April 1904): 515–19; (May 1904): 602–06.
"Twentieth Anniversary of the Federal Children's Bureau." *National Conference of Social Work* (1932): 33–40.
"Vocational Scholarships." *Child Labor Bulletin* 5 (May 1916): 7–8.
Wald, Lillian D., and Frances Alice Kellor. "Construction Camps of the People." *Survey* 23 (January 1, 1910): 449–65.
————, and Henry Moscowitz. "Taking Stock in New York's Factories." *Survey* 27 (March 16, 1912): 1928–29.
Wales, Marguerite. *Public Health Nurse in Action.* New York: Macmillan, 1941. (Introduction written by Wald.)
"What Keeps the Nurses Going?" *Survey* 68 (November 15, 1932): 590–91.

Shorter Works About Lillian D. Wald

Alger, George W. "Lillian D. Wald: The Memories of an Old Friend." *Survey Graphic* 29 (October 1940): 512–14.
Amidon, B. "Crusaders." *New Republic* 97 (December 7, 1938): 152–53.
"Angel of Tenements." *Literary Digest* 121 (February 1, 1936): 34.
"Angel of the Tenements." *Scholastic* 28 (February 1, 1936): 23.
Beatty, Jerome. "She Never Gave Up." *Forum and Century* 96 (August 1936): 70–73.
Bondfield, Margaret. "Neighbors." *Survey* 52 (September 1924): 587–88.

Brandt, J. A. "Nursing Stands Taller Because of Lillian D. Wald (1867–1940)." *Chart* 68 (November 1971): 293–95.

Buhler, Wilkerson K. "Lillian Wald: Public Health Pioneer." *Nursing Research* 40 (September–October 1991): 316–17.

Christy, T. E. "Portrait of a Leader: Lillian D. Wald." *Nursing Outlook* 18 (March 1970): 50–54.

Cook, Blanche Wiesen. "Female Support Networks and Political Activism: Lillian Wald, Crystal Eastman, Emma Goldman." In *A Heritage of Her Own: Toward a New Social History of American Women*, edited by Nancy F. Cott and Elizabeth H. Pleck. New York: Simon & Schuster, 1979.

_____. "Female Support Networks and Political Activism: Lillian Wald, Crystal Eastman, Emma Goldman." In *Women's America: Refocusing the Past*, edited by Linda Kerber and Jane DeHart-Matthews. New York: Oxford University Press, 1987.

Daniels, Doris. "Building a Winning Coalition: The Suffrage Fight in New York State." *New York History* 60 (1979): 59–80.

Eiseman, Alberta. *Rebels and Reformers: Biographies of Four Jewish Americans.* Garden City, NY: Zenith, 1976.

Erickson, G. P. "Public Health Nursing Initiatives: Guideposts for Future Practice." *Public Health Nursing* 4 (December 1987): 202–11.

"Forty Years on Henry Street." *Survey* 69 (May 1933): 192.

Frachel, R. R. "A New Profession: The Evolution of Public Health Nursing." *Public Health Nursing* 5 (June 1988): 86–90.

Gillis, Adolph, and Roland Ketchum, eds. *Our America.* Boston: Little, Brown, 1936.

"Giving." *American Mercury* (January 1938): 61.

Handlin, Oscar, ed. *This Was America: True Accounts of People and Places, Manners and Customs...* Cambridge, MA: Harvard University Press, 1949. Reissued with a new preface. Cambridge, MA: Harvard University Press, 1969.

Hanson, C. M., and E. Hilde. "Faculty Mentorship: Support for Nurse Practitioner Students and Staff Within the Rural Community Health Setting." *Journal of Community Health Nursing* 6 (1989): 73–81.

Hill, R. W. "Papers of Lillian D. Wald." *Social Service Review* 36 (December 1962): 462–63.

Howe, Irving. *World of Our Fathers.* New York: Harcourt Brace Jovanovich, 1976.

Hunting, H. B. "Lillian Wald – Crusading Nurse." In *Distinguished American Jews*, edited by Philip H. Lotz. New York: Association Press, 1945.

Johnson, James. "The Role of Women in the Founding of the United States Children's Bureau." In *Remember the Ladies: New Perspectives in American History*, edited by Carol V. R. George. Syracuse, NY: Syracuse University Press, 1975.

Kellogg, P. U. "Settler and Trail Blazer." *Survey* 57 (May 15, 1927): 777–80.

_____. "What About This Miss Wald?" *Survey* 63 (November 1, 1929): 182–83.

Kelly, D. N. "A Nurse in the Hall of Fame." *Supervisor-Nurse* 2 (November 1971): 9–11.

Lagemann, E. C. *A Generation of Women.* Cambridge, MA: Harvard University Press, 1979.

"Lillian D. Wald: A Great Neighbor." *Survey Graphic* 26 (April 1937): 223.

"Miss Wald and Henry Street Settlement Have Birthdays." *American Journal of Public Health* 23 (May 1933): 521–22.

Mottus, Jane E. *New York Nightingales.* Ann Arbor, MI: UMI Research Press, 1981.

Nutting, M. Adelaide, and Lavinia L. Dock. *A History of Nursing.* New York: G. P. Putnam's Sons, 1912.

"Our First Public Health Nurse." *Nursing Outlook* 19 (October 1971): 659–60.

"Pioneer of the City's Frontier." *Public Health Nurse* 20 (January 1928): 3.

Popiel, E. S. "Lillian Wald, Community Nurse. Try to Remember Our Heritage." *Colorado Nurse* 68 (January 1968): 3–5.

Reynolds, Moira Davison. *Women Champions of Human Rights: Eleven U.S. Leaders of the Twentieth Century.* Jefferson, NC: McFarland, 1991.

Riis, Jacob A. "Real Story of Miss Wald." *Survey* 30 (July 26, 1913): 551–52.

Roberts, Mary M. *American Nursing.* New York: Macmillan, 1954.

Robinson, Victor. *White Caps.* Philadelphia: Lippincott, 1946.

Rosenberg, J. A. "Child Health Nurses — Caring for Our Nation's Youth. The Origin of School Nursing in the U.S.: A Reflection of the Past Helps the Future." *Florida Nurse* 36 (November–December 1988): 10.

Schutt, G. B. "A Prophet Honored: Lillian D. Wald." *American Journal of Nursing* 17 (January 1971): 53.

Siegel, Beatrice. "Family of Nurses Fight for Justice — Lillian Wald and Henry Street Settlement." *New Directions for Women* 12 (March–April 1983): 13.

Silverstein, N. G. "Lillian Wald at Henry Street, 1893–1895." *ANS* 7 (January 1985): 1–12.

Smith, Helena Huntington. "Rampant But Respectable." *New Yorker* (December 14, 1929): 32.

Stillman, C. G. "Portrait of Lillian Wald." *Nation* (November 26, 1938): 569–70.

Wagenknecht, Edward. *Daughters of the Covenant.* Amherst: University of Massachusetts Press, 1983.

Wallace, E. "Three Pioneer Women." *Outlook* 112 (February 9, 1916): 346–47.

Waters, Y. *Visiting Nursing in the United States.* New York: William F. Fell, 1909.

Weinstein, Gregory. *Reminiscences of An Interesting Decade.* New York: International Press, 1928.

Wintz, L. "Career Paths of Nurses: When Is a Nurse No Longer a Nurse?" *Journal of Nursing Administration* 17 (April 1987): 33–37.

Woods, Robert A., and Albert J. Kennedy, eds. *Handbook of Settlements.* New York: Charities Publications Committee, 1911.

_____, and _____. *The Settlement Horizon.* New York: Russell Sage Foundation, 1922. Reprint. New Brunswick, NJ: Transaction, 1990.

Woolf, B. J. "Miss Wald at 70 Sees Her Dreams Realized." *New York Times Magazine* (March 7, 1937): 9.

Yost, Edna. *American Women of Nursing.* Philadelphia: Lippincott, 1947. Revised Edition. Philadelphia: Lippincott, 1965.

Young, M. R. "Inspiration." *Public Health Nursing* 25 (December 1933): 639–41.

Other Works About Lillian D. Wald

Play

"Lillian Wald: At Home on Henry Street." In *Lillian D. Wald: Progressive Activist*, edited by Clare Coss. New York: Feminist Press at the City University of New York, 1989.

Theses

Fastenau, Maureen Karen. "Maternal Government: The Social Settlement Houses and the Politicization of Women's Sphere, 1889–1920." Ph.D. diss., Duke University, 1982.

Gannon, Joseph Anthony. "Lillian Wald: A Study of Education at the Henry Street Settlement Based on Her Writings and Papers." Ph.D. diss., Fordham University School of Education, 1979.

Kersten, Evelyn Smith. "Industrial Nursing from 1895 to 1942: Development of a Specialty." Ed.D. diss., Columbia University Teacher's College, 1984.

Reznick, Allen E. "Lillian D. Wald: The Years at Henry Street." Ph.D. diss., University of Wisconsin, 1973.

Williams, Katherine Roulston. "Major Trends in Public Health Nursing 1902 to 1925: The Transition from Specialized to Generalized Practice." Ed.D. diss., Columbia University Teacher's College, 1981.

Primary Source Materials Relating to Lillian D. Wald

American Journal of Nursing Company, Inc. ca. 1900–1960s. Extent of collection: 47 boxes and 18 vols. Finding aids: Not listed. Location: Boston University, Mugar Memorial Library, Special Collections, History of Nursing, 771 Commonwealth Avenue, Boston, Massachusetts 02215. Scope of collection: Includes manuscripts and papers for corporation as well as biographical history and manuscripts of Wald.

Archives of the Department of Nursing Education. 1899–ca. 1965. Extent of collection: 145 ft. Finding aids: Published guide. Location: Columbia University Teacher's College Library, Adelaide Nutting History of Nursing Collection, 525 W. 120 St., New York, New York 10027. Scope of collection: Includes papers of department and Adelaide Nutting as well as clippings and correspondence pertaining to Wald.

Cornell University. New York Hospital School of Nursing. 1877–? Extent of collection: 160 ft. Finding aids: Published guide. Location: New York Hospital, Cornell Medical Center, 1300 York Avenue, New York, New York 10021. Scope of collection: Includes student records of Wald.

Jane Addams. Papers. 1838–1959. Extent of collection: 59 ft. Finding aids: Catalog of correspondence and checklist in library. Also published guide. Location: Friends Historical Library of Swarthmore College, Peace Collection, Swarthmore College, Swarthmore, Pennsylvania 19081. Scope of collection: Addams was social welfare activist and longstanding friend and colleague of Wald, who is listed as "important to the collection" of these papers.

Lillian D. Wald. Papers. Extent of collection: ca. 30,000 items. Finding aids: Not

listed. Location: Columbia University Libraries, Rare Book and Manuscript Library, 801 Butler Library, 535 West 114 Street, New York, New York 10027. Scope of collection: Papers concerning establishment and administration of Henry Street Settlement and other social causes in which Wald was involved.
Lillian D. Wald. Papers. ca. 1918–1940. Extent of collection: 60 items. Finding aids: Not listed. Location: Rare Book and Manuscripts Division, New York Public Library, Astor, Lenox, and Tilden Foundations, Fifth Avenue at 42nd Street, New York, New York 10018. Scope of collection: Correspondence sent to Wald as well as correspondence and other papers relating to Henry Street Visiting Nurse Society.
Social Welfare History Archives. Extent of collection: 10,134 books, 4,213 lin. ft. Finding aids: Published guide. Location: University of Minnesota, 101 Walter Library, 117 Pleasant St. SE, Minneapolis, Minnesota 55455. Scope of collection: Contains papers of many organizations and persons with whom Wald was closely associated.

(THE ABOVE ENTRY WAS CONTRIBUTED BY DOROTHY S. TAO)

65. *Ida Bell Wells-Barnett*
(1862–1931)
Journalist; lecturer; advocate for
African American rights; and antilynching crusader

BIOGRAPHICAL INFORMATION

Chronological Biography

Born a slave July 16, 1862, in Holly Springs, Mississippi, eldest of eight children of slave parents Elizabeth Bell (Warrenton) and James Wells.
1878–1883: Parents and youngest sibling died in yellow fever epidemic. At 14, secured teaching job in rural school to help support five brothers and sisters. **1883–1884:** Moved to Memphis, Tennessee; taught at first in nearby school and then in city's black schools. Attended Fisk University and Lemoyne Institute. Ordered by railroad conductor to move to car reserved for colored passengers; refused and was forcibly removed. Sued railroad and won. **1887:** Tennessee supreme court reversed 1884 circuit court decision and ruled against her. **1889:** Became reporter for, and bought one-third interest in, *Memphis Free Speech and Headlight*, small Memphis weekly. Elected secretary of National Colored Press Association. **1891:** Dismissed from teaching job for writing articles critical of education given to black children. **1892:** Became half owner of *Memphis Free Speech*. **March 9, 1892:**

After three black male friends were lynched by mob, began editorial antilynching campaign that lead to sacking of newspaper's office during her absence on May 27, 1892. **1892:** Moved to New York City on May 26th and became staff writer for *New York Age.* Founded Women's Loyal Union, antilynching society, in New York. **1893:** Moved to Chicago. Organized Ida B. Wells Women's Club, first black women's civic club in Chicago. **1893 and 1894:** Invited to speak in Great Britain; helped found antilynching and antisegregation society there. Conducted antilynching speaking tours in U.S. as well. **June 27, 1895:** Married Ferdinand Lee Barnett, black lawyer, journalist and editor of *Chicago Conservator,* first black newspaper in Illinois. Became editor, publisher and business manager of paper. **1895:** Published *A Red Record,* statistical account of lynchings for years 1892 to 1894 and history of lynching since Emancipation thirty years before. **1896:** Son, Charles, born. **1897:** Son, Herman, born. **1898:** Led delegation to see President William McKinley to protest lynchings. **1898–1902:** Served as secretary of National Afro-American Council, forerunner of National Association for the Advancement of Colored People (NAACP). **1901:** Daughter, Ida, born. **1904:** Daughter, Alfreda, born. **1906 and 1909:** Took part in meetings of Niagara Movement, militant group whose purpose was to provide forum for discussion of racial topics and to agitate for change. **1908?:** Founded and became first president of Negro Fellowship League, settlement house and community center for southern migrants in Chicago. **1910:** Gave antilynching address as principal speaker at National Negro Conference at which NAACP was formed. **1913:** Founded Alpha Suffrage Club, first black women's suffrage group, organized on January 13th. Marched in suffrage parade on March 3rd in Washington, D. C., on eve of Woodrow Wilson's first inaugural. **1913–1916:** Served as adult probation officer for Chicago municipal court, first woman to hold job in that city. **January 3, 1915:** Elected vice president of Chicago Branch of National Independent Equal Rights League. **June 1916:** Led Alpha Suffrage Club of Chicago in famous Chicago suffrage parade to Republican National Convention. **1918:** Denied passport to go to Versailles Peace Conference. **1918?–1927:** Went to East St. Louis and Arkansas to investigate reports of antiblack riots. Faced Chicago race riot. Lectured, presided at meetings and protested discrimination nationally and locally. **1920:** Negro Fellowship League closed due to lack of money. **1928:** Began to write autobiography, *Crusade for Justice.* **1929–1930:** Onset of depression turned her concern to unemployment in Chicago's black ghetto. **1930:** Ran as Republican candidate for Illinois state senate against two men; came in third. **March 25, 1931:** Died of uremia in Chicago hospital at age of 68; buried in Oakwood Cemetery. **1940:** Ida B. Wells housing project in Chicago dedicated in commemoration. **1950:** Named by Chicago one of 25 outstanding women in history of city. **July 16, 1987:** Historical marker dedicated by Memphis

Community Relations Commission at former site of *Free Speech* offices. 1990: United States Postal Service issued stamp in her honor during Black History Month.

Background Information

Parents: Elizabeth Bell (Warrenton) and James Wells. Mother had been sold by slave trader and was purchased by Bolling family before Civil War. Father grew up on plantation in nearby Tippah County and was son of his master and slave woman named Peggy. **Siblings:** Seven (Known names: Eugenia, James, George, Annie and Lily). **Children:** Four (Charles, Herman, Ida, Alfreda). **Influences:** Ferdinand Lee Barnett. **Ethnicity:** African American. **Also known as:** Wells; Iola. **Historical sites, landmarks, etc.:** Gravesite, Oakwood Cemetery, Chicago, Illinois; Historical Marker at former site of *Free Speech* offices, Memphis, Tennessee; Ida B. Wells Housing Project, Chicago, Illinois; U.S. Postage Stamp.

BIBLIOGRAPHICAL INFORMATION

Biographical Sketches About Ida Bell Wells-Barnett

Belford, Barbara. *Brilliant Bylines: A Biographical Anthology of Notable Newspaperwomen in America.* New York: Columbia University Press, 1986.

James, Edward T., ed. *Notable American Women 1607–1950: A Biographical Dictionary.* Cambridge, MA: Belknap Press of Harvard University Press, 1971.

Logan, Rayford W., and Michael R. Winston, eds. *Dictionary of American Negro Biography.* New York: W. W. Norton, 1982.

McHenry, Robert, ed. *Famous American Women: A Biographical Dictionary from Colonial Times to the Present.* Mineola, NY: Dover, 1983.

Smith, Jessie Carney, ed. *Notable Black American Women.* Detroit: Gale Research, 1992.

Toppin, Edgar A. *A Biographical History of Blacks in America Since 1528.* New York: David McKay, [1971]. (Listed as Wells, Ida B.)

Whitman, Alden, ed. *American Reformers: An H. W. Wilson Biographical Dictionary.* New York: H. W. Wilson Company, 1985.

Books by Ida Bell Wells-Barnett

Addams, Jane, and Ida B. Wells. *Lynching and Rape: An Exchange of Views.* Edited and with an introduction by Bettina Aptheker. New York: American Institute for Marxist Studies, 1979.

The Arkansas Race Riot. Chicago: [Hume Job Print, 1920].
Crusade for Justice: The Autobiography of Ida B. Wells. Edited by Alfreda M.
Duster. Chicago: University of Chicago Press, [1970].
Mob Rule in New Orleans. Chicago: Wells-Barnett, 1900.
On Lynchings. Salem, NH: Ayer, 1987.
On Lynchings: Southern Horrors, A Red Record, Mob Rule in New Orleans. New
York: Arno, 1969.
*The Reason Why the Colored American Is Not in the World's Columbian Exposi-
tion: The Afro-American's Contribution to Columbian Literature.* Chicago:
Ida B. Wells, [1893].
*A Red Record: Tabulated Statistics and Alleged Causes of Lynchings in the United
States, 1892-1893-1894.* Chicago: Donohue & Henneberry, [1895].
Southern Horrors: Lynch Law in All Its Phases. New York: New York Age Print,
1892.

Books About Ida Bell Wells-Barnett

Thompson, Mildred I. *Ida B. Wells-Barnett: An Exploratory Study of An American
Black Woman, 1893-1930.* Brooklyn: Carlson, 1990.

Shorter Works About Ida Bell Wells-Barnett

Aptheker, Bettina. "The Suppression of the Free Speech: Ida B. Wells and the
Memphis Lynching, 1892." *San Jose Studies* 3 (November 1977): 34-40.
Burt, Olive W. *Black Women of Valor.* New York: J. Messner, [1974].
Campbell, Karlyn Kohrs. "Style and Content in the Rhetoric of Early Afro-
American Feminists." *Quarterly Journal of Speech* 72 (November 1986):
434-45.
Davidson, Sue. *Getting the Real Story: Nellie Bly and Ida B. Wells.* Seattle: Seal,
1982.
Giddings, P. "Woman Warrior." *Essence* 18 (February 1988): 75-76 +.
Gifford, Carolyn De Swarte. "Women in Social Reform Movements." In *Women
and Religion in America,* Vol. 1, edited by Rosemary Radford Ruether and
Rosemary Skinner Keller. San Francisco: Harper & Row, 1981.
Gozemba, Patricia A., and Marilyn L. Humphries. "Women in the Anti-Ku Klux
Klan Movement, 1865-1984." *Women's Studies International Forum* 12
(1989): 35-40.
"Great Women in Negro History." *Sepia* 7 (February 1959): 70.
Holt, T. C. "The Lonely Warrior: Ida B. Wells-Barnett and the Struggle for Black
Leadership." In *Black Leaders of the Twentieth Century,* edited by John H.
Franklin and August Meier. Champaign, IL: University of Illinois Press,
1982.
"Honoring Black Journalists: Exhibit of Portraits of 12 Black Journalists Goes on
National Tour." *Editor & Publisher* 120 (February 21, 1987): 20 +.
"In the Quiet, Undisputed Dignity of My Womanhood: Black Feminist Thought

After Emancipation." In *Reconstructing Womanhood,* by Hazel V. Carby. Oxford: Oxford University Press, 1987.

King, A. "Family Tree: Ida B. Wells Barnett: Crusading Journalist." *Essence* 7 (October 1976): 50.

Loewenberg, Bert James, and Ruth Bogin, eds. *Black Women in Nineteenth-Century American Life: Their Words, Their Thoughts, Their Feelings.* University Park: Pennsylvania State University Press, 1976.

Marable, Manning. "Groundings with My Sisters: Patriarchy and the Exploitation of Black Women." *Journal of Ethnic Studies* 11 (1983): 1–19.

Morris, Gloria C. *Two Black Women in Media: A Minority Within a Minority.* Paper presented at the Annual Meeting of the Association for Education in Journalism (60th, Madison, Wisconsin, August 21–24, 1977), 1977. [ED155694]

Peavy, Linda S., and Ursula Smith. *Women Who Changed Things.* New York: Scribner, 1983.

Rudwick, Elliott M., and August Meier. "Black Man in the 'White City': Negroes and the Columbian Exposition, 1893." *Phylon* 26 (Winter 1965): 354–61.

Sewell, George. "Ida B. Wells: Black, Female, Liberated, Militant Crusader." *Black Collegian* 6 (May–June 1976): 20 + .

Sterling, Dorothy. *Black Foremothers: Three Lives.* Old Westbury, NY: Feminist Press, 1979. Reprint. New York: Feminist Press, 1988.

————, ed. *We Are Your Sisters: Black Women in the 19th Century.* New York: W. W. Norton, 1984.

Townes, E. M. "Ida B. Wells-Barnett: An Afro-American Prophet." *Christian Century* 106 (March 15, 1989): 285–86.

Tucker, D. M. "Miss Ida B. Wells and Memphis Lynching." *Phylon* 32 (Summer 1971): 112–22.

Wolseley, Roland E. "Ida B. Wells-Barnett: Princess of the Black Press." *Encore American & Worldwide News* 5 (April 5, 1976): 2.

"Woman Suffrage and the Crusade Against Lynching, 1890–1920." In *Woman's Legacy: Essays on Race, Sex, and Class in American History,* by Bettina Aptheker. Amherst, MA: University of Massachusetts Press, 1982.

Other Works About Ida Bell Wells-Barnett

Theses

Braxton, Joanne Margaret. "Autobiography by Black American Women: A Tradition Within a Tradition." Ph.D. diss., Yale University, 1984.

Brown, Karen Fitzgerald. "The Black Press of Tennessee: 1865–1980." Ph.D. diss., University of Tennessee, 1982.

Cash, Floris Loretta Barnett. "Womanhood and Protest: The Club Movement Among Black Women, 1892–1922." Ph.D. diss., State University of New York at Stony Brook, 1986.

Holland, Endesha Ida Mae. "The Autobiography of a Parader Without a Permit (The South, African-American Women, Theater, Civil Rights Movement)." Ph.D. diss., University of Minnesota, 1986.

Hutton, Mary Magdelene Boone. "The Rhetoric of Ida B. Wells: The Genesis of the Anti-Lynch Movement." Ph.D. diss., Indiana University, 1975.

Thompson, Mildred I. "Ida B. Wells-Barnett: An Exploratory Study of an American Black Woman, 1893–1930." Ph.D. diss., George Washington University, 1979.

Media Materials About Ida Bell Wells-Barnett

Sound Recordings

Brannon, Jean Marilyn, ed. *The Negro Woman.* Folkways Records FH5523, 1966. 1 disc; 33 ⅓ rpm; mono; 12 in.

Primary Source Materials Relating to Ida Bell Wells-Barnett

Black Women Oral History Project. Interviews. 1976–1981 (inclusive). Extent of collection: 72 interview transcripts. Finding aids: Unpublished finding aid. Location: Schlesinger Library, Radcliffe College, Cambridge, Massachusetts 02138. Scope of collection: Tapes and transcripts of oral histories and supporting documentation. Audiotape available.

Jeannine Dobbs. Class Essays, 1977. Extent of collection: 2 folders. Finding aids: Unpublished finding aid. Location: Schlesinger Library, Radcliffe College, Cambridge, Massachusetts 02138. Scope of collection: Photocopies of class essays on notable American women including Wells-Barnett.

(THE ABOVE ENTRY WAS CONTRIBUTED BY AMY DIBARTOLO ROCKWELL)

66. *Margaret Bush Wilson*
(1919–)

Advocate for African American rights; lawyer; community leader; and former chair of NAACP National Board of Directors

BIOGRAPHICAL INFORMATION

Chronological Biography

Born January 30, 1919, in St. Louis, Missouri, to Margaret Berenice (Casey) and James Thomas Bush, Sr. One of three children in prominent, middle class family. Although located in drab ghetto area, family home was beautiful and gracious; parents had strong sense of family. Attended public schools. Parents very active in National Association for the Advancement of Colored People (NAACP). Mother served on executive committee of St. Louis NAACP in 1920s and 1930s. Father was longtime member of organization, first successful black real estate broker in city and founding president of Real Estate Brokers Association of St. Louis, which organized city's black realtors. Sister, Ermine, was NAACP "Baby of the Year" in 1924. Brother James, Jr., later became active member.

1935: Graduated with honors from Sumner High School. **1940:** Earned B.A. cum laude from Talladega College in Alabama, majoring in economics and mathematics. During senior year in college was Juliette Derricotte Fellow, travel study fellowship with trip around world. Returned to St. Louis; father preferred that she enter one of "female" professions such as nursing, teaching or social work, but she was determined not to do so. Decided to become lawyer as she felt legal efforts important way to fight racism. **1940–1943:** Attended Lincoln University School of Law in St. Louis. School had been founded in 1939 after U.S. Supreme Court ruled that state had to admit blacks to University of Missouri Law School or make equal facilities available. (Later merged with University of Missouri School of Law.) Graduated with LL.B.; admitted to Missouri bar same year. Acted as counsel for father's Brokers Association in obtaining its corporate charter. **1943–1945:** United States attorney with legal division of Rural Electrification Administration in U.S. Department of Agriculture. **March 19, 1944:** Married Robert E. Wilson, Jr., whom she had met while both were in law school. **1947:** Admitted to Illinois bar. **1947–1965:** Practiced law in St. Louis, specializing in real estate law, as partner in firm of Wilson & Wilson. **1948:** United States Supreme Court outlawed racially restrictive covenants in real estate contracts; father had been moving force behind landmark *Shelley vs. Kramer* case. Unsuccessfully ran on Progressive party ticket for U.S. House of Representatives. First black woman to run for Congress in Missouri. **1956:** Helped establish Job Opportunities Council of St. Louis NAACP branch and served as secretary; organization worked to persuade white businessmen to hire blacks. Participated in picketing, although her preferred method was to reason with people. Elected to executive committee of St. Louis branch of NAACP. **1958:** Became first woman president of 6,000 member St. Louis branch of NAACP. **Early 1960s:** Organized first state-wide conference of NAACP in Missouri. **1961–1962:** Served as an assistant attorney general of Missouri. **1962:** Travelled extensively throughout state as president of Missouri State Conference of NAACP Branches. **August 1963:** Participated in "March on Washington" organized by Martin Luther King, Jr. **1963:** Elected to NAACP National Board of Directors. Received Bishop's award of Episcopal diocese of Missouri. **1965–1967:** Implemented Johnson administration's antipoverty program while employed as legal services specialist with State Technical Assistance Office. **1966:** Admitted to bar of U.S. Supreme Court. **1967–1968:** Administrator of community services and continuing education programs of 1965 Higher Education Act for Missouri Department of Community Affairs. **1968:** Divorced from husband. **1968–1969:** Deputy director, acting director, and one of founders of St. Louis Model City Program Agency. As acting director, testified before Senate Special Committee on Aging regarding usefulness of model cities program to elderly. **1969–1972:** Assistant director of St. Louis Lawyers for Housing. **1971:** Taught civil procedure in St. Louis University School of Law through Council on Legal Education Opportunities Institute. **1971–1984:** Treasurer of NAACP National Housing Corporation. **1972:** As NAACP board member, participated in hearing that overturned Atlanta branch's compromise permitting schools to remain partially segregated; believed commitment to principle of integration and equal opportunity prohibited condoning plan for reasons of expediency. Resumed private law practice in St. Louis. **1972–1977:** Member of Missouri Council on Criminal Justice. **1973:** Elected chair of NAACP annual convention; served as chief parliamentarian during 1973 and 1974 conventions. **1974:** Chaired NAACP committee and participated in writing its statement which demanded impeachment of President Richard M. Nixon for his role in Watergate scandal. **January 13, 1975:** Elected first black woman to chair of 64 member NAACP National Board of Directors; other three candidates were male. Only other woman to chair board had been one of organization's founders in 1909, Mary White Ovington, white woman who had been chair from 1917 to 1932. Achieved national recognition, regularly appearing on television network interview shows and being quoted in press on issues of special interest to blacks. As highest officer of 440,000 member group, her goals for NAACP included modernizing operations, hiring more professionals, establishing groups to keep close watch on national issues of interest to black community and involving persons from all walks of life in organization's activities. She felt increasing participation of young people in organization to be primary goal (as many had been drawn to militant organizations) and that this could be accomplished by stressing relevance of NAACP to civil rights problems. **1975–1976:** Chair of St. Louis Land Reutilization Authority. **May 21, 1979:** As NAACP Board chair, testified at House hearings concerning economic sanctions against Rhodesia. **October 1979:** Presented paper at annual conference of National Association of College Admissions Counselors regarding inequality of educational opportunity. **January 1981:** Named to Gateway National Bank board of directors. Believed that economic issues should be of primary concern to blacks in 1980s, as she saw economic aspect of black life as unfinished agenda of civil rights. **May 1983–January 1984:** Suspended executive director, Benjamin L. Hooks, because he refused to turn over requested internal records that she wanted to support her assertion of his incompetent management of NAACP. Friction had existed between them for years and each had supporters and detractors.

Dispute ensued over her authority to take such action and much national attention resulted. She reinstated Hooks eight days later. Board asked her to resign, but she declined to do so. They stripped her of all powers except to chair meetings and she completed her term of office in December. She then ran for board membership but was not elected, possibly due to procedural irregularities.   **1984:** Elected chair of board of trustees of Mutual Real Estate Investment Trust of New York.   **1985:** Began working with Howard University Partnership Institute, funded by U.S. Housing and Urban Development Department (HUD). Served as chair of committee advising institute on project that aimed to provide technical assistance and support services to encourage more economic development in black community. Felt this was extension of what she had been trying to accomplish with NAACP, but NAACP did not move quickly enough.   **1985–1987:** Chair of Intergroup Corporation.   **October 1988:** Elected chair of board of trustees of Talladega College.   **Present:** Senior partner in law firm of Wilson & Associates in St. Louis. Recipient of many awards and member of numerous boards, commissions and organizations including Talladega College, Association of Episcopal Churches, Afro-American Company of Baltimore City, etc. Continues to work for full civil rights for blacks and other minorities.

Background Information

Parents: Margaret Berenice (Casey) and James Thomas Bush, Sr.   **Siblings:** Two (Ermine, James).   **Children:** One (Robert Edmund III).   **Influences:** None.   **Ethnicity:** African American.   **Also known as:** None known.   **Historical sites, landmarks, etc.:** None known.

BIBLIOGRAPHICAL INFORMATION

Biographical Sketches About Margaret Bush Wilson

Dains, Mary K., ed. *Show Me Missouri Women: Selected Biographies*. Kirksville, MO: Thomas Jefferson University Press, 1989.

Jackson, George F. *Black Women, Makers of History: A Portrait*. Oakland, CA: GRT Book Printing, 1985.

Moritz, Charles, ed. *Current Biography Yearbook*. New York: H. W. Wilson Company, 1975.

Ploski, Harry A., and James Williams, eds. *The Negro Almanac: A Reference Work on the African American*. Detroit: Gale Research, 1989.

Smith, Jessie Carney, ed. *Notable Black American Women*. Detroit: Gale Research, 1992.

Books by Margaret Bush Wilson

A New Challenge: The Disadvantaged. Chicago: Public Personnel Association, 1969.

Shorter Works by Margaret Bush Wilson

"American Judiciary in Historical Perspective." *Crisis* 89 (February 1982): 37–40.
"Black Voters Can Make a Difference." *Crisis* 89 (June–July 1982): 6.
"Building on a Legacy." *Crisis* 87 (October 1980): 287–88. ·
"Call to Arms." *Crisis* 89 (August–September 1982): 14–16.
"The Decision Is Not Yours." *Journal of the National Association of College Admissions Counselors* 24 (January 1980): 7–12.
"Dialogue on Energy." *Crisis* 87 (February 1980): 41–43.
"Energy Policy Development: Assessment of Impact and Future Implications. Symposium." *Howard Law Journal* 24 (1981): 197–99.
"Mission to Lead." *Crisis* 86 (October 1979): 334–37 +.
"NAACP Position on Rhodesian Sanctions." *Crisis* 86 (October 1979): 352–54.
"A New Birth of Liberty: The Role of Thurgood Marshall's Civil Rights and Contribution." *Black Law Journal* 6 (1978): 67–87.
"Promise and Peril." *Crisis* 87 (December 1980): 465–66.
"Real NAACP Stands Up—NAACP v. LDF." *Crisis* 89 (May 1982): 10–15.
"This, Too, Will Pass Away." *Crisis* 88 (August–September 1981): 334 +.
"Tribute to Emmitt J. Douglas." *Crisis* 88 (July 1981): 290.
Wilson, Margaret Bush, and Benjamin L. Hooks. "Statement by Margaret Bush Wilson and Benjamin L. Hooks Following Address by President Reagan to NAACP Convention June 29, 1981." *Crisis* 88 (August–September 1981): 349.

Shorter Works About Margaret Bush Wilson

"American Jewish Congress Honors Mrs. Wilson." *Crisis* 85 (October 1978): 284.
Coleman, Milton. "Buoyed by Victories, Beset by Feuding, NAACP Mulls Its Future." *Washington Post* (June 3, 1983): A3.
————. "NAACP Chairman Reinstates Hooks." *Washington Post* (May 27, 1983): A1.
————. "NAACP Chairman Tells of Dispute Over Audit." *Washington Post* (June 9, 1983): A2.
————. "NAACP Displaces Chairman: Board Repudiates Her Suspension of Hooks as Director." *Washington Post* (June 12, 1983): A1.

Current, Gloster B. "NAACP—Soul of '76." *Crisis* 83 (1976): 271–79.

————. "'Our New Day Begun'—The Transition Convention." *Crisis* 84 (October 1977): 387+.

Ebert, A. "The Woman I Thought I'd Be." *Essence* 6 (August 1975): 42+.

Gilliam, Dorothy. "Feminism." *Washington Post* (July 18, 1983): B1.

Hornblower, Margot. "Outgoing Chief Blasts NAACP Board: Dead Man's Election Keeps Her Off Panel." *Washington Post* (January 10, 1984): A2.

Horning, Jay. "Former Head of NAACP Now Tackles 'Unfinished Agenda'." *St. Petersburg Times* (July 21, 1985): 9A.

Hunter, Charlayne. "New N.A.A.C.P. Head." *New York Times* (January 14, 1975): 30.

"Leading Voices: Our Style of Protest." *Essence Magazine* 13 (October 1982): 78.

McGill, Douglas C. "N.A.A.C.P. Leader Says She's Unaware of Meeting." *New York Times* (May 25, 1983): 11.

Magnuson, Ed. "He Didn't Give Us Anything." *Time* 118 (July 13, 1981): 11.

"Margaret Bush Wilson: NAACP's New Head." *Crisis* 82 (March 1975): 80–82.

"Margaret Wilson Cries Foul in NAACP Board Vote." *Jet* 65 (January 23, 1984): 6.

May, Lee. "NAACP Board Actions 'Sexist,' Chairman Charges, Backs Jackson." *Los Angeles Times* (November 27, 1983): 24.

"NAACP Board Head Says 'Colored' Stays in Name." *Jet* 43 (April 3, 1975): 9.

"NAACP Board Scraps 'Sour Grapes' Charges Against Benjamin Hooks." *Jet* 64 (June 27, 1983): 8.

"NAACP Hits Reagan's Economic Emancipation as New Black Bondage." *Jet* 60 (July 16, 1981): 6.

"The NAACP: Hooks Is Back." *Newsweek* 101 (June 6, 1983): 37.

"New Board Chairman." *Crisis* 82 (March 1975): 77.

"New NAACP Chairman Is Study in Determination." *Jet* 47 (January 30, 1975): 48–49.

Penn, William H. "70th NAACP Annual Convention." *Crisis* 86 (October 1979): 323–28+.

"Power Play: Mutiny at the N.A.A.C.P." *Time* 121 (May 30, 1983): 22.

Prince, Richard E. "NAACP Adopts Resolutions on Veterans Benefits, Youth." *Washington Post* (July 4, 1975): A4.

"Reagan Hosts Key Black Republican 'Rap' Session." *Jet* 60 (July 23, 1981): 5.

"Reagan Woos Blacks in Capitol Hill Budget Row." *Jet* 60 (July 9, 1981): 50.

Reese, Michael, and D. Camper. "The NAACP Suspends Hooks." *Newsweek* 101 (May 30, 1983): 61.

Rule, Sheila. "Board of N.A.A.C.P. Decides to Strip Chairman of Powers." *New York Times* (June 12, 1983): 1.

————. "Ex–N.A.A.C.P. Official Threatens to Sue Board." *New York Times* (January 10, 1984): 9.

————. "N.A.A.C.P. Board Rebuffs Chairman in Her Battle with Hooks." *New York Times* (July 12, 1983): 9.

Shales, Tom. "New Struggles on the Long Journey; Margaret Wilson Breaks Her Silence on Women's Rights and the NAACP." *Washington Post* (November 28, 1983): C1.

"Suspends Benjamin Hooks as NAACP Executive Director." *Jet* 64 (June 6, 1983): 4.

White, Jack E. "'Twilight Zone' for the N.A.A.C.P." *Time* 120 (July 12, 1982): 16.

"Woman Lawyer Is Elected Chairman of NAACP Board." *Washington Post* (January 14, 1975): A3.
"Women at the Top: By Accepting Challenges and Sidestepping Obstacles, These Women Have Reached the Pinnacle of Their Careers." *Ebony* 37 (August 1982): 146.
"Women Power at the NAACP." *Ebony* 30 (April 1975): 88–90 + .

Media Materials by Margaret Bush Wilson

Sound Recordings

Conference of Blacks, Presidential Politics, and Public Policy, Howard University, 1979. Washington, D. C.: Department of Political Science, Howard University, 1979. Side 1 and 2 of tape cassette; 62 min.
[Margaret Bush Wilson, Speaking at a Joint Meeting of the Michigan Bicentennial Commission and the Michigan Civil Rights Commission, Traces the History of Civil Rights Legislation in America]. Broadcast on WKAR, East Lansing, May 27, 1976. Sound tape reel; 12 min.; 7.5 ips; mono; 7 in. ¼ in. tape.

Media Materials About Margaret Bush Wilson

Sound Recordings

[Margaret Bush Wilson Observes Black Press Week by Talking About the Black Press in America and About Roy Wilkins, Thomas Fortune, and W.E.B. DuBois]. Broadcast on NET (National Press Club), March 19, 1976. Sound tape reel; 7 min.; 7.5 ips; mono; 7 in. ¼ in. tape.
Conversations from Wingspread. *The NAACP.* Racine, WI: Johnson Foundation, 1977. Side 1 of tape cassette; 28 min., 15 sec.

Video Recordings

Black Perspective on the News, Series 8. Philadelphia: WHYY-TV, PBSV, 1975–76. Video; 29 min.; color.

67. Sarah Winnemucca
(1844?–1891)

Advocate for Native American rights; peacemaker; and educator

BIOGRAPHICAL INFORMATION

Chronological Biography

Second daughter, and fourth of nine children, of important Northern Paiute (also spelled Piute) leader, Winnemucca. Mother's name was Tuboitonie.

Born in Humboldt Sink area, now part of state of Nevada. At that time, only a few white trappers and explorers had yet arrived in area. Indian name was Thoc-me-tony (Tocmetone), "Shell-Flower." Occasionally called Sallie instead of Sarah.

1850–1860: Along with others, taken by grandfather to work on ranch in San Joaquin Valley in California. He had previously guided John C. Fremont across Sierra-Nevada mountain range and had been favorably impressed by white ways. Added Spanish and English to three Indian languages she knew. Returned to Nevada and spent year as companion to daughter of white stage coach company agent at Mormon trading post near Genoa. Adopted name of Sarah; somewhat accepted Christianity, but also retained Native American religious beliefs.   **1860:** Because dying grandfather wanted her to attend school, sent to St. Mary's Convent School in San Jose, California. Wealthy white parents of students objected to her presence and she was sent home after only three weeks, despite being excellent student. White settlers had entered area in increasing numbers and clashes became more frequent. Paiute War resulted in Native Americans being placed on reservation at Pyramid Lake, north of what is now the city of Reno. Native Americans exploited by corrupt agents and left starving and destitute.   **1865–1866:** Starving Native Americans stole cattle. Baby brother killed during raid on Native American camp by retaliating soldiers. Mother and sister also died during this period, intensifying her hatred of Native American agents.   **1866:** Went to live with brother, Natchez, at Pyramid Lake.   **1868:** Along with brother, very instrumental in negotiation of peace treaty with Oregon superintendent.   **1868?–1871:** Interpreter at Camp McDermitt in northeastern Nevada as many poverty-stricken Paiutes turned to army for food rations. Respected by settlers, army and Paiutes, worked to keep peace and help her people.   **1870:** Met with General John M. Schofield in San Francisco to protest treatment of her people. He was unable to help because he had no jurisdiction in area. Went to Gold Hill, Nevada, to speak with Senator John P. Jones but he would not intervene. Wrote to commissioner of Indian Affairs concerning problems between Native American agents and Paiutes; gave assurance that Paiutes would be law-abiding members of community if she could guarantee them permanent home on own land, no encroachment by whites and opportunty for education.   **1871:** Married Lt. Edward C. Bartlett; left him about year later due to his drunkenness. Married Paiute man sometime later, but left him due to abuse.   **1872–1876:** Paiutes sent to Malheur reservation in southeastern Oregon. Conditions somewhat improved due to Native American agent Samuel Parrish. Served as interpreter for Parrish from 1875 to 1876; also taught at agency school. Appointment of new agent, William Rinehart, renewed problems. Evicted from reservation by him after she reported his unfair treatment of Native Americans. Many Paiutes left and joined Bannocks tribe in Idaho who were ready to fight to protest their terrible treatment. **June 1878:** Offered to act as scout, interpreter and peacemaker for army when Bannock War began because she and many other Paiutes felt army (unlike agents) had treated them fairly and would continue to do so. Persuaded Paiutes not to fight during war. No Native American or white man would enter hostile area, so she volunteered to do so after learning that father, brother and others may have been forced by Bannocks to join with them. Alone, without sleep and little food or water, travelled over 100 miles in three days and two nights to locate Bannock camp. Managed to free or persuade father and companions to leave Bannocks and returned to army base with valuable information. Continued to serve as scout, guide and interpreter to General Oliver O. Howard. After war, Paitues, who had remained peaceful, sent on months-long winter trek to Yakima reservation in Washington, along with warring Bannocks. Men were given overcoats, women nothing. Many died in freezing weather; no provisions had been made at Yakima reservation for them where all 543 were forced to share one building. **1879:** Lectured in San Francisco, exposing injustices to Paiutes, moving many to tears with expressive oratory. Press supported her efforts with considerable coverage; some agents and their friends tried to discredit her with vicious remarks, calling her a liar and drunken prostitute, but she persevered. **January 1880:** Invited to come to Washington, D. C., at government expense, she, father and other tribe members met with President Rutherford B. Hayes and Secretary of Interior Carl Schurz. Schurz issued orders that Paiutes would be returned to Oregon and be given land, but Yakima agent would not act, fearing white settlers' retaliation. **1880:** Disheartened, wrote to Gen. Howard who asked her to come to Vancouver, Washington, to teach Native American children at army post he headed. **January 9, 1882?:** Married Lt. Lambert H. Hopkins. **Early 1880s:** Paiutes' land had not been returned and other injustices continued. Accompanied by husband, toured Massachusetts, Rhode Island, Connecticut, New York, Pennsylvania, Maryland and western Nevada, lecturing on behalf of Paiutes. Received warm welcome, helped by support of Gen. Howard and others. **1883:** *Life Among the Paiutes: Their Wrongs and Claims* published; only book at time written or controlled in any way by Native American (and one of few nineteenth-century histories). Book remains important primary source for information on Paiute/white relations. Sold book at lectures to help finance tour during which she obtained thousands of signatures on petition calling for government to honor its promises to Paiutes. **1883–1886 or 1885–1887:** Despite poor health, opened school financed by Boston friends at brother's ranch near Lovelock, Nevada, to bring education to Paiute children. School was partially sponsored by Elizabeth Palmer Peabody, noted pioneer in kindergarten education. Taught for three years. **1884:** Congress passed bill to return land, but Interior Secretary Henry M. Teller refused to act. **October 18, 1887:** Husband died of tuberculosis. Suffering from rheumatism and recurrent fevers, retired to sister's home in Monida, Montana. **1887:** Strongly supported Dawes Severalty Act, feeling that private ownership of homestead was necessary step in process of Native Americans' achievement of legal and cultural parity. **October 16, 1891:** Died at about age 47 from tuberculosis. Dedicated activist for Native American self-determination and equal rights, highly regarded for her heroic, although mostly unsuccessful, efforts on behalf of her people. Called the "most famous Indian woman of the Pacific Coast."

Background Information

Parents: Mother, Tuboitonie; father, Winnemucca. **Siblings:** Eight (Known names: Natchez, Lee, Tom, Elma and Mary). **Children:** None known. **Influences:** None. **Ethnicity:** Native American (Paviotso-Paiute). **Also known as:** Hopkins; Thoc-me-tony; Shell Flower. **Historical sites, landmarks, etc.:** Marker, Circle Drive Around Fort McDermitt Reservation, McDermitt, Nevada, Erected in 1971; first historical marker in Nevada honoring a woman.

BIBLIOGRAPHICAL INFORMATION

Biographical Sketches About Sarah Winnemucca

Dockstader, Frederick J. *Great North American Indians.* New York: Van Nostrand Reinhold, 1977.

Hodge, Frederick Webb, ed. *Handbook of American Indians North of Mexico.* Washington, D. C.: GPO, 1910.

James, Edward T., ed. *Notable American Women 1607–1950: A Biographical Dictionary.* Cambridge, MA: Belknap Press of Harvard University Press, 1971.

McHenry, Robert, ed. *Famous American Women.* New York: Dover, 1980.

Mainiero, Lina, ed. *American Women Writers.* New York: Frederick Ungar, 1980. (Listed as Sarah Winnemucca Hopkins.)

Malone, Dumas, ed. *Dictionary of American Biography.* New York: Charles Scribner's Sons, 1964.

Zophy, Angela Howard. *Handbook of American Women's History.* New York: Garland, 1990. (Listed as Hopkins, Sarah Winnemucca.)

Books by Sarah Winnemucca

Life Among the Piutes; Their Wrongs and Claims. Ed. by Mrs. Horace Mann, and Printed for the Author. Boston: For Sale by Cupples, Upham & Co., G. P. Putnam's Sons, New York, and By the Author, 1883.

Reproduction of Life Among the Piutes: Their Wrongs and Claims. Edited by Mrs. Horace Mann. With Preface by M. R. Harrington. Introduction by Russ and Anne Johnson. Bishop, CA: Printed and Distributed by Chalfant Press, [1969].

Books About Sarah Winnemucca

Canfield, Gae Whitney. *Sarah Winnemucca of the Northern Paiutes.* Norman: University of Oklahoma Press, 1983.

Gehm, Katherine. *Sarah Winnemucca: Most Extraordinary Woman of the Paiute Nation.* Phoenix: O'Sullivan Woodside, 1975.

Kloss, Doris. *Sarah Winnemucca.* Minneapolis: Dillon, 1981.

Morrison, Dorothy Nafus. *Chief Sarah: Sarah Winnemucca's Fight for Indian Rights.* New York: Atheneum, 1980. Reprint. Portland: Oregon Historical Society Press, 1990.

Morrow, Mary Frances. *Sarah Winnemucca.* Milwaukee: Raintree, 1990.

Peabody, Elizabeth Palmer. *The Piutes. Second Report of the Model School of Sarah Winnemucca, 1886–1887.* Cambridge, MA: John Wilson and Son, 1887.

_____. *Sarah Winnemucca's Practical Solution of the Indian Problem.* Cambridge, MA: John Wilson and Son, 1886.

Shorter Works by Sarah Winnemucca

"The Father Assumes All His Wife's Work." In *I Am the Fire of Time: The Voices of Native American Women,* edited by Jane B. Katz. New York: E. P. Dutton, 1977. (Written under the name of Sarah Winnemucca Hopkins.)

"In the Spirit-Land." In *I Am the Fire of Time: The Voices of Native American Women,* edited by Jane B. Katz. New York: E. P. Dutton, 1977. (Written under the name of Sarah Winnemucca Hopkins.)

Jackson, Helen Hunt. *A Century of Dishonor: A Sketch of the United States Government's Dealings with Some of the Indian Tribes.* New York: Harper & Bros., 1881. (Includes letter in appendix from Winnemucca to Major H. Douglas.)

"Life Among the Piutes; Their Wrongs and Claims." In *Let Them Speak for Themselves: Women in the American West, 1849–1900,* edited by Christiane Fischer. Hamden, CT: Archon Books, 1977. (Written under the name of Sarah Winnemucca Hopkins.)

"My People Teach Their Children." In *I Am the Fire of Time: The Voices of Native American Women,* edited by Jane B. Katz. New York: E. P. Dutton, 1977. (Written under the name of Sarah Winnemucca Hopkins.)

"My Poor People Died Off Very Fast." In *I Am the Fire of Time: The Voices of Native American Women,* edited by Jane B. Katz. New York: E. P. Dutton, 1977. (Written under the name of Sarah Winnemucca Hopkins.)

"The Pah-Utes." *Californian* 6 (1882): 252–56. (Written under the name of Sarah Winnemucca Hopkins.)

"We Do Not Want Any Other Home." In *I Am the Fire of Time: The Voices of Native American Women*, edited by Jane B. Katz. New York: E. P. Dutton, 1977. (Written under the name of Sarah Winnemucca Hopkins.)

"The Women Know as Much as the Men." In *I Am the Fire of Time: The Voices of Native American Women*, edited by Jane B. Katz. New York: E. P. Dutton, 1977. (Written under the name of Sarah Winnemucca Hopkins.)

Shorter Works About Sarah Winnemucca

Beck, Nicholas. "The Vanishing Californians: The Education of Indians in the Nineteenth Century." *Southern California Quarterly* 69 (1987): 33–50.

Brimlow, George F. "The Life of Sarah Winnemucca, the Formative Years." *Oregon Historical Quarterly* 53 (June 1952): 103 + .

————, ed. "Two Cavalrymen's Diaries of the Bannock War, 1878." *Oregon Historical Quarterly* 68 (1967): 221–58.

D'Azevedo, Warren L., ed. *Handbook of North American Indians*. Washington, D. C.: Smithsonian Institution, 1986.

Egan, Ferol. *Sand in a Whirlwind: The Paiute Indian War of 1860*. Garden City, NY: Doubleday, 1972. Reprint. Reno: University of Nevada Press, 1985.

Fowler, Catherine S. "Sarah Winnemucca Northern Paiute, 1844–1891." In *American Indian Intellectuals*, edited by Margot Liberty. St. Paul: West Publishing, 1978.

Geer, Emily Apt. "Lucy W. Hayes and the New Women of the 1880's." *Hayes Historical Journal* 3 (1980): 18–26.

Haine, J. J. F. "A Belgian in the Gold Rush: California Indians." *California Historical Society Quarterly* 38 (June 1959): 141–55.

Howard, Oliver Otis. *Famous Indian Chiefs I Have Known*. New York: Century Co., 1912. Reprint. Lincoln: University of Nebraska Press, 1989.

————. "Famous Indian Chiefs: Winnemucca, Chief of the Piutes." *St. Nicholas* 35 (July 1908): 815–22.

————. *My Life and Experiences Among Our Hostile Indians; A Record of Personal Observations, Adventures, and Campaigns Among the Indians of the Great West, with Some Account of Their Life, Habits, Traits, Religion, Ceremonies, Dress, Savage Instincts, and Customs in Peace and War*. Hartford: A. D. Worthington & Company, [1907]. Reprint. With a New Introduction. New York: Da Capo Press, 1972.

————. "Toc-me-to-ne, An Indian Princess." *St. Nicholas* 35 (July 1908): 818–20.

Lieser, Julia F. *Famous American Indians and Tribes*. Indianapolis: Saturday Evening Post, 1977.

Luchetti, Cathy Lee. *Women of the West*. St. George, UT: Antelope Island Press, 1982.

"The Preliterate Traditions at Work: White Bull, Two Leggings, and Sarah Winnemucca." In *American Indian Autobiography*, by H. David Brumble. Berkeley: University of California Press, 1988.

Richey, Elinor. *Eminent Women of the West*. Berkeley: Howell-North Books, 1975.

————. "Sagebrush Princess with a Cause: Sarah Winnemucca." *American West* 12 (November 1975): 30–33 + .

"Sarah Winnemucca: Army Scout." In *American Indian Women*, by Marion E. Gridley. New York: Hawthorn, 1975.

"Sarah Winnemucca: The Cinderella Princess." In *Red Man Calling on the Great White Father*, by Katherine Charlotte Turner. Norman: University of Oklahoma Press, [1951].

Scherer, Joanna Cohan. "The Public Faces of Sarah Winnemucca." *Cultural Anthropology* 3 (May 1988): 178–204.

Scholten, Pat Creech. "Exploitation of Ethos: Sarah Winnemucca and Bright Eyes on the Lecture Tour." *Western Journal of Speech Communication* 41 (February 1977): 233–44.

Stewart, Patricia. "Sarah Winnemucca." *Nevada Historical Society Quarterly* 14 (Winter 1971): 23–38.

Truman, Margaret. *Women of Courage*. New York: Morrow, 1976.

Wood, Charles Erskine Scott. "Princess Sarah." *St. Nicholas* 35 (July 1908): 820–22.

_____. "Private Journal, 1878." *Oregon Historical Quarterly* 70 (1969): 5–38.

Media Materials About Sarah Winnemucca
Sound Recordings

Sarah Winnemucca. Boulder: National Center for Audio Tapes, 1966. Audiotape; 15 min.; 3 ¾ ips; 1 track; mono.

Other Works About Sarah Winnemucca
Theses

Haupt, Carol Magdelene. "The Image of the American Indian Female in the Biographical Literature and Social Studies Textooks of the Elementary Schools." ED.D. diss., Rutgers the State University of New Jersey–New Brunswick, 1984.

Primary Source Materials Relating to Sarah Winnemucca

Betty Lougaris Soldo. Papers. 1974. Extent of collection: 95-page item. Finding aids: Not listed. Location: Nevada Historical Society, Museum Research Library, 1650 N. Virginia St., Reno, Nevada 89503-1799. Scope of collection: M.A. thesis written by Soldo.

Bureau of Indian Affairs. Records. Extent of collection: Not listed. Finding aids: Not listed. Location: National Archives and Records Administration, Seventh Street and Pennsylvania Avenue N.W., Washington, D. C. 20408. Scope of collection: Special File #286 is of particular importance for pertinent archival materials.

Peabody, Mann, and Hawthorne Families. Papers. 1790–1938. Extent of collection: 14 vols. Finding aids: Unpublished guide. Location: Antioch College, Olive Kettering Library, Antiochiana, Yellow Springs, Ohio 45387-1694. Scope of collection: Collection of correspondence concerns education of women, women's rights and Winnemucca.

68. Addie L. Wyatt
(1924-   )

Advocate for African American rights and
women's rights; labor leader

BIOGRAPHICAL INFORMATION

Chronological Biography

Born March 8, 1924, in Brookhaven, Mississippi, second of eight children, and oldest daughter, to Maggie (Nolan) and Ambrose Cameron. Responsible from early age to help care for younger siblings. Parents encouraged children to believe in themselves and that they could be whatever they wished. Segregation was way of life. Family moved to Chicago when she was about six. Excellent student, attended public and private schools. Mother, father and grandmother worked to help support family, but finances were very strained.

May 12, 1940: At age 16, married the Rev. Claude S. Wyatt, Jr., after graduation from high school.   **1941:** First son born. In December, at age 17, needing to work because husband's cleaning plant salary was small, hired over telephone for typist position at Armour & Company, but was sent to work in canning department packing stew for U.S. Army and slicing bacon because company did not hire blacks for office positions. Became aware that office workers earned less and had poorer working conditions than unionized factory workers. Also discovered that rates of pay were not same for black and white typists in companies that hired blacks for office positions.   **1942:** Job changed to putting lids on cans, which she preferred, but newly hired white woman was then given that task. She protested, and with union's backing was reinstated. As result, joined Local 56 of United Packinghouse, Food & Allied Workers (merged with Amalgamated Meat Cutters, and later United Food and Commercial Workers International). At first union meeting, greatly impressed at seeing workers—old, young, women, men, various ethnic groups—all banding together to solve their common problems. Union became very important to women as they shared experiences trying to juggle family and job responsibilities.   **Mid 1940s:** Mother became seriously ill and died at about age 39; father died short time later. Took five younger siblings and raised them with own two sons beginning at barely 20 years of age. Husband was drafted in service, so she had to raise children as well as work in plant. Need for day care centers emphasized by own situation and sparked her continuing dedication to this cause.   **1945–1955:** Couple were volunteer youth leaders for Altgeld Gardens, Chicago Housing Authority **1951:** Participated in rally in Chicago stockyards for increased wages with over 10,000 other workers; her sign read "Equal Pay For Women." **1953–1955:** Speaking skills and ability to work well with others increasingly brought her attention; elected vice president and then first woman president of packinghouse local. **1954–1974:** Left job to work full time for union; duties included negotiating terms of contracts with company representatives in her district. Fought to improve conditions, especially for blacks and women who were discriminated against in hiring and salary. Union worked to eliminate wage differential between women and men and between workers in north and south of United States. Served as one of five international union representatives. As education director for all unions in district, planned schools and conference to train people for better jobs and union leadership. Raised funds, made speeches, participated in strikes, etc. **Spring 1965:** Supported voter registration drive in Selma, Alabama, by marching with others from labor movement in Dr. Martin Luther King, Jr.'s campaign. Returned to Chicago to raise funds for cause. Husband had become minister after working in post office for many years and was coordinator of Chicago ministers' group that worked under Dr. King; she served as coordinator for labor groups. King later came to Chicago to begin campaign to improve housing for blacks; she arranged meetings for him with labor representatives, as well as conferences and luncheons to raise funds. Was injured by brick thrown at marchers during one of nonviolent demonstrations. **1966:** Recommended to King that the Rev. Jesse Jackson head Operation Breadbasket, program to plan economic improvement for blacks. Continued to serve as advisor to Jackson throughout years. **1970:** Organized conference to bring black rank and file union members together to talk about problems and plan solutions. **1971:** Helped Jackson start organization, People United to Save Humanity (PUSH); served as advisor to organization's Project EXCEL, program to help black teens achieve in high school; husband was national secretary of PUSH. **1973:** Several trade union women who were active in labor movement felt need for women to join together to represent own interests and share experiences. Despite some predictions that women would not respond, she headed a planning committee that instituted regional meetings gauging desire for coalition; strong response prompted founding conference in March 1974. Received Image Award from League of Black Women. **January 19, 1974:** Keynote speaker at First Trade Union Women's Conference in New York City, attended by nearly 700 women representing 59 unions. Called for equal opportunities for women in jobs and leadership roles in unions. **March 1974:** Elected national vice president of Coalition of Labor Union Women (CLUW), which she helped found, becoming highest ranking black woman in trade union movement. Organization was first trade union women's organization of its kind in country. First conference in Chicago, at which she was both keynote and closing speaker, drew over 3,200 people, representing 58 unions, most paying own expenses; only 1,500 had been expected to attend. Local chapters were formed throughout country. Organization's goals are to strengthen role and participation of women in unions and in country, obtain equal rights for women in hiring and other areas and unionize presently unorganized women workers. Has had success in having women promoted to traditional "male" jobs which are higher paying and frequently easier. Felt strongly that for changes to occur in women's work lives, women must take leadership roles in trade unions. **1974–1978:** Appointed first director of AMCBW's newly formed Women's Affairs Department. **October 20, 1975:** Witness before joint House and Senate committee concerning jobs and prices in Chicago. **1975:** Received International Women's Year Award from University of Michigan. **January 5, 1976:** Picture appeared on cover of *Time* magazine as one of 12 "Women of the Year," first union leader ever so honored. **June 1976:** Unanimously elected international vice president of Amalgamated Meat Cutters and Butcher Workmen (later United Food and Commercial Workers International Union) of AFL-CIO. First woman to hold position in 550,000 member union of which 20 percent was female. **1976:** Received honorary Doctor of Law degree from Anderson College, service award from women's board of National Association for the Advancement of Colored People (NAACP) and Distinguished Labor Leader award from Woodlawn Organization, Chicago. **September 1977:** Elected executive vice president of CLUW at third convention. Calling for solidarity of all women, spoke at first national convention of Women for Racial and Economic Equality held in Chicago. **1977:** Appointed to national commission on observance of International Women's Year. Received Outstanding Woman in Western Region award from Iota Phi Lambda; named one of ten women of year by *Ladies' Home Journal* magazine; received Black Book award, *Ebony* magazine citation, and award from Urban Ministries, Inc. **1977–1988:** Member-at-large from Illinois to Democratic National Committee. **September 10–15, 1978:** Represented United States at conference on women in labor unions in Bogota, Colombia. **1978:** Recipient of honorary Doctor of Humane Letters degree from Columbia College. Appointed first director of AMCBW's Human Rights Department, formed by merger of Civil Rights Department and Women's Affairs Department (which she had headed since 1974). Member of National Advisory Commission for Women. **1978–1979:** Advisor and instructor of labor at Roosevelt University in Chicago. Member of labor advisory committee of Chicago Urban League. **1980:** Received *Ebony* magazine citation. Called for labor movement to voice disapproval regarding U.S. actions toward South Africa; felt banks should not lend funds, companies should not open factories there, etc. until South African blacks had full rights. **1981:** Recipient of Dr. Martin Luther King, Jr. Labor award. **1981, 1982 and 1983:** Named one of 100 most outstanding black women in America by *Ebony* magazine. **November 1, 1983:** Testified at House hearing regarding pension equity for women, representing United Food and Commercial Workers International Union. **August 18, 1984:** Gave keynote address at Warren, Ohio, conference on HR-5814, congressional bill regarding full employment. **September 30, 1984:** Retired as vice president of United Food and Commercial Workers Union. Also resigned as director of union's Civil Rights and Women's Department. Returned to Chicago where husband was pastor; continues to be active in civil rights, labor and women's issues. During long career, served as labor advisor to Dr. Martin Luther King, Jr., Dr. Ralph Abernathy and the Rev. Jesse L. Jackson and worked with them in civil rights causes. Served on numerous boards, committees and commissions and received many honors and awards. **1985:** Honored by Coalition of Labor Union Women for her contributions to American labor movement.

Background Information

Parents: Maggie (Nolan) and Ambrose Cameron. Mother was seamstress, father tailor. **Siblings:** Seven (Known names: Emmett, Willie, Bluet, Audrey and Maude). **Children:** Two (Renaldo, Claude S., III. Also raised five sisters and brothers). **Influences:** None. **Ethnicity:** African American. **Also known as:** Addie Lorraine. **Historical sites, landmarks, etc.:** None known.

BIBLIOGRAPHICAL INFORMATION

Biographical Sketches About Addie L. Wyatt

Leavitt, Judith A. *American Women Managers and Administrators: A Selective Biographical Dictionary of Twentieth-Century Leaders in Business, Education, and Government.* Westport, CT: Greenwood, 1985.
O'Neill, Lois Decker, ed. *The Women's Book of World Records and Achievements.* Garden City, NY: Anchor Press/Doubleday, 1979.

Shorter Works by Addie L. Wyatt

"Our Goal Is Human Survival." *Labor Today* 23 (October 1984): 2.
"Support South African Workers' Struggles." *Labor Today* 19 (November 1980): 1.

Shorter Works About Addie L. Wyatt

"Addie Wyatt." In *Particular Passions*, by Lynn Gilbert and Gaylen Moore. New York: Clarkson N. Potter, 1981.

"Addie Wyatt Given High Honor." *Butcher Workman* 62 (February 1976): 9.
Biddle, Marcia McKenna. *Labor.* Minneapolis: Dillon Press, 1979. Reprint. Minneapolis: Dillon Press, 1981.
"Dozen Who Made a Difference." *Time* 107 (January 5, 1976): 20.
Eason, Yla. "Today's Emerging Black Woman." *Chicago Tribune* (October 21, 1973): 4.
Foner, Philip S. *Women and the American Labor Movement: From World War I to the Present.* New York: Free Press, 1980.
Jackson, David. "The Gene Pool." *Chicago* 37 (November 1988): 172.
"Labor Group Cited Three Black Women." *Jet* 68 (March 25, 1985): 23.
"Labor Union Pioneer Addie Wyatt Retires." *Jet* 66 (August 27, 1984): 34.
Shanahan, Eileen. "3,000 Delegates at Chicago Meeting Organize a National Coalition of Labor Union Women." *New York Times* (March 25, 1974): 27.
"She's a Fighter on Three Fronts." *Ebony* 32 (August 1977): 70 + .
"Union Women Must Build for Participation." *Labor Today* 16 (March 1977): 3.
"Women of the Year 1977." *Ladies' Home Journal* 94 (June 1977): 77.
"Women's Affairs Director: Addie Wyatt." *Butcher Workman* 61 (May 1975): 2–3 + .
"Women's Conference Held in Bogota." *Butcher Workman* 64 (December–January 1978–1979): 21.

Media Materials by Addie L. Wyatt

Sound Recordings

National Education Association. *Convention Materials: NEA Annual Meeting—1981.* Washington, D. C. : National Education Association, 1981. 4 cassettes.

Media Materials About Addie L. Wyatt

Video Recordings

Great Women in Politics: News Conference with Addie L. Wyatt. Produced by MSU Media System's Educational Resource Center in Cooperation with the Political Science Department. Mankato State University, 1976. Videoreel; 32 min.; black and white.

APPENDICES

Appendix A: Birthplace

England
Counterslip
Blackwell, Elizabeth

Guatemala
[city unknown]
Moreno, Luisa

Hungary
Budapest
Schwimmer, Rosika

Lithuania
Kovno
Goldman, Emma

New Zealand
Clutha River
Cameron, Donaldina Mackenzie

Poland
Augustow
Stokes, Rose Harriet Pastor

Puerto Rico
Mayaguez
Bracetti, Mariana

Santurce
Maymi, Carmen Rosa

United States

Alabama
Birmingham
Davis, Angela

Marion
King, Coretta Scott

Tuskegee
Parks, Rosa

Arizona
Sonora
Olivarez, Graciela (Grace)

Arkansas
Huttig
Bates, Daisy

Colorado
LaSalle
Baca, Polly B.

Connecticut
New Haven
Motley, Constance Baker

Georgia
Atlanta
Robinson, Ruby Doris Smith

DaKalb County
Felton, Rebecca Ann Latimer

Illinois
Chicago
Fiorito, Eunice

Kansas
Ottawa County
O'Hare, Kate Richards

[427]

Louisiana
New Orleans
Dunbar-Nelson, Alice

Maryland
Princess Anne
Fauset, Crystal Dreda Bird

Massachusetts
Amherst
Jackson, Helen Maria Fiske Hunt

Boston
Hutchins, Grace
Ruffin, Josephine St. Pierre

Jamaica Plain
Balch, Emily Greene

Salem
Sanders, Elizabeth Elkins

Mississippi
Brookhaven
Wyatt, Addie L.

Holly Springs
Wells-Barnett, Ida Bell

Ruleville
Hamer, Fannie Lou Townsend

Missouri
St. Louis
Wilson, Margaret Bush

Nebraska
Bellevue
La Flesche, Susette

Friend
Strong, Anna Louise

Geneva
Barnard, Kate

Nevada
Humboldt Sink Area
Winnemucca, Sarah

New Hampshire
Concord
Flynn, Elizabeth Gurley

New York
Bronx
Apuzzo, Virginia M.

Brooklyn
Chisholm, Shirley

Brooklyn Heights
Day, Dorothy

Buffalo
Kuhn, Margaret E.

Elmira
Converse, Harriet Maxwell

Hamilton
Bonney, Mary L.

Jamesville
Quinton, Amelia Stone

Mariners Harbor
Bloor, Ella Reeve

New York
Hernandez, Aileen Clarke

Phelps
Emery, Sarah Elizabeth Van De Vort

Plymouth
Todd, Marion Marsh

Royalton Township
Lockwood, Belva Ann Bennett McNall

Staten Island
Lifton, Betty Jean

North Carolina
Salisbury
Koontz, Elizabeth Duncan

Ohio
Cincinnati
Wald, Lillian D.

Oberlin
Talbert, Mary Burnett

Ravenna
Upton, Harriet Taylor

Oklahoma
Alluwe
Lawson, Roberta Campbell

Lawton
Hayden, Iola M. Pohocsucut

Tullahassee
Robertson, Alice Mary

Pennsylvania
Cochran Mills
Seaman, Elizabeth Cochrane

Ridgway
Lease, Mary Elizabeth Clyens

South Carolina
Mayesville
Bethune, Mary McLeod

Sumter
Bass, Charlotta A. Spears

South Dakota
Yankton Sioux Agency
Bonnin, Gertrude Simmons

Tennessee
Memphis
Terrell, Mary Eliza Church

Nashville
Berry, Mary Frances

Texas
Houston
Jordan, Barbara

San Antonio
Tenayuca, Emma

Virginia
[city unknown, state is uncertain]
Pleasant, Mary Ellen

Richmond
Height, Dorothy I.

Washington, D.C.
Norton, Eleanor Holmes

Wisconsin
Keshena
Deer, Ada

Appendix B: Chronological by Date of Birth

Sanders, Elizabeth Elkins (1762–1851)
Pleasant, Mary Ellen (1812?–1904)
Bonney, Mary L. (1816–1900)
Blackwell, Elizabeth (1821–1910)
Jackson, Helen Maria Fiske Hunt (1830?–1885)
Lockwood, Belva Ann Bennett McNall (1830–1917)
Quinton, Amelia Stone (1833–1926)
Felton, Rebecca Ann Latimer (1835–1930)
Converse, Harriet Maxwell (1836–1903)
Emery, Sarah Elizabeth Van De Vort (1838–1895)
Bracetti, Mariana (ca. 1840–1904?)

Todd, Marion Marsh (1841–1914?)
Ruffin, Josephine St. Pierre (1842–1924)
Winnemucca, Sarah (1844?–1891)
Lease, Mary Elizabeth Clyens (1850?–1933)
Upton, Harriet Taylor (1853–1945)
La Flesche, Susette (1854–1903)
Robertson, Alice Mary (1854–1931)
Bloor, Ella Reeve (1862–1951)
Wells-Barnett, Ida Bell (1862–1931)
Terrell, Mary Eliza Church (1863–1954)
Talbert, Mary Burnett (1866–1923)
Balch, Emily Greene (1867–1961)

Seaman, Elizabeth Cochrane
(1867–1922)
Wald, Lillian D. (1867–1940)
Cameron, Donaldina Mackenzie
(1869–1968)
Goldman, Emma (1869–1940)
Barnard, Kate (1874?–1930)
Bethune, Mary McLeod (1875–1955)
Dunbar-Nelson, Alice (1875–1935)
Bonnin, Gertrude Simmons (1876?–
1938)
O'Hare, Kate Richards (1877–1948)
Schwimmer, Rosika (1877–1948)
Lawson, Roberta Campbell (1878–
1940)
Stokes, Rose Harriet Pastor (1879–
1933)
Bass, Charlotta A. Spears (1880?–
1969)
Hutchins, Grace (1885–1969)
Strong, Anna Louise (1885–1970)
Flynn, Elizabeth Gurley (1890–1964)
Fauset, Crystal Dreda Bird (1893?–
1965)
Day, Dorothy (1897–1980)
Kuhn, Margaret E. (1905–)
Moreno, Luisa (1907–1990?)
Height, Dorothy I. (1912–)

Parks, Rosa (1913–)
Tenayuca, Emma (1916–)
Hamer, Fannie Lou Townsend
(1917–1977)
Koontz, Elizabeth Duncan (1919–
1989)
Wilson, Margaret Bush (1919–)
Bates, Daisy (1920?–)
Motley, Constance Baker (1921–)
Chisholm, Shirley (1924–)
Wyatt, Addie L. (1924–)
Hernandez, Aileen Clarke (1926–)
Lifton, Betty Jean (1926–)
King, Coretta Scott (1927–)
Olivarez, Graciela (Grace) (1928–
1987)
Fiorito, Eunice (1930–)
Hayden, Iola M. Pohocsucut (1934–)
Deer, Ada (1935–)
Jordan, Barbara (1936–)
Norton, Eleanor Holmes (1937–)
Berry, Mary Frances (1938–)
Maymi, Carmen Rosa (1938–)
Apuzzo, Virginia M. (1941–)
Baca, Polly B. (1941–)
Robinson, Ruby Doris Smith
(1941?–1967)
Davis, Angela (1944–)

Appendix C: Ethnicity

African American
Bass, Charlotta A. Spears
Bates, Daisy
Berry, Mary Frances
Bethune, Mary McLeod
Chisholm, Shirley
Davis, Angela
Dunbar-Nelson, Alice
Fauset, Crystal Dreda Bird
Hamer, Fannie Lou Townsend
Height, Dorothy I.
Hernandez, Aileen Clarke
Jordan, Barbara
King, Coretta Scott

Koontz, Elizabeth Duncan
Maymi, Carmen Rosa
Motley, Constance Baker
Norton, Eleanor Holmes
Parks, Rosa
Pleasant, Mary Ellen
Robinson, Ruby Doris Smith
Ruffin, Josephine St. Pierre
Talbert, Mary Burnett
Terrell, Mary Eliza Church
Wells-Barnett, Ida Bell
Wilson, Margaret Bush
Wyatt, Addie L.

American Indian *see* **Native American**

Black *see* **African American**

Chicana/Chicano *see* **Hispanic American**

Dutch American
Bloor, Ella Reeve
Emery, Sarah Elizabeth Van De Vort

English
Blackwell, Elizabeth

English American
Balch, Emily Greene
Bloor, Ella Reeve
Felton, Rebecca Ann Latimer
Hutchins, Grace
Jackson, Helen Maria Fiske Hunt
Quinton, Amelia Stone
Robertson, Alice Mary
Strong, Anna Louise

French American
Bloor, Ella Reeve
La Flesche, Susette

German American
Fiorito, Eunice
Kuhn, Margaret E.

Guatemalan
Moreno, Luisa

Hispanic American *see also* **Spanish American**
Baca, Polly B.
Maymi, Carmen Rosa
Olivarez, Graciela (Grace)
Tenayuca, Emma

Hungarian
Schwimmer, Rosika

Irish American
Barnard, Kate
Day, Dorothy
Felton, Rebecca Ann Latimer
Flynn, Elizabeth Gurley
Lease, Mary Elizabeth Clyens
Olivarez, Graciela (Grace)

Italian American
Apuzzo, Virginia M.

Jewish
Goldman, Emma
Schwimmer, Rosika
Stokes, Rose Harriet Pastor

Jewish American
Lifton, Betty Jean
Wald, Lillian D.

Latina/Latino *see* **Hispanic American**

Lithuanian
Goldman, Emma

Mexican American *see* **Hispanic American**

Native American
Bonnin, Gertrude Simmons (Sioux)
Deer, Ada (Menominee)
Hayden, Iola M. Pohocsucut (Comanche)
La Flesche, Susette (Omaha)
Lawson, Roberta Campbell (Delaware)
Winnemucca, Sarah (Paviotso-Paiute)

Polish
Stokes, Rose Harriet Pastor

Polish American
Fiorito, Eunice

Puerto Rican
Bracetti, Mariana
Maymi, Carmen Rosa

Scottish American
Converse, Harriet Maxwell
Day, Dorothy
Felton, Rebecca Ann Latimer
Lawson, Roberta Campbell
Robertson, Alice Mary

Spanish American *see also* **Hispanic American**
Olivarez, Graciela (Grace)

Appendix D: Fields of Activity

abolition *see also* African
American rights
Blackwell, Elizabeth
Pleasant, Mary Ellen

adoptee rights/adoption rights
Lifton, Betty Jean

African American rights *see also*
abolition; antilynching; civil
rights; human rights; minority
rights
Bass, Charlotta A. Spears
Bates, Daisy
Berry, Mary Frances
Bethune, Mary McLeod
Chisholm, Shirley
Davis, Angela
Dunbar-Nelson, Alice
Fauset, Crystal Dreda Bird
Hamer, Fannie Lou Townsend
Height, Dorothy I.
Hernandez, Aileen Clarke
Jordan, Barbara
King, Coretta Scott
Koontz, Elizabeth Duncan
Maymi, Carmen Rosa
Moreno, Luisa
Motley, Constance Baker
Norton, Eleanor Holmes
Olivarez, Graciela (Grace)
Parks, Rosa
Pleasant, Mary Ellen
Robinson, Ruby Doris Smith
Ruffin, Josephine St. Pierre
Sanders, Elizabeth Elkins
Talbert, Mary Burnett
Terrell, Mary Eliza Church
Wells-Barnett, Ida Bell
Wilson, Margaret Bush
Wyatt, Addie L.

aged rights *see* older adult rights

American Indian rights *see* Native
American/Indigenous rights

anarchism
Goldman, Emma

antilynching *see also* African
American rights
Bass, Charlotta A. Spears
Dunbar-Nelson, Alice
Talbert, Mary Burnett
Wells-Barnett, Ida Bell

birth control/sex education
Blackwell, Elizabeth
Goldman, Emma
Lease, Mary Elizabeth Clyens
Stokes, Rose Harriet Pastor

black rights *see* African
American rights

blind *see* differently abled rights

Chicana/Chicano rights *see*
Hispanic American rights

child welfare/child labor/children's
rights *see also* labor/labor
organizer/unions
Barnard, Kate
Bethune, Mary McLeod
Blackwell, Elizabeth
Cameron, Donaldina Mackenzie
Chisholm, Shirley
Hutchins, Grace
Koontz, Elizabeth Duncan
Kuhn, Margaret E.
Maymi, Carmen Rosa
Norton, Eleanor Holmes
Olivarez, Graciela (Grace)
Parks, Rosa
Ruffin, Josephine St. Pierre
Sanders, Elizabeth Elkins
Schwimmer, Rosika
Seaman, Elizabeth Cochrane
Strong, Anna Louise
Talbert, Mary Burnett
Upton, Harriet Taylor
Wald, Lillian D.
Wyatt, Addie L.

Chinese women's rights *see also* **women's rights**
Cameron, Donaldina Mackenzie

civic affairs *see* community action/community affairs/civic affairs

civil rights *see also* adoptee rights/adoption rights; African American rights; Chinese women's rights; differently-abled rights; farmers rights/farm workers rights; Hispanic American rights; human rights; individual rights; lesbian rights/gay rights; minority rights; Native American/Indigenous rights; older adult rights; women's rights/women's suffrage
Berry, Mary Frances
Day, Dorothy
Flynn, Elizabeth Gurley
Hernandez, Aileen Clarke
Hutchins, Grace
Jordan, Barbara
King, Coretta Scott
Koontz, Elizabeth Duncan
Kuhn, Margaret E.
Maymi, Carmen Rosa
Moreno, Luisa
Norton, Eleanor Holmes
Olivarez, Graciela (Grace)
Parks, Rosa

clubwomen
Dunbar-Nelson, Alice
Lawson, Roberta Campbell
Ruffin, Josephine St. Pierre
Talbert, Mary Burnett
Terrell, Mary Eliza Church
Wells-Barnett, Ida Bell

communism
Bloor, Ella Reeve
Davis, Angela
Flynn, Elizabeth Gurley
Hutchins, Grace
Stokes, Rose Harriet Pastor

Strong, Anna Louise
Tenayuca, Emma

community action/community affairs/civic affairs
Bass, Charlotta A. Spears
Bates, Daisy
Blackwell, Elizabeth
Davis, Angela
Deer, Ada
Fauset, Crystal Dreda Bird
Hayden, Iola M. Pohocsucut
Hernandez, Aileen Clarke
Lawson, Roberta Campbell
Lease, Mary Elizabeth Clyens
Maymi, Carmen Rosa
Motley, Constance Baker
Olivarez, Graciela (Grace)
Parks, Rosa
Pleasant, Mary Ellen
Ruffin, Josephine St. Pierre
Strong, Anna Louise
Talbert, Mary Burnett
Tenayuca, Emma
Terrell, Mary Eliza Church
Wald, Lillian D.
Wells-Barnett, Ida Bell
Wilson, Margaret Bush
Wyatt, Addie L.

consumer rights
Apuzzo, Virginia M.
Barnard, Kate
Kuhn, Margaret E.

criminal justice *see* prisons/penology/criminal justice

differently abled rights
Fiorito, Eunice
Koontz, Elizabeth Duncan
Kuhn, Margaret E.
Norton, Eleanor Holmes

disabled rights *see* differently abled rights

economic opportunity/economic reform
Baca, Polly B.

poverty/homelessness/housing
Barnard, Kate
Blackwell, Elizabeth
Day, Dorothy
King, Coretta Scott
Kuhn, Margaret E.
Moreno, Luisa
Motley, Constance Baker
Norton, Eleanor Holmes
O'Hare, Kate Richards
Olivarez, Graciela (Grace)
Sanders, Elizabeth Elkins
Seaman, Elizabeth Cochrane
Tenayuca, Emma
Wilson, Margaret Bush
Winnemucca, Sarah
Wyatt, Addie L.

prisons/penology/criminal justice
Barnard, Kate
Felton, Rebecca Ann Latimer
O'Hare, Kate Richards
Olivarez, Graciela (Grace)
Sanders, Elizabeth Elkins
Seaman, Elizabeth Cochrane
Wilson, Margaret Bush

Prohibition *see* **temperance/ Prohibition**

race relations
Bethune, Mary McLeod
Dunbar-Nelson, Alice
Fauset, Crystal Dreda Bird
Height, Dorothy I.
Koontz, Elizabeth Duncan
Kuhn, Margaret E.
Ruffin, Josephine St. Pierre
Talbert, Mary Burnett

radicalism *see* **socialism/radicalism**

retiree rights *see* **older adult rights**

senior citizen rights *see* **older adult rights**

settlement houses
Balch, Emily Greene

Cameron, Donaldina Mackenzie
Strong, Anna Louise
Wald, Lillian D.
Wells-Barnett, Ida Bell

sex education *see* **birth control/sex education**

social action/social activism/social reform
Balch, Emily Greene
Barnard, Kate
Bass, Charlotta A. Spears
Cameron, Donaldina Mackenzie
Davis, Angela
Day, Dorothy
Dunbar-Nelson, Alice
Flynn, Elizabeth Gurley
Height, Dorothy I.
Hutchins, Grace
King, Coretta Scott
Kuhn, Margaret E.
Lease, Mary Elizabeth Clyens
Robinson, Ruby Doris Smith
Sanders, Elizabeth Elkins
Seaman, Elizabeth Cochrane
Strong, Anna Louise
Talbert, Mary Burnett
Tenayuca, Emma
Terrell, Mary Eliza Church
Wells-Barnett, Ida Bell

social work/social welfare
Balch, Emily Greene
Cameron, Donaldina Mackenzie
Deer, Ada
Fiorito, Eunice
Height, Dorothy I.
Olivarez, Graciela (Grace)
Ruffin, Josephine St. Pierre
Wald, Lillian D.

socialism/radicalism
Balch, Emily Greene
Bloor, Ella Reeve
Day, Dorothy
Flynn, Elizabeth Gurley
Goldman, Emma
Hutchins, Grace

Appendix E: Geographic Location of Civil Rights Activity

Davis, Angela
Hernandez, Aileen Clarke
Jackson, Helen Maria Fiske Hunt
Moreno, Luisa
O'Hare, Kate Richards
Pleasant, Mary Ellen
Todd, Marion Marsh

Colorado
Baca, Polly B.
Jackson, Helen Maria Fiske Hunt

Delaware
Dunbar-Nelson, Alice

Florida
Bethune, Mary McLeod

Georgia
Felton, Rebecca Ann Latimer
Robinson, Ruby Doris Smith

Illinois
Maymi, Carmen Rosa
Todd, Marion Marsh
Wells-Barnett, Ida Bell
Wyatt, Addie L.

Kansas
Lease, Mary Elizabeth Clyens

Maryland
Terrell, Mary Eliza Church

Massachusetts
Balch, Emily Greene
Ruffin, Josephine St. Pierre
Sanders, Elizabeth Elkins

Michigan
Todd, Marion Marsh

Mississippi
Hamer, Fannie Lou Townsend

Missouri
Wilson, Margaret Bush

Nebraska
La Flesche, Susette

Nevada
Winnemucca, Sarah

New Mexico
Olivarez, Graciela (Grace)

New York
Apuzzo, Virginia M.
Blackwell, Elizabeth
Chisholm, Shirley
Converse, Harriet Maxwell
Day, Dorothy
Fiorito, Eunice
Goldman, Emma
Height, Dorothy I.
Hutchins, Grace
Motley, Constance Baker
Norton, Eleanor Holmes
Seaman, Elizabeth Cochrane
Stokes, Rose Harriet Pastor
Talbert, Mary Burnett
Wald, Lillian D.
Wells-Barnett, Ida Bell

North Carolina
Koontz, Elizabeth Duncan

Ohio
Upton, Harriet Taylor

Oklahoma
Barnard, Kate
Hayden, Iola M. Pohocsucut
Lawson, Roberta Campbell
Robertson, Alice Mary

Pennsylvania
Bonney, Mary L.
Dunbar-Nelson, Alice
Fauset, Crystal Dreda Bird
Kuhn, Margaret E.
Quinton, Amelia Stone

Puerto Rico
Bracetti, Mariana

Tennessee
Wells-Barnett, Ida Bell

Texas
Jordan, Barbara
Moreno, Luisa
Tenayuca, Emma

Washington, D. C.
Berry, Mary Frances

Bonnin, Gertrude Simmons
Jordan, Barbara
Koontz, Elizabeth Duncan
Lockwood, Belva Ann Bennett
  McNall
Maymi, Carmen Rosa

Norton, Eleanor Holmes
Olivarez, Graciela (Grace)
Terrell, Mary Eliza Church

Wisconsin
Deer, Ada

Appendix F: Name Cross References

A Lady   *see*   Sanders, Elizabeth Elkins
Anise   *see*   Strong, Anna Louise
Apuzzo, Ginny   *see*   Apuzzo, Virginia M.
Baca-Barragan, Polly   *see*   Baca, Polly B.
Barragan, Polly   *see*   Baca, Polly B.
Bedy-Schwimmer, Rosika   *see* Schwimmer, Rosika
Bethune, Mary Jane   *see*   Bethune Mary McLeod
Bly, Nellie   *see*   Seaman, Elizabeth Cochrane
Bly, Nelly   *see*   Seaman, Elizabeth Cochrane
Bonney-Rambaut, Mary   *see*   Bonney, Mary L.
Braceti, Mariana   *see*   Bracetti, Mariana
Bracetti, Ana Maria   *see*   Bracetti, Mariana
Brazo de Oro   *see*   Bracetti, Mariana
Bright Eyes   *see*   La Flesche, Susette
Brooks, Emma   *see*   Tenayuca, Emma
Cochran, Elizabeth   *see*   Seaman, Elizabeth Cochrane
Cochrane, Elizabeth   *see*   Seaman, Elizabeth Cochrane
Cohen, Ella   *see*   Bloor, Ella Reeve
Cuevas, Mariana   *see*   Bracetti, Mariana
Cunningham, Kate   *see*   O'Hare, Kate Richards
Dunbar, Alice   *see*   Dunbar-Nelson, Alice
Fahn Quai   *see*   Cameron, Donaldina Mackenzie
Faucet, Crystal Bird   *see*   Fauset, Crystal Dreda Bird
Fauset, Crystal Byrd   *see*   Fauset, Crystal Dreda Bird
Gale   *see*   Strong, Anna Louise
H. H.   *see*   Jackson, Helen Maria Fiske Hunt
Hopkins, Sarah   *see*   Winnemucca, Sarah
Hunt, Helen   *see*   Jackson, Helen Maria Fiske Hunt
Inshata Theumba   *see*   La Flesche, Susette
Jackson, Helen   *see*   Jackson, Helen Maria Fiske Hunt
Jackson, Helen Hunt   *see*   Jackson, Helen Maria Fiske Hunt
Kuhn, Maggie   *see*   Kuhn, Margaret E.
Labiosa, Mariana   *see*   Bracetti, Mariana
Lady, A   *see*   Sanders, Elizabeth Elkins
Lease, Mary Ellen   *see*   Lease, Mary Elizabeth Clyens
Leese, Mary Elizabeth Clyens   *see*   Lease, Mary Elizabeth Clyens

Lo Mo   *see*   Cameron, Donaldina Mackenzie
Marah   *see*   Jackson, Helen Maria Fiske Hunt
Moore, Alice   *see*   Dunbar-Nelson, Alice
Musidora   *see*   Converse, Harriet Maxwell
Nellie Bly   *see*   Seaman, Elizabeth Cochrane
Nelly Bly   *see*   Seaman, Elizabeth Cochrane
Nelson, Alice Dunbar   *see*   Dunbar-Nelson, Alice
No Name   *see*   Jackson, Helen Maria Fiske Hunt
Observer   *see*   Stokes, Rose Harriet Pastor
Olivares, Graciela (Grace)   *see*   Olivarez, Graciela (Grace)
Omholt, Ella   *see*   Bloor, Ella Reeve
Pleasant, Mammy   *see*   Pleasant, Mary Ellen
Pleasants, Mammy   *see*   Pleasant, Mary Ellen
Pleasants, Mary Ellen   *see*   Pleasant, Mary Ellen
Rambaut, Mary   *see*   Bonney, Mary L.
Red Bird   *see*   Bonnin, Gertrude Simmons
Reeve, Ella   *see*   Bloor, Ella Reeve
Rip Van Winkle   *see*   Jackson, Helen Maria Fiske Hunt
Robertson, Alice   *see*   Robertson, Alice Mary
Robertson, Mary Alice   *see*   Robertson, Alice Mary
Robinson, Rubye   *see*   Robinson, Ruby Doris Smith
Rojas, Mariana   *see*   Bracetti, Mariana
Salome   *see*   Converse, Harriet Maxwell
Sasha   *see*   Stokes, Rose Harriet Pastor
Saxe Holm   *see*   Jackson, Helen Maria Fiske Hunt
Shell Flower   *see*   Winnemucca, Sarah
Shubin, Anna Louise   *see*   Strong, Anna Louise
Smith, Ruby Doris   *see*   Robinson, Ruby Doris Smith
Talbert, Mary   *see*   Talbert, Mary Burnett
Talbert, Mary Morris   *see*   Talbert, Mary Burnett
Terrell, Mollie   *see*   Terrell, Mary Eliza Church
Thocmetony   *see*   Winnemucca, Sarah
Tibbles, Susette   *see*   La Flesche, Susette
Ware, Ella   *see*   Bloor, Ella Reeve
Wells, Ida B.   *see*   Wells-Barnett, Ida Bell
Wells-Barnett, Iola   *see*   Wells-Barnett, Ida Bell
Wieslander, Rose Harriet Pastor   *see*   Stokes, Rose Harriet Pastor
Wyatt, Addie Lorraine   *see*   Wyatt, Addie L.
Zelda   *see*   Stokes, Rose Harriet Pastor
Zitkala-Sa   *see*   Bonnin, Gertrude Simmons
Zitkala-Sha   *see*   Bonnin, Gertrude Simmons

Appendix G:
Occupation/Field/Other Pursuits

administrative assistant
Robinson, Ruby Doris Smith

ambassador
Schwimmer, Rosika

anthropologist
Converse, Harriet Maxwell

artist
Stokes, Rose Harriet Pastor

author *see also* editor; journalist
Apuzzo, Virginia M.
Balch, Emily Greene
Barnard, Kate
Bass, Charlotta A. Spears
Bates, Daisy
Berry, Mary Frances
Bethune, Mary McLeod
Blackwell, Elizabeth
Bloor, Ella Reeve
Bonnin, Gertrude Simmons
Cameron, Donaldina Mackenzie
Chisholm, Shirley
Converse, Harriet Maxwell
Davis, Angela
Day, Dorothy
Deer, Ada
Dunbar-Nelson, Alice
Emery, Sarah Elizabeth Van De Vort
Fauset, Crystal Dreda Bird
Felton, Rebecca Ann Latimer
Fiorito, Eunice
Flynn, Elizabeth Gurley
Goldman, Emma
Hamer, Fannie Lou Townsend
Height, Dorothy I.
Hernandez, Aileen Clarke
Hutchins, Grace
Jackson, Helen Maria Fiske Hunt
Jordan, Barbara
King, Coretta Scott

Koontz, Elizabeth Duncan
Kuhn, Margaret E.
La Flesche, Susette
Lawson, Roberta Campbell
Lease, Mary Elizabeth Clyens
Lifton, Betty Jean
Lockwood, Belva Ann Bennett McNall
Maymi, Carmen Rosa
Moreno, Luisa
Motley, Constance Baker
Norton, Eleanor Holmes
O'Hare, Kate Richards
Olivarez, Graciela (Grace)
Parks, Rosa
Quinton, Amelia Stone
Robertson, Alice Mary
Ruffin, Josephine St. Pierre
Sanders, Elizabeth Elkins
Schwimmer, Rosika
Seaman, Elizabeth Cochrane
Stokes, Rose Harriet Pastor
Strong, Anna Louise
Talbert, Mary Burnett
Tenayuca, Emma
Terrell, Mary Eliza Church
Todd, Marion Marsh
Upton, Harriet Taylor
Wald, Lillian D.
Wells-Barnett, Ida Bell
Wilson, Margaret Bush
Winnemucca, Sarah
Wyatt, Addie L.

bookkeeper
Schwimmer, Rosika

broadcaster/television/radio
Jordan, Barbara
King, Coretta Scott
Lawson, Roberta Campbell
Norton, Eleanor Holmes
Olivarez, Graciela (Grace)

businesswoman
Seaman, Elizabeth Cochrane

clerk
Parks, Rosa
Robertson, Alice Mary

community services specialist
Maymi, Carmen Rosa

congresswoman *see also* politician; senator; state legislator
Chisholm, Shirley
Jordan, Barbara
Norton, Eleanor Holmes
Robertson, Alice Mary

cook
Pleasant, Mary Ellen

copywriter
Lifton, Betty Jean

economist
Balch, Emily Greene
Hutchins, Grace

editor *see also* author; journalist
Baca, Polly B.
Balch, Emily Greene
Bass, Charlotta A. Spears
Bates, Daisy
Berry, Mary Frances
Bloor, Ella Reeve
Bonnin, Gertrude Simmons
Dunbar-Nelson, Alice
Emery, Sarah Elizabeth Van De Vort
Felton, Rebecca Ann Latimer
Goldman, Emma
Hernandez, Aileen Clarke
Hutchins, Grace
Jordan, Barbara
Kuhn, Margaret E.
La Flesche, Susette
Lease, Mary Elizabeth Clyens
Lifton, Betty Jean
Moreno, Luisa
O'Hare, Kate Richards
Quinton, Amelia Stone
Ruffin, Josephine St. Pierre

Schwimmer, Rosika
Stokes, Rose Harriet Pastor
Strong, Anna Louise
Todd, Marion Marsh
Upton, Harriet Taylor
Wells-Barnett, Ida Bell

educator
Apuzzo, Virginia M.
Balch, Emily Greene
Barnard, Kate
Bates, Daisy
Berry, Mary Frances
Bethune, Mary McLeod
Blackwell, Elizabeth
Bonney, Mary L.
Bonnin, Gertrude Simmons
Cameron, Donaldina Mackenzie
Chisholm, Shirley
Davis, Angela
Deer, Ada
Dunbar-Nelson, Alice
Emery, Sarah Elizabeth Van De Vort
Fauset, Crystal Dreda Bird
Felton, Rebecca Ann Latimer
Fiorito, Eunice
Hamer, Fannie Lou Townsend
Hayden, Iola M. Pohocsucut
Height, Dorothy I.
Hernandez, Aileen Clarke
Hutchins, Grace
Jordan, Barbara
King, Coretta Scott
Koontz, Elizabeth Duncan
La Flesche, Susette
Lease, Mary Elizabeth Clyens
Lockwood, Belva Ann Bennett McNall
Norton, Eleanor Holmes
O'Hare, Kate Richards
Olivarez, Graciela (Grace)
Quinton, Amelia Stone
Robertson, Alice Mary
Talbert, Mary Burnett
Tenayuca, Emma
Terrell, Mary Eliza Church

Todd, Marion Marsh
Wald, Lillian D.
Wells-Barnett, Ida Bell
Wilson, Margaret Bush
Winnemucca, Sarah
Wyatt, Addie L.

elevator operator
Tenayuca, Emma

employment counselor
Maymi, Carmen Rosa

factory worker
Goldman, Emma
Hutchins, Grace
Moreno, Luisa
Stokes, Rose Harriet Pastor
Strong, Anna Louise
Wyatt, Addie L.

feminist
Apuzzo, Virginia M.
Balch, Emily Greene
Goldman, Emma
Hernandez, Aileen Clarke
Norton, Eleanor Holmes
Schwimmer, Rosika
Stokes, Rose Harriet Pastor
Strong, Anna Louise
Terrell, Mary Eliza Church
Upton, Harriet Taylor
Wells-Barnett, Ida Bell

government official/government worker
Apuzzo, Virginia M.
Baca, Polly B.
Barnard, Kate
Bates, Daisy
Berry, Mary Frances
Bethune, Mary McLeod
Fauset, Crystal Dreda Bird
Fiorito, Eunice
Hayden, Iola M. Pohocsucut
Height, Dorothy I.
Hernandez, Aileen Clarke
Hutchins, Grace
Jackson, Helen Maria Fiske Hunt

Jordan, Barbara
Koontz, Elizabeth Duncan
Lease, Mary Elizabeth Clyens
Maymi, Carmen Rosa
Motley, Constance Baker
Norton, Eleanor Holmes
O'Hare, Kate Richards
Olivarez, Graciela (Grace)
Robertson, Alice Mary
Wells-Barnett, Ida Bell
Wilson, Margaret Bush

guide
Winnemucca, Sarah

historian
Berry, Mary Frances

housekeeper
Pleasant, Mary Ellen

illustrator
La Flesche, Susette

interpreter *see* **translator/interpreter**

journalist *see also* **author; editor**
Balch, Emily Greene
Barnard, Kate
Bass, Charlotta A. Spears
Bates, Daisy
Berry, Mary Frances
Bethune, Mary McLeod
Blackwell, Elizabeth
Bloor, Ella Reeve
Bonnin, Gertrude Simmons
Cameron, Donaldina Mackenzie
Chisholm, Shirley
Converse, Harriet Maxwell
Davis, Angela
Day, Dorothy
Deer, Ada
Dunbar-Nelson, Alice
Emery, Sarah Elizabeth Van De Vort
Fauset, Crystal Dreda Bird
Felton, Rebecca Ann Latimer
Fiorito, Eunice
Goldman, Emma

Height, Dorothy I.
Hernandez, Aileen Clarke
Hutchins, Grace
Jackson, Helen Maria Fiske Hunt
Jordan, Barbara
King, Coretta Scott
Koontz, Elizabeth Duncan
Kuhn, Margaret E.
La Flesche, Susette
Lawson, Roberta Campbell
Lease, Mary Elizabeth Clyens
Lifton, Betty Jean
Lockwood, Belva Ann Bennett
  McNall
Maymi, Carmen Rosa
Moreno, Luisa
Motley, Constance Baker
Norton, Eleanor Holmes
Olivarez, Graciela (Grace)
Quinton, Amelia Stone
Robertson, Alice Mary
Ruffin, Josephine St. Pierre
Sanders, Elizabeth Elkins
Schwimmer, Rosika
Seaman, Elizabeth Cochrane
Stokes, Rose Harriet Pastor
Strong, Anna Louise
Talbert, Mary Burnett
Tenayuca, Emma
Terrell, Mary Eliza Church
Upton, Harriet Taylor
Wald, Lillian D.
Wells-Barnett, Ida Bell
Wilson, Margaret Bush
Winnemucca, Sarah
Wyatt, Addie L.

judge
Motley, Constance Baker

labor/labor organizer/unions
Balch, Emily Greene
Bloor, Ella Reeve
Flynn, Elizabeth Gurley
Hernandez, Aileen Clarke
Hutchins, Grace
Lease, Mary Elizabeth Clyens
Maymi, Carmen Rosa

Moreno, Luisa
Stokes, Rose Harriet Pastor
Tenayuca, Emma
Todd, Marion Marsh
Wald, Lillian D.
Wilson, Margaret Bush
Wyatt, Addie L.

lawyer
Berry, Mary Frances
Jordan, Barbara
Lease, Mary Elizabeth Clyens
Lockwood, Belva Ann Bennett
  McNall
Motley, Constance Baker
Norton, Eleanor Holmes
Olivarez, Graciela (Grace)
Todd, Marion Marsh
Wilson, Margaret Bush

lecturer/orator/public speaker
Apuzzo, Virginia M.
Berry, Mary Frances
Blackwell, Elizabeth
Bloor, Ella Reeve
Bonnin, Gertrude Simmons
Davis, Angela
Dunbar-Nelson, Alice
Emery, Sarah Elizabeth Van De
  Vort
Fauset, Crystal Dreda Bird
Felton, Rebecca Ann Latimer
Goldman, Emma
Height, Dorothy I.
Jordan, Barbara
King, Coretta Scott
Kuhn, Margaret E.
La Flesche, Susette
Lawson, Roberta Campbell
Lease, Mary Elizabeth Clyens
Lockwood, Belva Ann Bennett
  McNall
O'Hare, Kate Richards
Quinton, Amelia Stone
Robertson, Alice Mary
Schwimmer, Rosika
Stokes, Rose Harriet Pastor
Strong, Anna Louise

Talbert, Mary Burnett
Tenayuca, Emma
Terrell, Mary Eliza Church
Todd, Marion Marsh
Upton, Harriet Taylor
Wells-Barnett, Ida Bell
Winnemucca, Sarah
Wyatt, Addie L.

lobbyist
Lockwood, Belva Ann Bennett
  McNall

management consultant
Baca, Polly B.
Hernandez, Aileen Clarke

midwife
Goldman, Emma

missionary
Cameron, Donaldina Mackenzie

musician/singer
Bonnin, Gertrude Simmons
Dunbar-Nelson, Alice
Fiorito, Eunice
King, Coretta Scott
Lawson, Roberta Campbell

nun
Apuzzo, Virginia M.

nurse
Day, Dorothy
Goldman, Emma
Talbert, Mary Burnett
Wald, Lillian D

office worker *see also* **secretary**
Schwimmer, Rosika

orator *see* **lecturer/orator/public speaker**

organization executive secretary
Robinson, Ruby Doris Smith

parole officer *see also* **probation officer**
Dunbar-Nelson, Alice

party worker/party official
Apuzzo, Virginia M.

Baca, Polly B.
Balch, Emily Greene
Bass, Charlotta A. Spears
Bates, Daisy
Bethune, Mary McLeod
Bloor, Ella Reeve
Davis, Angela
Deer, Ada
Dunbar-Nelson, Alice
Emery, Sarah Elizabeth Van De
  Vort
Fauset, Crystal Dreda Bird
Fiorito, Eunice
Flynn, Elizabeth Gurley
Hamer, Fannie Lou Townsend
Hernandez, Aileen Clarke
Hutchins, Grace
Jordan, Barbara
Lawson, Roberta Campbell
Lease, Mary Elizabeth Clyens
Lockwood, Belva Ann Bennett
  McNall
O'Hare, Kate Richards
Stokes, Rose Harriet Pastor
Tenayuca, Emma
Terrell, Mary Eliza Church
Todd, Marion Marsh
Upton, Harriet Taylor
Wald, Lillian D.

peacemaker
Winnemucca, Sarah

philanthropist
Bonney, Mary L.
Pleasant, Mary Ellen
Quinton, Amelia Stone
Ruffin, Josephine St. Pierre
Sanders, Elizabeth Elkins

physician
Blackwell, Elizabeth

pioneer
Pleasant, Mary Ellen

playwright
Lifton, Betty Jean
Stokes, Rose Harriet Pastor

poet
Jackson, Helen Maria Fiske Hunt
Lease, Mary Elizabeth Clyens
Stokes, Rose Harriet Pastor
Strong, Anna Louise

politician *see also* **congress-woman; senator; state legislator**
Apuzzo, Virginia M.
Baca, Polly B.
Barnard, Kate
Bass, Charlotta A. Spears
Bloor, Ella Reeve
Chisholm, Shirley
Davis, Angela
Deer, Ada
Fauset, Crystal Dreda Bird
Felton, Rebecca Ann Latimer
Flynn, Elizabeth Gurley
Hutchins, Grace
Jordan, Barbara
Lease, Mary Elizabeth Clyens
Lockwood, Belva Ann Bennett
    McNall
Motley, Constance Baker
Norton, Eleanor Holmes
O'Hare, Kate Richards
Robertson, Alice Mary
Stokes, Rose Harriet Pastor
Todd, Marion Marsh
Upton, Harriet Taylor
Wells-Barnett, Ida Bell

postmistress
Robertson, Alice Mary

probation officer *see also* **parole officer**
Wells-Barnett, Ida Bell

production assistant
Lifton, Betty Jean

public affairs consultant *see also* **public relations consultant**
Hernandez, Aileen Clarke

public relations consultant *see also* **public affairs consultant**
Baca, Polly B.
Hernandez, Aileen Clarke

public speaker *see* **lecturer/orator/public speaker**

publisher
Bass, Charlotta A. Spears
Bates, Daisy
Bethune, Mary McLeod
Bonnin, Gertrude Simmons
Day, Dorothy
Felton, Rebecca Ann Latimer
Goldman, Emma
O'Hare, Kate Richards
Strong, Anna Louise
Wells-Barnett, Ida Bell

race relations worker
Bethune, Mary McLeod
Dunbar-Nelson, Alice
Fauset, Crystal Dreda Bird
Height, Dorothy I.
Koontz, Elizabeth Duncan
Kuhn, Margaret E.
Ruffin, Josephine St. Pierre
Talbert, Mary Burnett

radio *see* **broadcaster/television/radio**

research assistant
Hernandez, Aileen Clarke

restaurant owner
Pleasant, Mary Ellen
Robertson, Alice Mary

revolutionary
Bracetti, Mariana

saleswoman
Hernandez, Aileen Clarke
Parks, Rosa
Stokes, Rose Harriet Pastor

scriptwriter
Lifton, Betty Jean

scout
Winnemucca, Sarah

seamstress
Bracetti, Mariana
Parks, Rosa

secretary   *see also*   office worker
Lifton, Betty Jean
Olivarez, Graciela (Grace)
Robertson, Alice Mary

senator   *see also*   congresswoman;
   politician; state legislator
Felton, Rebecca Ann Latimer

sharecropper
Hamer, Fannie Lou Townsend

singer   *see*   musician/singer

social action worker
Kuhn, Margaret E.
Robinson, Ruby Doris Smith

social worker
Balch, Emily Greene
Cameron, Donaldina Mackenzie
Deer, Ada
Dunbar-Nelson, Alice
Fiorito, Eunice
Height, Dorothy I.
Robertson, Alice Mary
Strong, Anna Louise

sociologist
Balch, Emily Greene

state legislator   *see also*   congress-
   woman; politician; senator
Baca, Polly B.
Barnard, Kate

Chisholm, Shirley
Fauset, Crystal Dreda Bird
Jordan, Barbara
Motley, Constance Baker

tailor's assistant
Parks, Rosa

teacher/teaching   *see*   educator

technical advisor
Strong, Anna Louise

television   *see*   broadcaster/televi-
   sion/radio

translator/interpreter
La Flesche, Susette
Lawson, Roberta Campbell
Olivarez, Graciela (Grace)
Schwimmer, Rosika
Stokes, Rose Harriet Pastor
Winnemucca, Sarah

unions   *see*   labor/labor organizer/
   unions

urban affairs consultant
Hernandez, Aileen Clarke
Maymi, Carmen Rosa
Olivarez, Graciela (Grace)

writer   *see*   author; editor;
   journalist

Appendix H: Religious Affiliation

Baptist
Bonney, Mary L.
Jordan, Barbara
King, Coretta Scott
Lawson, Roberta Campbell
Quinton, Amelia Stone
Robinson, Ruby Doris Smith

Campbellite
Lease, Mary Elizabeth Clyens

Christian Scientist
Lease, Mary Elizabeth Clyens

Episcopalian
Bonney, Mary L.
Converse, Harriet Maxwell
Koontz, Elizabeth Duncan
Ruffin, Josephine St. Pierre
Upton, Harriet Taylor

Jewish
Wald, Lillian D.

Methodist
Felton, Rebecca Ann Latimer

Presbyterian
Cameron, Donaldina Mackenzie

Roman Catholic
Apuzzo, Virginia M.
Barnard, Kate
Day, Dorothy
Fiorito, Eunice

Lease, Mary Elizabeth Clyens
Olivarez, Graciela (Grace)
Pleasant, Mary Ellen

Theosophist
Lease, Mary Elizabeth Clyens

Unitarian
Balch, Emily Greene
Sanders, Elizabeth Elkins

Universalist
Emery, Sarah Elizabeth Van De
 Vort
Todd, Marion Marsh

Appendix I: Schools Attended

Abbott School, New York, New York
Jackson, Helen Maria Fiske Hunt

Alabama State College, Montgomery, Alabama
Parks, Rosa

American Indian Law Program, University of New Mexico, Albuquerque
Deer, Ada

American University, Washington, D. C.
Baca, Polly B.

Antioch College, Yellow Springs, Ohio
King, Coretta Scott
Norton, Eleanor Holmes

Atlanta University, Atlanta, Georgia
Koontz, Elizabeth Duncan

Barnard College, New York, New York
Lifton, Betty Jean

Bay Ridge High School, Brooklyn, New York
Hernandez, Aileen Clarke

Bell Lane Free School, London, England
Stokes, Rose Harriet Pastor

Bible Institute for Home and Foreign Missions, Chicago, Illinois
Bethune, Mary McLeod

Booker T. Washington High School (Montgomery, Alabama?)
Parks, Rosa

Boston Conservatory of Music, Boston, Massachusetts
Bonnin, Gertrude Simmons

Boston Normal School, Boston, Massachusetts
Fauset, Crystal Dreda Bird

Boston University Law School, Boston, Massachusetts
Jordan, Barbara

Bowdoin School, Boston, Massachusetts
Ruffin, Josephine St. Pierre

Brackenridge High School, San Antonio, Texas
Tenayuca, Emma

Brandeis University,Waltham, Massachusetts
Davis, Angela

Brooklyn College, Brooklyn, New York
Chisholm, Shirley

Bryn Mawr College, Bryn Mawr, Pennsylvania
Balch, Emily Greene
Hutchins, Grace
Strong, Anna Louise

Carrie A. Tuggle Elementary School, Birmingham, Alabama
Davis, Angela

Case Western Reserve University, Cleveland, Ohio
Kuhn, Margaret E.

Castelar Elementary School, Santurce, Puerto Rico
Maymi, Carmen Rosa

Castleman School for Girls, San Jose, California
Cameron, Donaldina Mackenzie

Clinton Liberal Institute, Clinton, New York
Emery, Sarah Elizabeth Van De Vort

Colorado State University, Fort Collins, Colorado
Baca, Polly B.

Columbia University, New York, New York
Chisholm, Shirley
Deer, Ada
Dunbar-Nelson, Alice
Fauset, Crystal Dreda Bird
Fiorito, Eunice
Hutchins, Grace
Koontz, Elizabeth Duncan
Motley, Constance Baker

Convent of the Holy Names, Oakland, California
Moreno, Luisa

Cornell University, Ithaca, New York
Dunbar-Nelson, Alice

Cortland Academy, Homer, New York
Quinton, Amelia Stone

DePaul University, Chicago, Illinois
Maymi, Carmen Rosa

Dunbar High School, Washington, D. C.
Norton, Eleanor Holmes

Earlham College, Richmond, Indiana
Bonnin, Gertrude Simmons

Elisabeth Irwin High School, New York, New York
Davis, Angela

Elizabeth Institute for Young Ladies, Elizabeth, New Jersey
La Flesche, Susette

Elmira College, Elmira, New York
Robertson, Alice Mary

Emma Willard's Female Seminary, Troy, New York
Bonney, Mary L.

Falmouth Female Seminary, Falmouth, Massachusetts
Jackson, Helen Maria Fiske Hunt

Felix Adler's Summer School of Applied Ethics (location not known)
Balch, Emily Greene

Fisk University, Nashville, Tennessee
Berry, Mary Frances
Motley, Constance Baker
Wells-Barnett, Ida Bell

Fort Sill Indian High School, Lawton, Oklahoma
Hayden, Iola M. Pohocsucut

Gasport Academy, Gasport, New York
Lockwood, Belva Ann Bennett McNall

Genesee College, Lima, New York
Lockwood, Belva Ann Bennett McNall

Genesee Wesleyan Seminary, Lima, New York
Lockwood, Belva Ann Bennett McNall

Geneva Medical College, Geneva, New York
Blackwell, Elizabeth

Girls High School, Brooklyn, New York
Chisholm, Shirley

Good Counsel High School, Chicago, Illinois
Fiorito, Eunice

Greeley High School, Greeley, Colorado
Baca, Polly B.

Hamilton Academy, Hamilton, New York
Bonney, Mary L.

Hardin College, Mexico, Missouri
Lawson, Roberta Campbell

Harvard Institute of Politics, JFK School of Government, Cambridge,
  Massachusetts
Deer, Ada

Hastings Law College, San Francisco, California
Todd, Marion Marsh

Hôpital de la Maternité, Paris, France
Blackwell, Elizabeth

Hospital Training School for Nurses, New York, New York
Wald, Lillian D.

Howard University, Washington, D.C.
Berry, Mary Frances
Hernandez, Aileen Clarke

Indiana University, Bloomington, Indiana
Koontz, Elizabeth Duncan

International Ladies' Garment Workers' Union Labor College (location not
  known)
Hernandez, Aileen Clarke

International School of Social Economy (location not known)
O'Hare, Kate Richards

Ipswich Female Seminary, Ipswich, Massachusetts
Jackson, Helen Maria Fiske Hunt

Ivy Hall Seminary (Bridgeton, New Jersey?)
Bloor, Ella Reeve

Johann Wolfgang von Goethe University, Frankfurt, Germany
Davis, Angela

L. J. Price High School, Atlanta, Georgia
Robinson, Ruby Doris Smith

LaSalle College, Philadelphia, Pennsylvania
Kuhn, Margaret E.

Lemoyne Institute (Memphis, Tennessee?)
Wells-Barnett, Ida Bell

Lincoln School, Marion, Alabama
King, Coretta Scott

Lincoln University School of Law, St. Louis, Missouri
Wilson, Margaret Bush

Livingstone College, Salisbury, North Carolina
Koontz, Elizabeth Duncan

Los Angeles Normal School, Los Angeles, California
Cameron, Donaldina Mackenzie

Los Angeles State College, Los Angeles, California
Hernandez, Aileen Clarke

Loyola University, Chicago, Illinois
Fiorito, Eunice

Madison Female College, Madison, Georgia
Felton, Rebecca Ann Latimer

Miss Catherine Ireland's, Boston, Massachusetts
Balch, Emily Greene

**Miss Cruttenden's English-French Boarding and Day School for Young
   Ladies and Little Girls,** Rochester, New York
Wald, Lillian D.

Miss Hayes, Oxford, Georgia
Felton, Rebecca Ann Latimer

Model School, Yellow Springs, Ohio
Terrell, Mary Eliza Church

Montgomery Industrial School for Girls, Montgomery, Alabama
Parks, Rosa

National University Law School (Washington, D.C.?)
Lockwood, Belva Ann Bennett McNall

New England Conservatory of Music, Boston, Massachusetts
King, Coretta Scott

New Haven High School, New Haven, Connecticut
Motley, Constance Baker

New York School of Social Work, New York, New York
Height, Dorothy I.
Hutchins, Grace

New York University, New York, New York
Height, Dorothy I.
Hernandez, Aileen Clarke
Motley, Constance Baker

North Carolina State College, Durham, North Carolina
Koontz, Elizabeth Duncan

Oberlin College, Oberlin, Ohio
Strong, Anna Louise
Talbert, Mary Burnett
Terrell, Mary Eliza Church

Oklahoma State University, Stillwater, Oklahoma
Hayden, Iola M. Pohocsucut

Oklahoma University, Norman, Oklahoma
Hayden, Iola M. Pohocsucut

Pearl High School, Nashville, Tennessee
Berry, Mary Frances

Pennsylvania School of Industrial Art, Philadelphia, Pennsylvania
Dunbar-Nelson, Alice

Philander Smith College, Little Rock, Arkansas
Bates, Daisy

Phillis Wheatley High School, Houston, Texas
Jordan, Barbara

Price High School, Salisbury, North Carolina
Koontz, Elizabeth Duncan

Public School 176, Brooklyn, New York
Hernandez, Aileen Clarke

Rankin High School, Rankin, Pennsylvania
Height, Dorothy I.

Royalton Academy, Royalton, New York
Lockwood, Belva Ann Bennett McNall

St. Elizabeth's Academy, Allegany, New York
Lease, Mary Elizabeth Clyens

St. Joseph's Academy, Oklahoma City, Oklahoma
Barnard, Kate

St. Mary's Convent School, San Jose, California
Winnemucca, Sarah

San Francisco Theological Seminary, San Anselmo, California
Kuhn, Margaret E.

Scotia Seminary, Concord, North Carolina
Bethune, Mary McLeod

Shorter College, Little Rock, Arkansas
Bates, Daisy

Sorbonne, Paris, France
Balch, Emily Greene
Davis, Angela

Spelman College, Atlanta, Georgia
Robinson, Ruby Doris Smith

Springler Institute, New York, New York
Jackson, Helen Maria Fiske Hunt

Straight College, New Orleans, Louisiana
Dunbar-Nelson, Alice

Sumner High School, St. Louis, Missouri
Wilson, Margaret Bush

Talladega College, Talladega, Alabama
Wilson, Margaret Bush

Temple University, Philadelphia, Pennsylvania
Kuhn, Margaret E.

Texas Southern University, Houston, Texas
Jordan, Barbara

University of California at Los Angeles, Los Angeles, California
Hernandez, Aileen Clarke

University of California at San Diego, San Diego, California
Davis, Angela

University of Chicago, Chicago, Illinois
Maymi, Carmen Rosa
Strong, Anna Louise

University of Hawaii (Honolulu, Hawaii?)
Kuhn, Margaret E.

University of Illinois, Chicago, Illinois
Maymi, Carmen Rosa

University of Illinois (location not known)
Lifton, Betty Jean

University of Illinois, Urbana, Illinois
Day, Dorothy

University of Michigan, Ann Arbor, Michigan
Berry, Mary Frances

University of Notre Dame, Notre Dame, Indiana
Olivarez, Graciela (Grace)

University of Oslo, Oslo, Norway
Hernandez, Aileen Clarke

University of Pennsylvania, Philadelphia, Pennsylvania
Bloor, Ella Reeve
Dunbar-Nelson, Alice

University of Southern California, Los Angeles, California
Hernandez, Aileen Clarke
Kuhn, Margaret E.

University of Wisconsin, Madison, Wisconsin
Deer, Ada

Waller High School, Chicago, Illinois
Day, Dorothy

Warren High School, Warren, Ohio
Upton, Harriet Taylor

Wells High School, Chicago, Illinois
Maymi, Carmen Rosa

West High School, Cleveland, Ohio
Kuhn, Margaret E.

White's Indiana Manual Institute, Wabash, Indiana
Bonnin, Gertrude Simmons

Women's Medical College of New York Infirmary, New York, New York
Wald, Lillian D.

Yale University, New Haven, Connecticut
Norton, Eleanor Holmes

Ypsilanti State Normal School, Ypsilanti, Michigan
Todd, Marion Marsh

Appendix J: Tribal Membership

Comanche
Hayden, Iola M. Pohocsucut

Delaware
Lawson, Roberta Campbell

Menominee
Deer, Ada

Omaha
La Flesche, Susette

Paviotso-Paiute
Winnemucca, Sarah

Sioux
Bonnin, Gertrude Simmons

INDEX

References are to **entry** number, not page number.